MORAL
ISSUES

MORAL ISSUES

Edited by
JAN NARVESON

Toronto   New York
OXFORD UNIVERSITY PRESS
1983

CANADIAN CATALOGUING IN PUBLICATION DATA
Main entry under title:
Moral issues

Bibliography: p.
ISBN 0-19-540426-2

1. Social ethics — Addresses, essays, lectures.
2. Ethics — Addresses, essays, lectures.
I. Narveson, Jan, 1936-

HM216.M67   170   C83-098152-7

COVER ART: The pedigree of King Henry VIII (London, 1561)
adapted by Heather Delfino.

Acknowledgements

RANDY E. BARNETT. "The Justice of Restitution" from *The American Journal of Jurisprudence*, Vol. 25, 1980. © The Natural Law Institute, Notre Dame Law School. Reprinted by permission. HUGO ADAM BEDAU. "Capital Punishment and Social Defense" abridged from *Matters of Life and Death: New Introductory Essays in Moral Philosophy*, ed. by Tom Regan © 1980 Random House, Inc. Reprinted by permission of the publisher. WILLIAM T. BLACKSTONE. "Freedom and Women" from *Ethics*, Vol. 85, 1975. © 1975 by The University of Chicago Press. All rights reserved. Reprinted by permission. W. E. COOPER. "What is Sexual Equality and Why Does Tey Want It?" from *Ethics*, Vol. 85, no. 3, 1975. © 1975 by The University of Chicago Press. All rights reserved. Reprinted by permission. SIMONE DE BEAUVOIR. "What Is a Woman?" from *The Second Sex* by Simone de Beauvoir, trans. by H.M. Parshley. © 1952 Alfred A. Knopf, Inc. Reprinted by permission of the publishers. WILLIAM EARLE. "In Defense of War". Copyright © 1973, *The Monist*, La Salle, Illinois. Reprinted from Vol. 57, no. 4, Oct. 1973 by permission. JOEL FEINBERG. "A Question about Potentiality" abridged from "The Potentiality Argument" from *Matters of Life and Death: New Introductory Essays in Moral Philosophy*, ed. by Tom Regan © 1980 Random House, Inc. Reprinted by permission of the publisher. PHILIPPA FOOT. "Euthanasia" from *Philosophy & Public Affairs*, Vol. 6, no. 2, 1977. Reprinted by permission of Philippa Foot. MARILYN FRYE. "Male Chauvinism: A Conceptual Analysis". Reprinted by permission of Prometheus Books from *Philosophy and Sex*, ed. by Robert Baker and Frederick Elliston, copyright 1975 by Prometheus Books. ROBERT S. GERSTEIN. "Capital Punishment — 'Cruel and Unusual'?: A Retributivist Response" from *Ethics*, Vol. 84, 1974. © 1974 by The University of Chicago Press. All rights reserved. Reprinted by permission. JONATHAN GLOVER. "Suicide and Gambling with Life" from Chapter 13 from Jonathan Glover: *Causing Death & Saving Lives* (Pelican Books 1977) pp. 170-81. Copyright © Jonathan Glover, 1977. Reprinted by permission of Penguin Books Ltd. TRUDY GOVIER. "What Should We Do About Future People?" from *The American Philosophical Quarterly*, 1979. Reprinted by permission. GARRETT HARDIN. "Living on a Lifeboat" abridged from *BioScience*. © 1975 by the American Institute of Biological Sciences. Reprinted by permission. SIDNEY HOOK. "The Death Sentence" from *The Death Penalty in America*. Reprinted by permission of Sidney Hook. JAMES M. HUMBER. "Abortion: The Avoidable Moral Dilemma" abridged from *The Journal of Value Inquiry*, Vol. 9, 1975. Reprinted by permission. JOHN HUNTER. "Sex and Personal Intimacy" from *Thinking About Sex and Love* by J.F.M. Hunter. Copyright © 1980 by J.F.M. Hunter. Reprinted by permission of Macmillan of Canada A Division of Gage Publishing Limited. THOMAS HURKA. "Rights and Capital Punishment" abridged from *Dialogue*, XXI, no. 4, December 1982. Reprinted by permission. GREGORY S. KAVKA. "Some Paradoxes of Deterrence" from *The Journal of Philosophy*, Vol. LXXV, no. 6 (June 1978). Reprinted by permission. SARA ANN KETCHUM. "Evidence, Statistics and Rights: A Reply to Simon" from *Analysis*, Vol. 39, no. 3, June 1979. Reprinted by permission of Sara Ann Ketchum. DOUGLAS P. LACKEY. "Missiles and Morals: A Utilitarian Look at Nuclear Deterrence" abridged from *Philosophy & Public Affairs*, Vol. 11, no. 3 (Summer 1982). Copyright (1982) by Princeton University Press.

ALISTAIR M. MACLEOD. "Equality of Opportunity" reprinted by permission of Alistair M. Macleod. ROBERT M. MARTIN. "Suicide and False Desires" from *Suicide: The Philosophical Issues*, ed. by M. Pabst Battin and David J. Mayo, St Martin's Press, Inc., New York. Copyright © 1980 by M. Pabst Battin and David J. Mayo. Reprinted by permission of the publisher. WALLACE MATSON. "Justice: A Funeral Oration", abridged. By permission of Wallace Matson. RICHARD D. MOHR. "Gay Rights" from *Social Theory & Practise*, Vol. 8, no. 1, Spring 1982. © *Social Theory & Practise*. Reprinted by permission. JAN NARVESON. "In Defense of Peace" © Jan Narveson. LISA NEWTON. "Reverse Discrimination as Unjustified" from *Ethics*, Vol. 83, 1973. © by the University of Chicago Press. All rights reserved. Reprinted by permission. ROBERT NOZICK. "Equality" abridged from "Equality, Envy, Exploitation, Etc." from *Anarchy, State, and Utopia* by Robert Nozick, copyright © 1974 by Basic Books, Inc., New York. Reprinted by permission of the publisher. ONORA O'NEILL. "Lifeboat Earth" from *Philosophy & Public Affairs*, Vol. 4, no. 3 (Spring 1975). Copyright © 1975 by Princeton University Press. DEREK PARFIT. "Future Generations", abridged. By permission of Derek Parfit. JAMES RACHELS. "Killing and Starving to Death" from *Philosophy*, Vol. 54, 1979. Cambridge University Press; "Active and Passive Euthanasia". Reprinted by permission of *The New England Journal of Medicine*, Vol. 292, pp. 78-80, 1975. STEVEN L. ROSS. "Abortion and the Death of the Fetus", from *Philosophy & Public Affairs*, Vol. 11, no. 3 (Summer 1982). Copyright © 1982 by Princeton University Press. ROBERT L. SIMON. Reprinted by permission of Robert L. Simon: "Statistical Justifications of Discrimination" from *Analysis*, Vol. 38, no. 1, January 1978; "Rights, Groups and Discrimination: A Reply to Ketchum" from *Analysis*, Vol. 40, no. 2, March 1980. PETER SINGER. "Is Racial Discrimination Arbitrary?" from *Philosophia*. Reprinted by permission. WAYNE SUMNER. "A Third Way" from L.W. Sumner, *Abortion and Moral Theory* copyright © 1981 by Princeton University Press, chapter 4 adapted by permission of Princeton University Press. MICHAEL TOOLEY. "In Defense of Abortion and Infanticide" reprinted by permission of Michael Tooley. RUSSELL VANNOY. "Erotic Love, a Final Appraisal". Reprinted by permission of Prometheus Books from *Sex Without Love*, by Russell Vannoy, copyright 1980. RICHARD WASSERSTROM. Reprinted by permission of Richard Wasserstrom: "A Defense of Programs of Preferential Treatment" from *National Forum*, Vol. 58, no. 1, Winter 1978; "Is Adultery Immoral?" from *Today's Moral Problems* (1975).

Every effort has been made to determine copyright owners. In the case of any omissions, the publishers will be pleased to make suitable acknowledgements in future editions.

Contents

IX. FUTURE PEOPLE

Introduction

This volume brings together essays on nine varied moral issues. Within its fairly compact format is ample material to serve as the sourcebook for those courses in moral philosophy—now so common as to be nearly standard—that stimulate thought about ethics by looking at concrete issues rather than abstract theories. As readers will soon find, however, it is scarcely possible to keep the "concrete" and the "abstract" separate in this realm. The difference between anthologies of readings on concrete issues and anthologies or texts on ethical theory is one of direction, not of real subject matter. Nevertheless, the direction *is* different.

What, then, are "moral issues"? Some anthologies use the word "problems" where this one uses "issues." "Problem" suggests a question of know-how, that is, a situation in which you know what needs to be accomplished but do not know quite how to do it. Moral issues are not like that. Of course we do have moral problems: whenever we are convinced that a certain course of action is right, but do not know how to get ourselves to follow it, we face a problem. Yet concerning matters such as abortion or nuclear disarmament, the question of what to do is itself the subject of wide and serious disagreement. If there is a "problem," it is what stand or position to take, and not how to act according to the position we choose. I have therefore selected essays that present the contrary views befitting "issues."

As a result, students will find much disagreement in these pages. They will not find an elaborate introduction to guide them through the issues, subtly helping them to make up their minds. There are several reasons for this. In the first place, the aim of *Moral Issues*, and of the kind of course it is likely to be used in, is to get students to think through the issues themselves. However, few students can derive maximum benefit from a set of readings without guidance from an instructor who has been trained to think philosophically, and has brought this training to bear on the issues at hand. If students read carefully they will have many questions that cannot be dealt with, let alone resolved, in an introduction. What they need is the kind of discussion and close examination that only the trained philosopher can provide.

Two interrelated difficulties have to be solved in making the final selection for any anthology of this kind: which issues to include, and which articles on each issue. The nine issues here have been chosen primarily with an eye to interest and variety. All are of major current interest to the general public as well as to professional philosophers and university students. Furthermore, each one has given rise to an abundance of challenging articles. The range of philosophical viewpoints, arguments, and principles is extensive; all, however, are part of Anglo/North American philosophy. It should also be noted that the articles themselves vary greatly in degree of sophistication. While every section contains some selections that will be readily comprehensible to the beginner, most also include articles that will challenge the advanced student. In addition, I have endeavored to strike a balance between "contemporary classics" that have already been widely anthologized and new material that is certain not to have been (several of the articles had not been previously published at all; however, none was solicited for this volume). The final section is of special interest, I think, as it introduces puzzles of a particularly intractable kind regarding an issue of undoubtedly major importance. It is well to end a volume about moral issues with a look at some of the uncharted territory that lies ahead. The combination of unresolved questions and new areas to explore should impart a healthy appreciation of the special and complex nature of moral philosophy.

Moral Issues concludes with a modest list of recommendations for further reading. Given the vast amount of material available, this could have been far longer, but experience as a teacher suggests that a short list has some chance of being used, whereas a lengthy one is almost sure to be ignored. The serious student will have no difficulty in following up any or all of these issues in the current literature.

I am grateful to the many people who offered advice and suggestions in the course of assembling this collection, particularly Thomas Hurka. I have no doubt that *Moral Issues* is greatly the better for their efforts; responsibility for the idiosyncrasies that remain is, of course, my own. In addition, I would like to acknowledge the assistance provided by my editors at the Oxford University Press, Richard Teleky and Sally Livingston.

JAN NARVESON

The University of Waterloo
January 1983

MORAL
ISSUES

I

EUTHANASIA AND SUICIDE

Active and Passive Euthanasia

JAMES RACHELS

The distinction between active and passive euthanasia is thought to be crucial for medical ethics. The idea is that it is permissible, at least in some cases, to withhold treatment and allow a patient to die, but it is never permissible to take any direct action designed to kill the patient. This doctrine seems to be accepted by most doctors, and it is endorsed in a statement adopted by the House of Delegates of the American Medical Association on December 4, 1973:

> The intentional termination of the life of one human being by another—mercy killing—is contrary to that for which the medical profession stands and is contrary to the policy of the American Medical Association.
> The cessation of the employment of extraordinary means to prolong the life of the body when there is irrefutable evidence that biological death is imminent is the decision of the patient and/or his immediate family. The advice and judgment of the physician should be freely available to the patient and/or his immediate family.

However, a strong case can be made against this doctrine. In what follows I will set out some of the relevant arguments, and urge doctors to reconsider their views on this matter.

To begin with a familiar type of situation, a patient who is dying of incurable cancer of the throat is in terrible pain, which can no longer be satisfactorily alleviated. He is certain to die within a few days, even if present treatment is continued, but he does not want to go on living for those days since the pain is unbearable. So he asks the doctor for an end to it, and his family joins in the request.

Suppose the doctor agrees to withhold treatment, as the conventional doctrine says he may. The justification for his doing so is that the patient is in terrible agony, and since he is going to die anyway, it would be wrong to prolong his suffering needlessly. But now notice this. If one simply withholds treatment, it may take the patient longer to die, and so he may suffer more than he would if more direct action were taken and a lethal injection given. This fact provides strong reason for thinking that, once the initial decision not to prolong his agony has been made, active euthanasia is actually preferable to passive euthanasia, rather than the reverse. To say otherwise is to endorse the option that leads to more suffering rather than less, and is contrary to the humanitarian impulse that prompts the decision not to prolong his life in the first place.

Part of my point is that the process of being "allowed to die" can be relatively slow and painful, whereas being given a lethal injection is relatively quick and painless. Let me give a different sort of example. In the United States about one in 600 babies is born with Down's syndrome. Most of these babies are otherwise healthy—that is, with only the usual pediatric care, they will proceed to an otherwise normal infancy. Some, however, are born with congenital defects such as intestinal obstructions that require operations if they are to live. Sometimes, the parents and the doctor will decide not to operate, and let the infant die. Anthony Shaw describes what happens then:

> When surgery is denied [the doctor] must try to keep the infant from suffering while natural forces sap the baby's life away. As a surgeon whose natural inclination is to use the scalpel to fight off death, standing by and watching a salvageable baby die is the most emotionally exhausting experience I know. It is easy at a conference, in a theoretical discussion to decide that such infants should be allowed to die. It is altogether different to stand by in the nursery and watch as dehydration and infection wither a tiny being over hours and days. This is a terrible ordeal for me and the hospital staff—much more so than for the parents who never set foot in the nursery.[1]

I can understand why some people are opposed to all euthanasia, and insist that such infants must be allowed to live. I think I can also understand why other people favor destroying these babies quickly and painlessly. But why should anyone favor letting "dehydration and infection wither a tiny being over hours and days"? The doctrine that says that a baby may be allowed to dehydrate and wither, but may not be given an injection that would end its life without suffering, seems so patently cruel as to require no further refutation. The strong language is not intended to offend, but only to put the point in the clearest possible way.

My second argument is that the conventional doctrine leads to decisions concerning life and death made on irrelevant grounds.

Consider again the case of the infants with Down's syndrome who need operations for congenital defects unrelated to the syndrome to live. Sometimes, there is no operation, and the baby dies, but when there is no such defect, the baby lives on. Now, an operation such as that to remove an intestinal obstruction is not prohibitively difficult. The reason why such operations are not performed in these cases is, clearly, that the child has Down's syndrome and the parents and the doctor judge that because of that fact it is better for the child to die.

But notice that this situation is absurd, no matter what view one takes of the lives and potentials of such babies. If the life of such an infant is worth preserving what does it matter if it needs a simple operation? Or, if one thinks it better that such a baby should not live on, what difference does it make that it happens to have an unobstructed intestinal tract? In either case, the matter of life and death is being decided on irrelevant grounds. It is the Down's syndrome, and not the intestines, that is the issue. The matter should be decided, if at all, on that basis, and not be allowed to depend on the essentially irrelevant question of whether the intestinal tract is blocked.

What makes this situation possible, of course, is the idea that when there is an intestinal blockage, one can "let the baby die," but when there is no such defect there is nothing that can be done, for one must not "kill" it. The fact that this idea leads to such results as deciding life or death on irrelevant grounds is another good reason why the doctrine would be rejected.

One reason why so many people think that there is an important moral difference between active and passive euthanasia is that they think killing someone is morally worse than letting someone die. But is it? Is killing, in itself, worse than letting die? To investigate this issue, two cases may be considered that are exactly alike except that one involves killing whereas the other involves letting someone die. Then, it can be asked whether this difference makes any difference to the moral assessments. It is important that the cases be exactly alike, except for this one difference, since otherwise one cannot be confident that it is this difference and not some other that accounts for any variation in the assessments of the two cases. So, let us consider this pair of cases:

In the first, Smith stands to gain a large inheritance if anything should happen to his six-year-old cousin. One evening while the child is taking his bath, Smith sneaks into the bathroom and drowns the child, and then arranges things so that it will look like an accident.

In the second, Jones also stands to gain if anything should happen to his six-year-old cousin. Like Smith, Jones sneaks in planning to drown the child in his bath. However, just as he enters the bathroom Jones sees the child slip and hit his head, and fall face down in the water. Jones is delighted; he stands by, ready to push the child's head back under if it is necessary, but it is not necessary. With only a little thrashing about, the child drowns all by himself, "accidentally," as Jones watches and does nothing.

Now Smith killed the child, whereas Jones "merely" let the child die. That is the only difference between them. Did either man behave better, from a moral point of view? If the difference between killing and letting die were in itself a morally important matter, one should say that Jones's behavior was less reprehensible than Smith's. But does one really want to say that? I think not. In the first place, both men acted from the same motive, personal gain, and both had exactly the same end in view when they acted. It may be inferred from Smith's conduct that he is a bad man, although that judgment may be withdrawn or modified if certain further facts are learned about him—for example, that he is mentally deranged. But would not the very same thing be inferred about Jones from his conduct? And would not the same further considerations also be relevant to any modification of this judgment? Moreover, suppose Jones pleaded, in his own defense, "After all, I didn't do anything except just stand there and watch the child drown. I didn't kill him; I only let him die." Again, if letting die were in itself less bad than killing, this defense should have at least some weight. But it does not. Such a "defense" can only be regarded as a grotesque perversion of moral reasoning. Morally speaking, it is no defense at all.

Now, it may be pointed out, quite properly, that the cases of euthanasia with which doctors are concerned are not like this at all. They do not involve personal gain or the destruction of normal healthy children. Doctors are concerned only with cases in which the patient's life is of no further use to him, or in which the patient's life has become or will soon become a terrible burden. However, the point is the same in these cases: the bare difference between killing and letting die does not, in itself, make a moral difference. If a doctor lets a patient die, for humane reasons, he is in the same moral position as if he had given the patient a lethal injection for humane reasons. If his decision was wrong—if, for example, the patient's illness was in fact curable—the decision would be equally regrettable no matter which method was used to carry it out. And if the doctor's decision was the right one, the method used is not in itself important.

The AMA policy statement isolates the crucial issue very well; the crucial issue is "the intentional termination of the life of one human being by another." But after identifying this issue, and forbidding "mercy killing," the statement goes on to deny that the cessation of treatment is the intentional termination of a life. This is where the mistake comes in, for what is the cessation of treatment, in these circumstances, if it is not "the intentional termination of the life of one human being by another"? Of course it is exactly that, and if it were not, there would be no point to it.

Many people will find this judgment hard to accept. One reason, I think, is that it is very easy to conflate the question of whether killing is, in itself, worse than letting die, with the very different question of whether most actual cases of killing are more reprehensible than most actual cases of letting die. Most actual cases of killing are clearly terrible (think, for example, of all the murders reported in the newspapers), and one hears of such cases every day. On the other hand, one hardly ever hears of a case of letting die, except for the actions of doctors who are motivated by humanitarian reasons. So one learns to think of killing in a much worse light than of letting die. But this does not mean that there is something about killing that makes it in itself worse than letting die, for it is not the bare difference between killing and letting die that makes the difference in these cases. Rather, the other factors—the murderer's motive of personal gain, for example, contrasted with the doctor's humanitarian motivation—account for different reactions to the different cases.

I have argued that killing is not in itself any worse than letting die; if my contention is right, it follows that active euthanasia is not any worse than passive euthanasia. What arguments can be given on the other side? The most common, I believe, is the following:

> The important difference between active and passive euthanasia is that, in passive euthanasia, the doctor does not do anything to bring about the patient's death. The doctor does nothing, and the patient dies of whatever ills already afflict him. In active euthanasia, however, the doctor does something to bring about the patient's death: he kills him. The doctor who gives the patient with cancer a lethal injection has himself caused his patient's death; whereas if he merely ceases treatment, the cancer is the cause of the death.

A number of points need to be made here. The first is that it is not exactly correct to say that in passive euthanasia the doctor does nothing, for he does do one thing that is very important: he lets the patient die. "Letting someone die" is certainly different, in some respects, from other types of action—mainly in that it is a kind of action that one may perform by way of not performing certain other actions. For example, one may let a patient die by way of not giving medication, just as one may insult someone by way of not shaking his hand. But for any purpose of moral assessment, it is a type of action nonetheless. The decision to let a patient die is subject to moral appraisal in the same way that a decision to kill him would be subject to moral appraisal: it may be assessed as wise or unwise, compassionate or sadistic, right or wrong. If a doctor deliberately let a patient die who was suffering from a routinely curable illness, the doctor would certainly be to blame if he had needlessly killed the patient. Charges against him would be appropriate. If so, it would be no defense at all for him to insist that he didn't "do anything." He would have done something very serious indeed, for he let his patient die.

Fixing the cause of death may be very important from a legal point of view, for it may determine whether criminal charges are brought against the doctor. But I do not think that this notion can be used to show a moral difference between active and passive euthanasia. The reason why it is considered bad to be the cause of someone's death is that death is regarded as a great evil—and so it is. However, if it has been decided that euthanasia—even passive euthanasia—is desirable in a given case, it has also been decided that in this instance death is no greater an evil than the patient's continued existence. And if this is true, the usual reason for not wanting to be the cause of someone's death simply does not apply.

Finally, doctors may think that all of this is only of academic interest—the sort of thing that philosophers may worry about but that has no practical bearing on their own work. After all, doctors must be concerned about the legal consequences of what they do, and active euthanasia is clearly forbidden by the law. But even so, doctors should also be concerned with the fact that the law is forcing upon them a moral doctrine that may be indefensible, and has a considerable effect on their practices. Of course, most doctors are not now in the position of being coerced in this matter, for they do not regard themselves as merely going along with what the law requires. Rather, in statements such as the AMA policy statement that I have quoted they are endorsing this doctrine as a central point of medical ethics. In that statement, active euthanasia is condemned not merely as illegal but as "contrary to that for which the medical profession stands," whereas passive euthanasia is approved. However, the preceding considerations suggest that there is really no moral difference between the two, considered in themselves (there may be important moral differences in some cases in their *consequences*, but, as I pointed out, these differences may make active euthanasia, and not passive euthanasia, the morally preferable option). So, whereas doctors may have to discriminate between active and passive euthanasia to satisfy the law, they should not do any more than that. In particular, they should not give the distinction any added authority and weight by writing it into official statements of medical ethics.

NOTE

1 Anthony Shaw, "Doctor, Do We Have a Choice?" *The New York Times Magazine*, 30 January 1972, 54.

Euthanasia

PHILIPPA FOOT

The widely used *Shorter Oxford English Dictionary* gives three meanings for the word "euthanasia": the first, "a quiet and easy death"; the second, "the means of procuring this"; and the third, "the action of inducing a quiet and easy death." It is a curious fact that no one of the three gives an adequate definition of the word as it is usually understood. For "euthanasia" means much more than a quiet and easy death, or the means of procuring it, or the action of inducing it. The definition specifies only the manner of the death, and if this were all that was implied a murderer, careful to drug his victim, could claim that his act was an act of euthanasia. We find this ridiculous because we take it for granted that in euthanasia it is death itself, not just the manner of death, that must be kind to the one who dies.

To see how important it is that "euthanasia" should not be used as the dictionary definition allows it to be used, merely to signify that a death was quiet and easy, one has only to remember that Hitler's "euthanasia" program traded on this ambiguity. Under this program, planned before the War but brought into full operation by a decree of 1 September 1939, some 275,000 people were gassed in centers which were to be a model for those in which Jews were later exterminated. Anyone in a state institution could be sent to the gas chambers if it was considered that he could not be "rehabilitated" for useful work. As Dr. Leo Alexander reports, relying on the testimony of a neuropathologist who received 500 brains from one of the killing centers,

> In Germany the exterminations included the mentally defective, psychotics (particularly schizophrenics), epileptics and patients suffering from infirmities of old age and from various organic neurological disorders such as infantile paralysis, Parkinsonism, multiple sclerosis and brain tumors. . . . In truth, all those unable to work and considered nonrehabilitable were killed.[1]

These people were killed because they were "useless" and "a burden on society"; only the manner of their deaths could be thought of as relatively easy and quiet.

Let us insist, then, that when we talk about euthanasia we are talking about a death understood as a good or happy event for the one who dies. This stipulation follows etymology, but is itself not exactly in line with current usage, which would be captured by the condition that the death should *not* be an evil rather than that it *should* be a good. That this is how people talk is shown by the fact that the case of Karen Ann Quinlan and others in a state of permanent coma is often discussed under the heading of "euthanasia." Perhaps it is not too late to object to the use of the word "euthanasia" in this sense. Apart from the break with the Greek origins of the word there are other unfortunate aspects of this extension of the term. For if we say that the death must be supposed to be a good to the subject we can also specify that it shall be for his sake that an act of euthanasia is performed. If we say merely that death shall not be an evil to him, we cannot stipulate that benefiting him shall be the motive where euthanasia is in question. Given the importance of the question, For whose sake are we acting? it is good to have a definition of euthanasia which brings under this heading only cases of opting for death for the sake of the one who dies. Perhaps what is most important is to say either that euthanasia is to be for the good of the subject or at least that death is to be no evil to him, thus refusing to talk Hitler's language. However, in this paper it is the first condition that will be understood, with the additional proviso that by an act of euthanasia we mean one of inducing or otherwise opting for death for the sake of the one who is to die.

A few lesser points need to be cleared up. In the first place it must be said that the word "act" is not to be taken to exclude omission: we shall speak of an act of euthanasia when someone is deliberately allowed to die, for his own good, and not only when positive measures are taken to see that he does. The very general idea we want is that of a choice of action or inaction directed at another man's death and causally effective in the sense that, in conjunction with actual circumstances, it is a sufficient condition of death. Of complications such as overdetermination, it will not be necessary to speak.

A second, and definitely minor, point about the definition of an act of euthanasia concerns the question of fact versus belief. It has already been implied that one who performs an act of euthanasia thinks that death will be merciful for the subject since we have said that it is on account of this thought that the act is done. But is it enough that he acts with this thought, or must things actually be as he thinks them to be? If one man kills another, or allows him to die, thinking that he is in the last stages of a terrible disease, though in fact he could have been cured, is this an act of euthanasia or not? Nothing much seems to hang on our decision about this. The same condition has got to enter into the definition whether as an element in reality or only as an element in the agent's belief. And however we define an act of euthanasia culpability or justifiability will be the same: if a man acts through ignorance his ignorance may be culpable or it may not.[2]

These are relatively easy problems to solve, but one that is dauntingly difficult has been passed over in this discussion of the definition and must now be faced. It is easy to say, as if this raised no problems, that an act of euthanasia is by definition one aiming at the *good* of the one whose death is in question, and that it is *for his sake* that his death is desired. But how is this to be explained? Presumably we are thinking of some evil already with him or to come on him if he continues to live, and death is thought of as a release from this evil. But this cannot be enough. Most people's lives contain evils such as grief or pain, but we do not therefore think that death would be a blessing to them. On the contrary life is generally supposed to be a good even for someone who is unusually unhappy or frustrated. How is it that one can ever wish for death for the sake of the one who is to die? This difficult question is central to the discussion of euthanasia, and we shall literally not know what we are talking about if we ask whether acts of euthanasia defined as we have defined them are ever morally permissible without first understanding better the reason for saying that life is a good, and the possibility that it is not always so.

If a man should save my life he would be my benefactor. In normal circumstances this is plainly true; but does one always benefit another in saving his life? It seems certain that he does not. Suppose, for instance, that a man were being tortured to death and was given a drug that lengthened his sufferings; this would not be a benefit but the reverse. Or suppose that in a ghetto in Nazi Germany a doctor saved the life of someone threatened by disease, but that the man once cured was transported to an extermination camp; the doctor might wish for the sake of the patient that he had died of the disease. Nor would a longer stretch of life always be a benefit to the person who was given it. Comparing Hitler's camps with those of Stalin, Dmitri Panin observes that in the latter the method of extermination was made worse by agonies that could stretch out over months.

> Death from a bullet would have been bliss compared with what many millions had to endure while dying of hunger. The kind of death to which they were condemned has nothing to equal it in treachery and sadism.[3]

These examples show that to save or prolong a man's life is not always to do him a service: it may be better for him if he dies earlier rather than later. It must therefore be agreed that while life is normally a benefit to the one who has it, this is not always so.

The judgment is often fairly easy to make—that life is or is not a good to someone—but the basis for it is very hard to find. When life is said to be a benefit or a good, on what grounds is the assertion made?

The difficulty is underestimated if it is supposed that the problem arises from the fact that one who is dead has nothing, so that the good someone gets from being alive cannot be compared with the amount he would otherwise have had. For why should this particular comparison be necessary? Surely it would be enough if one could say whether or not someone whose life was prolonged had more good than evil in the extra stretch of time. Such estimates are not always possible, but frequently they are; we say, for example, "He was very happy in those last years," or, "He had little but unhappiness then." If the balance of good and evil determined whether life was a good to someone we would expect to find a correlation in the judgments. In fact, of course, we find nothing of the kind. First, a man who has no doubt that existence is a good to him may have no idea about the balance of happiness and unhappiness in his life, or of any other positive and negative factors that may be suggested. So the supposed criteria are not always operating where the judgment is made. And secondly the application of the criteria gives an answer that is often wrong. Many people have more evil than good in their lives; we do not, however, conclude that we would do these people no service by rescuing them from death.

To get around this last difficulty Thomas Nagel has suggested that experience itself is a good which must be brought in to balance accounts.

> . . . life is worth living even when the bad elements of experience are plentiful, and the good ones too meager to outweigh the bad ones on their own. The additional positive weight is supplied by experience itself, rather than by any of its contents.[4]

This seems implausible because if experience itself is a good it must be so even when what we experience is wholly bad, as in being tortured to death. How should one decide how much to count for this experiencing; and why count anything at all?

Others have tried to solve the problem by arguing that it is a man's desire for life that makes us call life a good: if he wants to live then anyone who prolongs his life does him a benefit. Yet someone may cling to life where we would say confidently that it would be better for him if he died, and he may admit it too. Speaking of those same conditions in which, as he said, a bullet would have been merciful, Panin writes,

> I should like to pass on my observations concerning the absence of suicides under the extremely severe conditions of our concentration camps. The more that life became desperate, the more a prisoner seemed determined to hold onto it.[5]

One might try to explain this by saying that hope was the ground of this wish to survive for further days and months in the camp. But there is nothing unintelligible in the idea that a man might cling to life though he knew those facts about his future which would make any charitable man wish that he might die.

The problem remains, and it is hard to know where to look for a solution. Is there a conceptual connection between *life* and *good*? Because life is not always a good we are apt to reject this idea, and to think that it must be a contingent fact that life is usually a good, as it is a contingent matter that legacies are usually a benefit, if they are. Yet it seems not to be a contingent matter that to save someone's life is ordinarily to benefit him. The problem is to find where the conceptual connection lies.

It may be good tactics to forget for a time that it is euthanasia we are discussing and to see how *life* and *good* are connected in the case of living beings other than men. Even plants have things done to them that are harmful or beneficial, and what does them good must be related in some way to their living and dying. Let us therefore consider plants and animals, and then come back to human beings. At least we shall get away from the temptation to think that the connection between life and benefit must everywhere be a matter of happiness and unhappiness or of pleasure and pain; the idea being absurd in the case of animals and impossible even to formulate for plants.

In case anyone thinks that the concept of the beneficial applies only in a secondary or analogical way to plants, he should be reminded that we speak quite straightforwardly in saying, for instance, that a certain amount of sunlight is beneficial to most plants. What is in question here is the habitat in which plants of particular species flourish, but we can also talk, in a slightly different way, of what does them good, where there is some suggestion of improvement or remedy. What has the beneficial to do with sustaining life? It is tempting to answer, "everything," thinking that a healthy condition just is the one apt to secure survival. In fact, however, what is beneficial to a plant may have to do with reproduction rather than the survival of the individual member of the species. Nevertheless there is a plain connection between the beneficial and the life-sustaining even for the individual plant; if something makes it better able to survive in conditions normal for that species it is *ipso facto* good for it. We need go no further, and could go no further, in explaining why a certain environment or treatment is good for a plant than to show how it helps this plant to survive.[6]

This connection between the life-sustaining and the beneficial is reasonably unproblematic, and there is nothing fanciful or zoomorphic in speaking of benefiting or doing good to plants. A connection with its survival can make something beneficial to a plant. But this is not, of course, to say that we count life as a good to a plant. We may save its life by giving it what is beneficial; we do not benefit it by saving its life.

A more ramified concept of benefit is used in speaking of animal life. New things can be said, such as that an animal is better or worse off for something that happened, or that it was a good or bad thing for it that it did happen. And new things count as benefit. In the first place, there is comfort, which often is, but need not be, related to health. When loosening a collar which is too tight for a dog we can say, "That will be better for it." So we see that the words "better for it" have two different meanings which we mark when necessary by a difference of emphasis, saying "better *for* it" when health is involved. And secondly an animal can be benefited by having its life saved.

"Could you do anything for it?" can be answered by, "Yes, I managed to save its life." Sometimes we may understand this, just as we would for a plant, to mean that we had checked some disease. But we can also do something for an animal by scaring away its predator. If we do this, it is a good thing for the animal that we did, unless of course it immediately meets a more unpleasant end by some other means. Similarly, on the bad side, an animal may be worse off for our intervention, and this not because it pines or suffers but simply because it gets killed.

The problem that vexes us when we think about euthanasia comes on the scene at this point. For if we can do something for an animal— can benefit it—by relieving its suffering but also by saving its life, where does the greater benefit come when only death will end pain? It seemed that life was a good in its own right; yet pain seemed to be an evil with equal status and could therefore make life not a good after all. Is it only life without pain that is a good when animals are concerned? This does not seem a crazy suggestion when we are thinking of animals, since unlike human beings they do not have suffering as part of their normal life. But it is perhaps the idea of ordinary life that matters here. We would not say that we had done anything for an animal if we had merely kept it alive, either in an unconscious state or in a condition where, though conscious, it was unable to operate in an ordinary way; and the fact is that animals in severe and continuous pain simply do not operate normally. So we do not, on the whole, have the option of doing the animal good by saving its life though the life would be a life of pain. No doubt there are borderline cases, but that is no problem. We are not trying to make new judgments possible, but rather to find the principle of the ones we do make.

When we reach human life the problems seem even more troublesome. For now we must take quite new things into account, such as the subject's own view of his life. It is arguable that this places extra constraints on the solution: might it not be counted as a necessary condition of life's being a good to a man that he should see it as such? Is there not some difficulty about the idea that a benefit might be done to him by the saving or prolonging of his life even though he himself wished for death? Of course he might have a quite mistaken view of his own prospects, but let us ignore this and think only of cases where it is life as he knows it that is in question. Can we think that the prolonging of this life would be a benefit to him even though he would rather have it end than continue? It seems that this cannot be ruled out. That there is no simple incompatibility between life as a good and the wish for death is shown by the possibility that a man should wish himself dead, not for his own sake, but for the sake of someone else. And if we try to amend the thesis to say that life cannot be a good to one who wishes *for his own sake* that he should die, we find the crucial concept slipping through our fingers. As Bishop Butler pointed out long ago not all ends are either benevolent or self-interested. Does a man wish for death for his own sake in the relevant sense if, for instance, he wishes to revenge himself on another by his death? Or what if he is proud and refuses to stomach dependence or incapacity even though there are many good things left in life for him? The truth seems to be that the wish for death is sometimes compatible with life's being a good and sometimes not, which is possible because the description "wishing for death" is one covering diverse states of mind from that of the determined suicide, pathologically depressed, to that of one who is surprised to find that the thought of a fatal accident is viewed with relief. On the one hand, a man may see his life as a burden but go about his business in a more or less ordinary way; on the other hand, the wish for death may take the form of a rejection of everything that is in life, as it does in severe depression. It seems reasonable to say that life is not a good to one permanently in the latter state, and we must return to this topic later on.

When are we to say that life is a good or a benefit to a man? The dilemma that faces us is this. If we say that life as such is a good we find ourselves refuted by the examples given at the beginning of this discussion. We therefore incline to think that it is as bringing good things that life is a good, where it is a good. But if life is a good only because it is the condition of good things why is it not equally an evil when it brings bad things? And how can it be a good even when it brings more evil than good?

It should be noted that the problem has here been formulated in terms of the balance of good and evil, not that of happiness and unhappiness, and that it is not to be solved by the denial (which may be reasonable enough) that unhappiness is the only evil or happiness the only good. In this paper no view has been expressed about the nature of goods other than life itself. The point is that on any view of the goods and evils that life can contain, it seems that a life with more evil than good could still itself be a good.

It may be useful to review the judgments with which our theory must square. Do we think that life can be a good to one who suffers a lot of pain? Clearly we do. What about severely handicapped people; can life be a good to them? Clearly it can be, for even if someone is almost completely paralyzed, perhaps living in an iron lung, perhaps able to move things only by means of a tube held between his lips, we do not rule him out of order if he says that some benefactor saved his life. Nor is it different with mental handicap. There are many fairly severely handicapped people—such as those with Down's syndrome (mongolism)—for whom a simple affectionate life is possible. What about senility? Does this break the normal connection between life and good? Here we must surely distinguish between forms of senility. Some forms leave a life which we count someone as better off having than not having, so that a doctor who prolonged it would benefit the person concerned. With some kinds of senility this is however no longer true. There are some in geriatric wards who are barely conscious, though they can move a little and swallow food put into their mouths. To prolong such a state, whether in the old or in the very severely mentally handicapped, is not to do them a service or confer a benefit. But of course it need not be the reverse: only if there is suffering would one wish for the sake of the patient that he should die.

It seems, therefore, that merely being alive even without suffering is not a good, and that we must make a distinction similar to that which we made when animals were our topic. But how is the line to be drawn in the case of men? What is to count as ordinary human life in the relevant sense? If it were only the very senile or very ill who were to be said not to have this life it might seem right to describe it in terms of *operation*. But it will be hard to find the sense in which the men described by Panin were not operating, given that they dragged themselves out to the forest to work. What is it about the life that the prisoners were living that makes us put it on the other side of the dividing line from that of most of the physically or mentally handicapped and of some severely ill or suffering patients? It is not that they were in captivity, for life in captivity can certainly be a good. Nor is it merely the unusual nature of their life. In some ways the prisoners were living more as other men do than the patient in an iron lung.

The idea we need seems to be that of life which is ordinary human life in the following respect—that it contains a minimum of basic human goods. What is ordinary in human life—even in very hard lives—is that a man is not driven to work far beyond his capacity; that he has the support of a family or community; that he can more or less satisfy his hunger; that he has hopes for the future; that he can lie down to rest at night. Such things were denied to the men in the Vyatlag camps described by Panin; not even rest at night was allowed them when they were tormented by bed-bugs, by noise and stench, and by routines such as body-searches and bath-parades—arranged for the night time so that work norms would not be reduced. Disease too can so take over a man's life that the normal human goods disappear. When a patient is so overwhelmed by pain or nausea that he cannot eat with pleasure, if he can eat at all, and is out of the reach of even the most loving voice, he no longer has ordinary human life in the sense in which the words are used here. And we may now pick up a thread from an earlier part of the discussion by remarking that crippling depression can destroy the enjoyment of ordinary goods as effectively as external circumstances can remove them.

The suggested solution to the problem is, then, that there is a certain conceptual connection between *life* and *good* in the case of human beings as in that of animals and even plants. Here, as there, however, it is not the mere state of being alive that can determine, or itself count as, a good, but rather life coming up to some standard of normality. It was argued that it is as part of ordinary life that the elements of good that a man may have are relevant to the question of whether saving his life counts as benefiting him. Ordinary human lives, even very hard lives, contain a minimum of basic goods, but when these are absent the idea of life is no longer linked to that of good. And since it is in this way that the elements of good contained in a man's life are relevant to the question of whether he is benefited if his life is preserved, there is no reason why it should be the balance of good and evil that counts.

It should be added that evils are relevant in one way when, as in the examples discussed above, they destroy the possibility of ordinary goods, but in a different way when they invade a life from which the goods are already absent for a different reason. So, for instance, the connection between *life* and *good* may be broken because consciousness has sunk to a very low level, as in extreme senility or severe brain damage. In itself this kind of life seems to be neither good nor evil, but if suffering sets in one would hope for a speedy end.

This, admittedly inadequate, discussion of the sense in which life is normally a good, and of the reasons why it may not be so in some particular case, completes the account of what euthanasia is here taken to be. An act of euthanasia, whether literally act or rather omission, is attributed to an agent who opts for the death of another because in his case life seems to be an evil rather than a good. The question now to be asked is whether acts of euthanasia are ever justifiable. But there are two topics here rather than one. For it is one thing to say that some acts of euthanasia considered only in themselves and their results are morally unobjectionable, and another to say that it would be all right to legalize them. Perhaps the practice of euthanasia would allow too many abuses, and perhaps there would be too many mistakes. Moreover the practice might have very important and highly undesirable side-effects, because it is unlikely that we could change our principles about the treatment of the old and the ill without changing fundamental emotional attitudes and social relations. The topics must, therefore, be treated separately. In the next part of the discussion, nothing will be said about the social consequences and possible abuses of the practice of euthanasia, but only about acts of euthanasia considered in themselves.

What we want to know is whether acts of euthanasia, defined as we have defined them, are ever morally permissible. To be more accurate, we want to know whether it is ever sufficient justification of the choice of death for another that death can be counted a benefit rather than harm, and that this is why the choice is made.

It will be impossible to get a clear view of the area to which this topic belongs without first marking the distinct grounds on which objection may lie when one man opts for the death of another. There are two different virtues whose requirements are, in general, contrary to such actions. An unjustified act of killing, or allowing to die, is contrary to justice or to charity, or to both virtues, and the moral failings are distinct. Justice has to do with what men *owe* each other in the way of noninterference and positive service. When used in this wide sense, which has its history in the doctrine of the cardinal virtues, justice is not especially connected with, for instance, law courts but with the whole area of rights, and duties corresponding to rights. Thus murder is one form of injustice, dishonesty another, and wrongful failure to keep contracts a third; chicanery in a law court or defrauding someone of his inheritance are simply other cases of injustice. Justice as such is not directly linked to the good of another, and may require that something be rendered to him even where it will do him harm, as Hume pointed out when he remarked that a debt must be paid even to a profligate debauchee who "would rather receive harm than benefit from large possessions."[7] Charity, on the other hand, is the virtue which attaches us to the good of others. An act of charity is in question only where something is not demanded by justice, but a lack of charity and of justice can be shown where a man is denied something which he both needs and has a right to; both charity and justice demand that widows and orphans are not defrauded, and the man who cheats them is neither charitable nor just.

It is easy to see that the two grounds of objection to inducing death are distinct. A murder is an act of injustice. A culpable failure to come to the aid of someone whose life is threatened is normally contrary, not to justice, but to charity. But where one man is under contract, explicit or implicit, to come to the aid of another injustice too will be shown. Thus injustice may be involved either in an act or an omission, and the same is true of a lack of charity; charity may demand that someone be aided, but also that an unkind word not be spoken.

The distinction between charity and justice will turn out to be of the first importance when voluntary and nonvoluntary euthanasia are distinguished later on. This is because of the connection between justice and rights, and something should now be said about this. I believe it is true to say that wherever a man acts unjustly he has infringed a right, since justice has to do with whatever a man is owed, and whatever he is owed is his as a matter of right. Something should therefore be said about the different kinds of rights. The distinction commonly made is between having a right in the sense of having a liberty, and having a "claim-right" or "right of recipience."[8] The best way to understand such a distinction seems to be as follows. To say that a man has a right in the sense of a liberty is to say that no one can demand that he do not do the thing which he has a right to do. The fact that he has a right to do it consists in the fact that a certain kind of objection does not lie against his doing it. Thus a man has a right in this sense to walk down a public street or park his car in a public parking space. It does not follow that no one else may prevent him from doing so. If for some reason I want a certain man not to park in a certain place I may lawfully park there myself or get my friends to do so, thus preventing him from doing what he has a right (in the sense of a liberty) to do. It is different, however, with a claim-right. This is the kind of right which I have in addition to a liberty when, for example, I have a private parking space; now others have duties in the way of noninterference, as in this case, or of service, as in the case where my claim-right is to goods or services promised to me. Sometimes one of these rights gives other people the duty of securing to me that to which I have a right, but at other times their duty is merely to refrain from interference. If a fall of snow blocks my private parking space there is normally no obligation for anyone else to clear it away. Claim-rights generate duties; sometimes these duties are duties of noninterference; sometimes they are duties of service. If your right gives me the duty not to interfere with you I have "no right" to do it; similarly if your right gives me the duty to provide something for you I have "no right" to refuse to do it. What *I* lack is the right which is a liberty; I am not "at liberty" to interfere with you or to refuse the service.

Where in this picture does the right to life belong? No doubt people have the right to live in the sense of a liberty, but what is important is the cluster of claim-rights brought together under the title of the right to life. The chief of these is, of course, the right to be free from interferences that threaten life. If other people aim their guns at us or try to pour poison into our drink we can, to put it mildly, demand that they desist. And then there are the services we can claim from doctors, health officers, bodyguards, and firemen; the rights that depend on contract or public arrangement. Perhaps there is no particular point in saying that the duties these people owe us belong to the right to life; we might as well say that all the services owed to anyone by tailors, dressmakers, and couturiers belong to a right called the right to be elegant. But contracts such as those understood in the patient-doctor relationship come in in an important way when we are discussing the rights and wrongs of euthanasia, and are therefore mentioned here.

Do people have the right to what they need in order to survive, apart from the right conferred by special contracts into which other people have entered for the supplying of these necessities? Do people in the underdeveloped countries in which starvation is rife have the right to the food they so evidently lack? Joel Feinberg, discussing this question, suggests that they should be said to have "a claim," distinguishing this from a "valid claim," which gives a claim-right.

> The manifesto writers on the other side who seem to identify needs, or at least basic needs, with what they call "human rights," are more properly described, I think, as urging upon the world community the moral principle that *all* basic human needs ought to be recognized as *claims* (in the customary *prima facie* sense) worthy of sympathy and serious consideration right now, even though, in many cases, they cannot yet plausibly be treated as *valid* claims, that is, as grounds of any other people's duties. This way of talking avoids the anomaly of ascribing to all human beings now, even those in pre-industrial societies, such "economic and social rights" as "periodic holidays with pay."[9]

This seems reasonable, though we notice that there are some actual rights to service which are not based on anything like a contract, as for instance the right that children have to support from their parents and parents to support from their children in old age, though both sets of rights are to some extent dependent on existing social arrangements.

Let us now ask how the right to life affects the morality of acts of euthanasia. Are such acts sometimes or always ruled out by the right to life? This is certainly a possibility; for although an act of euthanasia is, by our definition, a matter of opting for death for the good of the one who is to die, there is, as we noted earlier, no simple connection between that to which a man has a right and that which is for his good. It is true that men have the right only to the kind of thing that is, in general, a good: we do not think that people have the right to garbage or polluted air. Nevertheless, a man may have the right to something which he himself would be better off without; where rights exist it is a man's will that counts not his or anyone else's estimate of benefit or harm. So the duties complementary to the right to life—the general duty of noninterference and the duty of service incurred by certain persons—are not affected by the quality of a man's life or by his prospects. Even if it is true that he would be, as we say, "better off dead," so long as he wants to live this does not justify us in killing him and may not justify us in deliberately allowing him to die. All of us have the duty of noninterference, and some of us may have the duty to sustain his life. Suppose, for example, that a retreating army has to leave behind wounded or exhausted soldiers in the wastes of an arid or snowbound land where the only prospect is death by starvation or at the hands of an enemy notoriously cruel. It has often been the practice to accord a merciful bullet to men in such desperate straits. But suppose that one of them demands that he should be left alive? It seems clear that his comrades have no right to kill him, though it is a quite different question as to whether they should give him a life-prolonging drug. The right to life can sometimes give a duty of positive service, but does not do so here. What it does give is the right to be left alone.

Interestingly enough we have arrived by way of a consideration of the right to life at the distinction normally labeled "active" versus "passive" euthanasia, and often thought to be irrelevant to the moral issue.[10] Once it is seen that the right to life is a distinct ground of objection to certain acts of euthanasia, and that this right creates a duty of noninterference more widespread than the duties of care there can be no doubt about the relevance of the distinction between passive and active euthanasia. Where everyone may have the duty to leave someone alone, it may be that no one has the duty to maintain his life, or that only some people do.

Where then do the boundaries of the "active" and "passive" lie? In some ways the words are themselves misleading, because they suggest the difference between act and omission which is not quite what we want. Certainly the act of shooting someone is the kind of thing we were talking about under the heading of "interference," and omitting to give him a drug a case of refusing care. But the act of turning off a respirator should surely be thought of as no different from the decision not to start it; if doctors had decided that a patient should be allowed to die, either course of action might follow, and both should be counted as passive rather than active euthanasia if euthanasia were in question. The point seems to be that interference in a course of treatment is not the same as other interference in a man's life, and particularly if the same body of people are responsible for the treatment and for its discontinuance. In such a case we could speak of the disconnecting of the apparatus as killing the man, or the hospital as allowing him to die. By and large, it is the act of killing that is ruled out under the heading of noninterference, but not in every case.

Doctors commonly recognize this distinction, and the grounds on which some philosophers have denied it seem untenable. James Rachels, for instance, believes that if the difference between active and passive is relevant anywhere, it should be relevant everywhere, and he has pointed to an example in which it seems to make no difference which is done. If someone saw a child drowning in a bath it would seem just as bad to let it drown as to push its head under water.[11] If "it makes no difference" means that one act would be as iniquitous as the other this is true. It is not that killing is *worse* than allowing to die, but that the two are contrary to distinct virtues, which gives the possibility that in some circumstances one is impermissible and the other permissible. In the circumstances invented by Rachels, both are wicked: it is contrary to justice to push the child's head under the water—something one has no right to do. To leave it to drown is not contrary to justice, but it is a particularly glaring example of lack of charity. Here it makes no practical difference because the requirements of justice and charity coincide; but in the case of the retreating army they did not: charity would have required that the wounded soldier be killed had not justice required that he be left alive.[12] In such a case it makes all the difference whether a man opts for the death of another in a positive action, or whether he allows him to die. An analogy with the right to property will make the point clear. If a man owns something he has the right to it even when its possession does him harm, and we normally have no right to take it from him. But if one day it should blow away, maybe nothing requires us to get it back for him; we could not deprive him of it, but we may allow it to go. This is not to deny that it will often be an unfriendly act or one based on an arrogant judgment when we refuse to do what he wants. Nevertheless, we would be within our rights, and it might be that no moral objection of any kind would lie against our refusal.

It is important to emphasize that a man's rights may stand between us and the action we would dearly like to take for his sake. They may, of course, also prevent action which we would like to take for the sake of others, as when it might be tempting to kill one man to save several. But it is interesting that the limits of allowable interference, however uncertain, seem stricter in the first case than the second. Perhaps there are no cases in which it would be all right to kill a man against his will *for his own sake* unless they could equally well be described as cases of allowing him to die, as in the example of turning off the respirator. However, there are circumstances, even if these are very rare, in which one man's life would justifiably be sacrificed to save others, and "killing" would be the only description of what was being done. For instance, a vehicle which had gone out of control might be steered from a path on which it would kill more than one man to a path on which it would kill one.[13] But it would not be permissible to steer a vehicle towards someone in order to kill him, against his will, for his own good. An analogy with property rights again illustrates the point. One may not destroy a man's property against his will on the grounds that he would be better off without it; there are however circumstances in which it could be destroyed for the sake of others. If his house is liable to fall and kill him that is his affair; it might, however, without injustice be destroyed to stop the spread of a fire.

We see then that the distinction between active and passive, important as it is elsewhere, has a special importance in the area of euthanasia. It should also be clear why James Rachels' other argument, that it is often "more humane" to kill than to allow to die, does not show that the distinction between active and passive euthanasia is morally irrelevant. It might be "more humane" in this sense to deprive a man of the property that brings evils on him, or to refuse to pay what is owed to Hume's profligate debauchee; but if we say this we must admit that an act which is "more humane" than its alternative may be morally objectionable because it infringes rights.

So far we have said very little about the right to service as opposed to the right to noninterference, though it was agreed that both might be brought under the heading of "the right to life." What about the duty to preserve life that may belong to special classes of persons such as bodyguards, firemen, or doctors? Unlike the general public they are not within their rights if they merely refrain from interfering and do not try to sustain life. The subject's claim-rights are two-fold as far as they are concerned and passive as well as active euthanasia may be ruled out here if it is against his will. This is not to say that he has the right to any and every service needed to save or prolong his life: the rights of other people set limits to what may be demanded, both because they have the right not to be interfered with and because they may have a competing right to services. Furthermore one must inquire just what the contract or implicit agreement amounts to in each case. Firemen and bodyguards presumably have a duty which is simply to preserve life, within the limits of justice to others and of reasonableness to themselves. With doctors it may however be different, since their duty relates not only to preserving life but also to the relief of suffering. It is not clear what a doctor's duties are to his patient if life can be prolonged only at the cost of suffering or suffering relieved only by measures that shorten life. George Fletcher has argued that what the doctor is under contract to do depends on what is generally done, because this is what a patient will reasonably expect.[14] This seems right. If procedures are part of normal medical practice then it seems that the patient can demand them however much it may be against his interest to do do. Once again it is not a matter of what is "most humane."

That the patient's right to life may set limits to permissible acts of euthanasia seems undeniable. If he does not want to die no one has the right to practice active euthanasia on him, and passive euthanasia may also be ruled out where he has a right to the services of doctors or others.

Perhaps few will deny what has so far been said about the impermissibility of acts of euthanasia, simply because we have so far spoken about the case of one who positively wants to live, and about his rights, whereas those who advocate euthanasia are usually thinking either about those who wish to die or about those whose wishes cannot be ascertained either because they cannot properly be said to have wishes or because, for one reason or another, we are unable to form a reliable estimate of what they are. The question that must now be asked is whether the latter type of case, where euthanasia though not *in*voluntary would again be *non*voluntary, is different from the one discussed so far. Would we have the right to kill someone for his own good so long as we had no idea that he positively wished to live? And what about the life-prolonging duties of doctors in the same circumstances? This is a very difficult problem. On the other hand, it seems ridiculous to suppose that a man's right to life is something which generates duties only where he has signaled that he wants to live; as a borrower does indeed have a duty to return something lent on indefinite loan only if the lender indicates that he wants it back. On the other hand, it might be argued that there is something illogical about the idea that a right has been infringed if someone incapable of saying whether he wants it or not is deprived of something that is doing him harm rather than good. Yet on the analogy of property we would say that a right has been infringed. Only if someone had earlier told us that in such circumstances he would not want to keep the thing could we think that his right had been waived. Perhaps if we could make confident judgments about what anyone in such circumstances would wish, or what he would have wished beforehand had he considered the matter, we could agree to consider the right to life as "dormant," needing to be asserted if the normal duties were to remain. But as things are we cannot make any such assumption; we simply do not know what most people would want, or would have wanted, us to do unless they tell us. This is certainly the case so far as active measures to end life are concerned. Possibly it is different, or will become different, in the matter of being kept alive, so general is the feeling against using sophisticated procedures on moribund patients, and so much is this dreaded by people who are old or terminally ill. Once again the distinction between active and passive euthanasia has come on the scene, but this time because most people's attitudes to the two are so different. It is just possible that we might presume, in the absence of specific evidence, that someone would not wish, beyond a certain point, to be kept alive; it is certainly not possible to assume that he would wish to be killed.

In the last paragraph we have begun to broach the topic of voluntary euthanasia, and this we must now discuss. What is to be said about the case in which there is no doubt about someone's wish to die: either he has told us beforehand that he would wish it in circumstances such as he is now in, and has shown no sign of a change of mind, or else he tells us now, being in possession of his faculties and of a steady mind. We should surely say that the objections previously urged against acts of euthanasia, which it must be remembered were all on the ground of rights, had disappeared. It does not seem that one would infringe someone's right to life in killing him with his permission and in fact at his request. Why should someone not be able to waive his right to life, or rather, as would be more likely to happen, to cancel some of the duties of noninterference that this right entails? (He is more likely to say that he should be killed by this man at this time in this manner, than to say that anyone may kill him at any time and in any way.) Similarly someone may give permission for the destruction of his property, and request it. The important thing is that he gives a critical permission, and it seems that this is enough to cancel the duty normally associated with the right. If someone gives you permission to destroy his property it can no longer be said that you have no right to do so, and I do not see why it should not be the same with taking a man's life. An objection might be made on the ground that only God has the right to take life, but in this paper religious as opposed to moral arguments are being left aside. Religion apart, there seems to be no case to be made out for an infringement of rights if a man who wishes to die is allowed to die or even killed. But of course it does not follow that there is no moral objection to it. Even with property, which is after all a relatively small matter, one might be wrong to destroy what one had the right to destroy. For, apart from its value to other people, it might be valuable to the man who wanted it destroyed, and charity might require us to hold our hand where justice did not.

Let us review the conclusion of this part of the argument, which has been about nonvoluntary and voluntary euthanasia and the right to life. It has been argued that from this side come stringent restrictions on the acts of euthanasia that could be morally permissible. Active nonvoluntary euthanasia is ruled out by that part of the right to life which creates the duty of noninterference though passive nonvoluntary euthanasia is not ruled out, except where the right to life-preserving action has been created by some special condition such as a contract between a man and his doctor. Voluntary euthanasia is another matter: as the preceding paragraph suggested, no right is infringed if a man is allowed to die or even killed at his own request.

Turning now to the other objection that normally holds against inducing the death of another, that it is against charity, or benevolence, we must tell a very different story. Charity is the virtue that gives attachment to the good of others, and because life is normally a good, charity normally demands that it should be saved or prolonged. But as we so defined an act of euthanasia that it seeks a man's death for his own sake—for his good—charity will normally speak in favor of it. This is not, of course, to say that charity can require an act of euthanasia which justice forbids, but if an act of euthanasia is not contrary to justice—that is, it does not infringe rights—charity will rather be in its favor than against.

Once more the distinction between nonvoluntary and voluntary euthanasia must be considered. Could it ever be compatible with charity to seek a man's death although he wanted to live, or at least had not let us know that he wanted to die? I have argued that in such circumstances active euthanasia would infringe his right to life, but passive euthanasia would not do so, unless he had some special right to life-preserving service from the one who allowed him to die. What would charity dictate? Obviously when a man wants to live there is a presumption that he will be benefited if his life is prolonged, and if it is so the question of euthanasia does not arise. But it is, on the other hand, possible that he wants to live where it would be better for him to die: perhaps he does not realize the desperate situation he is in, or perhaps he is afraid of dying. So, in spite of a very proper resistance to refusing to go along with a man's own wishes in the matter of life and death, someone might justifiably refuse to prolong the life even of someone who asked him to prolong it, as in the case of refusing to give the wounded soldier a drug that would keep him alive to meet a terrible end. And it is even more obvious that charity does not always dictate that life should be prolonged where a man's own wishes, hypothetical or actual, are not known.

So much for the relation of charity to nonvoluntary passive euthanasia, which was not, like nonvoluntary active euthanasia, ruled out by the right to life. Let us now ask what charity has to say about voluntary euthanasia both active and passive. It was suggested in the discussion of justice that if of sound mind and steady desire a man might give others the *right* to allow him to die or even to kill him, where otherwise this would be ruled out. But it was pointed out that this would not settle the question of whether the act was morally permissible, and it is this that we must now consider. Could not charity speak against what justice allowed? Indeed it might do so. For while the fact that a man wants to die suggests that his life is wretched, and while his rejection of life may itself tend to take the good out of the things he might have enjoyed, nevertheless his wish to die might here be opposed for his own sake just as it might be if suicide were in question. Perhaps there is hope that his mental condition will improve. Perhaps he is mistaken in thinking his disease incurable. Perhaps he wants to die for the sake of someone else on whom he feels he is a burden, and we are not ready to accept this sacrifice whether for ourselves or others. In such cases, and there will surely be many of them, it could not be for his own sake that we kill him or allow him to die, and therefore euthanasia as defined in this paper would not be in question. But this is not to deny that there could be acts of voluntary euthanasia both passive and active against which neither justice nor charity would speak.

We have now considered the morality of euthanasia both voluntary and nonvoluntary, and active and passive. The conclusion has been that nonvoluntary active euthanasia (roughly, killing a man against his will or without his consent) is never justified; that is to say, that a man's being killed for his own good never justifies the act unless he himself has consented to it. A man's rights are infringed by such an action, and it is therefore contrary to justice. However, all the other combinations, nonvoluntary passive euthanasia, voluntary active euthanasia, and voluntary passive euthanasia are sometimes compatible with both justice and charity. But the strong condition carried in the definition of euthanasia adopted in this paper must not be forgotten; an act of euthanasia as here understood is one whose purpose is to benefit the one who dies.

In the light of this discussion let us look at our present practices. Are they good or are they bad? And what changes might be made, thinking now not only of the morality of particular acts of euthanasia but also of the indirect effects of instituting different practices, of the abuses to which they might be subject and of the changes that might come about if euthanasia became a recognized part of the social scene.

The first thing to notice is that it is wrong to ask whether we should introduce the practice of euthanasia as if it were not something we already had. In fact we do have it. For instance it is common, where the medical prognosis is very bad, for doctors to recommend against measures to prolong life, and particularly where a process of degeneration producing one medical emergency after another has already set in. If these doctors are not certainly within their legal rights this is something that is apt to come as a surprise to them as to the general public. It is also obvious that euthanasia is often practiced where old people are concerned. If someone very old and soon to die is attacked by a disease that makes his life wretched, doctors do not always come in with life-prolonging drugs. Perhaps poor patients are more fortunate in this respect than rich patients, being more often left to die in peace; but it is in any case a well-recognized piece of medical practice, which is a form of euthanasia.

No doubt the case of infants with mental or physical defects will be suggested as another example of the practice of euthanasia as we already have it, since such infants are sometimes deliberately allowed to die. That they are deliberately allowed to die is certain; children with severe spina bifida malformations are not always operated on even where it is thought that without the operation they will die; and even in the case of children with Down's syndrome who have intestinal obstructions the relatively simple operation that would make it possible to feed them is sometimes not performed.[15] Whether this is euthanasia in our sense or only as the Nazis understood it is another matter. We must ask the crucial question, "Is it for the sake of the child himself that the doctors and parents choose his death?" In some cases the answer may really be yes, and what is more important it may really be true that the kind of life which is a good is not possible or likely for this child, and that there is little but suffering and frustration in store for him.[16] But this must presuppose that the medical prognosis is wretchedly bad, as it may be for some spina bifida children. With children who are born with Down's syndrome it is, however, quite different. Most of these are able to live on for quite a time in a reasonably contented way, remaining like children all their lives but capable of affectionate relationships and able to play games and perform simple tasks. The fact is, of course, that the doctors who recommend against life-saving procedures for handicapped infants are usually thinking not of them but rather of their parents and of other children in the family or of the "burden on society" if the children survive. So it is not for their sake but to avoid trouble to others that they are allowed to die. When brought out into the open this seems unacceptable: at least we do not easily accept the principle that adults who need special care should be counted too burdensome to be kept alive. It must in any case be insisted that if children with Down's syndrome are deliberately allowed to die this is not a matter of euthanasia except in Hitler's sense. And for our children, since we scruple to gas them, not even the manner of their death is "quiet and easy"; when not treated for an intestinal obstruction a baby simply starves to death. Perhaps some will take this as an argument for allowing active euthanasia, in which case they will be in the company of an S.S. man stationed in the Warthgenau who sent Eichmann a memorandum telling him that "Jews in the coming winter could no longer be fed" and submitting for his consideration a proposal as to whether "it would not be the most humane solution to kill those Jews who were incapable of work through some quicker means."[17] If we say we are *unable* to look after children with handicaps we are no more telling the truth than was the S.S. man who said that the Jews could not be fed.

Nevertheless if it is ever right to allow deformed children to die because life will be a misery to them, or not to take measures to prolong for a little the life of a newborn baby whose life cannot extend beyond a few months of intense medical intervention, there is a genuine problem about active as opposed to passive euthanasia. There are well-known cases in which the medical staff has looked on wretchedly while an infant died slowly from starvation and dehydration because they did not feel able to give a lethal injection. According to the principles discussed in the earlier part of this paper they would indeed have had no right to give it, since an infant cannot ask that it should be done. The only possible solution—supposing that voluntary active euthanasia were to be legalized—would be to appoint guardians to act on the infant's behalf. In a different climate of opinion this might not be dangerous, but at present, when people so readily assume that the life of a handicapped baby is of no value, one would be loath to support it.

Finally, on the subject of handicapped children, another word should be said about those with severe mental defects. For them too it might sometimes be right to say that one would wish for death for their sake. But not even severe mental handicap automatically brings a child within the scope even of a possible act of euthanasia. If the level of consciousness is low enough it could not be said that life is a good to them, any more than in the case of those suffering from extreme senility. Nevertheless if they do not suffer it will not be an act of euthanasia by which someone opts for their death. Perhaps charity does not demand that strenuous measures are taken to keep people in this state alive, but euthanasia does not come into the matter, any more than it does when someone is, like Karen Ann Quinlan, in a state of permanent coma. Much could be said about this last case. It might even be suggested that in the case of unconsciousness this "life" is not the life to which "the right to life" refers. But that is not our topic here.

What we must consider, even if only briefly, is the possibility that euthanasia, genuine euthanasia, and not contrary to the requirements of justice or charity, should be legalized over a wider area. Here we are up against the really serious problem of abuse. Many people want, and want very badly, to be rid of their elderly relatives and even of their ailing husbands or wives. Would any safeguards ever be able to stop them describing as euthanasia what was really for their own benefit? And would it be possible to prevent the occurrence of acts which were genuinely acts of euthanasia but morally impermissible because infringing the rights of a patient who wished to live, or whose wishes were unknown?

Perhaps the furthest we should go is to encourage patients to make their own contracts with a doctor by making it known whether they wish him to prolong their life in case of painful terminal illness or of incapacity. A document such as the Living Will seems eminently sensible, and should surely be allowed to give a doctor following the previously expressed wishes of the patient immunity from legal proceedings by relatives.[18] Legalizing active euthanasia is, however, another matter. Apart from the special repugnance doctors feel towards the idea of a lethal injection, it may be of the very greatest importance to keep a psychological barrier up against killing. Moreover it is active euthanasia which is the most liable to abuse. Hitler would not have been able to kill 275,000 people in his "euthanasia" program if he had had to wait for them to need life-saving treatment. But there are other objections to active euthanasia, even voluntary active euthanasia. In the first place it would be hard to devise procedures that would protect people from being persuaded into giving their consent. And secondly the possibility of active voluntary euthanasia might change the social scene in ways that would be very bad. As things are, people do, by and large, expect to be looked after if they are old or ill. This is one of the good things that we have, but we might lose it, and be much worse off without it. It might come to be expected that someone likely to need a lot of looking after should call for the doctor and demand his own death. Something comparable could be good in an extremely poverty-stricken community where the children genuinely suffered from lack of food; but in rich societies such as ours it would surely be a spiritual disaster. Such possibilities should make us very wary of supporting large measures of euthanasia, even where moral principle applied to the individual act does not rule it out.

NOTES

I would like to thank Derek Parfit and the editors of *Philosophy & Public Affairs* for their very helpful comments.

1. Leo Alexander, "Medical Science under Dictatorship," *New England Journal of Medicine*, 14 July 1949, 40.

2. For a discussion of culpable and nonculpable ignorance see Thomas Aquinas, *Summa Theologica*, First Part of the Second Part, Question 6, article 8, and Question 19, articles 5 and 6.

3. Dmitri Panin, *The Notebooks of Sologdin* (London, 1976), 66-7.

4. Thomas Nagel, "Death," in James Rachels, ed., *Moral Problems* (New York, 1971), 362.

5. Panin, *Sologdin*, 85.

6. Yet some detail needs to be filled in to explain why we should not say that a scarecrow is beneficial to the plants it protects. Perhaps what is beneficial must either be a feature of the plant itself, such as protective prickles, or else must work on the plant directly, such as a line of trees which give it shade.

7. David Hume, *Treatise*, Book III, Part II, Section 1.

8. See, for example, D. D. Raphael, "Human Rights Old and New," in D. D. Raphael, ed., *Political Theory and the Rights of Man* (London, 1967), and Joel Feinberg, "The Nature and Value of Rights," *The Journal of Value Inquiry* 4, no. 4 (Winter 1970), 243-57. Reprinted in Samuel Gorovitz, ed., *Moral Problems in Medicine* (Englewood Cliffs, N.J., 1976).

9. Feinberg, "Human Rights," *Moral Problems in Medicine*, 465.

10. See, for example, James Rachels, "Active and Passive Euthanasia," *New England Journal of Medicine*, 292, no. 2 (9 January 1975), 78-80. [Reprinted in the present volume, 1-6.]

11. *Ibid.*

[12] It is not, however, that justice and charity conflict. A man does not lack charity because he refrains from an act of injustice which would have been for someone's good.

[13] For a discussion of such questions, see my article "The Problem of Abortion and the Doctrine of Double Effect," *Oxford Review,* no. 5 (1967); reprinted in Rachels, *Moral Problems,* and Gorovitz, *Moral Problems in Medicine.*

[14] George Fletcher, "Legal Aspects of the Decision Not to Prolong Life," *Journal of the American Medical Association* 203, no. 1 (1 January 1968), 119-22. Reprinted in Gorovitz.

[15] I have been told this by a pediatrician in a well-known medical centre in the United States. It is confirmed by Anthony M. Shaw and Iris A. Shaw, "Dilemma of Informed Consent in Children," *New England Journal of Medicine* 289, no. 17 (25 October 1973), 885-90. Reprinted in Gorovitz.

[16] It must be remembered, however, that many of the social miseries of spina bifida children could be avoided. Professor R. B. Zachary is surely right to insist on this. See, for example, "Ethical and Social Aspects of Spina Bifida," *The Lancet,* 3 August 1968, 274-6. Reprinted in Gorovitz.

[17] Quoted by Hannah Arendt, *Eichmann in Jerusalem* (London, 1963), 90.

[18] Details of this document are to be found in J.A. Behnke and Sissela Bok, eds., *The Dilemmas of Euthanasia* (New York, 1975), and in A. B. Downing, ed., *Euthanasia and the Right to Life: The Case for Voluntary Euthanasia* (London, 1969).

Suicide and Gambling with Life

JONATHAN GLOVER

> *I'm sure most of us, confronted with the sight of a man walking towards the edge of a precipice, would rugger tackle him first and seek to dissuade him second. But how about the man who is patently drinking himself to death? How about the man who, faced with the statistics, still elects to smoke? Should we also legislate to tie them down, lock them away because of these life-threatening habits? And if we did, how long before we were passing further laws against those who lead too sedentary a life—for the same reason?*
>
> —Ian Martin: "Slow Motion Suicide,"
> *New Society*, October 1974

It was once common to think of a person who killed himself with strong moral disapproval. In England, suicide was illegal right up to 1961. The arguments for the traditional moral condemnation varied. Sometimes the appeal was simply to the sanctity of life, sometimes it was to the view that the right of life and death belongs, not to the person himself, but to God, or even the king or the state. Of these arguments, the only one to be touched on here is the assertion that a man must not usurp God's right to decide the time of his death. This one is interesting only because of the elegance of its decisive refutation by David Hume:

> Were the disposal of human life so much reserved as the peculiar province of the Almighty that it were an encroachment on his right, for men to dispose of their own lives; it would be equally criminal to act for the preservation of life as for its destruction. If I turn aside a stone which is falling upon my head, I disturb the course of nature, and I invade the peculiar province of the Almighty by lengthening out my life beyond the period which by the general laws of matter and motion he had assigned it.[1]

The view that suicide is morally wrong has been held so strongly that some have treated it as one of the purest cases of an obviously wrong kind of act. Wittgenstein said,

> If suicide is allowed then everything is allowed. If anything is not allowed then suicide is not allowed. This throws a light on the nature of

ethics, for suicide is, so to speak, the elementary sin. And when one inves-tigates it it is like investigating mercury vapour in order to comprehend the nature of vapours. Or is even suicide in itself neither good nor evil?[2]

But in the sixty years since these remarks were made, it has come to seem less obvious that suicide is wrong at all, even to people who are far from holding that everything is allowed.

The reaction against responding to suicide with horror and con-demnation has made widespread the view that the question is not in any way a moral one. Suicide is sometimes thought of as an irrational symptom of mental disturbance and so as a "medical" problem. On a different view, it is a matter for each person's free choice: other peo-ple should have nothing to say about it, and the question for someone contemplating it is simply one of whether his future life will be worth living. Against these views, it will be argued here that consideration of a possible act of suicide raises moral questions, for the person himself and for other people, of the same complexity as other acts of killing. (It does not, of course, follow from this that it would in some cases be a good thing to revert to traditional attitudes of disapproval towards those who have attempted suicide.) It will also be argued here that the moral case which justifies some acts of intervention to prevent a sui-cide has implications for social policy on a wider range of issues than is at first apparent.

I

THE VARIETY OF SUICIDAL AND NEAR-SUICIDAL ACTS

There are many different kinds of suicidal act. The act of someone whose life is fundamentally a happy one but who tries to kill himself in a state of severe but temporary depression differs from the act of someone who, after prolonged deliberation, decides to kill himself rather than face any more of his incurable illness. And the case is dif-ferent again when people kill themselves for reasons that we, even if not Durkheim, can call "altruistic," perhaps because they do not want to be a burden to others, or as a protest against some political or social evil, or as a gesture in support of some cause. Here distinguishable but related acts vary from voluntary acceptance of a martyr's death at the hands of others, to slow suicide by hunger strike, and public and dramatic suicide (such as that of Jan Palach in Czechoslovakia or some of the Buddhist suicides in Vietnam).

Apart from these, there is a whole range of acts on the border of suicide. Some of the most interesting work on the explanation of sui-cide is that of Professor Stengel and others suggesting that many apparent attempts at suicide may not have been intended to succeed.[3] Comparison of those "attempts" which end in death and those which do not shows some significant differences. More men than women make attempts ending in death, while more women than men make "attempts" which they survive. The peak age for fatal attempts is between fifty-five and sixty-four, while the peak age for non-fatal ones is between twenty-four and forty-four. Such discrepancies make it plausible to suggest that not all "attempts" are the result of an equally firm decision to die. Some may be a cry for help without any real intention to die. Others may be made in a state of mind where a gamble is taken with some risk of death and some chance of survival followed by help.

As well as the dramatic case of a suicide "attempt," there are other instances where people gamble with their lives. People in wars volunteer for high-risk missions, sometimes out of altruism or duty, but sometimes because they do not value their lives much, or even half want to die. The same may be true of some who take on dangerous jobs, such as soldier or war correspondent, or some of those who like dangerous sports. Then there are those who drink or smoke heavily, or who eat too much and exercise too little, all in the knowledge of the earlier death that will probably result.

In the cases mentioned, we would not count a course of action as even near-suicidal unless the risk of death was welcomed, or at least accepted with indifference. A member of a bomb-disposal squad may very much want to live, and do his work out of public spirit: it would be quite inappropriate to call him suicidal. And the same is true of heavy smokers who want a long life but who cannot escape their addiction.

But in all cases where people opt for the risk or certainty of their own death, whether or not with suicidal intent, it is possible to raise two moral questions. Ought they to risk their lives? Should other people intervene to prevent them? One reason for thinking that to raise the question of the morality of an act of suicide is inappropriate is the belief that an act of suicide must be done in such a state of disturbance that moral considerations stand no chance of influencing the decision. But thinking about the variety of suicidal and near-suicidal acts should cast doubt on this belief.

II

QUESTIONS FOR THE PERSON THINKING OF SUICIDE

Where someone contemplating suicide is sufficiently in control of himself to deliberate about his course of action, two factors are relevant to the decision. What would his own future life be like, and would it be worth living? What effect would his decision (either way) have on other people?

The difficulties in answering the question about one's own future life are obvious. If life is at present sufficiently bad to make a person think suicide may be in his own interest, he will need to have some idea of how likely or unlikely is any improvement in his state. This is often hard to predict (except in cases where the blight on his life is an absolutely incurable illness). Most of us are bad at giving enough weight to the chances of our lives changing for better or worse. And people sometimes contemplate suicide without exploring the possibility of less radical steps to deal with their problems. Someone who would normally not even consider such upheavals as leaving his family, changing his job, emigrating, or seeking psychiatric help, should not absolutely rule out any of them once he enters the region where killing himself is not ruled out either. And, since many of us are bad at predicting our own futures, it is worth talking to other people who may see the thing differently, whether friends or the Samaritans.

The other difficulty is deciding what sort of life is worth living. One test has to do with the amount of life for which you would rather be unconscious. Most of us prefer to be an anesthetized for a painful operation. If most of my life were to be on that level, I might opt for permanent anesthesia, or death. But complications arise. It may be that we prefer to be anesthetized for an operation only because we have plenty of other times to experience life without pain. It may be worth putting up with a greater degree of pain where the alternative is no life at all. And, even if we can decide about when we would rather be unconscious, the question whether a life is worth living cannot be decided simply by totting up periods of time to see if more than half our waking life is below zero in this way. Some brief periods of happiness may be of such intensity as to justify much longer periods of misery. (Equally, some brief periods of agony or despair may outweigh longer periods of mild cheerfulness.)

Our estimates of the quality of our lives are especially vulnerable to temporary changes of mood, so that the only reasonable way to reach a serious evaluation is to consider the question over a fairly long stretch of time. Even this has limitations, because of the difficulty of giving the right weight to estimates made at different times and in different moods, but anything less is hopelessly inadequate.

The other question to be answered is about the effects on other people of a decision for or against the suicide. No doubt there are some people whose lives are so desperately bad that their own interests should come before any loss to other people. But sometimes an act of suicide can shatter the lives of others (perhaps parents) to a degree the person might never have suspected. Suicide cannot be seen to be the right thing to do without the most careful thought about the effects on all those emotionally involved. There is also the question of the loss of any general contribution the person might make to society.

To kill oneself can sometimes be the right thing to do, but much less often than may at first sight appear. (Evidence of a reasonably respectable kind could come from studies of the later lives of those whose "attempts" fail and of the lives of families after one member kills himself.) To suggest that some acts of suicide may be morally wrong is not to advocate that those who make failed "attempts" ought to be responded to with condemnation or reproach: it is obvious that the last thing that is helpful is any pressure of this kind.

It is interesting that the case against suicide is also a case against gambling with one's life. There are familiar stories of the wives of racing-car drivers pleading with their husbands to retire. This kind of thing is not just a marginal feature of dangerous jobs or sports, but something which ought to be considered very seriously before starting on them.

III

INTERVENTION: THE PROBLEMS

The moral question for the person contemplating suicide is simply whether his being dead would be a better state of affairs for himself and others or a worse one. ("Simply" does not imply that this question is easy.) But for other people contemplating intervention to prevent a suicide, the matter is more complicated. They have to ask the same question about whether the death would on the whole be a good or a bad thing. But, if they decide it would be a bad thing, they also must ask the further question, whether it would be right for them to intervene. This will seem not to be a separate question only to someone who thinks that we are always entitled to interfere in other people's lives where they would otherwise do something wrong.

The question of intervention can take various forms. Are we entitled to use our powers of persuasion in an attempt to stop someone killing himself? If our persuasion fails, or we have no opportunity to use it, may we then use coercion? If we can use some coercion, how far may we go? (This problem is clearly illustrated by the use of forcible feeding on people killing themselves by hunger strike.) If someone arrives in hospital after a suicide attempt, should doctors make efforts to revive him?

These questions are related to others not involving suicide: to what extent ought there to be persuasion, social pressure or legislation of a paternalist kind, to try to stop people risking their lives? These questions arise about matters such as seat belts in cars, drugs, smoking, obesity, dangerous sports or safety standards in houses.

IV

INTERVENTION: A POLICY

Apart from consideration of side-effects, the guiding principles to be applied are two. It is desirable where possible to save a worthwhile life. It is desirable where possible to respect a person's autonomy. The prevention of suicide is obviously a place where these two principles will sometimes conflict, and I have no general formula for deciding priorities. The policy to be suggested here is that there should be an attempt to save the maximum number of worthwhile lives compatible with using paternalist restrictions of autonomy only temporarily in the case of sane adults. Some people may accept the same general principles, but strike a different balance between them where they conflict.

Where we think someone bent on suicide has a life worth living, it is always legitimate to reason with him and to try to persuade him to stand back and think again. There is no case against reasoning, as it in no way encroaches on the person's autonomy. There is a strong case in its favor, as where it succeeds it will prevent the loss of a worthwhile life. (If the person's life turns out not to be worthwhile, he can always change his mind again.) And if persuasion fails, the outcome is no worse than it would otherwise have been.

Where someone has decided that his life is not worth living and is not deflected from his decision for suicide by persuasion, it is legitimate to restrain him by force from his first attempt, or even several attempts. (I do not attempt to draw any precise boundary here.) This legitimacy depends on our belief that his life will be worth living: those of us who do not believe in the sanctity of life will not agree to overriding someone's autonomy in order to make him endure a life not worth living. And we ought to limit severely the number of times we use force to frustrate a person's decision to kill himself, because a persistent policy of forcible prevention is a total denial of his autonomy in the matter. If we prevent him once or a few times this gives him a chance to reconsider, and the decision later is still his own. Even those who do not set any independent value on autonomy may feel in the case of a rational person that his persistent suicide attempts cast doubt on their own judgment that his life is worth living.

The endorsement of limited coercion given here does not extend to the forcible feeding of those on hunger strike. Someone set on a slow death of this kind has plenty of time to reconsider the decision, and so the justification of temporary intervention does not apply. In addition, much stronger justification would be needed for imposing the pain and humiliation that normally accompany forcible feeding than for the relatively harmless methods of frustrating a normal suicide attempt.

The question of forcible prevention is easier to answer in the case of a rational person calmly deciding that his life is not worth living than it is in the case of someone prone to bouts of suicidal depression. In the case of the rational person we intervene to give him a chance to think again, but should ultimately respect his decision. But should we equally respect the decision for suicide taken in a temporary but recurring mood of despair?

There is no difficulty in justifying intervention in the case of someone in a suicidal mood for the only time in his life. He is given time to think again, and he never again decides to kill himself. His life has been saved at minimal cost to his autonomy. But what are we to say of someone whose emotional life is a constant series of ups and downs, who alternates between very much wanting to go on living and moods of suicidal depression? If we treat him on a par with the person who calmly and rationally contemplates suicide, we will, after frustrating a few attempts, allow him to go ahead. But the rightness of this seems much more doubtful where moods of temporary depression are involved.

This is partly because a sustained and reflective preference for suicide seems much better evidence that a person's life is not worth living than are frequent changes of mind about it. And it is also because overriding a decision that is the product of a passing mood is less disrespectful of autonomy than overriding a preference that plays a stable role in a person's outlook. Where someone fluctuates between optimism and pessimism about his life, there may be no neutral vantage point from which he can take a "rational" decision. In such a case, he does not fully possess the desire either to live or to die, in the dispositional sense of "possess" that is relevant to the autonomy principle. It is hard to see in such a case that we can decide about intervention on any basis other than our views about the likely quality of his future life, together with any side effects we think relevant. (If we are unable to judge whether his future life is likely on balance to be worth living, we may allow the scale to be tipped by the effects of his suicide on his family.)

Some decisions about intervention have to be taken largely in ignorance of the state of mind and reasons behind the person's decision to kill himself. A mere passer-by may be in a position to intervene, or, more often, a doctor in a hospital may be in a position to revive someone after an attempt. In all such cases, the intervention is justified. This is for the same reason that intervention is justified in any first attempt. There is the chance of saving a worthwhile life at the cost of only a temporary interference with autonomy: there is a very strong chance that someone calmly determined to kill himself will have other opportunities.

V

PATERNALISM AND GAMBLING WITH LIFE

To what extent is intervention justified when someone places his own life at risk? When ought we to try to persuade people not to run risks or even compel them by law not to do so? These questions again do not have simple answers. We need to take into account the benefits that may result from running the risks, the degree of risk involved and the drawbacks of the different kinds of intervention. Whether or not persuasion should be used may also vary in individual cases according to the likely side-effects of a death. If someone volunteers for a highly useful but dangerous job, such as bomb-disposal, it may not be right to try to argue him out of this. But the position changes if he has a large family and there are plenty of bachelor volunteers. (The arguments for intervention are not all paternalist ones.)

As the benefits from a risky course of action decrease and the risk increases, so the case for trying to persuade someone to change his mind increases. And there comes a point where the risks are so disproportionate to the benefits that, if persuasion is unsuccessful, there is justification for stronger pressure, and perhaps legislation. So much injury and loss of life results from the failure to wear seat belts in cars that it is right for the law to make wearing them compulsory. Those who resist this proposed legislation use arguments appealing to people's freedom from paternalist interference and say that persuasion is better than compulsion. So it is, but freedom from such a trivial piece of compulsion is purchased at too great a cost in lives and happiness.

We rightly value having a large area of our lives free from fussy state interference. And for the state to intervene to prevent us taking any risk to life, however small, would involve an officious paternalism which nearly everyone would find not worthwhile. But when the risks increase, the objections should diminish. Against this, we have to set the benefits for which the risks are run. Having to spend a moment putting on a seat belt is an extremely trivial disadvantage to weigh against avoiding a high risk. But having to give up an activity like mountaineering might be a large sacrifice for those who like it, and so a much larger degree of risk would be necessary to justify banning it.

I do not know where the boundaries of legislation should be. A great deal of investigation and argument is needed. But is is at least fairly clear that our intuitive responses to this question probably need to be revised. Social traditions grow up in which some things are thought of as outside the scope of legislation simply because they have never been legally controlled. We are used to paternalist laws making motorcyclists wear crash helmets, but the idea of laws forbidding people to smoke cigarettes shocks us as an infringement of traditional liberties. Yet our location of smoking within the realm of individual free decisions is a tradition that grew up before we knew the facts about its effects. A rational social policy would be concerned with striking a balance between minimizing risks and minimizing the kinds of restrictions that frustrate people in things that really matter to them. It is not at all clear that our traditional frontiers of legislation achieve this.

The argument here is that reasons for preventing suicides are also reasons for social policies of risk reduction, if necessary by legislation. To some it may appear odd that I have argued in favor of legislation to prevent people taking certain risks with their lives, but have not argued for the re-introduction of legislation against suicide. The reason for this is that suicide is a special case. Legislation seems, hardly surprisingly, to be of little use in reducing the suicide rate, and its main effect was to impose an additional ordeal on those who survived their suicide attempts. There is also the thought that some suicide decisions are quite rational, being taken by people with a very clear assessment of their future lives, so that interference is unjustified. And the appeal to autonomy has much more force where the person's decision is of such importance to him than it has when it concerns a person's decision not to bother to put on his seat belt. There is nothing to be said for a substantial erosion of autonomy that is also ineffective. There is a lot to be said for saving many people who want to live, but who, for trivial advantages, thoughtlessly gamble with their lives.

NOTES

[1] David Hume, "Of Suicide," in his *Essays*.
[2] Ludwig Wittgenstein, *Notebooks*, 1914-16, concluding paragraphs.
[3] Erwin Stengel, *Suicide and Attempted Suicide* (Harmondsworth, 1964).

Suicide and False Desires

ROBERT M. MARTIN

Is killing himself ever one's real aim? We can't deny that (at least) most people want to go on living. But it is sometimes claimed that all, or at least many, who seem bent on killing themselves do not *really* want to die—that death is not *really* in their interests. These claims are often part of an attempt to justify the policy of forceful intervention to prevent suicide, on the grounds that this would be doing people the favor of saving them from the death they don't really want.

Two parts of this argument are questionable: the claim that suicide is always or usually a *false desire* in some sense; and the implied premise that we are justified in interfering when someone is acting against his true interests or desires. I think there are *certain* cases when we might be justified in interfering in some mild ways when someone is about to act against his real interests or desires, though I won't go into the difficult question of exactly when this sort of paternalistic intervention is permissible. I shall argue that claims that suicide is always or usually a false desire are unfounded, and that we are not justified in interfering in even those cases in which the desire for death is a false one.

One sort of argument for intervention on the grounds that suicide isn't really desired is based on the claim that suicidal people are always or usually mentally ill, or at least pathologically disturbed or irrational. One does not want to make these claims trivial because they are definitionally true, by defining irrationality or mental illness to include suicidal desires or behaviors; for this argument to be any good, there have to be independent grounds for these claims. Professional opinion varies here. Some argue that being suicidal is not a symptom of mental illness at all.[1] Others want to distinguish people who are irrationally suicidal from those whose suicidal impulses spring from a "realistic assessment of life situations."[2] Still others claim that rational suicide is an extreme rarity, and that most suicidal individuals "are suffering from clinically recognizable psychiatric illnesses."[3] The debate is a complicated one, often involving questionable psychological theories, assertions about matters of fact one wishes were supported by more empirical observation, and the interesting problem that notions like *health* and *rationality* and their opposites skip around among descriptive, theoretical, and rather arbitrarily evaluative uses. Going further into these questions is beyond the scope of this paper, but I'll note the following: It is the suicidal desires of the *sane* I'm interested in here, and almost everyone admits that it's possible for sane people to have these desires. Nevertheless, it's not at all obvious that mentally ill or irrational people ought, in general, to be prevented from acting on their desires, or that they should be paternalistically forced to act in accord with what we think their desires ought to be. Furthermore, even if there *are* occasions when ill or irrational people ought, for their own good, to be prevented from doing what they think they want to, there are special considerations (which I'll raise later) which make it inappropriate to treat suicidal desires in particular this way.

An argument for intervention in suicide of the sane is based on the claim that suicides are always (or often) ambivalent, and thus don't really want death:

> Individuals who are intent on killing themselves still wish very much to be rescued or to have their deaths prevented. Suicide prevention consists essentially in recognizing that the potential victim is "in balance" between his wishes to live and his wishes to die, then throwing one's efforts on the side of life.[4]

It is not clear why this author speaks of the contrary wishes of the suicidal individual as "in balance" while assuming that he is about to kill himself; one would imagine that the individual about to act this way has desires to die that have *outweighed* the contrary ones (especially if he is "*intent*" on killing himself). Perhaps what is really meant here is that suicides are "ambivalent" in the sense that although on balance they wish to die, still strong residual doubts and contrary feelings remain. But why is this supposed to justify intervention? We all continue to harbor doubts whenever we make up our minds about any difficult choice; but this hardly means that we don't *really* want to do what we've decided, or that someone else is then justified in stopping us.

There are, however, four legitimate senses in which we may be said to have false desires—to think we want what we really don't, or to desire something that's not really in our interests:

> *Sense 1:* Someone sincerely says she wants to become famous; after she does succeed at this, however, she discovers that fame doesn't have the charms she thought it would, and has its own agonies. She says, "I thought I wanted to be famous, but I really didn't." This is a case of incomplete or mistaken information about the object desired.
>
> *Sense 2:* Someone believes falsely that a tidal wave will flood his home town. He sells his house at a great loss, and quits his good job. Although he understood fully the nature and implications of his desired actions (selling and quitting), he discovers that those actions were not what he really wanted to do—that they were not really in his interests—when he finds out that there will be no tidal wave. Here there is false or incomplete information about circumstances.

Sense 3: Someone thinks that the only way to get good grades at school is to bribe her instructors, but later finds out that a bit of studying instead would have resulted in better grades at less cost. Her wanting to bribe her instructors wasn't in accord with her real interests because of false or incomplete information about alternatives.

Sense 4: Someone has a bad day at the office, and suddenly and uncharacteristically decides the business world is not for him. Later he regrets having thrown his career away; he feels that his earlier dissatisfaction, while it was real enough at the time, was false in the sense that it was fleeting and not representative of his enduring personality.

Now, desire to kill oneself may be false desire in any of these four senses. Someone may want to kill himself because (*sense 1*) he falsely believes he will go to a land of everlasting bliss after death; or because (*sense 2*) he falsely believes he is suffering from a terminal and debilitating disease; or because (*sense 3*) he isn't aware that there are forms of therapy which can cure his growing depressions; or because (*sense 4*) he feels a serious but atypical and fleeting suicidal urge. We can say of all these people that they don't *really* want to die, or that death is not congruent with their *real* values or interests.

Clearly, there have been suicides because of false desires like these, though I wouldn't want to guess what proportion of suicidal desires are false. George Murphy claims that the percentage of suicidal desires that are false in *sense 4* is large:

> We can confidently predict recovery from [the suicidal] urge in the great majority of cases, when other symptoms of depression lift. The desire to terminate one's life is usually transient. The "right" to suicide is a "right" desired only temporarily.[5]

Louise Horowitz, in an article which otherwise strongly opposes interference with suicide, argues that

> one can distinguish between suicides which are appropriate and those which are the result of misinterpretations or failures to see the alternative courses of action. . . . We . . . have the right in the interest of rationality to point out alternative courses of action which we believe [the suicidal person] may have overlooked. But the individual contemplating suicide is not obliged to defend his decision, only to discuss it in order to avoid making a mistake.[6]

It seems to me that it is *sometimes* appropriate to interfere with the carrying out of false nonsuicide desires in the mild ways Horowitz indicates, especially when the person involved is a friend, has asked our advice, and the like. But I shall argue that intervention is *never* appropriate when the false desire is for suicide, because suicide desires are importantly different from others.

When (if ever) do we feel justified in intervening to prevent someone's actions? I should think that the justification for this could be that what the person was about to do was not *for his own good* (I ignore the other valid reason: when others would be harmed). Now, something is incompatible with the agent's own good when it conflicts either with his current interests and desires or when it will conflict with future interests and desires. The examples of nonsuicidal false desire, previously mentioned, are cases in which a current desire has consequences that will conflict with the agent's future interests and desires. (I am assuming here that something counts as harm for an individual only if it or its consequences conflict with some value or desire of that individual himself.) Intervention is (perhaps sometimes) justified, because it would spare the agent future grief.

But suppose that someone never is in position to suffer conflict with his real desires as a result of acting on false desires. Suppose, for example, that the woman who wanted to be famous (*case 1*, above) had felt satisfied with her life as she worked toward fame, but died before she became famous enough to find out that it was not what she thought it would be. What justification would there have been for preventing her from acting on her false desire? None, because she never did suffer conflict with her real values and desires as a result of her actions. Had she lived, she would have regretted her efforts to become famous; but her life, as actually lived, was satisfying to her and congruent with all her felt wishes and values.

Now let us examine the false desire for suicide. Suicide results in death, of course, and we normally count death as a harm. But we do because we value our life. However, if someone wants to die, death does not count as a harm *for him*. But what if the desire for death is a false desire? When we intervene in what would otherwise be a successful suicide, we *never* save the agent from a future state incompatible with any of his desires or values, from any grief or regret as a consequence of his actions. The man who believes that death will bring him to paradise will not be disappointed—not because he will go to paradise, but because there won't be any *him* left after his death to be disappointed. The person who kills himself because of the false belief that he has a terminal disease won't regret his decision. The man who killed himself unaware that therapy could have helped his depression won't be worse off than had we intervened, because after his death he won't be *any* way; and because before death he desired death and got it. And the man who had the fleeting desire for death won't suffer when he returns to more stable and characteristic contrary desires, because he won't return.

The point here is that suicide is the act of putting one's self out of existence—an obvious point, but one that seems to have been widely ignored in the discussion of the subject. We can't then make the usual sorts of judgment about acts and their consequences for the agent, because death is the only consequence for him, and after that there is no more agent. A false desire for death is, after all, a desire for death; suicide achieves that desire, and the agent does not live to suffer the normal consequences of acting on false desires.

It is this argument I referred to above when talking about insane or irrational suicidal desires. They are *desires*, after all, and thus have a *prima facie* claim for satisfaction: and if no agent will suffer bad consequences, why is it benevolent to interfere?

For these reasons I think that although false desires may sometimes justify intervention, in the case of suicide they never do. I do think, but for reasons I shall not argue here, that considerations related to our duties to others may show suicide to be sometimes immoral, and when these duties are so strong as to override an agent's valid claim to do what he wants to do, we are justified in interfering in suicide. But when such considerations are not relevant (and I think occasions when they are relevant are rare), we must not interfere in suicide.

NOTES

The author expresses his gratitude to his colleague, Dr. Susan Sherwin, and to the editors of *Suicide: The Philosophical Issues*, for helpful suggestions on preliminary drafts of this article.

[1] Thomas S. Szasz, "The Ethics of Suicide," in M. P. Mattin and D. J. Mayo, eds., *Suicide: The Philsophical Issues* (New York, 1980).

[2] Jerome A. Motto, "The Right to Suicide: A Psychiatrist's View," in *Suicide: The Philosophical Issues*.

[3] George E. Murphy, "Suicide and the Right to Die," *American Journal of Psychiatry*, 130, no. 4 (April 1973), editorial, 472.

[4] Edwin S. Shneidman, "Preventing Suicide," *American Journal of Nursing* 65, no. 5 (1965), 10.

[5] Murphy, "Suicide and the Right to Die," 472.

[6] Louise Horowitz, "The Morality of Suicide," *Journal of Critical Analysis* III, no. 4 (January 1972), 164-5.

II

WAR

In Defense of War

WILLIAM EARLE

A philosophical consideration of political affairs has the disadvantage of being incapable, in and of itself, of implying any specific practical action or policy. It would, then, seem useless except for the accompanying reflection that specific policy undertaken without any attention to principles, is mindless; and mindless action can have no expectation either of practical effect or of intellectual defense. No doubt the relation of principles to action is complex indeed; but at least it can be said that practical principles without reference to possible action are vacuous, and action which can not be clarified by principle is aimless commotion. Principled action offers us then the best that can be hoped for. That, however, is the work not of philosophy but of statesmanship, a faculty which is as theoretically clear as it need be but also skilled by experience in reading the existing political scene. Accordingly my present remarks aim only at some principles involved in the understanding of war, focussing on those which seem conspicuously absent in contemporary discussion, and not at defending any specific judgments about the current war. Examples of incoherent principles will be drawn from present discussions; but any other war might have served equally well. No judgment about the present war can be derived from these remarks on principles; and if most of the false principles are quoted from the antiwar side, it is only because that side has been more vocal.

The villain of the present essay is *pacifism*, by which I mean a principled opposition to all war. Since it is a principled opposition, any appropriate opposition to pacifism must itself be a matter of principles. That pacifism is a principle and not a specific opposition to this war is sufficiently indicated by the suffix "ism," as well as by the arguments it mounts to make its principle plausible: it is war itself which is evil, and peace itself good under no matter what terms. Pacifism thinks it is sufficient to declare these ideals to win all hearts and minds; and if to some these pacifist principles seem impractical or indeed immoral, that can only be because the unconverted are hard of heart, slow of comprehension, or the world itself not yet ready for such a glory. That pacifism itself is practically absurd and morally deplorable is the chief burden of these present remarks. The argument will be by way of excavating the presuppositions and tracing the consequences of pacifism, and exhibiting them to the reader for his free choice. That pacifism itself is evil does *not*, needless to say, imply that the *persons* who hold that view are evil; a radical distinction between the character of persons and the character of their articulated views is the very basis of this or any other civilized discussion. If human beings could not be decent while their views are absurd, then all of us would fall into the abyss.

In any event, the first casualty of the present war seems to have been philosophy itself. The transition was easy: from an opposition to the war on whatever ground, a portion of the public mind rose to what it thought was the proper principle of that opposition: pacifism, the sentiment that war was itself evil. And its arguments proceeded down from that height. Flattering itself for its "idealism," it could only survey the home reality it had left with high indignation: *we were killing!* Children were trotted forth on TV to ask: why must men kill one another? Can we not all love one another, the child asks, having immediately forgotten his fight with his brother off-screen. Having been illuminated by the purity and innocence of children, the new pacifist can but flagellate himself in public remorse. Not merely must this war be stopped at once, but all war and forever; we must recompense our enemies for the damage wrought upon them; we must ask their forgiveness, for are they not really our friends and our friends our enemies? and as the confusion multiplies and moral passion inflames itself, nothing appears as too severe a punishment for ourselves; impeachment of our leaders and finally the impeachment of ourselves and our history seem too gentle. These public outbursts of moral self-hatred are, of course, not unknown in history; let Savonarola stand for them all. Today the uproar is orchestrated by retired baby-doctors, neurotic poets and novelists, psychoanalysts, ministers and confused philosophers, each of whom, armed with the authority of his special "insight," seeks to speak for suffering humanity. The message to be read through the tear-stained faces is the same: we must stop killing! Regardless of how one reads the present war, what is *said* publicly for or most usually against it, presents something like the eclipse of political thought. And with the eclipse of thought, we are left with some of the most preposterous slogans ever to find utterance. When supported by high passion, parades and demonstrations, insults in loud voices, we find ourselves once again in the theater of the absurd.

I

WHY WAR?

Why indeed, asks the child? Why can not everyone love one another? Settle all disputes "rationally," so that all men could live as brothers, already having forgotten the first brothers, Cain and Abel? Thrashing around for "explanations" of the horrid fact that men can indeed be hostile to one another, the sloganeer with a smattering of pop-culture finds some answers ready to hand. War has a biological origin; it arises from an excess of testosterone in the male; maybe there is a biological solution, something like castration? That Indira Gandhi and Golda Meir have conducted their wars very successfully, is already forgotten. Or maybe they are men in disguise? Or the impulse to fight arises from some distorted family history, a son conditioned by a father who in turn was conditioned by his father to conceive war as particularly masculine, an expression of *machismo*; but that could be remedied by "treatment." Perhaps drugs, suggested a recent president of the American Psychological Society. Or perhaps war arises from selfishness, a moral flaw which could be remedied by a turn of the heart, that hoped for by a Quaker who during World War II looked Hitler straight in the eye and said: Thou art an evil man! If there is a warlike "instinct," maybe it could be diverted into harmless games like chess or the Olympics. And then maybe there is no such instinct? Animals like the gazelle or lamb may be found which are not particularly aggressive; why not take them for our ideal? Or, if not an animal "instinct," then surely it is generated by the capitalist society, which as everyone knows, fosters aggression, competition, acquisitiveness, imperialism. But then even the most casual glance sees that communist societies are even more imperialist and aggressive than the capitalist. And does not the stock market fall with each new bombing? Or, finally, it is all caused by presidents, who wish to be mentioned in the history books, or be reelected by the Veterans of Foreign Wars. The presidency should, accordingly, be abolished; policy should be turned over to the people. But which people? Those people who have been treated, have had a change of heart, who take flowers and gentle animals for their ideal, in a word, the saving remnant who through their dictatorship, will save the world from every war except that against themselves.

The generating assumption of this system of explanations is of course that there can be no *moral justification* for war at all. It is simply an evil; and since man is "naturally good," one must look for a "cause" of his distorted conduct. If war were morally justifiable, then that justification would remove any occasion for looking for pathological explanations. If one does not seek for "causes" for a man doing good works other than the goodness of the work itself, neither need one seek biological, psychological, cultural, sociopolitical causes for a justifiable war. The justification *is* the cause in this case.

And so then the question, why war? would be answered if any moral justification for it were forthcoming. A "justifiable war"? Is that not a contradiction in terms, or is it the pacifist who represents a living contradiction in terms?

This first answer to the question, why war, assumes at the start that it *is* evil, assumes that men are or could be "naturally good," meaning "peaceful," but since in point of fact they are not, the "explanation" is to be found in an artificial distortion of their passionate nature. The elimination of war will result from a correction of that passionate nature, through treatment whether physiological, psychological, social or rhetorical. In a word, either their bodies or their characters must be changed by whatever treatment promises success. The lion will lie down with the lamb, indeed will be indistinguishable from him. He will abandon pride, greed, egotism, the desire to display power, to intimidate, to coerce; he will at the end of history at last be good. But, of course, absolutely *all* men must be good; for if even a few are left who do *not* so envisage the good, our "good" men will be, of course, good-for-nothing, and their peace will be the peace determined by the wicked. Unwilling to fight for their lives or ideals, they are suppressed and at that point the whole of human history recommences as if there had been no interlude, or at best an interlude within common sense. The lamb who lies down with the lion may indeed be good for the lion when his appetites return; and if he is good in any other sense, it could only be on a mystic plane not exactly pertinent to the practical moral plane of existence. It is not surprising then that advocates in the church of the kingdom of heaven, do indeed place it in heaven, but never advocate it as political policy. After all, by definition, heaven has already expelled or refused admittance to the wicked, hence is hardly faced with problems commensurate with ours on earth. What does a lion *eat* in heaven? Men, needless to say, are not animals *simpliciter*, but rational or spirited animals; but neither reasons nor spirit so long as they remain living can *contradict* animal needs.

That rational animals engage in hostilities unto death has always seemed a scandal to those philosophers who neglect existence. If one stamp of moralist finds both the cause and solution to war in some alteration in body or character, many philosophers of abstractions find both the cause and solution to war in *thought* to be corrected by right reasoning. If rational men still fight, and if war is irrational, then there must be a rational solution to it. The medium of reason is the word, so we can expect this stamp of pacifist to praise the verbal solution to hostilities: the treaty. Would it not be reasonable to prevent or terminate hostilities by calculation, agreements, and solemnly pledged words? It is easy to forgive philosophers and the educated in general for their touching confidence in the power of words; they exercise a magical power in and over the mind; but perhaps that is their proper place. However, it is an outrageous neglect to fancy that they have any power except that over the mind, mind moreover which itself has the *obligation* to superintend the very existential conditions of its own life. Who then is surprised when he reads that in the last 350 years, something like 85 percent of the treaties signed in the Western world have been broken? But the treaty theory of peace can then congratulate itself on the fact that now a culprit can be identified, declared to be an aggressor, and, while the aggressor is condemned by the "enlightened goodwill of mankind," he nevertheless proceeds to enjoy his dinner, and later may be celebrated as a benefactor of mankind; he will certainly not hesitate to sign new treaties. Our question is what to do: wring one's hands over men's irrationality or rethink the meaning of war? In all of this, one can easily agree that treaties exercise some slight restraining power over the more rapacious inclinations; but would it not be criminal neglect to entrust the security of one's country to treaties? And in fact, does any responsible leader ever do it? No doubt, the lambs, since they have nothing better to work with.

And eventually, as the final rational "solution" to the problem of war, there is the idea of a single superstate, whether an enlargement of one of those now extant, such as the USA, Russia or China—or conceived as a super United Nations. This convulsive, "final solution" to the war problem particularly appeals to those who have little "negative capability" as Keats put it, little tolerance for the uncertain, for risk, for in fact the most fundamental characteristics of free human life. When put in the form of a super United Nations, it almost looks harmless. But it can more properly be put in uglier terms; if it were indeed to be a Super State, it could be nothing short of a Super Totalitarianism. The historical totalitarianisms we have all witnessed would be as nothing compared with this monstrosity; and, as has often been remarked, they grew in precisely the same spiritual soil, a certain inability to face risk, death, war or confusion, in a word, the existential conditions of a free life with dignity. Everything must be put *in order!* And if the World is not now in order and never has been, then the order will be imposed, imposed in fact by the very Force which once seemed so odious. A new order of the World; but now *its* dissidents become World-enemies and where are they to flee? Do they have a right to life itself? Are they not enemies of the World? In this abstract fantasia, the first thing lost sight of is a small annoying matter, a point of logic: any Order is also only itself a *specific* order. Law and Order, of course, are only universal abstractions, whose proper medium of existence is the word. In existence itself, it is always this or that order, that is, *somebody's* order; and then there is always a somebody else, who believes honestly in another order, one perhaps more favorable to himself or his ideal. Again the eternal hostilities break out, now however with a difference: hostilities between nations have not been eliminated, but only redubbed: each is now a *civil* war within the World State. Perhaps the candid observer will be excused if he fails to perceive the difference, except in the new savagery now morally permitted. And as for the individual? He has been forgotten for a long time in his prison or madhouse. He must be given therapy.

Many serious persons, of course, are sensitive to these paradoxes, and yet finally in desperation cling to the solution of a world state or world dictatorship as the only preventative of world destruction through nuclear holocaust. It is one thing to be willing to give one's own life for one's nation, but it is qualitatively different to destroy the habitable parts of the globe for "nothing but" freedom and dignity. For our present discussion, we shall assume that some such thing is possible now or in the not-too-distant future. The possibility raises questions, obviously, of an ultimate order. But I do not think it unambiguously true that some such possible world catastrophe compels assent to world totalitarianism. In any event, for the moment, it might seem that here, at last, pacifism becomes sanity; and that any acceptance of world destruction is the very essence of evil and immorality. I shall revert to this question at the end and touch upon it now only to complete this first part surveying various sentiments which find war, as such and in principle, intolerable with the ensuing effort to formulate a solution or eliminate the cause.

II

THE JUSTIFICATION OF WAR

The attitudes so far considered begin, as we have seen, by assuming war to be unjustifiable; *if* it is unjustifiable, then its cause must be found, in biological, psychological, social or moral distortions of an inherently peace-loving human nature; the cure is always some form of therapy. Or those who conduct war must have reasoned badly or given up the hope that rational discussion with its eventual treaty would be effective. Wars are "irrational," no philosophical justification of any is possible; thought will find the rational "solution." But on the other hand, if war is justifiable, then the search for its causes in either distortions of the passionate nature of man, or in errors or failures of reason, is downright foolish. The justification removes the premise of the search for causes and cures. The justification removes the premise of the search for causes and cures. The justification of war as a form of moral and rational excellence may seem scandalous to the pacifist, and yet it is that scandal I should like to defend. And as for talk about the greater or lesser of two evils, I shall try to avoid this ambiguous, slippery and ultimately meaningless effort to calculate the incalculable. The justification of war aims at showing both its morality and its rationality; if therefore there are occasions when a moral and rational man must fight, then a proscription of war in principle must be itself irrational and ethically deplorable.

In a word, the justification of war is existence; to will to exist is to affirm war as its means and condition. But perhaps the term "existence" puts the matter too abstractly. In the present context, and in its most abstract sense, existence is a synonym for life, and nonexistence for death. Wars then are justified as means taken to assure life and death. And yet little has been said; the life and death of what? Bare life measured by the beating of the heart, is hardly life at all; it would be prized only as the supporter and condition of a life *worth living*. Obviously men have always thought it justifiable to fight not merely to preserve their physical being, but also for those additional things which make that life worth living, fertile lands, access to the sea, minerals, a government of their choice, laws and customs and religions, and finally peace itself. Existence then is hardly bare survival but an existence in the service of all those concrete values which illuminate and glorify existence. They too must exist; it is almost by definition that values, in and of their intrinsic meaning, *demand existence*. Justice would misunderstand itself if it were content to remain abstract and merely ideal.

So much might easily be granted until another reflection arises, that perhaps the goods of existence could be shared by all men. This utopian notion is much beloved of *philosophers* or *art critics* who look upon the diversities of thought and cultural style as so many advantages and opportunities for spiritual growth. And indeed they are; but then those values are not exactly what war is about. If the library can house every book in peaceful coexistence, or if the museum can calmly exhibit the styles of the world, why must men themselves fight? Could the world not be like an international congress of philosophy or perhaps a quieter meeting of UNESCO: would this not be the civilized thing? Would it not be better if nations conducted themselves according to the model of a genteel conversation, where views are advanced and withdrawn without anger, and where men say "excuse me for interrupting"?

But elementary reflection is sufficient to dispel these dreams. Existence or life individuates itself; when it can speak it says "I," and what it possesses, "mine." Nothing is changed logically in this respect when the I becomes a We, and mine, Ours. That I am not you, or we are not they, is the ineluctable ground of war; individuation is essential to existence. That which is not individuated does not exist, but subsists as a universal or abstract meaning. Consequently the meaning of a book or cultural artifact can be shared by all; but the existent book or existent painting can not, and could supply a ground for conflict. No wonder philosophers or scientists or critics, accustomed to living in the domain of abstractions and ideal meanings which are not, like quantities of matter, diminished progressively by each man who partakes of them, find something scandalous and primitive about war or anything else appropriate in the domain of existence and life. Nothing is easier than for the spirit to neglect the conditions of its own existence, or indeed be outraged by them.

I have used the term "existential" intentionally in spite of its abstractness to avoid at all costs what might seem to be its more common equivalent, "material." Some sentimental pacifists think it sufficient to prove that a nation has gone to war for "material" interests to conclude, with cheers from their audience, that such a war is *immoral*. That idealism should find itself opposed to "matter," or its equivalent, life and existence, would certainly not have surprised the Buddha or Nietzsche, both of whom accurately perceived that the only surcease of war and public sorrow is in nothingness, Nirvana or eternity. And, as President Truman remarked, those who can not stand the heat should get out of the kitchen.

But, of course, what the sentimental pacifist wants is nothing so radical as the genuine alternative of a Buddha; he wants an *existent* heaven, perpetual peace-on-earth, a mishmash which has never been or never will be seen, violating as it does patent ontological differences subsisting between existence and the abstract. The exposure of this error is not difficult. At what precise point do material interests become ideal? Is the health of a nation "material" or "ideal"? But its health depends, of course, upon its wealth; is the pursuit of that wealth ideal or materialistic and crass? Is the culture of a nation an ideal or a material value? and is its culture dependent or not upon the wealth available for education and leisure? Is the wealth devoted to such tasks materialistic or idealistic? Money versus human life! All these false contrasts need not be multiplied to perceive the vacuity of any argument against war based upon "idealistic" as opposed to "materialistic" principles.

Functioning according to the same false logic is another simplistic contrast, also beloved of pacifists: that thought to exist between egoism and altruism. The high-minded rhetoric poured out against "selfishness" is laughable indeed when not taken seriously. Is it "selfish" for me to protect my own life, or those of my family, friends, or compatriots? And, moreover, not merely our physical existence, but our human life with its wealth, customs, laws, institutions, languages, religions, our autonomy? Or to protect the "material," i.e., economic conditions which support all these values? To affirm any form of life at all is at the same time to affirm the means to it; what *could* be more confused than to will our life and also to will the life opposed to it? The ultimate pacifist who would do nothing even to protect his own life for fear of killing another, is simply a case of self-hatred; but both nature and logic combine to guarantee that this particular illness never becomes widespread. Has or could there ever be a defense for the idea that everyone else's life is preferable to my own, particularly when adopted in turn by everyone else? To be bound together in friendship is certainly preferable to being torn apart by hostility; but is it not clear that neither the friendship of all nor the hostility of all is possible; the line to be drawn which assures the provisional existence of any state is to be drawn by practical statesmanship judging in its time for its time, and not by abstract, would-be idealistic principles, which by hoping to be valid for all times are pertinent to none.

Excursus on Equality. No doubt it will have been noted that war here has *not* been justified as a means of securing justice or equality. It has been justified as a means necessary to any nation to secure or preserve its own social good, and as such, is held to be eminently reasonable and honorable. However, the social life of a nation is not itself to be further judged by means of abstract categories such as justice or equality. Hasty thought frequently identifies justice with equality, particularly since justice is elusive and protean in its applications, whereas the notion of equality, being mathematical and abstract, is within the grasp of all. I either do or do not have as much as another; if I do not, am I not wronged? Can not anyone see this? and indeed they can, but what can not be so immediately seen is whether such inequality is also *ipso facto* unjust.

These confusions pour into those discussions which, for example, would justify any war at all against the United States; since we have more than anyone else, we could never have a right to defend that more. To have more is to be guilty before the abstract bar of Equality. But this last gasp of the French Revolution, amplified by Marxist bellows, blows against certain existential realities. Those realities are simply that the earth itself is differentiated by rivers, climates, flora and fauna, mountains, valleys and plains. Not all can live everywhere nor is this an injustice to them. And, to belabor the obvious, men are not equal, having very different temperaments, tastes, ideals, and histories. Not merely are men not equal, they are not unequal either, the category of "equality" being quantitative whereas a man or a nation is not a quantity of anything, but rather an individual or communal person aiming at a definite form of excellent life. Since nations and men are always already in a differentiated possession of the goods of the world, differentiated forms of excellence, differentiated histories and memories, the desire to equalize all is equivalent to the desire to obliterate history as well as the individuated free choices of nations and men. Computerized thought might delight in such simplicities, but is there any a priori reason why a truly just mind must accept it?

If I have not used the notion of justice in any abstract form to justify war, again, it is for the simple reason that it leads nowhere. Wars are fought *over* differing notions of justice; does any party to war ever think itself unjust? Justice in the abstract therefore is useless for purposes of condemnation or justification. Victory in war equally does not decide what is abstractly just, but which form of justice will prevail.

III

OBJECTIONS TO WAR

1. What the "people" think of war. I shall use this title for a slippery mass of appeals increasingly popular in the mass media. Reporters, seemingly getting the "objective" facts, can always ask some fleeing peasants: "do you want war?" Of course, the bewildered peasant replies that he only wishes to live in peace, that war has destroyed his family, his rice fields, that it is caused by "government," that he could live equally well under any regime, that in fact he does not know the enemy, or does, having relatives among them, etc., all of which is pathetic as much for the sufferings of the peasant as for the mindlessness of the reporter who imagines himself to be presenting an ultimate argument based upon "humanity."

Television, since it can not picture any thought about war, is confined to showing what can be shown: the dismembered, burned, legless, eyeless, as if to say: this is what war really is. And when the dead or wounded are little children, women, or old men, the very heart recoils; the argument is decisive. But not yet: the soldiers must be asked; have they not seen it first hand, fought it with their lives, seen their comrades fall before their very eyes? Any number can be rounded up to swear they haven't the faintest idea what all the killing is about, that it must be immoral or absurd, probably conducted by munition makers or politicians seeking reelection, in a word by all that "establishment" in which they never had much participation even during peace. Their own virtue is to be resigned or, if they "think," to wearing peace symbols.

As for the ideal component in war, the honor and courage of the soldier, that too is immediately debunked. "There's nothing heroic about war" says the soldier who may just yesterday have risked his life to save a comrade. War is nothing but living in the mud and rain, with poor food, disease, fatigue, danger and boredom; is that heroic? His reticence about "heroism" is admirable; but we need not believe what he says. Since heroism is doing one's duty or going beyond it under extreme conditions, it is difficult to see how the difficulties diminish the accomplishment; without those difficulties, genuine heroism would be nothing but parade-ground heroics. But let us look in more detail at these arguments of the people.

The "People": who are they? They are either citizens of their country or not; if not, they have no political right to complaint. If so, then their government is indeed theirs, and they have every political duty to observe its decisions or try to alter them legally. In any event, the people are all the people, not merely the peasants, and they are in their collective capacity *already* represented by their government, whose decisions they must respect as made by their legal representatives. If the people are in no way represented by their government, then the question shifts itself away from war to that of forming a representative government. In any event, war and peace are decisions which obviously fall to the national government and not to miscellaneous groups, random interests, or *ad hoc* political rallies. Nor, least of all, to the private opinions of reporters interviewing a few people, usually those with the least opportunity to consider and weigh what is at stake. To suggest opinion polls or referenda on these questions every month or so, simply offers us the idea of another form of government altogether, an unheard-of-populism which in effect negates representative government altogether and substitutes for it the ever-shifting voice of the street. And since that in turn clearly reflects the overwhelming influence of propaganda, immediate "democracy" of this order shifts the decision from government to the directors and voices of "news" media. It is hardly surprising that this prospect delights the media, but it is surprising that so many otherwise sensible citizens wish to shift their allegiance from their own duly elected representatives to the directors of news media whom they have not elected and for the most part hardly know, all the while imagining that this offers them an opportunity themselves to direct the course of events.

The truth is, unwelcome as it may be, that the "people," ordinary housewives, factory workers, farmers, etc., as fine as they may be personally, are in no position whatsoever to consider the wisdom of that very politics upon which their own lives depend. It is, naturally, for this reason that very few nations at all, and none of any importance, are run on any such scheme. It is precisely the responsibility of representatives of the people to occupy themselves with such questions, inform themselves and circumspectly weigh the possibilities. The limits of experience and political habits of thought which more or less make the ordinary private citizen private, at the same time warn us against encouraging any immediate or undue influence of his opinions on matters of state. What the people think is simply the repetition of slogans derived either from campaigning politicians or their favorite newspaper. For some researchers, the popular mind is a pool of infinite wisdom and goodness; the truth is it is nothing but an ephemeral reflection of popular songs, sandwich-board slogans, newspaper headlines and clichés. For the popular mind "thought" is what can be written on a placard or shouted at a rally; for the reflective, thought is precisely what eludes this form of expression. Who has the wind to shout a *qualified* thought?

Nothing could be more dangerous than the enthusiasms of the people. Mad joy at the beginning of hostilities; and rage when the bodies are brought in, the expenses reckoned up. But of course this is precisely what is to be expected from the people, suggestible, flighty, and unused to either foresight or circumspection. As for the shallow notion that the people want only peace, that all peoples love one another as brothers, and that war therefore is imposed upon them from above—could one find any stretch of history or any segment of the world where these notions are significantly illustrated? The natural brotherhood of man? The natural goodness of the people? Indeed! One could far better argue that there is nothing whatsoever "natural" in man; the natural is exactly what man *decides.*

When we substitute for the people, the common soldier, all the same applies. Their experience is always tempting to novelists, looking for the "reality" of war. The reality in question, it should be remembered, is the one they are best equipped to express with vividness: the day-to-day life in the foxhole, or in the pouring rain, the mudholes, the terror, sickness, ambiguities of fighting life. It is easy for novelists to enter into the mind of the G.I. who is presented as seeing only what lies before his eyes: a dead friend. *That* is the reality of war; meanwhile at headquarters, the colonels are arrogant, incompetent, not really suffering but instead well provided with booze and whores, no doubt profiteering from the PX, and in cahoots with the government, known to be corrupt. No doubt all this is true enough from time to time, and no doubt anyone at all can sympathize with the sentiments involved. And no doubt at all, the same structure can easily be found in any civil society that ever was in peace time as well. The question however concerns the exact pertinence of such considerations, to the justification or lack of it for any given war. Since wars are not fought in the first place to make common soldiers comfortable, nor to make generals live the same lives as privates, nor to remove corruption in the armies involved, the only pertinence of such observations when true would be to improve the army, not to stop the war. And that a platoon leader does not know the whole strategy from his experience, that a general can not perform his legitimate functions in the same state of exhaustion as the G.I., nor carry his maps and codes into the foxholes, nor subject himself to the same risks as the ordinary soldier, is all obvious but no doubt at times escapes the full approval of the G.I. which is why the G.I. is not a general.

Related, is the curious popular objection that war is immoral because the soldier does not know his enemy *personally.* A German soldier of World War I in *All Quiet on the Western Front* receives a shock when after killing a Frenchman, he realizes he never knew him personally. However he would have received a greater shock upon recovering his wits when he realized that if he *had* known him personally and acted out of personal rage, his act would be radically transformed in meaning. From being a soldier doing his *duty,* he would be transformed into a *murderer.* But no doubt this distinction is too fine for those who love to talk of war as "mass murder," oblivious to all distinctions between on the one hand the legitimate duties of the police and soldiers, and on the other punishable murder. This essential distinction is obliterated in that higher pacifistic fog where all "taking of human life" is immoral. There could hardly be anything more obscurantist than the desire to obliterate all distinctions of roles and offices of men into that warm, personal, brotherly unity of "the personal." Generals receive criticism for not taking a "personal" interest in each of their troops; I, for one, would demote any who did. If some such thing is the philosophy of the best seller, it is easy to predict that of the worst seller: the wise general and the stupid G.I. In all of this, it would hardly take a Nietzsche to perceive the influence of that old, popular motive, the resentment of authority. In the present instance it feeds pacifism.

Popular thought loves to "psych" its political leaders. In this, has it not been aided and abetted by the rise of psychological novels where the plot sinks into insignificance and the psychological analysis of motives occupies the stage, usually a popular version of Freud. Psychologizing has, undoubtedly, a limited relevance to political decision; national policies are at the same time policies of leaders, whose characters and temperaments are significant factors in their actions and reactions. Roosevelt and Churchill both considered the personalities of Hitler and Stalin in this fashion, and if their judgments left something to be desired, at least the pertinence of the question is undeniable; political personality is unquestionably a factor in objective policy. Which items in announced policy are sticking points, and which negotiable? Which remarks made to the inner constituency, and which to the outer world? Generals also try to sense the temperament of their opponents, as one factor in the whole.

On the other hand, what could be more ludicrous than the popular effort to assess policy through a judgment of the character and assumed private motives of the initiators of that policy? Antiwar finds nothing but reprehensible private motives at the root of the matter; prowar finds nothing but heroic strength; reflection finds both irrelevant. Wars are neither justifiable nor unjustifiable in terms of the private motives of the leaders; wars are not personal acts of rage and revenge, but as von Clausewitz showed, an extension of policy by other means. Policies are measured by their probable costs and effects, and not by the motives of the agents.

The weighing of policy properly belongs in the hands of those responsible and thoughtful men who are experienced in such matters. It is not in any conspicuous sense the experience of pastors in their morality, poets with their sensitivity, the young with their "idealism," psychoanalysts with their probings of emotions, or news reporters with their "scoops."

The distressing thing about popular psychologizing is its confidence; it *knows* the black heart inside the political leader, and is certain that anything more complex or even favorable is "naive." All of which reflects the failure of both psychology and the psychological novel to make their point; should not popular wisdom at least be sensitive to the difficulties and ambiguities of searching out the motives of the human heart? If I can only seldom if ever be confident I know my own motives, how can I be so sure I know those of others?

I conclude that the "people" must take their chances in war, do not represent a pool of persons separate from the organized body of citizens with a government, and that their perception, judgment and analysis of public policy is sound only by accident. Public policy is beyond the scope of private people; since it is, the common people revert to something they imagine themselves to be expert in, the psychological motives of leaders; but alas, even that is beyond their or anyone else's proper grasp. At which point we have nothing to do but return to where we should never have left, the objective consideration of policy by those competent to consider it.

2. *The Sufferings of the People.* A final set of criticisms against war again purports to rest upon humanitarian or idealistic grounds: its argument is the simple exhibition of death, injuries, disease, poverty, destruction, the ravaging of both countryside and cities. Television makes it as vivid as possible, and the color photographs in *Life* magazine are almost enough to sicken the heart of the bravest and to shake the firmest judgment. Indeed this is their overt intention, and it is not long before they end up on pacifist posters as ultimate arguments. But of course arguments they are not, at best facts to be considered; but then who hasn't already considered them? Is there anyone who imagines war to be anything but killing? The decision to fight is the decision to kill; such a decision, needless to say, is never easy although it may frequently be justified. *If justified,* what service is performed by such direct appeals to vital instinct and sentiment? At best they would enfeeble our powers of judgment, never too strong, so that we would choose the unjustifiable rather than the wise course.

These images thought to be decisive, are in reality nothing but kicks below the belt and from behind; reasonable moral judgment can never be a simple reaction to our emotions and sentiments; the emotions and sentiments themselves are more than enough for that; but it is the role of policy and judgment to judge *over* these forces. The job is no doubt the most difficult man faces; it is hardly made easier by the daily flood of images of suffering in the media.

The image in itself is no argument against anything. It would be easy indeed by vivid color photographs, accompanied by recordings of screaming, wailing and crying, to sicken anyone of the very project of living. Surgical operations would never be undertaken, women would be afraid to give birth to children; images of the old, sick and senile would convince us that life itself is folly; and some such thing is the conclusion of transcendental ascetics. But then such an ethic, by intention, is not pertinent to public policy, necessarily committed to not merely life, but the good life.

The humanitarian argument drawn from ruins and suffering, aims at a higher idealism; but with a suddenness which would have delighted Hegel, turns into its opposite, a crass materialism. If human life is justifiable in terms of its excellence, where is the idealism in locating that excellence in a clinging to cities and fields? Or finally, in clinging to mere life itself as our highest value? The founder of Western philosophy, Socrates, disdained to use arguments resting upon such sympathies in his own defense, and did *not* bring his wife and children to court to plead for him. Nor did he conjure up imaginative pictures of his own suffering. No doubt, this is old-fashioned. . . .

Since one dies anyway, the sole question would seem to be *how* one dies, with honor or not. There is no moral obligation to live at all costs and under any conditions; there is no moral obligation to live at all; there is a moral obligation to live honorably if one lives at all. What that obligation dictates under specific historical concrete circumstances clearly can not be decided for all and in general; but it can dictate that under some circumstances, some men must find their honor in defending unto death what they take to be more valuable than sheer existence, namely a human life dedicated to excellence and dignity. Human lives whose chief moral defense is that they have kept themselves alive, have at the same stroke lost *all* moral defense. Such is the age-old paradox of life.

Traditionally, the man who chose life and personal safety under any conditions was regarded as a coward, and his condition that of a slave. Do we now have new reasons for reversing this decision? Which is not to say that some have not tried; what other judgment could be pronounced upon the current rash of movies and novels all celebrating the *antihero* as a new form of excellence; sometimes it is even thought to be "authentic" or "existential"! What is it but mediocrity and cowardice? It follows that some are authentic cowards, but need we admire them? A footnote to the present confusion is the argument that war "brutalizes" the troops. The brutalization is rarely spelled out although hovering around the attack is the suspicion that troops are brutalized in their coarse speech, their terms of contempt for the enemy, their failure personally to consider the "justice" of every order, to bring their superiors before the bar of their own private conscience, their fondness for booze and camp followers above lectures and the opera. Well! But if brutalization means a willingness to kill the enemy, I for one fail to perceive the fault; that's what they are there for in the first place, and who is closer to the brute, a man afraid to kill the enemy, or one who will kill and die to preserve the freedom and dignity of himself or his compatriots?

There will always be occasions when human freedom and dignity are threatened; there will always be occasions then for a justifiable war, and the pacifistic argument fails. To attack the very idea of war is to attack something fundamental to the preservation of any honorable life, and to offer under the flag of idealism or humanitarianism, the very substance of cowardice. Having already denounced Soviet injustice, what could be a worse capitulation than Bertand Russell's slogan: "Better Red than dead"?

IV

WHAT WAR DECIDES

Needless to say, victory does not always fall to the just. And if not, then victory is no measure of the justice of the cause, a truth commonly recognized by the respect accorded to the defeated. For while they were indeed defeated with regard to the immediate occasion of the dispute, they were not defeated, if they fought well, with regard to something far more important, that infinite self-respect which defines their humanity. The morale of a nation, that is, its self-respect, is certainly tested by the war, and is that factor which nullifies the old Chinese warlord "solution" to the problem of war, much beloved of computer thinkers. Why not, the argument goes, have the leaders meet on a neutral ground, calculate their resources, and decide victory without bloodshed, as the story says the warlords did. Is this not the essense of "rationality"? If the idea seems preposterous is it not because there remains one *incalculable* factor, the morale of the troops and the nations behind them? No doubt, this factor was negligible when the troops in question were mercenaries without any morale whatsoever except that for their pay or "professional" reputation. And no doubt one can easily find battles when the odds are so unequal as to render armed resistance suicidal. But even such "suicidal" resistances *win something*, namely, the enacted courage unto death of the men fighting them; to think nothing of this or to regard it as pure folly is itself a judgment proceeding out of little but crass materialism. To offer it as a rational *idealism* is a betrayal of everything noble in the defeated. A man is not necessarily ignoble because he was defeated; but he is if there is nothing he will fight for except his own skin.

Courage then, about which little is said today without an accompanying smirk, is a virtue whose analysis quickly carries us into transcendental realms. It looks like madness or vanity or an "ego-trip" to those who imagine the issues of life settled, and settled into the values of biology, economics, or fundamentally *pleasure*. But courage puts all those values into question, discloses that as always, men today put to themselves a goal and destiny which has no common measure with mere life, mere well-being, or mere comfort. These things may properly be fought over, but they are not *in themselves* the full story of what is involved. That full story can never be told, but at very least it must include what here is called the transcendental, the domain of freedom and dignity which is never compromised by mere death, poverty, or defeat; but most certainly is compromised by a certain deafness to its claims. Wars are not fought to prove courage, but they do prove it all the same.

In Defense of Peace

JAN NARVESON

Wars continue to blemish the escutcheon of humanity—both actual wars and prospective ones. We have long since accustomed ourselves to the possibility of thermonuclear war, but the prospect has been with us so long that we are either bored or fatigued by it; and in either case, the effect is that we simply don't take it into account very much in our daily lives. It hangs about like a dark cloud at the back of our consciousnesses, subtly making our lives worse, but not making them impossible or even disrupting them all that much, except in special cases. Even the very real effect which we could discern, if we were so inclined, on our tax bills is scarcely noted by we individuals who bear that burden. One might almost say that the danger of war is like the weather: everbody talks about it, but nobody does anything about it. Except that this wouldn't quite be right—we don't even talk about it all that much; and more interestingly, it can hardly be true that *no*body does *any*thing about it, for are not wars fought, threatened, and prepared for by people? Were no one doing anything about them, how could they be the threat they are?

What must be meant is not that nobody can do anything about war, but instead something like this: either (A) that no individual can do anything about it, by himself, or (B) that none of the people, such as you and I, who would like very much to have utter and lasting peace, can do anything about it. There is a good deal to be said for both of these options. Option A is not *quite* true, perhaps, for there are some few people, quite likely, who could push the appropriate button and cause a great deal of trouble. But even those people can't actually start a whole war, for that requires that somebody on the other side push the appropriate buttons in response, and then we already have many people acting in concert, or at least in response to each other. And on the other hand, we can't completely rule out the possibility that some really extraordinary person might have enough personal magnetism to be able to influence those who are in positions of power to lay down their arms. Miracles do happen. It's just that, being miracles, they are inherently unreliable. Option B is also very near to being true, without quite being so. Again, of course, no one ordinary person by himself (or herself) can do much; but a great many of them acting together could do quite a lot. Indeed, in the end wars are fought by a great many ordinary people, people much like you and I, who go from families and friends to battlefields and war-planning rooms as routinely as we go off to offices, workshops and fields. It isn't even like Jekyll and Hyde, who at least did not know each other very well. No, the moral monstrosities of war, if that is what they are, are committed by the very same people who help their wives with the grocery shopping, take the kids to the park, and engage in all the other ordinary relations of ordinary life. In this, as will be pondered further below, there is surely occasion for wonder. Meanwhile, it remains that not even *they* can, any one of them, do very much about wars by themselves, even though, obviously (since they are the very people who fight them) they could, acting together, do a great deal about them.

So it is not quite true that people are literally powerless to do anything about war, even if we only count the overwhelming portion of mankind who are not in the most powerful positions in their various countries. But I expect that most of us think it very close to the truth. How close, and why, is important, and I shall say a bit more about that directly. But when that is said, we will still face an urgent question about values and principles; I will move to those matters for the remainder of this paper.

What is the main source of the feeling of powerlessness which nearly everyone, quite understandably, has regarding so major a subject as war? I suggest that the general answer to this is, in a word, Bureaucracy. Bureaucracy, we may say, unleashes two of the most powerful forces in human nature—cowardice and lack of imagination. Both deserve some comment.

1. The connections between bureacracy and cowardice are mainly two. In the first place, those who act as part of a large organization will generally owe their jobs to various particular people on higher rungs of that organization, especially on the next higher rung. This will motivate the bureaucrat to smother his or her conscience in the interests of job security. (Even if the organization is not one in which people's livelihoods are involved, it will be one in which various kinds of prestige are; but the livelihood factor is so prominent and so powerful that we shall go on as though it were the only one.) That is, it would motivate him to smother it if he has one in the first place. And well he might; indeed, it's even probable that he does have one, at least a modest one. That, however, is where the other factor, lack of imagination, comes into the picture. Meanwhile we have the other way in which bureaucracy and cowardice go hand in hand. For bureaucracy enables one to shrink from the need to act by offering the excuse that it's really somebody else's job. In a sizable organization, there is always somebody else to blame, especially when one is, as nearly all are, on the middle or lower organizational rungs. The coward in us all will seize on such opportunities with alacrity, indeed glee. And thus, nothing out of the way will ever get done, except in those rare cases where truly remarkable people are involved.

2. It needs hardly be mentioned that bureaucracy stimulates, shall we say, the antiimagination. It does, of course, stifle imagination, but on top of that, it positively promotes and encourages the reverse of imagination. The psychological distance between the bureaucrat and the events he is ultimately causing in the outside world is inversely proportional to the number of desks between him and it (weighted by the amount of paper on each, perhaps). The question of what it is *like* to be immolated by napalm or ravaged by leukemia caused by radiation is not one which readily arises in a paper environment, let alone an environment of computer terminals, with cool data neatly flicking on and off them. One need be neither cowardly nor without conscience and humanity to be the cause, or part of the cause, of the most monstrous horrors and evils if one is sufficiently immunized to the real consequences of one's actions (or inactions, as the case may be) to be acting nearly in a sort of moral fog.

To put a lot of blame on bureaucracy, as I call it, is not to take all the blame off the rest of us. To a degree, no doubt, bureaucracy is our fault. In some measure, and in some sense, it is we who cause and encourage it. And I mean to ascribe the bureaucratic habit as much to those of us who uncomplainingly put up with it as to the bureaucrats themselves. Unfortunately, it is hard to be anything but gloomy about the trends in this respect. Bureaucracy is on the increase, and it is not easy to imagine that it will be reversed. This should make us very uncomfortable. The prospects of peace are not too good so long as the bureaucratic vices are on the loose, and the likelihood of their being effectively suppressed on the scale required to keep them from working industriously and insidiously for the general misery is unhappily low.

I should add that I take the idea of bureaucracy to be closely related to another idea which has often, and rightly, been pointed to as importantly responsible for the frequency of wars, namely the State. It is pretty clear that war, at least on anything like its modern scale (and "modern" here goes back a few centuries for this purpose), is virtually impossible without the State. Only the existence of an agency with more or less unlimited powers and very vague or nonexistent responsibility will enable hundreds of thousands of people to be harnessed to the chariots of war. Even an exceedingly large and "powerful" non-State organization, such as the General Motors Corporation, would have no real chance of mounting a genuine war without the support of the State. We have heard a lot from the Left about the warmongering propensities of capitalism; but I wonder whether even the most enthusiastic proponent of such theories has set back and asked himself seriously whether he would invest in a war, if he really had his choice in the matter. Moved only by considerations of profit, and not at all by obscurer motives of honor, glory, and the Spirit of the Nation, would we be willing to put up the kind of sums required for even a rather modest war by current standards? Not likely. Capitalists may jump at the chance to provide arms for the market created by governments, but I daresay they'd have quite a different view if they genuinely had to bear the risks and the costs of war themselves. Now, the standard theory of the State which we are accustomed to hearing is that it is justified because it has, somehow, the consent of us all, or that it is a good deal from the point of view of each of us, providing protection and all sorts of vital services and whatnot. But what rational being would convey unlimited power on an agency which was merely providing him with a service for which he is *willing* to pay? No: I suspect that the popularity of government, apart from being thoroughgoingly habitual for most people, is due in major measure to our far worse habit of crediting some people under some circumstances with *authority*. Indeed, it seems pretty clear that no State could last a day without this habit. But isn't recognition of authority really a bureaucratic habit? Were we to make a genuine cost-benefit analysis of what we are supposedly trying to get out of government, would authority get into the act at any point? I suspect not. Or rather, it would enter as a cost, not a benefit. To regard authority as basically justified, rather than an inevitable evil or organization, is to have absorbed the bureaucratic outlook on things into one's soul.

Having said all that, however, I remain uneasy. The frequency of war is not sufficiently explained on the hypothesis that it's all an unfortunate byproduct of poorly designed societal structures. Nor is its intensity, the amazing resoluteness and will with which it is so often pursued. We need a deeper inquiry to satisfy ourselves on that subject. But of course our major concern here is not simply explanation. What we really want to know is whether war is ever *justified*; and the relation between the question of explanation and justification in a matter of this kind is not clear, nor is it likely to be simple when it becomes clear, if it ever does.

But I hope that we can help matters along here by focussing on a somewhat narrower issue. Instead of asking whether war is ever justified, let us instead ask whether it is ever *rational*. Can we accuse those who participate in them of real irrationality? This, of course, does require that we have a reasonably clear notion of what it is to be rational, and it can reasonably be objected that that is no easy matter. But I am not sure that it can reasonably be objected that it is just as difficult as the original question about justification *simpliciter*. At very least, I am quite sure that we can pretty well identify the notion of rationality as it is very widely and normally conceived. The view of rationality in question I have in mind goes nowadays under the name of "Maximization." Let us pause for a moment to set down the essentials of this view.

The theory of maximization is currently encapsulated in the statement that "A rational agent tries to maximize his utility"; or more precisely, that a rational agent *maximizes his expected utility*. Three notions need to be explained: utility, expected utility, and maximization. Let's take them in order. (1) The question of just what *utility* is has received lots of perplexed and perplexing attention from philosophers, but the dominant notion nowadays is this: a state of affairs has *utility* for a given agent, *A,* to the extent that *A prefers* it to its alternatives. Of course, we are interested in appraising the actions of an agent with this theory, so we are really only interested in those states of affairs that the agent could possibly try to bring about, or at least could possibly try to bring about. This brings up notion (2): *expected* utility. Suppose I am trying to bring about a given state of affairs, *S*. In the hope of doing so, I perform an action, *X*. Well, expectedness is simply the probability I attach, in the light of my information (or: best information, perhaps) to the proposition that if I do *X*, then *S* will result. And expected utility, then, is simply the probability-weighted utility, that is, how much utility or value *A* would realize if *S* did come about, times the probability that it will come about if *A* does *X*. This leads to the toughest one of the lot, (3): Maximization. To say that *A* "maximizes" his expected utility is to say that among the alternative actions *A could* perform—*X, T, Z,* etc., let's call them—the one he does perform (chooses to perform) is the one which produces the maximally preferred outcome, the highest utility, when weighted by the probability that it will indeed come about.

What is important about this general conception of rationality is that it takes, in some sense which is rather difficult to explain clearly, the values of the agent as *given*. This has often been advanced as a criticism of the view, but I think it is actually its strength, for present purposes. A couple of notes on this matter are in order. First, the view is intended to make the question of the agent's *information* relevant, in two respects. One: I have talked only of "preferring a state of affairs to its alternatives"; but of course, the agent might have a inadequate appreciation of what those alternatives are. Information about that is going to be relevant to the agent, in general; for he can hardly fail to be interested in the possibility that there is a possible state of affairs he would prefer even more, if only he knew about it, to the ones he knows he prefers now to the alternatives he now knows about. And two: it plainly makes information about the probabilities relating actions to outcomes relevant to the agent. Again, of course, he might attach a certain probability to an outcome which there is really very little reason to attach to it, or even very good reason not to attach to it. This information will plainly be relevant to him. We might extend the theory a little to say that an ideally rational agent would act in the light of perfect information of this, or of both, kinds. But in general, we don't adopt quite that high a standard. Generally, we evaluate an agent's rationality on the basis of the information which he actually has, or the information which he has good reason to know that he could acquire in the light of the information he does have.

The second note I want to make is that no other criticisms about the agent's general line of action are *rational* criticisms on this view. We can criticize the agent for having acted poorly in the light of the information he has, or for not having good enough information. But we cannot criticize him for having the "wrong values," just like that—not unless they are values which he would not have if only he knew more than he does. Values are, in a word, wants or preferences, on this view, at bottom; and no more. This is not to say that I can't criticize you at all in that way. It is only to say that any such criticisms are not ones which impugn your rationality, whatever else they might do. They might impugn your humanity, for instance, or your taste: but it is not clear that someone who is inhuman or has bad taste is *irrational*. (The situation is complicated, though, as will shortly be seen.)

Now how, initially, will we evaluate the rationality, given this theory, of those who make war? (We need not distinguish, just yet, between those who start it and those who fight back against an agressor.) Clearly, we will ask what he is trying to achieve. That is, we will try to assess his utility schedules or functions, as they are called: in other words, try to figure out what his general preferences are insofar as they are relevant to appraising his participation in war. And then we will try to assess his information base: was it reasonable for him to suppose that the probability that he would win the war (for instance) was high enough to make his participation rational in relation to his ends? Our assessment of the former dimension might lead to the conclusion that war simply was not a sensible way to try to secure the values he was trying to secure. Given his known preferences, the costs of making war were very high, what he had to gain from it even if he did win were not really very important to him, and in any case alternative ways of trying to get it would clearly, in his case, be at least equally likely to get him what he wanted. In that case, war would clearly be contra-rational.

Now, the pacifist is the person who thinks that war (either aggressive *or* defensive) will never get us what we really want. (Or anyway, one sort of pacifist may take that line.) *Whatever* we want, war is not worth the risk, says the sort of pacifist I have in mind here. Or does he say that? Doesn't he instead say something more like "whatever, deep down inside, we *really* want, war isn't worth the risk"? If so, of course, the question arises how he knows *that*. Perhaps when he says we "really" want something, he means only that it is what he wishes we wanted; and that might be another story altogether! Still, he could instead mean something close to the restrictions of our theory; perhaps he is claiming that if we only knew more clearly what the options were, or envisaged more alternative possible situations, then we would see that we wanted some of those more than any of the ones we currently conceive of; and then if he could show that war was just not a way of achieving those, his case would be made out. Or if he could show that the costs of war inevitably outweighed those other objectives' advantages, if any, then we would see that war wasn't a good choice.

Unfortunately, it is by no means clear that we could prove either, let alone both, of those claims as being true of just *any* agent. The trouble is that people's preferences do seem to *differ* a great deal. It is by no means certain that Napoleon's preferences would on the whole have been better served if he had, like the later Candide, merely stayed home and cultivated his garden. Now, I don't, let me hasten to say, really know very much about Napoleon's motives. In part, I suppose, he was fighting for the "glory" of France. In part, he may merely have enjoyed the military art; or he may have liked bringing his enemies to their knees, simply for its own sake. If either of the latter were the case, then it is surely not easy to say that all that fighting wasn't worth it *to him*!

Now there is another dimension to all this which, I think, gives us peacemongers (as I suppose that most of us are) a pretty strong case, even on this very restricted theory of rationality. But before trying to make that case, I want to focus some attention on a most interesting, challenging, and, to me anyway, upsetting essay tending in the opposite direction. The essay in question is by a philosopher, William Earle, and is appropriately entitled "In Defense of War."[1] It is far too easy for most of us to gloss over or ignore what Professor Earle has to say, and at any rate I do not think we can or should do so. I shall therefore try to take up his challenge, and try to show that it is rational for us to condemn war quite generally—although, in fairness to Earle, I should note that I have no intention of defending the view he is primarily concerned to attack, namely pacifism. Having previously criticized that doctrine—the doctrine that we are never justified in fighting, even in defense of ourselves or others—I have no intention of defending it now. But I take it that Earle's view cuts quite a lot deeper than that; at least, it may be construed as doing so, and it is that deeper challenge which I hope to be able to meet here.

Since I do not wish to defend pacifism, I had best begin by saying precisely what I do wish to defend, and what I take Earle to be denying. The view I wish to defend is that whenever there is a war, at least one party to it is, objectively, morally unjustified. I do not mean that at least one must be acting irrationally, nor even unreasonably, and I certainly don't mean that at least one party must be acting inexcusably. I claim only that there is a rational conception of morality which makes the above true; and I believe that that conception, or something like it, is the only feasible basis for any prospect of long-term peace at the global level. And I take it that Earle denies this.

According to Earle, "In a word, the justification of war is existence; to will to exist is to affirm war as its means and condition" (49).[2] To exist is to be a *particular* individual with distinct interests, aspirations, needs, passions. And I take it that Earle is insisting that an individual *must* be moved by *his* interests, when he says, for instance, "Existence or life individuates itself; when it can speak it says 'I', and what it possesses, 'mine' " (49). And this is true; moreover, it is incorporated into the theory of rational behavior outlined above. But do we get from there to the conclusion, for instance, that "the only surcease of war and public sorrow is in nothingness, Nirvana or eternity" (50), as Buddha and Nietszche thought?

Earle observes that "war here has *not* been justified as a means of securing justice or equality. It has been justified as a means necessary to any nation to secure or preserve its own social good, and as such, is held to be eminently reasonable and honorable" (51). In an important extension of this line of thought, he insists that using "the notion of justice in any abstract form . . . . leads nowhere. Wars are fought *over* differing notions of justice; does any party to war ever think itself unjust?" (52) These passages are of great importance, indeed contain, I suspect, the nub of the matter. But we need to distinguish three components which might be involved in them. (*A*) First, there is the claim that what promotes the social good of a particular nation justifies any actions taken toward that end, including war. Next there follows an assertion about justice; but it is not entirely clear which of at least two distinct claims about it is being made. We shall separate them now. (*B*) Second, then, there is a possible claim to the effect that justice is *relative:* that justice "in the abstract" is useless for resolving the disagreements which lead to war, because, each party having his own view about justice and there being no way to decide which is correct because there just is no "correct" notion of it, it follows that each can justifiably pursue a war in the only sense of "justifiable" there can be here, namely that it is justified by the theory of justice which the party in question holds. (*C*) Third, however, there is a different possible claim, though it might have much the same practical effect. This is simply that people inevitably differ as to which acts are just and which aren't, even though ultimate abstract justice might be the same for all.

Some comments on each are in order. Regarding claim *A*, we should note first that of course it assumes that the social goods of differing nations may really differ sufficiently, and be sufficiently irreconcilable, that they would lead to war; and next, of course, it asserts that that is the only kind of justification a nation needs. Whether either of these is true remains to be seen, and will be considered further in a bit. Meanwhile, we can move to claim *B* which, I believe, is false. There are very basic considerations which lead to that conclusion, but I might first note that it implies something which is, I believe, plainly false *to fact*. The nations of the world, when they invoke principles in support of their actions, do not generally invoke principles which are unrecognizable and irreconcilable on the face of it. For example, no nation would admit to being an *aggressor,* just like that. Nations whom we believe to be aggressors at least do not admit this in their public utterances. In addition to this, I believe it can be shown that the whole idea of justice is such as to make subscription to relativism simply nonsensical. Why? Because justice is, inherently, concerned with the adjudication of conflicting *claims*. The whole point of a theory of justice is to say who is right and who is wrong when claims conflict, and to do so in a way that is independent of and superior to the interested points of view of the parties themselves. There *cannot*, as a matter of logic, be two conflicting theories of justice which are both true—any more than there can be two conflicting theories of anything else which are both true. But I shall not dwell on this here. Instead, let us consider claim *C* for as noted it could, if true, have the same effect as *B*. Is there any inherent reason, any inevitable reason, why people must differ in the application of principles of justice, even though they agree as to what those principles are? As a proposition of psychology, this is a difficult one. There are, of course, many sources of possible bias in these matters, and it is not terribly surprising that these sources often win out. But is there any good reason to think that they must *inevitably* do so? Can't a source of bias be detected, after all, with a modest amount of patience and care, plus of course the assistance which we are very likely to get from the jeers of the opposite parties in our disputes?

It will be useful to pause here for a moment to dwell on an example—quite an important one in the current world—of a theory which allegedly would make the kind of disputes Earle may have in mind inevitable. I have in mind the Marxist doctrine that one's position in the class structure of society, which in turn is rooted in its "material base," make antagonistic theories of justice (more generally, "ideologies") inevitable. This view has had a very powerful influence on many people, and certainly deserves to be carefully considered if only for that reason. But one no sooner begins to consider it than it begins to crumble before one's very eyes. For one thing, the vital details have never been made very clear. Is it claimed that the teaching of moral and social ideas in any nation is necessarily tightly controlled by its rulers? That is contrary to fact, for one thing. And for another, if one's ideas are controlled by one's social position, then why should it even be *possible* for teachers to inculcate ideas which are contrary to our supposed class interests, as they obviously must if the rulers are to succeed? Does the theory hold that it is impossible for a member of social class *X* to come to hold ideas favorable to social class *Y*? Well, for one thing what about people like Marx and Engels themselves, neither of whom *belonged*, by the usual criteria of the theory, to the class (viz., the working class) which their social theory most strongly identifies with? And they *invented* the theory, for goodness' sake! Some enthusiasts reply that one's ideas are determined not by the class one literally belongs to, but rather by the class one identifies with! I leave to the reader the task of lifting the corner of the carpet which that reply tries to sweep the problem under. Meanwhile, I conclude that neither this theory nor any other has much prospect of demonstrating the *inevitability* of bias. But it may well be admitted that disagreements are unsurprising among beings so diverse as we humans, whether or not they are literally inevitable; what I do want to insist is only that once we have agreement on the most general principles of justice, it is surely unreasonable to insist that any further or more detailed agreement in their application is utterly impossible. Better to say, merely, that reaching detailed agreement requires patience, skill, and a genuine concern to reach it.

We return, then to the important claim which I tabled a couple of paragraphs back. Is a nation justified in doing anything necessary to promote its social good? The question is surely paralleled at the individual level. Is an individual justified in doing anything necessary to promote his personal good? I suspect, indeed, that the answer at the national level cannot be plausible if it is not the same at the individual level. Indeed, Professor Earle's argument seems couched fundamentally at the individual level. Surely he is not going to argue that individuals ought to submerge their own individualities in some faceless general good; and if not, then he can hardly insist that individuals ought to go along with a nationally conceived good, no matter what its relation to their own.

At this point, though, we come up against what might seem to be a stone wall. For the theory of rational behavior which I have outlined awhile back seems to dictate an affirmative answer to our question. Surely, once the "good" of an individual has been identified by himself, nothing in this theory can prevent the outcome that it might justify anything at all, including the kind of acts of which wars are made: namely, violence and aggression. How can this be escaped?

But we have to remember that our primary question is whether such actions can be *morally* justified; though of course we do not want that question answered in such a way as to make morality a matter of utter indifference to the individual. We want the morality in question to be a rational morality. And what is that? It is a morality which it is rational to espouse and support. If such a morality leads to the result about justice which I am concerned to defend—namely, that in any dispute on the scale of war, at least one party must be in the wrong— then there is a basis, and even a hope, of peace—perhaps. Whereas if both parties in war can be genuinely justified in pursuing it, then there is not much.

What, then, might be such a basis? The general argument for it was provided by Hobbes; but Hobbes supposed that it led to political conclusions of a well-known type, and in this I believe he was wrong. I shall instead take his argument as a ground for a public and rational morality. As such, the argument is fairly straightforward. Consider the situation in which neither we nor others acknowledge any principled constraints on their behavior. People do whatever they perceive to be to their advantage; and they know that others act likewise. If so, what must happen? Well, if people don't just happen to have a distaste for violence (and too many do not), and if there are things we want which are in short enough supply so that we can't all have them without an extensive scheme of cooperation, then in the absence of any internalized constraints on our behavior, the situation will rapidly degenerate into one of war. Nobody will be able to trust anybody, and nothing of what anybody wants will be achieved, almost no matter what it is—with the exception that those who *want* war will get plenty of that. Such an exceptional individual pays an interestingly high price: namely, he cannot rely on being alive for very long. For the rest of us, though, we can have a lot to gain by being alive; and this is true even if our particular interests and desires are exceedingly idiosyncratic and shared by no one else. Even of such an eccentric it will be true that he is better off alive than dead, provided only that others will leave him to pursue his idiosyncratic desires in peace. For nearly everyone, though, the rewards are still greater, for we also get the benefit of being able to pursue our individual goals in peace, but we also get the benefit of cooperation, which is now possible. All these benefits, in exchange for one very small price: renunciation of the unlimited freedom to pursue our ends in just any way we please. The restriction is that we will refrain from violence to others. This and renunciation of the freedom to ignore what one has voluntarily taken upon oneself to do in return for benefits from others—except that this is hardly a different principle, but really just a ramification of the main one.

Now, one who publicly insists that he must be allowed to do *whatever* is necessary to achieve his ends, *whatever* they are is in a very difficult position *vis-à-vis* his fellow man. He is saying, in effect, "You must be subservient to me on all those occasions when it serves my interest for you to be so." How could anyone else rationally accept a proposition like that? Clearly he can't. But that's not all. We have ample reason to deal with anyone who genuinely meant any such thing in the most extreme manner, for he is obviously a danger to the rest of us. We would, in fact, have to be admitted by such people to be perfectly justified in *killing* them. How could they complain? For we are supposing that there are as yet *no* rules. Someone who complains is assuming that there *are* rules. And normally, of course, he is right. Normal people do acknowledge rules: in particular, this very basic and very obvious rule that we will renounce *unlimited* pursuit of our ends, confining ourselves to behavior of the type that others can rationally accept. There is, of course, a corollary, as Hobbes says: namely, that if others won't do that, then we are entitled to use "all the helps and advantages of war."

Hobbes thought that this reasoning led to the necessity to acknowledge obedience to the State, no matter what the State might be like. If that were so, then it would also be easy to see that world peace would depend upon a Super State being established, a World State so powerful as to be able to keep everyone else in line. Professor Earle thinks that this would be of necessity a totalitarian state, and that that would be awful—worse than the continued prospect of war. I am not sure that it would have to be any more totalitarian than most States already are; but that is quite awful enough for me. Fortunately, however, I don't believe that it is necessary. What is not necessary, in particular, is this: it is not necessary for all of us (or any of us) to accept an absolute obligation to the State, either our own or a supposed World State. What is necessary is only that we almost all of us accept the general principle, the principle to abide by those restrictions which all rational men must require of all others.

One splendid example of how not to proceed is mentioned by Earle himself. War, he says, is not justified in the name of justice and Equality, but of the securing and preservation of any nation's own social good. Now in respect of justice, what he says is false. War is justified in the name of justice, and *only* in that name. All rational men must accept the right of each to defend himself against the very type of behavior which it is the business of the social agreement to proscribe. But as pointed out, that precisely means that this other behavior must be proscribed, and interestingly enough, the "securing of any nation's own social good," if no restrictions are placed on what that "good" might consist in, is one of the very things thus proscribed and put beyond the pale of justice. But let's take Equality, which is another matter. It is popular in some quarters to take equality as the very hall-mark of justice. But that is true only in the sense that all of us must acknowledge the *same principles,* and nobody can pretend to special favor from those principles. What is not true is that justice, conceived along the lines laid down above, is concerned about any *further* equality than that. On the contrary. Given any sort of good, we may be sure that some will have more than others: by nature in some respects, as a result of good fortune in other respects, and as a result of the ordinary workings of human relations in still others. To insist that those who have more must surrender it as a condition of peace is equivalent to insisting on war. For that *would* be to ask us not to be who we are, to require us to convert ourselves into somebody else. And I think there is little doubt but that the confusion of justice and equality is responsible for major portions of the threats to peace which now confront the world. Those who shoot the kneecaps off upholders of "the bourgeois order," those who sow terror in order to bring about the communist utopia, are not just misguidedly pursuing the right goals of social justice in the wrong way. They are pursuing the *wrong goals of social justice*. Neither the poor nor the rich have any rational interest in a social order which would force the rich, or the talented, or the lucky, to give to the poor, untalented, and unfortunate. I believe that this is susceptible of philosophical demonstration. And if it is, nothing could be more important to our current world situation, for in that case the main premise on which the main threat to world peace now rests would be rationally insupportable.

Well, it may be said, grant all this sort of thing, and what does it really prove against an argument such as Earle's? Something, I think. For one thing, I believe it shows why the starting-point of his argument, the sheer particularity of human existence, does not prove that war is necessary. A further point is that it does not allow references to courage and honor, to freedom and dignity, to obscure matters as they do, I think, at the conclusion of his essay. "There is no moral obligation to live at all costs and under any conditions," he observes; indeed, as he says, "there is no moral obligation to live at all; there is a moral obligation to live honorably if one lives at all" (57). Granting all this, it hardly shows that warmongers exemplify the category of honor. Again, he insists that those who die in a just cause, "while they were indeed defeated with regard to the immediate occasion of the dispute . . . were not defeated, if they fought well, with regard to something far more important, that infinite self-respect which defines their humanity" (58). Let us accept all this too: but it does not show that those who die in an *un*just cause, or who die for what turns out in fact to be no good reason whatever, have won the said infinite self-respect. Instead, I suggest, their lives have been tragically wasted, and this though they fall positively reeking with courage. Now Earle concludes his essay with the thought that "Wars are not fought to prove courage, but they do prove it all the same" (59). Well, to take an example from a recent movie, so does Russian Roulette, which quite possibly *is* played simply to prove courage, of a sort. But if it is nevertheless "courage" of a damn fool, we will not do well to speak of it as a manifestation of the "transcendental." Courage, as Earle implicitly agrees, I believe, is a virtue when, but *only* when, it is exercised in some honorable cause. And injustice is never honorable. So if I am right in claiming—along with the rest of mankind—that one side or the other in any war must be acting unjustly, then we must conclude that the fact that wars are occasions for courage does not justify them.

But equally, as I have insisted, we cannot accept pacifism either. If Earle is only insisting that to resist injustice is in its turn justifiable and that there are some causes for which we ought to be willing to die, then we must agree with this. Undoubtedly he is likewise right in pointing out that both sides in most wars will insist that they have justice on their sides. But this, I think, really shows that what is needed is clearer thought and better understanding. And it may be admitted that the prospect for those things has never been exactly overwhelming among humans. Let us hope that the awesome nature of the consequences of bad thinking in today's world will help those prospects along, if nothing else will.

NOTES

This paper was first presented at the Conference on the Prospects for World Peace held at Florida Atlantic University in August 1979.

1 William Earle, "In Defense of War," *The Monist,* October 1973, 561-9. Reprinted in the present volume, 43-59.

2 Numbers refer to pages in this book.

Some Paradoxes of Deterrence

GREGORY S. KAVKA

Deterrence is a parent of paradox. Conflict theorists, notably Thomas Schelling, have pointed out several paradoxes of deterrence: that it may be to the advantage of someone who is trying to deter another to be irrational, to have fewer available options, or to lack relevant information.[1] I shall describe certain new paradoxes that emerge when one attempts to analyze deterrence from a moral rather than a strategic perspective. These paradoxes are presented in the form of statements that appear absurd or incredible on first inspection, but can be supported by quite convincing arguments.

Consider a typical situation involving deterrence. A potential wrongdoer is about to commit an offense that would unjustly harm someone. A defender intends, and threatens, to retaliate should the wrongdoer commit the offense. Carrying out retaliation, if the offense is committed, could well be morally wrong. (The wrongdoer could be insane, or the retaliation could be out of proportion with the offense, or could seriously harm others besides the wrongdoer.) The moral paradoxes of deterrence arise out of the attempt to determine the moral status of the defender's *intention* to retaliate in such cases. If the defender knows retaliation to be wrong, it would appear that this intention is evil. Yet such "evil" intentions may pave the road to heaven, by preventing serious offenses and by doing so without actually harming anyone.

Scrutiny of such morally ambiguous retaliatory intentions reveals paradoxes that call into question certain significant and widely accepted moral doctrines. These doctrines are what I call *bridge principles.* They attempt to link together the moral evaluation of actions and the moral evaluation of agents (and their states) in certain simple and apparently natural ways. The general acceptance, and intuitive appeal, of such principles, lends credibility to the project of constructing a consistent moral system that accurately reflects our firmest moral beliefs about both agents and actions. By raising doubts about the validity of certain popular bridge principles, the paradoxes presented here pose new difficulties for this important project.

I

In this section, a certain class of situations involving deterrence is characterized, and a plausible normative assumption is presented. In the following three sections, we shall see how application of this assumption to these situations yields paradoxes.

The class of paradox-producing situations is best introduced by means of an example. Consider the balance of nuclear terror as viewed from the perspective of one of its superpower participants, nation N. N sees the threat of nuclear retaliation as its only reliable means of preventing nuclear attack (or nuclear blackmail leading to world domination) by its superpower rival. N is confident such a threat will succeed in deterring its adversary, provided it really intends to carry out that threat. (N fears that, if it bluffs, its adversary is likely to learn this through leaks or espionage.) Finally, N recognizes it would have conclusive moral reasons *not* to carry out the threatened retaliation, if its opponent were to obliterate N with a surprise attack. For although retaliation would punish the leaders who committed this unprecedented crime and would prevent them from dominating the postwar world, N knows it would also destroy many millions of innocent civilians in the attacking nation (and in other nations), would set back postwar economic recovery for the world immeasurably, and might add enough fallout to the atmosphere to destroy the human race.

Let us call situations of the sort that nation N perceives itself as being in, *Special Deterrent Situations* (SDSs). More precisely, an agent is in an SDS when he reasonably and correctly believes that the following conditions hold. First, it is likely he must intend (conditionally) to apply a harmful sanction to innocent people, if an extremely harmful and unjust offense is to be prevented. Second, such an intention would very likely deter the offense. Third, the amounts of harm involved in the offense and the threatened sanction are very large and of roughly similar quantity (or the latter amount is smaller than the former). Finally, he would have conclusive moral reasons not to apply the sanction if the offense were to occur.

The first condition in this definition requires some comment. Deterrence depends only on the potential wrongdoer's *beliefs* about the prospects of the sanction being applied. Hence, the first condition will be satisfied only if attempts by the defender to bluff would likely be perceived as such by the wrongdoer. This may be the case if the defender is an unconvincing liar, or is a group with a collective decision procedure, or if the wrongdoer is shrewd and knows the defender quite well. Generally, however, bluffing will be a promising course of action. Hence, although it is surely logically and physically possible for an SDS to occur, there will be few actual SDSs. It may be noted, though, that writers on strategic policy frequently assert that nuclear deterrence will be effective only if the defending nation really intends to retaliate.[2] If this is so, the balance of terror may fit the definition of an SDS, and the paradoxes developed here could have significant practical implications.[3] Further, were there no actual SDSs, these paradoxes would still be of considerable theoretical interest. For they indicate that the validity of some widely accepted moral doctrines rests on the presupposition that certain situations that could arise (i.e., SDSs) will not.

Turning to our normative assumption, we begin by noting that any reasonable system of ethics must have substantial utilitarian elements. The assumption that produces the paradoxes of deterrence concerns the role of utilitarian considerations in determining one's moral duty in a narrowly limited class of situations. Let the *most useful* act in a given choice situation be that with the highest expected utility. Our assumption says that the most useful act should be performed whenever a very great deal of utility is at stake. This means that, if the difference in expected utility between the most useful act and its alternatives is extremely large (e.g., equivalent to the difference between life and death for a very large number of people), other moral considerations are overridden by utilitarian considerations.

This assumption may be substantially weakened by restricting in various ways its range of application. I restrict the assumption to apply only when (i) a great deal of *negative* utility is at stake, and (ii) people will likely suffer serious injustices if the agent fails to perform the most useful act. This makes the assumption more plausible, since the propriety of doing one person a serious injustice, in order to produce positive benefits for others, is highly questionable. The justifiability of doing the same injustice to prevent a utilitarian disaster which itself involves grave injustices, seems more in accordance with our moral intuitions.

The above restrictions appear to bring our assumption into line with the views of philosophers such as Robert Nozick, Thomas Nagel, and Richard Brandt, who portray moral rules as "absolutely" forbidding certain kinds of acts, but acknowledge that exceptions might have to be allowed in cases in which such acts are necessary to prevent catastrophe.[4] Even with these restrictions, however, the proposed assumption would be rejected by supporters of genuine Absolutism, the doctrine that there are certain acts (such as vicarious punishment and deliberate killing of the innocent) that are always wrong, whatever the consequences of not performing them. (Call such acts *inherently evil.*) We can, though, accommodate the Absolutists. To do so, let us further qualify our assumption by limiting its application to cases in which (iii) performing the most useful act involves, at most, a small *risk* of performing an inherently evil act. With this restriction, the assumption still leads to paradoxes, yet is consistent with Absolutism (unless that doctrine is extended to include absolute prohibitions on something other than doing acts of the sort usually regarded as inherently evil).[5] The triply qualified assumption is quite plausible; so the fact that it produces paradoxes is both interesting and disturbing.

II

The first moral paradox of deterrence is:

> (*P1*) There are cases in which, although it would be wrong for an agent to perform a certain act in a certain situation, it would nonetheless be right for him, knowing this, to form the intention to perform that act in that situation.

At first, this strikes one as absurd. If it is wrong and he is aware that it is wrong, how could it be right for him to form the intention to do it? *P1* is the direct denial of a simple moral thesis, the Wrongful Intentions Principle (WIP): *To intend to do what one knows to be wrong is itself wrong.*[6] WIP seems so obvious that, although philosophers never call it into question, they rarely bother to assert it or argue for it. Nevertheless, it appears that Abelard, Aquinas, Butler, Bentham, Kant, and Sidgwick, as well as recent writers such as Anthony Kenny and Jan Narveson, have accepted the principle, at least implicitly.[7]

Why does WIP seem so obviously true? First, we regard the man who fully intends to perform a wrongful act and is prevented from doing so solely by external circumstances (e.g., a man whose murder plan is interrupted by the victim's fatal heart attack) as being just as bad as the man who performs a like wrongful act. Second, we view the man who intends to do what is wrong, and then changes his mind, as having corrected a moral failing or error. Third, it is convenient, for many purposes, to treat a prior intention to perform an act, as the beginning of the act itself. Hence, we are inclined to view intentions as parts of actions and to ascribe to each intention the moral status ascribed to the act "containing" it.

It is essential to note that WIP appears to apply to conditional intentions in the same manner as it applies to nonconditional ones. Suppose I form the intention to kill my neighbor if he insults me again, and fail to kill him only because, fortuitously, he refrains from doing so. I am as bad, or nearly as bad, as if he had insulted me and I had killed him. My failure to perform the act no more erases the wrongness of my intention, than my neighbor's dropping dead as I load my gun would negate the wrongness of the simple intention to kill him. Thus the same considerations adduced above in support of WIP seem to support the formulation: If it would be wrong to perform an act in certain circumstances, then it is wrong to intend to perform that act on the condition that those circumstances arise.

Having noted the source of the strong feeling that *P1* should be rejected, we must consider an instantiation of *P1*:

> (*P1'*) In an SDS, it would be wrong for the defender to apply the sanction if the wrongdoer were to commit the offense, but it is right for the

defender to form the (conditional) intention to apply the sanction if the wrongdoer commits the offense.

The first half of P_I', the wrongness of applying the sanction, follows directly from the last part of the definition of an SDS, which says that the defender would have conclusive moral reasons not to apply the sanction. The latter half of P_I', which asserts the rightness of forming the intention to apply the sanction, follows from the definition of an SDS and our normative assumption. According to the definition, the defender's forming this intention is likely necessary, and very likely sufficient, to prevent a seriously harmful and unjust offense. Further, the offense and the sanction would each produce very large and roughly commensurate amounts of negative utility (or the latter would produce a smaller amount). It follows that utilitarian considerations heavily favor forming the intention to apply the sanction, and that doing so involves only a small risk of performing an inherently evil act.[8] Applying our normative assumption yields the conclusion that it is right for the defender to form the intention in question.

This argument, if sound, would establish the truth of P_I', and hence P_I, in contradiction with WIP. It suggests that WIP should not be applied to *deterrent intentions*, i.e., those conditional intentions whose existence is based on the agent's desire to thereby deter others from actualizing the antecedent condition of the intention. Such intentions are rather strange. They are, by nature, self-stultifying: if a deterrent intention fulfills the agent's purpose, it ensures that the intended (and possibly evil) act is not performed, by preventing the circumstances of performance from arising. The unique nature of such intentions can be further explicated by noting the distinction between intending to do something, and desiring (or intending) to intend to do it. Normally, an agent will form the intention to do something because he either desires doing that thing as an end in itself, or as a means to other ends. In such cases, little importance attaches to the distinction between intending and desiring to intend. But, in the case of deterrent intentions, the ground of the desire to form the intention is entirely distinct from any desire to carry it out. Thus, what may be inferred about the agent who seeks to form such an intention is this. He desires *having the intention* as a means of deterrence. Also, he is willing, in order to prevent the offense, to accept a certain *risk* that, in the end, he will apply the sanction. But this is entirely consistent with his having a strong desire not to apply the sanction, and no desire at all to apply it. Thus, while the object of his deterrent intention might be an evil act, it does not follow that, in desiring to adopt that intention, he desires to do evil, either as an end or as a means.

WIP ties the morality of an intention exclusively to the moral qualities of its object (i.e., the intended act). This is not unreasonable since, typically, the only significant effects of intentions are the acts of the agent (and the consequences of these acts) which flow from these intentions. However, in certain cases, intentions may have *autonomous effects* that are independent of the intended act's actually being performed. In particular, intentions to act may influence the conduct of other agents. When an intention has important autonomous effects, these effects must be incorporated into any adequate moral analysis of it. The first paradox arises because the autonomous effects of the relevant deterrent intention are dominant in the moral analysis of an SDS, but the extremely plausible WIP ignores such effects.[9]

III

P1' implies that a rational moral agent in an SDS should want to form the conditional intention to apply the sanction if the offense is committed, in order to deter the offense. But will he be able to do so? Paradoxically, he will not be. He is a captive in the prison of his own virtue, able to form the requisite intention only by bending the bars of his cell out of shape. Consider the preliminary formulation of this new paradox:

> (*P2'*) In an SDS, a rational and morally good agent cannot (as a matter of logic) have (or form) the intention to apply the sanction if the offense is committed.[10]

The argument for *P2'* is as follows. An agent in an SDS recognizes that there would be conclusive moral reasons not to apply the sanction if the offense were committed. If he does not regard these admittedly conclusive moral reasons as conclusive reasons for him not to apply the sanction, then he is not moral. Suppose, on the other hand, that he does regard himself as having conclusive reasons not to apply the sanction if the offense is committed. If, nonetheless, he is disposed to apply it, because the reasons for applying it motivate him more strongly than do the conclusive reasons not to apply it, then he is irrational.

But couldn't our rational moral agent recognize, in accordance with *P1'*, that he ought to form the intention to apply the sanction? And couldn't he then simply grit his teeth and pledge to himself that he will apply the sanction if the offense is committed? No doubt he could, and this would amount to trying to form the intention to apply the sanction. But the question remains whether he can succeed in forming that intention, by this or any other process, while remaining rational and moral. And it appears he cannot. There are, first of all, psychological difficulties. Being rational, how can he dispose himself to do something that he knows he would have conclusive reasons not to do, when and if the time comes to do it? Perhaps, though, some exceptional people can produce in themselves dispositions to act merely by pledging to act. But even if one could, in an SDS, produce a disposition to apply the sanction in this manner, such a disposition would not count as a *rational intention* to apply the sanction. This is because, as recent writers on intentions have suggested, it is part of the concept of rationally intending to do something, that the disposition to do the intended act be caused (or justified) in an appropriate way by the agent's view of reasons for doing the act.[11] And the disposition in question does not stand in such a relation to the agent's reasons for action.

It might be objected to this that people sometimes intend to do things (and do them) for no reason at all, without being irrational. This is true, and indicates that the connections between the concepts of intending and reasons for action are not so simple as the above formula implies. But it is also true that intending to do something for no reason at all, in the face of recognized significant reasons not to do it, would be irrational. Similarly, a disposition to act in the face of the acknowledged preponderance of reasons, whether called an "intention" or not, could not qualify as rational. It may be claimed that such a disposition, in an SDS, is rational in the sense that the agent knows it would further his aims to form (and have) it. This is not to deny the second paradox, but simply to express one of its paradoxical features. For the point of $P2'$ is that the very disposition that *is* rational in the sense just mentioned, is at the same time irrational in an equally important sense. It is a disposition to act in conflict with the agent's own view of the balance of reasons for action.

We can achieve some insight into this by noting that an intention that is deliberately formed, resides at the intersection of two distinguishable actions. It is the beginning of the act that is its object and is the end of the act that is its formation. As such, it may be assessed as rational (or moral) or not, according to whether either of two different acts promotes the agent's (or morality's) ends. Generally, the assessments will agree. But, as Schelling and others have noted, it may sometimes promote one's aims *not* to be disposed to act to promote one's aims should certain contingencies arise. For example, a small country may deter invasion by a larger country if it is disposed to resist any invasion, even when resistance would be suicidal. In such situations, the assessment of the rationality (or morality) of the agent's intentions will depend upon whether these intentions are treated as components of their object-acts or their formation-acts. If treated as both, conflicts can occur. It is usual and proper to assess the practical rationality of an agent, at a given time, according to the degree of correspondence between his intentions and the reasons he has for performing the acts that are the objects of those intentions. As a result, puzzles such as $P2'$ emerge when, for purposes of moral analysis, an agent's intentions are viewed partly as components of their formation-acts.

Let us return to the main path of our discussion by briefly summarizing the argument for $P2'$. A morally good agent regards conclusive moral reasons for action as conclusive reasons for action *simpliciter*. But the intentions of a rational agent are not out of line with his assessment of the reasons for and against acting. Consequently, a rational moral agent cannot intend to do something that he recognizes there are conclusive moral reasons not to do. Nor can he intend conditionally to do what he recognizes he would have conclusive reasons not to do were that condition to be fulfilled. Therefore, in an SDS, where one has conclusive moral reasons not to apply the sanction, an originally rational and moral agent cannot have the intention to apply it without ceasing to be fully rational or moral; nor can he form the intention (as this entails having it).

We have observed that forming an intention is a process that may generally be regarded as an action. Thus, the second paradox can be reformulated as:

(P2) There are situations (namely SDSs) in which it would be right for agents to perform certain actions (namely forming the intention to apply the sanction) and in which it is possible for some agents to perform such actions, but impossible for rational and morally good agents to perform them.

$P2$, with the exception of the middle clause, is derived from the conjunction of $P1'$ and $P2'$ by existential generalization. The truth of the middle clause follows from consideration of the vengeful agent, who desires to punish those who commit seriously harmful and unjust offenses, no matter what the cost to others.

$P2$ is paradoxical because it says that there are situations in which rationality and virtue preclude the possibility of right action. And this contravenes our usual assumption about the close logical ties between the concepts of right action and agent goodness. Consider the following claim. *Doing something is right if and only if a morally good man would do the same thing in the given situation.* Call this the Right-Good Principle. One suspects that, aside from qualifications concerning the good man's possible imperfections or factual ignorance, most people regard this principle, which directly contradicts $P2$, as being virtually analytic. Yet the plight of the good man described in the second paradox does not arise out of an insufficiency of either knowledge or goodness. $P2$ says there are conceivable situations in which virtue and knowledge combine with rationality to preclude right action, in which virtue is an obstacle to doing the right thing. If $P2$ is true, our views about the close logical connection between right action and agent goodness, as embodied in the Right-Good Principle, require modifications of a sort not previously envisioned.

IV

A rational moral agent in an SDS faces a cruel dilemma. His reasons for intending to apply the sanction if the offense is committed are, according to $P1'$, conclusive. But they outrun his reasons for doing it. Wishing to do what is right, he wants to form the intention. However, unless he can substantially alter the basic facts of the situation or his beliefs about those facts, he can do so only by making himself less morally good; that is, by becoming a person who attaches grossly mistaken weights to certain reasons for and against action (e.g., one who prefers retribution to the protection of the vital interests of innocent people).[12] We have arrived at a third paradox:

> (*P3*) In certain situations, it would be morally right for a rational and morally good agent to deliberately (attempt to) corrupt himself.[13]

P3 may be viewed in light of a point about the credibility of threats which has been made by conflict theorists. Suppose a defender is worried about the credibility of his deterrent threat, because he thinks the wrongdoer (rightly) regards him as unwilling to apply the threatened sanction. He may make the threat more credible by passing control of the sanction to some *retaliation-agent*. Conflict theorists consider two sorts of retaliation-agents: people known to be highly motivated to punish the offense in question, and machines programmed to retaliate automatically if the offense occurs. What I wish to note is that future selves of the defender himself are a third class of retaliation-agents. If the other kinds are unavailable, a defender may have to create an agent of this third sort (i.e., an altered self willing to apply the sanction), in order to deter the offense. In cases in which applying the sanction would be wrong, this could require self-corruption.

How would a rational and moral agent in an SDS, who seeks to have the intention to apply the sanction, go about corrupting himself so that he may have it? He cannot form the intention simply by pledging to apply the sanction; for, according to the second paradox, his rationality and morality preclude this. Instead, he must seek to initiate a causal process (e.g., a reeducation program) that he hopes will result in his beliefs, attitudes, and values changing in such a way that he can and will have the intention to apply the sanction should the offense be committed. Initiating such a process involves taking a rather odd, though not uncommon attitude toward oneself: viewing oneself as an object to be molded in certain respects by outside influences rather than by inner choices. This is, for example, the attitude of the lazy but ambitious student who enrolls in a fine college, hoping that some of the habits and values of his highly motivated fellow students will "rub off" on him.

We can now better understand the notion of "risking doing *X*" which was introduced in section I. For convenience, let *X* be "killing." Deliberately risking killing is different from risking deliberately killing. One does the former when one rushes an ill person to the hospital in one's car at unsafe speed, having noted the danger of causing a fatal accident. One has deliberately accepted the risk of killing by accident. One (knowingly) risks deliberately killing, on the other hand, when one undertakes a course of action that one knows may, by various causal processes, lead to one's later performing a deliberate killing. The mild-mannered youth who joins a violent street gang is an example. Similarly, the agent in an SDS, who undertakes a plan of self-corruption in order to develop the requisite deterrent intention, knowingly risks deliberately performing the wrongful act of applying the sanction.

The above description of what is required of the rational moral agent in an SDS, leads to a natural objection to the argument that supports P_3. According to this objection, an attempt at self-corruption by a rational moral agent is very likely to fail. Hence, bluffing would surely be a more promising strategy for deterrence than trying to form retaliatory intentions by self-corruption. Three replies may be given to this objection. First, it is certainly *conceivable* that, in a particular SDS, undertaking a process of self-corruption would be more likely to result in effective deterrence than would bluffing. Second, and more important, bluffing and attempting to form retaliatory intentions by self-corruption will generally not be mutually exclusive alternatives. An agent in an SDS may attempt to form the retaliatory intention while bluffing, and plan to continue bluffing as a "fall-back" strategy, should he fail. If the offense to be prevented is disastrous enough, the additional expected utility generated by following such a combined strategy (as opposed to simply bluffing) will be very large, even if his attempts to form the intention are unlikely to succeed. Hence, P_3 would still follow from our normative assumption. Finally, consider the rational and *partly corrupt* agent in an SDS who already has the intention to retaliate. (The nations participating in the balance of terror may be examples.) The relevant question about him is whether he ought to act to become less corrupt, with the result that he would lose the intention to retaliate. The present objection does not apply in this case, since the agent already has the requisite corrupt features. Yet, essentially the same argument that produces P_3 leads, when this case is considered, to a slightly different, but equally puzzling, version of our third paradox:

> (P_3*) In certain situations, it would be morally wrong for a rational and partly corrupt agent to (attempt to) reform himself and eliminate his corruption.

A rather different objection to P_3 is the claim that its central notion is incoherent. This claim is made, apparently, by Thomas Nagel, who writes:

> The notion that one might sacrifice one's moral integrity justifiably, in the service of a sufficiently worthy end, is an incoherent notion. For if one were justified in making such a sacrifice (or even morally required to make it), then one would not be sacrificing one's moral integrity by adopting that course: one would be preserving it (132-3).

Now the notion of a justified sacrifice of moral virtue (integrity) would be incoherent, as Nagel suggests, if one could sacrifice one's virtue only by doing something wrong. For the same act cannot be both morally justified and morally wrong. But one may also be said to sacrifice one's virtue when one deliberately initiates a causal process that one expects to result, and does result, in one's later becoming a less virtuous person. And, as the analysis of SDSs embodied in P_1' and P_2' implies, one may, in certain cases, be justified in initiating such a process (or even be obligated to initiate it). Hence, it would be a mistake to deny P_3 on the grounds advanced in Nagel's argument.

There is, though, a good reason for *wanting* to reject P_3. It conflicts with some of our firmest beliefs about virtue and duty. We regard the promotion and preservation of one's own virtue as a vital responsibility of each moral agent, and self-corruption as among the vilest of enterprises. Further, we do not view the duty to promote one's virtue as simply one duty among others, to be weighed and balanced against the rest, but rather as a special duty that encompasses the other moral duties. Thus, we assent to the Virtue Preservation Principle: *It is wrong to deliberately lose (or reduce the degree of) one's moral virtue.* To many, this principle seems fundamental to our very conception of morality.[14] Hence the suggestion that duty could require the abandonment of virtue seems quite unacceptable. The fact that this suggestion can be supported by strong arguments produces a paradox.

This paradox is reflected in the ambivalent attitudes that emerge when we attempt to evaluate three hypothetical agents who respond to the demands of SDSs in various ways. The first agent refuses to try to corrupt himself and allows the disastrous offense to occur. We respect the love of virtue he displays, but are inclined to suspect him of too great a devotion to his own purity relative to his concern for the well-being of others. The second agent does corrupt himself to prevent disaster in an SDS. Though we do not approve of his new corrupt aspects, we admire the person that he *was* for his willingness to sacrifice what he loved—part of his own virtue—in the service of others. At the same time, the fact that he succeeded in corrupting himself may make us wonder whether he was entirely virtuous in the first place. Corruption, we feel, does not come easily to a good man. The third agent reluctantly but sincerely tries his best to corrupt himself to prevent disaster, but fails. He may be admired both for his willingness to make such a sacrifice and for having virtue so deeply engrained in his character that his attempts at self-corruption do not succeed. It is perhaps characteristic of the paradoxical nature of the envisioned situation, that we are inclined to admire most the only one of these three agents who fails in the course of action he undertakes.

V

It is natural to think of the evaluation of agents, and of actions, as being two sides of the same moral coin. The moral paradoxes of deterrence suggest they are more like two separate coins that can be fused together only by significantly deforming one or the other. In this concluding section, I shall briefly explain this.

Our shared assortment of moral beliefs may be viewed as consisting of three relatively distinct groups: beliefs about the evaluation of actions, beliefs about the evaluation of agents and their states (e.g., motives, intentions, and character traits), and beliefs about the relationship between the two. An important part of this last group of beliefs is represented by the three bridge principles introduced above: the Wrongful Intentions, Right-Good, and Virtue Preservation principles. Given an agreed upon set of bridge principles, one could go about constructing a moral system meant to express coherently our moral beliefs in either of two ways: by developing principles that express our beliefs about act evaluation and then using the bridge principles to derive principles of agent evaluation—or vice versa. If our bridge principles are sound and our beliefs about agent and act evaluation are mutually consistent, the resulting systems would, in theory, be the same. If, however, there are underlying incompatibilities between the principles we use to evaluate acts and agents, there may be significant differences between moral systems that are *act-oriented* and those which are *agent-oriented*. And these differences may manifest themselves as paradoxes which exert pressure upon the bridge principles that attempt to link the divergent systems, and the divergent aspects of each system, together.

It seems natural to us to evaluate acts at least partly in terms of their consequences. Hence, act-oriented moral systems tend to involve significant utilitarian elements. The principle of act evaluation usually employed in utilitarian systems is: in a given situation, one ought to perform the most useful act, that which will (or is expected to) produce the most utility. What will maximize utility depends upon the facts of the particular situation. Hence, as various philosophers have pointed out, the above principle could conceivably recommend one's (i) acting from nonutilitarian motives, (ii) advocating some nonutilitarian moral theory, or even (iii) becoming a genuine adherent of some nonutilitarian theory.[15] Related quandaries arise when one considers, from an act-utilitarian viewpoint, the deterrent intention of a defender in an SDS. Here is an intention whose object-act is anti-utilitarian and whose formation-act is a utilitarian duty that cannot be performed by a rational utilitarian.

A utilitarian might seek relief from these quandaries in either of two ways. First, he could defend some form of rule-utilitarianism. But then he would face a problem. Shall he include, among the rules of his system, our normative assumption that requires the performance of the most useful act, whenever an enormous amount of utility is at stake (and certain other conditions are satisfied)? If he does, the moral paradoxes of deterrence will appear within his system. If he does not, it would seem that his system fails to attach the importance to the consequences of particular momentous acts that any reasonable moral, much less utilitarian, system should. An alternative reaction would be to stick by the utilitarian principle of act evaluation, and simply accept P_1-P_3, and related oddities, as true. Taking this line would require the abandonment of the plausible and familiar bridge principles that contradict P_1-P_3. But this need not bother the act-utilitarian, who perceives his task as the modification, as well as codification, of our moral beliefs.

Agent-oriented (as opposed to act-oriented) moral systems rest on the premise that what primarily matters for morality are the internal states of a person: his character traits, his intentions, and the condition of his will. The doctrines about intentions and virtue expressed in our three bridge principles are generally incorporated into such systems. The paradoxes of deterrence may pose serious problems for some agent-oriented systems. It may be, for example, that an adequate analysis of the moral virtues of justice, selflessness, and benevolence, would imply that the truly virtuous man would feel obligated to make whatever personal sacrifice is necessary to prevent a catastrophe. If so, the moral paradoxes of deterrence would arise within agent-oriented systems committed to these virtues.

There are, however, agent-oriented systems that would not be affected by our paradoxes. One such system could be called Extreme Kantianism. According to this view, the only things having moral significance are such features of a person as his character and the state of his will. The Extreme Kantian accepts Kant's dictum that morality requires treating oneself and others as ends rather than means. He interprets this to imply strict duties to preserve one's virtue and not to deliberately impose serious harms or risks on innocent people. Thus, the Extreme Kantian would simply reject P_1-P_3 without qualm.

Although act-utilitarians and Extreme Kantians can view the paradoxes of deterrence without concern, one doubts that the rest of us can. The adherents of these extreme conceptions of morality are untroubled by the paradoxes because their viewpoints are too one-sided to represent our moral beliefs accurately. Each of them is closely attentive to certain standard principles of agent *or* act evaluation, but seems too little concerned with traditional principles of the other sort. For a system of morality to reflect our firmest and deepest convictions adequately, it must represent a middle ground between these extremes by seeking to accommodate the valid insights of both act-oriented and agent-oriented perspectives. The normative assumption set out in section I was chosen as a representative principle that might be incorporated into such a system. It treats utilitarian considerations as relevant and potentially decisive, while allowing for the importance of other factors. Though consistent with the absolute prohibition of certain sorts of acts, it treats the distinction between harms and risks as significant and rules out absolute prohibitions on the latter as unreasonable. It is an extremely plausible middle-ground principle; but, disturbingly it leads to paradoxes.

That these paradoxes reflect conflicts between commonly accepted principles of agent and act evaluation, is further indicated by the following observation. Consider what initially appears a natural way of viewing the evaluation of acts and agents as coordinated parts of a single moral system. According to this view, reasons for action determine the moral status of acts, agents, and intentions. A right act is an act that accords with the preponderance of moral reasons for action. To have the right intention is to be disposed to perform the act supported by the preponderance of such reasons, because of those reasons. The virtuous agent is the rational agent who has the proper substantive values, i.e., the person whose intentions and actions accord with the preponderance of moral reasons for action. Given these considerations, it appears that it should always be possible for an agent to go along intending, and acting, in accordance with the preponderance of moral reasons; thus ensuring both his own virtue and the rightness of his intentions and actions. Unfortunately, this conception of harmonious coordination between virtue, right intention, and right action, is shown to be untenable by the paradoxes of deterrence. For they demonstrate that, in any system that takes consequences plausibly into account, situations can arise in which the rational use of moral principles leads to certain paradoxical recommendations: that the principles used, and part of the agent's virtue, be abandoned, and that wrongful intentions be formed.

One could seek to avoid these paradoxes by moving in the direction of Extreme Kantianism and rejecting our normative assumption. But to do so would be to overlook the plausible core of act-utilitarianism. This is the claim that, in the moral evaluation of acts, how those acts affect human happiness often is important—the more so as more happiness is at stake—and sometimes is decisive. Conversely, one could move toward accommodation with act-utilitarianism. This would involve qualifying, so that they do not apply in SDSs, the traditional moral doctrines that contradict $P1$-$P3$. And, in fact, viewed in isolation, the considerations adduced in section II indicate that the Wrongful Intentions Principle ought to be so qualified. However, the claims of $P2$ and $P3$, that virtue may preclude right action and that morality may require self-corruption, are not so easily accepted. These notions remain unpalatable even when one considers the arguments that support them.

Thus, tinkering with our normative assumption or with traditional moral doctrines would indeed enable us to avoid the paradoxes, at least in their present form. But this would require rejecting certain significant and deeply entrenched beliefs concerning the evaluation either of agents or of actions. Hence, such tinkering would not go far toward solving the fundamental problem of which the paradoxes are symptoms: the apparent incompatability of the moral principles we use to evaluate acts and agents. Perhaps this problem can be solved. Perhaps the coins of agent and act evaluation can be successfully fused. But it is not apparent how this is to be done. And I, for one, do not presently see an entirely satisfactory way out of the perplexities that the paradoxes engender.

NOTES

An earlier version of this paper was presented at Stanford University. I am grateful to several, especially Robert Merrihew Adams, Tyler Burge, Warren Quinn, and Virginia Warren, for helpful comments on previous drafts. My work was supported, in part, by a Regents' Faculty Research Fellowship from the University of California.

1 *The Strategy of Conflict* (New York, 1960), Chaps. 1-2; and *Arms and Influence* (New Haven, Conn., 1966), Chap. 2.

2 See, for example, Herman Kahn, *On Thermonuclear War*, 2nd ed. (Princeton, 1960), 185; and Anthony Kenny, "Counterforce and Countervalue," in Walter Stein, ed., *Nuclear Weapons: A Catholic Response* (London, 1965), 162-4.

3 See, for example, note 9, below.

4 Nozick, *Anarchy, State, and Utopia* (New York, 1974) 30-1 n.; Nagel, "War and Massacre," *Philosophy & Public Affairs* 1, no. 2 (Winter 1972), 123-44, p. 126; Brandt, "Utilitarianism and the Rules of War," *ibid.*, 145-65, p. 147, especially n. 3.

5 Extensions of Absolutism that would block some or all of the paradoxes include those which forbid intending to do what is wrong, deliberately making oneself less virtuous, or intentionally risking performing an inherently evil act. (An explanation of the relevant sense of "risking performing an act" will be offered in section IV.)

6 I assume henceforth that, if it would be wrong to do something, the agent knows this. (The agent, discussed in section IV, who has become corrupt may be an exception.) This keeps the discussion of the paradoxes from getting tangled up with the separate problem of whether an agent's duty is to do what is actually right, or what he believes is right.

7 See *Peter Abelard's Ethics*, D. E. Luscombe, trans. (New York, 1971), 5-37; Thomas Aquinas, *Summa Theologica*, 1a2ae. 18-20; Joseph Butler, "A Dissertation on the Nature of Virtue," in *Five Sermons* (Indianapolis, 1950), 83; Immanuel Kant, *Foundations of the Metaphysics of Morals*, first section; Jeremy Bentham, *An Introduction to the Principles of Morals and Legislation*, Chap. 9, secs. 13-16; Henry Sidgwick, *The Methods of Ethics* (New York, 1907), 60-1, 201-4; Kenny, "Counterforce and Countervalue," 159, 162; and Jan Narveson, *Morality and Utility* (Baltimore, Md., 1967), 106-8.

8 A qualification is necessary. Although having the intention involves only a small risk of applying the threatened sanction to innocent people, it follows, from points made in section IV, that forming the intention might also involve risks of performing *other* inherently evil acts. Hence, what really follows is that forming the intention is right in those SDSs in which the composite risk is small. The limitation in the scope of $P1'$ is to be henceforth understood. It does not affect $P1$, $P2$, or $P3$, since each is governed by an existential quantifier.

9 In *Nuclear Weapons*, Kenny and others use WIP to argue that nuclear deterrence is immoral because it involves having the conditional intention to kill innocent people. The considerations advanced in this section suggest that this argument, at best, is inconclusive, since it presents only one side of a moral paradox, and, at worst, is mistaken, since it applies WIP in just the sort of situation in which its applicability is most questionable.

10 "Rational and morally good" in this and later statements of the second and third paradoxes, means rational and moral in the given situation. A person who usually is

rational and moral, but fails to be in the situation in question, could, of course, have the intention to apply the sanction. $P2'$ is quite similar to a paradox concerning utilitarianism and deterrence developed by D. H. Hodgson in *Consequences of Utilitarianism* (Oxford, 1967), Chap. 4.

[11] See, for example, S. Hampshire and H.L.A. Hart, "Decision, Intention and Certainty," *Mind* LXVII.1, 265 (January 1958), 1-12; and G.E.M. Anscombe, *Intention* (Ithaca, N.Y.,1966).

[12] Alternatively, the agent could undertake to make himself into an *irrational* person whose intentions are quite out of line with his reasons for action. However, trying to become irrational, in these circumstances, is less likely to succeed than trying to change one's moral beliefs, and furthermore, might itself constitute self-corruption. Hence, this point does not affect the paradox stated below.

[13] As Donald Regan has suggested to me, $P3$ can be derived directly from our normative assumption: imagine a villain credibly threatening to kill very many hostages unless a certain good man corrupts himself. I prefer the indirect route to $P3$ given in the text, because $P1$ and $P2$ are interesting in their own right and because viewing the three paradoxes together makes it easier to see what produces them.

[14] Its supporters might, of course, allow exceptions to the principle in cases in which only the agent's feelings, and not his acts or dispositions to act, are corrupted. (For example, a doctor "corrupts himself" by suppressing normal sympathy for patients in unavoidable pain, in order to treat them more effectively.) Further, advocates of the doctrine of double effect might consider self-corruption permissible when it is a "side effect" of action rather than a means to an end. For example, they might approve of a social worker's joining a gang to reform it, even though he expects to assimilate some of the gang's distorted values. Note, however, that neither of these possible exceptions to the Virtue Preservation Principle (brought to my attention by Robert Adams) applies to the agent in an SDS who corrupts his *intentions* as a chosen *means* of preventing an offense.

[15] See Hodgson, *Consequences*. Also, Adams, "Motive Utilitarianism," *The Journal of Philosophy* 73, no. 14 (12 August 1976), 467-81; and Bernard Williams, "A Critique of Utilitarianism, " in J.J.C. Smart and Williams, *Utilitarianism: For and Against* (New York, 1973), sec. 6.

Missiles and Morals:
A Utilitarian Look
at Nuclear Deterrence

DOUGLAS P. LACKEY

Though American foreign policy since 1945 has oscillated between conciliation and confrontation, American military policy at the strategic level has remained firmly tied to the notion of nuclear deterrence. After Hiroshima and Nagasaki, it was apparent that the effects of nuclear weapons were so terrible that their future use could never be condoned. But the threat to use nuclear weapons need not require their use, and such threats, in themselves, might prevent great evils. For those worried about Soviet expansion, a credible threat to use nuclear weapons might hold Soviet power in check. For those worried about future nuclear wars, the threat to use the bomb in retaliation might prevent nuclear wars from beginning. For an American public eager for demobilization, nuclear threats provided an appealing substitute for foot soldiering on foreign soil.[1] The stance of deterrence, of threat without use, appeared to both liberals and conservatives to command an overwhelming moral and prudential case. Small wonder, then, that after several abortive, perhaps deliberately abortive,[2] attempts at the internationalization of atomic weapons, the United States opted for unilateral development of nuclear weapons and delivery systems. Whatever residual qualms policy makers felt about the possession of nuclear arms were effectively silenced by the explosion of the first Soviet bomb in 1949. That the Soviets should possess nuclear weapons when the United States did not was politically unthinkable. Thirty-two years and ten thousand American nuclear weapons later, it still is.

Nevertheless it was arguable almost from the first that the case for deterrence was weaker than it seemed. The effectiveness of nuclear threats as a deterrent to Soviet aggression or Communist expansion was and remains barely credible. If the threat to use nuclear weapons did not prevent the subversion of Czechoslovakia, the blockade of Berlin, the collapse of Chiang Kai-shek, the fall of Dienbienphu, or the invasion of Hungary, all of which occurred before the Soviet Union could effectively deter an American nuclear strike with nuclear weapons and missiles of its own, how much less effective must nuclear threats have been towards deterring the Soviet invasion of Czechoslovakia in 1968 and the invasion of Afghanistan in 1979, and how little effect could such threats have as a deterrent to the much discussed but little expected invasion of West Germany by forces of the Warsaw pact?[3]

Since there have been no uses of nuclear weapons in war since 1945, the case for nuclear threats as a deterrent to first uses of nuclear weapons seems a bit stronger. Nevertheless the role that nuclear deterrence has played in keeping the world free of nuclear war is a matter for debate. In the case of wars in progress, nuclear weapons have not been introduced in many cases because they cannot be effectively deployed relative to overall military objectives. The Israelis cannot use nuclear weapons on the Golan for fear of polluting the Kennerit; the Iraquis could not use them against Jerusalem without destroying the mosques they seek to liberate. The United States could not use nuclear weapons in South Vietnam without contaminating the countryside of our own allies; the Soviets could not use them against Prague and Budapest without destroying the industries they seek to exploit. As for the prevention through deterrence of large-scale nuclear war, it can be argued that every decrease in the chance of a nuclear first strike that results from fear of a retaliatory second strike is matched by an increase in the chance of a nuclear first strike that results from accident or mistake, human or mechanical failure; that every decrease in the chance that innocent millions will die from an undeterred first strike is matched by an increase in the chance that innocent millions will die from a nuclear second strike that cannot be stopped after initial deterrence has failed. To these dangers we should add the consideration that the American argument, "the United States must have the bomb if the Soviet Union has one," is replicable by every nation state, producing pressure for proliferation which in turn increases the chance of war, and the consideration that no degree of threat can deter a nuclear terrorist who prefers to be dead rather than blue, or red, or green, and who has built his bomb with the help of weapons technology developed by states that are sworn "to deterrence only." There is little, at least in a preliminary survey of the evidence, that supports the idea that the construction of nuclear weapons for the purpose of issuing nuclear threats has contributed to the prevention of nuclear wars since 1945, or will contribute towards preventing them in the future. Whatever the game theorists say, the common-sense view that you cannot prevent wars by building bombs still has some weight.

The argument that nuclear deterrence can replace the war of soldiers on the ground with a war of threats in the air has also seen hard sledding since 1945. The need for retaining conventional forces has been apparent since the Berlin blockade, and the effect that reliance on nuclear deterrence has had on the quality of conventional forces is by now well known. It is no accident that the last successful American military operation (Inchon) preceded the development of ICBMs, and the increasing ineptitude of American conventional forces exhibited in the successively botched Son Tay, Mayaguez, and Iranian rescue attempts is too obvious to bear comment. There is no necessary connection between nuclear strength and conventional weakness, but in a world of limited resources the development of strategic forces has twisted military budgets in favor of high technology, and the result has been complicated guns that won't shoot and complicated planes that can't fly.[4] The idea that the nation's "first line" of defense consists of radar towers and missiles rather than men on the battlefield must inevitably weaken the morale of the Army and the Marines. However plausible it may have seemed to John Foster Dulles, there is little support now for the view that nuclear threats can substitute in any way for the painful sacrifices of conventional war.

The moral and prudential case for deterrence seems overcome by events. But there is a rejoinder to these criticisms that many find decisive: deterrence is bad, but disarmament is worse. Elected officials remember well that the only Presidential candidate since 1945 with a kind word for nuclear disarmament was humiliated in 1972 and voted out of the Senate in 1980. Fortunately moral philosophers do not stand for election and are free to examine all the options regardless of practical constraints. This is what I propose to do, with the important limitation that the moral systems I shall bring to bear upon the subject are all utilitarian systems. In normal circumstances one may have one's doubts about utilitarianism, but if nuclear war is among the results of policies under consideration, the gravity of the consequences carries all else before.

I

FOUR DECISION RULES

The agreeable utilitarian idea that the moral worth of acts and policies is to be measured in the value of their consequences has been troubled from the beginning by the problem that the consequences of policies are often uncertain. Suppose that Policy 1 will produce either A or B, that Policy 2 will produce either C or D, and that by some accepted standard of value A is better than C but B is worse than D. The rule that the best policy is the one with the best consequences will not tell us which policy to choose, and there is no consensus among utilitarian theorists as to how the general rule should be modified in order to generate the morally right choice. Nevertheless there are many ingenious suggestions about how to deal with choice under uncertainty, and in this essay we will deploy four different principles of choice: Minimax, Dominance, Disaster Avoidance, and Expected Value Maximization. Each principle will be used twice over, first for the utilitarian calculation, which we will call the moral calculation; second, for a prudential calculation, which will indicate, from the standpoint of the United States, what the prudential course of action might be.

Each prudential and moral calculation requires a standard of value, and in the essay the usual standard of value will be the satisfaction of preferences. In the utilitarian calculation, we will consider outcome A to be better than outcome B if the vast majority of persons in this and in several future generations would prefer A to B. In the prudential calculation, we will consider outcome A to be better than outcome B if the vast majority of Americans in this and in several future genera- tions would prefer A to B. Given the subject matter of nuclear war, for many problems value can be equated with human lives, and outcome A can be considered better than outcome B if fewer people are killed by war in A than are killed by war in B. But considering that at least some Americans are on record as preferring being dead to being red, and since many Americans (I think) would prefer a small chance of nuclear attack to a very large chance of Soviet world domination, the equation of value with human lives cannot always be relied upon, especially in the prudential calculation.

In all four models of choice we confine our inquiry to just two nations—the United States and the Soviet Union. These are the pri- mary protagonists in the nuclear drama, and we will argue in a later section that conclusions reached about the bilateral case can also be applied straightforwardly to the multilateral case. Furthermore, we will apply our four models of choice to just three strategies, *Superior- ity*, *Equivalence*, and *Nuclear Disarmament*. Though there are many stra- tegies for nuclear armament, these three have been at the center of the strategic debate at least since the late 1950s:

> S: Maintain second-strike capacity; seek first-strike capacity; threaten first and second strikes ("Superiority").
> E: Maintain second-strike capacity; do not seek first-strike capacity; threaten second strikes only ("Equivalence").
> ND: Do not seek to maintain second-strike capacity ("Nuclear Disarma- ment").

In the statement of these strategies the terminology is standard: Nation A is presumed to have *first-strike capacity* against B if A can launch a nuclear attack on B without fear of suffering unacceptable damage from B's subsequent counterstrike; nation A is said to have *second-strike capacity* against B if A is capable of inflicting unacceptable damage on B after having suffered a nuclear first strike by B.

Strategy S has been the favored strategy of hard-line anticommun- ists ever since the early 1950s. In its original form, as we find it in John Foster Dulles, the Superiority Strategy called for threats of American first strikes against Russian cities in retaliation for what American policy defined as Soviet acts of aggression. In its present form, as it is developed by Paul Nitze, Colin Gray, and others, the Superiority Strategy calls for threats, or implied threats, of American first strikes against Soviet military forces, combined with large-scale increases in American strategic arms.[5]

The Superiority Strategy, however, is not the exclusive property of doctrinaire anticommunists or hard-line "forward" strategists. Since aiming one's missiles at enemy missiles implies a desire to destroy those missiles before they are launched, that is, a desire to launch a first strike, all retargeting of American missiles from Soviet cities to Soviet missiles, up to and including President Carter's Directive 59 in the summer of 1980, imply partial endorsement of Strategy S.[6] Such "counterforce" as opposed to "countervalue" targetings are entailed by Strategy S even if they do not in fact bring first-strike capacity; Strategy S as defined implies that the United States will *seek* first-strike capacity, not that it will in fact obtain it. Strategy S advocates steps which will produce first-strike capacity unless new countermeasures are developed by the Soviet Union to cancel them out.

Strategy E, the "equivalence" strategy, enshrines the Wohlstetter-McNamara doctrine of Mutual Assured Destruction, and includes both massive retaliations against massive strikes and flexible responses against lesser strikes.[7] The possibility and permanence of Strategy E seemed assured by SALT I in 1972, since negotiated restrictions on the deployment of antiballistic missiles seemed to guarantee permanent second-strike capacity to both sides. Unfortunately, SALT I did not limit the development and deployment of MIRVs (multiple independently targeted reentry vehicles), and the deployment of MIRVs through the 1970s has led to cries on both sides that mutual second-strike capacity is dissolving and mutual first-strike capacity is emerging.[8]

Notice that although Strategy E permits bilateral arms control, it actually prohibits substantial reductions in nuclear arms. The delicate balance of mutual second-strike capacity becomes increasingly unstable as arms levels are lowered, and sooner or later, mutual disarmament brings a loss of second-strike capacity on one side and the emergence of first-strike capacity on the other, contrary to E.

Strategy ND calls for a unilateral halt in the development of American nuclear weapons and delivery systems, even if such a halt eventuates in Soviet first-strike capacity. Strategy ND is a policy of *nuclear* disarmament; it does *not* call for the abandonment of conventional weapons and should not be equated with pacifism or confused with general and complete disarmament. In fact, increases in conventional weapons levels are compatible with Strategy ND.

II

MINIMAX

Considering the hundreds of billions of dollars the United States has spent on strategic weapons since 1945, it is remarkable how little anyone knows about what would happen should these weapons be used. In an unsettling account of the present state of national defense James Fallows writes:

> There has never been a nuclear war, and nobody knows what a nuclear war would mean . . . . No one knows how these weapons would perform if they were fired; whether they would hit the targets at which they are aimed; whether human society would be set back for decades, centuries as a result . . . . Most strategic arguments (are) disputes of faith rather than fact.[9]

Fallows's gloomy judgment is confirmed by a report presented to Congress in 1979 by the Office of Technology Assessment:

> The effects of nuclear war that cannot be calculated are at least as important as those for which calculations are attempted. Moreover even these very limited calculations are subject to large uncertainties . . .This is particularly true for indirect effects such as deaths resulting from injuries and the unavailability of medical care, or for economic damage resulting from disruptions and disorganization rather than direct disruption.[10]

Fallows and the OTA do not exaggerate. To date no Minuteman missile has been test-fired from an operational silo; no American ICBM has been properly tested on a North-South trajectory, and missile accuracy reports are a guessing game subject to vagaries of wind, gravitational anomaly, and fratricidal interference from other "friendly" missiles. On top of all this, the entire defense communications network and all electronic guidance systems may be disrupted by the electromagnetic pulses that emanate from thermonuclear blasts.[11]

Anyone who accepts such estimates of the depth of our ignorance about nuclear war will be encouraged to use a principle of choice that does not require knowledge of the probabilities that a given nuclear policy will produce a given result. Of such principles, perhaps the most widely used in both prudential and moral calculation is the Minimax Principle:

> Choose any policy the worst outcome of which is at least as good as the worst outcome of any other policy.

Let us do the Minimax moral calculation first. The worst outcome of both the Superiority Strategy and the Equivalence Strategy is a large-scale thermonuclear exchange in which both sides launch as many of their missiles as possible. The worst outcome of the Nuclear Disarmament Strategy is a unilateral nuclear strike on the United States by the Soviet Union followed by whatever increases in Soviet power such a strike might bring. (I list a unilateral Soviet nuclear attack as an outcome of ND not because ND makes such attacks likely but because they are physically possible given ND. Minimax pays no heed to probabilities.) Since the vast majority of persons (especially Russian persons) in this and several future generations would prefer a one-sided attack on the United States to all-out nuclear war between the United States and the Soviet Union, the utilitarian Minimax Principle declares that the morally right policy is Nuclear Disarmament.

The prudential calculation is not so straightforward. Americans as a group will agree with people at large as to the worst outcome associated with each policy. But it is not so clear that Americans will agree that an outcome in which the Soviet Union attacks an unresponding United States is preferable to an outcome in which the Soviet Union attacks and the United States responds. A reasonable survey of prevailing American sentiments would probably report (i) that a substantial number of Americans would prefer one-sided destruction to two-sided destruction, even if the destroyed side happens to be the American side, on grounds that more lives are saved if only one side is destroyed, and (ii) that a substantial number of Americans would prefer two-sided destruction to one-sided destruction, on the grounds that if the Soviet Union attacks the United States, the Soviet Union deserves to be punished. If these are the genuine American preferences, the Minimax Principle yields no verdict in the prudential case. For the record, we might also note that Minimax reasoning fails to distinguish, either morally or prudentially, between the Equivalence Strategy and the Superiority Strategy, since the same disaster is the worst outcome in either case.

III

DOMINANCE

Like Minimax, Dominance is a principle of choice under uncertainty which makes no reference to probabilities of outcomes:

> Choose a policy (if any) yielding results which cannot be improved, no matter what the opposition or nature may choose to do.

Obviously such policies are rarely found, but many writers feel that such a dominant strategy is available in the arena of nuclear choice. For simplicity, let us consider only the Equivalence Strategy and the Nuclear Disarmament Strategy, and let us assume that the only variable in the environment is the Soviet choice between E and ND. Since each side has two options, there are four outcomes.:

1. The United States arms; the Soviet Union disarms;
2. The United States and the Soviet Union both disarm;
3. The United States and the Soviet Union both arm; and
4. The United States disarms; the Soviet Union arms.

If we suppose (as most students of strategy do) that the vast majority of American people prefer these outcomes in the order in which they are presented, then prudentially the United States should remain armed, no matter what the Soviet Union does.[12] By the Dominance Principle, then, the United States should stick with Equivalence.

Since these ratings are made from the national point of view, the conclusion thus far is strictly prudential. The moral argument yields surprisingly different results. Presumably a large majority of people in the world prefer 2 to 1, that is, they prefer neither side having nuclear arms to one side having them. This suffices to show that Equivalence does not dominate from the moral point of view. Furthermore, if we assume that a large majority of people in the world, fearful of all-out nuclear war, prefer that the United States practice ND even if the Soviet Union does not, it is Nuclear Disarmament that dominates from the moral point of view.

We have the consistent but disagreeable result that, if we follow Dominance, prudence dictates one policy while morality dictates another. We could challenge this conclusion by making different assessments of preferences. But there are other grounds which might lead us to conclude that the real problem here is not the assessment of preferences but the Dominance Principle itself.

IV

CONCEPTUAL PROBLEMS

Both the Minimax and the Dominance Principles are examples of game-theoretical strategic principles that treat each outcome as the result of equally permissible and equally possible moves in a gamelike situation. Rapoport, Green, and others in the past have criticized certain aspects of the game-theoretical approach;[13] its tendency, for example, to treat situations of nuclear strategy as zero-sum games in which cooperation is impossible, rather than as constant-sum games in which it can be prudent to cooperate. But the game-theoretical approach is inadequate in a way that cannot be remedied by shifting to broader principles and a wider range of games. In the standard logic of games each alternative is taken as given, and there is no room for calculating how the threat to make one move will influence the chance that another move is made, a consideration which is at the heart of the argument for deterrence. Consider the following argument, which proceeds on the basis of fixed alternatives: "The logical possibilities are that either the Soviets will attack or they will not attack. If they attack, there is no point in threatening to counterattack, since the whole point of the threat was to prevent the attack. If they do not attack, there is no point in threatening to counterattack, since there is no initial attack for the threat to deter: we conclude, therefore, nuclear threats are futile, or they are otiose." The notion that threats might diminish the chance of attack goes by the board. Perhaps we should dispense with deterrence, but the argument for dispensing with it cannot be this easy!

Even worse difficulties can be generated by combining information about outcomes with the dominance principle. Suppose that Americans prefer outcomes 1 through 4 as stated in the previous section, and suppose that it is given information that (i) whenever the United States arms, the Soviet Union will arm, and that (ii) whenever the United States disarms, the Soviet Union will disarm. Since Americans prefer mutual disarmament to mutual armament, the preferred strategy in the light of the given information is for the United States to disarm. But game-theoretical reasoning still insists that the preferred strategy is to remain armed. Even if the Soviets will disarm when the United States disarms, it remains true that they will either arm or disarm. If they arm, it is better for the United States to arm. If they disarm, it is better for the United States to arm. Therefore the United States should arm in any event. The result will be mutual armament, a situation worse than that which could confidently be achieved by the choice of disarmament. It is not possible here to review all the systems devised in recent years by game theorists attempting to cope with this problem. Suffice it to say that there is a consensus that something must be done but no consensus about what to do, and the state of the field is sufficiently unsettled to warrant serious investigation of more information-sensitive decision principles.[14]

V

DISASTER AVOIDANCE

Let us suppose that one type of information that we *do* have about nuclear war is information pertaining to the ordering of the probabilities of the various outcomes. For example, most people would agree that the chance of nuclear war on the Superiority Strategy is greater than the chance of war on the Equivalence Strategy, though what quantitative probabilities are, in either case, is difficult to say. If this type of information is all the information we have, and if there are outcomes all parties identify as disastrous, the rational course of action, Gregory Kavka suggests, is dictated by what he calls the Disaster Avoidance Principle:

> When choosing between potential disasters under two dimensional uncertainty, it is rational to select the alternative that minimizes the probabiltiy of disaster occurrence.[15]

Kavka does not advance the Avoidance Principle as a solution for all problems of two dimensional uncertainty, but he recommends its use in situations in which nine special conditions are satisfied. Use of the Avoidance Principle is rational if and only if: (i) quantitative probabilities and utilities are unknown; (ii) conditional probabilities are known; (iii) all disastrous outcomes are extremely unacceptable; (iv) all disastrous outcomes are roughly the same order of magnitude; (v) the chooser regards the difference in utility between nondisastrous outcomes to be small compared to the difference between disastrous outcomes and nondisastrous outcomes; (vi) the choice is unique, that is, not one of a series of choices; (vii) the probabilities of the disasters are not thought to be insignificant; (viii) the probability of the greater disaster is not thought to be very large; and (ix) the probabilities of the disasters are not thought to be very close to equal.

Kavka argues that all nine of these conditions are satisfied by the problem of nuclear choice, and proceeds to apply the Disaster Avoidance Principle to the choice between Equivalence and Nuclear Disarmament. (He does not consider the Superiority Strategy.) Arguing that:

> We can be confident that the likelihood of Soviet domination if the U.S. disarms is greater than the likelihood of war if the U.S. practices deterrence,[16]

he concludes that the rational choice is the Equivalence Strategy. Since there is no place in the calculations for differences between the preferences of Americans and the preferences of all people, it follows from Kavka's reasoning that the Equivalence Strategy is the morally preferred choice—at least for utilitarians.

This is not the place for full theoretical analysis of Kavka's Avoidance Principle, which supplies a principle of rational choice to problems beset by what Daniel Ellsberg called "ambiguity," as opposed to "risk."[17] For our purposes, let us agree that the principle *does* represent a principle of rational choice *if* all nine of Kavka's qualifying conditons are satisfied. What is more at issue is whether the conditions are in fact satisfied in the case of nuclear choice and whether the principle has been properly applied to this particular problem.

Kavka's fourth condition is that "disastrous outcomes must be roughly of the same order of magnitude." Obviously if one outcome is hundreds of times more disastrous than the other, and the probabilities of the disasters are not known, minimax reasoning should prevail. Kavka argues that the disaster which might be produced by the Equivalence Strategy is nuclear war, and the disaster which might be produced by nuclear disarmament is Soviet domination. For Kavka these are disasters "roughly equal in magnitude," which shows that, for Kavka, "roughly equal" is very rough indeed. But it would be useless to belabor the comparison of nuclear war with Soviet domination, since in fact the comparision is irrelevant. The main catastrophe of the Equivalence Strategy is *all-out* nuclear war; the main catastrophe of Nuclear Disarmament is a *one-sided* nuclear war. Are *these* disasters roughly equal in magnitude?

Clearly a two-sided nuclear war would be rated by everyone as a "great disaster" and a one-sided nuclear war would be rated by everyone as a "great disaster." This might tempt us to conclude that these are disasters roughly equal in magnitude. Indeed, most people are not capable of discriminating finely between nuclear wars, a psychological fact that advocates of limited nuclear war are given to deplore. But let us suppose that 20,000,000 Americans will die in a one-sided nuclear war and that 60,000,000 Americans and 60,000,000 Russians will die in a two-sided nuclear war, figures which are not unreasonable and which reflect the fact that a Soviet first strike would be relatively smaller against an America practicing nuclear disarmament. If we shake the Strangelovian dizziness out of our heads, we can make a serious attempt to compare the magnitude of 20,000,000 deaths and 120,000,000 deaths. If we take the comparison to be *six to one*, we might agree with Kavka that the two disasters are "roughly equal in magnitude." But this is obviously not the proper way to make the comparison. We must ask whether X and Y should be rated roughly equal in magnitude given that X and Y are quite the same *except* that in Y there are 100,000,000 more deaths than in X. Certainly 100,000,000 dead as opposed to no dead at all is a matter of very great magnitude, and thus Kavka's assumption that there is no difference between the magnitude of the disaster produced by deterrence and the magnitude of the disaster produced by disarmament is false— even if it makes the disaster produced by disarmament much *greater* than he assumes it to be.

Even more disturbing than Kavka's claim that his nine conditions are satisfied is his final deduction of the result that disarmament is irrational. The major premise of this argument is the Avoidance Principle; the minor premise—a crucial step in the deduction—is the claim that the likelihood of disaster under disarmament is greater than the likelihood of disaster under deterrence. This empirical claim is presented as a proposition of which "we can be confident," but I feel no confidence whatsoever about it, and it is asserted without argument or evidence.[18] Not a single author who has discussed nuclear deterrence feels that the risk of nuclear war resulting from the practice of deterrence is negligible, and there are many—the whole staff of the *Bulletin of Atomic Scientists*, for example—who consider it to be substantial. In discussion of nuclear disarmament, there are many who feel that the Soviet Union might *attempt* nuclear blackmail if it gained first-strike capacity, but there are not many who are sure that such attempts at blackmail would succeed. The sole evidence which history provides on this subject is the sobering fact that the period of nuclear supremacy for the United States was precisely the period of greatest communist expansion in the world (1945-49). One can only speculate that Kavka, like many authors who dismiss nuclear disarmament as unwise and impractical, has blurred together the effects of *nuclear* disarmament and the effects of *general and complete* disarmament.[19] As a result, he has illicitly upgraded the chance of Soviet domination resulting from the strategy of *nuclear* disarmament and begs the question in favor of Equivalence.

VI

EXPECTED VALUE

Perhaps the most natural of all responses to the problem of uncertainty is to discount the weight of consequences by whatever chance there is that they will not occur. To compute the "expected value" of a policy, then, we should consider each possible outcome of the policy, multiply the utility of that outcome by the probability that it will occur, and take the sum of all these products. In the area of nuclear strategy we cannot supply precise numbers for the probabilities of the outcomes, nor can we attempt to supply precise figures for the corresponding utilities. Nevertheless, we *do* have much more information about these subjects than the orderings of probabilities to which we were restricted in the Disaster Avoidance model, and what imprecision there is in our information can be respected by stating the information in the form of approximations. For example, we can classify the probability of outcomes as "negligible," "small but substantial," "fifty-fifty," "very likely," and "almost certain," and we can classify outcomes as "extremely bad," "bad," "neutral," and so forth. In considering the products of utilities and outcomes, we can neglect all outcomes of negligible probability, and all outcomes of small but substantial probability *except* those classified as extremely good or extremely bad. In many cases, use of such estimates will yield surprisingly definite results.

Now, what are the "outcomes" the probabilities of which we ought to consider? Given the traditionally assumed goals of deterrence, we should certainly consider the effects of each policy on the probability

TABLE I

	One-sided Strike*	All-out Nuclear War	Soviet Aggression	Very High Military Spending
Superiority	Fifty-fifty [a]	Fifty-fifty [b]	Small [c]	Certain [d]
Equivalence	Small [e]	Small [f]	Small [g]	Fifty-fifty [h]
Nuclear Disarmament	Small [i]	Zero [j]	Small [k]	Small [l]

*A "one-sided strike" is a first strike that may or may not be answered by a second strike. A comparison of the probability of one-sided strikes and two-sided strikes in a given row indicates that a first strike will lead to an all-out nuclear war.

of nuclear war, the probability of Soviet nonnuclear aggression, and the probability of Soviet nuclear blackmail. As we have noted, in considering the probability of nuclear war, it is essential to distinguish the probability of a one-sided nuclear strike from the probability of all-out nuclear war. Among other outcomes, we will consider only the effects of nuclear strategies on military spending, since the impact of policies on spending can be determined with little controversy. Since we have four outcomes and three policies to consider, the probabilities can be represented on a three-by-four grid (see Table 1). Each probability assessment will be defended in turn.

Value of the Superiority Strategy

1. Strategists disagree about the probability of Soviet or American first strike under the Superiority Strategy. All students of the subject rate it as having at least a small but substantial probability. I believe that it is more reasonable to rate the probability as fifty-fifty within a time frame of about fifty years, since (i) every real or presumed step towards first-strike capacity by either side raises the chance of a pre-emptive first strike by the side falling behind; (ii) the concentration on technological development prompted by the Superiority Strategy raises that chance of a technological breakthrough that might destabilize the balance of power; (iii) the increasing technological complexity of weapons required by the Superiority Strategy raises the chance of a first strike as a result of accident or mistake; (iv) the constant changes of weaponry required by the Superiority Strategy creates pressure for proliferation, either because obsolete weapons are constantly disposed of on the international arms market or because wealthy developing countries, dazzled by new weapons, make buys to keep up with appearances.

2. Under Superiority, the chance of an American second strike—given a Soviet first strike—is practically the same as the chance of a Soviet first strike. Though it is always possible that the President or his survivor will not respond to a Soviet first strike, the military and technological systems installed under the Superiority Strategy are geared for belligerence. Accordingly the chance of an American failure to respond is negligible.

3. Even in the face of the Superiority Strategy, the chance of Soviet nonnuclear aggression (an invasion of West Germany or Iran, for example) must be rated as small but not negligible. The prospect of an American first strike in response to a Soviet conventional attack may not be taken seriously by the Soviets, especially if Soviet military personnel think that they can deter any American first strike with the prospect of a massive Soviet second strike.

4. The sums of money required to sustain the Superiority Strategy are staggering. The Reagan administration's rejection of SALT and its apparent acceptance of the Superiority Strategy will produce an increase in the fraction of the American gross national product

devoted to defense from five to six and one-half percent: an increase of over $150 billion per year over the Carter projections, which were largely keyed to the Equivalence Strategy.

Value of the Equivalence Strategy

5. Most students of strategy agree that the chance of an American or Soviet first strike under the Equivalence Strategy is small but substantial. The peculiar pressures for a first strike listed under the Superiority Strategy are absent, but there is still the chance of a first strike through accident, mistake, human folly, or a suicidal leadership.

6. Since the chance of a first strike is less under Equivalence than under Superiority, there is less chance of an all-out nuclear war under Equivalence than under Superiority. The chance of a first strike under Equivalence is small, and the chance of all-out war following a first strike is smaller still. Since the primary aim of the Equivalence Strategy is not to "defeat" the Soviet Union or to develop a first-strike capacity, but to deter a Soviet first strike, it may be obvious to the President or his survivor that once a Soviet first strike is actually launched, there is no point whatsoever in proceeding with an American second strike. If the chance that the President will fail to respond is substantial, the chance of an all-out war under Equivalence is considerably less than the chance of a first strike under Equivalence.[20] On the other hand, the credibility of the American deterrent to a first strike depends on the perception by Soviet planners that an American second strike is inevitable once a Soviet first strike is launched, and the President and his defense strategists may decide that the only convincing way to create this perception is to make the American second strike a *semi-automatic* response. Thus it might be difficult to stop an American second strike even if the President wished to forgo it. On balance, it seems reasonable to rate the chance of the second strike as greater than one-half the chance that the Soviet first strike will be launched. This would make the chance small but still substantial.

7. Over the years two arguments have been proposed to show that Superiority provides a more effective deterrent against Soviet aggression than does Equivalence.

(a) The Superiority Strategy requires constant technological innovation, and technological innovation is an area in which the United States possesses a relative advantage. If the United States presses forward with strategic weapons development, the Soviet Union will be so exhausted from the strain of keeping up with the United States that it will have little money or energy left over for nonnuclear aggression. In the end, the strain such competition will exert on the Soviet economy might produce food riots like those in Poland in 1970, and might even bring down the Soviet socioeconomic system.

But since "the strain of keeping up" did not stop the Soviets from invading Hungary, Czechoslovakia, and Afghanistan, the level of expenditure needed to produce truly effective strain is unknown.

Furthermore, the assumption of *relative* economic stress is undemonstrated: at least one economist who has seriously studied the subject has argued on various grounds that a unit of military spending by the United States disrupts the American economy far more than the equivalent military spending by the Soviet Union.[21]

(b) It is occasionally argued that the Soviets will take the possibility of an American second strike more seriously under the Superiority Strategy than under the Equivalence Strategy, since the Superiority Strategy gives the United States something closer to first-strike capacity and therefore something less to fear from a Soviet second strike.

But in the game of nuclear strategy one cannot "almost" have first-strike capacity; one either has it or one doesn't. There is no reason to think that the Superiority Strategy will ever yield first-strike capacity, since the Soviet Union will feel forced to match the United States step for step. The Soviets know that the President will never be confident enough in American striking capacity to risk the survival of the United States on a nuclear response to Soviet nonnuclear aggression. Consequently, there is no reason to think that Superiority provides a better deterrent against Soviet aggression than does Equivalence. The chance of serious nonnuclear Soviet aggression under Equivalence is small.

8. In the presence of serious efforts at arms control, expenditures for strategic weapons will be much less under Equivalence than under Superiority. If efforts at arms control fail, then expenditures will remain very high. The chance of very high expenditures under Equivalence would best be put at about fifty-fifty.

Value of the Nuclear Disarmament Strategy

9. Most strategists are agreed that the chance of a Soviet first strike under the Equivalence Strategy is small. I believe that the chance of a Soviet first strike is small even under the strategy of Nuclear Disarmament.

(a) Since under Nuclear Disarmament at most one side retains nuclear arms, the chance of nuclear war occurring by accident is reduced at least by one half, relative to the Equivalence Strategy. Since only half the technology is deployed, there is only half the chance of a mechanical malfunction leading to war.

(b) Since at most one side remains armed, there is considerably less chance under Nuclear Disarmament that a nuclear war will occur by mistake. The principal mistake that might cause a nuclear war is the mistake of erroneously thinking that the other side is about to launch a nuclear attack. Such mistakes create enormous pressure for the launching of preemptive strikes, in order to get one's weapons in the air before they are destroyed on the ground. There is no chance that this mistake can occur under Nuclear Disarmament. The side that remains armed (if any) need not fear that the other side will launch a nuclear attack. The side that chooses to disarm cannot be tempted to launch a preemptive strike no matter what it believes the other side is doing, since it has no weapons with which to launch the strike.

(c) Even the opponents of Nuclear Disarmament describe the main peril of nuclear disarmament as nuclear blackmail by the Soviet Union. Opponents of disarmament apparently feel that after nuclear disarmament, nuclear threats are far more probable than nuclear disasters.

(d) Though nuclear weapons are not inherently more destructive than other sorts of weapons, conceived or actual (the napalm raids on Tokyo in March 1945 caused more deaths than Hiroshima or Nagasaki), nuclear weapons are universally *perceived* as different in kind from nonnuclear weapons. The diplomatic losses a nation would incur upon using even tactical nuclear weapons would be immense.

(e) A large-scale nuclear attack by the Soviet Union against the United States might contaminate the American and Canadian Great Plains, a major source of Soviet grain imports. The Soviets could still turn to Argentina, but the price of grain after the attack would skyrocket, and no combination of Argentinean, Australian, or other grain sources could possibly compensate for American or Canadian losses.

(f) The Soviets will find it difficult to find actual military situations in which it will be practical to use atomic weapons against the United States, or against anyone else. Nuclear weapons proved superfluous in the Soviet invasions of Hungary and Czechoslovakia, and they do not seem to be practicable in Afghanistan, where the human costs of the Soviet attempt to regain control are high. If the Soviets did not use nuclear weapons against China between 1960 and 1964 in order to prevent the development of Chinese nuclear capacity, it is hardly likely that they could use them against a nonnuclear United States. Of course it is always *possible* that the Soviet Union might launch a nuclear attack against a nonnuclear United States, perhaps as an escalatory step in a conventional conflict, but it is also *possible* that the Soviet Union will launch a nuclear attack on the United States *right now*, despite the present situation of Equivalence. The point is that there is no such thing as a guarantee against nuclear attack, but the probability of an actual attack is small under either strategy.

10. The chance of all-out nuclear war under the Equivalence Strategy is slight, but the chance of all-out nuclear war under Nuclear Disarmament is zero. There cannot be a two-sided nuclear war if only one side possesses nuclear arms.

11. In considering the threat of Soviet nonnuclear aggression under Nuclear Disarmament, we must consider Soviet nuclear threats—usually called "nuclear blackmail"—as well as possible uses of conventional arms by the Soviets.

(a) Suppose that the United States unilaterally gives up second-strike capacity. What are the odds that the Soviet Union would attempt to influence Amercian behavior through nuclear threats? Obviously, one's views about the chances for successful nuclear blackmail depends on one's views about the chances of a Soviet first strike against a nonnuclear United States. If the chances of a Soviet first strike are slight, then the chances of successful blackmail will also be slight. We have already argued on a variety of grounds that chances of a Soviet first strike under ND are small. I would suggest that the ability of the Soviet Union to manipulate a nonnuclear United States would be the same as the ability of the United States to manipulate the Soviet Union from 1945 to 1949, when strategic conditions were reversed. Anyone who reflects on events from 1945 to 1949 will conclude that nuclear threats have little effect on nations capable of acting with resolve.

There is always the chance that the Soviet Union will carry out its nuclear threats, but there is always the chance that the Soviet Union will carry out its threats even if the United States retains nuclear weapons. There is no device that provides a guarantee against nuclear blackmail. Consequently it cannot be argued that Equivalence provides a guarantee against blackmail that Nuclear Disarmament does not.

The foregoing dismissal of nuclear blackmail violates conventional strategic wisdom, which is concerned with nuclear blackmail almost to obsession. Numerous authors, for example, cite the swift fall of Japan after Hiroshima as evidence of the strategic usefulness of nuclear weapons and nuclear threats. The case of Japan is worth considering. Contrary to the canonical view certified by Secretary Stimson in his famous (and self-serving) *Harper's* article in 1947,[22] I believe that the bombings of Hiroshima and Nagasaki had almost no effect on events leading to the surrender of Japan. If so, the force of the Japanese precedent, which still influences strategic thought, is greatly attenuated.

Obviously the bombings of Hiroshima and Nagasaki had no effect on the popular desire for peace in Japan, since the Japanese public did not know of the atomic bombings until the war was over. What is more surprising is that the bombings do not seem to have influenced either the Emperor or the military command in making the decision to sue for peace. The Emperor, as is now well known, had decided for peace as early as January 1945, and if he was set on peace in January, he did not need the bombings of August to make up his mind. The military, on the other hand, do not seem to have desired peace even after the bombs were dropped; the record shows that the military (i) correctly surmised that the United States had a small supply of these bombs, (ii) debated improved antiaircraft measures to prevent any further bombs from being delivered, and (iii) correctly inferred that bombs of this type could not be used to support a ground invasion, which they felt they could repulse with sufficient success to secure a conditional surrender. What tipped the political scales so that the

Emperor could find his way to peace was not the bombing of Naga-saki on 9 August, but the Russian declaration of war on 8 August. Unaware of Stalin's commitment at Yalta to enter the war against Japan, the Japanese had hoped through the spring and summer of 1945 that the Soviets would mediate a negotiated settlement between the United States and Japan rather than send the Red Army into a new theater of war. When the Russians invaded Manchuria on 9 August, Premier Suzuki, according to reports, cried, "The game is over," and when the Emperor demanded surrender from the Council of Elders on 10 August, he never mentioned atomic bombs as the occasion of his demand for peace.[23] Little can be inferred from such evidence about the effectiveness of nuclear threats.

(b) The strategy of Nuclear Disarmament does not forbid uses of conventional arms in response to acts of aggression. Since there is no reason to believe that adoption of the strategy of Nuclear Disarmament by the United States will make acts of Soviet aggression any more palatable than they are at present, in all probability the American government under ND will appropriate funds for conventional arms sufficient to provide a deterrent to Soviet aggression roughly comparable to the deterrent provided by nuclear arms under S and E. This argument assumes that the deterrent effects of the American strategic nuclear arsenal (whatever they are) can be obtained with a developed arsenal of modern conventional weapons. A review of the difficulties involved in the use of strategic nuclear weapons in con-crete situations may convince the reader that conventional weapons can match the deterrent effect of nuclear weapons. Indeed, the whole development of "flexible response" systems during the McNamara era testifies to the widespread recognition that strategic nuclear weap-ons provide little leverage to nations who would seek to control the flow of world events.

12. Since it is impossible to predict how much money must be spent on conventional forces in order to supply a deterrent equal to the present (nuclear) deterrent against Soviet nonnuclear aggression, it is possible that levels of military spending under ND will be greater than levels under E. But it is also possible that the levels of spending will be much less. The technical equipment needed to maintain E is fantasti-cally expensive, but the labor costs of training and improving conven-tional forces can also be staggering. All things considered, it is still likely that spending will be less under ND than under E, especially if the draft is revived.

Comparison of Superiority and Equivalence

The chance of a Soviet first strike is greater under Superiority than under Equivalence, and the chance of all-out nuclear war is greater under Superiority than under Equivalence. The ability of Equiva-lence to deter Soviet nonnuclear aggression is equal to the ability of

Superiority to deter such aggression, and the Equivalence strategy costs less. Thus Equivalence is preferable to Superiority from both the prudential and the moral point of view.

Comparison of Equivalence and Nuclear Disarmament

We have argued that Nuclear Disarmament and Equivalence are equal in their ability to deter Soviet nonnuclear aggression. In the category of military spending Nuclear Disarmament is preferable to Equivalence. In the category of "all-out war" ND is clearly superior to E, and in the category of "first strikes," ND seems to be about equal to E. Thus we have what seems to be a decisive prudential and moral argument in favor of Nuclear Disarmament: in every category, ND is either equal to or superior to E.

NOTES

[1] In the sequence of these things, the idea of nuclear threats as a deterrent to nuclear war seems, oddly, to have come first. As early as 1946, Bernard Brodie wrote:

> The first and most vital step in any American security program for the age of atomic bombs is to take measures to guarantee to ourselves in case of attack the possibility of retaliation in kind. The writer in making this statement is not for the moment concerned about who will win the next war in which atomic bombs have been used. Thus far the chief purpose of our military establishment has been to win wars. From now on its chief purpose must be to avert them. It can have almost no other useful purpose (Bernard Brodie, ed., *The Absolute Weapon* [New York, 1946], 76).

> But the idea of nuclear retaliation as a deterrent to nonnuclear aggression followed soon after, and to this date the United States has persistently and repeatedly refused to announce a policy of "no first use."

[2] The case that the 1946 Baruch Plan for the internationalization of atomic weapons was deliberately designed to be nonnegotiable is persuasively made by Gregg Herken, *The Winning Weapon: The Atomic Bomb in the Cold War* (New York, 1980). According to Herken the earlier Acheson-Lilienthal plan might have been negotiable.

[3] Nigel Calder in *Nuclear Nightmares: An Investigation into Possible Wars* (New York, Viking, 1980), 42 notes that the NATO concept of deterring a Warsaw pact invasion of West Germany with NATO nuclear retaliation assumes that NATO will not be deterred from this nuclear first strike by the thought of a massive Soviet second strike in return. Calder correctly observes that this is odd thinking, since the possibility of an American second strike is supposed to be the threat which deters a Soviet first strike. Apparently the tacticians believe that the thought of destruction of Russian cities will deter the Soviets in a way that the thought of the destruction of American cities will not deter NATO. Since this belief is very probably false, we have a paradox: either nuclear deterrence will deter nonnuclear aggression but not nuclear aggression, or it will deter nuclear aggression but not nonnuclear aggression. Thus deterrence in the European theater cannot simultaneously do the two jobs for which it was originally designed: deterring Soviet aggression, and deterring nuclear war.

[4] The gun is the M-16 and the plane is the F-111. For the tragic history of the M-16 see James Fallows, *National Defense* (New York, 1981), Chap. 4.

[5] On "massive retaliation" see John Foster Dulles, Dept. of State Bulletin 30, 791, 25

January 1954. For Superiority policy in the 1960s see, for example, Barry Goldwater, *Why Not Victory?* (New York, 1962), 162:

We must stop lying to ourselves and our friends about disarmament. We must stop advancing the cause of the Soviet Union by playing along with Communist inspired deception.

"Disarmament," for Goldwater, includes arms control, since he warns against the danger of "disarmament, or arms control, as the 87th Congress cutely puts it" (99). For a recent interpretation of Superiority see Colin Gray and Keith Payne, "Victory Is Possible," *Foreign Policy* 39 (Summer 1980), 14-27, and Colin Gray, "Nuclear Strategy: The Case for a Theory of Victory," *International Security* 4 (Summer 1979), 54-87.

[6] The uproar caused by the announcement of Directive 59 on 25 July 1980 prompted administration defenders to make the discomfiting revelation that counterforce retargetings are regarded by the Defense Department as matters of course. See for example, Walter Slocombe, "The Countervailing Strategy," *International Security* 5, no. 4 (Spring 1981).

[7] Crudely speaking, Wohlstetter sold the strategy in the 1950s and McNamara bought it in the 1960s. See especially Albert Wohlstetter, "The Delicate Balance of Terror," *Foreign Affairs,* January 1959, and Robert McNamara, *The Essence of Security* (London, 1968).

[8] The much discussed Soviet threat to American land-based missiles does *not* imply Soviet progress towards a first strike, given the invulnerability of American nuclear submarines. But the development of the American MIRV, combined with the vulnerability of Soviet missile submarines, most of which remain in port and all of which, apparently, can be tracked by American anti-submarine forces, *does* imply the development of *American* first-strike capacity. Under current conditions my estimate is that the United States can pursue strategy E only by abandoning some fraction of its antisubmarine surveillance. For a recent study of vulnerability of land-based missiles see Eliot Marshall, "A Question of Accuracy," *Science,* 11 September 1981, 1230-1.

[9] Fallows, *National Defense,* 139-40.

[10] "The Effects of Nuclear War," U.S. Congress, Office of Technology Assessment, 1979, 3.

[11] On the electromagnetic pulse or EMP, see Janet Raloff, "EMP: A Sleeping Dragon," *Science News*, 9 May 1981, 300-2, and 16 May 1981, 314-15.

[12] Technically, it might be possible to develop a prudential case for nuclear disarmament as follows: (a) take all alleged preferences for two-sided destruction, (b) subtract from these all preferences based on the idea that a second strike against Russia is needed to deter their first strike; this idea is illicit since the preference poll in all cases assumes that the first strike has already occurred, and (c) subtract all preferences based on considerations of retributive justice on the grounds that these are political preferences rather than personal evaluations of the utility present in the situations judged. (For the distinction between political preferences and personal preferences see Ronald Dworkin, "What is Equality? Part 1: Equality of Welfare," *Philosophy & Public Affairs* 10, no. 3 [Summer 1981]: 197-8.) The residue of support for nuclear retaliation might be small enough for us to judge that the American people prudentially prefer disarmament.

[13] For criticisms of the zero-sum approach to nuclear strategy see Anatol Rapoport, *Strategy and Conscience* (New York, 1964); and Philip Green, *Deadly Logic* (Columbus, Ohio, 1966).

[14] For approaches which attempt to break out of the static analyses which have pre-

vailed since von Neumann and Morgenstern see Nigel Howard, *Paradoxes of Rationality* (Cambridge, Mass., 1971); Michael Taylor, *Anarchism and Cooperation* (New
York, 1976); and Steven Brams and Donald Wittman, "Nonmyopic Equilibria in a 2
× 2 Games" (forthcoming). Howard, Taylor, and Brams and Wittman all note that
the prudential argument for armament presented here for the United States will
lead Soviet strategists to the same result, and thus individual prudence produces a
collective result (mutual armament), which is less liked by each side than mutual disarmament. In sum, all these authors assume that nuclear arms races are Prisoners'
Dilemmas. Howards's theory of metagames, Taylor's theory of supergames, and the
Brams/Wittman theory of moves all try to show that a proper theory of games will
establish that the mutually preferred solution is an equilibrium from which prudent
players will not depart. I find it impossible to connect Howard's metagame equilibria
with the psychology of the players; see, *contra* Howard, John Harsanyi, "Communi-
cation," *American Political Science Reveiw* 68 (1974), 729-31; 1692-5. Taylor's super-
game equilibria require repeated plays of the game, and for obvious reasons
repeated plays of games involving nuclear war have little relation to reality. Furthermore, Taylor's equilibria require low discount rates, and in most thought about
nuclear war, long run payoffs are highly discounted in favor of such short run
results as political intimidation or war prevention. Brams's theory of moves is not
affected by discount rates, but it provides no clue as to how to move to the cooperative solution when history has trapped players in a noncooperative equilibrium. A
far better approach to escaping the Prisoners' Dilemma is to never enter into it, and I
have suggested ("Ethics and Nuclear Deterrence," in *Moral Problems* 2nd ed., James
Rachels, ed. [New York, 1975], 332-45) that nuclear arms races in particular are not
Prisoners' Dilemmas if the payoffs are properly evaluated.

[15] Gregory Kavka, "Deterrence, Utility, and Rational Choice," *Theory and Decision* 12
(1980), 50.

[16] *Ibid.*, 51.

[17] Daniel Ellsberg, "Risk, Ambiguity, and the Savage Axioms," *Quarterly Journal of Economics* 75 (1961), 643-9.

[18] Kavka, "Deterrence," 45, writes, "This appears to be the way things stand with
respect to expert opinion, as seen from the point of view of the United States. (See,
e.g., Levine 1963, Herzog 1965, and Van Cleave 1973.)" Unpaginated footnotes are
a curse, and I cannot find passages in the books cited that defend Kavka's case.
Levine and Herzog, throughout, seem to be leaning to the opposite view. Van Cleave
is summarizing and takes no stand of his own. See Arthur Herzog, *The War-Peace
Establishment* (New York, 1965); Arthur Levine, *The Arms Debate* (Cambridge, Mass.,
1963); and Van Cleave's chapter in *American Defense Policy,* 3rd ed., Richard Head
and Ervin Bakke, eds., (Baltimore, Md., 1973).

[19] The speculation that Kavka has confused nuclear with general and complete disarmament is not idle. On p. 44 he writes of "unilateral nuclear disarmament," but on
pp. 45 and 51, in the thick of the argument, he speaks only of "unilateral disarmament."

[20] The thought that an American President may lack the nerve to destroy civilization
depresses the military mind. In stating the requirements of deterrence, General
Maxwell Taylor writes, "So understood, deterrence depends essentially on an
assured destruction capability, a strong communications net, and a strong President
unlikely to flinch from his responsibility. . . . Such reflections emphasize the importance of the character and will of the President as a factor adding to the deterrent
effect of our weapons. Since the attitude of the President will be strongly influenced
by that of the people whom he represents, national character also participates in the
effectiveness and stability of deterrence. . . . In addition to the moral [*sic*] qualities of

the President and the nation there are a number of other factors which may stabilize or undermine deterrence" (Maxwell Taylor, *Precarious Security* [New York, 1976], 68-9). On the other hand, some military figures, at least in their public statements, are entirely confident that the President will respond and launch the second strike. General George Seignious, former director of the joint staff of the Joint Chiefs of Staff, testified in 1979, "I find such a surrender scenario irresponsible—for it sends the wrong message to the Soviets. We have not built and maintained our strategic forces—at the cost of billions—in order to weaken their deterrent impact by telling the Russians and the world that we would back down—when, in fact, we would not" (quoted in Herbert Scoville, *MX: Prescription for Disaster* [Cambridge, Mass., 1981], 82).

[21] See Seymour Melman, *Our Depleted Society* (New York, 1965), and *Pentagon Capitalism* (New York, 1970).

[22] Stimson's "The Decision to Use the Atomic Bomb" appeared in *Harper's Magazine*, February 1947, 97-107. Typical of Stimson's *post hoc ergo propter hoc* is:

We believed that our attacks struck cities which must certainly be important to the Japanese military leaders, both Army and Navy, and we waited for a result. We waited one day.

[23] For the Emperor's active attempts to obtain peace see Herbert Feis, *The Atomic Bomb and the End of World War II* (Princeton, 1966), 66. For the military response to the atomic bombings see Hanson Baldwin, *Great Mistakes of the War* (New York, 1950), 87-107. For Suzuki's remark that "The game is over" see W. Craig, *The Fall of Japan* (New York, 1967), 107. One interesting suggestion about the special effectiveness of the atomic bomb against Japan is found in a remark made by General Marshall to David Lilienthal in 1947, "We didn't realize its value to give the Japanese such a shock that they could surrender without loss of face" (quoted in Feis, *The Atomic Bomb*, 6). Marshall's remark is *prima facie* reasonable, but I can find nothing in the documents on the Japanese side that supports it.

III

PUNISHMENT

Capital Punishment and Social Defense

HUGO ADAM BEDAU

THE ANALOGY WITH SELF-DEFENSE

Capital punishment, it is sometimes said, is to the body politic what self-defense is to the individual. If the latter is not morally wrong, how can the former be morally wrong? In order to assess the strength of this analogy, we need to inspect rather closely the morality of self-defense.

Except for the absolute pacifists, who believe it is morally wrong to use violence even to defend themselves or others from unprovoked and undeserved aggression, most of us believe that it is not morally wrong and may even be our moral duty to use violence to prevent aggression. The law has long granted persons the right to defend themselves against the unjust aggressions of others, even to the extent of killing a would-be assailant. It is very difficult to think of any convincing argument that would show it is never rational to risk the death of another in order to prevent death or grave injury to oneself or to others. Certainly self-interest dictates the legitimacy of self-defense. So does concern for the well-being of others. So also does justice. If it is unfair for one person to attempt violence on another, then it is hard to see why morality compels the victim to acquiesce in the attempt by another to hurt him or her, rather than to resist it, even if that resistance may involve injury to the assailant.

The foregoing account assumes that the person acting in self-defense is innocent of any provocation of the assailant. It also assumes that there is no alternative to victimization except resistance. In actual life, both assumptions—especially the second—are often false, because there may be a third alternative: escape, or removing oneself from the scene of danger and imminent aggression. Hence, the law imposes on us the so-called "duty to retreat." Before we use violence to resist aggression, we must try to get out of the way, lest unnecessary violence be used to resist aggression. Now suppose that unjust aggression is imminent, and there is no path open for escape. How much violence may justifiably be used to ward off aggression? The answer is: No more violence than is necessary to prevent the aggressive assault. Violence beyond that is unnecessary and therefore unjustified. We may restate the principle governing the use of violence in self-defense in terms of the use of "deadly force" by the police in the discharge of their duties. The rule is this: Use of deadly force is justified only to prevent loss of life in immediate jeopardy where a lesser use of force cannot reasonably be expected to save the life that is threatened.

In real life, violence in self-defense in excess of the minimum necessary to prevent aggression is often excusable. One cannot always tell what will suffice to deter or prevent becoming a victim, and the law looks with a certain tolerance upon the frightened and innocent would-be victim who turns upon a vicious assailant and inflicts a fatal injury even though a lesser injury would have been sufficient. What is not justified is deliberately using far more violence than is necessary to prevent becoming a victim. It is the deliberate, not the impulsive, use of violence that is relevant to the death-penalty controversy, since the death penalty is enacted into law and carried out in each case only after ample time to weigh alternatives. Notice that we are assuming that the act of self-defense is to protect one's person or that of a third party. The reasoning outlined here does not extend to the defense of one's property. Shooting a thief to prevent one's automobile from being stolen cannot be excused or justified in the way that shooting an assailant charging with a knife pointed at one's face can be. In terms of the concept of "deadly force," our criterion is that deadly force is never justified to prevent crimes against property or other violent crimes not immediately threatening the life of a person.

The rationale for self-defense as set out above illustrates two moral principles of great importance to our discussion. . . . One is that if a life is to be risked, then it is better that it be the life of someone who is guilty (in our context, the initial assailant) rather than the life of someone who is not (the innocent potential victim). It is not fair to expect the innocent prospective victim to run the added risk of severe injury or death in order to avoid using violence in self-defense to the extent of possibly killing his assailant. It is only fair that the guilty aggressor run the risk.

The other principle is that taking life deliberately is not justified so long as there is any feasible alternative. One does not expect miracles, of course, but in theory, if shooting a burglar through the foot will stop the burglary and enable one to call the police for help, then there is no reason to shoot to kill. Likewise, if the burglar is unarmed, there is no reason to shoot at all. In actual life, of course, burglars are likely to be shot at by aroused householders because one does not know whether they are armed, and prudence may dictate the assumption that they are. Even so, although the burglar has no right to commit a felony against a person or a person's property, the attempt to do so does not give the chosen victim the right to respond in whatever way he or she pleases in retaliation, and then to excuse or justify such conduct on the ground that he or she was "only acting in self-defense." In these ways the law shows a tacit regard for the life of even a felon and discharges the use of unnecessary violence even by the innocent; morality can hardly do less.

PREVENTING CRIME VERSUS DETERRING CRIME

The analogy between capital punishment and self-defense requires us to face squarely the empirical questions surrounding the preventive and deterrent effects of the death penalty. Let us distinguish first between preventing and deterring crime. Executing a murderer in the name of punishment can be seen as a crime-*preventive* measure just to the extent it is reasonable to believe that if the murderer had not been executed he or she would have committed other crimes (including, but not necessarily confined to, murder). Executing a murderer can be seen as a crime *deterrent* just to the extent it is reasonable to believe that by the example of the execution other persons are frightened off from committing murder. Any punishment can be a crime preventive without being a crime deterrent, and it can be a deterrent without being a preventive. It can also be both or neither. Prevention and deterrence are theoretically independent because they operate by different methods. Crimes can be prevented by taking guns out of the hands of criminals, by putting criminals behind bars, by alerting the public to be less careless and less prone to victimization, and so forth. Crimes can be deterred only by making would-be criminals frightened of being arrested, convicted, and punished for crimes—that is, making persons overcome their desire to commit crimes by a stronger desire to avoid the risk of being caught and punished.

THE DEATH PENALTY AS A CRIME PREVENTIVE

Capital punishment is unusual among penalties because its preventive effects limit its deterrent effects. The death penalty can never deter the executed person from further crimes. At most, it can prevent him or her from committing them. Popular discussions of the death penalty are frequently confused and misleading because they so often involve the assumption that the death penalty is a perfect and infallible deterrent so far as the executed criminal is concerned, whereas nothing of the sort is true. It is even an exaggeration to think that in any given case of execution the death penalty has proved to be an infallible crime preventive. What is obviously true is that once a person has been executed, it is physically impossible for him or her to commit any further crimes. But this does not prove that by executing a murderer society has in fact prevented any crimes. To prove this, one would need to know what crimes the executed criminal would have committed if he or she had not been executed and had been punished only in some less severe way (e.g., by imprisonment).

What is the evidence that the death penalty is an effective crime preventive? From the study of imprisonment, and parole and release records, it is clear that in general, if the murderers and other criminals who have been executed are like the murderers who were convicted but not executed, then (i) executing all convicted murderers would have prevented few crimes, but not many murders (less than one convicted murderer in a hundred commits another murder); and (ii) convicted murderers, whether inside prison or outside after release, have at least as good a record of no further criminal activity as does any other class of convicted felon.

These facts show that the general public tends to overrate the danger and threat to public safety constituted by the failure to execute every murderer who is caught and convicted. While one would be in error to say that there is no risk such criminals will repeat their crimes—or similar ones—if they are not executed, one would be equally in error to say that by executing every convicted murderer we know that many horrible crimes will never be committed. All we know is that a few such crimes will never be committed; we do not know how many or by whom they would have been committed. (Obviously, if we did we could have prevented them.) This is the nub of the problem. There is no way to know in advance which if any of the incarcerated or released murderers will kill again. It is useful in this connection to remember that the only way to guarantee that no horrible crimes ever occur is to execute *everyone* who might conceivably commit such a crime. Similarly, the only way to guarantee that no convicted murderer ever commits another murder is to execute them all. No society has ever done this, and for 200 years our society has been moving steadily in the opposite direction.

These considerations show that our society has implicitly adopted an attitude toward the risk of murder rather like the attitude it has adopted toward the risk of fatality from other sources, such as automobile accidents, lung cancer, or drowning. Since no one knows when or where or upon whom any of these lethal events will befall, it would be too great an invasion of freedom to undertake the severe restrictions that alone would suffice to prevent any of them from occurring. It is better to take the risks and keep our freedom than to try to eliminate the risks altogether and lose our freedom in the process. Hence, we have lifeguards at the beach, but swimming is not totally prohibited; smokers are warned, but cigarettes are still legally sold; pedestrians may be given the right of way in a crosswalk, but marginally competent drivers are still allowed to operate motor vehicles. Some risk is therefore imposed on the innocent; in the name of our right to freedom, our other rights are not protected by society at all costs.

THE DEATH PENALTY AS A CRIME DETERRENT

Determining whether the death penalty is an effective deterrent is even more difficult than determining its effectiveness as a crime preventive. In general, our knowledge about how penalties deter crimes and whether in fact they do—whom they deter, from which crimes, and under what conditions—is distressingly inexact. Most people nevertheless are convinced that punishments do deter, and that the more severe a punishment is the better it will deter. For more than a generation, social scientists have studied the question of whether the death penalty is a deterrent and of whether it is a better deterrent than the alternative of imprisonment. Their verdict, while not unanimous, is fairly clear. Whatever may be true about the deterrence of lesser crimes by other penalties, the deterrence achieved by the death penalty for murder is not measurably greater than the deterrence achieved by long-term imprisonment. In the nature of the case, the evidence is quite indirect. No one can identify for certain any crimes that did not occur because the would-be offender was deterred by the threat of the death penalty and that would not have been deterred by a lesser threat. Likewise, no one can identify any crimes that did occur because the offender was not deterred by the threat of prison even though he would have been deterred by the threat of death. Nevertheless, such evidence as we have fails to show that the more severe penalty (death) is really a better deterrent than the less severe penalty (imprisonment) for such crimes as murder.

If the conclusion stated above is correct, and the death penalty and long-term imprisonment are equally effective (or ineffective) as deterrents to murder, then the argument for the death penalty on grounds of deterrence is seriously weakened. One of the moral principles identified earlier comes into play and requires us to reject the death penalty on moral grounds. This is the principle that unless there is a good reason for choosing a more rather than a less severe punishment for a crime, the less severe penalty is to be preferred. This principle obviously commends itself to anyone who values human life and who concedes that, all other things being equal, less pain and suffering is always better than more. Human life is valued in part to the degree that it is free of pain, suffering, misery, and frustration, and in particular that it is free of such experiences when they serve no purpose. If the death penalty is not a more effective deterrent than imprisonment, then its greater severity than imprisonment is gratuitous, purposeless suffering and deprivation.

A COST/BENEFIT ANALYSIS OF THE
DEATH PENALTY

A full study of the costs and benefits involved in the practice of capital punishment would not be confined solely to the question of whether it is a better deterrent or preventive of murder than imprisonment. Any thoroughgoing utilitarian approach to the death-penalty controversy would need to examine carefully other costs and benefits as well, because maximizing the balance of social benefits over social costs is the sole criterion of right and wrong according to utilitarianism. Let us consider, therefore, some of the other costs and benefits to be calculated. Clinical psychologists have presented evidence to suggest that the death penalty actually incites some persons of unstable mind to murder others, either because they are afraid to take their own lives and hope that society will punish them for murder by putting them to death, or because they fancy that they, too, are killing with justification analogously to the justified killing involved in capital punishment. If such evidence is sound, capital punishment can serve as a counter-preventive or an incitement to murder, and these incited murders become part of its social cost. Imprisonment, however, has not been known to incite any murders or other crimes of violence in a comparable fashion. (A possible exception might be found in the imprisonment of terrorists, which has inspired other terrorists to take hostages as part of a scheme to force the authorities to release their imprisoned comrades.) The risks of executing the innocent are also part of the social cost. The historical record is replete with innocent persons indicted, convicted, sentenced, and occasionally legally executed for crimes they did not commit, not to mention the guilty persons unfairly convicted, sentenced to death, and executed on the strength of perjured testimony, fraudulent evidence, subornation of jurors, and other violations of the civil rights and liberties of the accused. Nor is this all. The high costs of a capital trial, of the inevitable appeals, the costly methods of custody most prisons adopt for convicts on "death row," are among the straightforward economic costs that the death penalty incurs. No scientifically valid cost/benefit analysis of capital punishment has ever been conducted, and it is impossible to predict exactly what such a study would show. Nevertheless, based on such evidence as we do have, it is quite possible that a study of this sort would favor abolition of all death penalties rather than their retention.

WHAT IF EXECUTIONS DID DETER?

From the moral point of view, it is quite important to determine what one should think about capital punishment if the evidence clearly showed that the death penalty is a distinctly superior method of social defense by comparison with less severe alternatives. Kantian moralists, as we have seen, would have no use for such knowledge, because their entire case for the morality of the death penalty rests on the way it is thought to provide just retribution, not on the way it is thought to provide social defense. For a utilitarian, however, such knowledge would be conclusive. Those who follow Locke's reasoning would also be gratified, because they defend the morality of the death penalty both on the ground that it is retributively just and on the ground that it provides needed social defense.

What about the opponents of the death penalty, however? To oppose the death penalty in the face of incontestable evidence that it is an effective method of social defense seems to violate the moral principle that where grave risks are to be run, it is better that they be run by the guilty than by the innocent. Consider in this connection an imaginary world in which by executing a murderer the victim is invariably restored to life, whole and intact, as though the murder had never occurred. In such a miraculous world, it is hard to see how anyone could oppose the death penalty on moral grounds. Why shouldn't a murderer die if that will infallibly bring the victim back to life? What could possibly be morally wrong with taking the murderer's life under such conditions? It would turn the death penalty into an instrument of perfect restitution, and it would give a new and better meaning to *lex talionis,* "a life for a life." The whole idea is fanciful, of course, but it shows better than anything else how opposition to the death penalty cannot be both moral and wholly unconditional. If opposition to the death penalty is to be morally responsible, then it must be conceded that there are conditions (however unlikely) under which that opposition should cease.

But even if the death penalty were known to be a uniquely effective social defense, we could still imagine conditions under which it would be reasonable to oppose it. Suppose that in addition to being a slightly better preventive and deterrent than imprisonment, executions also have a slight incitive effect (so that for every ten murders an execution prevents or deters, it also incites another murder). Suppose also that the administration of criminal justice in capital cases is inefficient, unequal, and tends to secure convictions of murderers who least "deserve" to be sentenced to death (including some death sentences and a few executions of the innocent). Under such conditions, it would still be reasonable to oppose the death penalty, because on the facts supposed more (or not fewer) innocent lives are being threatened and lost by using the death penalty than would be risked by abolishing it. It is important to remember throughout our evaluation of the deterrence controversy that we cannot ever apply the principle . . . that advises us to risk the lives of the guilty in order to save the lives of the innocent. Instead, the most we can do is weigh the risk for the general public against the execution of those who are *found* guilty by an imperfect system of criminal justice. These hypothetical factual assumptions illustrate the contingencies upon which the morality of opposition to the death penalty rests. And not only the morality of opposition; the morality of any defense of the death penalty rests on the same contingencies. This should help us understand why, in resolving the morality of capital punishment one way or the other, it is so important to know, as well as we can, whether the death penalty really does deter, prevent, or incite crime, whether the innocent really are ever executed, and whether any of these things are likely to occur in the future.

HOW MANY GUILTY LIVES IS ONE INNOCENT LIFE WORTH?

The great unanswered question that utilitarians must face concerns the level of social defense that executions should be expected to achieve before it is justifiable to carry them out. Consider three possible situations: (A) At the level of a hundred executions per year, each additional execution of a convicted murderer reduces the number of murder victims by ten. (B) Executing every convicted murderer reduces the number of murders to 5,000 victims annually, whereas executing only one out of ten reduces the number to 5,001. (C) Executing every convicted murderer reduces the murder rate no more than does executing one in a hundred and no more than a random pattern of executions does.

Many people contemplating situation A would regard this as a reasonable trade-off: The execution of each further guilty person saves the lives of ten innocent ones. (In fact, situation A or something like it may be taken as a description of what most of those who defend the death penalty on grounds of social defense believe is true.) But suppose that, instead of saving 10 lives, the number dropped to 0.5, i.e., one victim avoided for each two additional executions. Would that be a reasonable price to pay? We are on the road toward the situation described in situation B, where a drastic 90 percent reduction in the number of persons executed causes the level of social defense to drop by only 0.0002 percent. Would it be worth it to execute so many more murderers at the cost of such a slight decrease in social defense? How many guilty lives is one innocent life worth? In situation C, of course, there is no basis for executing all convicted murderers, since there is no gain in social defense to show for each additional murderer executed after the first out of each hundred murderers has been executed. How, then, should we determine which out of each hundred convicted murderers is the unlucky one to be put to death?

It may be possible, under a complete and thoroughgoing cost/benefit analysis of the death penalty, to answer such questions. But an appeal merely to the moral principle that if lives are to be risked then let it be the lives of the guilty rather than the lives of the innocent will not suffice. (We have already noticed that this abstract principle is of little use in the actual administration of criminal justice, because the police and the courts do not deal with the guilty as such but only with those *judged* guilty.) Nor will it suffice to agree that society deserves all the crime prevention and deterrence it can get by inflicting severe punishments. These principles are consistent with too many different policies. They are too vague by themselves to resolve the choice on grounds of social defense when confronted with hypothetical situations like those proposed above.

Since no adequate cost/benefit analysis of the death penalty exists, there is no way to resolve these questions from this standpoint at the present time. Moreover, it can be argued that we cannot have such an analysis without already establishing in some way or other the relative value of innocent lives versus guilty lives. Far from being a product of a cost/benefit analysis, this comparative evaluation of lives would have to be brought into any such analysis. Without it, no cost/benefit analysis can get off the ground. Finally, it must be noted that we have no knowledge at present that begins to approximate anything like the situation described above in *A,* whereas it appears from the evidence we do have that we achieve about the same deterrent and preventive effects whether we punish murder by death or by imprisonment. Therefore, something like the situation in *B* or in *C* may be correct. If so, this shows that the choice between the two policies of capital punishment and life imprisonment for murder will probably have to be made on some basis other than social defense; on that basis the two policies are equivalent and therefore equally acceptable.

CONCLUSION

Our discussion of the death penalty from the moral point of view shows that there is no one moral principle the validity of which is paramount and that decisively favors one side to the controversy. Rather, we have seen how it is possible to argue either for or against the death penalty, and in each case to be appealing to moral principles that derive from the worth, value, or dignity of human life. We have also seen how it is impossible to connect any of these abstract principles with the actual practice of capital punishment without a close study of sociological, psychological, and economic factors. By themselves, the moral principles that are relevant are too abstract and uncertain in application to be of much help. Without the guidance of such principles, of course, the facts (who gets executed, and why) are of little use, either.

My own view of the controversy is that on balance, given the moral principles we have identified in the course of our discussion (including the overriding value of human life), and given the facts about capital punishment and crimes against the person, the side favoring abolition of the death penalty has the better of the argument. And there *is* an alternative to capital punishment: long-term imprisonment. Such a punishment is retributive and can be made appropriately severe to reflect the gravity of the crime for which it is the punishment. It gives adequate (though hardly perfect) protection to the public. It is free of the worst defect to which the death penalty is liable: execution of the innocent. It tacitly acknowledges that there is no way for a criminal, alive or dead, to make amends for murder or other grave crimes against the person. Finally, it has symbolic significance. The death penalty, more than any other kind of killing, is done in the name of society and on its behalf. Each of us has a hand in such a killing, and unless such killings are absolutely necessary they cannot really be justified. Thus, abolishing the death penalty represents extending the hand of life even to those who by their crimes have "forfeited" any right to live. It is a tacit admission that we must abandon the folly and pretence of attempting to secure perfect justice in an imperfect world.

Searching for an epigram suitable for our times, in which governments have launched vast campaigns of war and suppression of internal dissent by means of methods that can only be described as savage and criminal, Camus was prompted to admonish: "Let us be neither victims nor executioners." Perhaps better than any other, this exhortation points the way between forbidden extremes if we are to respect the humanity in each of us without trespassing on the humanity of others.

Rights and Capital Punishment

THOMAS HURKA

Discussions of the morality of capital punishment, and indeed discussions of the morality of punishment in general, usually assume that there are two possible justifications of punishment, a deterrence justification associated with utilitarianism and other consequentialist moral theories, and a retributive justification associated with deontological moral theories. But now that rights-based theories are attracting the increasing attention of moral philosophers it is worth asking whether these theories may not employ a different justification of punishment, with different consequences for the morality of particular forms of punishment. I will argue that rights theories do employ a different justification of punishment, and that this justification combines many of the attractive features of the deterrence and retributive justifications while avoiding their unattractive features. In particular, I will argue that the rights-based justification has more attractive consequences for the morality of capital punishment than either the deterrence or retributive justifications.[1]

Rights-based moral theories hold that persons have certain natural rights, and the fact that these rights are natural is often expressed by saying that persons would possess them "in the state of nature." Among the rights which persons are usually said to possess in the state of nature is the right to punish those who violate the rights of others. In section 7 of the *Second Treatise*, Locke says that the state of nature has a Law of Nature to govern it, and that "everyone has a right to punish the transgressors of the Law to such a Degree, as may hinder its Violation." [2] Nozick too includes a right to punish among those he grants in *Anarchy, State, and Utopia*, quoting Locke's description of this right with approval, and devoting an entire section to a discussion of "the right of all to punish."[3] If persons have a right to punish in the state of nature, then they are permitted to punish the violators of rights if they want to, but they are also permitted to refrain from punishing them if they do not want to. . . .

The right to punish which persons have in the state of nature is not a primitive right, but derives from another more general right which they possess. Whenever persons in the state of nature have a natural right they also have the right to *enforce* that right, that is, the right to use coercion against other persons to prevent them from violating it.[4] The most familiar form of coercion is the use of force, and persons in the state of nature therefore have the right to use force to defend themselves against would-be violators of their rights, and also to defend third parties. But this right of self- (and other-) defense is not the only enforcement right which they possess. The making of threats is also a form of coercion, and persons in the state of nature therefore also have the right to threaten others with certain harms if they succeed in violating their rights, or succeed in violating the rights of third parties. It is from this second enforcement-right that the right to punish derives. If persons in the state of nature have the right to threaten others with harms if they succeed in violating rights, then they surely also have the right to inflict these harms on them once the relevant rights have been violated. But this is just what the right to punish is: a right to inflict harms on persons who have successfully violated the rights of others.[5]

Although Locke and Nozick include a right to punish among those possessed in the state of nature they do not provide any justification of this right. They do not show *why* rights theories should contain a right to punish, or even why they should contain enforcement rights in general, but simply include these rights on a list of those possessed in the state of nature. There is one kind of rights theory, however, which in a somewhat stricter usage of the term than is usual I will call a "libertarian" rights theory, which can provide such a justification. A libertarian rights theory holds that there is really only one natural right, namely the equal right of all persons to the most extensive liberty compatible with a like liberty for other persons, and that all other natural rights are species or instances of the right to liberty. They are all rights to exercise liberty in certain specified areas, and impose on other persons the duty not to interfere with liberty in those areas.[6] Because these rights are instances of a right to the *most extensive* liberty we are to identify them by identifying the most extensive right to liberty possible. Comparing the extent of different liberties in the way this requires involves some obvious difficulties, but the following should be uncontroversial. If one liberty contains another as a proper part, so that exercising the second liberty always involves exercising the first, but exercising the first liberty does not always involve exercising the second, then the first liberty is more extensive than the second (some examples: the liberty to buy property in Canada is more extensive than the liberty to buy property in Alberta, for it contains it as a proper part; the liberty to move either of one's arms freely is more extensive than the liberty to move one's left arm freely, for it contains it as a proper part, and so on). But this is all we need to show why a libertarian rights theory has to contain enforcement rights. Let us imagine that we have discovered that L is the most extensive liberty not containing the liberty to do any enforcing such that every person can have an equal right to exercise all the liberties in L, and no one person's right conflicts with that of any other. Then in deciding whether to grant enforcement rights we are deciding whether to add to L the liberty of removing from other persons the liberty of removing liberties in L from other persons. We have every reason to do this and no reason not to. If we add this liberty—and it is once again best described as the liberty to remove from other persons the liberty of removing liberties in L from other persons—we will be creating a new liberty L', which contains L as a proper part, and is therefore more extensive than it. But at the same time we will not be subtracting liberties from any other person's liberty L. Although the liberty we are adding conflicts with some liberties of other persons these are all liberties which have already been excluded from L, and have therefore already been excluded from the protection of their natural right to liberty. Allowing enforcement rights enables us to extend the scope of everyone's right to liberty—which is just what a libertarian rights theory requires us to do—without detracting in any way from the right to liberty of others. And if this is the case, then a libertarian rights theory can give exactly the same justification for these rights as for any other rights it grants.

This justification of enforcement rights, which I have presented so far in a fairly abstract way, applies most directly to the right of self- (or other-) defense. If we give persons the right to use force to prevent rights violations then we are obviously extending the scope of their right to liberty without limiting the right to liberty of anyone else, for no one has the right to violate rights. But it also applies to the right to make and carry out threats which lies behind the right to punish. When we threaten a person with harms if he successfully violates rights we do not remove from him the liberty of violating rights as such. But we do remove from him the more complex liberty of violating rights and not having those harms inflicted on him afterwards. If he does not have the right to exercise the simple liberty he does not have the right to exercise the more complex one either, and in giving other persons the right to remove the more complex liberty from him a libertarian rights theory is once again extending the scope of their right to liberty without in any way detracting from his.

Because it derives the right to punish from a right to make certain threats, the rights-based justification has two attractive consequences which also follow from the retributive justification. The first is that it is never permissible to punish persons who have not violated, or who have not been found by reliable proceedings to have violated, the rights of other persons. Guilt, in other words, is a necessary condition of the permissibility of punishment on the rights-based view. The reasoning leading up to this consequence should be fairly evident. The right to use coercion to prevent others from violating rights only entitles us to make a very specific threat, namely the threat to inflict certain harms on them if they actually succeed in violating rights, and we could not claim to be carrying out this threat if we inflicted harms on someone whom we did not have reliable reasons to think had violated rights. This first consequence also follows from the retributive justification, but it is a well-known objection to the deterrence justification that no such consequence follows from it. Critics of the deterrence justification often point out that it could license the framing and "punishment" of an innocent man if this would be sufficiently effective in deterring future crimes. The rights-based justification is not open to this objection for it holds, along with the retributive justification, that guilt is always a necessary condition of the permissibility of punishment. The second consequence is that it is never permissible to punish persons for rights violations unless our intention to punish persons for those violations has been publicly announced in the past. The reasoning leading up to this consequence should also be evident. If punishment is only permissible because it is the carrying out of a permissible threat, then it is only permissible when that threat has actually been made. Punishments for the violation of secret laws, or for the violation of retroactive laws, are never permissible on the rights-based view, though we can easily imagine circumstances in which they would be permissible and even required on the deterrence view, and perhaps even on some retributive views as well.

The rights-based justification, then, has some attractive consequences in common with the retributive justification for the question when punishment is permissible. But when it turns to the question how much punishment is permissible, or how severe a punishment is permissible, it has some consequences in common with the retributive justification and some in common with the deterrence justification. The important thing to realize here is that the enforcement rights which persons have in the state of nature are not unqualified. They are subject to at least two qualifications, and these qualifications place limits on the severity of the punishments which they may inflict in the state of nature, and which their governments may inflict in civil society. To set out these qualifications I will begin by examining some particular cases involving self-defense where I think their intuitive attractiveness is especially evident, and then give them a theoretical justification. I will conclude by showing what the implications of these qualifications are for questions about the morality of punishment, and in particular for questions about the morality of capital punishment.

Let us begin by imagining the following case. One person X is trying to violate a fairly unimportant right of another person Y, say, the right not to be tickled,[7] and Y is considering how to prevent this. Y is not nearly as strong as X, so he cannot hope to stop X just by resisting him physically. Nor will any threat of Y's deter X. But Y does have in his hands a pistol with which he can kill X. If killing X is the only way Y can prevent X from violating his right not to be tickled, is it permissible for Y to use his pistol? . . . We would insist that there is an upper limit on the amount of coercion persons can use to enforce their rights, and that this limit is lower the less important the rights are which they are enforcing. For Y to kill X just to prevent him from tickling him is for Y quite clearly to overstep a limit which is, in the case of a very unimportant right like the right not to be tickled, very low indeed.

Reflection on this case suggests what I will call an *upper limit* qualification on persons' enforcement rights. The most natural way for a rights theory to express this qualification is as follows. Although Y's right to enforce his right to ϕ entitles him to act in ways which would otherwise involve violating some rights of X's, it does not entitle him to act in ways which would otherwise involve violating any rights of X's which are more important than his own right to ϕ. In the course of enforcing his right to ϕ Y can act in ways which would otherwise involve violating X's right to ϕ, or any rights of X's which are less important than his right to ϕ. So if X is trying to kill him Y can kill X in self-defense, or assault him or tie him up. But he cannot act in ways which would otherwise involve violating any rights of X's which are more important than his right to ϕ. For an important right like the right to life this will not be much of a restriction but for other less important rights it will be. For a very unimportant right like the right not to be tickled, for instance, the upper limit qualification will rule out anything more than the very smallest amount of coercion to enforce it.[8]

Now let us imagine another case. X is attacking Y with the intention of killing him, and Y is considering how to prevent this. He has in one hand a pistol, with which he can kill X, and in the other hand a tranquilizer gun, with which he can sedate X long enough to make his escape but with which he will not do X any permanent damage. The two weapons will be equally effective in repelling X's attack and Y knows this. Is it permissible for Y to use his pistol and kill X? Although Y's killing X would not violate the upper limit qualification I think most of us would agree that it is not permissible. We would insist that there is another limitation on the amount of coercion Y can use to enforce his rights, one which requires him never to use more than the minimum amount of coercion necessary to prevent the violation of his rights. In this case Y's killing X would involve more than the minimum amount of coercion, for he can also use the tranquilizer gun on X, and killing him is therefore impermissible.

This second case suggests another qualification on persons' enforcement rights, one which I will call a *minimum necessary* qualification, and which it is most natural for a rights theory to express as follows. Although Y's right to enforce his right to ϕ sometimes entitles him to act in ways which would otherwise involve violating X's right to ψ, it only does so when it is not possible for Y to prevent the violation of his right to ϕ just as effectively by acting in ways which would otherwise involve violating only rights of X's which are less important than his right to ψ. (If it is possible for Y to prevent the violation of his right to ϕ by acting in ways which would not otherwise involve violating any of X's rights, e.g. by running away, this qualification requires him to run away.)[9] . . .

In discussing the upper limit and minimum necessary qualifications I have made extensive use of the notion of the *importance* of a natural right, and there will no doubt be questions about exactly what this notion involves. In speaking of the importance of a right I have intended in the first place to speak of something intuitive. We all have, I trust, an intuitive sense that the right to life is more important than the right not to be physically assaulted, which in turn is more important than the right not to be tickled. But the notion can also be given a formal representation in a libertarian rights theory of the kind we have been discussing. If every right is an instance of the right to liberty, then it seems natural to say that one right is more important than another whenever it is a right to a more extensive liberty than the other. And although comparing the extent of some liberties raises obvious difficulties the following should once again be uncontroversial. If one liberty contains another as a proper part, so that exercising the second liberty always involves exercising the first, but exercising the first liberty does not always involve exercising the second, then the first liberty is more extensive than the second. The ranking procedure which these two suggestions yield is perhaps most usefully put as follows: one right is more important than another whenever violating the first right always involves violating the second, but violating the second right does not always involve violating the first (an example: the right to buy property in Canada is more important than the right to buy property in Alberta because preventing a person from buying property in Canada always involves preventing him from buying it in Alberta, but preventing him from buying it in Alberta does not always involve preventing him from buying it in Canada.) This ranking procedure does not generate anything like a complete ordering over rights. It only generates a partial ordering, but the ordering is not so partial as to be useless. It has, for instance, some clear results about a number of rights that are important for questions about self-defense. It holds that the right not to be both tied up and beaten is more important than the right simply not to be tied up, that the right not to have both arms broken is more important than the right not to have one's left arm broken, and that the right not to have property valued at $100 destroyed is more important than the right not to have property valued at $1 destroyed. It also has some clear results about a number of rights that are important for questions about punishment. It holds that the right not to be imprisoned for ten years is more important than the right not to be imprisoned for five years, and that the right not to be fined $100 is more important than the right not to be fined $1. Most importantly for our concerns, however, it has clear results about the right which is most centrally involved in questions about capital punishment, namely the right to life. On a libertarian view the right to life is the right to exercise the liberty of choosing life over death, and imposes on others the duty not to remove that liberty, as they would do if they forcibly chose death for us. But this means that the right to life has to be the most important natural right there is. Choosing life is choosing to exercise all the liberties we do exercise when we are alive, while choosing death is choosing to exercise no further liberties at all. A person who removes the liberty of choosing life from us is therefore removing all our other liberties from us. In violating our right to life he is violating all our other rights as well, for he is leaving us in a position where we can never exercise those rights again. Although the proper part ranking procedure has clear results in these areas it does not have clear results in certain others. It does not say anything determinate about the relative importance of property rights and rights not to be physically assaulted, for instance, or of property rights and rights not to be imprisoned. These gaps in the ordering it generates weaken but they do not prevent the operation of the upper limit and minimum necessary qualifications. If property rights and rights not to be physically assaulted are unranked with respect to each other then neither is more important than the other, and persons may if necessary use force against others to prevent them from destroying their property, and destroy others' property to prevent them from assaulting them. Far from being an unwanted result this is one which I think we ought to welcome, for our intuitions seem to support the view that in most cases these two forms of self-defense are, if necessary, permissible.[10] . . .

Although the upper limit and minimum necessary qualifications are intuitively appealing we will not be fully entitled to accept them until we have provided them with some kind of theoretical justification. We can do this by extending the libertarian justification of enforcement rights which we have already constructed. This justification says that by adding to the liberty L protected by every person's right to liberty the liberty of removing from other persons the liberty of removing liberties in L from other persons we extend the scope of every person's right to liberty without detracting from the right to liberty of anyone else. But things are not quite as simple as this. When we enforce our rights (or those of a third party) against another person we usually remove from him, not only the liberty of removing liberties in L from other persons, but also certain other liberties. In fending off his attack we may prevent him from killing us but we also break his arm; in interfering with his robbery attempt we may prevent him from stealing our neighbor's jewelry but we also confiscate his gun, and so on. These are not reasons for denying the existence of enforcement rights—the argument for that remains intact—but they are reasons for placing certain qualifications on them to ensure that their exercise does not do more to interfere with liberty than it needs to, or more to interfere with liberty than it does to protect it. The most obvious such qualification is the minimum necessary qualification. A person whose enforcement rights are subject to this qualification still always has those enforcement rights. He still always has the right to remove from other persons the liberty of removing liberties in L from other persons, but he is now required to make sure that, whenever he exercises this right, he removes as few other liberties from these persons as he can. The minimum necessary qualification does not detract in any way from his right to liberty, for it does not take away from him any of the enforcement rights which the libertarian justification says he has. But it does extend the right to liberty of other persons by making certain interferences with their liberty impermissible. The more difficult qualification to justify is the upper limit qualification, for this qualification does take away some of the enforcement rights which the libertarian justification seems to say a person has. Someone whose enforcement rights are subject to the upper limit qualification rights does not really have those rights when the only way of exercising them would involve infringing rights of other persons which are more important than the ones he is trying to protect (as when the only way of preventing another from tickling him is by shooting him dead). But I think the upper limit qualification can still be shown to follow from the basic principle of a libertarian rights theory. If this principle says that every person has a right to the most extensive liberty compatible with a like liberty for others it will hardly want to allow persons who are enforcing rights to remove more liberty from others than they are trying to protect themselves. But this is just what enforcement rights without the upper limit qualification would allow. They would allow a person protecting a very narrow liberty of his own (say, the liberty to choose not to be tickled) to remove much more extensive liberties from another person, and even to remove all his liberties by shooting him dead. Enforcement rights without the upper limit qualification would sometimes cost more in terms of liberty removed than they would gain in terms of liberty protected, and a theory which wants us to have a right to the most extensive liberty possible will therefore surely insist on the qualification.

Having discussed the upper limit and minimum necessary qualifications in a general way let us now see what their implications are for questions about punishment. The qualifications place limits on the severity of the punishments which persons are permitted to inflict in the state of nature, and which their governments are permitted to inflict in civil society. It follows from the upper limit qualification that they are never permitted to inflict punishments which infringe rights that are more important than the ones which the offender has violated, and which they are therefore enforcing. And it follows from the minimum necessary qualification that they are never permitted to inflict punishments which infringe rights that are more important than is necessary to prevent further violations of the right which they are enforcing. If two punishments will be equally effective in deterring violations of this right, they have a duty to impose the less severe punishment; and if no punishments will be effective in deterring violations, they have a duty to impose no punishment at all. . . .

Of these two consequences the one which follows from the upper limit qualification also follows from many versions of the retributive justification. Many retributive theorists also hold that there is an upper limit on the severity of the punishments we can inflict for certain crimes, and that we do wrong if we exceed this limit. But no such consequence follows from the deterrence justification. The deterrence justification permits and even requires as severe a punishment as will best promote the over-all good of society, and this punishment can sometimes be very severe indeed. It might well be the case that capital punishment would be an effective deterrent to the crime of shoplifting, and that the benefits to society as a whole of the huge reduction in shoplifting resulting from its imposition would far outweigh the harms to the one or two individuals foolish enough to be caught and executed for shoplifting. Most of us do not think, however, that it could ever be permissible to impose capital punishment for the crime of shoplifting, and take it to be a serious objection to the deterrence justification that it could sometimes require it. The consequence which follows from the minimum necessary qualification also follows from the deterrence justification, but it does not follow from the retributive justification. The retributive justification can require us to impose severe punishments when no further rights violations will be prevented by them, and indeed when no further social good will result from them at all. Some retributive theorists like Kant have of course revelled in this fact, but I think most of us find it repugnant. We think that punishment is only permissible when it does something to promote social good, and take it to be a serious objection to the retributive justification that it requires it even when it does nothing to promote social good.

What are the consequences of the rights-based justification for the special case of capital punishment? Capital punishment infringes the right to life of a criminal, and the right to life is the most important right there is. This means that, given the upper limit qualification, the rights-based justification will only allow capital punishment to be imposed on persons who have violated the right to life of another, that is, it will only allow capital punishment to be imposed for the crime of murder. At the same time, however, given the minimum necessary qualification, the rights-based justification will only allow capital punishment to be imposed for the crime of murder if there is no other less severe punishment which is equally effective at deterring murder. Extensive criminological studies have failed to produce any evidence that capital punishment is a more effective deterrent to murder than life imprisonment, and the rights-based justification will therefore hold that, until such evidence is produced, the imposition of capital punishment for any crime at all is impermissible.[11] This is in my view an attractive consequence, and it is one which also follows from the deterrence justification. But it is not bought at the cost of the many unattractive consequences of the deterrence justification. Many of us believe that if capital punishment is not an effective deterrent to murder then it ought not to be imposed. But we would not want this view to commit us to the simple deterrence justification, with all the unattractive consequences which that justification has. We would not want it to commit us to the view that capital punishment could be a permissible or even a required punishment for shoplifting, and we would not want it to commit us to the view that it could be permissible or even required to frame and "punish" an innocent man. The rights-based justification allows us to give some weight to the question of deterrence in assessing the morality of capital punishment, without giving it the overwhelming weight which it has in the deterrence justification.

Perhaps the distinctive consequences of the rights-based justification for the morality of capital punishment can best be summarized as follows. Assuming that a retributive calculus will find capital punishment a "fitting" punishment for the crime of murder, the retributive justification holds that it is a necessary and sufficient condition for the permissibility (and even requiredness) of imposing capital punishment on a person that he be guilty of murder. The rights-based justification agrees that this is a necessary condition but denies that it is sufficient; for a punishment to be permissible, it maintains, it must have some independent deterrent effect. The deterrence justification, by contrast, holds that it is a necessary and sufficient condition for the permissibility (and even requiredness) of imposing capital punishment on a person that this punishment have some independent deterrent effect. The rights-based justification once again agrees that this is a necessary condition but denies that it is sufficient; for a punishment to be permissible the person who undergoes it must be guilty of a crime, and guilty of a crime which violated rights at least as important as those which his punishment will infringe. In the rights-based justification conditions which are individually both necessary and sufficient in the deterrence and retributive justifications are made individually necessary but only jointly sufficient, and for this reason the rights-based justification can be said to combine the attractive features of the other two justifications while avoiding their unattractive features. The view that the conditions focussed on by the deterrence and retributive justifications are individually necessary but only jointly sufficient for the permissibility of punishment has of course been defended by a number of philosophers. But I think it is only in the context of a rights-based moral theory that this view can be given a theoretical justification, and the attractive features of the deterrence and retributive justifications combined in a manner that is principled rather than *ad hoc*.

NOTES

[1] Some philosophers have argued that we should apply the deterrence justification to the institution of punishment and the retributive justification to particular acts within this institution; for classic statements of this "mixed" view see John Rawls, "Two Concepts of Rules," *Philosophical Review* 64 (1955), 3-32, and H.L.A. Hart, "Prolegomenon to the Principles of Punishment," in his *Punishment and Responsibility* (Oxford, 1968), 1-13. But these arguments seem to me to rely on a dubious distinction between an institution and the acts of which it is composed. The rights-based justification I will defend has many of the same attractive consequences as this mixed view without relying on its dubious assumptions about institutions.

[2] John Locke, *Two Treatises of Government*, ed. Peter Laslett, 2nd ed. (New York, 1967).

[3] Robert Nozick, *Anarchy, State, and Utopia* (New York, 1974), 10, 137-42.

[4] On this see H.L.A. Hart, "Are There Any Natural Rights?", *Philosophical Review* 64 (1955), 175-91.

[5] Enforcement rights are often said to include not only a right of self- (and other-) defense and a right to punish but also a right to exact compensation, where this right to exact compensation is sometimes exercised alongside the right to punish and sometimes exercised when it would be wrong to punish. The right to exact compensation, however, need not be regarded as a separate enforcement right. If we say that alongside their ordinary rights persons have more complex rights not to be harmed without compensation being paid them afterwards, we can say that exacting compensation prevents the violation of these rights in exactly the same way that self-defense prevents the violation of simpler rights. Why compensation sometimes can and sometimes cannot be accompanied by punishment—and what distinguishes the two cases—is an extremely difficult question, which lies outside the scope of this paper. For a discussion see Robert Nozick, *Anarchy, State, and Utopia* (New York, 1974), 57-73.

[6] A libertarian rights theory of this kind is presented in Immanuel Kant, *The Metaphysical Elements of Justice: Part I of the Metaphysics of Morals*, John Ladd, trans. (Indianapolis, 1965), and discussed by Hart in "Are There Any Natural Rights?".

[7] Those who do not believe there is a right not to be tickled as such can imagine that X is trying to violate all the (fairly unimportant) rights that he would violate if he tickled Y without his consent.

[8] In *Anarchy, State, and Utopia*, 62, Nozick gives a different version of this upper limit qualification, using the notion of harm, and saying that the upper limit on the harm we can inflict on an attacker is some function $f(H)$ of the harm H which he is threatening to visit on us, where $f(H) > H$, or at least $f(H) \geq H$. If the notion of harm which Nozick is using here is the ordinary utilitarian notion (as it certainly seems to be—see especially the remarks on 58 and 75) then I am not sure that it is the appropriate one to be using at this point in a rights theory, and I am not sure that, if it is used, it will always yield the right results. I will argue below that the right not to be physically assaulted is not less important than the property right which a person has who owns a weapon, and that as a result my version of the upper limit qualification always allows the victim of an assault to destroy his attacker's weapon if that is the only way he can prevent himself from being physically beaten. Nozick's version, however, does not always allow this. Whether I can destroy my attacker's weapon or not depends at least in part on how much he will be harmed by its destruction. If my attacker is not going to do me a very great harm (I already have one broken arm so another will not be much of an added inconvenience), and if he is very fond of his weapon (it is a family heirloom and its destruction will cause him untold misery),

then Nozick's version of the upper limit qualification says I cannot destroy his weapon to prevent him from breaking my arm. This is surely not what a libertarian rights theory ought to say.

9 Nozick discusses a (different) version of this minimum necessary qualification in his "Moral Complications and Moral Structures," *Natural Law Forum* 13 (1968), 1-50. See especially the discussion of Principle VII.

10 In "The Paradox of Punishment," *Philosophy and Public Affairs* 9 (1979-80), 42-58, Alan H. Goldman worries that something like the upper limit qualification forbids us to imprison persons for crimes against property, even though imprisoning these persons is necessary if our laws protecting property are to be effective. This worry only arises because Goldman's version of the upper limit qualification is incorrect. "If we ask which rights are forfeited in violating the rights of others," he says, "it is plausible to answer just those rights that one violates (or an equivalent set)," where equivalence "is to be measured in terms of some average or normal preference scale, much like the one used by the utilitarian when comparing and equating utilities and disutilities," (45). Since most people would prefer losing several thousand dollars to spending five years in prison, Goldman concludes that the upper limit qualification forbids us to give five-year prison terms for thefts of several thousand dollars. Goldman's problem here is similar to Nozick's: he is trying to generate a ranking of rights using concepts which belong properly in a utilitarian rather than a rights-based theory. If he used genuine rights concepts he would find that property rights and rights not to be imprisoned are not ranked with respect to each other, and that the upper limit qualification permits imprisonment for crimes against property.

11 As is often pointed out, the studies have not produced evidence that capital punishment is *not* a deterrent to murder either. But the onus of proof in this question is surely on the defenders of capital punishment to show that it is.

The Death Sentence

SIDNEY HOOK

Since I am not a fanatic or absolutist, I do not wish to go on record as being categorically opposed to the death sentence in all circumstances. I should like to recognize two exceptions. A defendant convicted of murder and sentenced to life should be permitted to choose the death sentence instead. Not so long ago a defendant sentenced to life imprisonment made this request and was rebuked by the judge for his impertinence. I can see no valid grounds for denying such a request out of hand. It may sometimes be denied, particularly if a way can be found to make the defendant labor for the benefit of the dependents of his victim as is done in some European countries. Unless such considerations are present, I do not see on what reasonable ground the request can be denied, particularly by those who believe in capital punishment. Once they argue that life imprisonment is either a more effective deterrent or more justly punitive, they have abandoned their position.

In passing, I should state that I am in favor of permitting *any* criminal defendant, sentenced to life imprisonment, the right to choose death. I can understand why certain jurists, who believe that the defendant wants thereby to cheat the state out of its mode of punishment, should be indignant at the idea. They are usually the ones who believe that even the attempt at suicide should be deemed a crime—in effect saying to the unfortunate person that if he doesn't succeed in his act of suicide, the state will punish him for it. But I am baffled to understand why the absolute abolitionist, dripping with treacly humanitarianism, should oppose this proposal. I have heard some people actually oppose capital punishment in certain cases on the ground that: "Death is too good for the vile wretch! Let him live and suffer to the end of his days." But the absolute abolitionist should be the last person in the world to oppose the wish of the lifer, who regards this form of punishment as torture worse than death, to leave our world.

My second class of exceptions consists of those who having been sentenced once to prison for premeditated murder, murder again. In these particular cases we have evidence that imprisonment is not a sufficient deterrent for the individual in question. If the evidence shows that the prisoner is so psychologically constituted that, without being insane, the fact that he can kill again with impunity may lead to further murderous behavior, the court should have the discretionary power to pass the death sentence if the criminal is found guilty of a second murder.

In saying that the death sentence should be *discretionary* in cases where a man has killed more than once, I am *not* saying that a murderer who murders again is more deserving of death than the murderer who murders once. Bluebeard was not twelve times more deserving of death when he was finally caught. I am saying simply this: that in a sub-class of murderers, i.e., those who murder several times, there may be a special group of sane murderers who, knowing that they will not be executed, will not hesitate to kill again and again. For *them* the argument from deterrence is obviously valid. Those who say that there must be no exceptions to the abolition of capital punishment cannot rule out the existence of such cases on a priori grounds. If they admit that there is a reasonable probability that such murderers will murder again or attempt to murder again, a probability which usually grows with the number of repeated murders, and still insist they would *never* approve of capital punishment, I would conclude that they are indifferent to the lives of the human beings doomed, on their position, to be victims. What fancies itself as a humanitarian attitude is sometimes an expression of sentimentalism. The reverse coin of sentimentalism is often cruelty.

Our charity for all human beings must not deprive us of our common sense. Nor should our charity be less for the future or potential victims of the murderer than for the murderer himself. There are crimes in this world which are, like acts of nature, beyond the power of men to anticipate or control. But not all or most crimes are of this character. So long as human beings are responsible and educable, they will respond to praise and blame and punishment. It is hard to imagine it but even Hitler and Stalin were once infants. Once you *can* imagine them as infants, however, it is hard to believe that they were already monsters in their cradles. Every confirmed criminal was once an amateur. The existence of confirmed criminals testifies to the defects of our education—where they can be reformed—and of our penology—where they cannot. That is why we are under the moral obligation to be intelligent about crime and punishment. Intelligence should teach us that the best educational and penological system is the one which prevents crimes rather than punishes them; the next best is one which punishes crime in such a way as to prevent it from happening again.

NOTE

Because of the rapid increase in major crimes of violence, the author believes it is now justifiable to extend the range of classes of capital crimes for which capital punishment may be merited (1983).

Capital Punishment—
"Cruel and Unusual"?:
A Retributivist Response

ROBERT S. GERSTEIN

Thomas Long, in his article "Capital Punishment—'Cruel and Unusual'?"[1] canvasses the various arguments made for the view that capital punishment is cruel and unusual punishment and comes to the conclusion that the only argument with substantial merit is that which holds that capital punishment is unconstitutional because the pain and suffering it involves cannot be shown to be justified by its effectiveness as a deterrent. It must therefore be regarded as an irrational imposition of pain and suffering until such time as it can be shown that it is a more effective deterrent than less severe punishments would be. He then goes on to admit that this argument has its "sinister" aspects: it is probably true that no punishment could meet the burden of proof required by this standard of rationality. The force of the argument then is to undermine the justification for punishment generally.

I would suggest that Long arrives at this surprising result largely because he has chosen to restrict his consideration of the legitimacy of capital punishment to utilitarian considerations. The key to understanding this restriction is to be found, I believe, in his decision to disregard the retributivist view because "nonretributive views are today predominant among theoreticians of crime and punishment."[2] Having rejected retributivism, and any consideration of whether people "deserve" certain sorts of punishments or not, he is left with a classic utilitarian calculus in which the pain caused to the criminal is to be balanced against the benefits society would gain from the example his punishment sets to others. The dilemma in which he finds himself at the end of his indecisive calculations serves to underline Kant's warning to the penologist who stops being concerned with giving people what they deserve and instead "rummages around in the winding paths of a theory of happiness"[3] for guidance.

It is true that many judges and scholars simply reject retributivism out of hand.[4] It is also true, however, that there has in recent years been a revival of interest in retributive theory.[5] I would like to suggest that the rejection of retributivism is largely a product of misunderstanding and that, properly understood, the retributive view offers a more plausible basis for the solution of the problems surrounding cruel and unusual punishment generally, and capital punishment in particular, than do utilitarian views such as Long's.

The most common way of misunderstanding retributivism is to take it to be a fancy word for revenge. Those who assume that it is simply a rationalization for the venting of our passion for vengeance[6] quite rightly conclude that retributivism can offer us little help in deciding what is cruel and unusual punishment. Obviously this passion is not subject to any inherent limits on cruelty: it has been known to lead people to kill not only wrongdoers, but their whole families as well; it has led to boilings in oil and burnings at the stake. Others who connect retributivism with revenge construe it as a kind of utilitarian argument. In this view the retributivist is not one who justifies the urge to vengeance, but one who thinks that punishment is useful because it allows people to vent this emotion in a (relatively) harmless and orderly way.[7] People who see retributivism in this way also quite rightly come to the conclusion that it offers us no help in deciding what kinds of punishments should be ruled out as cruel and unusual.

These misunderstandings have at their heart the equation of vengeance with retribution. The equation is made understandable by the fact that there are connections, historical and conceptual, between these two ideas. It is mistaken because it misses the enormous and crucial differences between them.

Vengefulness is an emotional response to injuries done to us by others: we feel a desire to injure those who have injured us. Retributivism is not the idea that it is good to have and satisfy this emotion. It is rather the view that there are good arguments for including that kernel of rationality to be found in the passion for vengeance as a part of any just system of laws. Assuming the existence of a generally just legal system, the argument for making retributive punishment a part of it has been succinctly stated in this way:

> In order to enjoy the benefits that a legal system makes possible, each man must be prepared to make an important sacrifice—namely, the sacrifice of obeying the law even when he does not desire to do so. Each man calls on others to do this, and it is only just or fair that he bear a comparable burden when his turn comes. Now if the system is to remain just, it is important to guarantee that those who disobey will not thereby gain an unfair advantage over those who obey voluntarily. Criminal punishment thus attempts to maintain the proper balance between benefit and obedience by insuring that there is no profit in criminal wrongdoing.[8]

It has been seen that some critics of retributivism regard it as a theory that would lead us to use criminals as objects upon which to vent our emotions, as scapegoats to be dealt with without regard to their value as people. In fact, nothing could be further from the truth. It is a major tenet of the standard form of retributivism that "a human being can never be manipulated merely as a means to the purposes of someone else."[9] Punishment is not, in this view, a matter of injuring people because it is useful to us but of dealing with them in the way they deserve to be dealt with. The question for the retributivist is not: what will be the most advantageous way of disposing of this criminal? Rather it is: what is the just way to treat one of our fellow citizens who has willfully taken unjust advantage of the rest of us?

It is especially surprising that critics suggest that retributivism leads to the destruction of all limits on the severity of punishment. Retributivism in its classic form has within it a standard which measures out the severity of the punishment with great care: *lex talionis*.[10] Indeed, if the purpose of punishment is to restore the balance of advantages necessary to a just community, then punishment must be proportioned to the offense: any unduly severe punishment would unbalance things in the other direction.

In fact, one of the great advantages of retributivism over other views is that it serves not only as a justification for punishment but also as a guide to the appropriate kind of punishment and a limit on the severity of punishment. Most other views require us to balance various utilitarian considerations against each other to come to our conclusions. So, for example, a very harsh punishment might be warranted for a particular crime from the point of view of the needs of deterrence, but we might decide to mitigate it because it would simply be too painful to those that would undergo it. Understood from this perspective, the problem of deciding whether some particular punishment was cruel and unusual would, of course, be a matter of weighing the social advantages to be derived from it against the pain it would cause the criminal. A variety of policies, including deterrence, security, and rehabilitation, must all be taken into account.

In retributivism, on the other hand, we have a single coherent perspective from which to make a principled judgment as to the punishment appropriate for this offense and this person. Because punishment is justified as the deserved response of the community to a member who has acted unjustly, it is essential that the punishment meted out to him be consistent with his position as a member of the community. He is not to be treated as an object or even as an enemy. Our duty to treat him justly is no less stringent than that which we have toward any other member of the community. The purpose of punishment is to restore the balance of justice within the community, not further to derange it.

What then would retributivism regard as cruel and unusual punishment? Clearly, any punishment the severity of which was out of proportion with the offense. But further, any punishment which would be inconsistent with the criminal's status as a member of the community whose capacity for a sense of justice (a capacity of which he did not make use when he committed his crime)[11] is worthy of our respect. This is not to say that we may not cause him pain, and even very great pain. To say that punishment is justified is to say that a man with the capacity for a sense of justice ought to feel guilty and recognize that he should suffer for what he has done. The line is not to be drawn in terms of the degree, but in terms of the kind of suffering that is inflicted. As Plato pointed out, it can never be the business of a just man to make another man less just than he was.[12] An affliction which undermines a man's self-respect rather than awakening his conscience, which impairs his capacity for justice rather than stimulating it, could not serve as just punishment.

In fact, one of the most widely accepted views of the meaning of "cruel and unusual punishment," that developed by Justice Brennan,[13] fits very well into the retributivist perspective. Brennan argues that cruel and unusual punishments are those which "treat members of the human race as non-humans, as objects to be toyed with and discarded."[14] He sums up his view in terms of the "primary principle . . . that a punishment must not in its severity be degrading to human dignity."[15] Brennan's position gains both force and clarity when it is seen in the context of retributivism. In this context the distinction between punishments which destroy human dignity and those which do not becomes more plausible because the theory shows us how we can justify the imposition of some afflictive punishments on a person while giving full respect to his human dignity. The idea of human dignity is also given content when it is explicated in terms of the capacity for a sense of justice. Just as we justify punishment as a response to those who abuse this capacity, so we shape and limit punishment out of the desire to preserve and stimulate it.

How does capital punishment fit into this scheme? The retributivist view, to the extent it is dealt with at all, is dealt with only as providing arguments in favor of capital punishment.[16] This is, first, because it does offer a justification for punishment in general, and, second, because the *lex talionis* can be seen as a justification for capital punishment in particular: "life for life, eye for eye, tooth for tooth." Of course, this should make it clear that retributivism would almost certainly rule out as cruel and unusual the use of capital punishment for rape, or for any other crime but murder. But is the retributivist committed to the support of capital punishment for murder? Kant argued that because there is "no sameness of kind between death and remaining alive even under the most miserable conditions" only capital punishment can restore the balance of justice where murder has been committed.[17]

The retributive theory contains the foundation of a very different sort of argument, however.[18] It can lead us to ask how it is possible for us to continue to respect the moral capacity of another while we prepare for and carry out his execution. The answer to this question might depend on attitudes that do change over time. Perhaps the people involved in the ceremony surrounding the public beheading of a nobleman in the eighteenth century could continue to have profound respect for him as a moral being.[19] But ceremonial public executions would not be tolerated among us today. Given our surreptitious and mechanical approach to execution, it is hard to see that the condemned are treated as anything more than "objects to be . . . discarded." The condemned man's physical suffering may be minimized, but that is no more than we would do for a domestic animal to be disposed of. It is not the degree of suffering which might lead the retributivist to regard capital punishment as cruel and unusual, but its dehumanizing character, its total negation of the moral worth of the person to be executed.

I have not attempted here to give a justification of retributivism but only to establish that it would be a serious mistake not to include it among the alternative positions to be considered in gaining a full understanding of the issues involved in declaring the death penalty unconstitutional. Retributivism does offer a coherent and intuitively sound approach to understanding what the phrase "cruel and unusual punishment" can be taken to mean. It is not subject to the difficulties that beset positions like that developed by Long. And if it does not give us an easy answer to the question whether the death penalty is cruel and unusual, it does present the question to us in a form which presses us to make a principled judgment of the most serious sort: when, if ever, can we say that a person whom we continue to respect as a fellow member of a community founded on the principles of justice is deserving of death at our hands?

NOTES

[1] *Ethics* 83 (April 1973), 214-23.

[2] *Ibid.*, 220, n. 21.

[3] Immanuel Kant, *The Metaphysical Elements of Justice*, John Ladd, trans. (Indianapolis, 1965), 100.

[4] See Furman v. Georgia, 92 S. Ct. 2726, 2779-80 (Marshall, J., concurring 1972), and the authorities cited at 2780, no. 86.

[5] See W. H. Moberly, *The Ethics of Punishment* (London, 1968); Herbert Morris, "Persons and Punishment," *The Monist* 52 (October 1968), 475; Jeffrey Murphy, "Three Mistakes about Retributivism," *Analysis* 31 (April 1971), 166.

[6] See Furman v. Georgia, 92 S.Ct., 2726, 2779 (Marshall, J., concurring 1972).

[7] *Ibid.*, at 2761 (Stewart, J., concurring), 2836 (Powell, J., dissenting); Goldberg and Dershowitz, "Declaring the Death Penalty Unconstitutional," *Harvard Law Review* 83 (June 1970), 1773, 1796.

[8] Murphy, 166.

[9] Kant, 100.

[10] *Ibid.*, 101.

[11] The concept of the capacity for a sense of justice is developed in Rawls, "The Sense of Justice," *Philosophical Review* 72 (1963), 281.

[12] *Republic*, F. Cornford, trans. (Oxford, 1941), 13.

[13] Concurring in Trop v. Dulles, 356 U.S. 86, 102 (1958), and Furman v. Georgia, 92 S.Ct., 2726, 2742-8 (1972).

[14] Furman v. Georgia, at 2743.

[15] *Ibid.*, at 2748.

[16] See *ibid.*, 92 S.Ct. 2726, 2779 (Marshall, J., concurring), 2761 (Stewart, J., concurring), 2836 (Powell, J., dissenting).

[17] Kant, 102.

[18] Moberly, on whose view I have drawn extensively here, is one leading retributivist who opposes capital punishment (see *The Ethics of Punishment*, 296-9).

[19] See Kant, 103, where such an execution is used as an example.

The Justice of Restitution

RANDY E. BARNETT

A restitutive theory of justice is a rights-based approach to criminal sanctions that views a crime as an offense by one individual against the rights of another calling for forced reparations by the criminal to the victim. This is a sharp departure from the two predominant sanctioning theories—retribution and crime prevention. Rights-based analysts have criticized this approach for failing to include *mens rea*, or criminal intent into the calculation of sanctions, thereby ignoring the traditional distinction between crime and tort. Such a distinction is problematic, however, since punishment for an evil mind cannot be made compatible with a coherent individual rights framework. To do so would require the existence of a right to certain thoughts of others, a morally and theoretically objectionable position.

To understand the argument for a restitutive remedy for rights violations one must posit what a crime is: an unjust redistribution of entitlements by force that requires for its rectification a redistribution of entitlements by force if necessary from the offender to the victim. Certain common objections to such an approach are considered, including the difficulty of measuring damages, the impossibility of reparation and the problem of criminal attempts.

I

Restitution to victims of crimes is a subject that has received increasing attention recently. Almost all treatments, however, have concerned how such a scheme might be implemented or how restitution has fared in other cultures and times.[1] What remains to be considered is the sort of justice theory that properly underlies such an approach and how this theory compares to more familiar formulations of criminal justice. In two recent articles, I have attempted to show that the principle that should animate any system of justice is a restitutive one.[2] Here I intend to expand upon the ground already covered by first considering the argument of two critics of a restitutive theory. Examining their thoughtful attack will highlight much of what is at stake in the debate and the theoretical superiority of the restitutive approach. After that I will explore more fully what a restitutive theory of justice should look like and how one might deal with some criticisms likely to be made of it.

Before proceeding, it might be useful to review what is meant by restitutive justice: "Restitution refers to monies or services paid by the *offender* to the victim, whether directly to the victim or through intermediaries such as insurance companies."[3] This is to be distinguished from compensation which "refers to monies paid by the *State* to the victim or . . . by the offender to the State."[4] I have said that a restitutive theory of justice "views crime as an offense by one individual against the rights of another. The victim has suffered a loss. Justice consists of the culpable offender making good the loss he has caused. . . . His debt, therefore, is not to society; it is to the victim."[5] Such a theory "recognizes rights in the victim and this is a principal source of its strength. The nature and limit of the victim's right to restitution at the same time defines the nature and limit of the criminal liability. In this way, the aggressive action of the criminal creates a *debt* to the victim."[6] An implication of such an approach is the collapse for most purposes of the traditional distinction between crime and tort with their merger into a single theory of corrective justice that looks to the conduct, broadly defined, of the parties to a case with a view toward enforcing individual rights while obtaining whatever incidental maximization of certain moral goals may be possible. It is on this unifying characteristic of restitutive justice that the two critics have focussed.

In "Crime and Tort: Old Wine in Old Bottles,"[7] Richard A. Epstein argues that the traditional distinction between tort law and criminal law can only be understood by examining the essential purposes of each institution. He concludes by drawing the following distinction: While the tort and criminal law both deal with volitional[8] invasions of one individual's rights by another, here the similarity ends. The differences in the *prima facie* cases in each system and the remedies imposed can only be explained by their different functions. The purpose of the (civil) tort law is to compensate individuals who have been harmed by a rights invasion; the purpose of the criminal law is to punish individuals who have revealed a *mens rea* or bad intention to invade rights by an overt act which attempts (successfully or not) to carry out this intention. For Epstein, then, the function of the civil law is to restore the victim while the criminal law is based on "the view that the state should punish any person whose own conduct is worthy of moral condemnation,"[9] regardless of whether a victim has been harmed. As he puts it, "the actual harm itself is immaterial to the criminal law."[10] Epstein goes on to show how only this distinction can explain the differences between the civil and criminal systems.

It is interesting to note that Professor Epstein never considers the actual historical separation of the two systems. Though the question has yet to be settled, many have convincingly argued that it was the rise of the English monarchy and the King's desire for increased power (and a share of the reparations) that led to the fissure rather than any theoretical distinction.[11] The rationalization of the split came centuries later. Such an observation, if true, does not, however, resolve the theoretical challenge. Even if Epstein's distinction between tort and crime is correct, as it may well be, it must still be justified and any attempt to do so will face at least two main difficulties, which at this point I shall merely list.

The first is that if the purpose of the criminal law is to punish only those who are worthy of moral condemnation, it is difficult to see why the bad intention must necessarily be linked to an (overt) act. Is it merely a practical problem (viz., that we can't read minds) that prevents punishing people's thoughts or is it a theoretical one? For on Epstein's view, "if the accused believes that property he is about to take belongs to another, it should make no difference in the application of the criminal law that by some fluke or confusion the property is unowned, that the accused happens to own it [!], that a gift was about to be made or that the owner has not communicated a subjective consent to allow the accused to use it."[12]

A second, somewhat related problem is whether and how a rights approach, within which Epstein works, gives the state (or anyone else) a right to punish offenders that would justify a separate system devoted to this end. Where does such a right come from and how does it relate to the rights enforced in Epstein's civil system? Though for Epstein the purpose of the criminal law is "moral condemnation" of the offender, it needs to be shown that *punishment* is a justifiable form of condemnation consistent with a theory of individual rights.

This discussion must be seen in its proper context. I do not mean to deny that some rights violators deserve to be "punished" as the term may be used—the deliberate infliction of *unpleasantness* for the purpose of moral condemnation. Neither do I criticize the distinctions made by retributivists as to who is deserving of punishment and who is not. Rather, my argument would be that utilitarian considerations are illegitimate to support such practices and that the retributive argument from desert is insufficient to justify the *forcible* imposition of suffering on an offender. The remaining alternative is nonviolent punishment—approbation, isolation, and even banishment,[13] which though nonviolent may prove to be very harsh. As Joel Feinberg has suggested, a

> ... skeptic might readily concede that the reprobative symbolism of punishment is necessary to, and justified by, [its] ... various derivative functions [of disavowal, nonacquiescence, vindication, and absolution]. Indeed, he may even add deterrence to the list, for condemnation is likely to make it clear, where it would not otherwise be so, that a penalty is not a mere price tag. Granting that point, however, this kind of skeptic would have us consider whether the ends that justify public condemnation of criminal conduct might not be achieved equally well by means of less painful symbolic machinery. . . . Isn't there a way to stigmatize without inflicting any further (pointless) pain to the body, to family, to creative capacity?

One can imagine an elaborate public ritual, exploiting the most trust-worthy devices of religion and mystery, music and drama, to express in the most solemn way the community's condemnation of a criminal for his das-tardly deed. Such a ritual might condemn so very emphatically that there could be no doubt of its genuineness, thus rendering symbolically super-fluous any further hard physical treatment. Such a device would preserve the condemnatory function of punishment while dispensing with its usual physical media—incarceration and corporal mistreatment. . . . The prob-lem of justifying punishment, when it takes this form, may really be that of justifying our particular symbols of infamy.[14]

Epstein does not consider such questions except for a single vague mention of retributive theory.[15] His objective is simply to rationalize the traditional distinction between crime and tort, and while he argu-ably succeeds in this endeavor, this limited scope weakens his defense of that distinction. As a result, his criticism that a restitutive approach fails to take notice of the proper differences between crime and tort is severely undercut.

Fortunately we do not have to look to Epstein alone for a defense of his position, for Roger Pilon, operating within the same theoretical framework, has dealt with precisely these issues in his excellent "Criminal Remedies: Restitution, Punishment, or Both?"[16] He attempts to show how a rights-based theory of justice demands both civil sanctions (restitution) and criminal sanctions (punishments). His argument is based on the contention that a restitutive approach fails to capture "the whole of what is at issue in the criminal transaction." "To be sure," he says, ". . . criminal acts of the kind under consider-ation do involve harms to victims—hence our first concern ought to be to make victims whole again. But is that all they involve?"[17] Pilon concludes, with Epstein, that what a criminal act involves (and there-fore what the criminal law is justified in punishing) is the *mens rea* or bad intent of the offender. "For we punish some moral offense, some action that involves a guilty mind."[18] In other words, ". . . the criminal act includes both the 'wrongs' of the tort act and the *morally* wrong aspect—the guilty mind."[19]

This formulation avoids, or seems to, the first question I raised above—why punish only the *mens rea* that is evidenced by an overt act apart from practical considerations? Here it appears that the intent is not being punished; rather the intent colors the act, somehow chang-ing the act from a morally neutral one (perhaps justifying restitution) to a morally objectionable one justifying punishment. In this way the act and intention are apparently inextricably joined—theoretically inseparable. Now there is nothing particularly novel or unreasonable about such a construction and it might indeed answer the first ques-tion.[20] I do not agree with Pilon, however, that this formulation avoids the second problem, and it is to this I now turn.

The problem, put simply, is how punishment can be made comfort-able within a context of individual rights, for Pilon, no less than Epstein (or I), wishes to focus "attention upon the parties directly involved, upon the rights violated and the obligations now owing."[21] Pilon qualifiedly stays within what he terms the "state of nature" and assumes ". . . with Nozick . . . that no institutional rights (e.g., rights of the state) can be justified except as they are grounded first in individuals."[22] The right to punish must reside, therefore, in the parties to a crime, i.e., the victims. To this point Pilon is entirely within the individual rights context. But he must then ask how a right to punish comes to reside in the victim.

Pilon argues that by using ". . . the victim for his own ends, and against the victim's will . . . the criminal alienated his own right against being similarly treated by the victim. . . . The original act thus creates a right in the victim (or his surrogate) to use the criminal as he himself was used."[23] Intention is again the key, for an unintentional harm cannot justify an intentional harm in return, but only compensation (restitution). An intentional harm gives the victim a right to intentionally harm (punish) the criminal, for only in this way does the remedy "mirror" the offense. Pilon contends that a right to restitution is parasitic on a more fundamental right to a remedy which duplicates or, to use his phrase, reflects the criminal act as closely as possible. At this point a serious problem arises: Does such a general principle follow from a rights approach and is it even consistent with it? Such a proposition must be closely considered to see if it can do the work that Pilon intends for it.

To say that a victim's remedy must mirror the wrong, Pilon must assert the following:

(1) If A violates B's rights, B's remedy must mirror the nature of the rights violation.
(2) If A acted unintentionally, B's only remedy is restitution.
(3) If A acted intentionally, B also has an additional right to punish A.
(4) B may punish A, therefore, if and only if A had the requisite mental state (*mens rea*) at the time of the offense.
(5) The existence of this mental state at the time of the act creates, therefore, in B a right that he would not possess were it not present.
(6) Since a remedy must mirror the extent and nature of the rights violation, the existence of this mental state must violate an additional right in the victim, such that an additional remedy is justified.

The only right which could account for (6) would be a right to have others think a particular, i.e., nonaggressive, way (about you?). B, on this view, has a right to a certain mental state in A, such that he may punish A if this attitude is not maintained. B, therefore, has a right not to be harmed (giving rise to a remedy of restitution) and a further right not to have others, here A, intend to harm him (giving rise to a further right to punishment). Notice that I am not contending that Pilon must justify the punishment of bare intentions with no overt act.[24] Rather, even if it is assumed that for some reason the right to a peaceful mental state in others giving rise if violated to a right to punish can only arise in combination with a harmful act, this additional (though conditioned) right must still be supported. Put another way, Pilon and Epstein must show that the existence of an intent to violate a right (and not all morally objectionable intentions) has violated an additional right in the victim that the volitional, harmful act unaccompanied by such an intention does not.[25]

Professor Epstein doesn't deal with this problem but Pilon does. In the case of an intentional crime: "The criminal," Pilon suggests, "has not simply harmed you. *He has affronted your dignity*."[26] Now whatever else this might mean, here it can only mean that you have a right to dignity such that violations of it give you a right to some form of rectification (and, presumably self-defense as well). While conceding that ". . . dignity is a difficult idea to come to grips with,"[27] Pilon attempts to explain how such a right might exist. He says that rights are ". . . grounded in and derived from human dignity. A dignity rich enough to generate rights must surely figure in the remedy for violations of those rights."[28] But surely the second sentence does not follow easily from the first. For if it is true (as it may well be) that *rights flow from* dignity, this doesn't imply *a right to* dignity itself whatever this might mean. And if "dignity" is not a right, why should it "figure in the remedy" at all?

There is reason to believe that dignity is not and cannot be a right in the traditional sense. The sort of dignity which Pilon's formulation requires is the right to a certain attitude or opinion in the minds of *others* since he seeks to punish mental states. I suggest that Pilon has jumped from the proposition that "people who intend to harm others and do some act in furtherance of that intent (though the source of this proviso remains obscure) are morally worse people than those without this intention" to the proposition that "this moral difference invades additional rights generating thereby additional remedies." The latter does not follow from the former and the requisite connecting proposition—that evil intentions violate rights or that a person has a right to be free from others thinking harmful thoughts about them—is a troublesome position to contemplate much less defend.

Another approach would be to ask whether, assuming that a bad act coupled with a bad intent violates *more* rights than the volitional act alone, does the same act coupled with a noble purpose or intent violate *fewer* rights? It would seem that the thrust of a rights thesis is that persons have rights regardless of how others view them and if it is to be suggested that this precludes considering only good intentions and not bad, then such asymmetry must be explained.[29]

Moreover, even if such a right could be posited and justified, this would not get Pilon as far as he would like, for the ultimate question at issue—should a remedy be restorative and reparative or should it be destructive of an equal right in the offender?—is not resolved by establishing that a right to dignity has been violated. The question remains why the harming of a victim gives him a right to equally harm the offender rather then some form of restitution, monetary or otherwise. In other words, if it is conceded, as Pilon does, that restitution is the appropriate remedy for all other rights violations including intangible ones, then why does violating a right to dignity bring about an entirely different *form* of remedy? This problem is not solved by making its resolution the victim's concern as Pilon suggests[30] since our enterprise is to determine the limit of victim discretion compatible with individual rights including the rights of the offender.

Those who seek to defend a dual system of justice—restitutive (civil) and punitive (criminal)—must show that they both follow from a rights thesis or that one or both is justified on some other ground. If one accepts the rights thesis, then both systems must be consistent with it. This, as I have tried to show, is a difficult task.

II

How might the argument for a restitutive remedy for rights violation be structured? First, it is necessary to posit what, after all, a rights violation is: an interference with the use of one's person or property provided that use is not itself harming others. While a theory of rights is required to specify those actions that are permissible and those that are not, when a right once specified is violated what has occurred is an appropriation by someone of the use of what belongs to another. Thus, if I force you out of your house, I have interfered with your use of your body, house, and land. I am acting as though I own your body, house, and land though I do not. While I am acting as owner, your right to unobstructed use of what is yours gives you an absolute right to regain control of your property however necessary. This is self-defense. But once the incident is over, what then? Self-defense is inappropriate since there is nothing presently to defend against. A wrongful distribution has taken place and it is a *fait accompli*.

What must be done is to rectify that wrongful distribution somehow, however imperfectly this may be done. A redistribution of rights, then, must take place. The offender must give something to the victim, by force if necessary. That what was interfered with may have been intangible does not make it any less a "harm" or rights invasion. It is no less an unjust distribution. If an intangible can be sold, as we know it can, surely it can be stolen or destroyed as well. A theory of rights, therefore, involves a theory of just distribution of rights and a crime is a wrongful interference with that distribution; it is an unjustified redistribution which necessitates, if the victim desires,[31] another redistribution to rectify.

To appreciate the sort of concrete remedies such an approach suggests (and precludes), consider the example of arson. *A* burns down *B*'s house. What *A* has done is interfered with *B*'s ownership of his house as though he, *A*, owned it. He has treated *B*'s house in a manner inconsistent with *B*'s rights to his house. A redistribution from *A* to *B* would involve the building of another house or, if *B* prefers, money payments sufficient to accomplish this. The act of burning down A's house (if A has one) redistributes nothing to B.[32] Such a right would be inconsistent with A's legitimate right to *his* house. It is misleading and wrong to say that by burning B's house A has given up all rights to his own house. What A has incurred is an obligation to redistribute that which was unjustly taken—he must repair B's house and A has given up any rights which may be necessary to accomplish this task. Justice, then, on the rights thesis must be redistributive, not retributive:

> [C]ompensation protects just distributions, and the rights they involve, by undoing, insofar as possible, actions that disturb such distributions. Put briefly, justice is a matter of people having those things that they deserve, are entitled to, or otherwise ought to have, and compensation serves justice by preventing and undoing actions that would prevent people from having these things.[33]

A restitutive approach considers neither the desert or merit of the victim, nor the desert of the criminal. Rather, a restitutive theory is concerned with the *entitlements* disturbed by the criminal act and the entitlements to restitution consequently created in the victim. It is not that the victim deserves compensation on account of some quality he may possess, but that he is entitled to restitution on account of an injury he has received at the hands of a criminal.[34] Since a properly understood theory of restitution is not concerned with desert, it is neither impermissibly asymmetric nor inappropriately future-oriented.

It is important to note that a restitutive theory does not measure damages by what it would take to please the victim *now*. To do so would make the criminal act of minimal, if any, relevance. Instead, we would need to consider how outraged the victim is and just what it would take to appease his anger. Or, conversely, we might consider how indifferent the victim is and might ask whether he needs to be appeased at all.[35] The same trouble would attach to considering the victim's merit or desert.

Such an approach, apart from its obvious practical difficulties, seems to be inconsistent with the proper focus of justice. What the offender is liable for is not the mental attitude—vengeful or benign—of the victim, but the harmful consequences of his criminal act. Such consequences might include mental anguish, but this form of suffering is distinct from the desire (or lack of it) for harsh revenge. While the line dividing the two categories may be fine, it is a very real one nonetheless. Moreover, this last argument strengthens the case against retribution, for some, though not all, theories of retribution are based on the need to appease or satisfy the victim and therefore could only be incidental to a redistribution of rights.

With this notion of restitutive justice in mind, it should be illuminating to consider a few of the objections most often made of it.

A prominent criticism of a restitutive theory is that it is impossible to adequately measure the appropriate restitution for a crime. A retributivist would claim that this is a failing his theory successfully avoids. Thus a murder obviously calls for the death penalty and the loss of, say, an eye naturally calls for a loss of the criminal's eye. While this apparent symmetry is attractive, it is also deceiving. Commensurability, it may be shown, actually presents as great a problem for the retributivist as it does for the restitutivist.

Let us say, to stay with the example of arson, that I deliberately burn down your house. We saw that a restitituve theory calls for me to rebuild the house or have it rebuilt or, in the alternative, any other form of restitution the parties might negotiate. A retributivist would have to say that you (only) have the right to burn down my house. But what if I don't have a house? Can you compel me to build one so that you can burn it down? But what if I don't care if you burn down the house I built? Or what if my house is worth less than yours; or I don't care about mine at all; or you didn't really like the house I burned down and it didn't bother you much, but burning down my house would really bother me? A retributivist who wants to match pain with pain would have considerable difficulty with each of these examples. And one who seeks to match act for act would have similar problems with the case, for example, of a blind man who puts out the eye of another. What is its moral equivalent?

This line of argument does not undermine the *theoretical* case for retribution, but only its claim to *practical* superiority.[36] The effort to match hurt for hurt or act for act is as fraught with difficulties as the measurement of damages. Even when personal injury is considered, retributive sanctions are not easy to locate. If you are raped, must you confine your retribution to a similar rape of the offender with similar damages? Do I have to perform it myself (difficult for a woman) or must I find someone who will do it?

To highlight the problems of a retributive approach is not to suggest that a restitutive theory does not present measurement difficulties of its own. But at least a restitutive standard concerns the subjective mental state of the parties far less than retribution and, where it does, it compensates for an already existing mental state (pain and suffering) and not a prediction of future satisfaction (to the victim) or hurt (to the criminal). Nor does it force the victim to devise a retaliation of equal and possibly horrific magnitude. Rather, where, for example, a woman has been raped, justice mandates that the criminal repair his acts by paying for hospital care, psychiatric counselling, and a cash award for suffering. If the victim didn't want anything from the rapist, she could, if she wishes, have the cash value of her benefits assigned to a rape crisis unit. While any theory of justice will present some problems of measurement, it would seem that those facing a restitutive theory are far fewer and less extreme.

With this in mind, let me now consider what seems to be the main obstacle to accepting a restitutive view. How can money damages, in any sense, make up for a criminal act?[37] If restitution is a chimera, then there can be no restitutive theory of justice. In part this problem presents itself because of an overemphasis placed on money damages by proponents of a restitutive theory (myself included). The rights invasion does not immediately call for money damages, but for reparation: for the criminal to restore as best he can what was taken from or deprived the victim. Money damages may or may not be the most appropriate form of restitution. Personal services of some kind may be another. Perhaps a variety of acts could constitute restitution, provided they serve the legitimate end of restoring the victim and not (unless wholly incidentally) some other illegitimate end, such as punishment or crime prevention.

The objection that *nothing* can repair a criminal act must be answered on several levels. Insofar as it means that the event cannot be erased, the criticism is misplaced. For if this is the thrust, then on this ground a leaky roof cannot be repaired since the leak has already occurred and cannot be "unleaked." This is not how we normally think of repairing something. At another level it might be objected that some crimes are so heinous that they are beyond repair. To this comes the two-part reply that many or even most crimes do not fall into this category, and that because those that do cannot be *completely* repaired does not mean that they cannot be repaired *at all*. Surely some restitution is more just than none.[38]

Finally, the criticism is nonunique, not because the alternatives— utilitarianism and retribution—cannot restore the victim since this is not their goal, but because neither theory can perfectly achieve *its* objectives, whether utilitarian or retributive. Does utilitarianism perfectly deter? Does retribution perfectly balance the score? An approach need not work perfectly to be justified.

The last objection I will consider is raised by both Epstein and John Hospers. Epstein contends that only a "punishment for bad intention" rationale from criminal law can explain punishment of unsuccessful attempts to commit a crime.[39] If this is correct, then the status of attempts is uncertain in a restitutive theory which views intention as irrelevant to the calculation of a just sanction. "If you don't penalize [unsuccessful] attempts," argues Hospers, "more attempts will be made, and more are likely to succeed. Besides, the man who attempts to kill you deserves a penalty; some would even say he deserves as great a penalty as if he had succeeded."[40]

While I have examined this issue elsewhere,[41] a brief discussion here might serve to clarify the issues. The question of attempts is interesting for if we reject punishing criminal desert, then it would seem that a criminal who intends to commit a crime, but fails in his attempt, cannot be sanctioned. Retributive theory, however, itself does not satisfactorily deal with the problem of unsuccessful attempts. For if it is desert that we punish and not the effects of a criminal act (justifying, thereby, punishment where there are no effects), why are attempts punished less severely than the crime itself? Why, for example, is attempted murder considered less serious and punished less severely than murder when the desert is presumably the same?[42]

The real question becomes, or is all along, whether an attempt is a crime. The rights theorist must ask whether an unsuccessful attempt to violate a right violates any right? Put this way, the question appears to answer itself in the negative. What the rights theorist must decide, then, is not whether an unsuccessful attempt is a crime—it isn't—but instead when an attempt becomes a *threat* such that it is subject to the prohibition on the use or threatened use of force. Unsuccessful attempts, therefore, may only be sanctionable if they are successful threats. Such an inquiry, as it concerns what constitutes a breach within a theory of rights and not how breaches are to be dealt with when they occur, is outside a theory of restitutive justice. Such a theory posits that *any* rights violation is a harm giving rise to a right in the victim to restitution. The *application* of this theory must await the outcome of the discussion, but the restitutive theory itself is in no way affected by that outcome:

> . . . for until it is settled what conduct is to be legally denounced and discouraged we have not settled from what we are to *deter* people, or who are to be considered *criminals* from whom we are to exact *retribution* [or restitution], or on whom we are to wreak *vengeance*, or whom we are to *reform*.[43]

It should now be apparent that those who defend the forcible punishment of criminals beyond restitution are hard pressed to make such a program consistent with individual rights. The significance of such a difficulty is considerable for it means that the restitutive theory of justice or, at the very least, the rejection of punishment is not only consistent with an individual rights approach, it is required by it. And if this is true many will face an uncomfortable (and some an easy) choice between individual rights on the one hand and punishment on the other—a choice that is not currently thought to be necessary.

In this article I have attempted to outline the justice of the restitutive theory I have described elsewhere. To this end it was useful to examine criticisms made by others operating within much the same philosophical context as I. The arguments presented here do little, however, to answer the criticisms made by those who do not share a rights-based approach to criminal sanctions.[44] Such a worthwhile project must, regrettably, be left to future work.

NOTES

[1] See, generally, Stephen Schafer, *Compensation and Restitution to Victims of Crime*, 2nd ed., enl. (Montclair, N.J., 1970); Joe Hudson and Burt Galaway, eds., *Considering the Victim: Readings in Restitution and Victim Compensation* (Springfield, Ill., 1975), and *Restitution in Criminal Justice* (Lexington, Mass., 1977).

2 In "Restitution: A New Paradigm of Criminal Justice," *Ethics* 87, no. 4 (July 1977), 279-301, I argued that the existing paradigm of criminal justice—punishment—has failed (in the Kuhnian sense) to solve the problems it was in part responsible for creating; that the justifications traditionally offered—deterrence, disablement (or incapacitation), and reformation—are inadequately served by punishment and that, alone or in combination, they are inappropriate and problematic justification for the deliberate, forcible infliction of suffering on a criminal offender. I also suggested that proportionality, rehabilitation, and victim compensation were attempts to salvage the punishment paradigm and, though they have ultimately been undercut by the paradigm itself, they point in the direction of a new paradigm—restitution. In "Assessing the Criminal: Restitution, Retribution and the Legal Process," in *Assessing the Criminal*, Randy E. Barnett and John Hagel III, ed. (Cambridge, Mass., 1977), 1-31, with John Hagel I outlined a restitutive theory albeit in a conclusory manner. The theory as formulated revolved around the distinction between moral rights and moral goals. Moral rights are those actions which may never be interfered with. The purpose of a system of justice is to rectify infringements of moral rights and nothing more. Crime prevention, whether by deterrence, disablement, reformation, or rehabilitation, is a highly desirable (moral) goal which may be well served by the course of justice but has no place in the calculation of sanctions for rights violations.

3 Laura Nader and Elaine Combs-Schilling, "Restitution in Cross-cultural Perspective," *Restitution in Criminal Justice,* 28. (Emphasis in original.)

4 *Ibid.*, 27-8. (Emphasis in original.)

5 Barnett, *op. cit.*, 287-8.

6 *Ibid.*, 291. (Emphasis in original.)

7 In *Assessing the Criminal*, 231-57.

8 For a discussion of what he means by "volition," see his excellent "A Theory of Strict Liability," *Journal of Legal Studies* 2 (1973), 166-8.

9 Epstein, "Crime and Tort," 248.

10 *Ibid.*

11 See Schafer; Richard E. Laster, "Criminal Restitution: A Survey of its Past History and an Analysis of its Present Usefulness," *University of Richmond Law Review* 5 (1970), 71-80; Bruce Jacobs, "The Concept of Restitution: An Historical Overview," in *Restitution in Criminal Justice*, 45-62; for a general historical background, see Fredrick Pollack and Fredric William Maitland, *The History of English Law* (Cambridge, 1898), 460; A. S. Diamond, *Primitive Law* (London, 1935), 148, 316, n. 5; Heinrich Oppenheimer, *The Rationale of Punishment* (London, 1913), 162-3, 173-4; Nader and Combs-Schilling, 27-44; and William F. McDonald, "The Role of the Victim in America," in *Assessing the Criminal*, 295-8.

12 Epstein, *op. cit.*, 251.

13 More easily handled where common areas are privately owned, for example, shopping centers. For a historical perspective, see Leonard P. Liggio, "The Transportation of Criminals: A Brief Political-Economic History," in *Assessing the Criminal*, 273-94.

14 Joel Feinberg, *Doing and Deserving* (Princeton, 1970), 115-16.

15 *Ibid.*, 248.

16 Roger Pilon, "Criminal Remedies: Restitution, Punishment, or Both?" *Ethics* 88, no. 4 (July 1978), 348-57.

17 *Ibid.*, 350.

18 *Ibid.*, 355.

19 *Ibid.* (Emphasis in original.)

20 About this some doubt still remains. See also, for example, Max Atkinson, "Justified

and Deserved Punishments," *Mind* 78 (July 1969), 364. There he contends that
". . . the requital of evil conduct would, if taken as the basis for punishing a type of
conduct, justify official punishment of lying and other forms of immorality. . . ."

21 Pilon, 349.

22 *Ibid.*, 352, n. 7. See Robert Nozick, *Anarchy, State, and Utopia* (New York, 1974), 6,
137-42. But see Jeffrie G. Murphy, "A Paradox in Locke's Theory of Natural
Rights," *Dialogue* 9 (Summer 1969), 256-71, for the contrary (and I believe incorrect)
view that *no one* in the state of nature properly may punish.

23 Pilon, 355-6.

24 Though this may be a consequence of his position. For the problems raised by such a
proposal, see Herbert Morris, "Punishment for Thoughts," *The Monist* 48, no. 3 (July
1965), 342-76.

25 To illustrate what must be established, consider the following: I swing a sword at you
and cut you severely. Your rights have been violated—viz., the right to be free in
your person or property from the unjustified use of force. Now add to this act the
fact that I intended to harm you. Since the remedy of restitution entirely satisfies the
first act (less the intention) that violated the right to be free from the unjustified use
of force, the intentional act must violate an *additional* right, viz., the right to a particular (peaceful) mental state in others.

26 Pilon, 351-2. (Emphasis in original.)

27 *Ibid.*, 352.

28 *Ibid.*

29 Walter Kaufman has remarked that while many freely speculate about the proper
proportionate punishment commensurate with desert, "[s]peculation about proportionate rewards, on the other hand, has remained a rather barren affair." (Kaufman,
"Retribution and the Ethics of Punishment," in *Assessing the Criminal*, 228).

30 Pilon, 356.

31 If the victim does not desire a redistribution, then he has made a gift.

32 It may be argued that a right "to burn down *A*'s house" has been distributed to *B*, but
this cannot be since this is not the right that *A* appropriated. *A* has stolen *B*'s house
and in the process destroyed it. What he has taken is the house; this, and nothing
less, is what must be returned.

33 James W. Nickel, "Justice in Compensation," *William and Mary Law Review* 18 (Winter
1976), 382. I would confine the discussion to entitlements.

34 For a discussion of the distinction, see Nozick; see also Feinberg, 55-87. Feinberg
speaks of "desert of reparation" as a polar (two party) form of desert (74-5), but
there seems to be no reason why reparations might not also be thought of as an entitlement as he employs the distinction.

35 The so-called "poor criminal/rich victim," "rich criminal/poor victim" and "rich crim-
inal/rich victim" dilemmas are species of this type of inappropriate concern with victim satisfaction. See, for example, Pilon, 351.

36 This point is made by Jeffrie G. Murphy, "Three Mistakes About Retributivism,"
Analysis 31 (April 1971), 166-9: "[T]his objection as Hegel rightly sees, is superficial.
Surely the principle *jus talionis*, though requiring likeness of punishment, does not
require *exact* likeness in all respects. There is no reason *in principle (though there are
always practical difficulties* [my emphasis]) against trying to specify in a general way
what the costs in life and labour of certain kinds of criminal might be, and how the
costs of punishment might be calculated, so that retribution could be understood as
preventing criminal profit" (168).

37 "The past is not a blackboard, the slate cannot be wiped clean, and what is done cannot be undone" (Kaufman, 230).

38 It is curious that while the victim of a property crime is often conceded to be entitled to restitution, a victim of a more serious crime who suffers much more is usually excluded from a restitution scheme. It would seem, to the contrary, that a more serious injury entitles the victim to more extensive restitution not less.

39 Epstein, 248-53.

40 John Hospers, "Retribution: The Ethics of Punishment," in *Assessing the Criminal*, 205.

41 Barnett, "Restitution: A New Paradigm of Criminal Justice," as it appears in *Assessing the Criminal*, 375-8. Part of my argument there, which is tentatively offered, is that while intent is immaterial to the calculation of a just sanction, it may be material at other stages of inquiry, most notably in determining justified self-defense in a legal action by the aggressor against the victim who used force to ward off an attack.

42 This objection is raised by Gerald Dworkin and David Blumenfeld in "Punishment for Intentions," *Mind* 75 (1966), 396-404, and again by H.L.A. Hart in "Intention and Punishment," *Oxford Review* 4 (February 1967), 5-22, reprinted in *Punishment and Responsibility*, 111-35. The contention of both articles is that retributive and utilitarian theories cannot justify different treatment of attempts. Paul J. Dietl, however, in "On Punishing Attempts," *Mind* 79 (January 1970), 130-2, shows that utilitarian analysis can withstand such a criticism: "It is perfectly conceivable that a person might think that committing a crime was worth the risk of the penalty for success but not worth undertaking at all if, should he fail, he would still be punished" (130). A similar attempt by John Marshall to defend retributive theory in "Punishment for Intentions," *Mind* 80 (October 1971), 597-8, meets with considerably less success: "To the question 'Why don't we punish *X* as severely as *Y*?' [where *X* has failed in his attempt and *Y* has succeeded] it is only to be expected that the retributivist *qua* retributivist will have no answer. He will say that, since *X* and *Y* *ex hypothesi* have the same moral worth, they deserve equal punishment, but this does not preclude his also saying on the basis of some general moral theory that there might be good reasons (non-retributive but not, therefore, non-moral reasons) for treating *X* differently than *Y*" (598).

43 Hart, *Punishment and Responsibility*, 8. My earlier discussion of attempts cited at n. 41 may be deficient for failing to make this point clear.

44 See, for example, Franklin G. Miller, "Restitution and Punishment: A Reply to Barnett," *Ethics* 88, no. 4 (July 1977), 358-60; Stanley S. Kleinberg, "Criminal Justice and Private Enterprise," *Ethics* 90 (January 1980), 270-82; and Richard Dagger, "Restitution, Punishment, and Debts to Society," in Joe Hudson and Burt Galaway, eds., *Victims, Offenders and Alternative Sanctions* (Lexington, Mass., 1980), 3-13.

IV

FEEDING THE HUNGRY

Killing and Starving to Death

JAMES RACHELS

Although we do not know exactly how many people die each year of malnutrition or related health problems, the number is very high, in the millions.[1] By giving money to support famine relief efforts, each of us could save at least some of them. By not giving, we let them die.

Some philosophers have argued that letting people die is not as bad as killing them, because in general our "positive duty" to give aid is weaker than our "negative duty" not to do harm.[2] I maintain the opposite: letting die is just as bad as killing.[3] At first this may seem wildly implausible. When reminded that people are dying of starvation while we spend money on trivial things, we may feel a bit guilty, but certainly we do not feel like murderers. Philippa Foot writes:

> Most of us allow people to die of starvation in India and Africa, and there is surely something wrong with us that we do; it would be nonsense, however, to pretend that it is only in law that we make a distinction between allowing people in the underdeveloped countries to die of starvation and sending them poisoned food. There is worked into our moral system a distinction between what we owe people in the form of aid and what we owe them in the way of non-interference.[4]

No doubt this would be correct if it were intended only as a description of what most people believe. Whether this feature of "our moral system" is rationally defensible is, however, another matter. I shall argue that we are wrong to take comfort in the fact that we "only" let these people die, because our duty not to let them die is equally as strong as our duty not to kill them, which, of course, is very strong indeed.

Obviously, this Equivalence Thesis is not morally neutral, as philosophical claims about ethics often are. It is a radical idea which, if true, would mean that some of our "intuitions" (our prereflective beliefs about what is right and wrong in particular cases) are mistaken and must be rejected. Neither is the view I oppose morally neutral. The idea that killing is worse than letting die is a relatively conservative thesis which would allow those same intuitions to be preserved. However, the Equivalence Thesis should not be dismissed merely because it does not conform to all our prereflective intuitions. Rather than being perceptions of the truth, our "intuitions" might sometimes signify nothing more than our prejudices or selfishness or cultural conditioning. Philosophers often admit that, in theory at least, some intuitions might be unreliable—but usually this possibility is not taken seriously, and conformity to prereflective intuition is used uncritically as a test of the acceptability of moral theory. In what follows I shall argue that many of our intuitions concerning killing and letting die *are* mistaken, and should not be trusted.

I

We think that killing is worse than letting die, not because we overestimate how bad it is to kill, but because we underestimate how bad it is to let die. The following chain of reasoning is intended to show that letting people in foreign countries die of starvation is very much worse than we commonly assume.

Suppose there were a starving child in the room where you are now—hollow eyed, belly bloated, and so on—and you have a sandwich at your elbow that you don't need. Of course you would be horrified; you would stop reading and give her the sandwich, or better, take her to a hospital. And you would not think this an act of supererogation: you would not expect any special praise for it, and you would expect criticism if you did not do it. Imagine what you would think of someone who simply ignored the child and continued reading, allowing her to die of starvation. Let us call the person who would do this Jack Palance, after the very nice man who plays such vile characters in the movies. Jack Palance indifferently watches the starving child die; he cannot be bothered even to hand her the sandwich. There is ample reason for judging him very harshly; without putting too fine a point on it, he shows himself to be a moral monster.

When we allow people in far-away countries to die of starvation, we may think, as Mrs. Foot puts it, that "there is surely something wrong with us." But we most emphatically do not consider ourselves moral monsters. We think this, in spite of the striking similarity between Jack Palance's behavior and our own. He could easily save the child; he does not; and the child dies. We could easily save some of those starving people; we do not; and they die. If we are not monsters, there must be some important difference between him and us. But what is it?

One obvious difference between Jack Palance's position and ours is that the person he lets die is in the same room with him, while the people we let die are mostly far away. Yet the spatial location of the dying people hardly seems a relevant consideration.[5] It is absurd to suppose that being located at a certain map coordinate entitles one to treatment which one would not merit if situated at a different longitude or latitude. Of course, if a dying person's location meant that we *could not* help, that would excuse us. But, since there are efficient famine relief agencies willing to carry our aid to the far-away countries, this excuse is not available. It would be almost as easy for us to send these agencies the price of the sandwich as for Palance to hand the sandwich to the child.

The location of the starving people does make a difference, psychologically, in how we feel. If there were a starving child in the same room with us, we could not avoid realizing, in a vivid and disturbing way, how it is suffering and that it is about to die. Faced with this realization our consciences probably would not allow us to ignore the child. But if the dying are far away, it is easy to think of them only abstractly, or to put them out of our thoughts altogether. This might explain why our conduct would be different if we were in Jack Palance's position even though, from a moral point of view, the location of the dying is not relevant.

There are other differences between Jack Palance and us, which may seem important, having to do with the sheer numbers of people, both affluent and starving, that surround us. In our fictitious example Jack Palance is one person, confronted by the need of one other person. This makes his position relatively simple. In the real world our position is more complicated, in two ways: first, in that there are millions of people who need feeding, and none of us has the resources to care for all of them; and second, in that for any starving person we *could* help there are millions of other affluent people who could help as easily as we.

On the first point, not much needs to be said. We may feel, in a vague sort of way, that we are not monsters because no one of us could possibly save *all* the starving people—there are just too many of them, and none of us has the resources. This is fair enough, but all that follows is that, individually, none of us is responsible for saving everyone. We may still be responsible for saving someone, or as many as we can. This is so obvious that it hardly bears mentioning; yet it is easy to lose sight of, and philosophers have actually lost sight of it. In his article "Saving Life and Taking Life,"[6] Richard Trammell says that one morally important difference between killing and letting die is "dischargeability." By this he means that, while each of us can discharge completely a duty not to kill anyone, no one among us can discharge completely a duty to save everyone who needs it. Again, fair enough; but all that follows is that, since we are only bound to save those we can, the class of people we have an obligation to save is much smaller than the class of people we have an obligation not to kill. It does *not* follow that our duty with respect to those we can save is any less stringent. Suppose Jack Palance were to say: "I needn't give this starving child the sandwich because, after all, I can't save everyone in the world who needs it." If this excuse will not work for him, neither will it work for us with respect to the children we could save in India or Africa.

The second point about numbers was that, for any starving person we *could* help, there are millions of other affluent people who could help as easily as we. Some are in an even better position to help since they are richer. But by and large these people are doing nothing. This also helps to explain why we do not feel especially guilty for letting people starve. How guilty we feel about something depends, to some extent, on how we compare with those around us. If we were surrounded by people who regularly sacrificed to feed the starving, and we did not, we would probably feel ashamed. But because our neighbors do not do any better than we, we are not so ashamed.

But again, this does not imply that we should not feel more guilty or ashamed than we do. A psychological explanation of our feelings is not a moral justification of our conduct. Suppose Jack Palance were only one of twenty people who watched the child die; would that decrease his guilt? Curiously, I think many people assume it would. Many people seem to feel that if twenty people do nothing to prevent a tragedy, each of them is only one-twentieth as guilty as he would have been if he had watched the tragedy alone. It is as though there is only a fixed amount of guilt, which divides. I suggest, rather, that guilt multiplies, so that each passive viewer is fully guilty, if he could have prevented the tragedy but did not. Jack Palance watching the girl die alone would be a moral monster; but if he calls in a group of his friends to watch with him, he does not diminish his guilt by dividing it among them. Instead, they are all moral monsters. Once the point is made explicit, it seems obvious.

The fact that most other affluent people do nothing to relieve hunger may very well have implications for one's own obligations. But the implication may be that one's own obligations *increase* rather than decrease. Suppose Palance and a friend were faced with two starving children, so that, if each did his "fair share," Palance would only have to feed one of them. But the friend will do nothing. Because he is well-off, Palance could feed both of them. Should he not? What if he fed one and then watched the other die, announcing that he has done *his* duty and that the one who died was his friend's responsibility? This shows the fallacy of supposing that one's duty is only to do one's fair share, where this is determined by what would be sufficient *if* every one else did likewise.

To summarize: Jack Palance, who refuses to hand a sandwich to a starving child, is a moral monster. But we feel intuitively that we are not so monstrous, even though we also let starving children die when we could feed them almost as easily. If this intuition is correct, there must be some important difference between him and us. But when we examine the most obvious differences between his conduct and ours—the location of the dying, the differences in numbers—we find no real basis for judging ourselves less harshly than we judge him. Perhaps there are some other grounds on which we might distinguish our moral position, with respect to actual starving people, from Jack Palance's position with respect to the child in my story. But I cannot think of what they might be. Therefore, I conclude that if he is a monster, then so are we—or at least, so are we after our rationalizations and thoughtlessness have been exposed.

This last qualification is important. We judge people, at least in part, according to whether they can be expected to realize how well or how badly they behave. We judge Palance harshly because the consequences of his indifference are so immediately apparent. By contrast, it requires an unusual effort for us to realize the consequences of our indifference. It is normal behavior for people in the affluent countries not to give to famine relief, or if they do give, to give very little. Decent people may go along with this normal behavior pattern unthinkingly, without realizing, or without comprehending in a clear way, just what this means for the starving. Thus, even though those decent people may act monstrously, we do not judge them monsters. There is a curious sense, then, in which moral reflection can transform decent people into indecent ones: for if a person thinks things through, and realizes that he is, morally speaking, in Jack Palance's position, his continued indifference is more blameworthy than before.

The preceding is not intended to prove that letting people die of starvation is as bad as killing them. But it does provide strong evidence that letting die is much worse than we normally assume, and so that letting die is much *closer* to killing than we normally assume. These reflections also go some way towards showing just how fragile and unreliable our intuitions are in this area. They suggest that, if we want to discover the truth, we are better off looking at arguments that do not rely on unexamined intuitions.

II

Before arguing that the Equivalence Thesis is true, let me explain more precisely what I mean by it. I take it to be a claim about what does, or does not, count as a morally good reason in support of a value judgment: the bare fact that one act is an act of killing, while another act is an act of "merely" letting someone die, is not a morally good reason in support of the judgment that the former is worse than the latter. Of course there may be *other* differences between such acts that are morally significant. For example, the family of an irreversibly comatose hospital patient may want their loved one to be allowed to die, but not killed. Perhaps the reason for their preference is religious. So we have at least one reason to let the patient die rather than to kill him—the reason is that the family prefers it that way. This does not mean, however, that the distinction between killing and letting die *itself* is important. What is important is respecting the family's wishes. (It is often right to respect people's wishes even if we think those wishes are based on false beliefs.) In another sort of case, a patient with a painful terminal illness may want to be killed rather than allowed to die because a slow, lingering death would be agonizing. Here we have a reason to kill and not let die, but once again the reason is not that one course is intrinsically preferable to the other. The reason is, rather, that the latter course would lead to more suffering.

It should be clear, then, that I will *not* be arguing that every act of letting die is equally as bad as every act of killing. There are lots of reasons why a particular act of killing may be morally worse than a particular act of letting die, or vice versa. If a healthy person is murdered, from a malicious motive, while a person in irreversible coma is allowed to die upon a calm judgment that maintaining him alive is pointless, certainly this killing is very much worse than this letting die. Similarly, if an ill person who could be saved is maliciously allowed to die, while a terminal patient is killed, upon his request, as an act of kindness, we have good reason to judge the letting die worse than the killing. All that I want to argue is that, whatever reasons there may be for judging one act worse than another, the simple fact that one is killing, whereas the other is only letting die, is not among them.

The first stage of the argument is concerned with some formal relations between moral judgments and the reasons that support them. I take it to be a point of logic that moral judgments are true only if good reasons support them; for example, if there is no good reason why you ought to do some action, it cannot be true that you ought to do it. Moreover, when there is a choice to be made from among several possible actions, the preferable alternative is the one that is backed by the strongest reasons.

But when are the reasons for or against one act stronger than those for or against another act? A complete answer would have to include some normative theory explaining why some reasons are intrinsically weightier than others. Suppose you are in a situation in which you can save someone's life only by lying: the normative theory would explain why "Doing A would save someone's life" is a stronger reason in favor of doing A than "Doing B would be telling the truth" is in favor of doing B.

However, there are also some purely formal principles that operate here. The simplest and least controversial such principle is this:

(1) If there are the *same* reasons for or against A as for or against B, then the reasons in favor of A are neither stronger nor weaker than the reasons in favor of B; and so A and B are morally equivalent—neither is preferable to the other.

Now, suppose we ask why killing is morally objectionable. When someone is killed, there may of course be harmful effects for people other than the victim himself. Those who loved him may grieve, and those who were depending on him in one way or another may be caused hardship because, being dead, he will be unable to perform as expected. However, we cannot explain the wrongness of killing purely, or even mainly, in terms of the bad effects for the survivors. The primary reason why killing is wrong is that something very bad is done to the victim himself: he ends up dead; he no longer has a good—his life—which he possessed before. But notice that exactly the same can be said about letting someone die. The primary reason why it is morally objectionable to let someone die, when we could save him, is that he ends up dead; he no longer has a good—his life—which he possessed before. Secondary reasons again have to do with harmful effects on those who survive. Thus, the explanation of why killing is bad mentions features of killing that are also features of letting die, and vice versa. Since there are no comparably general reasons in favor of either, this suggests that:

(2) There are the same reasons for and against letting die as for and against killing.

And if this is true, we get the conclusion:

(3) Therefore, killing and letting die are morally equivalent—neither is preferable to the other.

The central idea of this argument is that there is no morally relevant difference between killing and letting die, that is, no difference which may be cited to show that one is worse than the other. The argument therefore contains a premise—(2)—that is supported only inductively. The fact that the explanation of why killing is wrong applies equally well to letting die, and vice versa, provides strong evidence that the inductive generalization is true. Nevertheless, no matter how carefully we analyze the matter, it will always be possible that there is some subtle, morally relevant difference between the two that we have overlooked. In fact, philosophers who believe that killing is worse than letting die have sometimes tried to identify such differences. I believe that these attempts have failed; here are three examples:

1. The first is one that I have already mentioned. Trammell urges that there is an important difference in the "dischargeability" of duties not to kill and not to let die. We can completely discharge a duty not to kill anyone; but we cannot completely discharge a duty to save everyone who needs aid. This is obviously correct, but it does not show that the Equivalence Thesis is false, for two reasons. In the first place, the difference in dischargeability only shows that the class of people we have a duty to save is smaller than the class of people we have a duty not to kill. It does not show that our duty with respect to

those we *can* save is any less stringent. In the second place, if we *cannot* save someone, and that person dies, then we do not let him die. It is not right to say that I let Josef Stalin die, for example, since there is no way I could have saved him. So if I cannot save everyone, then neither can I let everyone die.

2. It has also been urged that, in killing someone, we are *doing* something—namely, killing him—whereas, in letting someone die, we are not doing anything. In letting people die of starvation, for example, we only *fail* to do certain things, such as sending food. The difference is between action and inaction; and somehow, this is supposed to make a moral difference.[7]

There are also two difficulties with this suggestion. First, it is misleading to say, without further ado, that in letting someone die we do nothing. For there is one very important thing that we do: we let someone die. "Letting someone die" is different, in some ways, from other sorts of actions, mainly in that it is an action we perform *by way of* not performing other actions. We may let someone die by way of not feeding him, just as we may insult someone by way of not shaking his hand. (If it is said, "I didn't do anything; I simply refrained from taking his hand when he offered it," it may be replied "You did do one thing—you insulted him.") The distinction between action and inaction is relative to a specification of *what* actions are or are not done. In insulting someone, we may *not* smile, speak, shake hands, and so on—but we *do* insult or snub the person. And in letting someone die, the following may be among the things that are not done: we do not feed the person, we do not give medication, and so on. But the following is among the things that are done: we let him die.

Second, even if letting die were only a case of inaction, why should any moral conclusion follow from *that* fact? It may seem that a significant conclusion follows if we assume that we are not responsible for inactions. However, there is no general correlation between the action-inaction distinction and any sort of moral assessment. We ought to do some things, and we ought not do others, and we can certainly be morally blameworthy for not doing things as well as for doing them—Jack Palance was blameworthy for not feeding the child. (In many circumstances we are even legally liable for not doing things: tax fraud may involve only "inaction"—failing to report certain things to the Department of Internal Revenue—but what of it?) Moreover, failing to act can be subject to all the other kinds of moral assessment. Not doing something may, depending on the circumstances, be right, wrong, obligatory, wise, foolish, compassionate, sadistic, and so on. Since there is no general correlation between the action-inaction distinction and *any* of these matters, it is hard to see how anything could be made out of this distinction in the present context.

3. My final example is from Trammell again. He argues that "optionality" is a morally relevant difference between killing and let-

ting die. The point here is that if we fail to save someone, we leave open the option for someone else to save him; whereas if we kill, the victim is dead and that is that. This point, I think, has little significance. For one thing, while "optionality" may mark a difference between killing and *failing to save*, it does not mark a comparable difference between killing and *letting die*. If X fails to save Y, it does not follow that Y dies; someone else may come along and save him. But if X lets Y die, it does follow that Y dies; Y is dead and that is that.[8] When Palance watches the child die, he does not merely fail to save the child; he lets her die. And when we fail to send food to the starving, and they die, we let them die—we do not merely fail to save them.

The importance of "optionality" in any particular case depends on the actual chances of someone else's saving the person we do not save. Perhaps it is not so bad not to save someone if we know that someone else *will* save him. (Although even here, we do not behave as we ought; for we ought not simply to leave what needs doing to others.) And perhaps it even gets us off the hook a little if there is the *strong chance* that someone else will step in. But in the case of the world's starving, we know very well that no person or group of persons is going to come along tomorrow and save all of them. We know that there are at least some people who will *not* be saved, if we do not save them. So, as an excuse for not giving aid to the starving, the "optionality" argument is clearly in bad faith. To say of those people, after they are dead, that someone else *might* have saved them, in the very weak sense in which that will be true, does not excuse us at all. The others who might have saved them, but did not, are as guilty as we, but that does not diminish our guilt—as I have already remarked, guilt in these cases multiplies, not divides.

III

I need now to say a few more things about the counter-intuitive nature of the Equivalence Thesis.

The fact that this view has radical implications for conduct has been cited as a reason for rejecting it. Trammell complains that "Denial of the distinction between negative and positive duties leads straight to an ethic so strenuous that it might give pause even to a philosophical John the Baptist."[9] Suppose John is about to buy a phonograph record, purely for his enjoyment, when he is reminded that with this five dollars a starving person could be fed. On the view I am defending, he ought to give the money to feed the hungry person. This may not seem exceptional until we notice that the reasoning is reiterable. Having given the first five dollars, John is not free to use another five to buy the record. For the poor are always with him: there is always *another* starving person to be fed, and then another, and then another. "The problem," Trammell says, "is that, even though fulfilment of one particular act of aid involves only minimal effort, it sets a precedent for millions of such efforts."[10] So we reach the bizarre conclusion that it is almost always immoral to buy phonograph records! And the same goes for fancy clothes, cars, toys, and so on.

This sort of *reductio* argument is of course familiar in philosophy. Such arguments may be divided into three categories. The strongest sort shows that a theory entails a contradiction, and, since contradictions cannot be tolerated, the theory must be modified or rejected. Such arguments, when valid, are of course devastating. Second, an argument may show that a theory has a consequence which, while not inconsistent, is nevertheless demonstrably false—that is, an independent proof can be given that the offensive consequence is unacceptable. Arguments of this second type, while not quite so impressive as the first, can still be irresistible. The third type of *reductio* is markedly weaker than the others. Here, it is merely urged that some consequence of a theory is counter-intuitive. The supposedly embarrassing consequence is perfectly consistent, and there is no proof that it is false; the complaint is only that it goes against our unreflective, pretheoretical beliefs. Now sometimes even this weak sort of argument can be effective, especially when we have not much confidence in the theory, or when our confidence in the pretheoretical belief is unaffected by the reasoning which supports the theory. However, it may happen that *the same reasoning which leads one to accept a theory also persuades one that the pretheoretical beliefs were wrong.* (If this did not happen, philosophy would always be in the service of what we already think; it could never challenge and change our beliefs, and would be, in an important sense, useless.) The present case, it seems to me, is an instance of this type. The same reasoning which leads to the view that we are as wicked as Jack Palance, and that killing is no worse than letting die, also persuades (me, at least) that the prereflective belief in the rightness of our affluent life-style is mistaken.[11]

So, I want to say about all this what H.P. Grice once said at a conference when someone objected that his theory of meaning had an unacceptable implication. Referring to the supposedly embarrassing consequence, Grice said, "See here, that's not an *objection* to my theory—*that's* my theory!"[12] Grice not only accepted the implication, he claimed it as an integral part of what he wanted to say. Similarly, the realization that we are morally wrong to spend money on inessentials, when that money could go to feed the starving, is an integral part of the view I am defending. It is not an embarrassing consequence of the view; it is (part of) the view itself.

There is another way in which the counter-intuitive nature of the Equivalence Thesis may be brought out. It follows from that thesis that if the *only* difference between a pair of acts is that one is killing, while the other is letting die, those actions are equally good or bad—neither is preferable to the other. Defenders of the distinction between positive and negative duties have pointed out that in such cases our intuitions often tell us just the opposite: killing seems obviously worse. Here is an example produced by Daniel Dinello:

> Jones and Smith are in a hospital. Jones cannot live longer than two hours unless he gets a heart transplant. Smith, who has had one kidney removed, is dying of an infection in the other kidney. If he does not get a kidney transplant, he will die in about four hours. When Jones dies, his one good kidney can be transplanted to Smith, or Smith could be killed and his heart transplanted to Jones . . . it seems clear that it would, in fact, be wrong to kill Smith and save Jones, rather than letting Jones die and saving Smith.[13]

And another from Trammell:

> If someone threatened to steal $1000 from a person if he did not take a gun and shoot a stranger between the eyes, it would be very wrong for him to kill the stranger to save his $1000. But if someone asked from that person $1000 to save a stranger, it would seem that his obligation to grant this request would not be as great as his obligation to refuse the first demand—even if he has good reason for believing that without his $1000 the stranger would certainly die. . . . In this particular example, it seems plausible to say that a person has a greater obligation to refrain from killing someone, even though the effort required of him ($1000) and his motivation toward the stranger be assumed identical in both cases.[14]

The conclusion we are invited to draw from these examples is that, contrary to what I have been arguing, the bare difference between killing and letting die *must be* morally significant.

Now Dinello's example is badly flawed, since the choice before the doctor is not a choice between killing and letting die at all. If the doctor kills Smith in order to transplant his heart to Jones, he will have killed Smith. But if he waits until Jones dies, and then transfers the kidney to Smith, he will *not* have "let Jones die." The reason is connected with the fact that not every case of not saving someone is a case of letting him die. (Josef Stalin died, and I did not save him, but I did not let Stalin die.) Dinello himself points out that, in order for it to be true that X lets Y die, X must be "in a position" to save Y, but not do so.[15] (I was never in a position to save Stalin.) Now the doctor is in a position to save Jones only if there is a heart available for transplantation. But no such heart is available—Smith's heart, for example, is not available since Smith is still using it. Therefore, since the doctor is not in a position to save Jones, he does not let Jones die.[16]

Trammell's example is not quite so easy to dismiss. Initially, I share the intuition that it would be worse to kill someone to prevent $1000 from being stolen than to refuse to pay $1000 to save someone. Yet on reflection I have not much confidence in this feeling. What is at stake in the situation described is the person's $1000 and the stranger's life. But we end up with the *same* combination of lives and money, no matter which option the person chooses: if he shoots the stranger, the stranger dies and he keeps his $1000; and if he refuses to pay to save the stranger, the stranger dies and he keeps his $1000. It makes no difference, either to the person's interests or to the stranger's interests, which option is chosen; why, then, do we have the curious intuition that there is a big difference here?

I conceded at the outset that most of us believe that in letting people die we are not behaving as badly as if we were to kill them. I think I have given good reasons for concluding that this belief is false. Yet giving reasons is often not enough, even in philosophy. For if an intuition is strong enough, we may continue to rely on it and assume that *something* is wrong with the arguments opposing it, even though we are not sure exactly what is wrong. It is a familiar remark: "X is more certain than any argument that might be given against it." So in addition to the arguments, we need some account of why people have the allegedly mistaken intuition and why it is so persistent. Why do people believe so firmly that killing is so much worse than letting die, both in fictitious cases such as Trammell's, and in the famine relief cases in the real world? In some ways the explanation of this is best left to the psychologists; the distinctly philosophical job is accomplished when the intuition is shown to be false. However, I shall hazard a hypothesis, since it shows how our intuitions can be explained without assuming that they are perceptions of the truth.

Human beings are to some degree altruistic, but they are also to a great degree selfish, and their attitudes on matters of conduct are largely determined by what is in their own interests, and what is in the interests of the few other people they especially care about. In terms of both the costs and the benefits, it is to their own advantage for people in the affluent countries to regard killing as worse than letting die. First, the *costs* of never killing anyone are not great: we can live very well without ever killing. But the cost of not allowing people to die, when we could save them, would be very great. For any one of us to take seriously a duty to save the starving would require that we give up our affluent life-styles; money could no longer be spent on luxuries while others starve. On the other side, we have much more to *gain* from a strict prohibition on killing than from a like prohibition on letting die. Since we are not in danger of starving, we will not suffer if people do not regard feeding the hungry as so important; but we would be threatened if people did not regard killing as very, very bad. So, both the costs and the benefits encourage us, selfishly, to view killing as worse than letting die. It is to our own advantage to believe this, and so we do.

NOTES

1 For an account of the difficulties of getting reliable information in this area, see Nick Eberstadt, "Myths of the Food Crisis," *New York Review of Books*, 19 February 1976, 32-7.

2 Richard L. Trammell, "Saving Life and Taking Life," *Journal of Philosophy* 72 (1975), 131-7, is the best defense of this view of which I am aware.

3 This article is a companion to an earlier one, "Active and Passive Euthanasia," *New England Journal of Medicine* 292 (9 January 1975), 78-80 [reprinted in the present volume, 1-6], in which I discuss the (mis)use of the killing/letting die distinction in medical contexts. But nothing in this article depends on the earlier one.

[4] Philippa Foot, "The Problem of Abortion and the Doctrine of the Double Effect," *Oxford Review* no. 5 (1967); reprinted in James Rachels, ed., *Moral Problems*, 2nd ed. (New York, 1975), 66.

[5] On this point, and more generally on the whole subject of our duty to contribute for famine relief, see Peter Singer, "Famine, Affluence, and Morality," *Philosophy & Public Affairs* 1 (Spring 1972), 232.

[6] Trammell, 133.

[7] This argument is suggested by Paul Ramsey in *The Patient as Person* (New Haven, Conn., 1970), 151.

[8] This difference between failing to save and letting die was pointed out by David Sanford in a very helpful paper, "On Killing and Letting Die," read at the Western Division meeting of the American Philosophical Association, in New Orleans, on 30 April 1976.

[9] Trammell, 133.

[10] *Ibid.*, 134.

[11] There is also some independent evidence that this prereflective belief is mistaken; see Singer, "Famine, Affluence, and Morality."

[12] Grice made this remark several years ago at Oberlin. I do not remember the surrounding details of the discussion, but the remark seems to me an important one which applies to lots of "objections" to various theories. The most famous objections to act-utilitarianism, for example, are little more than descriptions of the theory, with the question-begging addendum, "Because it says *that*, it can't be right."

[13] Daniel Dinello, "On Killing and Letting Die," *Analysis* 31, no. 3 (January 1971), 83, 86.

[14] Trammell, 131.

[15] Dinello, 85.

[16] There is another way to meet Dinello's counter-example. A surprisingly strong case can be made that it would *not* be any worse to kill Smith than to "let Jones die." I have in mind adapting John Harris's argument in "The Survival Lottery," *Philosophy* 50 (1975), 81-7.

Living on a Lifeboat

GARRETT HARDIN

Susanne Langer[1] has shown that it is probably impossible to approach an unsolved problem save through the door of metaphor. Later, attempting to meet the demands of rigor, we may achieve some success in cleansing theory of metaphor, though our success is limited if we are unable to avoid using common language, which is shot through and through with fossil metaphors. (I count no less than five in the preceding two sentences.)

Since metaphorical thinking is inescapable it is pointless merely to weep about our human limitations. We must learn to live with them, to understand them, and to control them. "All of us," said George Eliot in Middlemarch, "get our thoughts entangled in metaphors, and act fatally on the strength of them." To avoid unconscious suicide we are well advised to pit one metaphor against another. From the interplay of competitive metaphors, thoroughly developed, we may come closer to metaphor-free solutions to our problems.

No generation has viewed the problem of the survival of the human species as seriously as we have. Inevitably, we have entered this world of concern through the door of metaphor. Environmentalists have emphasized the image of the earth as a spaceship—Spaceship Earth. Kenneth Boulding[2] is the principal architect of this metaphor. It is time, he says, that we replace the wasteful "cowboy economy" of the past with the frugal "spaceship economy" required for continued survival in the limited world we now see ours to be. The metaphor is notably useful in justifying pollution control measures.

Unfortunately, the image of a spaceship is also used to promote measures that are suicidal. One of these is a generous immigration policy, which is only a particular instance of a class of policies that are in error because they lead to the tragedy of the commons.[3] These suicidal policies are attractive because they mesh with what we unthinkingly take to be the ideals of "the best people." What is missing in the idealistic view is an insistence that rights and responsibilities must go together. The "generous" attitude of all too many people results in asserting inalienable rights while ignoring or denying matching responsibilities.

For the metaphor of a spaceship to be correct the aggregate of people on board would have to be under unitary sovereign control.[4] A true ship always has a captain. It is conceivable that a ship could be run by a committee. But it could not possibly survive if its course were determined by bickering tribes that claimed rights without responsibilities.

What about Spaceship Earth? It certainly has no captain, and no executive committee. The United Nations is a toothless tiger, because the signatories of its charter wanted it that way. The spaceship metaphor is used only to justify spaceship demands on common resources without acknowledging corresponding spaceship responsibilities.

An understandable fear of decisive action leads people to embrace "incrementalism"—moving toward reform by tiny stages. As we shall see, this strategy is counterproductive in the area discussed here if it means accepting rights before responsibilities. Where human survival is at stake, the acceptance of responsibilities is a precondition to the acceptance of rights, if the two cannot be introduced simultaneously.

LIFEBOAT ETHICS

Before taking up certain substantive issues let us look at an alternative metaphor, that of a lifeboat. In developing some relevant examples the following numerical values are assumed. Approximately two-thirds of the world is desperately poor, and only one-third is comparatively rich. The people in poor countries have an average per capita GNP (Gross National Product) of about $200 per year; the rich, of about $3,000. (For the United States it is nearly $5,000 per year.) Metaphorically, each rich nation amounts to a lifeboat full of comparatively rich people. The poor of the world are in other, much more crowded lifeboats. Continuously, so to speak, the poor fall out of their lifeboats and swim for a while in the water outside, hoping to be admitted to a rich lifeboat, or in some other way to benefit from the "goodies" on board. What should the passengers on a rich lifeboat do? This is the central problem of "the ethics of a lifeboat."

First we must acknowledge that each lifeboat is effectively limited in capacity. The land of every nation has a limited carrying capacity. The exact limit is a matter for argument, but the energy crunch is convincing more people every day that we have already exceeded the carrying capacity of the land. We have been living on "capital"— stored petroleum and coal—and soon we must live on income alone.

Let us look at only one lifeboat—ours. The ethical problem is the same for all, and is as follows. Here we sit, say 50 people in a lifeboat. To be generous, let us assume our boat has a capacity of 10 more, making 60. (This, however, is to violate the engineering principle of the "safety factor." A new plant disease or a bad change in the weather may decimate our population if we don't preserve some excess capacity as a safety factor.)

The 50 of us in the lifeboat see 100 others swimming in the water outside, asking for admission to the boat, or for handouts. How shall we respond to their calls? There are several possibilities.

One. We may be tempted to try to live by the Christian ideal of being "our brother's keeper," or by the Marxian ideal[5] of "from each according to his abilities, to each according to his needs." Since the needs of all are the same, we take all the needy into our boat, making a total of 150 in a boat with a capacity of 60. The boat is swamped, and everyone drowns. Complete justice, complete catastrophe.

Two. Since the boat has an unused excess capacity of 10, we admit just 10 more to it. This has the disadvantage of getting rid of the safety factor, for which action we will sooner or later pay dearly. Moreover, *which* 10 do we let in? "First come, first served?" The best 10? The neediest 10? How do we *discriminate?* And what do we say to the 90 who are excluded?

Three. Admit no more to the boat and preserve the small safety factor. Survival of the people in the lifeboat is then possible (though we shall have to be on our guard against boarding parties).

The last solution is abhorrent to many people. It is unjust, they say. Let us grant that it is.

"I feel guilty about my good luck," say some. The reply to this is simple: *Get out and yield your place to others.* Such a selfless action might satisfy the conscience of those who are addicted to guilt but it would not change the ethics of the lifeboat. The needy person to whom a guilt-addict yields his place will not himself feel guilty about his sudden good luck. (If he did he would not climb aboard.) The net result of conscience-striken people relinquishing their unjustly held positions is the elimination of their kind of conscience from the lifeboat. The lifeboat, as it were, purifies itself of guilt. The ethics of the lifeboat persist, unchanged by such momentary aberrations.

This then is the basic metaphor within which we must work out our solutions. Let us enrich the image step by step with substantive additions from the real world.

REPRODUCTION

The harsh characteristics of lifeboat ethics are heightened by reproduction, particularly by reproductive differences. The people inside the lifeboats of the wealthy nations are doubling in numbers every 87 years; those outside are doubling every 35 years, on the average. And the relative difference in prosperity is becoming greater.

Let us, for a while, think primarily of the U.S. lifeboat. As of 1973 the United States had a population of 210 million people, who were increasing by 0.8% per year, that is, doubling in number every 87 years.

Although the citizens of rich nations are outnumbered two to one by the poor, let us imagine an equal number of poor people outside our lifeboat—a mere 210 million poor people reproducing at a quite different rate. If we imagine these to be the combined populations of Colombia, Venezuela, Ecuador, Morocco, Thailand, Pakistan, and the Philippines, the average rate of increase of the people "outside" is 3.3% per year. The doubling time of this population is 21 years.

Suppose that all these countries, and the United States, agreed to live by the Marxian ideal, "to each according to his needs," the ideal of most Christians as well. Needs, of course, are determined by population size, which is affected by reproduction. Every nation regards its rate of reproduction as a sovereign right. If our lifeboat were big enough in the beginning it might be possible to live *for a while* by Christian-Marxian ideals. *Might.*

Initially, in the model given, the ratio of non-Americans to Americans would be one to one. But consider what the ratio would be 87 years later. By this time Americans would have doubled to a population of 420 million. The other group (doubling every 21 years) would now have swollen to 3,540 million. Each American would have more than eight people to share with. How could the lifeboat possibly keep afloat?

All this involves extrapolation of current trends into the future, and is consequently suspect. Trends may change. Granted: but the change will not necessarily be favorable. If—as seems likely—the rate of population increase falls faster in the ethnic group presently inside the lifeboat than it does among those now outside, the future will turn out to be even worse than mathematics predicts, and sharing will be even more suicidal.

RUIN IN THE COMMONS

The fundamental error of the sharing ethics is that it leads to the tragedy of the commons. Under a system of private property the man (or group of men) who own property recognize their responsibility to care for it, for if they don't they will eventually suffer. A farmer, for instance, if he is intelligent, will allow no more cattle in a pasture than its carrying capacity justifies. If he overloads the pasture, weeds take over, erosion sets in, and the owner loses in the long run.

But if a pasture is run as a commons open to all, the right of each to use it is not matched by an operational responsibility to take care of it. It is no use asking independent herdsmen in a commons to act responsibly, for they dare not. The considerate herdsman who refrains from overloading the commons suffers more than a selfish one who says his needs are greater. (As Leo Durocher says, "Nice guys finish last.") Christian-Marxian idealism is counterproductive. That it *sounds* nice is no excuse. With distribution systems, as with individual morality, good intentions are no substitute for good performance.

A social system is stable only if it is insensitive to errors. To the Christian-Marxian idealist a selfish person is a sort of "error." Prosperity in the system of the commons cannot survive errors. If *everyone* would only restrain himself, all would be well; but it takes *only one less than everyone* to ruin a system of voluntary restraint. In a crowded world of less than perfect human beings—and we will never know any other—mutual ruin is inevitable in the commons. This is the core of the tragedy of the commons.

One of the major tasks of education today is to create such an awareness of the dangers of the commons that people will be able to recognize its many varieties, however disguised. There is pollution of the air and water because these media are treated as commons. Further growth of population and growth in the per capita conversion of natural resources into pollutants require that the system of the commons be modified or abandoned in the disposal of "externalities."

The fish populations of the oceans are exploited as commons, and ruin lies ahead. No technological invention can prevent this fate: in fact, all improvements in the art of fishing merely hasten the day of complete ruin. Only the replacement of the system of the commons with a responsible system can save oceanic fisheries.

The management of western range lands, though nominally rational, is in fact (under the steady pressure of cattle ranchers) often merely a government-sanctioned system of the commons, drifting toward ultimate ruin for both the rangelands and the residual enterprisers.

WORLD FOOD BANKS

In the international arena we have recently heard a proposal to create a new commons, namely an international depository of food reserves to which nations will contribute according to their abilities, and from which nations may draw according to their needs. Nobel laureate Norman Borlaug has lent the prestige of his name to this proposal.

A world food bank appeals powerfully to our humanitarian impulses. We remember John Donne's celebrated line, "Any man's death diminishes me." But before we rush out to see for whom the bell tolls let us recognize where the greatest political push for international granaries comes from, lest we be disillusioned later. Our experience with Public Law 480 clearly reveals the answer. This was the law that moved billions of dollars worth of U.S. grain to food-short, population-long countries during the past two decades. When P.L. 480 first came into being, a headline in the business magazine *Forbes*[6] revealed the power behind it: "Feeding the World's Hungry Millions: How it will mean billions for U.S. business."

And indeed it did. In the years 1960 to 1970 a total of $7.9 billion was spent on the "Food for Peace" program, as P.L. 480 was called. During the years 1948 to 1970 an additional $49.9 billion were extracted from American tax-payers to pay for other economic aid programs, some of which went for food and food-producing machinery. (This figure does *not* include military aid.) That P.L. 480 was a give-away program was concealed. Recipient countries went through the motions of paying for P.L. 480 food—with IOU's. In December 1973 the charade was brought to an end as far as India was concerned when the United States "forgave" India's $3.2 billion debt.[7] Public announcement of the debt was delayed for two months: one wonders why.

"Famine—1975!"[8] is one of the few publications that points out the commercial roots of this humanitarian attempt. Though all U.S. taxpayers lost by P.L. 480, special interest groups gained handsomely. Farmers benefited because they were not asked to contribute the grain—it was bought from them by the taxpayers. Besides the direct benefit there was the indirect effect of increasing demand and thus raising prices of farm products generally. The manufacturers of farm machinery, fertilizers, and pesticides benefited by the farmers' extra efforts to grow more food. Grain elevators profited from storing the grain for varying lengths of time. Railroads made money hauling it to port, and shipping lines by carrying it overseas. Moreover, once the machinery for P.L. 480 was established an immense bureaucracy had a vested interest in its continuance regardless of its merits.

Very little was ever heard of these selfish interests when P.L. 480 was defended in public. The emphasis was always on its humanitarian effects. The combination of multiple and relatively silent selfish interest with highly vocal humanitarian apologists constitutes a powerful lobby for extracting money from taxpayers. Foreign aid has become a habit that can apparently survive in the absence of any known justification. A news commentator in a weekly magazine,[9] after exhaustively going over all the conventional arguments for foreign aid—self-interest, social justice, political advantage, and charity—and concluding that none of the known arguments really held water, concluded: "So the search continues for some logically compelling reasons for giving aid. . ." In other words, *Act now, Justify later*—if ever. (Apparently a quarter of a century is too short a time to find the justification for expending several billion dollars yearly.)

The search for a rational justification can be short-circuited by interjecting the word "emergency." Borlaug uses this word. We need to look sharply at it. What is an "emergency"? It is surely something like an accident, which is correctly defined as *an event that is certain to happen, though with a low frequency.*[10] A well-run organization prepares for everything that is certain, including accidents and emergencies. It budgets for them. It saves for them. It expects them—and mature decision-makers do not waste time complaining about accidents when they occur.

What happens if some organizations budget for emergencies and others do not? If each organization is solely responsible for its own well-being, poorly managed ones will suffer. But they should be able to learn from experience. They have a chance to mend their ways and learn to budget for infrequent but certain emergencies. The weather, for instance, always varies and periodic crop failures are certain. A wise and competent government saves out of the production of the good years in anticipation of bad years that are sure to come. This is not a new idea. The Bible tells us that Joseph taught this policy to Pharaoh in Egypt more than 2,000 years ago. Yet it is literally true that the vast majority of the governments of the world today have no such policy. They lack either the wisdom or the competence, or both. Far more difficult than the transfer of wealth from one country to another is the transfer of wisdom between sovereign powers or between generations.

"But it isn't their fault! How can we blame the poor people who are caught in an emergency? Why must we punish them?" The concepts of blame and punishment are irrelevant. The question is, what are the operational consequences of establishing a world food bank? If it is open to every country every time a need develops, slovenly rulers will not be motivated to take Joseph's advice. Why should they? Others will bail them out whenever they are in trouble.

Some countries will make deposits in the world food bank and others will withdraw from it: there will be almost no overlap. Calling such a depository-transfer unit a "bank" is stretching the metaphor of *bank* beyond its elastic limits. The proposers, of course, never call attention to the metaphorical nature of the word they use.

THE RATCHET EFFECT

An "international food bank" is really, then, not a true bank but a disguised one-way transfer device for moving wealth from rich countries to poor. In the absence of such a bank, in a world inhabited by individually responsible sovereign nations, the population of each nation would repeatedly go through a cycle of the sort shown in Figure 1. P_2 is greater than P_1, either in absolute numbers or because a deterioration of the food supply has removed the safety factor and produced a dangerously low ratio of resources to population. P_2 may be said to represent a state of overpopulation, which becomes obvious upon the appearance of an "accident," e.g., a crop failure. If the "emergency" is not met by outside help, the population drops back to the "normal" level—the "carrying capacity" of the environment—or even below. In the absence of population control by a sovereign, sooner or later the population grows to P_2 again and the cycle repeats. The long-term population curve[11] is an irregularly fluctuating one, equilibrating more or less about the carrying capacity.

A demographic cycle of this sort obviously involves great suffering in the restrictive phase, but such a cycle is normal to any independent country with inadequate population control. The third century theologian Tertullian[12] expressed what must have been the recognition of many wise men when he wrote: "The scourges of pestilence, famine, wars, and earthquakes have come to be regarded as a blessing to overcrowded nations, since they serve to prune away the luxuriant growth of the human race."

Only under a strong and farsighted sovereign—which theoretically

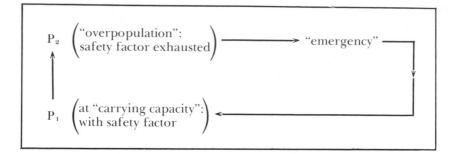

Figure 1
The population cycle of a nation that has no effective, conscious population control, and which receives no aid from the outside. P_2 is greater than P_1.

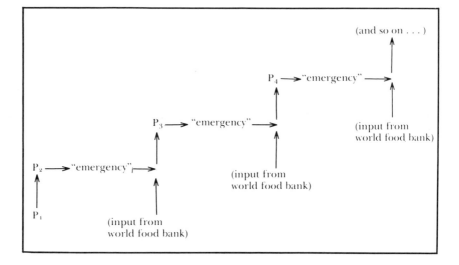

Figure 2
The population escalator. Note that input from a world food bank acts like the pawl of a ratchet, preventing the normal population cycle shown in Figure 1 from being completed. P_{n+1} is greater than P_n, and the absolute magnitude of the "emergencies" escalates. Ultimately the entire system crashes. The crash is not shown, and few can imagine it.

could be the people themselves, democratically organized—can a population equilibrate at some set point below the carrying capacity, thus avoiding the pains normally caused by periodic and unavoidable disasters. For this happy state to be achieved it is necessary that those in power be able to contemplate with equanimity the "waste" of surplus food in times of bountiful harvests. It is essential that those in power resist the temptation to convert extra food into extra babies. On the public relations level it is necessary that the phrase "surplus food" be replaced by "safety factor."

But wise sovereigns seem not to exist in the poor world today. The most anguishing problems are created by poor countries that are governed by rulers insufficiently wise and powerful. If such countries can draw on a world food bank in times of "emergency," the population *cycle* of Figure 1 will be replaced by the population *escalator* of Figure 2. The input of food from a food bank acts as the pawl of a ratchet, preventing the population from retracing its steps to a lower level. Reproduction pushes the population upward, inputs from the world bank prevent its moving downward. Population size escalates, as does the absolute magnitude of "accidents" and "emergencies." The process is brought to an end only by the total collapse of the whole system, producing a catastrophe of scarcely imaginable proportions.

Such are the implications of the well-meant sharing of food in a world of irresponsible reproduction.

I think we need a new word for systems like this. The adjective "melioristic" is applied to systems that produce continual improvement; the English word is derived from the Latin *meliorare*, to become or make better. Parallel with this it would be useful to bring in the word *pejoristic* (from the Latin *pejorare*, to become or make worse). This word can be applied to those systems which, by their very nature, can be relied upon to make matters worse. A world food bank coupled with sovereign state irresponsibility in reproduction is an example of a pejoristic system.

This pejoristic system creates an unacknowledged commons. People have more motivation to draw from than to add to the common store. The license to make such withdrawals diminishes whatever motivation poor countries might otherwise have to control their populations. Under the guidance of this ratchet, wealth can be steadily moved in one direction only, from the slowly-breeding rich to the rapidly-breeding poor, the process finally coming to a halt only when all countries are equally and miserably poor.

All this is terribly obvious once we are acutely aware of the pervasiveness and danger of the commons. But many people still lack this awareness and the euphoria of the "benign demographic transition"[13] interferes with the realistic appraisal of pejoristic mechanisms. As concerns public policy, the deductions drawn from the benign demographic transition are these:

1. If the per capita GNP rises the birth rate will fall; hence, the rate of population increase will fall, ultimately producing ZPG (Zero Population Growth).
2. The long-term trend all over the world (including the poor countries) is of a rising per capita GNP (for which no limit is seen).
3. Therefore, all political interference in population matters is unnecessary; all we need to do is foster economic "development"—*note the metaphor*—and population problems will solve themselves.

Those who believe in the benign demographic transition dismiss the pejoristic mechanism of Figure 2 in the belief that each input of food from the world outside fosters development within a poor country thus resulting in a drop in the rate of population increase. Foreign aid has proceeded on this assumption for more than two decades. Unfortunately it has produced no indubitable instance of the asserted effect. It has, however, produced a library of excuses. The air is filled with plaintive calls for more massive foreign aid appropriations so that the hypothetical melioristic process can get started.

The doctrine of demographic *laissez-faire* implicit in the hypothesis of the benign demographic transition is immensely attractive. Unfortunately there is more evidence against the melioristic system than there is for it.[14] On the historical side there are many counter-examples. The rise in per capita GNP in France and Ireland during the past century has been accompanied by a rise in population growth. In the 20 years following the Second World War the same positive correlation was noted almost everywhere in the world. Never in world history before 1950 did the worldwide population growth reach 1% per annum. Now the average population growth is over 2% and shows no signs of slackening.

On the theoretical side, the denial of the pejoristic scheme of Figure 2 probably springs from the hidden acceptance of the "cowboy economy" that Boulding castigated. Those who recognize the limitations of a spaceship, if they are unable to achieve population control at a safe and comfortable level, accept the necessity of the corrective feedback of the populaton cycle shown in Figure 1. No one who knew in his bones that he was living on a true spaceship would countenance political support of the population escalator shown in Figure 2.

ECO-DESTRUCTION VIA THE GREEN REVOLUTION

The demoralizing effect of charity on the recipient has long been known. "Give a man a fish and he will eat for a day: teach him how to fish and he will eat for the rest of his days." So runs an ancient Chinese proverb. Acting on this advice the Rockefeller and Ford Foundations have financed a multipronged program for improving agriculture in the hungry nations. The result, known as the "Green Revolution," has been quite remarkable. "Miracle wheat" and "miracle rice" are splendid technological achievements in the realm of plant genetics.

Whether or not the Green Revolution can increase food production is doubtful,[15] but in any event not particularly important. What is missing in this great and well-meaning humanitarian effort is a firm grasp of fundamentals. Considering the importance of the Rockefeller Foundation in this effort it is ironic that the late Alan Gregg, a much-respected vice-president of the Foundation, strongly expressed his doubts of the wisdom of all attempts to increase food production some two decades ago. (This was before Borlaug's work—supported by Rockefeller—had resulted in the development of "miracle wheat.") Gregg[16] likened the growth and spreading of humanity over the surface of the earth to the metastasis of cancer in the human body, wryly remarking that "Cancerous growths demand food; but, as far as I know, they have never been cured by getting it."

"Man does not live by bread alone"—the scriptural statement has a rich meaning even in the material realm. Every human being born constitutes a draft on all aspects of the environment—food, air, water, unspoiled scenery, occasional and optional solitude, beaches, contact with wild animals, fishing, hunting—the list is long and incompletely known. Food can, perhaps, be significantly increased: but what about forests, and solitude? If we satisfy the need for food in a growing population we necessarily decrease the supply of other goods, and thereby increase the difficulty of equitably allocating scarce goods.[17]

The present population of India is 600 million, and it is increasing by 15 million per year. The environmental load of this population is already great. The forests of India are only a small fraction of what they were three centuries ago. Soil erosion, floods, and the psychological costs of crowding are serious. Every one of the net 15 million lives added each year stresses the Indian environment more severely. *Every life saved this year in a poor country diminishes the quality of life for subsequent generations.*

Observant critics have shown how much harm we wealthy nations have already done to poor nations through our well-intentioned but misguided attempts to help them.[18] Particularly reprehensible is our failure to carry out post-audits of these attempts.[19] Thus have we shielded our tender consciences from knowledge of the harm we have done. Must we Americans continue to fail to monitor the consequences of our external "do-gooding?" If, for instance, we thoughtlessly make it possible for the present 600 million Indians to swell to 1,200 millions by the year 2001—as their present growth rate promises—will posterity in India thank *us* for facilitating an even greater destruction of *their* environment? Are good intentions ever a sufficient excuse for bad consequences?

NOTES

Footnotes have been renumbered—Ed.

[1] Susanne Langer, *Philosophy in a New Key* (Cambridge, Mass., 1942).

[2] Kenneth Boulding, "The Economics of the Coming Spaceship Earth," in H. Jarrett, ed., *Edvironmental Quality in a Growing Economy* (Baltimore, Md., 1966).

[3] Garrett Hardin, "The Tragedy of the Commons," *Science* 162 (1968), 1243-8.

[4] W. Ophuls, "The Scarcity Society," *Harpers* 248 (1974), 47-52.

[5] Karl Marx, "Critique of the Gotha Program," in R. C. Tucker, ed., *The Marx-Engels Reader* (New York, 1972), 388.

[6] See W.C. Paddock, "How Green is the Green Revolution?" *BioScience* 20 (1970) 897-902.

[7] *The Wall Street Journal*, 19 February 1974.

[8] W. C. Paddock and P. Paddock, *Famine 1975!* (Boston, 1967).

[9] K. Lansner, "Should Foreign Aid Begin at Home?" *Newsweek*, 11 February 1974, 32.

[10] Hardin, *Exploring New Ethics for Survival: The Voyage of the Spaceship* Beagle (New York, 1972), 81-2.

[11] Hardin, in *Biology: Its Principles and Implications,* 2nd ed. (San Francisco, 1966), Chap. 9.

[12] Hardin, *Population, Evolution, and Birth Control* (San Francisco, 1969), 18.

[13] Hardin, *Stalking the Wild Taboo* (Los Altos, Cal., 1973), Chap. 23.

[14] K. Davis, "Population," *Scientific American* 209, no. 3 (1963), 62-71.

[15] M. Harris, "How Green the Revolution," *Natural History* 81, no. 3 (1972), 28-30; W.C. Paddock, "How Green is the Green Revolution?"; H.G. Wilkes, "The Green Revolution," *Environment* 14, no. 8, 32-9.

[16] A. Gregg, "A Medical Aspect of the Population Problem," *Science* 121 (1955), 681-2.

[17] Hardin, "The Economics of Wilderness," *Natural History* 78, no. 6 (1969), 20-7, and "Preserving Quality on Spaceship Earth," in J.B. Trefethen, ed., *Transactions of the Thirty-Seventh North American Wildlife and Natural Resources Conference* (Washington, D.C., 1972).

[18] W. Paddock and E. Paddock, *We Don't Know How* (Ames, Iowa, 1973).

[19] M.T. Farvar and J.P. Milton, *The Careless Technology* (Garden City, N.Y., 1972).

Lifeboat Earth

ONORA O'NEILL

If in the fairly near future millions of people die of starvation, will those who survive be in any way to blame for those deaths? Is there anything which people ought to do now, and from now on, if they are to be able to avoid responsibility for unjustifiable deaths in famine years? I shall argue from the assumption that persons have a right not to be killed unjustifiably to the claim that we have a duty to try to prevent and postpone famine deaths. A corollary of this claim is that if we do nothing we shall bear some blame for some deaths.

JUSTIFIABLE KILLING

I shall assume that persons have a right not to be killed and a corresponding duty not to kill. I shall make no assumptions about the other rights persons may have. In particular, I shall not assume that persons have a right not to be allowed to die by those who could prevent it or a duty to prevent others' deaths whenever they could do so. Nor will I assume that persons lack this right.

Even if persons have no rights other than a right not to be killed, this right can justifiably be overridden in certain circumstances. Not all killings are unjustifiable. I shall be particularly concerned with two sorts of circumstances in which the right not to be killed is justifiably overridden. The first of these is the case of unavoidable killings; the second is the case of self-defense.

Unavoidable killings occur in situations where a person doing some act causes some death or deaths which he could not avoid. Often such deaths will be unavoidable because of the killer's ignorance of some relevant circumstance at the time of his decision to act. If B is driving a train, and A blunders onto the track and is either unnoticed by B or noticed too late for B to stop the train, and B kills A, then B could not have avoided killing A, given his decision to drive the train. Another sort of case of unavoidable killing occurs when B could avoid killing A or could avoid killing C, but cannot avoid killing one of the two. For example, if B is the carrier of a highly contagious and invariably fatal illness, he might find himself so placed that he cannot avoid meeting and so killing either A or C, though he can choose which of them to meet. In this case the unavoidability of B's killing someone is not relative to some prior decision B made. The cases of unavoidable killings with which I want to deal here are of the latter sort, and I shall argue that in such cases B kills justifiably if certain further conditions are met.

A killing may also be justifiable if it is undertaken in self-defense. I shall not argue here that persons have a right of self-defense which is independent of their right not to be killed, but rather that a minimal right of self-defense is a corollary of a right not to be killed. Hence the notion of self-defense on which I shall rely is in some ways different from, and narrower than, other interpretations of the right of self-defense. I shall also assume that if A has a right to defend himself against B, then third parties ought to defend A's right. If we take seriously the right not to be killed and its corollaries, then we ought to enforce others' rights not to be killed.

The right of self-defense which is a corollary of the right not to be killed is a right to take action to prevent killings. If I have a right not to be killed then I have a right to prevent others from endangering my life, though I may endanger their lives in so doing only if that is the only available way to prevent the danger to my own life. Similarly if another has the right not to be killed then I should, if possible, do something to prevent others from endangering his life, but I may endanger their lives in so doing only if that is the only available way to prevent the danger to his life. This duty to defend others is *not* a general duty of beneficence but a very restricted duty to enforce others' rights not to be killed.

The right to self-defense so construed is quite narrow. It includes no right of action against those who, though they cause or are likely to cause us harm, clearly do not endanger our lives. (However, specific cases are often unclear. The shopkeeper who shoots a person who holds him up with a toy gun was not endangered, but it may have been very reasonable of him to suppose that he was endangered.) And it includes no right to greater than minimal preventive action against a person who endangers one's life. If B is chasing A with a gun, and A could save his life either by closing a bullet-proof door or by shooting B, then if people have only a right not to be killed and a minimal corollary right of self-defense, A would have no right to shoot B. (Again, such cases are often unclear—A may not know that the door is bullet-proof or not think of it or may simply reason that shooting B is a better guarantee of prevention.) A right of proportionate self-defense which might justify A in shooting B, even were it clear that closing the door would have been enough to prevent B, is not a corollary of the right not to be killed. Perhaps a right of proportionate retaliation might be justified by some claim such as that aggressors lose certain rights, but I shall take no position on this issue.

In one respect the narrow right of self-defense, which is the corollary of a right not to be killed, is more extensive than some other interpretations of the right of self-defense. For it is a right to take action against others who endanger our lives whether or not they do so intentionally. A's right not to be killed entitles him to take action not only against aggressors but also against those "innocent threats"[1] who endanger lives without being aggressors. If B is likely to cause A's death inadvertently or involuntarily, then A has, if he has a right not to be killed, a right to take whatever steps are necessary to prevent B from doing so, provided that these do not infringe B's right not to be killed unnecessarily. If B approaches A with a highly contagious and invariably lethal illness, then A may try to prevent B from getting near him even if B knows nothing about the danger he brings. If other means fail, A may kill B in self-defense, even though B was no aggressor.

This construal of the right of self-defense severs the link between aggression and self-defense. When we defend ourselves against innocent threats there is no aggressor, only somebody who endangers life. But it would be misleading to call this right a right of self-preservation. For self-preservation is commonly construed (as by Locke) as including a right to subsistence, and so a right to engage in a large variety of activities whether or not anybody endangers us. But the right which is the corollary of the right not to be killed is a right only to prevent others from endangering our lives, whether or not they intend to do so, and to do so with minimal danger to their lives. Only if one takes a Hobbesian view of human nature and sees others' acts as always completely threatening will the rights of self-defense and self-preservation tend to merge and everything done to maintain life be done to prevent its destruction. Without Hobbesian assumptions the contexts where the minimal right of self-defense can be invoked are fairly special, yet not, I shall argue, rare.

There may be various other circumstances in which persons' rights not to be killed may be overridden. Perhaps, for example, we may justifiably kill those who consent to us doing so. I shall take no position on whether persons can waive their rights not to be killed or on any further situations in which killings might be justifiable.

JUSTIFIABLE KILLINGS ON LIFEBOATS

The time has come to start imagining lurid situations, which is the standard operating procedure for this type of discussion. I shall begin by looking at some sorts of killings which might occur on a lifeboat and shall consider the sorts of justifications which they might be given.

Let us imagine six survivors on a lifeboat. There are two possible levels of provisions:

(1) Provisions are on all reasonable calculations sufficient to last until rescue. Either the boat is near land, or it is amply provisioned or it has gear for distilling water, catching fish, etc.

(2) Provisions are on all reasonable calculations unlikely to be sufficient for all six to survive until rescue.

We can call situation (1) *the well-equipped lifeboat situation*; situation (2) *the under-equipped lifeboat situation*. There may, of course, be cases where the six survivors are unsure which situation they are in, but for simplicity I shall disregard those here.

On a well-equipped lifeboat it is possible for all to survive until rescue. No killing could be justified as unavoidable, and if someone is killed, then the justification could only be self-defense in special situations. Consider the following examples:

(1a) On a well-equipped lifeboat with six persons, *A* threatens to jettison the fresh water, without which some or all would not survive till rescue. *A* may be either hostile or deranged. *B* reasons with *A*, but when this fails, shoots him. *B* can appeal to his own and the others' right of self-defense to justify the killing. "It was him or us," he may reasonably say, "for he would have placed us in an under-equipped lifeboat situation." He may say this both when *A* acts to harm the others and when *A* acts as an innocent threat.

(1b) On a well-equipped lifeboat with six persons, *B*, *C*, *D*, *E*, and *F* decide to withhold food from *A*, who consequently dies. In this case they cannot appeal to self-defense—for all could have survived. Nor can they claim that they merely let *A* die—"We didn't *do* anything"—for *A* would not otherwise have died. This was not a case of violating the problematic right not to be allowed to die but of violating the right not to be killed, and the violation is without justification of self-defense or of unavoidability.

On an under-equipped lifeboat it is not possible for all to survive until rescue. Some deaths are unavoidable, but sometimes there is no particular person whose death is unavoidable. Consider the following examples:

(2a) On an under-equipped lifeboat with six persons, *A* is very ill and needs extra water, which is already scarce. The others decide not to let him have any water, and *A* dies of thirst. If *A* drinks, then not all will survive. On the other hand it is clear that *A* was killed rather than allowed to die. If he had received water he might have survived. Though some death was unavoidable, *A*'s was not and selecting him as the victim requires justification.

(2b) On an under-equipped lifeboat with six persons, water is so scarce that only four can survive (perhaps the distillation unit is designed for supplying four people). But who should go without? Suppose two are chosen to go without, either by lot or by some other method, and consequently die. The others cannot claim that all they did was to allow the two who were deprived of water to die—for these two might otherwise have been among the survivors. Nobody had a greater right to be a survivor, but given that not all could survive, those who did not survive were killed justifiably if the method by which they were chosen was fair. (Of course, a lot needs to be said about what would make a selection procedure fair.)

(2c) The same situation as in (2b) holds, but the two who are not to drink ask to be shot to ease their deaths. Again the survivors cannot claim that they did not kill but at most that they killed justifiably. Whether they did so is not affected by their shooting rather than dehydrating the victims, but only by the unavoidability of some deaths and the fairness of procedures for selecting victims.

(2d) Again the basic situation is as in (2b). But the two who are not to drink rebel. The others shoot them and so keep control of the water. Here it is all too clear that those who died were killed, but they too may have been justifiably killed. Whether the survivors kill justifiably depends neither on the method of killing nor on the victims' cooperation, except insofar as cooperation is relevant to the fairness of selection procedures.

Lifeboat situations do not occur very frequently. We are not often confronted starkly with the choice between killing or being killed by the application of a decision to distribute scarce rations in a certain way. Yet this is becoming the situation of the human species on this globe. The current metaphor "spaceship Earth" suggests more drama and less danger; if we are feeling sober about the situation, "lifeboat Earth" may be more suggestive.

Some may object to the metaphor "lifeboat Earth." A lifeboat is small; all aboard have equal claims to be there and to share equally in the provisions. Whereas the earth is vast and while all may have equal rights to be there, some also have property rights which give them special rights to consume, while others do not. The starving millions are far away and have no right to what is owned by affluent individuals or nations, even if it could prevent their deaths. If they die, it will be said, this is a violation at most of their right not to be allowed to die. And this I have not established or assumed.

I think that this could reasonably have been said in times past. The poverty and consequent deaths of far-off persons was something which the affluent might perhaps have done something to prevent, but which they had (often) done nothing to bring about. Hence they had not violated the right not to be killed of those living far off. But the economic and technological interdependence of today alters this situation.[2] Sometimes deaths are produced by some persons or groups of persons in distant, usually affluent, nations. Sometimes such persons and groups of persons violate not only some persons' alleged right not to be allowed to die but also their more fundamental right not to be killed.

We tend to imagine violations of the right not to be killed in terms of the killings so frequently discussed in the United States today: confrontations between individuals where one directly, violently, and intentionally brings about the other's death. As the lifeboat situations have shown, there are other ways in which we can kill one another. In any case, we do not restrict our vision to the typical mugger or murderer context. B may violate A's right not to be killed even when

(a) B does not act alone.

(b) *A*'s death is not immediate.
(c) It is not certain whether *A* or another will die in consequence of *B*'s action.
(d) *B* does not intend *A*'s death.

The following set of examples illustrates these points about killings:

(aa) *A* is beaten by a gang consisting of *B*, *C*, *D*, etc. No one assailant single-handedly killed him, yet his right not to be killed was violated by all who took part.

(bb) *A* is poisoned slowly by daily doses. The final dose, like earlier ones, was not, by itself, lethal. But the poisoner still violated *A*'s right not to be killed.

(cc) *B* plays Russian roulette with *A*, *C*, *D*, *E*, *F*, and *G*, firing a revolver at each once, when he knows that one firing in six will be lethal. If *A* is shot and dies, then *B* has violated his right not to be killed.

(dd) Henry II asks who will rid him of the turbulent priest, and his supporters kill Becket. It is reasonably clear that Henry did not intend Becket's death, even though he in part brought it about, as he later admitted.

These explications of the right not to be killed are not too controversial taken individually, and I would suggest that their conjunction is also uncontroversial. Even when *A*'s death is the result of the acts of many persons and is not an immediate consequence of their deeds, nor even a certain consequence, and is not intended by them, *A*'s right not to be killed may be violated.

FIRST CLASS VERSUS STEERAGE ON LIFEBOAT EARTH

If we imagine a lifeboat in which special quarters are provided for the (recently) first-class passengers, and on which the food and water for all passengers are stowed in those quarters, then we have a fair, if crude, model of the present human situation on lifeboat Earth. For even on the assumption that there is at present sufficient for all to survive, some have control over the means of survival and so, indirectly, over others' survival. Sometimes the exercise of control can lead, even on a well-equipped lifeboat, to the starvation and death of some of those who lack control. On an ill-equipped lifeboat some must die in any case and, as we have already seen, though some of these deaths may be killings, some of them may be justifiable killings. Corresponding situations can, do, and will arise on lifeboat Earth, and it is to these that we should turn our attention, covering both the presumed present situation of global sufficiency of the means of survival and the expected future situation of global insufficiency.

Sufficiency Situations

Aboard a well-equipped lifeboat any distribution of food and water which leads to a death is a killing and not just a case of permitting a death. For the acts of those who distribute the food and water are the causes of a death which would not have occurred had those agents either had no causal influence or done other acts. By contrast, a person whom they leave in the water to drown is merely allowed to die, for his death would have taken place (other things being equal) had those agents had no causal influence, though it could have been prevented had they rescued him.[3] The distinction between killing and allowing to die, as here construed, does not depend on any claims about the other rights of persons who are killed. The death of the shortchanged passenger of example (1b) violated his property rights as well as his right not to be killed, but the reason the death was classifiable as a killing depended on the part which the acts of the other passengers had in causing it. If we suppose that a stowaway on a lifeboat has no right to food and water and is denied them, then clearly his property rights have not been violated. Even so, by the above definitions he is killed rather than allowed to die. For if the other passengers had either had no causal influence or done otherwise, his death would not have occurred. Their actions—in this case distributing food only to those entitled to it—caused the stowaway's death. Their acts would be justifiable only if property rights can sometimes override the right not to be killed.

Many would claim that the situation on lifeboat Earth is not analogous to that on ordinary lifeboats, since it is not evident that we all have a claim, let alone an equal claim, on the earth's resources. Perhaps some of us are stowaways. I shall not here assume that we do all have some claim on the earth's resources, even though I think it plausible to suppose that we do. I shall assume that even if persons have unequal property rights and some people own nothing, it does not follow that B's exercise of his property rights can override A's right not to be killed.[4] Where our activities lead to others' deaths which would not have occurred had we either done something else or had no causal influence, no claim that the activities were within our economic rights would suffice to show that we did not kill.

It is not far-fetched to think that at present the economic activity of some groups of persons leads to others' deaths. I shall choose a couple of examples of the sort of activity which can do so, but I do not think that these examples do more than begin a list of cases of killing by economic activities. Neither of these examples depends on questioning the existence of unequal property rights; they assume only that such rights do not override a right not to be killed. Neither example is one for which it is plausible to think that the killing could be justified as undertaken in self-defense.

Case one might be called the *foreign investment* situation. A group of investors may form a company which invests abroad—perhaps in a plantation or in a mine—and so manage their affairs that a high level of profits is repatriated, while the wages for the laborers are so minimal that their survival rate is lowered, that is, their expectation of life is lower than it might have been had the company not invested there.

In such a case the investors and company management do not act alone, do not cause immediate deaths, and do not know in advance who will die; it is also likely that they intend no deaths. But by their involvement in the economy of an underdeveloped area they cannot claim, as can another company which has no investments there, that they are "doing nothing." On the contrary, they are setting the policies which determine the living standards which determine the survival rate. When persons die because of the lowered standard of living established by a firm or a number of firms which dominate a local economy and either limit persons to employment on their terms or lower the other prospects for employment by damaging traditional economic structures, and these firms could either pay higher wages or stay out of the area altogether, then those who establish these policies are violating some persons' rights not to be killed. Foreign investment which *raises* living standards, even to a still abysmal level, could not be held to kill, for it causes no additional deaths, unless there are special circumstances, as in the following example.

Even when a company investing in an underdeveloped country establishes high wages and benefits and raises the expectation of life for its workers, it often manages to combine these payments with high profitability only by having achieved a tax-exempt status. In such cases the company is being subsidized by the general tax revenue of the underdeveloped economy. It makes no contribution to the infrastructure—e.g. roads and harbors and airports—from which it benefits. In this way many underdeveloped economies have come to include developed enclaves whose development is achieved in part at the expense of the poorer majority.[5] In such cases, government and company policy combine to produce a high wage sector at the expense of a low wage sector; in consequence, some of the persons in the low wage sector, who would not otherwise have died, may die; these persons, whoever they may be, are killed and not merely allowed to die. Such killings may sometimes be justifiable—perhaps, if they are outnumbered by lives saved through having a developed sector—but they are killings nonetheless, since the victims might have survived if not burdened by transfer payments to the developed sector.

But, one may say, the management of such a corporation and its investors should be distinguished more sharply. Even if the management may choose a level of wages, and consequently of survival, the investors usually know nothing of this. But the investors, even if ignorant, are responsible for company policy. They may often fail to exercise control, but by law they have control. They choose to invest in a company with certain foreign investments; they profit from it; they can, and others cannot, affect company policy in fundamental ways. To be sure the investors are not murderers—they do not intend to bring about the deaths of any persons; nor do the company managers usually intend any of the deaths company policies cause. Even so, investors and management acting together with the sorts of results just described do violate some persons' rights not to be killed and usually cannot justify such killings either as required for self-defense or as unavoidable.

Case two, where even under sufficiency conditions some persons' economic activities result in the deaths of other persons, might be called the *commodity pricing* case. Underdeveloped countries often depend heavily on the price level of a few commodities. So a sharp drop in the world price of coffee or sugar or cocoa may spell ruin and lowered survival rates for whole regions. Yet such drops in price levels are not in all cases due to factors beyond human control. Where they are the result of action by investors, brokers, or government agencies, these persons and bodies are choosing policies which will kill some people. Once again, to be sure, the killing is not single-handed, it is not instantaneous, the killers cannot foresee exactly who will die, and they may not intend anybody to die.

Because of the economic interdependence of different countries, deaths can also be caused by rises in the prices of various commodities. For example, the present near-famine in the Sahelian region of Africa and in the Indian subcontinent is attributed by agronomists partly to climatic shifts and partly to the increased prices of oil and hence of fertilizer, wheat, and other grains.

> The recent doubling in international prices of essential foodstuffs will, of necessity, be reflected in higher death rates among the world's lowest income groups, who lack the income to increase their food expenditures proportionately, but live on diets near the subsistence level to begin with.[6]

Of course, not all of those who die will be killed. Those who die of drought will merely be allowed to die, and some of those who die because less has been grown with less fertilizer will also die because of forces beyond the control of any human agency. But to the extent that the raising of oil prices is an achievement of Arab diplomacy and oil company management rather than a windfall, the consequent deaths are killings. Some of them may perhaps be justifiable killings (perhaps if outnumbered by lives saved within the Arab world by industrialization), but killings nonetheless.

Even on a sufficiently equipped earth some persons are killed by others' distribution decisions. The causal chains leading to death-producing distributions are often extremely complex. Where they can be perceived with reasonable clarity we ought, if we take seriously the right not to be killed and seek not merely to avoid killing others but to prevent third parties from doing so, to support policies which reduce deaths. For example—and these are only examples—we should support certain sorts of aid policies rather than others; we should oppose certain sorts of foreign investment; we should oppose certain sorts of commodity speculation, and perhaps support certain sorts of price support agreements for some commodities (e.g. those which try to maintain high prices for products on whose sale poverty-stricken economies depend).

If we take the view that we have no duty to enforce the rights of others, then we cannot draw so general a conclusion about our duty to support various economic policies which might avoid some unjustifiable killings. But we might still find that we should take action of certain sorts either because our own lives are threatened by certain economic activities of others or because our own economic activities threaten others' lives. Only if we knew that we were not part of any system of activities causing unjustifiable deaths could we have no duties to support policies which seek to avoid such deaths. Modern economic causal chains are so complex that it is likely that only those who are economically isolated and self-sufficient could know that they are part of no such systems of activities. Persons who believe that they are involved in some death-producing activities will have some of the same duties as those who think they have a duty to enforce others' rights not to be killed.

Scarcity Situations

The last section showed that sometimes, even in sufficiency situations, some might be killed by the way in which others arranged the distribution of the means of subsistence. Of far more importance in the long run is the true lifeboat situation—the situation of scarcity. We face a situation in which not everyone who is born can live out the normal span of human life and, further, in which we must expect today's normal life-span to be shortened. The date at which serious scarcity will begin is not generally agreed upon, but even the more optimistic prophets place it no more than decades away.[7] Its arrival will depend on factors such as the rate of technological invention and innovation, especially in agriculture and pollution control, and the success of programs to limit human fertility.

Such predictions may be viewed as exonerating us from complicity in famine deaths. If famine is inevitable, then—while we may have to choose whom to save—the deaths of those whom we do not or cannot save cannot be seen as killings for which we bear any responsibility. For these deaths would have occurred even if we had no causal influence. The decisions to be made may be excruciatingly difficult, but at least we can comfort ourselves that we did not produce or contribute to the famine.

However, this comforting view of famine predictions neglects the fact that these predictions are contingent upon certain assumptions about what people will do in the prefamine period. Famine is said to be inevitable *if* people do not curb their fertility, alter their consumption patterns, and avoid pollution and consequent ecological catastrophes. It is the policies of the present which will produce, defer, or avoid famine. Hence if famine comes, the deaths that occur will be results of decisions made earlier. Only if we take no part in systems of activities which lead to famine situations can we view ourselves as choosing whom to save rather than whom to kill when famine comes. In an economically interdependent world there are few people who can look on the approach of famine as a natural disaster from which they may kindly rescue some, but for whose arrival they bear no responsibility. We cannot stoically regard particular famine deaths as unavoidable if we have contributed to the emergence and extent of famine.

If we bear some responsibility for the advent of famine, then any decision on distributing the risk of famine is a decision whom to kill. Even a decision to rely on natural selection as a famine policy is choosing a policy for killing—for under a different famine policy different persons might have survived, and under different prefamine policies there might have been no famine or a less severe famine. The choice of a particular famine policy may be justifiable on the grounds that once we have let it get to that point there is not enough to go around, and somebody must go, as on an ill-equipped lifeboat. Even so, the famine policy chosen will not be a policy of saving some but not all persons from an unavoidable predicament.

Persons cannot, of course, make famine policies individually. Famine and prefamine policies are and will be made by governments individually and collectively and perhaps also by some voluntary organizations. It may even prove politically impossible to have a coherent famine or prefamine policy for the whole world; if so, we shall have to settle for partial and piecemeal policies. But each person who is in a position to support or oppose such policies, whether global or local, has to decide which to support and which to oppose. Even for individual persons, inaction and inattention are often a decision—a decision to support the famine and prefamine policies, which are the status quo whether or not they are "hands off" policies. There are large numbers of ways in which private citizens may affect such policies. They do so in supporting or opposing legislation affecting aid and foreign investment, in supporting or opposing certain sorts of charities or groups such as Zero Population Growth, in promoting or opposing ecologically conservative technology and lifestyles. Hence we have individually the onus of avoiding killing. For even though we

(a) do not kill single-handedly those who die of famine
(b) do not kill instantaneously those who die of famine
(c) do not know which individuals will die as the result of the prefamine and famine policies we support (unless we support something like a genocidal famine policy)
(d) do not intend any famine deaths

we nonetheless kill and do not merely allow to die. For as the result of our actions in concert with others, some will die who might have survived had we either acted otherwise or had no causal influence.

FAMINE POLICIES AND PREFAMINE POLICIES

Various principles can be suggested on which famine and prefamine policies might reasonably be based. I shall list some of these, more with the aim of setting out the range of possible decisions than with the aim of stating a justification for selecting some people for survival. One very general policy might be that of adopting whichever more specific policies will lead to the fewest deaths. An example would be going along with the consequences of natural selection in the way in which the allocation of medical care in situations of great shortage does, that is, the criteria for relief would be a high chance of survival if relief is given and a low chance otherwise—the worst risks would be abandoned. (This decision is analogous to picking the ill man as the victim on the lifeboat in 2a.) However, the policy of minimizing deaths is indeterminate, unless a certain time horizon is specified. For the policies which maximize survival in the short run—e.g. preventive medicine and minimal living standards—may also maximize population increase and lead to greater ultimate catastrophe.[8]

Another general policy would be to try to find further grounds which can justify overriding a person's right not to be killed. Famine policies adopted on these grounds might permit others to kill those who will forgo their right not to be killed (voluntary euthanasia, including healthy would-be suicides) or to kill those whom others find dependent and exceptionally burdensome, e.g. the unwanted sick or aged or unborn or newborn (involuntary euthanasia, abortion, and infanticide). Such policies might be justified by claims that the right not to be killed may be overridden in famine situations if the owner of the right consents or if securing the right is exceptionally burdensome.

Any combination of such policies is a policy of killing some and protecting others. Those who are killed may not have their right not to be killed violated without reason; those who set and support famine policies and prefamine policies will not be able to claim that they do not kill, but if they reason carefully they may be able to claim that they do so without justification.

From this vantage point it can be seen why it is not relevant to restrict the right of self-defense to a right to defend oneself against those who threaten one's life but do not do so innocently. Such a restriction may make a great difference to one's view of abortion in cases where the mother's life is threatened, but it does not make much difference when famine is the issue. Those who might be chosen as likely victims of any famine policy will probably be innocent of contributing to the famine, or at least no more guilty than others; hence the innocence of the victims is an insufficient ground for rejecting a policy. Indeed it is hard to point a finger at the guilty in famine situations. Are they the hoarders of grain? The parents of large families? Inefficient farmers? Our own generation?

In a sense we are all innocent threats to one another's safety in scarcity situations, for the bread one person eats might save another's life. If there were fewer people competing for resources, commodity prices would fall and starvation deaths be reduced. Hence famine deaths in scarcity situations might be justified on grounds of the minimal right of self-defense as well as on grounds of the unavoidability of some deaths and the reasonableness of the policies for selecting victims. For each famine death leaves fewer survivors competing for whatever resources there are, and the most endangered among the survivors might have died—had not others done so. So a policy which kills some may be justified on the grounds that the most endangered survivors could have been defended in no other way.

Global scarcity is not here yet. But its imminence has certain implications for today. If all persons have a right not to be killed and a corollary duty not to kill others, then we are bound to adopt prefamine policies which ensure that famine is postponed as long as possible and is minimized. And a duty to try to postpone the advent and minimize the severity of famine is a duty on the one hand to minimize the number of persons there will be and on the other to maximize the means of subsistence.[9] For if we do not adopt prefamine policies with these aims we shall have to adopt more drastic famine policies sooner.

So if we take the right not to be killed seriously, we should consider and support not only some famine policy for future use but also a population and resources policy for present use. There has been a certain amount of philosophical discussion of population policies.[10] From the point of view of the present argument it has two defects. First, it is for the most part conducted within a utilitarian framework and focusses on problems such as the different population policies required by maximizing the total and the average utility of a population. Secondly this literature tends to look at a scarcity of resources as affecting the quality of lives but not their very possibility. It is more concerned with the question, How many people should we add? than with the question, How few people could we lose? There are, of course, many interesting questions about population policies which are not relevant to famine. But here I shall consider only population and resource policies determined on the principle of postponing and minimizing famine, for these are policies which might be based on the claim that persons have a right not to be killed, so that we have a duty to avoid or postpone situations in which we shall have to override this right.

Such population policies might, depending upon judgments about the likely degree of scarcity, range from the mild to the draconian. I list some examples. A mild population policy might emphasize family planning, perhaps moving in the direction of fiscal incentives or measures which stress not people's rights but their duties to control their bodies. Even a mild policy would require a lot both in terms of invention (e.g. the development of contraceptives suitable for use in poverty-stricken conditions) and innovation (e.g. social policies which reduce the incentives and pressures to have a large family).[11] More draconian policies would enforce population limitation—for example, by mandatory sterilization after a certain number of children were born or by reducing public health expenditures in places with high net reproduction rates to prevent death rates from declining until birth rates do so. A policy of completely eliminating all further births (e.g. by universal sterilization) is also one which would meet the requirement of postponing famine, since extinct species do not suffer famine. I have not in this argument used any premises which show that a complete elimination of births would be wrong, but other premises might give reasons for thinking that it is wrong to enforce sterilization or better to have some persons rather than no persons. In any case the political aspects of introducing famine policies make it likely that this most austere of population policies would not be considered.

There is a corresponding range of resource policies. At the milder end are the various conservation and pollution control measures now being practiced or discussed. At the tougher end of the spectrum are complete rationing of energy and materials consumption. If the aim of a resources policy is to avoid killing those who are born, and adequate policy may require both invention (e.g. solar energy technology and better waste retrieval techniques) and innovation (e.g. introducing new technology in such a way that its benefits are not quickly absorbed by increasing population, as has happened with the green revolution in some places).

At all events, if we think that people have a right not to be killed, we cannot fail to face up to its long-range implications. This one right by itself provides ground for activism on many fronts. In scarcity situations which we help produce, the defeasibility of the right not to be killed is important, for there cannot be any absolute duty not to kill persons in such situations but only a commitment to kill only for reasons. Such a commitment requires consideration of the condition or quality of life which is to qualify for survival. Moral philosophers are reluctant to face up to this problem; soon it will be staring us in the face.

NOTES

[1] Cf. Robert Nozick, *Anarchy, State and Utopia* (New York, 1974), 34. Nozick defines an innocent threat as "someone who is innocently a causal agent in a process such that he would be an aggressor had he chosen to become such an agent."

[2] Cf. Peter Singer, "Famine, Affluence, and Morality," *Philosophy & Public Affairs* 1, no. 3 (Spring 1972), 229-43, 232. I am in agreement with many of the points which Singer makes, but am interested in arguing that we must have some famine policy from a much weaker set of premises. Singer uses some consequentialist premises: starvation is bad; we ought to prevent bad things when we can do so without worse consequences; hence we ought to prevent starvation whether it is nearby or far off and whether others are doing so or not. The argument of this article does not depend on a particular theory about the grounds of obligation, but should be a corollary of any nonbizarre ethical theory which has any room for a notion of rights.

3 This way of distinguishing killing from allowing to die does not rely on distinguishing "negative" from "positive" acts. Such attempts seem unpromising since any act has multiple descriptions of which some will be negative and others positive. If a clear distinction is to be made between killing and letting die, it must hinge on the *difference* which an act makes for a person's survival, rather than on the description under which the agent acts.

4 The point may appear rather arbitrary, given that I have not rested my case on one theory of the grounds of obligation. But I believe that almost any such theory will show a right not to be killed to override a property right. Perhaps this is why Locke's theory can seem so odd—in moving from a right of self-preservation to a justification of unequal property rights, he finds himself gradually having to reinterpret all rights as property rights, thus coming to see us as the owners of our persons.

5 Cf. P.A. Baron, *The Political Economy of Growth* (New York, 1957), especially Chap. 5, "On the Roots of Backwardness"; or A.G. Frank, *Capitalism and Underdevelopment in Latin America* (New York, 1967). Both works argue that underdeveloped economies are among the products of developed ones.

6 Lester R. Brown and Erik P. Eckholm, "The Empty Breadbasket," *Ceres* (F.A.O. Review on Development), March-April 1974, 59. See also N. Borlaug and R. Ewell, "The Shrinking Margin," in the same issue.

7 For discussions of the time and extent of famine see, for example, P.R. Ehrlich, *The Population Bomb*, rev. ed. (New York, 1971); R.L. Heilbroner, *An Inquiry into the Human Prospect* (New York, 1974); *Scientific American*, September 1974, especially R. Freedman and B. Berelson, "The Human Population"; P. Demeny, "The Populations of the Underdeveloped Countries"; R. Revelle, "Food and Population."

8 See *Scientific American*, September 1974, especially A.J. Coale, "The History of the Human Population."

9 The failure of "right to life" groups to pursue these goals seriously casts doubt upon their commitment to the preservation of human lives. Why are they active in so few of the contexts where human lives are endangered?

10 For example, J.C.C. Smart, *An Outline of a System of Utilitarian Ethics* (Melbourne, 1961), 18, 44 ff.; Jan Narveson, "Moral Problems of Population," *The Monist* 57 (1973), 62-86; "Utilitarianism and New Generations," *Mind* 76 (1967), 62-72.

11 Cf. Mahmood Mamdani, *The Myth of Population Control* (New York, 1972), for evidence that high fertility can be based on rational choice rather than ignorance or incompetence.

V

ABORTION

A Third Way

L. WAYNE SUMNER

The practice of abortion confronts us with two different sets of moral questions belonging to two different decision contexts. The primary context is that in which a woman chooses whether to have an abortion and a physician chooses whether to perform it; here the focus is on the moral quality of abortion itself. Because this context is one of individual decision we will call the set of moral questions which it contains the *personal* problem of abortion. The secondary context is that in which a society chooses how, or whether, to regulate abortions; here the focus is on the merits of alternative abortion policies. Because this context is one of social decision we will call the set of moral questions which it contains the *political* problem of abortion.

Although the two kinds of problem raised by abortion are distinct, they are also connected. A complete view of the morality of abortion will therefore offer connected solutions to them. In most countries in the west public discussion of abortion has been distorted by the dominance of two such views. The liberal view, espoused by "pro-choice" groups, holds that (voluntary) abortion is always morally innocuous and (therefore) that the only acceptable abortion policy is one which treats abortion as another variety of minor elective surgery. The conservative view, espoused by "pro-life" groups, holds that abortion is always morally serious and (therefore) that the only acceptable abortion policy is one which treats abortion as another variety of homicide.

Because they define the extremities of the continuum of possible positions, and because each is sufficiently simple and forceful to be advocated by a powerful movement, these established views constitute the familiar reference points in our abortion landscape. Yet neither has managed to command the allegiance of more than a small minority of the public. For the rest of us who are unwilling to embrace either of the extreme options the problem has been the lack of a well-defined middle ground between them. In contrast to the power of the established views more moderate alternatives may appear both indistinct and indecisive.

Public distrust of the established views is well grounded: neither stands up under critical scrutiny.[1] If their demise is not to leave us without any credible view of abortion three tasks must be successfully completed. The first is to define a third way with abortion and to distinguish it from both of the views which it will supersede. The second is to give it an intuitive defense by showing that it coheres better than either of its predecessors with our considered moral judgments both on abortion itself and on closely related issues. Then, finally, the third way must be grounded in a moral theory. The first two of these tasks will be undertaken here; the more daunting theoretical challenge is confronted elsewhere.[2]

I

SPECIFICATIONS

Despite their opposition, the two established views suffer from similar defects. Collating their failures will provide us with some positive guidelines to follow in building a more satisfactory alternative. The central issue in the morality of abortion is the moral status of the fetus. Let us say that a creature has *moral standing* if, for the purpose of moral decision-making, it must be counted for something in its own right. To count for nothing is to have no moral standing; to count for as much as possible (as much, that is, as any creature does) is to have full moral standing. We may, for the purpose of the present discussion, make this rather vague notion more precise by adopting the rights vocabulary favored by both of the established views. We will suppose that having (some) moral standing is equivalent to having (some) right to life. The central issue in the morality of abortion is then whether fetuses have moral standing in this sense.[3]

The conservative view, and also the more naive versions of the liberal view, select a precise point (conception, birth, etc.) as the threshold of moral standing, implying that the transition from no standing to full standing occurs abruptly. In doing so they rest more weight on these sudden events than they are capable of bearing. A view that avoids this defect will allow full moral standing to be acquired gradually. It will therefore attempt to locate not a threshold point, but a threshold period or stage.

Both of the established views attribute a uniform moral status to all fetuses, regardless of their dissimilarities. Each, for example, counts a newly conceived zygote for precisely as much (or as little) as a full-term fetus, despite the enormous differences between them. A view that avoids this defect will assign moral status differentially, so that the threshold stage occurs sometime during pregnancy.

A consequence of the uniform approach adopted by both of the established views is that neither can attach any significance to the development of the fetus during gestation. Yet this development is the most obvious feature of gestation. A view that avoids this defect will base the (differential) moral standing of the fetus at least in part on its level of development. It will thus assign undeveloped fetuses a moral status akin to that of ova and spermatozoa, whereas it will assign developed fetuses a moral status akin to that of infants.

So far, then, an adequate view of the fetus must be gradual, differential, and developmental. It must also be derived from a satisfactory criterion of moral standing. Such a criterion must be general (applicable to beings other than fetuses), it must connect moral standing with the empirical properties of such beings, and it must be morally relevant. Its moral relevance is partly testable by appeal to intuition, for arbitrary or shallow criteria will be vulnerable to counterexamples. But the final test of moral relevance is grounding in a moral theory.

An adequate view of the fetus promises a morally significant division between early abortions (before the threshold stage) and late abortions (after the threshold stage). It also promises borderline cases (during the threshold stage). Wherever that stage is located, abortions that precede it will be private matters, since the fetus will at that stage lack moral standing. Thus the provisions of the liberal view will apply to early abortions: they will be morally innocent (as long as the usual conditions of maternal consent, etc., are satisfied) and ought to be legally unregulated (except for rules equally applicable to all other medical procedures). Early abortion will have the same moral status as contraception.

Abortions that follow the threshold stage will be interpersonal matters, since the fetus will at that stage possess moral standing. Thus the provisions of the conservative view will apply to late abortions: they must be assessed on a case-by-case basis and they ought to be legally permitted only on appropriate grounds. Late abortions will have the same moral status as infanticide, except for the difference made by the physical connection between fetus and mother.

A third way with abortion is thus a moderate and differential view, combining elements of the liberal view for early abortions with elements of (a weakened version of) the conservative view for late abortions. The policy that a moderate view will support is a moderate policy, permissive in the early stages of pregnancy and more restrictive (though not as restrictive as conservatives think appropriate) in the later stages. So far as the personal question of the moral evaluation of particular abortions is concerned, there is no pressing need to resolve the borderline cases around the threshold stage. But a workable abortion policy cannot tolerate this vagueness and will need to establish a definite time limit beyond which the stipulated grounds will come into play. Although the precise location of the time limit will unavoidably be somewhat arbitrary, it will be defensible as long as it falls somewhere within the threshold stage. Abortion on request up to the time limit and only for cause thereafter: these are the elements of a satisfactory abortion policy.

A number of moderate views may be possible, each of them satisfying all of the foregoing constraints. A particular view will be defined by selecting (i) a criterion of moral standing, (ii) the natural characteristics whose gradual acquisition during normal fetal development carries with it the acquisition of moral standing, and (iii) a threshold stage. Of these three steps, the first is the crucial one, since it determines both of the others.

II

A CRITERION OF MORAL STANDING

We are assuming that for a creature to have moral standing is for it to have a right to life. Any such right imposes duties on moral agents; these duties may be either negative (not to deprive the creature of life) or positive (to support the creature's life). Possession of a right to life implies at least some immunity against attack by others, and possibly also some entitlement to the aid of others. As the duties may vary in strength, so may the corresponding rights. To have some moral standing is to have some right to life, whether or not it may be overridden by the rights of others. To have full moral standing is to have the strongest right to life possessed by anyone, the right to life of the paradigm person. Depending on one's moral theory, this right may or may not be inviolable and indefeasible and thus may or may not impose absolute duties on others.

To which creatures should we distribute (some degree of) moral standing? On which criterion should we base this distribution? It may be easier to answer these questions if we begin with the clear case and work outward to the unclear ones. If we can determine why we ascribe full standing to the paradigm case, we may learn what to look for in other creatures when deciding whether or not to include them in the moral sphere.

The paradigm bearer of moral standing is an adult human being with normal capacities of intellect, emotion, perception, sensation, decision, action, and the like. If we think of such a person as a complex bundle of natural properties, then in principle we could employ as a criterion any of the properties common to all normal and mature members of our species. Selecting a particular property or set of properties will define a class of creatures with moral standing, namely, all (and only) those who share that property. The extension of that class will depend on how widely the property in question is distributed. Some putative criteria will be obviously frivolous and will immediately fail the tests of generality or moral relevance. But even after excluding the silly candidates, we are left with a number of serious ones. There are four that appear to be the most serious: we might attribute full moral standing to the paradigm person on the ground that he/she is (i) intrinsically valuable, (ii) alive, (iii) sentient, or (iv) rational. A intuitive test of the adequacy of any of these candidates will involve first enumerating the class of beings to whom it will distribute moral standing and then determining whether that class either excludes creatures that upon careful reflection we believe ought to be included or includes creatures that we believe ought to be excluded. In the former case the criterion draws the boundary of the moral sphere too narrowly and fails as a necessary condition of moral standing. In the latter case the criterion draws the boundary too broadly and fails as a sufficient condition. (A given criterion may, of course, be defective in both respects.)

Beings may depart from the paradigm along several different dimensions, each of which presents us with unclear cases that a criterion must resolve. These cases may be divided into seven categories: (a) inanimate objects (natural and artificial); (b) non-human terrestrial species of living things (animals and plants); (c) nonhuman extraterrestrial species of living things (should there be any); (d) artificial "life forms" (androids, robots, computers); (e) grossly defective human beings (the severely and permanently retarded or deranged); (f) human beings at the end of life (especially the severely and permanently senile or comatose); (g) human beings at the beginning of life (fetuses, infants, children). Since the last context is the one in which we wish to apply a criterion, it will here be set aside. This will enable us to settle on a criterion without tailoring it specially for the problem of abortion. Once a criterion has established its credentials in other domains, we will be able to trace out its implications for the case of the fetus.

The first candidate for a criterion takes a direction rather different from that of the remaining three. It is a commonplace in moral philosophy to attribute to (normal adult) human beings a special worth or value or dignity in virtue of which they possess (among other rights) a full right to life. This position implies that (some degree of) moral standing extends just as far as (some degree of) this intrinsic value, a higher degree of the latter entailing a higher degree of the former. We cannot know which things have moral standing without being told which things have intrinsic worth (and why)—without, that is, being offered a theory of intrinsic value. What is unique about this criterion, however, is that it is quite capable in principle of extending moral standing beyond the class of living beings, thus embracing such inanimate objects as rocks and lakes, entire landscapes (or indeed worlds), and artifacts. Of course, nonliving things cannot literally have a right to *life*, but it would be simple enough to generalize to a right to (continued) *existence*, where this might include both a right not to be destroyed and a right to such support as is necessary for that existence. A criterion that invokes intrinsic value is thus able to define a much more capacious moral sphere than is any of the other candidates.

Such a criterion is undeniably attractive in certain respects: how else are we to explain why it is wrong to destroy priceless icons or litter the moon even when doing so will never affect any living, sentient, or rational being? But it is clear that it cannot serve our present purpose. A criterion must connect moral standing with some property of things whose presence or absence can be confirmed by a settled, objective, and public method of investigation. The property of being intrinsically valuable is not subject to such verification. A criterion based on intrinsic value cannot be applied without a theory of intrinsic value. Such a theory will supply a criterion of intrinsic value by specifying the natural properties of things in virtue of which they possess such value. But if things have moral standing in virtue of having intrinsic value, and if they have intrinsic value in virtue of having some natural property, then it is that natural property which is serving as the real criterion of moral standing, and the middle term of intrinsic value is eliminable without loss. A theory of intrinsic value may thus entail a criterion of moral standing, but intrinsic value cannot itself serve as that criterion.

There is a further problem confronting any attempt to ground moral rights in the intrinsic worth of creatures. One must first be certain that this is not merely a verbal exercise in which attributing intrinsic value to things is just another way of attributing intrinsic moral standing to them. Assuming that the relation between value and rights is synthetic, there are then two possibilities: the value in question is moral or it is nonmoral. If it is moral, the criterion plainly fails to break out of the circle of moral properties to connect them with the nonmoral properties of things. But if it is nonmoral, it is unclear what it has to do with moral rights. If there are realms of value, some case must be made for deriving moral duties toward things from the nonmoral value of these things.

The remaining three candidates for a criterion of moral standing (life, sentience, rationality) all satisfy the verification requirement since they all rest standing on empirical properties of things. They may be ordered in terms of the breadth of the moral spheres they define. Since rational beings are a proper subset of sentient beings, which are a proper subset of living beings, the first candidate is the weakest and will define the broadest sphere, whereas the third is the strongest and will define the narrowest sphere.[4] In an interesting recent discussion, Kenneth Goodpaster has urged that moral standing be accorded to all living beings, simply in virtue of the fact that they are alive.[5] Although much of his argument is negative, being directed against more restrictive criteria, he does provide a positive case for including all forms of life within the moral sphere.[6]

Let us assume that the usual signs of life—nutrition, metabolism, spontaneous growth, reproduction—enable us to draw a tolerably sharp distinction between animate and inanimate beings, so that all plant and animal species, however primitive, are collected together in the former category. All such creatures share the property of being *teleological systems*: they have functions, ends, directions, natural tendencies, and so forth. In virtue of their teleology such creatures have needs, in a nonmetaphorical sense—conditions that must be satisfied if they are to thrive or flourish. Creatures with needs can be benefited or harmed; they are benefited when their essential needs are satisfied and harmed when they are not. It also makes sense to say that such creatures have a good: the conditions that promote their life and health are good for them, whereas those that impair their normal functioning are bad for them. But it is common to construe morality as having essentially to do with benefits and harms or with the good of creatures. So doing will lead us to extend moral standing to all creatures capable of being benefited and harmed, that is, all creatures with a good. But this condition will include all organisms (and systems of organisms), and so life is the only reasonable criterion of moral standing.

This extension of moral standing to plants and to the simpler animals is of course highly counterintuitive, since most of us accord the lives of such creatures no weight whatever in our practical deliberations. How could we conduct our affairs if we were to grant protection of life to every plant and animal species? Some of the more extreme implications of this view are, however, forestalled by Goodpaster's distinction between a criterion of inclusion and a criterion of comparison.[7] The former determines which creatures have (some) moral standing and thus locates the boundary of the moral sphere; it is Goodpaster's contention that life is the proper inclusion criterion. The latter is operative entirely within the moral sphere and enables us to assign different grades of moral standing to different creatures in virtue of some natural property that they may possess in different degrees. Since all living beings are (it seems) equally alive, life cannot serve as a comparison criterion. Goodpaster does not provide such a criterion, though he recognizes its necessity. Thus his view enables him to affirm that all living creatures have (some) moral standing but to deny that all such creatures have equal standing. Though the lives of all animate beings deserve consideration, some deserve more than others. Thus, for instance, higher animals might count for more than lower ones, and all animals might count for more than plants.

In the absence of a criterion of comparison, it is difficult to ascertain just what reforms Goodpaster's view would require in our moral practice. How much weight must human beings accord to the lives of lichen or grass or bacteria or insects? When are such lives more important than some benefit for a higher form of life? How should we modify our eating habits, for example? There is a problem here that extends beyond the incompleteness and indeterminacy of Goodpaster's position. Suppose that we have settled on a comparison criterion; let it be sentience (assuming that sentience admits of degrees in some relevant respect). Then a creature's ranking in the hierarchy of moral standing will be determined by the extent of its sentience: nonsentient (living) beings will have minimal standing, whereas the most sentient beings (human beings, perhaps) will have maximal standing. But then we are faced with the obvious question: if sentience is to serve as the comparison criterion, why should it not also serve as the inclusion criterion? Conversely, if life is the inclusion criterion, does it not follow that nothing else can serve as the comparison criterion, in which case all living beings have equal standing? It is difficult to imagine an argument in favor of sentience as a comparison criterion that would not also be an argument in favor of it as an inclusion criterion.[8] Since the same will hold for any other comparison criterion, Goodpaster's view can avoid its extreme implications only at the price of inconsistency.

Goodpaster's view also faces consistency problems in its claim that life is necessary for moral standing. Beings need not be organisms in order to be teleological systems, and therefore to have needs, a good, and the capacity to be benefited and harmed. If these conditions are satisfied by a tree (as they surely are), then they are equally satisfied by a car. In order to function properly most machines need periodic maintenance; such maintenance is good for them, they are benefited by it, and they are harmed by its neglect. Why then is being alive a necessary condition of moral standing? Life is but an (imperfect) indicator of teleology and the capacity to be benefited and harmed. But Goodpaster's argument then commits him to treating these deeper characteristics as the criterion of moral standing, and thus to according standing to many (perhaps most) inanimate objects.

This inclusion of (at least some) nonliving things should incline us to re-examine Goodpaster's argument—if the inclusion of all living things has not already done so. The connection between morality and the capacity to be benefited and harmed appears plausible, so what has gone wrong? We may form a conjecture if we again consider our paradigm bearer of moral standing. In the case of a fully normal adult human being, it does appear that moral questions are pertinent whenever the actions of another agent promise to benefit or threaten to harm such a being. Both duties and rights are intimately connected with benefits and harms. The kinds of acts that we have a (strict) duty not to do are those that typically cause harm, whereas positive duties are duties to confer benefits. Liberty-rights protect autonomy, which is usually thought of as one of the chief goods for human beings, and the connection between welfare-rights and benefits is obvious. But if we ask what counts as a benefit or a harm for a human being, the usual answers take one or both of the following directions:

1. *The desire model.* Human beings are benefited to the extent that their desires (or perhaps their considered and informed desires) are satisfied; they are harmed to the extent that these desires are frustrated.

2. *The experience model.* Human beings are benefited to the extent that they are brought to have experiences that they like or find agreeable; they are harmed to the extent that they are brought to have experiences that they dislike or find disagreeable.

We need not worry at this stage whether one of these models is more satisfactory than the other. On both models benefits and harms for particular persons are interpreted in terms of the psychological states of those persons, in terms, that is, of their interests or welfare. Such states are possible only for beings who are conscious or sentient. Thus, if morality has to do with the promotion and protection of interests or welfare, morality can concern itself only with beings who are conscious or sentient.[9] No other beings can be beneficiaries or victims *in the morally relevant way.* Goodpaster is not mistaken in suggesting that nonsentient beings can be benefited and harmed. But he is mistaken in suggesting that morality has to do with benefits and harms as such, rather than with a particular category of them. And that can be seen the more clearly when we realize that the broadest capacity to be benefited and harmed extends not only out to but beyond the frontier of life. Leaving my lawn mower out in the rain is bad for the mower, pulling weeds is bad for the weeds, and swatting mosquitoes is bad for the mosquitoes; but there are no moral dimensions to any of these acts unless the interests or welfare of some sentient creature is at stake. Morality requires the existence of sentience in order to obtain a purchase on our actions.

The failure of Goodpaster's view has thus given us some reason to look to sentience as a criterion of moral standing. Before considering this possibility directly, it will be helpful to turn to the much narrower criterion of rationality. The rational/nonrational boundary is more difficult to locate with certainty than the animate/inanimate boundary, since rationality (or intelligence) embraces a number of distinct but related capacities for thought, memory, foresight, language, self-consciousness, objectivity, planning, reasoning, judgment, deliberation, and the like.[10] It is perhaps possible for a being to possess some of these capacities and entirely lack others, but for simplicity we will assume that the higher-order cognitive processes are typically owned as a bundle.[11] The bundle is possessed to one extent or another by normal adult human beings, by adolescents and older children, by persons suffering from the milder cognitive disorders, and by some other animal species (some primates and cetaceans for example). It is not possessed to any appreciable extent by fetuses and infants, by the severely retarded or disordered, by the irreversibly comatose, and by most other animal species. To base moral standing on rationality is thus to deny it alike to most nonhuman beings and to many human beings. Since the implications for fetuses and infants have already been examined, they will be ignored in the present discussion. Instead we will focus on why one might settle on rationality as a criterion in the first place.

That rationality is sufficient for moral standing is not controversial (though there are some interesting questions to be explored here about forms of artificial intelligence). As a necessary condition, however, rationality will exclude a good many sentient beings—just how many, and which ones, to be determined by the kind and the stringency of the standards employed. Many will find objectionable this constriction of the sphere of moral concern. Because moral standing has been defined in terms of the right to life, to lack moral standing is not necessarily to lack all rights. Thus one could hold that, although we have no duty to (nonrational) animals to respect their lives, we do have a duty to them not to cause them suffering. For the right not to suffer, one might choose a different (and broader) criterion—sentience, for example. (However, if this is the criterion appropriate for that right, why is it not also the criterion appropriate for the right to life?) But even if we focus strictly on the (painless) killing of animals, the implications of the criterion are harsh. Certainly we regularly kill nonhuman animals to satisfy our own needs or desires. But the justification usually offered for these practices is either that the satisfaction of those needs and desires outweighs the costs to the animals (livestock farming, hunting, fishing, trapping, experimentation) or that no decent life would have been available for them anyway (the killing of stray dogs and cats). Although some of these arguments doubtless are rationalizations, their common theme is that the lives of animals do have some weight (however slight) in the moral scales, which is why the practice of killing is one that requires moral justification (raises moral issues). If rationality is the criterion of moral standing, and if (most) nonhuman animals are nonrational, killing such creatures could be morally questionable only when it impinges on the interests of rational beings (as where animals are items of property). In no case could killing an animal be a wrong against it. However callous and chauvinistic the common run of our treatment of animals may be, still the view that killing a dog or a horse is morally no more serious (*ceteris paribus*) than weeding a garden can be the considered judgment of only a small minority.

The standard that we apply to other species we must in consistency apply to our own. The greater the number of animals who are excluded by that standard, the greater the number of human beings who will also be excluded. In the absence of a determinate criterion it is unclear just where the moral line will be drawn on the normal/abnormal spectrum: will a right to life be withheld from mongoloids, psychotics, the autistic, the senile, the profoundly retarded? If so, killing such persons will again be no wrong *to them*. Needless to say, most such persons (in company with many animals) are sentient and capable to some extent of enjoyable and satisfying lives. To kill them is to deprive them of lives that are of value to them. If such creatures are denied standing, this loss will be entirely discounted in our moral reasoning. Their lack of rationality may ensure that their lives are less full and rich than ours, that they consist of simpler pleasures and more basic enjoyments. But what could be the justification for treating their deaths as though they cost them nothing at all?

There is a tradition, extending back at least to Kant, that attempts just such a justification. One of its modern spokesmen is A.I. Melden, who treats the capacity for moral agency as the criterion of moral standing.[12] This capacity is manifested by participation in a moral community—a set of beings sharing allegiance to moral rules and recognition of one another's integrity. Rights can be attributed only to beings with whom we can have such moral intercourse, thus only to beings who have interests similar to ours, who show concern for the well-being of others, who are capable of uniting in cooperative endeavors, who regulate their activities by a sense of right and wrong, and who display the characteristically moral emotions of indignation, remorse, and guilt.[13] Rationality is a necessary condition (though not a sufficient one) for possessing this bundle of capacities. Melden believes that of all living creatures known to us only human beings are capable of moral agency.[14] Natural rights, including the right to life, are thus human rights.

We may pass over the obvious difficulty of extending moral standing to all human beings on this basis (including the immature and abnormal) and focus on the question of why the capacity for moral agency should be thought necessary for possession of a right to life. The notion of a moral community to which Melden appeals contains a crucial ambiguity. On the one hand it can be thought of as a community of moral agents—the bearers of moral duties. Clearly to be a member of such a community one must be capable of moral agency. On the other hand a moral community can be thought of as embracing all beings to whom moral agents owe duties—the bearers of moral rights. It cannot simply be assumed that the class of moral agents (duty-bearers) is coextensive with the class of moral patients (right-bearers). It is quite conceivable that some beings (infants, nonhuman animals) might have rights though they lack duties (because incapable of moral agency). The capacity for moral agency is (trivially) a condition of having moral duties. It is not obviously also a condition of having moral rights. The claim that the criterion for rights is the same as the criterion for duties is substantive and controversial. The necessity of defending this claim is merely concealed by equivocating on the notion of a moral community.

Beings who acknowledge one another as moral agents can also acknowledge that (some) creatures who are not themselves capable of moral agency nonetheless merit (some) protection of life. The more we reflect on the function of rights, the stronger becomes the inclination to extend them to such creatures. Rights are securities for beings who are sufficiently autonomous to conduct their own lives but who are also vulnerable to the aggression of others and dependent upon these others for some of the necessaries of life. Rights protect the goods of their owners and shield them from evils. We ascribe rights to one another because we all alike satisfy these minimal conditions of autonomy, vulnerability, and dependence. In order to satisfy these conditions a creature need not itself be capable of morality: it need only possess interests that can be protected by rights. A higher standard thus seems appropriate for possession of moral duties than for possession of moral rights. Rationality appears to be the right sort of criterion for the former, but something less demanding (such as sentience) is better suited to the latter.

A criterion of life (or teleology) is too weak, admitting classes of beings (animate and inanimate) who are not suitable loci for moral rights; being alive is necessary for having standing, but it is not sufficient. A criterion of rationality (or moral agency) is too strong, excluding classes of beings (human and nonhuman) who are suitable loci for rights; being rational is sufficient for having standing, but it is not necessary. A criterion of sentience (or consciousness) is a promising middle path between these extremes. Sentience is the capacity for feeling or affect. In its most primitive form it is the ability to experience sensations of pleasure and pain, and thus the ability to enjoy and suffer. Its more developed forms include wants, aims, and desires (and thus the ability to be satisfied and frustrated); attitudes, tastes, and values; and moods, emotions, sentiments, and passions. Consciousness is a necessary condition of sentience, for feelings are states of mind of which their owner is aware. But it is not sufficient; it is at least possible in principle for beings to be conscious (percipient, for instance, or even rational) while utterly lacking feelings. If rationality embraces a set of cognitive capacities, then sentience is rooted in a being's affective and conative life. It is in virtue of being sentient that creatures have interests, which are compounded either out of their desires or out of the experiences they find agreeable (or both). If morality has to do with the protection and promotion of interests, it is a plausible conjecture that we owe moral duties to all those beings capable of having interests. But this will include all sentient creatures.

Like rationality, and unlike life, it makes sense to think of sentience as admitting of degrees. Within any given mode, such as the perception of pain, one creature may be more or less sensitive than another. But there is a further sense in which more developed (more rational) creatures possess a higher degree of sentience. The expansion of consciousness and of intelligence opens up new ways of experiencing the world, and therefore new ways of being affected by the world. More rational beings are capable of finding either fulfilment or frustration in activities and states of affairs to which less developed creatures are, both cognitively and affectively, blind. It is in this sense of a broader and deeper sensibility that a higher being is capable of a richer, fuller, and more varied existence. The fact that sentience admits of degrees (whether of sensitivity or sensibility) enables us to employ it both as an inclusion criterion and as a comparison criterion of moral standing. The animal kingdom presents us with a hierarchy of sentience. Non-sentient beings have no moral standing; among sentient beings the more developed have greater standing than the less developed, the upper limit being occupied by the paradigm of a normal adult human being. Although sentience is the criterion of moral standing, it is also possible to explain the relevance of rationality. The evolutionary order is one of ascending intelligence. Since rationality expands a creature's interests, it is a reliable indicator of the degree of moral standing which that creature possesses. Creatures less rational than human beings do not altogether lack standing, but they do lack full standing.

An analysis of degrees of standing would require a graded right to life, in which the strength of the right varied inversely with the range of considerations capable of overriding it. The details of any such analysis will be complex and need not be worked out here. However, it seems that we are committed to extending (some) moral standing at least to all vertebrate animals, and also to counting higher animals for more than lower.[15] Thus we should expect the higher vertebrates (mammals) to merit greater protection of life than the lower (fish, reptiles, amphibia, birds) and we should also expect the higher mammals (primates, cetaceans) to merit greater protection of life than the lower (canines, felines, etc.). Crude as this division may be, it seems to accord reasonably well with most people's intuitions that in our moral reasoning paramecia and horseflies count for nothing, dogs and cats count for something, chimpanzees and dolphins count for more, and human beings count for most of all.

A criterion of sentience can thus allow for the gradual emergence of moral standing in the order of nature. It can explain why no moral issues arise (directly) in our dealings with inanimate objects, plants, and the simpler forms of animal life. It can also function as a moral guideline in our encounters with novel life forms on other planets. If the creatures we meet have interests and are capable of enjoyment and suffering, we must grant them some moral standing. We thereby constrain ourselves not to exploit them ruthlessly for our own advantage. The kind of standing that they deserve may be determined by the range and depth of their sensibility, and in ordinary circumstances this will vary with their intelligence. We should therefore recognize as equals beings who are as rational and sensitive as ourselves. The criterion also implies that if we encounter creatures who are rational but nonsentient—who utterly lack affect and desire—nothing we can do will adversely affect such creatures (in morally relevant ways). We would be entitled, for instance, to treat them as a species of organic computer. The same obviously holds for forms of artificial intelligence; in deciding whether to extend moral standing to sophisticated machines, the question (as Bentham put it) is not whether they can reason but whether they can suffer.

A criterion of sentience also requires gentle usage of the severely abnormal. Cognitive disabilities and disorders may impair a person's range of sensibility, but they do not generally reduce that person to the level of a nonsentient being. Even the grossly retarded or deranged will still be capable of some forms of enjoyment and suffering and thus will still possess (some) moral standing in their own right. This standing diminishes to the vanishing point only when sentience is entirely lost or never gained in the first place. If all affect and responsivity are absent, and if they cannot be engendered, then (but only then) are we no longer dealing with a sentient creature. This verdict accords well with the contemporary trend toward defining death in terms of the permanent loss of cerebral functioning. Although such patients are in one obvious sense still alive (their blood circulates and is oxygenated), in the morally relevant sense they are now beyond our reach, for we can cause them neither good nor ill. A criterion of life would require us to continue treating them as beings with (full?) moral standing, whereas a criterion of rationality would withdraw that standing when reason was lost even though sensibility should remain. Again a criterion of sentience enables us to find a middle way.

Fastening upon sentience as the criterion for possession of a right to life thus opens up the possibility of a reasonable and moderate treatment of moral problems other than abortion, problems pertaining to the treatment of nonhuman animals, extraterrestrial life, artificial intelligence, "defective" human beings, and persons at the end of life. We need now to trace out its implications for the fetus.

III

THE MORALITY OF ABORTION

The adoption of sentience as a criterion determines the location of a threshold of moral standing. Since sentience admits of degrees, we can in principle construct a continuum ranging from fully sentient creatures at one extreme to completely nonsentient creatures at the other. The threshold of moral standing is that area of the continuum through which sentience fades into nonsentience. In phylogenesis the continuum extends from homo sapiens to the simple animals and plants, and the threshold area is the boundary between vertebrates and invertebrates. In pathology the continuum extends from the fully normal to the totally incapacitated, and the threshold area is the transition from consciousness to unconsciousness. Human ontogenesis also presents us with a continuum from adult to zygote. The threshold area will be the stage at which sentience first emerges, but where is that to be located?

A mental life is built upon a physical base. The capacity for sentience is present only when the necessary physiological structures are present. Physiology, and in particular neurophysiology, is our principal guide in locating a threshold in the phylogenetic continuum. Like a stereo system, the brain of our paradigm sentient being is a set of connected components. These components may be roughly sorted into three groups: forebrain (cerebral hemispheres, thalamus, hypothalamus, amygdala), midbrain (cerebellum), and brainstem (upper part of the spinal cord, pineal and pituitary glands). The brainstem and midbrain play no direct role in the individual's conscious life; their various parts regulate homeostasis (temperature, respiration, heartbeat, etc.), secrete hormones, make reflex connections, route nerves, coordinate motor activities, and so on. All of these functions can be carried on in the total absence of consciousness. Cognitive, perceptual, and voluntary motor functions are all localized in the forebrain, more particularly in the cerebral cortex. Sensation (pleasure/pain), emotion, and basic drives (hunger, thirst, sex, etc.) are controlled by subcortical areas in the forebrain. Although the nerves that transmit pleasure/pain impulses are routed through the cortex, their ultimate destination is the limbic system (amygdala, hypothalamus). The most primitive forms of sentience are thus possible in the absence of cortical activity.

Possession of particular neural structures cannot serve as a criterion of moral standing, for we cannot rule out encounters with sentient beings whose structures are quite different from ours. But in all of the species with which we are familiar, the components of the forebrain (or some analogues) are the minimal conditions of sentience. Thus the evolution of the forebrain serves as an indicator of the kind and degree of sentience possessed by a particular animal species. When we turn to human ontogenesis we may rely on the same indicator.

The normal gestation period for our species is 280 days from the onset of the last menstrual period to birth. This duration is usually divided into three equal trimesters of approximately thirteen weeks each. A zygote has no central nervous system of any sort. The spinal cord makes its first appearance early in the embryonic period (third week), and the major divisions between forebrain, midbrain, and brainstem are evident by the end of the eighth week. At the conclusion of the first trimester virtually all of the major neural components can be clearly differentiated and EEG activity is detectable. The months to follow are marked chiefly by the growth and elaboration of the cerebral hemispheres, especially the cortex. The brain of a seven-month fetus is indistinguishable, at least in its gross anatomy, from that of a newborn infant. Furthermore, by the seventh month most of the neurons that the individual's brain will contain during its entire lifetime are already in existence. In the newborn the brain is closer than any other organ to its mature level of development.

There is no doubt that a newborn infant is sentient—that it feels hunger, thirst, physical pain, the pleasure of sucking, and other agreeable and disagreeable sensations. There is also no doubt that a zygote, and also an embryo, are presentient. It is difficult to locate with accuracy the stage during which feeling first emerges in fetal development. The structure of the fetal brain, including the cortex, is well laid down by the end of the second trimester. But there is reason to expect the more primitive and ancient parts of that brain to function before the rest. The needs of the fetus dictate the order of appearance of neural functions. Thus the brainstem is established and functioning first, since it is required for the regulation of heartbeat and other metabolic processes. Since the mammalian fetus develops in an enclosed and protected environment, cognition and perception are not essential for survival and their advent is delayed. It is therefore not surprising that the cortex, the most complex part of the brain and the least important to the fetus, is the last to develop to an operational level.

Simple pleasure/pain sensations would seem to occupy a medial position in this priority ranking. They are localized in a part of the brain that is more primitive than the cortex, but they could have little practical role for a being that is by and large unable either to seek pleasurable stimuli or to avoid painful ones. Behavioral evidence is by its very nature ambiguous. Before the end of the first trimester, the fetus will react to unpleasant stimuli by flinching and withdrawing. However, this reaction is probably a reflex that is entirely automatic. How are we to tell when mere reflex has crossed over into consciousness? The information we now possess does not enable us to date with accuracy the emergence of fetal sentience. Of some judgments, however, we can be reasonably confident. First-trimester fetuses are clearly not yet sentient. Third-trimester fetuses probably possess some degree of sentience, however minimal. The threshold of sentience thus appears to fall in the second trimester. More ancient and primitive than cognition, the ability to discriminate simple sensations of pleasure and pain is probably the first form of consciousness to appear in the ontogenetic order. Further, when sentience emerges it does not do so suddenly. The best we can hope for is to locate a threshold stage or period in the second trimester. It is at present unclear just how far into that trimester this stage occurs.

The phylogenetic and pathological continua yield us clear cases at the extremes and unclear cases in the middle. The ontogenetic continuum does the same. Because there is no quantum leap into consciousness during fetal development, there is no clean and sharp boundary between sentient and nonsentient fetuses. There is therefore no precise point at which a fetus acquires moral standing. More and better information may enable us to locate the threshold stage ever more accurately, but it will never collapse that stage into a point. We are therefore inevitably confronted with a class of fetuses around the threshold stage whose sentience, and therefore whose moral status, is indeterminate.

A criterion based on sentience enables us to explain the status of other putative thresholds. Neither conception nor birth marks the transition from a presentient to a sentient being. A zygote has not one whit more consciousness than the gametes out of which it is formed. Likewise, although a neonate has more opportunity to employ its powers, it also has no greater capacity for sensation than a full-term fetus. Of thresholds located during gestation, quickening is the perception of fetal movement that is probably reflex and therefore preconscious. Only viability has some relevance, though at one remove. A fetus is viable when it is equipped to survive in the outside world. A being that is aware of, and can respond to, its own inner states is able to communicate its needs to others. This ability is of no use *in utero* but may aid survival in an extrauterine environment. A fetus is therefore probably sentient by the conventional stage of viability (around the end of the second trimester). Viability can therefore serve as a (rough) indicator of moral standing.

Our common moral consciousness locates contraception and infanticide in quite different moral categories. This fact suggests implicit recognition of a basic asymmetry between choosing not to create a new life in the first place and choosing to destroy a new life once it has been created. The boundary between the two kinds of act is the threshold at which that life gains moral protection. Since gametes lack moral standing, contraception (however it is carried out) merely prevents the creation of a new person. Since an infant has moral standing, infanticide (however it is carried out) destroys a new person. A second-trimester threshold of moral standing introduces this asymmetry into the moral assessment of abortion. We may define an early abortion as one performed sometime during the first trimester or early in the second and a late abortion as one performed sometime late in the second trimester or during the third. An early abortion belongs in the same moral category as contraception: it prevents the emergence of a new being with moral standing. A late abortion belongs in the same moral category as infanticide: it terminates the life of a new being with moral standing. The threshold of sentience thus extends the morality of contraception forward to cover early abortion and extends the morality of infanticide backward to cover late abortion. One of the sentiments voiced by many people who contemplate the problem of abortion is that early abortions are importantly different from late ones. The abortion techniques of the first trimester (the IUD, menstrual extraction, vacuum aspiration) are not to be treated as cases of homicide. Those employed later in pregnancy (saline induction, hysterotomy) may, however, have a moral quality approaching that of infanticide. For most people, qualms about abortion are qualms about late abortion. It is a virtue of the sentience criterion that it explains and supports this differential approach.

The moral issues raised by early abortion are precisely those raised by contraception. It is for early abortions that the liberal view is appropriate. Since the fetus at this stage has no right to life, early abortion (like contraception) cannot violate its rights. But if it violates no one's rights, early abortion (like contraception) is a private act. There are of course significant differences between contraception and early abortion, since the former is generally less hazardous, less arduous, and less expensive. A woman has, therefore, good prudential reasons for relying on contraception as her primary means of birth control. But if she elects an early abortion, then, whatever the circumstances and whatever her reasons, she does nothing immoral.[16]

The moral issues raised by late abortion are similar to those raised by infanticide. It is for late abortions that (a weakened form of) the conservative view is appropriate. Since the fetus at this stage has a right to life, late abortion (like infanticide) may violate its rights. But if it may violate the fetus' rights, then late abortion (like infanticide) is a public act. There is, however, a morally significant difference between late abortion and infanticide. A fetus is parasitic upon a unique individual in a manner in which a newborn infant is not. That parasitic relation will justify late abortion more liberally than infanticide, for they do not occur under the same circumstances.

Since we have already explored the morality of abortion for those cases in which the fetus has moral standing, the general approach to late abortions is clear enough. Unlike the simple and uniform treatment of early abortion, only a case-by-case analysis will here suffice. We should expect a serious threat to the woman's life or health (physical or mental) to justify abortion, especially if that threat becomes apparent only late in pregnancy. We should also expect a risk of serious fetal deformity to justify abortion, again especially if that risk becomes apparent (as it usually does) only late in pregnancy. On the other hand, it should not be necessary to justify abortion on the ground that pregnancy was not consented to, since a woman will have ample opportunity to seek an abortion before the threshold stage. If a woman freely elects to continue a pregnancy past that stage, she will thereafter need a serious reason to end it.

A differential view of abortion is therefore liberal concerning early abortion and conservative (in an extended sense) concerning late abortion. The status of the borderline cases in the middle weeks of the second trimester is simply indeterminate. We cannot say of them with certainty either that the fetus has a right to life or that it does not. Therefore we also cannot say either that a liberal approach to these abortions is suitable or that a conservative treatment of them is required. What we can say is that, from the moral point of view, the earlier an abortion is performed the better. There are thus good moral reasons, as well as good prudential ones, for women not to delay their abortions.

A liberal view of early abortion in effect extends a woman's deadline for deciding whether to have a child. If all abortion is immoral, her sovereignty over that decision ends at conception. Given the vicissitudes of contraception, a deadline drawn that early is an enormous practical burden. A deadline in the second trimester allows a woman enough time to discover that she is pregnant and to decide whether to continue the pregnancy. If she chooses not to continue it, her decision violates neither her duties nor any other being's rights. From the point of view of the fetus, the upshot of this treatment of early abortion is that its life is for a period merely probationary; only when it has passed the threshold will that life be accorded protection. If an abortion is elected before the threshold, it is as though from the moral point of view that individual had never existed.

Settling on sentience as a criterion of moral standing thus leads us to a view of the moral status of the fetus, and of the morality of abortion, which satisfies the constraints set out in Section I. It is gradual, since it locates a threshold stage rather than a point and allows moral standing to be acquired incrementally. It is differential, since it locates the threshold stage during gestation and thus distinguishes the moral status of newly conceived and full-term fetuses. It is developmental, since it grounds the acquisition of moral standing in one aspect of the normal development of the fetus. And it is moderate, since it distinguishes the moral status of early and late abortions and applies each of the established views to that range of cases for which it is appropriate.

IV

AN ABORTION POLICY

[For reasons of space, Professor Sumner's detailed recommendations have been omitted—Ed.]

There is, therefore, a third way with the abortion issue. Its superiority over the established views lies largely in its sensitivity to a factor which both of them are committed to ignoring: the manifest differences between a fetus at the beginning and at the end of its prenatal existance. Views which deny the relevance of this factor deserve to command no more than minority support. Those who, for this reason, can embrace neither of the established views need feel no diffidence about seeking a middle ground between them. A moderate and differential view of abortion is capable of drawing the common-sense distinction between early and late abortions, and of showing that such a distinction is neither shallow nor arbitrary. The view from the middle lacks of course the simplicity which has made it so easy to market its more extreme counterparts. But then why should we think that the moral problems raised by abortion are simple?

NOTES

This paper is a revised version of Chapter 4 of *Abortion and Moral Theory* (Princeton, 1981); [also reprinted in Joel Feinberg, ed., *The Problem of Abortion* (Belmont, Cal., 1983)—Ed.]

[1] I will not be defending this assessment in the present paper. For the arguments see *Abortion and Moral Theory*, Chaps. 2 and 3.

[2] *Abortion and Moral Theory*, Chaps. 5 and 6.

[3] The adoption of this working definition of moral standing should not be construed as a concession that rights are the appropriate category for dealing with the moral issues posed by abortion. But since both of the established views employ the rhetoric of rights, there is some point to showing how that rhetoric is equally available to a moderate view. For a generalized notion of moral standing freed from all connection with rights, see *Abortion and Moral Theory*, Section 23.

[4] Or so we shall assume, though it is certainly possible that some (natural or artificial) entity might display signs of intelligence but no signs of either sentience or life. We might, for instance, create forms of artificial intelligence before creating forms of artificial life.

[5] Kenneth E. Goodpaster, "On Being Morally Considerable," *Journal of Philosophy* 75, no. 6 (June 1978). Goodpaster speaks of "moral considerability" where we are speaking of moral standing. The notions are identical, except for the fact that Goodpaster explicitly refrains from restricting moral considerability to possession of rights, let alone the right to life. Nothing in my assessment of Goodpaster's view will hang on this issue of rights.

[6] In the paragraph to follow I have stated that case in my own words.

[7] These are my terms; Goodpaster distinguishes between a criterion of moral considerability and a criterion of moral significance (311). It is odd that when Goodpaster addresses the practical problems created by treating life as an inclusion criterion (324) he does not appeal to the inclusion/comparison distinction. Instead he invokes the quite different distinction between its being reasonable to attribute standing to a creature and its being (psychologically and causally) possible to act on that attribution. One would have thought the question is not what we *can* bring ourselves to do but what we *ought* to bring ourselves to do, and that the inclusion/comparison distinction is precisely designed to help us answer this question.

[8] Goodpaster does not defend separating the two criteria but merely says "we should not expect that the criterion for having 'moral standing' at all will be the same as the criterion for adjudicating competing claims to priority among beings that merit that standing" (311). Certainly inclusion and comparison criteria can be different, as in Mill's celebrated evaluation of pleasures. For Mill every pleasure has some value simply in virtue of being a pleasure (inclusion), but its relative value is partly determined by its quality or kind (comparison). All of this is quite consistent (despite claims to the contrary by some critics) because every pleasure has some quality or other. Goodpaster's comparison criterion threatens to be narrower than his inclusion criterion; it certainly will be if degrees of standing are based on sentience, since many living things have no sentience at all. It is inconsistent to base degrees of standing on (variations) in a property and also to extend (some) standing to beings who lack that property entirely.

[9] Goodpaster does not shrink from attributing interests to nonsentient organisms since he assumes that if a being has needs, a good, and a capacity to be benefited and harmed, then that being has interests. There is much support for this assumption in the dictionary definitions of both "interest" and "welfare," though talk of protecting the interests or welfare of plants seems contrived and strained. But philosophers and economists have evolved technical definitions of "interest" and "welfare" that clearly tie these notions to the psychological states of sentient beings. It is the existence of beings with interests or welfare *in this sense* that is a necessary condition of the existence of moral issues.

[10] Possession of a capacity at a given time does not entail that the capacity is being manifested or displayed at that time. A person does not lose the capacity to use language, for instance, in virtue of remaining silent or being asleep. The capacity remains as long as the appropriate performance could be elicited by the appropriate stimuli. It is lost only when this performance can no longer be evoked (as when the person has become catatonic or comatose). Basing moral standing on the possession of some capacity or set of capacities does not therefore entail silly results, such as that persons lose their rights when they fall asleep. This applies of course, not only to rationality but also to other capacities, such as sentience.

[11] The practical impact of basing moral standing on rationality will, however, depend on which particular capacities are treated as central. Practical rationality (the ability to adjust means to ends, and vice versa) is, for instance, much more widely distributed through the animal kingdom than is the use of language.

[12] A.I. Melden, *Rights and Persons* (Oxford, 1977).

[13] Melden rejects rationality as a criterion of standing (187), but only on the ground that a being's rationality does not ensure its possessing a sense of morality. Clearly rationality is a necessary condition of moral agency. Thus a criterion of moral agency will not extend standing beyond the class of rational beings.

[14] Whether or not this is so will depend on how strong the conditions of moral agency are. Certainly many nonhuman species display altruism, if we mean by this a concern for the well-being of conspecifics and a willingness to accept personal sacrifices for their good. On 199 Melden enumerates a number of features of our lives that are to serve as the basis of our possession of rights; virtually all mammals display all of these features.

[15] It is unclear at present whether invertebrates are capable of feeling pain, though the discovery of endorphins (opiates manufactured by the body) even in very simple organisms suggests that they may be. If so, then we are committed to extending (some) moral standing to invertebrates as well.

[16] Unless there are circumstances (such as extreme underpopulation) in which contraception would also be immoral.

In Defense of Abortion and Infanticide

MICHAEL TOOLEY

This essay deals with the question of the morality of abortion and infanticide. The fundamental ethical objection traditionally advanced against these practices rests on the contention that human fetuses and infants have a right to life. It is this claim which will be the focus of attention here. The basic issue to be discussed, then, is what properties a thing must possess in order to have a right to life. My approach will be to set out and defend a basic moral principle specifying a condition an organism must satisfy if it is to have a right to life. It will be seen that this condition is not satisfied by human fetuses and infants, and thus that they do not have a right to life. So unless there are other objections to abortion and infanticide which are sound, one is forced to conclude that these practices are morally acceptable ones.[1] In contrast, it may turn out that our treatment of adult members of some other species is morally indefensible. For it is quite possible that some nonhuman animals do possess properties that endow them with a right to life.

I

ABORTION AND INFANTICIDE

What reason is there for raising the question of the morality of infanticide? One reason is that it seems very difficult to formulate a completely satisfactory pro-abortion position without coming to grips with the infanticide issue. For the problem that the liberal on abortion encounters here is that of specifying a cutoff point which is not arbitrary: at what stage in the development of a human being does it cease to be morally permissible to destroy it, and why?

It is important to be clear about the difficulty here. The problem is not, as some have thought, that since there is a continuous line of development from a zygote to a newborn baby, one cannot hold that it is seriously wrong to destroy a newborn baby without also holding that it is seriously wrong to destroy a zygote, or any intermediate stage in the development of a human being. The problem is rather that if one says that it is wrong to destroy a newborn baby but not a zygote or some intermediate stage, one should be prepared to point to a *morally relevant* difference between a newborn baby and the earlier stage in the development of a human being.

Precisely the same difficulty can, of course, be raised for a person who holds that infanticide is morally permissible, since one can ask what morally relevant difference there is between an adult human being and a newborn baby. What makes it morally permissible to destroy a baby, but wrong to kill an adult? So the challenge remains. But I shall argue that in the latter case there is an extremely plausible answer.

Reflecting on the morality of infanticide forces one to face up to this challenge. In the case of abortion a number of events—quickening or viability, for instance—might be taken as cutoff points, and it is easy to overlook the fact that none of these events involves any morally significant change in the developing human. In contrast, if one is going to defend infanticide, one has to get very clear about what it is that gives something a right to life.

One of the interesting ways in which the abortion issue differs from most other moral issues is that the plausible positions on abortion appear to be extreme ones. For if a human fetus has a right to life, one is inclined to say that, in general, one would be justified in killing it only to save the life of the mother, and perhaps not even in that case.[2] Such is the extreme anti-abortion position. On the other hand, if the fetus does not have a right to life, why should it be seriously wrong to destroy it? Why would one need to point to special circumstances—such as the presence of genetic disease, or a threat to the woman's health—in order to justify such action? The upshot is that there does not appear to be any room for a moderate position on abortion such as one finds, for example, in the Model Penal Code recommendations.[3]

Aside from the light it may shed on the abortion question, the issue of infanticide is both interesting and important in its own right. The theoretical interest has been mentioned above: it forces one to face up to the question of what it is that gives something a right to life. The practical importance need not be labored. Most people would prefer to raise children who do not suffer from gross deformities or from severe physical, emotional, or intellectual handicaps. If it could be shown that there is no moral objection to infanticide, the happiness of society could be significantly and justifiably increased.

The suggestion that infanticide may be morally permissible is not an idea that many people are able to consider dispassionately. Even philosophers tend to react in a way which seems primarily visceral—offering no arguments, and dismissing infanticide out of hand.

Some philosophers have argued, however, that such a reaction is not inappropriate, on the ground that, first, moral principles must, in the final analysis, be justified by reference to our moral feelings, or intuitions, and secondly, infanticide is one practice that is judged wrong by virtually everyone's moral intuition. I believe, however, that this line of thought is unsound, and I have argued elsewhere that even if one grants, at least for the sake of argument, that moral intuitions are the final court of appeal regarding the acceptability of moral principles, the question of the morality of infanticide is not one that can be settled by an appeal to our intuitions concerning it.[4] If infanticide is to be rejected, an argument is needed, and I believe that the considerations advanced in this essay show that it is unlikely that such an argument is forthcoming.

II

WHAT SORT OF BEING CAN POSSESS A RIGHT TO LIFE?

The issues of the morality of abortion and of infanticide seem to turn primarily upon the answers to the following four questions:

1. What properties, other than potentialities, give something a right to life?
2. Do the corresponding potentialities also endow something with a right to life?
3. If not, do they at least make it seriously wrong to destroy it?
4. At what point in its development does a member of the biologically defined species *Homo sapiens* first possess those nonpotential properties that give something a right to life?

The argument to be developed in the present section bears upon the answers to the first two questions.

How can one determine what properties endow a being with a right to life? An approach that I believe is very promising starts out from the observation that there appear to be two radically different sorts of reasons why an entity may lack a certain right. Compare, for example, the following two claims:

1. A child does not have a right to smoke;
2. A newspaper does not have a right not to be torn up.

The first claim raises a substantive moral issue. People might well disagree about it, and support their conflicting views by appealing to different moral theories. The second dispute, in contrast, seems an unlikely candidate for moral dispute. It is natural to say that newspapers just are not the sort of thing that can have any rights at all, including a right not to be torn up. So there is no need to appeal to a substantive moral theory to resolve the question whether a newspaper has a right not to be torn up.

One way of characterizing this difference . . . is to say that the second claim, unlike the first, is true in virtue of a certain *conceptual* connection, and that is why no moral theory is needed in order to see that it is true. The explanation, then, of why it is that a newspaper does not have a right not to be torn up, is that there is some property P such that, first, newspapers lack property P, and secondly, it is a conceptual truth that only things with property P can be possessors of rights.

What might property P be? A plausible answer, I believe, is set out and defended by Joel Feinberg in his paper, "The Rights of Animals and Unborn Generations."[5] It takes the form of what Feinberg refers to as the *interest principle*: ". . . the sorts of beings who *can* have rights are precisely those who have (or can have) interests."[6] And then, since "interests must be compounded somehow out of conations,"[7] it follows that things devoid of desires, such as newspapers, can have neither interests nor rights. Here, then, is one account of the difference in status between judgments such as (1) and (2) above.

Let us now consider the right to life. The interest principle tells us that an entity cannot have any rights at all, and *a fortiori*, cannot have a right to life, unless it is capable of having interests. This in itself may be a conclusion of considerable importance. Consider, for example, a fertilized human egg cell. Someday it will come to have desires and interests. As a zygote, however, it does not have desires, nor even the *capacity* for having desires. What about interests? This depends upon the account one offers of the relationship between desires and interests. It seems to me that a zygote cannot properly be spoken of as a subject of interests. My reason is roughly this. What is in a thing's interest is a function of its present and future desires, both those it will actually have and those it could have. In the case of an entity that is not presently capable of any desires, its interest must be based entirely upon the satisfaction of future desires. Then, since the satisfaction of future desires presupposes the continued existence of the entity in question, anything which has an interest which is based upon the satisfaction of future desires must also have an interest in its own continued existence. Therefore something which is not presently capable of having any desires at all—like a zygote—cannot have any interests at all unless it has an interest in its own continued existence. I shall argue shortly, however, that a zygote cannot have such an interest. From this it will follow that it cannot have any interests at all, and this conclusion, together with the interest principle, entails that not all members of the species *Homo sapiens* have a right to life.

The interest principle involves, then, a thesis concerning a necessary condition which something must satisfy if it is to have a right to life, and it is a thesis which has important moral implications. It implies, for example, that abortions, if performed sufficiently early, do not involve any violation of a right to life. . . .

It is possible, however, that the interest principle does not exhaust the conceptual connections between rights and interests. It formulates only a very general connection: a thing cannot have any rights at all unless it is capable of having at least some interest. May there not be more specific connections, between particular rights and particular sorts of interests? . . .

. . . These . . . can be summed up, albeit somewhat vaguely, by the following, *particular-interests principle:*

> It is a conceptual truth that an entity cannot have a particular right, R, unless it is at least capable of having some interest, I, which is furthered by its having right R.

Given this particular-interests principle, certain familiar facts, whose importance has not often been appreciated, become comprehensible. Compare an act of killing a normal adult human being with an act of torturing one for five minutes. Though both acts are seriously wrong, they are not equally so. Here, as in most cases, to violate an individual's right to life is more seriously wrong than to violate his right not to have pain inflicted upon him. Consider, however, the corresponding actions in the case of a newborn kitten. Most people feel that it is seriously wrong to torture a kitten for five minutes, but not to kill it painlessly. How is this difference in the moral ordering of the two types of acts, between the human case and the kitten case, to be explained? One answer is that while normal adult human beings have both a right to life and a right not to be tortured, a kitten has only the latter. But why should this be so? The particular-interests principle suggests a possible explanation. Though kittens have some interests, including, in particular, an interest in not being tortured, which derives from their capacity to feel pain, they do not have an interest in their own continued existence, and hence do not have a right not to be destroyed. This answer contains, of course, a large promissory element. One needs a defense of the view that kittens have no interest in continued existence. But the point here is simply that there is an important question about the rationale underlying the moral ordering of certain sorts of acts, and that the particular-interests principle points to a possible answer. . . .

It would be widely agreed, I believe, both that rights impose obligations, and that the obligations they impose upon others are *conditional* upon certain factors. . . .

. . . The account which I now prefer, and which I have defended elsewhere,[8] is this:

"A has a right to X"

means the same as

> "A is such that it can be in A's interest to have X, and *either* (i) A is not capable of making an informed and rational choice whether to grant others permission to deprive him of X, in which case, if it is in A's interest not to be deprived of X, then, by that fact alone, others are under a *prima facie* obligation not to deprive A of X, or (ii) A is capable of making an informed and rational choice whether to grant others permission to deprive him of X, in which case others are under a *prima facie* obligation not to deprive A of X if and only if A has not granted them permission to do so."

And if this account, or something rather similar is correct, then so is the particular-interests principle.

What I now want to do is to apply the particular-interests principle to the case of the right to life. First, however, one needs to notice that the expression, "right to life," is not entirely happy, since it suggests that the right in question concerns the continued existence of a biological organism. That this is incorrect can be brought out by considering possible ways of violating an individual's right to life. Suppose, for example, that future technological developments make it possible to change completely the neural networks in a brain, and that the brain of some normal adult human being is thus completely reprogrammed, so that the organism in question winds up with memories (or rather, apparent memories), beliefs, attitudes, and personality traits totally different from those associated with it before it was subjected to reprogramming. (The pope is reprogrammed, say, on the model of Bertrand Russell.) In such a case, however beneficial the change might be, one would surely want to say that *someone* had been destroyed, that an adult human being's right to life had been violated, even though no biological organism had been killed. This shows that the expression, "right to life," is misleading, since what one is concerned about is not just the continued existence of a biological organism.

How, then, might the right in question be more accurately described? A natural suggestion is that the expression, "right to life," refers to the right of a subject of experiences and other mental states to continue to exist. It might be contended, however, that this interpretation begs the question against certain possible views. For someone might hold—and surely some people in fact do—that while continuing subjects of experiences and other mental states certainly have a right to life, so do some other organisms that are only potentially such continuing subjects, such as human fetuses. A right to life, on this view, is *either* the right of a subject of experiences to continue to exist, *or* the right of something that is only potentially a continuing subject of experiences to become such an entity.

This view is, I believe, to be rejected, for at least two reasons. In the first place, this view appears to be clearly incompatible with the interest principle, as well as with the particular-interests principle. Secondly, this position entails that the destruction of potential persons is, in general, *prima facie* seriously wrong, and I shall argue, in the next section, that the latter view is incorrect.

Let us consider, then, the right of a subject of experiences and other mental states to continue to exist. The particular-interests principle implies that something cannot possibly have such a right unless its continued existence can be in its interest. We need to ask, then, what must be the case if the continued existence of something is to be in its interest.

. . . The picture that emerges . . . is this. In the first place, nothing at all can be in an entity's interest unless it has desires at some time or other. But more than this is required if the continued existence of the entity is to be in its own interest. One possibility, which will generally be sufficient, is that the individual have, at the time in question, a desire for its own continued existence. Yet it also seems clear that an individual's continued existence can be in its own interest even when such a desire is not present. What is needed, apparently, is that the continued existence of the individual will make possible the satisfaction of some desires existing at other times. But not just any desires existing at other times will do. . . . It is crucial that they be desires that belong to one and the same subject of consciousness.

The critical question, then, concerns the conditions under which desires existing at different times can be correctly attributed to a single, continuing subject of consciousness. This question raises a number of difficult issues which cannot be considered here. Part of the rationale underlying the view I wish to advance will be clear, however, if one considers the role played by memory in the psychological unity of an individual over time. When I remember a past experience, what I know is not merely that there was a certain experience which someone or other had, but that there was an experience that belonged to the *same* individual as the present memory beliefs, and it seems clear that this feature of one's memories is, in general, a crucial part of what it is that makes one a continuing subject of experiences, rather than merely a series of psychologically isolated, momentary subjects of consciousness. This suggests something like the following principle:

> Desires existing at different times can belong to a single, continuing subject of consciousness only if that subject of consciousness possesses, at some time, the concept of a continuing self or mental substance.[9]

Given this principle, together with the particular-rights principle, one can set out the following argument in support of a claim concerning a necessary condition which an entity must satisfy if it is to have a right to life:

1. The concept of a right is such that an individual cannot have a right at time T to continued existence unless the individual is such that it can be in its interest at time T that it continue to exist.
2. The continued existence of a given subject of consciousness cannot be in that individual's interest at time T unless *either* that individual has a desire, at time T, to continue to exist as a subject of consciousness, *or* that individual can have desires at other times.
3. An individual cannot have a desire to continue to exist as a subject of consciousness unless it possesses the concept of a continuing self or mental substance.
4. An individual existing at one time cannot have desires at other times unless there is at least one time at which it possesses the concept of a continuing self or mental substance.

Therefore:

5. An individual cannot have a right to continued existence unless there is at least one time at which it possesses the concept of a continuing self or mental substance.

This conclusion is obviously significant. But precisely what implications does it have with respect to the morality of abortion and infanticide? The answer will depend upon what relationship there is between, on the one hand, the behavioral and neurophysiological development of a human being, and, on the other, the development of that individual's mind. . . .

If one [adopts] the view that there is a close relation between the behavioral and neurophysiological development of a human being, and the development of its mind, then the above conclusion has a very important, and possibly decisive implication with respect to the morality of abortion and infanticide. For when human development, both behavioral and neurophysiological, is closely examined, it is seen to be most unlikely that human fetuses, or even newborn babies, possess any concept of a continuing self.[10] And in the light of the above conclusion, this means that such individuals do not possess a right to life. . . .

III

IS IT MORALLY WRONG TO DESTROY POTENTIAL PERSONS?

In this section I shall consider the question of whether it can be seriously wrong to destroy an entity, not because of the nonpotential properties it presently possesses, but because of the properties it will later come to have, if it is not interfered with. First, however, we need to be clear why this is such a crucial question. We can do this by considering a line of thought that has led some people to feel that the anti-abortionist position is more defensible than that of the pro-abortionist. The argument in question rests upon the gradual and continuous development of an organism as it changes from a zygote into an adult human being. The anti-abortionist can point to this development, and argue that it is morally arbitrary for a pro-abortionist to draw a line at some point in this continuous process—such as at birth, or viability—and to say that killing is permissible before, but not after, that particular point.

The pro-abortionist reply would be, I think, that the emphasis upon the continuity of the process is misleading. What the anti-abortionist is really doing is simply challenging the pro-abortionist to specify what properties a thing must have in order to have a right to life, and to show that the developing organism does acquire those properties at the point in question. The pro-abortionist may then be tempted to argue that the difficulty he has in meeting this challenge should not be taken as grounds for rejecting his position. For the anti-abortionist cannot meet this challenge either; he is equally unable to say what properties something must have if it is to have a right to life.

Although this rejoinder does not dispose of the anti-abortionist argument, it is not without bite. For defenders of the view that abortion is almost always wrong have failed to face up to the question of the *basic* moral principles on which their position rests—where a basic moral principle is one whose acceptability does not rest upon the truth of any factual claim of a nonmoral sort.[11] They have been content to assert the wrongness of killing any organism, from a zygote on, if that organism is a member of the biologically defined species *Homo sapiens*. But they have overlooked the point that this cannot be an acceptable *basic* moral principle, since difference in species is not *in itself* a morally relevant difference.[12]

The anti-abortionist can reply, however, that it is possible to defend his position, but not a pro-abortion position, *without* getting clear about the properties a thing must possess if it is to have a right to life. For one can appeal to the following two claims. First, that there is a property, even if one is unable to specify what it is, that (i) is possessed by normal adult humans, and (ii) endows any being possessing it with a right to life. Secondly, that if there are properties which satisfy (i) and (ii), at least one of those properties will be such that any organism potentially possessing that property has a right to life even now, simply in virtue of that potentiality—where an organism possesses a property potentially if it will come to have it in the normal course of its development.

The second claim—which I shall refer to as the potentiality principle—is crucial to the anti-abortionist's defense of his position. Given that principle, the anti-abortionist can defend his position without grappling with the very difficult question of what nonpotential properties an entity must possess in order to have a right to life. It is enough to know that adult members of *Homo sapiens* do have such a right. For then one can employ the potentiality principle to conclude that any organism which belongs to the species *Homo sapiens*, from a zygote on—with the possible exception of those that suffer from certain gross neurophysiological abnormalities—must also have a right to life.

The pro-abortionist, in contrast, cannot mount a comparable argument. He cannot defend his position without offering at least a partial answer to the question of what properties a thing must possess in order to have a right to life.

The importance of the potentiality principle, however, goes beyond the fact that it provides support for an anti-abortion position. For it seems that if the potentiality principle is unsound, then there is no acceptable defense of an extreme conservative view on abortion.

The reason is this. Suppose that the claim that an organism's having certain potentialities is sufficient grounds for its having a right to life cannot be sustained. The claim that a fetus which is a member of *Homo sapiens* has a right to life can then be attacked as follows. The reason an adult member of *Homo sapiens* has a right to life, but an infant ape, say, does not, is that there are certain psychological properties which the former possesses and the latter does not. Now even if one is unsure exactly what the relevant psychological characteristics are, it seems clear that an organism in the early stages of development from a zygote into an adult member of *Homo sapiens* does not possess those properties. One need merely compare a human fetus with an ape fetus. In early stages of development, neither will have any mental life at all. (Does a zygote have a mental life? Does it have experiences? Or beliefs? Or desires?) In later stages of fetal development some mental events presumably occur, but these will be of a very rudimentary sort. The crucial point, however, is that given what we know through comparative studies of, on the one hand, brain development, and, on the other, behavior after birth, it is surely reasonable to hold that there are no significant differences in the respective mental lives of a human fetus and an ape fetus. There are, of course, physiological differences, but these are not in themselves morally significant. *If* one held that potentialities were relevant to the ascription of a right to life, one could argue that the physiological differences, though not morally relevant in themselves, are morally relevant in virtue of their causal consequences: they will lead to later psychological differences that are morally relevant, and for this reason the physiological differences are themselves morally significant. But if the potentiality principle is not available, this line of argument cannot be used, and there will then be no differences between a human fetus and an ape fetus that the anti-abortionist can use as grounds for ascribing a right to life to the former but not to the latter. . . .

The conclusion seems to be, then, that the anti-abortionist position is defensible only if the potentiality principle is sound. Let us now consider what can be said against that principle. One way of attacking it is by appealing to the conclusion advanced in the previous section, to the effect that an individual cannot have a right to continued existence unless there is at least one time at which it possesses the concept of a continuing self or mental substance. This principle entails the denial of the potentiality principle. Or more precisely, it does so in conjunction with the presumably uncontroversial empirical claim that a fertilized human egg cell, which does possess the relevant potentialities, does not possess the concept of a continuing self or mental substance.

Alternatively, one could appeal to the more modest claim involved in the interest principle, and use it to argue that since a fertilized human egg cell cannot have any interests at all, it cannot have any rights, and *a fortiori* cannot have a right to life. So potentialities alone cannot endow something with a right to life.

Given these lines of argument, is there any reason not to rest the case at this point? I want to suggest that there are at least two reasons why one needs to take a closer look at the potentiality principle. The first is that some people who are anti-abortionists may wish to reject not only the particular-interests principle, but also the more modest interest principle, and although I believe that this response to the above arguments is unsound, I think it is important to see whether there aren't other arguments that are untouched by this reply.

A second, and more important reason why it is unwise to base one's case against the anti-abortionist entirely upon an appeal to principles such as the interest principle is this. The anti-abortionist can modify his position slightly, and avoid the arguments in question. Specifically, he can abandon his claim that a human fetus has a right to life, but contend that it is nevertheless seriously wrong to kill it. Some philosophers would feel that such a modification cannot possibly be acceptable, on the ground that no action can be seriously wrong unless it violates someone's right to something. It seems to me, however, that this latter view is in fact mistaken.[13] In any case, let us consider the position that results from this modification. An anti-abortionist who is willing to adopt this position can then appeal, not to the potentiality principle, but to the following *modified potentiality principle:*

If there are properties possessed by normal adult human beings that endow any organism possessing them with a right to life, then at least one of those properties is such that it is seriously wrong to kill any organism that potentially possesses that property, simply in virtue of that potentiality.

Since this modified potentiality principle is not concerned with the attribution of rights to organisms, it cannot be attacked by appealing to the interest principle, or to the particular-interests principle, or to some analysis of the concept of a right.

Let us now consider how the case against the anti-abortionist position can be strengthened. I shall advance three arguments which are objections to both the original and the modified potentiality principles. Since the original potentiality principle cannot be correct unless the modified one is, it will suffice to consider only the modified principle. The basic issue, then, is this. Is there any property J which satisfies the following three conditions:

1. There is a property, K, such that any individual possessing property K has a right to life, and there is a scientific law, L, to the effect that any organism possessing property J will, in the normal course of events, come to possess property K at some later time;
2. Given the relationship just described between property J and property K, it is seriously wrong to kill anything possessing property J;
3. If property J were not related to property K in the way indicated, the fact that an organism possessed property J would not make it seriously wrong to kill it.

In short, the question is whether there is a property, *J*, that makes it seriously wrong to kill something *only because J* stands in a certain causal relation to a second property, *K*, which is such that anything possessing that property *ipso facto* has a right to life.

My first objection turns upon the claim that if one accepts the modified potentiality principle, one ought also to accept the following, *generalized potentiality principle:*

> If there are any properties possessed by normal adult human beings that endow any organism possessing them with a right to life, then at least one of those properties is such that it is seriously wrong to perform any action that will prevent some system, which otherwise would have developed the property, from doing so.

This generalized potentiality principle differs from the original and the modified potentiality principles in two respects. First, it applies to *systems* of objects, and not merely to organisms. I think that this first generalization is one that ought to be accepted by anyone who accepts either the original or the modified principle. For why should it make any difference whether the potentiality resides in a single organism, or in a system of organisms that are so interrelated that they will in the normal course of affairs, due to the operation of natural laws, causally give rise to something that possesses the property in question? Surely it is only the potentiality for a certain outcome that matters, and not whether there are one or more objects interacting and developing in a predetermined way to produce that outcome.

In thinking about this issue, it is important not to confuse *potentialities* with mere *possibilities*. The generalized potentiality principle does not deal with collections of objects that merely have the capacity to interact in certain ways. The objects must already be interrelated in such a way that in the absence of external interference the laws governing their future interaction and development will bring it about that the system will develop the property in question.

The second difference is that the original and modified potentiality principles deal only with the *destruction* of organisms, while the generalized principle deals with any action that prevents an organism, or a system, from developing the relevant property. I think that the anti-abortionist will certainly want to accept this generalization. . . .

Suppose, now, that artificial wombs have been perfected. A healthy, unfertilized human egg cell has been placed in one, along with a large number of spermatozoa. If the device is turned on, the spermatozoa will be carried, via a conveyor belt, to the unfertilized egg cell, where, we can assume, fertilization will take place. The device is such, moreover, that no outside assistance will be needed at any future stage, and nine months later a normal human baby will emerge from the artificial womb. Given these assumptions—all of which are certainly empirically possible—once such a device has been turned on, there will exist an active potentiality that will, if not interfered with, give rise to something that will become an adult human being, and so will have a right to life. But would it be seriously wrong to destroy that potentiality—as might be done, for example, by turning off the machine, or by cutting the conveyor belt, so that fertilization does not place? Most people, I believe, would certainly not think that such actions were seriously wrong. If that view is correct, the generalized potentiality principle must be rejected as unsound.

In short, the first argument against the modified potentiality principle, and hence against the original potentiality principle, is as follows. It is reasonable to accept the modified principle only if it is also reasonable to accept the generalized potentiality principle, because whether the potentialities reside in a single organism or in a system does not seem to be a morally significant difference. But to accept the generalized potentiality principle is to commit oneself to the view that interference with an artificial womb so as to prevent fertilization from taking place is just as seriously wrong as abortion, and for precisely the same reason. If, as seems plausible, this is not an acceptable view, then one cannot reasonably accept either the original or the modified potentiality principle.

Let us now turn to my second argument against the modified potentiality principle. This argument turns upon the following crucial claim:

> Let C be any type of causal process where there is some type of occurrence, E, such that processes of type C would possess no intrinsic moral significance were it not for the fact that they result in occurrences of type E.

Then:

> The characteristic of being an act of intervening in a process of type C which prevents the occurrence of an outcome of type E makes an action intrinsically wrong to precisely the same degree as does the characteristic of being an act of ensuring that a causal process of type C, which it was in one's power to initiate, does not get initiated.

This principle, which I shall refer to as the moral symmetry principle with respect to action, would be rejected by some philosophers. They would argue that there is an important distinction to be drawn between "what we owe people in the form of aid and what we owe them in the way of noninterference,"[14] and that the latter, "negative duties," are duties that it is more serious to neglect than the former, "positive" ones. This view arises from an intuitive response to examples such as the following. Even if it is wrong not to send food to starving people in other parts of the world, it is more wrong still to kill someone. And isn't the conclusion, then, that one's obligation to refrain from killing someone is a more serious obligation than one's obligation to save lives?

I want to argue that this is not the correct conclusion. . . . It is probably true, for example, that most cases of killing are morally worse than most cases of merely letting die. This, however, is not an objection to the moral symmetry principle, since that principle does not imply that, all things considered, acts of killing are, in general, morally on a par with cases of allowing someone to die. What the moral symmetry principle implies is rather that, *other things being equal*, it is just as wrong to fail to save someone as it is to kill someone. If one wants to test this principle against one's moral intuitions, one has to be careful to select pairs of situations in which all other morally relevant factors—such as motivation, and risk to the agent—are equivalent. And I have suggested that when this is done, the moral symmetry principle is by no means counterintuitive.[15]

My argument against the modified potentiality principle can now be stated. Suppose at some future time a chemical were to be discovered which when injected into the brain of a kitten would cause the kitten to develop into a cat possessing a brain of the sort possessed by humans, and consequently into a cat having all the psychological capabilities characteristic of normal adult humans. Such cats would be able to think, to use language, and so on. Now it would surely be morally indefensible in such a situation to hold that it is seriously wrong to kill an adult member of the species *Homo sapiens* without also holding that it is wrong to kill any cat that has undergone such a process of development: there would be no morally significant differences.

Secondly, imagine that one has two kittens, one of which has been injected with the special chemical, but which has not yet developed those properties that in themselves endow something with a right to life, and the other of which has not been injected with the special chemical. It follows from the moral symmetry principle that the action of injecting the former with a "neutralizing" chemical that will interfere with the transformation process and prevent the kitten from developing those properties that in themselves would give it a right to life is *prima facie* no more seriously wrong than the action of intentionally refraining from injecting the second kitten with the special chemical.

It perhaps needs to be emphasized here that the moral symmetry principle does not imply that neither action is morally wrong. Perhaps both actions are wrong, even seriously so. The moral symmetry principle implies only that if they are wrong, they are so to precisely the same degree.

Thirdly, compare a kitten that has been injected with the special chemical and then had it neutralized, with a kitten that has never been injected with the chemical. It is clear that it is no more seriously wrong to kill the former than to kill the latter. For although their bodies have undergone different processes in the past, there is no reason why the kittens need differ in any way with respect to either their present properties or their potentialities.

Fourthly, again consider two kittens, one of which has been injected with the special chemical, but which has not yet developed those properties that in themselves would give it a right to life, and the other of which has not been injected with the chemical. It follows from the

previous two steps in the argument that the combined action of injecting the first kitten with a neutralizing chemical and then killing it is no
more seriously wrong than the combined action of intentionally
refraining from injecting the second kitten with the special chemical
and then killing it.

Fifthly, one way of neutralizing the action of the special chemical is
simply to kill the kitten. And since there is surely no reason to hold
that it is more seriously wrong to neutralize the chemical and to kill
the kitten in a single step than in two successive steps, it must be the
case that it is no more seriously wrong to kill a kitten that has been
injected with the special chemical, but which has not developed those
properties that in themselves would give it a right to life, than it is to
inject such a kitten with a neutralizing chemical and then to kill it.

Next, compare a member of *Homo sapiens* that has not developed
far enough to have those properties that in themselves give something
a right to life, but which later will come to have them, with a kitten
that has been injected with the special chemical but which has not yet
had the chance to develop the relevant properties. It is clear that it
cannot be any more seriously wrong to kill the human than to kill the
kitten. The potentialities are the same in both cases. The only difference is that in the case of a human fetus the potentialities have
been present from the beginning of the organism's development,
while in the case of the kitten they have been present only from the
time it was injected with the special chemical. This difference in the
time at which the potentialities were acquired is not a morally relevant
one.

It follows from the previous three steps in the argument that it is no
more seriously wrong to kill a human being that lacks properties that
in themselves, and irrespective of their causal consequences, endow
something with a right to life, but which will naturally develop those
properties, than it would be to intentionally refrain from injecting a
kitten with the special chemical, and to kill it. But if it is the case that
normal adult humans do possess properties that in themselves give
them a right to life, it follows in virtue of the modified potentiality
principle that it is seriously wrong to kill any human organism that
will naturally develop the properties in question. Thus, if the modified potentiality principle is sound, we are forced by the above line of
argument to conclude that if there were a chemical that would transform kittens into animals having the psychological capabilities possessed by adult humans, it would be seriously wrong to intentionally
refrain from injecting kittens with the chemical, and to kill them
instead.

But is it clear that this final conclusion is unacceptable? I believe
that it is. It turns out, however, that this issue is *much* more complex
than most people take it to be.[16] Here, however, it will have to suffice
to note that the vast majority of people would certainly view this conclusion as unacceptable. For while there are at present no special

chemicals that will transform kittens in the required way, there are other biological organisms, namely unfertilized human egg cells, and special chemicals, namely human spermatozoa, that will transform those organisms in the required way. So if one were to hold that it was seriously wrong to intentionally refrain from injecting kittens with the special chemical, and instead to kill them, one would also have to maintain that it was *prima facie* seriously wrong to refrain from injecting human egg cells with spermatozoa, and instead to kill them. So unless the anti-abortionist is prepared to hold that any woman, married or unmarried, does something seriously wrong every month that she intentionally refrains from getting pregnant, he cannot maintain that it would be seriously wrong to refrain from injecting the kitten with the special chemical, and instead to kill it.

In short, the above argument shows that anyone who wants to defend the original or the modified potentiality principle must either argue against the moral symmetry principle, or hold that in a world in which kittens could be transformed into "rational animals," it would be seriously wrong to kill newborn kittens. But we have just seen that if one accepts the latter claim, one must also hold that it is seriously wrong to intentionally refrain from fertilizing a human egg cell, and to kill it instead. Consequently, it seems very likely that any anti-abortionist rejoinder to the present argument will be directed against the moral symmetry principle. In the present essay I have not attempted to offer a thorough defense of that principle, although I have tried to show that what is perhaps the most important objection to it—the one that appeals to a distinction between positive and negative duties—rests upon a superficial analysis of our moral intuitions. Elsewhere, however, I have argued that a thorough examination of the moral symmetry principle sustains the conclusion that that principle is in fact correct. . . .

To sum up, what I have argued in the present section is this. The anti-abortionist position is defensible only if some version of the potentiality principle is sound. The original version of that principle is incompatible, however, both with the particular-interests principle and with the interest principle, and also with the account of the concept of a right offered above. The modified potentiality principle avoids these problems. There are, however, at least three other serious objections which tell against both the original potentiality principle and the modified one. It would seem, therefore, that there are excellent reasons for rejecting the potentiality principle, and with it, the anti-abortionist position.

IV

SUMMARY AND CONCLUSIONS

In this paper I have advanced three main philosophical contentions:

1. An entity cannot have a right to life unless it is capable of having an interest in its own continued existence;
2. An entity is not capable of having an interest in its own continued existence unless it possesses, at some time, the concept of a continuing self, or subject of experiences and other mental states;
3. The fact that an entity will, if not destroyed, come to have properties that would give it a right to life does not in itself make it seriously wrong to destroy it.

If these philosophical contentions are correct, the crucial question is a factual one: At what point does a developing human being acquire the concept of a continuing self, and at what point is it capable of having an interest in its own continued existence? I have not examined this issue in detail here, but I have suggested that careful scientific studies of human development, both behavioral and neurophysiological, strongly support the view that even newborn humans do not have the capacities in question. If this is right, then it would seem that infanticide during a time interval shortly after birth must be viewed as morally acceptable.

But where is the line to be drawn? What is the precise cutoff point? If one maintained, as some philosophers do, that an individual can possess a concept only if it is capable of expressing that concept linguistically, then it would be a relatively simple matter to determine whether a given organism possessed the concept of a continuing subject of experiences and other mental states. It is far from clear, however, that this claim about the necessary connection between the possession of concepts and the having of linguistic capabilities is correct. I would argue, for example, that one wants to ascribe mental states of a conceptual sort—such as beliefs and desires—to animals that are incapable of learning a language, and that an individual cannot have beliefs and desires unless it possesses the concepts involved in those beliefs and desires. And if that view is right—if an organism can acquire concepts without thereby acquiring a way of expressing those concepts linguistically—then the question of whether an individual possesses the concept of a continuing self may be one that requires quite subtle experimental techniques to answer.

If this view of the matter is roughly correct, there are two worries that one is left with at the level of practical moral decisions, one of which may turn out to be deeply disturbing. The lesser worry is the question just raised: Where is the line to be drawn in the case of infanticide? This is not really a troubling question since there is no serious need to know the exact point at which a human infant acquires a right to life. For in the vast majority of cases in which infanticide is desirable due to serious defects from which the baby suffers, its desirability will be apparent at birth or within a very short time thereafter. Since it seems clear that an infant at this point in its development is not capable of possessing the concept of a continuing subject of experiences and other mental states, and so is incapable of having an interest in its own continued existence, infanticide will be morally permissible in the vast majority of cases in which it is, for one reason or another, desirable. The practical moral problem can thus be satisfactorily handled by choosing some short period of time, such as a week after birth, as the interval during which infanticide will be permitted.

The troubling issue which arises out of the above reflections concerns whether adult animals belonging to species other than *Homo sapiens* may not also possess a right to life. For once one allows that an individual can possess concepts, and have beliefs and desires, without being able to express those concepts, or those beliefs and desires, linguistically, then it becomes very much an open question whether animals belonging to other species do not possess properties that give them a right to life. Indeed, I am strongly inclined to think that adult members of at least some nonhuman species do have a right to life. My reason is that, first, I believe that some nonhuman animals are capable of envisaging a future for themselves, and of having desires about future states of themselves. Secondly, that anything which exercises these capacities has an interest in its own continued existence. And thirdly, that having an interest in one's own continued existence is not merely a necessary, but also a sufficient condition, for having a right to life.

The suggestion that at least some nonhuman animals have a right to life is not unfamiliar, but it is one that most of us are accustomed to dismissing very casually. The line of thought advanced here suggests that this attitude may very well turn out to be tragically mistaken. Once one reflects upon the question of the *basic* moral principles involved in the ascription of a right to life to organisms, one may find oneself driven to the conclusion that our everyday treatment of members of other species is morally indefensible, and that we are in fact murdering innocent persons.

NOTES

[1] My forthcoming book, *Abortion and Infanticide*, contains a detailed examination of other important objections.

[2] Judith Jarvis Thomson, in her article "A Defense of Abortion," *Philosophy & Public Affairs* 1, no. 1 (1971), 47-66, argues very forcefully for the view that this conclusion is incorrect. For a critical discussion of her argument, see Chapter 3 of *Abortion and Infanticide*.

[3] Section 230.3 of the American Law Institute's *Model Penal Code* (Phildelphia, 1962).

[4] *Abortion and Infanticide*, Chap. 10.

[5] In William T. Blackstone, ed., *Philosophy and Environmental Crisis* (Athens, Ga., 1974), 43-68.

[6] *Op. cit.*, 51.

[7] *Ibid.*, 49-50.

[8] *Op. cit.*, sect. 5.2.

[9] For a fuller discussion and defense of this principle, see *op. cit.*, sect. 5.3.

10 For a detailed survey of the scientific evidence concerning human development, see *op. cit.*, sect. 11.5.

11 Consider the belief that it is *prima facie* wrong to pull cats' tails. Here is a belief that is almost universally accepted, but very few people, if any, would regard it as a basic moral belief. For this belief rests upon a nonmoral belief, to the effect that pulling cats' tails causes them pain. If one came to believe that cats actually enjoy this, one would abandon the moral belief in question. So the belief, though widely and firmly accepted, is a derived moral belief, rather than a basic one.

12 For a much more extended discussion of this point, see, for example, Peter Singer's essay, "Animals and the Value of Life," in Tom Regan, ed., *Matters of Life and Death* (Philadelphia, 1980), or my own discussion in section 4.2 of *Abortion and Infanticide*.

13 *Op. cit.*, sect. 7.33.

14 Philippa Foot, "The Problem of Abortion and the Doctrine of the Double Effect," *The Oxford Review* 5 (1967), 5-15. See the discussion on pp. 11ff.

15 For a much more detailed defense of this view, see section 6.5 of *Abortion and Infanticide*.

16 A discussion of why this is so can be found in Chapter 7 of *Abortion and Infanticide*.

A Question about Potentiality

JOEL FEINBERG

THE STRICT POTENTIALITY CRITERION

[Let *C* stand for the whole *collection* of traits sufficient to confer commonsense personhood on any being that possesses it.] "All and only those creatures who either actually or potentially possess *C* (that is, who either have *C* now or would come to have *C* in the natural course of events) are moral persons now, fully protected by the rule against homicide." This criterion . . . permits one to draw the line of moral personhood in the human species right at the moment of conception, which will be counted by some as an advantage. It also has the undeniable advantage of immunity from one charge of arbitrariness since it will extend moral personhood to all beings in *any* species or category who possess *C*, either actually or potentially. It may also cohere with our psychological attitudes, since it can explain why it is that many people, at least, think of unformed or unpretty fetuses as precious. Zygotes and embryos in particular are treasured not for what they are but for what they are biologically "programmed" to become in the fullness of time: real people fully possessed of *C*.

The difficulties of this criterion are of two general kinds, those deriving from the obscurity of the concept of "potentiality," which perhaps can be overcome, and the more serious difficulties of answering the charge that merely potential possession of any set of qualifications for a moral status does not logically ensure actual possession of that status. Consider just one of the problems raised by the concept of potentiality itself.[1] How, it might be asked, can a mere zygote be a potential person, whereas a mere spermatozoon or a mere unfertilized ovum is not? If the spermatozoon and ovum we are talking about are precisely those that will combine in a few seconds to form a human zygote, why are they not potential zygotes, and thus potential people, *now*? The defender of the potentiality criterion will reply that it is only at the moment of conception that any being comes into existence with exactly the same chromosomal makeup as the human being that will later emerge from the womb, and it is *that* chromosomal combination that forms the potential person, not anything that exists before it comes together. The reply is probably a cogent one, but uncertainties about the concept of potentiality might make us hesitate, at first, to accept it, for we might be tempted to think of both the germ cell (spermatozoon or ovum) and the zygote as potentially a particular person, while holding that the differences between their potentials, though large and significant to be sure, are nevertheless differences in degree rather than kind. It would be well to resist that temptation, however, for it could lead us to the view that some of the entities and processes that combined still earlier to form a given spermatozoon were themselves potentially that spermatozoon and hence potentially the person that spermatozoon eventually became, and so on. At the end of that road is the proposition that everything is potentially everything else, and thus the destruction of all utility in the concept of potentiality. It is better to hold this particular line at the zygote.

The remaining difficulty for the strict potentiality criterion is much more serious. It is a logical error, some have charged, to deduce *actual* rights from merely *potential* (but not yet actual) qualification for those rights. What follows from potential qualification, it is said, is potential, not actual, rights; what entails actual rights is actual, not potential, qualification. As the Australian philosopher Stanley Benn puts it, "A potential president of the United States is not on that account Commander-in-Chief [of the U.S. Army and Navy]."[2] This simple point can be called "the logical point about potentiality." Taken on its own terms, I don't see how it can be answered as an objection to the strict potentiality criterion. It is still open to an antiabortionist to argue that merely potential commonsense personhood is a ground for *duties* we may have toward the potential person. But he cannot argue that it is the ground for the potential person's *rights* without committing a logical error.

THE MODIFIED OR GRADUALIST POTENTIALITY CRITERION

"Potential possession of *C* confers not a right, but only a claim, to life, but that claim keeps growing stronger, requiring ever stronger reasons to override it, until the point when *C* is actually possessed, by which time it has become a full right to life." This modification of the potentiality criterion has one distinct and important advantage. It coheres with the widely shared feeling that the moral seriousness of abortion increases with the age of the fetus. It is extremely difficult to believe on other than very specific theological grounds that a zygote one day after conception is the sort of being that can have any rights at all, much less the whole armory of "human rights" including "the right to life." But it is equally difficult for a great many people to believe that a full-term fetus one day before birth does not have a right to life. Moreover, it is very difficult to find one point in the continuous development of the fetus before which it is utterly without rights and after which it has exactly the same rights as any adult human being. Some rights in postnatal human life can be acquired instantly or suddenly; the rights of citizenship, for example, come into existence at a precise moment in the naturalization proceedings after an oath has been administered and a judicial pronouncement formally produced and certified. Similarly, the rights of husbands and wives come into existence at just that moment when an authorized person utters the words "I hereby pronounce you husband and wife." But the rights of the fetus cannot possibly jump in this fashion from nonbeing to being at some precise moment in pregnancy. The alternative is to think of them as growing steadily and gradually throughout the entire nine-month period until they are virtually "mature" at parturition. There is, in short, a kind of growth in "moral weight" that proceeds in parallel fashion with the physical growth and development of the fetus.

An "immature right" on this view is not to be thought of simply as no right at all, as if in morals a miss were as good as a mile. A better characterization of the unfinished right would be a "weak right," a claim with some moral force proportional to its degree of development, but not yet as much force as a fully matured right. The key word in this account is "claim." Elsewhere I have given an account of the difference between having a right (which I defined as a "valid claim") and having a claim that is not, or not quite, valid. What would the latter be like?

> One might accumulate just enough evidence to argue with relevance and cogency that one has a right . . . although one's case might not be overwhelmingly conclusive. The argument might be strong enough to entitle one to a hearing and fair consideration. When one is in this position, it might be said that one "has a claim" that deserves to be weighed carefully. Nevertheless the balance of reasons may turn out to militate against recognition of the claim, so that the claim is not a valid claim or right.[3]

Now there are various ways in which a claim can fail to be a right. There are many examples, particularly from the law, where *all* the claims to some property, including some that are relevantly made and worthy of respect, are rejected, simply because none of them is deemed strong enough to qualify as a right. In such cases, a miss truly is as good as a mile. But in other cases, an acknowledged claim of (say) medium strength will be strong enough to be a right *unless* a stronger claim appears on the scene to override it. For these conflict situations, card games provide a useful analogy. In poker, three-of-a-kind is good enough to win the pot unless one of the other players "makes claim" to the pot with a higher hand, say a flush or a full house. The player who claims the pot with three-of-a-kind "has a claim" to the pot that is overridden by the stronger claim of the player with the full house. The strongest claim presented will, by that fact, constitute a right to take the money. The player who withdrew with a four-flush had "no claim at all," but even that person's hand might have established a right to the pot if no stronger claim were in conflict with it.

The analogy applies to the abortion situation in the following way.

The game has at least two players, the mother and the fetus, though more can play, and sometimes the father and/or the doctor are involved too. For the first few weeks of its life, the fetus (zygote, embryo) has hardly any claim to life at all, and virtually any reason of the mother's for aborting it will be strong enough to override a claim made in the fetus's behalf. At any stage in the game, any reason the mother might have for aborting will constitute a claim, but as the fetus matures, its claims grow stronger requiring ever-stronger claims to override them. After three months or so, the fact that an abortion would be "convenient" for the mother will not be a strong enough claim, and the fetus's claim to life will defeat it. In that case, the fetus can be said to have a valid claim or right to life in the same sense that the poker player's full house gives him or her a right to the pot: It is a right in the sense that it is the strongest of the conflicting claims, not in the sense that it is stronger than any conflicting claim that could conceivably come up. By the time the fetus has become a neonate (a newborn child), however, it has a "right to life" of the same kind all people have, and no mere conflicting claim can override it. (Perhaps more accurately, only claims that other human persons make in self-defense to their own lives can ever have an equal strength.)

The modified potentiality criterion has the attractiveness characteristic of compromise theories when fierce ideological quarrels rage between partisans of more extreme views. It shares one fatal flaw, however, with the strict potentiality criterion: Despite its greater flexibility, it cannot evade "the logical point about potentiality." A highly developed fetus is much closer to being a commonsense person with all the developed traits that qualify it for moral personhood than is the mere zygote. But being almost qualified for rights is not the same thing as being partially qualified for rights; nor is it the same thing as being qualified for partial rights, quasi-rights, or weak rights. The advanced fetus is closer to being a person than is the zygote, just as a dog is closer to personhood than a jellyfish, but that is not the same thing as being "more of a person." In 1930, when he was six years old, Jimmy Carter didn't know it, but he was a potential president of the United States. That gave him no claim *then*, not even a very weak claim, to give commands to the U.S. Army and Navy. Franklin D. Roosevelt in 1930 was only two years away from the presidency, so he was a potential president in a much stronger way (the potentiality was much less remote) than was young Jimmy. Nevertheless, he was not actually president, and he had no more of a claim to the prerogatives of the office than did Carter. The analogy to fetuses in different stages of development is of course imperfect. But in both cases it would seem to be invalid to infer the existence of a "weak version of a right" from an "almost qualification" for the full right. In summary, the modified potentiality criterion, insofar as it permits the potential possession of C to be a *sufficient condition* for the actual possession of claims, and in some cases of rights, is seriously flawed in the same manner as the strict potentiality criterion.

NOTES

[Footnotes have been renumbered—Ed.]

1 These problems are discussed in more detail in Joel Feinberg, "The Rights of Animals and Future Generations" (Appendix: The Paradoxes of Potentiality), in W.T. Blackstone, ed., *Philosophy and Environmental Crisis* (Athens, Ga., 1974), 67-8.

2 Stanley I. Benn, "Abortion, Infanticide, and Respect for Persons," in J. Feinberg, ed., *The Problem of Abortion* (Belmont, Cal., 1973), 102.

3 Feinberg, *Social Philosophy* (Englewood Cliffs, N.J., 1973), 66.

Abortion and the Death of the Fetus

STEVEN L. ROSS

Abortion as it is presently practiced may simply be an unhappy compromise between two logically separable actions. An abortion (i) terminates a pregnancy, ending the physical dependency relationship the fetus[1] has to the mother, and (ii) terminates the life of the fetus, ending both its present functions as an organism and its ongoing development into a more complex one. Now performing (ii) will guarantee (i) in any state of affairs, as one cannot (logically) be pregnant unless one is keeping a fetus alive. And in current practice, we cannot perform (i) without simultaneously performing (ii). This however is not a matter of logic but of fact, and like many matters of fact, we can easily imagine it otherwise. It is quite possible, conceptually and practically, that we would be able to separate the fetus from the mother, even at the earliest stages, performing (i), but keep it alive until it is fully viable elsewhere, thereby *not* performing (ii). Abortion then would become skewered on its two struts. There would be abortion$_1$ where the pregnancy but not the life of the fetus would be ended, and abortion$_2$, where the fetus would be killed despite the fact that this was not at all necessary to our accomplishing (i). I will call current practice, where separation and death occur more or less simultaneously, abortion$_3$.

Separating abortion$_3$ into abortion$_1$ and abortion$_2$ seems to take an extremely contentious practice and leave us with two remarkably uncontentious ones. It is difficult to see how we could have any objections to abortion$_1$, and it seems equally difficult to see how we could possibly justify abortion$_2$. With abortion$_1$ everyone should be satisfied. The liberal achieves the termination of an unwanted pregnancy, without the result that so infuriates the conservative, the termination of what is surely in some sense an innocent life.[2] There is no reason to think of the death of the fetus as something the liberal passionately wants so much as something, given what he does want, he is prepared to accept. That is, his commitment to abortion$_1$ is strong enough to carry him over into a commitment to abortion$_3$, even though this brings with it the additional unpleasantries of abortion$_2$. The conservative starts at the other end and moves in the opposite direction: he is sufficiently repulsed by abortion$_2$ to oppose abortion$_3$, even though insofar as abortion₃ involves abortion₁, clearly there are some things that may be said in defense of it.

Some have said that if we abort early enough, that which is being terminated is so far from being anything remotely like a person that it just isn't worth getting terribly excited about. But even if this concept of the fetus is granted without qualification, and it is far from clear that it should be, on its own it can hardly justify our killing it. I am not talking about what you may or may not have a *right* to do, but what you can be said to have a good *reason* to do. You might have on your window ledge an utterly insignificant onion shoot, and you may have excellent reason to get it out of your house and throw it away. But if a neighbor begged you to let him have it instead, if he said it was of the utmost importance that you let him take the burden off your hands, if you saw he was quite sincere and so forth, what possible reason could you have to refuse? It may be said that no one could possibly care so much about something like an onion shoot. But this is indeed a weak excuse for destroying it. Add that this shoot will in a fairly short period become a person, and any mystery over someone else's concern instantly vanishes. Hence so long as we give an account remotely faithful to what the fetus is, it would seem we could give no good reason for destroying it if its survival elsewhere did not inconvenience us.

And if this is correct, it would seem we are faced with something like a fork: we either defend abortion₂ or ordinary elective abortions³ become permissible only because they are performed at a time when no other way of ending a pregnancy is available. I will set aside the question whether an argument like this would indeed constitute an acceptable defense or whether we are then left in an impossible position with respect to current practice. I will here grasp the first prong and defend abortion₂ ; that is, defend killing the fetus even where this could be avoided.

I

I want to begin by looking at what is surely one of the more powerful arguments in defense of present-day abortion, not because I am interested in assessing it in any detail—if I am right, we should attend instead to the less ambiguous practice I have called abortion₂—but because of an underlying assumption regarding abortion that is particularly relevant to my argument. This is the claim that a woman has a right to terminate a pregnancy, even if doing so results in a person's death, simply because anyone has a right to terminate any dependency relation he or she has not willingly entered. This view has been given its most dramatic expression in Judith Jarvis Thomson's now famous example of the violinist who needs our kidneys for nine months to survive.[4] Obviously, the argument goes, we are in no way obligated to remain attached; simply not wanting to suffer the inconvenience is more than enough justification for unplugging ourselves, even though we know that acting on this reason results in a person's death.

Now this example and what it is taken to prove cannot be quite so straightforward as all that. No less a philosopher than Kant is frequently criticized for (allegedly) requiring us to betray a stranger hiding in our house should the would-be murderer ask us the stranger's whereabouts, and the intuition behind this criticism seems to be that we sometimes *do* have an obligation to a dependent stranger even if we did not choose the dependency relationship. Whether Thomson's thesis is in any way undermined by intuitions such as these is not my concern because I hope to show that however right or wrong she may be, her argument is essentially irrelevant. Her strategy, however, is not. By granting that the fetus is a person, Thomson clearly believes she has been able to avoid a rather murky controversy regarding the fetus and personhood and defend our separating ourselves from the fetus (even should this cause its death) regardless of how this controversy is settled. In one sense, at least, she is clearly right. Her argument is certainly not vulnerable to the charge that the fetus is more of a person and so has more of a right to life than she allows. But Thomson is wrong to think that she has presented the status of the fetus in a way that leaves nothing to be desired from the standpoint of the traditional antiabortionist. Further, what has been left out is crucial to understanding the real nature of the abortion problem.

What lies on the other end of the kidney machine is indeed a person, but—and this brings us to what I take to be the underlying assumption here—this person is also a complete stranger to us. Our first impulse here might be to say, "But this is exactly as it should be; the fetus *is* like a stranger." There is no shared past, no ongoing interaction; in short, no relationship. However, this way of seeing the fetus is in the end insupportable. Holding to it leaves us unable to account for a certain range of emotions and attitudes the fetus characteristically elicits. And this inability is not an uncommon problem. All too often, a certain picture or idea of the fetus is put forward because such a picture is particularly good at doing whatever philosophical work is at hand. But if we say this is what the fetus *is*, we will be unable to explain many of the feelings we have towards it. I want instead to pursue a strategy of "reflective equilibrium" here, moving back and forth between our idea of the fetus and whatever corrections of this image our various feelings towards the fetus require. Thus, rather than say "what the fetus is" in terms of some independent assessment of, say, its volition, self-consciousness, or capacities, I believe we are better advised to look at how, given certain descriptions, it is understandably the object of a rather special range of emotions. Our ability to do this will go hand in hand with our ability to say what the fetus is; if we can say why the feelings we have are justified, an idea of what the fetus is will emerge. If we begin by putting forward first this, then that analogy for the fetus, invariably such a picture will not square with *all* the feelings the fetus in fact elicits. Such is the case here. If we say the fetus should be seen as a stranger (or, following Tooley, some lower order animal[5]), it is then incomprehensible why so many parents have special concern for and interest in the fetus they do. Choosing to bring the fetus to term is not at all like choosing to make those efforts required to keep a stranger alive. Here we choose to *have our child*. If, as most parents do, we allow the fetus to live, we may well be doing so with the anticipation of bringing someone into the world with whom we are then quite closely bound. And this possibility (or for most, inevitability) must enter into how we think of the fetus now. Hence intense long-range concern over all that awaits the object of our efforts once the physical dependency of pregnancy ends makes sense here in a way it simply cannot should the object be an animal or a stranger.

Yet if these models fail to account for the special solicitous concern the fetus often elicits, they also fail to account for an attitude we could not defend were the fetus the most remote of strangers, nay, were it a dog—the desire to have it dead. These two attitudes, being especially concerned for the welfare of the fetus and wanting it dead, which on the surface are so dissimilar, are in fact quite closely bound up with one another. Both stem from the same source: the fact that the fetus represents one of the potentially most central relationships possible to the one who carries it. In a sense, one could say this captures, in a thumbnail sort of way, what the fetus is. The fetus is the only thing that someone—a parent—may with equal comprehensibility and legitimacy care for or want dead. I now want to defend this claim.

II

On an analysis like Thomson's, of course, we *never* seek the death of the fetus. In seeking an abortion, we only seek (justly) to terminate a dependency we are in no way obligated to continue. The death of the fetus is an unfortunate consequence of something we have every right to do. It is certainly not in itself either what we have a right to do or even something we ought to want. Let us assume I have every right to terminate the dependency relation I have to the violinist I find myself plugged into. I certainly ought to *prefer* this did not cause his death. If he could be saved by other means, I ought to be delighted, and it would seem nothing short of monstrous to seek to frustrate these means if they did become available. Thomson makes this point explicitly when she says, "I have argued that you are not morally required to spend nine months in bed, sustaining the life of that violinist: but to say this is by no means to say that if, when you unplug yourself, there is a miracle and he survives, you then have a right to turn round and slit his throat."[6]

Clearly our desire for independence will always be comprehensible and, in some cases, justifiable. Our desire to see someone who means us no harm dead can never be either. Perhaps this would not be quite so monstrous if we say the fetus is not a person. But whatever differences we may hope for by this adjustment should not be exaggerated. Someone who claimed he had not violated the prohibition against killing bald eagles because he had in fact only destroyed their eggs would understandably be looked upon quite skeptically. In any event, to repeat an earlier query, What good reason can we have for wanting *any* complex organism dead when its being alive in no obvious way inconveniences us? Again, this suggests that the right to abortion$_3$ is really but the right to extrication, to what I have called abortion$_1$. Or, as one philosopher has argued, it is helpful to see the desire for abortion$_3$ as reducible without remainder to the desire for "early abandonment." In both cases it seems:

> the parent(s) (a) no longer wish to bestow their legal name upon the child . . . ; (b) no longer wish to retain the child in utero and, once born, as a legal heir to property; (c) no longer wish to provide support for the child in utero and, once born, as their own; and (d) no longer wish to retain any legal relationship to the child.[7]

I believe this view of abortion$_3$ as abandonment (an abandonment that happens to but need not lead to the death of the fetus) is inevitable to any analysis which defends abortion as the right to terminate a pregnancy. But this parallel, seductive as it is, appears to me radically to misrepresent the reasons for abortion many in fact have. If upon entering a clinic women were told, "We can take the fetus out of your womb without any harm to you or it, keep it alive elsewhere for nine months, and then see it placed in a good home," many would, understandably, be quite unsatisfied. What they want is not to be saved from "the inconvenience of pregnancy" or "the task of raising a certain (existing) child"; what they want is *not to be parents*, that is, they do not want there to *be* a child they fail or succeed in raising. Far from this being "exactly like" abandonment, they abort precisely to avoid being among those who later abandon. They cannot be satisfied *unless* the fetus is killed; nothing else will do. I do not want to argue that one *must* feel this way, only that it is understandable if one does. Are these people monsters? Hardly. Certainly anyone who wants the violinist they unplug themselves from, or a full-grown child they abandon, dead *is* incomprehensibly malicious. But it is precisely because our relationship to the fetus is not like either of these that the desire that it be dead makes sense.

Let us look a bit more closely at Thomson's violinist. If we keep the violinist alive, our relationship to him more or less terminates the moment his dependency on us ends. We may get the odd invitation to concerts, but this is of a very different order from what we go through should we bring our child home. However, not wanting any serious complications in our lives would seem the sort of thing covered by abandonment. As many antiabortionists say now, and doubtless many more would say given the possibility of abortion$_1$, you don't have to bring it home; you could very well abandon it and put it up for adoption. And of course they are right—we could. But this course of action would not stop our being parents, at least not in one rather obvious sense of the term. It would not in fact free our life of a certain kind of complication. Although we would not be bringing the child up, because someone else (let us assume) is all too gladly embracing those tasks, we do not want precisely this state of affairs to come about.[8]

At the risk of stating the obvious, there are two respects in which we can be a parent. There is the biological sense, in which we simply play whatever part nature has allotted to us required for the perpetuation of the species. It is very rare, outside the stud farm, that we speak of this as something that may be done well or badly. Certainly when we say someone is a good father, we don't mean that he is especially good at getting others with child. On the other hand there is something which, for lack of a better term, I will call the moral or personal sense in which we may be parents. This involves the far more complicated and, at least once we are past the first few months, uniquely human enterprise of interacting with our children in a variety of ways: being involved with their development, their inner lives, their moral education, and so on, all in an unusually intimate way. Our children rather quickly develop their own personalities, and it is with these, not the bodies that must be fed and clothed, that we are so deeply involved. Yet they are also deeply susceptible to whatever influences our characters and personalities may have on them, and so this is a relationship that is understandably cultivated with the greatest of care. Here we do speak of someone doing well or badly. To be a successful parent in this sense is justly regarded as a genuine and as one of the more genuinely satisfying accomplishments we may hope for. Now clearly these two respects in which one may be a parent are analytically distinct. One can simply donate one's sperm or bring a child to term and that can be the end of it. Alternatively, one can have the most rewarding of personal relationships imaginable with children one has adopted. But they are not quite so separate, or separable, for many of us in actual fact. It is usually important to us that the children we raise are the children we have had, and conversely—the more central concern in this discussion—that the children we bear are in fact raised by us. Undoubtedly, this desire is in part instinctual. But it would be a mistake to say it is entirely so; there are reasons for it. In part, it stems from the deep identification parents understandably develop with their children by virtue of the genetic carryover. But it also stems from the more subtle understanding that to raise a child is to influence him or her considerably in a particularly personal way, and that those who *are* so genetically tied to the child have the most legitimate claim to exercise this kind of influence. Thus one anticipates a certain and very special kind of involvement over time that will have this character at least in part because of the initial biological link.

One can of course have good reasons to bear one's child but waive this claim, handing the business of raising it over to another. But we can also have good reasons for avoiding this kind of choice and preventing its attendant difficulties from ever arising. One can, that is, simply want there to be no child at all. I do not for a moment deny that this desire may in some cases be animated by rather selfish or callous concerns; I am only concerned to argue that it need not be. A woman may feel very strongly that she and not anyone else ought to raise whatever children she brings into the world. Or, more likely, that she ought to do so only in conjunction with a supportive husband who is also (and not by chance) the father of the child. The "ought" here needs to be understood in a rather special way. It is clearly not the "ought" of rationality. But neither is it the moral "ought" understood impersonally. It is closer, in some ways, to a preference—"this is how I wish to lead *my* life"—but obviously, it is nothing like a wish or whim. It is a deeply felt personal preference subscribed to by some, yet intelligible to all. One has a certain picture of what parenting, and the context surrounding it, should be, an image grounded in a mixture of certain psychological assumptions and well-thought-out personal aspirations. Further, conforming to this image will be deeply bound up with the most central values the person holds: one wants very much to be a certain kind of *person*, that is, the sort who has children only when able to raise them oneself in an environment one finds right.[9] We see bearing children as one of the more important things we ever do, and we want to do it in a responsible way; that is, only when we can raise them ourselves in a loving, attentive, unambivalent fashion. The desire here is not to fail or be remiss with respect to this picture. For someone with these values, such failure would be a source of substantial—in part because it would be ongoing—shame and humiliation. Nor is this at all mysterious or surprising. There would always be in the world a person to whom one was failing to be a proper or full parent, and this is a failure one understandably dreads. Abortion for those with these values is best seen, I suggest, as the only means by which they can regain their situation antecedent to pregnancy where there simply was no child and consequently no one with whom to either succeed or fail as a parent.

I anticipate two kinds of objections here. Some will ask, How can we be said to fail as a parent if we see to it that the child we cannot take care of is placed in good hands? If I am on my deathbed or become incapacitated, surely it would be anything but a failure on my part to see my children well cared for by another. This is certainly true, but the parallel is misplaced. In this kind of example, we act as we do because of the bond or love we feel toward some existing person. The failure I am speaking of is the anticipation of failing to have these feelings when such a person comes to exist. We do not see ourselves as disposed to care along these lines in the first place. This brings me to the second objection. Some philosophers will claim a defense such as this one countenances the worst sort of preciousness on the mother's part. Of course we may sympathize with her plight, they will say, but only up to a point. We should not forget that it is hardly the fault of the fetus that the mother does not want it as she ought to, and so it hardly seems fair that the fetus die as a result of a remissness on her part. Gary Atkinson writes:

> It is implausible to say the least to suggest that either one may fulfill his obligations or make them null by killing the embryo he is obliged to love, especially when the evil consequences to the embryo *arise from the person's failure to meet his obligations*, i.e. to love the embryo.[10]

But I think examining this criticism only underscores my argument. It is patently absurd, so far as I can see, to speak of being "obliged to love." We can say that it is too bad that a father does not love his daughter despite her having been exemplary, or too bad that it is the other way round. But neither the father nor the daughter fails here to do what he or she is *obliged* to do. We may even say one *ought* to love the other, but this means only what we know already, that love would be the appropriate response here. We cannot, however, be obligated to have whatever emotional responses are appropriate to a situation. One may be obligated to serve in a time of crisis, but it is ridiculous to say one is obligated to feel patriotic. We can be obligated to do only that which we could conceivably be made to do. If I am obligated to repay you and fail, you may take me to court, and there I may be forced to mend my ways. But if I am 'obliged to love' and fail? This is not something we can be made to do, not because it is in some sense outside our competence to love in response to force (as it is outside our competence to fly in response to force) but because what can be done in response to force cannot be love. It cannot be a genuine response of *ours*, which, in order to be love (or patriotism), it must be. I have no intention of offering a detailed account of the concept of love here, but no analysis can afford to overlook the way in which it is in the deepest sense of the term self-expressive. It is entirely the subject's to give or withhold.[11] Care or concern may be delegated, as when someone is ordered to care for a foundling. Conversely, someone might come to love a child as a result of being asked to care for it. But the love is understood as something additional, precisely because it betokens a bond or response one has come to form on one's own. I do not mean to suggest in the least that love must be seen as stemming from some choice made in a vacuum; often it grows quite naturally out of certain situations, the normal one between parent and child being perhaps the clearest example. But it is just this that is seen as the problem. It is not the "absence of love" that is at stake here so much as whether the context is one in which love is likely to occur, or to occur at all happily. The mother (in my example) has reason to believe that the situation she faces will not have the love relation she hopes for as its natural concomitant. This is not something she "chooses to feel" so much as something she acknowledges given her situation and its relation to the nature of parenting. Finally, it is misleading even to say we ought to love the fetus where this means only that this is the response called for. We cannot, so far as I can see, love the fetus even if we wanted to, as we cannot be said to love anything we have not interacted with. The most we can ask a parent to do is hope to love it in the future. This is a hope the mother here very much wants to have but, because of certain circumstances, feels she cannot. It is precisely because the mother would very much prefer to love the child the fetus will become, rather than stand in whatever far less satisfactory relation to it she is destined to have, that she chooses abortion.

III

It is clear that I have assumed throughout that the fetus is not strictly identical to a person. Not only would the considerations I have here advanced fail to justify killing a person, they would, I think, fail even to make sense in that context. What we are seeking here is to prevent a certain potential person from becoming a person because once it achieves that status it achieves a good deal more as well. It is then that person we either decide to care for or to abandon, with neither of these alternatives being satisfactory. This assumption has gone undefended here only because it has been so well and so extensively defended elsewhere. It has been said that the fetus is no more a person than an acorn is an oak tree,[12] that the fetus lacks any conception of a self and so cannot think of itself in any future state or suffer the misfortune of death,[13] and so on. Philosophical considerations such as these are buttressed by our own everyday experience: a mother who loses her fetus in a miscarriage simply is not seen to have suffered the sort of loss suffered by someone who loses his eighteen-year-old son in war; the most vehement "right to lifer" does not seriously consider treating a woman who has had an abortion exactly as if she were guilty of murdering an adult, and so on.

The fetus then is not a person. But it is more than a potential person. Or, to put it more precisely, it is more than just *any* potential person; it is potentially some particular person's *child*. If we could somehow create people out of bacteria spores, there would be in the intermediate stages a potential person, but there would not be any potential parents. There would be no one who would have this special relationship to it once it became a person, and so, paradoxically, no one who could have any good reason not to want it to reach that stage. Being a potential person is in no way meaningless from the moral point of view. Far from it; if in fact that was *all* there were to the status of the fetus, it would be impossible to justify killing it. Returning to our example of the spores, I don't think we would see their malicious destruction as equivalent to the destruction of, say, some lower order animal, however biologically similar they might be in other ways. Similarly, if a psychopath could kill embryos *in utero* with a ray gun, we would not think this very far from murder. It is rarely noticed that only the parent's desire to see the fetus dead is ever taken seriously in the first place; no one else could possibly have a reason we would consider for a moment. I have tried to say something here as to why this desire (alone) might be justified. Of course, this special relationship the parent has to the fetus also accounts for those emotions, more commonly felt, at the other end of the spectrum: parents usually desire this potential person to reach maturity with an intensity that any observer of the life of a growing spore would find impossible to achieve. This is not the conviction that the fetus "deserves" or "ought" to reach maturity—though this desire may include this as well—but rather the hope that they will have *their child*. Sentiments analogous to these may be felt by others, as when a prospective adopting couple follows a woman's pregnancy with special hope and anticipation. But because the weight of the biological tie can never be dismissed or ignored, the feelings of the parents towards *this* fetus, whether of hope or dread, can never be duplicated elsewhere. The point is essentially this: if we see the fetus simply as something like a clump of tissue or a lower order animal, however great the biological resemblance relation might be, then we cannot account for the kind of interest and concern the parent will take in it at this point. But if we see it unconditionally as a person, or even as a potential person, then we cannot explain why this concern may understandably take the form of seeking its death. Only when we hold fast to the way an ongoing and uniquely binding relationship looms large from the start with this rapidly dividing group of cells do we provide the ground for a real concern and for a satisfactory defense of abortion.[14]

NOTES

I would like to thank Ruth Cigman of Iona College and James Muyskens of Hunter College for their comments and suggestions on this paper.

[1] By "fetus" I will throughout be referring only to the fetus (or embryo) in the earliest stages of pregnancy.

[2] Perhaps some extreme "naturalist" would object that all the same abortion₁ meddles with nature's course. But this view is too silly even to have found expression in the political spectrum.

[3] By "elective" abortions I mean those which are not performed for any clear reason regarding the health or safety of the mother or the fetus. I am dealing throughout with those cases where there is no danger to the mother if she continues the pregnancy, no defect in the fetus, nor where the mother is tragically young.

[4] Judith Jarvis Thomson, "In Defense of Abortion," *Philosophy & Public Affairs* 1, no. 1 (Fall 1971), 47-66.

[5] Michael Tooley, "Abortion and Infanticide," *Philosophy & Public Affairs* 2, no. 1 (Fall 1972), 37-65.

[6] Thomson, "In Defense of Abortion," 66.

[7] R.M. Herbenick, "Remarks on Abortion, Abandonment, and Adoption Options," *Philosophy & Public Affairs* 5, no. 1 (Fall 1975), 102.

8 Strictly speaking, there is no reason why either parent could not feel this way, though a condition of the kind of situation I have in mind here is that neither wants the child. Usually, however, a certain asymmetry between the sexes enters in: sometimes the mother discovers the pregnancy when she is no longer in contact with the father; in any event, it is her body that must suffer the operation and so it is a decision we understandably see as primarily hers, and so on. At some points I will speak of "the mother," at other points "the parent," depending on which seems more natural in the context at hand. But certainly the values that underlie this desire are not unavailable to men.

9 I am throughout assuming that one's behavior regarding contraception would be consistent with values such as these, and so the pregnancy would be of the sort incurred despite reasonable precautions.

10 G.M. Atkinson, "The Morality of Abortion," *International Philosophical Quarterly* 14, no. 3 (1974), 355.

11 See Stanley Cavell, "The Avoidance of Love," in his *Must We Mean What We Say?* (New York, 1969), 267-353.

12 Thomson, "In Defense of Abortion," 48.

13 Tooley, "Abortion and Infanticide," see especially 40-9.

14 I have been concerned here only with justifying a parent's, specifically a mother's, desire to see the fetus killed. I have said nothing about whether this desire translates into a *right*. This is an enormously complicated question involving us in various theories of rights and entitlement, and it is one I have intentionally set aside here. All I want to say is that if she does have a right to abortion₂ in the earliest stages of pregnancy (as I believe she does), she has it then because of the considerations I have mentioned. If she does not, it is despite these considerations having the weight they do.

Abortion: The Avoidable Moral Dilemma

JAMES M. HUMBER

Most of those arguing for and against abortion see the controversy as being one which can be resolved only by determining the proper use of "human." Those opposed to the procedure, for example, usually offer into evidence biological data which, they say, clearly indicate the fetus' humanity. If prenatal beings are known to be human, they then continue, such organisms must be seen as having the right to life. And since abortion is always the violation of that right, the procedure must be considered immoral.[1] In opposition to this "conservative" position, those favoring abortion use various ploys. Some try to show that "human" is ordinarily being used in such a way that it excludes at least some prenatal beings (e.g., zygotes and/or embryos) from its extension. Unfortunately, all such attempts fail, for with each definition offered, some commonly recognized group of human beings is denied human status.[2] Recognizing this fact, other abortion advocates seek to defend their view by appealing to the arbitrary character of definition. Basically, the argument takes two forms. The most radical position is represented by Mr. Garrett Hardin:

> Whether the fetus is or is not a human being is a matter of definition, not fact; and we can define any way we wish. In terms of the human problem involved, it would be unwise to define the fetus as human.[3]

The difficulty with this view, of course, is all too apparent. That is, if definition is *purely* arbitrary, we may classify any group of persons as non-human, just so long as we believe the procedure is warranted by the presence of some "human problem." Alcoholics, the senile, those on welfare, *any* group legitimately may be classed as non-human and dealt with as we please. Hardin recognizes the problem, but refuses to acknowledge its force:

> This is, of course, the well-known argument of "the camel's nose"—which says that if we let the camel put his nose in the tent, we will be unable to keep him from forcing his whole body inside. The argument is false. It is *always* possible to draw arbitrary lines *and enforce them*.[4]

Clearly, Hardin wants prenatal beings *alone* to be arbitrarily classed as non-human. But upon what basis can this preference be supported?

It is obvious that he could not seriously assert that embryonic organisms constitute the only group of beings posing a "human problem." What we are left with, then, is simply Hardin's "bare feeling" that arbitrary definition is proper if and only if the beings to be classified are *in utero*. But what makes this feeling more proper than the feeling, say, that alcoholics should be classed as non-human and exterminated? Hardin gives us no answer.

A less radical version of the arbitrary definition defense of abortion has been developed by Glanville Williams. Sensing Hardin's problem, Williams attempts to give rational support for Hardin's "feeling" that it is with prenatal beings alone that arbitrary non-human classification is legitimate:

> Do you wish to regard the microscopic fertilized ovum as a human being? You can if you want to. . . . But there are most important social arguments for *not* adopting this language. Moreover, *if you look at actual beliefs and behavior, you will find almost unanimous rejection of it.*[5]

In effect, the arbitrary classification of fetuses is now held to be proper, not merely because there are social arguments which make such action desirable, but even more importantly, because society's behavior indicates that the majority does not believe such entities are human anyway (e.g., women do not mourn the loss of a spontaneously aborted zygote as they do the death of a child, etc.).

The first thing which must be noted about Williams' attenuated version of the arbitrary definition defense is that it is not entirely clear. Is Williams claiming that, society's attitudes and behavior being what they are, fertilized ova have *already* been classified as non-human, and that it would be improper to disagree with majority opinion? Or is his view merely that the classificatory status of such organisms is in doubt, and that the available "social arguments," together with majority consent, provide us with good reasons for grouping pre-natal beings as non-human? Let us examine each possibility in turn.

If the first interpretation of Williams' meaning is accepted, his position must be rejected out of hand, for what it amounts to is simply the assertion that the majority is always right. But whether or not the proposition, "X is human," is true or not, is not something to be resolved by an appeal to majority opinion. In the late Middle Ages, for example, the majority's "actual beliefs and behavior" were such that children were not considered fully human.[6] Would Williams want to admit that one who killed a troublesome child in those days was acting in a morally acceptable manner? And what of the Salem witch hunts? Was witch killing "right for them," but not for us? Surely not; indeed, if the fact that the majority of the residents of Salem thought witch killing proper indicates anything, it is only that the majority of the people of that city were ignorant. The conclusion, then, seems clear: if Williams wants to show that fertilized ova are non-human (i.e., if he wants to prove that it is improper today to disagree with the majority concerning the status of pre-natal beings), he must provide us with some reasoned argument which demonstrates that fact. But no such argument is offered. Consequently, this interpretation of his position must be rejected.

Although the second construction of Williams' argument is stronger than the first, there seem to be two good reasons for concluding that it is unsound. First, if Williams takes majority doubt concerning classification plus the availability of "social arguments" as together providing a moral justification for dealing with certain groups of beings as non-human, various undesirable consequences follow. In both word and deed, for instance, we every day illustrate that the majority view in this country is that there are at least some criminals who are sub-human. Rapists and murderers are often referred to as "animals" and "mad dogs"; and when these men are caught, they are housed like wild animals in a zoo. Then too, the social arguments for getting rid of such misanthropes are numerous. Would Williams want to use these insights to develop a new argument for capital punishment?[7]

Although it is not likely that he would do so, it could be that Williams would be willing to accept the logical implications of his argument, and admit that capital punishment, euthanasia, the killing of mentally defectives, etc., are all moral. But even if this were done, Williams' defense of abortion must be rejected as it stands, for unless it is modified in some significant way, it can only be seen as fostering morally irresponsible action. To illustrate: let us say that we are deer hunting with some friends. One of our colleagues sees a movement in the bushes and fires. When we ask him why he acted as he did, he replies: (i) although he was not sure what had moved in the bushes, it was much more probable that it was a deer than a man and, (ii) if it were a deer he did not want it to get away, for his family needed the food, and the deer in this region had overpopulated and were destroying the crops of local farmers. Now even if we grant the truth of (i) and (ii), I doubt that anyone would accept these facts as a justification for our trigger-happy friend's behavior. True, we would not call our hunter immoral; but we *would* think him careless, and insist that he not be allowed to carry a loaded gun. And in the same vein, a woman who was not sure that the fertilized ovum within her was human, and thus decided to have an abortion simply because she wanted no more children, or would be subject to economic and/or psychological hardship given the child's birth, should not be held responsible enough to make that life and death decision.

In order to buttress Williams' argument, defenders of abortion could object to our hunter analogy on two grounds: (a) It could be said that it does not cover two very important cases, viz., that in which the life of the mother, and that in which the lives of the mother and her fetus are endangered; or, (b) it could be objected that it fails to note that there is a special relationship between a woman and the organism developing within her. Now both these criticisms appear well founded. Even when modified in the ways suggested, however, Williams' argument must be rejected.

First, *if* it were true that we could never be sure that prenatal beings were human, abortion would have to be considered morally acceptable whenever the conditions of (a) were in evidence. But the reason abortion would be permitted in these two special instances is not what Williams would have us believe. That is to say, in neither case would we arbitrarily define individual fetuses as non-human in order to legitimatize particular abortions. On the contrary, if only the mother's life were in jeopardy, we would reason that we *have* to act in order to save her, and that since the fetus is not known to be human, we would be justified in "playing the odds," hoping all the while that our actions were not destructive of a human being. If, on the other hand, the lives of both the mother and her fetus were endangered, the argument for abortion would be stronger—indeed, abortion in this case would be warranted even if the fetus were known to be human, for the only choice here would be between saving one life, or letting two persons die. If one were to accept Williams' version of the argument, however, he would be led to one of two ridiculous results: either fetuses would be non-human (in the two cases mentioned) and not non-human (in all other cases), or, because there would sometimes be good reasons for classifying fetuses as non-human, it could be argued that they should always be so categorized. Now the first alternative is so inconsistent that I should think even proponents of arbitrary definition would be unwilling to accept it. As for the second, it leads to moral absurdities. For example, an advocate of this view would have to claim that since a *starving* hunter is warranted in arbitrarily classifying a motion in the bushes as non-human and shooting, *all* movements in bushes may be thought of as being due to non-human causes, and all hunters may "fire at will."

Before a proper evaluation of (b) can be made, we must first get clear as to the exact nature of the "special relationship" to which it alludes. Surely it is not simply that of mother to child, for if our hunter analogy is amended so that the careless hunter is a woman who, at the moment of shooting, knew that the motion in the bushes must have been caused either by a deer or her child, we would think her *more* careless rather than less so in firing. If there is anything "special" about the relationship, then, it can only be that the embryonic organism exists as a parasite, and that when an abortion is effected, conditions which are both necessary for the continued life of the fetus and in some sense possessed (or "owned") by the mother, are removed.

Having clarified the nature of the relationship referred to in (b), a second question arises: how could abortion advocates use knowledge of this relationship's existence in order to demonstrate that persons seeking abortions are not morally irresponsible? Two alternatives present themselves. First, it could be argued that the parasitic status of the conceptus shows that it is not a "separate human being endowed with human rights."[8] Now although it may well be true that the fetus' total dependence upon the mother is one factor causing some to doubt its humanity, dependency can hardly be taken to prove that the fetus is non-human and without the right to life. To hold otherwise, one should have to accept the contention that it would be morally proper to cut the umbilical cord of a newborn baby who had not yet begun to breathe, and leave the child to die of suffocation and/or starvation. But this is clearly ridiculous. If knowledge of the parasitic status of the fetus is of any importance at all, then, it can only be in helping us to understand why some people doubt prenatal organisms' humanity. But our hunter analogy has all along assumed that the status of fetal beings is dubious, and the reasons for this doubt are (at least at this point in the development of our thesis) of no consequence. As a result, the first interpretation of (b) contains nothing which could allow Williams to avoid the charge of fostering moral irresponsibility.

The second version of (b) is better founded than the first, and it has been defended in detail by Professor Judith Jarvis Thomson.[9] Women have the right to abort, she says, because they have the right to control their own bodies. And *even if the fetus is a human and possessed of human rights,*

> . . . having a right to life does not guarantee having either a right to be given the use of or a right to be allowed continued use of another person's body—even if one needs it for life itself.[10]

Because Thomson assumes from the first that prenatal beings are human, I am, by conjoining her argument with that of Williams, strengthening it considerably. In addition, this action gives us a new defense of abortion—one which, I believe, makes the strongest possible case for abortion's morality. If, as Williams holds, we could never be sure that fetuses were human, and if, as Thomson says, women have a right to control their bodies, then *perhaps* an appeal to the right to control one's body would justify abortion. Quite frankly, I am not sure. Luckily, we need not face this issue, for the combined thesis may be invalidated on other grounds. Specifically, Williams' assumption concerning the uncertain classificatory status of embryonic organisms can be shown to be false; and with this demonstration, the two theses will be separated, Thomson's argument then having to stand or fall on its own.

As previously noted, most of the discussion surrounding abortion has centered upon attempts to determine the proper use of "human." Not only has this procedure been particularly unproductive, it has also failed to explain why those who oppose abortion usually wish to hold that human life begins at conception, rather than at some other point in gestation.[11] Both these failures can be overcome, however, if only one is willing to shift his focus of attention. What, after all, is the meaning of "conception?" As employed in ordinary language, the term appears to have three uses: (1) Sometimes it is used to mean "beginning," "start," or "creation" (as when we say, "The design has been faulty since its conception."). (2) Sometimes it is used to mean "act of conceiving," where "conceiving" means "to imagine" or "to form a notion or idea" (e.g., "Conception of his meaning was possible for me only after he gave an example."). (3) And finally, "conception" is often used to mean "notion" or "idea" (e.g., "I now have a conception of what must have happened yesterday."). Now which of these three uses is being employed when we discuss human conception? Surely it is the first; for when I say X "My conception occurred approximately nine months before I was born," I do not mean to say (as with use 2) that I imagined or thought of something at that time. Similarly, I do not mean to hold (as use 3 would require) that someone else—presumably my parents—had an idea or notion of me. Well then, if uses (2) and (3) are excluded, what else could X mean than that I had my beginning, start, or creation, about nine months before I was born? And note, it is I who got his start at the point thus denominated. This is extremely important, for if it is essential for me to be me that I be human (as surely it is), then what I am asserting when I assert X is that my creation *as a human* occurred nine months before my birth. And if this is so, the rationale for the "anti-abortion" position becomes clear: one can deny that human beings are created at conception, only by denying that they begin to exist when they begin to exist.

Having demonstrated that from conception on embryonic organisms are human, we can only conclude that Williams is in error when he holds that the classificatory status of these beings is uncertain. This being so, the combined Williams-Thomson argument must be rejected, and we are left with Thomson's argument alone. Now, can that reasoning stand by itself once the humanity of organisms *in utero* is admitted? In arguing that it can, Thomson constructs the following example: Assume, she says, that you are kidnapped by The Society of Music Lovers and connected via some medical equipment to a sick, unconscious, virtuoso violinist. The violinist has a rare, potentially fatal disease, which can be cured only if he remains connected to you for nine months. Only you can perform the life-giving function because you alone have the proper blood type. Given this as the situation, then, Thomson asks:

> Is it morally incumbent on you to accede to this situation? No doubt it would be very nice of you if you did. . . . But do you *have* to accede to it? What if it were not nine months, but nine years? Or longer still? . . . I imagine you would regard this as outrageous. . . .[12]

The conclusion seems clear: if the right to control one's body justifies "unplugging" the violinist, it must also legitimatize abortion—and this holds true regardless of whether the fetus is human or not.

Although Thomson's argument has immediate appeal, it is a relatively easy matter to show that her reasoning rests upon a confusion.[13] Consider the following counterexample: Let us say that I am involved in a shipwreck. After being thrown overboard, I manage to tie myself securely to a large piece of flotsam. As I am bobbing around in the water, a non-swimmer grabs my arm and asks that I help him get onto the piece of floating debris to which I have tied myself. To this I answer, "having a right to life does not guarantee having either a right to be given the use of or a right to be allowed continued use of another person's body." With that, I shake him loose from my arm and watch him go under for the third time.

Surely no one will doubt that in my example, I acted in an immoral manner. But why does the immorality show up so clearly here, and not in Thomson's paradigm? The answer, I think, lies in the degree of hardship being imposed upon the persons whose bodies are being used. In my example, for instance, it would have required very little effort for the one shipwrecked person to have saved the life of the other. In Thomson's analogy, however, we are asked to consider ourselves bedridden for months, even years. And as Aristotle long ago realized, anyone can "break" under pressure and do something which he realizes is wrong. Now in certain cases (i.e., when the pressure is so great that the average person could not reasonably be expected to withstand it), the man who "breaks" and acts immorally is said to have an excuse for his actions. But to excuse an act is not to say that it is morally right. Indeed, just the opposite is true, for unless an act is wrong, it hardly stands in need of an excuse. And if this is granted, two conclusions seem mandated: First, if Thomson's reasoning has some "convincing power," it is only because the reader has followed her in failing to distinguish between excused acts, and acts which are morally right. And second, if Thomson's argument shows anything at all about abortion, it is only that it is a morally wrong act which, like all other morally wrong acts, may sometimes be excused.

II

Professor Thomson's argument is not the only defense of abortion which proceeds upon the assumption that fetal beings are human. Two others have been constructed along similar lines; and if abortion is to be shown to be immoral, the indefensible character of these theses also must be demonstrated. . . .

To begin, some of those defending abortion argue that there is a distinction to be made between "human" and "human person," and that as a result, abortion of a human conceptus may be justified.[14] That is, even if human life begins at conception, these people say, no *individual* is present until sometime later in gestation. And if this is so,

> . . . then under some circumstances the welfare of actually existing persons might supersede the welfare of developing human tissue.[15]

Now there are two reasons why any defense constructed along these lines must fail. First, if there are formidable difficulties involved in trying to define "human," these problems must simply re-arise in attempts to define "human person." And if this is so, it must be impossible to distinguish a human from a human person. Even if we ignore this apparently irresolvable problem, however, what possibly could serve to justify the belief that an individual's rights may 'supersede' those of a human? That is, since the right to life is a human right rather than a personal one, fetuses must be seen as possessing that right even if they are not held to be true individuals. Why, then, do these proponents of abortion feel that a human's right to life may be negated whenever it conflicts with some right or rights possessed by an individual? Clearly there can be only one answer, viz., these abortion advocates must be assuming that it is more valuable, important, or worthy, to be a human person than to be human. But how could this presupposition be shown to be true? In some circumstances, perhaps (as when the mother-to-be is, say, a doctor on the verge of discovering a cure for cancer), a good case could be made that this woman should be allowed to abort rather than having to risk her life in childbirth. But what if the expectant mother is an alcoholic, on welfare, and a general burden to society? Would the abortion advocate allow us to turn the argument around and insist that this woman should not be allowed to abort her "innocent" fetus, even if her own life were in jeopardy? This seems highly unlikely. But if this is so, the question simply re-arises: what is there about being a person which, in itself, makes one better or more worthy than a being who is merely human? The abortion advocate gives us no answer. And this, I suspect, is because there is no answer to be given.

The last defense of abortion to be considered is not only the most philosophically sophisticated, it is also the most complex.[16] Reduced to its barest essentials, Professor Brandt's article presents us with two new defenses of abortion. As a first line of attack Brandt argues

> . . . that there is not an unrestricted *prima facie* obligation not to kill [humans], but only a *prima facie* obligation not to kill in certain types of cases; and . . . [to] tentatively suggest a general formulation of a restricted principle which would have the effect of not entailing that there is a *prima facie* obligation not to cause an abortion.[17]

As an example of a restricted principle which would not entail that it is *prima facie* wrong to have an abortion, Brandt offers the following:

> It is *prima facie* wrong to kill human beings, except those which are not sentient and have no desires, and except in reasonable defense of self or others against unjust assault.[18]

Now, if one accepts Brandt's principle and wishes to justify abortion, there are two avenues of attack open to him, depending upon which part of the principle he wishes to emphasize. First, one could claim that abortion may sometimes be justified as a "reasonable defense of self or others against unjust assault." If this were tried, however, it would have to be rejected, for even if a pregnant woman's life were in danger, a non-sentient fetus could hardly be held responsible for its actions. Further, since the fetus is merely growing without conscious purpose, it makes no sense at all to say that it is attempting to do anything, much less take the life of another human being. But if this is so, no self-defense justification of abortion is possible. After all, how could person X seriously hold that his or her killing of another (Y) was justified in terms of self-defense, and at the same time admit that Y was neither responsible for his actions, nor unjustly assaulting X?[19]

The second way one could use Brandt's principle to argue for abortion would be to claim that the procedure is justified by the fact that pre-natal beings are "not sentient and have no desires." Now if this ploy were used, the reply would be obvious: how can one accept this version of the principle and consistently maintain that it would be wrong to kill a person who was unconscious or in a coma? Brandt realizes that his thesis may be objected to in this way, and he replies that although his principle obviously needs amendment "It seems clear . . . that a restricted principle can be formulated along the suggested line . . ." (511). Now this statement of confidence is heartwarming, but it offers little in the way of practical help for one who wishes to amend the principle so as to allow for abortion without undesirable side-effects. How could the necessary changes be made? Unless I am mistaken, it is a relatively easy matter to show that no amendment is possible.

First, one must get clear as to what Brandt is really trying to do. Rather than holding that all humans have a *prima facie* right to life, and then arguing that to be human one must be sentient (as some have done), Brandt seeks to sidestep the discussion of "human" by using sentience (or the lack of it) as the defining characteristic for a special class of humans—viz., those to whom the right to life does not apply. But this is clearly illegitimate. After all, the right to life is ordinarily spoken of as a *human* right, i.e., it is not a personal right, nor is it a right which one possesses by virtue of his being a member of a special group or class of humans. To hold otherwise not only makes a mockery of ordinary language, it also undercuts morals completely, potentially justifying all sorts of horrors. In short, one cannot, as Brandt wishes to do, make the question concerning whether or not one has the right to life rest upon a determination of the particular type of human being the person in question is. If one is human he has, by definition, *all* human rights (including the right to life). And this remains true regardless of the *kind* of human being he is.

Brandt seems to sense that an objection of the above sort could be brought against his thesis. Thus, in order to demonstrate that there are "kinds of humans, such that it is not wrong to destroy them" (509), he constructs the following example:

> Suppose a human being has suffered massive brain damage in an accident. He is unconscious, and it is quite clear he will never regain consciousness—

his brain is beyond repair. His body, however, can be kept alive by means known to science, more or less indefinitely. Is there a *prima facie* obligation to keep this being alive, or to refrain from terminating its existence? I believe there is no such thing.[20]

Now I have no doubts that most of us believe that we have no *prima facie* duty to keep alive the being described by Brandt. But why is this? Is it because, as Brandt suggests, we see the unconscious being as a human of a special type, one to whom the right to life is no longer applicable? Or is it because we think the unconscious being is, for one reason or another, not fully human? I think the weight of evidence is clearly in favor of the latter view. For instance, do we not refer to beings of the sort Brandt has described as "vegetables?" And do we not say that entities of this kind are "as good as dead?" This being so, there should be nothing mysterious about why we believe that it would be proper to let Brandt's brain-damaged being die. Taking that being's non-human status for granted, we reason that there is nothing immoral about letting "it" die, for "it" is not human, and hence does not possess the right to life. If added evidence is needed, one need only refer to Brandt's own example. If it is true, as Brandt believes, that his paradigm illustrates that there are kinds of humans to whom we deny the right to life, why does he end the quoted passage by asking: "Is there an obligation to keep *this being* alive, or to refrain from terminating *its* existence?" I submit that the reasons for this statement are clear, and that they confirm the view that *we never* consider a being to be without the right to life, unless we have sincere doubts concerning his or her humanity.

Brandt's second defense of abortion is double-barreled. First, as an explication of "*A* is *prima facie* wrong," he offers the following:

A would be prohibited by a rule of the moral code which would be preferred, as a code to be current in their society, by all persons who

(a) expected to live a lifetime in that society,
(b) were rational at least in the sense that their preferences were fully guided by all relevant available knowledge, and
(c) were impartial in the sense that . . . their preference was uninfluenced by information which would specially advantage them as compared with any other person or group.[21]

Next, he asks, would these impartial choosers opt to prohibit abortion? He believes that they would not, and offers two arguments in support of this view. His first reason for holding as he does is that

. . . we are asked to determine what such an impartial being would choose in a moral system . . . if he *did not know* whether he was merely a fetus or a living human being. But is such ignorance about one's own status even possible? . . . [I]f a being is able to consider values, alternative biographies, and possible choices among moral systems . . . how could be possibly—assuming he knows the laws of science—be in doubt about whether he is a thinking human adult or merely an unborn fetus which might never be born?[22]

Now, if Brandt's ruminations are true, I would argue that we have a full demonstration of the fact that his explication of "*A* is *prima facie* wrong" is incorrect. The reasoning is simple. If it is true that the choosers of a moral system would be unable to function because they could not be ignorant of their status (if they could not be impartial in the sense required by c), then, for the same reason, they should not be able to form a sound moral policy on infanticide. Brandt admits as much, for he allows that ". . . there is a difficulty in allowing 'all persons' . . . to include young children, for the intellectual limitations of young children may be such that it is *causally impossible* for them to function in the required way . . . as choosers of a moral code."[23] But if this is true, how could a moral code chooser be in doubt about whether he was an adult or merely a newborn baby? For Brandt to be consistent, then, he must hold that his moral choosers could not decide whether or not infanticide is wrong. And if this is the case, I submit that we have good cause to reject his analysis of "*A* is *prima facie* wrong."

The second "barrel" of Brandt's argument is even more ingenious than the first. Supposing, for the sake of argument, that his moral code choosers could be impartial in the sense required, he holds that they would not opt to prohibit abortion because

> . . . such a chooser could not know that, even if all fetuses survived birth, *he* would survive, and hence he would not be motivated to choose the abortion-prohibiting moral system. . . .[24]

That is to say, it is Brandt's contention that one's personal identity extends back only to the moment of his birth, and that awareness of this fact would cause his impartial choosers to favor abortion. In order to support this view, he offers the following example:

> Suppose I were seriously ill and were told that, for a sizable fee . . . my brain would be removed to another body which could provide normal life, but the unfortunate result of the operation would be that my memory and learned abilities would be wholly lost, and that the forming of memory brain traces must begin again from scratch, as a newborn baby. . . . The question is whether I would take an interest in the continued existence of myself in *that* sense. It seems to me that I would not. . . .[25]

Accepting this analogy, Brandt feels that he has good reason to hold that an impartial moral code selector would choose to permit abortion. His reasoning on this point is as follows:

> The thought that the fetus to which he may be attached might issue in a conscious infant would interest him no more than just the thought that *somebody* will be born. On account of the memory-gap, he will feel no more interest in the birth of this fetus than I feel in the health and welfare of the body into which my brain is transferred.[26]

Now, if any credence at all is to be given our earlier analysis of "conception," this argument must be rejected; for as we have seen, everyday discourse shows clearly that it is conception rather than birth that marks the beginning of each human life. We need not rest our case upon our earlier argument, however, for it is an easy matter to prove Brandt wrong on other grounds. What, after all, is he saying? To be sure, he is in the general tradition of Locke, holding that one's identity extends back as far as his recollections. But this is not all: Brandt goes beyond Locke, assuming that one can remember as far back as his birth. But this is just not true. Try as I may, I cannot remember events before I was one or two years old. (I do not doubt that Professor Brandt has a phenomenal memory, but I still feel certain that even he cannot remember his birth or the events immediately following.) Thus, if Brandt is correct in holding that the existence of a "memory-gap" will cause his moral code choosers to favor abortion, he must also hold that it will lead them to condone infanticide. And unless one is willing to accept the view that the killing of newborn babies is not even *prima facie* wrong, Brandt's analysis must be rejected out of hand.

· · ·

Once people are educated to the point that their desire to be rational will (hopefully) cause them to want to avoid the abortion dilemma, action on several fronts is possible. If the statistics are to be believed, most women who seek abortions do so because they find themselves with unwanted pregnancies.[27] And women who have unwanted pregnancies turn to abortion for one or more of the following three reasons: (i) the woman is unmarried, the child illegitimate, and the mother wants to avoid showing her "sin" to society; (ii) the woman (especially the married woman) would agree to have the child and give it up for adoption, except that there is a social stigma attached to such action; and (iii) the mother simply does not want to put up with pregnancy and childbirth. Given these as the primary causes for abortion, then anti-abortion action along the following lines would seem to be indicated:

[For reasons of space, only one of Professor Humber's concluding recommendations is included here—Ed.]

Some women, it is true, simply do not want to suffer through pregnancy and childbirth. And where this is the case, our hope lies, not in changing social attitudes, but in doing our best to advance scientific research. At present, the process is being developed whereby a fertilized egg can be transplanted from one woman's womb into another's. If this procedure could be perfected so that it was both successful and relatively inexpensive, women—all women—would have a viable alternative to abortion.[28] Instead of abortion clinics, we could have transplant clinics. Women who wanted children could register, just as they now register for adoption; and when the need arose, they could be called up for service. Now what could be the objections to such a procedure? Certainly the formation of transplant clinics would raise various new moral and legal problems. But could the new moral problems be as grave as those we now face in abortion? And why could we not simply look upon transplantation as early adoption, thus minimizing the need for new legislation? Of course, there are also practical matters to be considered. Before uterine transplants could be used, for example, it would have to be shown that the procedure was safe, not only for the transplanted egg, but also for both the women involved. But if we are willing to spend the money for research, such safety could be secured. There remains, then, the matter of cost. How expensive would such an operation be? Frankly, I do not know. But it need not be as inexpensive as an abortion, for the cost could be split between the donor and donee. Also, why should it not be possible to obtain a small federal subsidy for such procedures? All in all, there appears to be nothing which would make it impossible in principle for uterine transplants to serve as an alternative to abortion.

NOTES

[Footnotes have been renumbered—Ed.]

Some of the ideas in this paper were expressed summarily in my "The Immorality of Abortion," a paper read at the Eastern A.P.A. meeting, December 1973.

[1] The two chief proponents of this view are Paul Ramsey, "The Morality of Abortion," in *Life or Death: Ethics and Options* (Seattle, 1968); and John T. Noonan Jr., "Abortion and the Catholic Church: A Summary History," *Natural Law Forum* 12 (1967). For a complete discussion of the failure of these analyses, see D. Callahan, *Abortion: Law, Choice and Morality* (London, 1970), 378-94.

[2] For example, Herman Schwartz ["The Parent or the Fetus," *Humanist* 27 (1967)], 126, contends that abortion is moral because the fetus is not ". . . a rational creature, with unique emotions and feelings, intellect and a personality, a being with whom we can identify." But this definition excludes (at least) newborn babies, and thus allows for infanticide.

[3] Garrett Hardin, "Abortion—or Compulsory Pregnancy?" *Journal of Marriage and the Family* 30 (May 1968), 250-1.

[4] G. Hardin, "Semantic Aspects of Abortion," *ETC.* (September 1967), 264.

[5] Glanville Williams, "The Legalization of Medical Abortion," *The Eugenics Review* 56 (April 1964), 21.

[6] See Philippe Ariès, *Centuries of Childhood*, Robert Baldick, trans. (New York, 1965), 38-9.

[7] My choice of criminals here was purely arbitrary. The argument would apply with equal force to the senile, children born with mental defects, etc.

[8] Although their statements are far from clear, when members of women's liberation argue for abortion on demand, they seem to be reasoning along these lines.

[9] Judith Jarvis Thomson, "A Defense of Abortion," *Philosophy & Public Affairs* 1 (1971).

[10] *Ibid.*, 56.

[11] This preference is evident even among those who admit that microgenetics cannot prove that human life begins at conception. See Paul Ramsey, "Abortion: A Review Article," *The Thomist* 37 (1973).

[12] Thomson, *op. cit.*, 49.

[13] Baruch Brody has challenged Professor Thomson's position by pointing out that she fails to distinguish between our duty to save someone's life, and our duty not to take it (B. Brody, "Thomson on Abortion," *Philosophy & Public Affairs* 1 [1972], 339-40).

There is some doubt, however, that the distinction Brody insists upon is ever properly made in morals (see R.B. Brandt, "The Morality of Abortion," *The Monist* 56 [1972], 509-10). This being the case, I have avoided these issues entirely, attacking Thomson via an alternate route.

14 Thomas L. Hayes, "A Biological View," *Commonweal* 85 (March 1967); Rudolph Ehrensing, "When is it Really Abortion?" *The National Catholic Reporter* (May 1966).

15 Ehrensing, *ibid.*, 4.

16 Brandt, *op. cit.*

17 *Ibid.*, 506.

18 *Ibid.*, 511.

19 For a more detailed version of this argument, see B. Brody, "Abortion and the Sanctity of Human Life," *American Philosophical Quarterly* 10 (1973).

20 Brandt, *op. cit.*, 509.

21 *Ibid.*, 513.

22 *Ibid.*, 523.

23 *Ibid.*, 515.

24 *Ibid.*, 523.

25 *Ibid.*, 524.

26 *Ibid.*, 525.

27 Callahan, *op. cit.*, 292-4. Alice S. Rossi, "Abortion Laws and Their Victims," *Trans-Action* (1966).

28 There is one possible exception to this statement. If a woman wanted an abortion because she knew that her child would be born deformed, it is almost certain that she would find no one willing to be a transplant recipient. This being so, the only way we can rid ourselves of abortions sought on these grounds is to find the cause of birth defects and eradicate them.

VI

SEX: WITH OR WITHOUT MARRIAGE

What Is a Woman?

SIMONE DE BEAUVOIR

. . . What is a woman?

To state the question is, to me, to suggest, at once, a preliminary answer. The fact that I ask it is in itself significant. A man would never get the notion of writing a book on the peculiar situation of the human male.[1] But if I wish to define myself, I must first of all say: "I am a woman"; on this truth must be based all further discussion. A man never begins by presenting himself as an individual of a certain sex; it goes without saying that he is a man. The terms *masculine* and *feminine* are used symmetrically only as a matter of form, as on legal papers. In actuality the relation of the two sexes is not quite like that of two electrical poles, for man represents both the positive and the neutral, as is indicated by the common use of *man* to designate human beings in general; whereas woman represents only the negative, defined by limiting criteria, without reciprocity. In the midst of an abstract discussion it is vexing to hear a man say: "You think thus and so because you are a woman"; but I know that my only defense is to reply: "I think thus and so because it is true," thereby removing my subjective self from the argument. It would be out of the question to reply: "And you think the contrary because you are a man," for it is understood that the fact of being a man is no peculiarity. A man is in the right in being a man; it is the woman who is in the wrong. It amounts to this: just as for the ancients there was an absolute vertical with reference to which the oblique was defined, so there is an absolute human type, the masculine. Woman has ovaries, a uterus; these peculiarities imprison her in her subjectivity, circumscribe her within the limits of her own nature. It is often said that she thinks with her glands. Man superbly ignores the fact that his anatomy also includes glands, such as the testicles, and that they secrete hormones. He thinks of his body as a direct and normal connection with the world, which he believes he apprehends objectively, whereas he regards the body of woman as a hindrance, a prison, weighed down by everything peculiar to it. "The female is a female by virtue of a certain *lack* of qualities," said Aristotle; "we should regard the female nature as afflicted with a natural defectiveness." And St. Thomas for his part pronounced woman to be an "imperfect man," an "incidental" being. This is symbolized in Genesis where Eve is depicted as made from what Bossuet called "a supernumerary bone" of Adam.

Thus humanity is male and man defines woman not in herself but as relative to him; she is not regarded as an autonomous being. Michelet writes: "Woman, the relative being. . . ." And Benda is most positive in his *Rapport d'Uriel:* "The body of man makes sense in itself quite apart from that of woman, whereas the latter seems wanting in significance by itself. . . . Man can think of himself without woman. She cannot think of herself without man." And she is simply what man decrees; thus she is called "the sex," by which is meant that she appears essentially to the male as a sexual being. For him she is sex—absolute sex, no less. She is defined and differentiated with reference to man and not he with reference to her; she is the incidental, the inessential as opposed to the essential. He is the Subject, he is the Absolute—she is the Other.[2]

The category of the *Other* is as primordial as consciousness itself. In the most primitive societies, in the most ancient mythologies, one finds the expression of a duality—that of the Self and the Other. This duality was not originally attached to the division of the sexes; it was not dependent upon any empirical facts. It is revealed in such works as that of Granet on Chinese thought and those of Dumézil on the East Indies and Rome. The feminine element was at first no more involved in such pairs as Varuna-Mitra, Uranus-Zeus, Sun-Moon, and Day-Night than it was in the contrasts between Good and Evil, lucky and unlucky auspices, right and left, God and Lucifer. Otherness is a fundamental category of human thought.

Thus it is that no group ever sets itself up as the One without at once setting up the Other over against itself. If three travelers chance to occupy the same compartments, that is enough to make vaguely hostile "others" out of all the rest of the passengers on the train. In small-town eyes all persons not belonging to the village are "strangers" and suspect; to the native of a country all who inhabit other countries are "foreigners"; Jews are "different" for the anti-Semite, Negroes are "inferior" for American racists, aborigines are "natives" for colonists, proletarians are the "lower class" for the privileged.

Lévi-Strauss, at the end of a profound work on the various forms of primitive societies, reaches the following conclusion: "Passage from the state of Nature to the state of Culture is marked by man's ability to view biological relations as a series of contrasts; duality, alternation, opposition, and symmetry, whether under definite or vague forms, constitute not so much phenomena to be explained as fundamental and immediately given data of social reality."[3] These phenomena would be incomprehensible if in fact human society were simply a *Mitsein* or fellowship based on solidarity and friendliness. Things become clear, on the contrary, if, following Hegel, we find in consciousness itself a fundamental hostility toward every other consciousness; the subject can be posed only in being opposed—he sets himself up as the essential, as opposed to the other, the inessential, the object.

But the other consciousness, the other ego, sets up a reciprocal claim. The native traveling abroad is shocked to find himself in turn regarded as a "stranger" by the natives of neighboring countries. As a matter of fact, wars, festivals, trading, treaties, and contests among tribes, nations, and classes tend to deprive the concept *Other* of its absolute sense and to make manifest its relativity; willy-nilly, individuals and groups are forced to realize the reciprocity of their relations. How is it, then, that this reciprocity has not been recognized between the sexes, that one of the contrasting terms is set up as the sole essential, denying any relativity in regard to its correlative and defining the latter as pure otherness? Why is it that women do not dispute male sovereignty? No subject will readily volunteer to become the object, the inessential; it is not the Other who, in defining himself as the Other, establishes the One. The Other is posed as such by the One in defining himself as the One. But if the Other is not to regain the status of being the One, he must be submissive enough to accept this alien point of view. Whence comes this submission in the case of woman?

There are, to be sure, other cases in which a certain category has been able to dominate another completely for a time. Very often this privilege depends upon inequality of numbers—the majority imposes its rule upon the minority or persecutes it. But women are not a minority, like the American Negroes or the Jews; there are as many women as men on earth. Again, the two groups concerned have often been originally independent; they may have been formerly unaware of each other's existence, or perhaps they recognized each other's autonomy. But a historical event has resulted in the subjugation of the weaker by the stronger. The scattering of the Jews, the introduction of slavery into America, the conquests of imperialism are examples in point. In these cases the oppressed retained at least the memory of former days; they possessed in common a past, a tradition, sometimes a religion or a culture.

The parallel drawn by Bebel between women and the proletariat is valid in that neither ever formed a minority or a separate collective unit of mankind. And instead of a single historical event it is in both cases a historical development that explains their status as a class and accounts for the membership of *particular individuals* in that class. But proletarians have not always existed, whereas there have always been women. They are women in virtue of their anatomy and physiology. Throughout history they have always been subordinated to men,[4] and hence their dependency is not the result of a historical event or a social change—it was not something that *occurred*. The reason why otherness in this case seems to be an absolute is in part that it lacks the contingent or incidental nature of historical facts. A condition brought about at a certain time can be abolished at some other time, as the Negroes of Haiti and others have proved; but it might seem that a natural condition is beyond the possibility of change. In truth, however, the nature of things is no more immutably given, once for all, than is historical reality. If woman seems to be the inessential which never becomes the essential, it is because she herself fails to bring about this change. Proletarians say "We"; Negroes also. Regarding themselves as subjects, they transform the bourgeois, the whites, into "others". But women do not say "We," except at some congress of feminists or similar formal demonstration; men say "women," and women use the same word in referring to themselves. They do not authentically assume a subjective attitude. The proletarians have accomplished the revolution in Russia, the Negroes in Haiti, the Indo-Chinese are battling for it in Indo-China; but the women's effort has never been anything more than a symbolic agitation. They have gained only what men have been willing to grant; they have taken nothing, they have only received.

The reason for this is that women lack concrete means for organizing themselves into a unit which can stand face to face with the correlative unit. They have no past, no history, no religion of their own; and they have no such solidarity of work and interest as that of the proletariat. They are not even promiscuously herded together in the way that creates community feeling among the American Negroes, the ghetto Jews, the workers of Saint-Denis, or the factory hands of Renault. They live dispersed among the males, attached through residence, housework, economic condition, and social standing to certain men—fathers or husbands—more firmly than they are to other women. If they belong to the bourgeoisie, they feel solidarity with men of that class, not with proletarian women; if they are white, their allegiance is to white men, not to Negro women. The proletariat can propose to massacre the ruling class, and a sufficiently fanatical Jew or Negro might dream of getting sole possession of the atomic bomb and making humanity wholly Jewish or black; but woman cannot even dream of exterminating the males. The bond that unites her to her oppressors is not comparable to any other. The division of the sexes is a biological fact, not an event in human history. Male and female stand opposed within a primordial *Mitsein*, and woman has not broken it. The couple is a fundamental unity with its two halves riveted together, and the cleavage of society along the line of sex is impossible. Here is to be found the basic trait of woman: she is the

Other in a totality of which the two components are necessary to one another.

NOTES

[Translated by H. M. Parshley.]

[1] The Kinsey Report (Alfred C. Kinsey *et al.*, *Sexual Behavior in the Human Male*, Philadelphia, 1948) is no exception, for it is limited to describing the sexual characteristics of American men, which is quite another matter.

[2] E. Lévinas expresses this idea most explicitly in his essay, *Temps et L'Autre*. "Is there no other case in which otherness, alterity [altérité] unquestionably marks the nature of a being, as its essence, an instance of otherness not consisting purely and simply in the opposition of two species of the same genus? I think that the feminine represents the contrary in its absolute sense, this contrariness being in no wise affected by any relation between it and its correlative and thus remaining absolutely other. Sex is not a certain specific difference . . . no more is the sexual difference a mere contradiction. . . . Nor does this difference lie in the duality of two complementary terms, for two complementary terms imply a pre-existing whole. . . . Otherness reaches its full flowering in the feminine, a term of the same rank as consciousness but of oppostie meaning."

I suppose that Lévinas does not forget that woman, too, is aware of her own consciousness, or ego. But it is striking that he deliberately takes a man's point of view, disregarding the reciprocity of subject and object. When he writes that woman is mystery, he implies that she is mystery for man. Thus his description, which is intended to be objective, is in fact an assertion of masculine privilege.

[3] See C. Lévi-Strauss, *Les Structures Elémentaires de la Parenté*. My thanks are due to C. Lévi-Strauss for his kindness in furnishing me with the proofs of his work.

[4] With rare exceptions, perhaps, like certain matriarchal rulers, queens, and the like [Translator's note].

Is Adultery Immoral?

RICHARD WASSERSTROM

Many discussions of the enforcement of morality by the law take as illustrative of the problem under consideration the regulation of various types of sexual behavior by the criminal law. It was, for example, the Wolfenden Report's recommendations concerning homosexuality and prostitution that led Lord Devlin to compose his now famous lecture, "The Enforcement of Morals." And that lecture in turn provoked important philosophical responses from H.L.A. Hart, Ronald Dworkin, and others.

Much, if not all, of the recent philosophical literature on the enforcement of morals appears to take for granted the immorality of the sexual behavior in question. The focus of discussion, at least, is whether such things as homosexuality, prostitution, and adultery ought to be made illegal even if they are immoral, and not whether they are immoral.

I propose in this paper to think about the latter, more neglected topic, that of sexual morality, and to do so in the following fashion. I shall consider just one kind of behavior that is often taken to be a case of sexual immorality—adultery. I am interested in pursuing at least two questions. First, I want to explore the question of in what respects adulterous behavior falls within the domain of morality at all: For this surely is one of the puzzles one encounters when considering the topic of sexual morality. It is often hard to see on what grounds much of the behavior is deemed to be either moral or immoral, for example, private homosexual behavior between consenting adults. I have purposely selected adultery because it seems a more plausible candidate for moral assessment than many other kinds of sexual behavior.

The second question I want to examine is that of what is to be said about adultery, without being especially concerned to stay within the area of morality. I shall endeavor, in other words, to identify and to assess a number of the major arguments that might be advanced against adultery. I believe that they are the chief arguments that would be given in support of the view that adultery is immoral, but I think they are worth considering even if some of them turn out to be nonmoral arguments and considerations.

A number of the issues involved seem to me to be complicated and difficult. In a number of places I have at best indicated where further philosophical exploration is required without having successfully conducted the exploration myself. The paper may very well be more useful as an illustration of how one might begin to think about the subject of sexual morality than as an elucidation of important truths about the topic.

Before I turn to the arguments themselves there are two preliminary points that require some clarification. Throughout the paper I shall refer to the immorality of such things as breaking a promise, deceiving someone, etc. In a very rough way, I mean by this that there is something morally wrong that is done in doing the action in question. I mean that the action is, in a strong sense of *"prima facie"*, *prima facie* wrong or unjustified. I do not mean that it may never be right or justifiable to do the action; just that the fact that it is an action of this description always does count against the rightness of the action. I leave entirely open the question of what it is that makes actions of this kind immoral in this sense of "immoral."

The second preliminary point concerns what is meant or implied by the concept of adultery. I mean by "adultery" any case of extramarital sex, and I want to explore the arguments for and against extramarital sex, undertaken in a variety of morally relevant situations. Someone might claim that the concept of adultery is conceptually connected with the concept of immorality, and that to characterize behavior as adulterous is already to characterize it as immoral or unjustified in the sense described above. There may be something to this. Hence the importance of making it clear that I want to talk about extramarital sexual relations. If they are always immoral, this is something that must be shown by argument. If the concept of adultery does in some sense entail or imply immorality, I want to ask whether that connection is a rationally based one. If not all cases of extramarital sex are immoral (again, in the sense described above), then the concept of adultery should either be weakened accordingly or restricted to those classes of extramarital sex for which the predication of immorality is warranted.

One argument for the immorality of adultery might go something like this: what makes adultery immoral is that it involves the breaking of a promise, and what makes adultery seriously wrong is that it involves the breaking of an important promise. For, so the argument might continue, one of the things the two parties promise each other when they get married is that they will abstain from sexual relationships with third persons. Because of this promise both spouses quite reasonably entertain the expectation that the other will behave in conformity with it. Hence, when one of the parties has sexual intercourse with a third person he or she breaks that promise about sexual relationships which was made when the marriage was entered into, and defeats the reasonable expectations of exclusivity entertained by the spouse.

In many cases the immorality involved in breaching the promise relating to extramarital sex may be a good deal more serious than that involved in the breach of other promises. This is so because adherence to this promise may be of much greater importance to the parties than is adherence to many of the other promises given or received by them in their lifetime. The breaking of this promise may be much more hurtful and painful than is typically the case.

Why is this so? To begin with, It may have been difficult for the nonadulterous spouse to have kept the promise. Hence that spouse may feel the unfairness of having restrained himself or herself in the absence of reciprocal restraint having been exercised by the adulterous spouse. In addition, the spouse may perceive the breaking of the promise as an indication of a kind of indifference on the part of the adulterous spouse. If you really cared about me and my feelings—the spouse might say—you would not have done this to me. And third, and related to the above, the spouse may see the act of sexual intercourse with another as a sign of affection for the other person and as an additional rejection of the nonadulterous spouse as the one who is loved by the adulterous spouse. It is not just that the adulterous spouse does not take the feelings of the spouse sufficiently into account, the adulterous spouse also indicates through the act of adultery affection for someone other than the spouse. I will return to these points later. For the present, it is sufficient to note that a set of arguments can be developed in support of the proposition that certain kinds of adultery are wrong just because they involve the breach of a serious promise which, among other things, leads to the intentional infliction of substantial pain by one spouse upon the other.

Another argument for the immorality of adultery focusses not on the existence of a promise of sexual exclusivity but on the connection between adultery and deception. According to this argument, adultery involves deception. And because deception is wrong, so is adultery.

Although it is certainly not obviously so, I shall simply assume in this paper that deception is always immoral. Thus the crucial issue for my purposes is the asserted connection between extramarital sex and deception. Is it plausible to maintain, as this argument does, that adultery always does involve deception and is on that basis to be condemned?

The most obvious person on whom deceptions might be practiced is the nonparticipating spouse; and the most obvious thing about which the nonparticipating spouse can be deceived is the existence of the adulterous act. One clear case of deception is that of lying. Instead of saying that the afternoon was spent in bed with A, the adulterous spouse asserts that it was spent in the library with B, or on the golf course with C.

There can also be deception even when no lies are told. Suppose, for instance, that a person has sexual intercourse with someone other than his or her spouse and just does not tell the spouse about it. Is that deception? It may not be a case of lying if, for example, the spouse is never asked by the other about the situation. Still, we might say, it is surely deceptive because of the promises that were exchanged at marriage. As we saw earlier, these promises provide a foundation for the reasonable belief that neither spouse will engage in sexual relationships with any other persons. Hence the failure to bring the fact of extramarital sex to the attention of the other spouse deceives that spouse about the present state of the marital relationship.

Adultery, in other words, can involve both active and passive deception. An adulterous spouse may just keep silent or, as is often the fact, the spouse may engage in an increasingly complex way of life devoted to the concealment of the facts from the nonparticipating spouse. Lies, half-truths, clandestine meetings, and the like may become a central feature of the adulterous spouse's existence. These are things that can and do happen, and when they do they make the case against adultery an easy one. Still, neither active nor passive deception is inevitably a feature of an extramarital relationship.

It is possible, though, that a more subtle but pervasive kind of deceptiveness is a feature of adultery. It comes about because of the connection in our culture between sexual intimacy and certain feelings of love and affection. The point can be made indirectly at first by seeing that one way in which we can, in our culture, mark off our close friends from our mere acquaintances is through the kinds of intimacies that we are prepared to share with them. I may, for instance, be willing to reveal my very private thoughts and emotions to my closest friends or to my wife, but to no one else. My sharing of these intimate facts about myself is from one perspective a way of making a gift to those who mean the most to me. Revealing these things and sharing them with those who mean the most to me is one means by which I create, maintain, and confirm those interpersonal relationships that are of most importance to me.

Now in our culture, it might be claimed, sexual intimacy is one of the chief currencies through which gifts of this sort are exchanged. One way to tell someone—particularly someone of the opposite sex— that you have feelings of affection and love for them is by allowing to them or sharing with them sexual behaviors that one doesn't share with the rest of the world. This way of measuring affection was certainly very much a part of the culture in which I matured. It worked something like this. If you were a girl, you showed how much you liked someone by the degree of sexual intimacy you would allow. If you liked a boy only a little, you never did more than kiss—and even the kiss was not very passionate. If you liked the boy a lot and if your feeling was reciprocated, necking, and possibly petting, was permissible. If the attachment was still stronger and you thought it might even become a permanent relationship, the sexual activity was correspondingly more intense and more intimate, although whether it would ever lead to sexual intercourse depended on whether the parties (and particularly the girl) accepted fully the prohibition on non-marital sex. The situation for the boy was related, but not exactly the same. The assumption was that males did not naturally link sex with affection in the way in which females did. However, since women did, males had to take this into account. That is to say, because a woman would permit sexual intimacies only if she had feelings of affection for the male and only if those feelings were reciprocated, the male had to have and express those feelings, too, before sexual intimacies of any sort would occur.

The result was that the importance of a correlation between sexual intimacy and feelings of love and affection was taught by the culture and assimilated by those growing up in the culture. The scale of possible positive feelings toward persons of the other sex ran from casual liking at the one end to the love that was deemed essential to and characteristic of marriage at the other. The scale of possible sexual behavior ran from brief, passionless kissing or hand-holding at the one end to sexual intercourse at the other. And the correlation between the two scales was quite precise. As a result, any act of sexual intimacy carried substantial meaning with it, and no act of sexual intimacy was simply a pleasurable set of bodily sensations. Many such acts were, of course, more pleasurable to the participants because they were a way of saying what the participants' feelings were. And sometimes they were less pleasurable for the same reason. The point is, however, that in any event sexual activity was much more than mere bodily enjoyment. It was not like eating a good meal, listening to good music, lying in the sun, or getting a pleasant back rub. It was behavior that meant a great deal concerning one's feelings for persons of the opposite sex in whom one was most interested and with whom one was most involved. It was among the most authoritative ways in which one could communicate to another the nature and degree of one's affection.

If this sketch is even roughly right, then several things become somewhat clearer. To begin with, a possible rationale for many of the rules of conventional sexual morality can be developed. If, for example, sexual intercourse is associated with the kind of affection and commitment to another that is regarded as characteristic of the marriage relationship, then it is natural that sexual intercourse should be thought properly to take place between persons who are married to each other. And if it is thought that this kind of affection and commitment is only to be found within the marriage relationship, then it is not surprising that sexual intercourse should only be thought to be proper within marriage.

Related to what has just been said is the idea that sexual intercourse ought to be restricted to those who are married to each other as a means by which to confirm the very special feelings that the spouses have for each other. Because the culture teaches that sexual intercourse means that the strongest of all feelings for each other are shared by the lovers, it is natural that persons who are married to each other should be able to say this to each other in this way. Revealing and confirming verbally that these feelings are present is one thing that helps to sustain the relationship; engaging in sexual intercourse is another.

In addition, this account would help to provide a framework within which to make sense of the notion that some sex is better than other sex. As I indicated earlier, the fact that sexual intimacy can be meaningful in the sense described tends to make it also the case that sexual intercourse can sometimes be more enjoyable than at other times. On this view, sexual intercourse will typically be more enjoyable where the strong feelings of affection are present than it will be where it is merely "mechanical." This is so in part because people enjoy being loved, especially by those whom they love. Just as we like to hear words of affection, so we like to receive affectionate behavior. And the meaning enhances the independently pleasurable behavior.

More to the point, moreover, an additional rationale for the prohibition on extramarital sex can now be developed. For given this way of viewing the sexual world, extramarital sex will almost always involve deception of a deeper sort. If the adulterous spouse does not in fact have the appropriate feelings of affection for the extramarital partner, then the adulterous spouse is deceiving that person about the presence of such feelings. If, on the other hand, the adulterous spouse does have the corresponding feelings for the extramarital partner but not toward the nonparticipating spouse, the adulterous spouse is very probably deceiving the nonparticipating spouse about the presence of such feelings toward that spouse. Indeed, it might be argued, whenever there is no longer love between the two persons who are married to each other, there is deception just because being married implies both to the participants and to the world that such a bond exists. Deception is inevitable, the argument might conclude, because the feelings of affection that ought to accompany any act of sexual intercourse can only be held toward one other person at any given time in one's life. And if this is so, then the adulterous spouse always deceives either the partner in adultery or the nonparticipating spouse about the existence of such feelings. Thus extramarital sex involves deception of this sort and is for this reason immoral even if no deception vis-à-vis the occurrence of the act of adultery takes place.

What might be said in response to the foregoing arguments? The first thing that might be said is that the account of the connection between sexual intimacy and feelings of affection is inaccurate. Not inaccurate in the sense that no one thinks of things that way, but in the sense that there is substantially more divergence of opinion than that account suggests. For example, the view I have delineated may describe reasonably accurately the concepts of the sexual world in which I grew up, but it does not capture the sexual *weltanschauung* of today's youth at all. Thus, whether or not adultery implies deception in respect to feelings depends very much on the persons who are involved and the way they look at the "meaning" of sexual intimacy.

Second, the argument leaves to be answered the question of whether it is desirable for sexual intimacy to carry the sorts of messages described above. For those persons for whom sex does have these implications, there are special feelings and sensibilities that must be taken into account. But it is another question entirely whether any valuable end—moral or otherwise—is served by investing sexual behavior with such significance. That is something that must be shown and not just assumed. It might, for instance, be the case that substantially more good than harm would come from a kind of demystification of sexual behavior: one that would encourage the enjoyment of sex more for its own sake and one that would reject the centrality both of the association of sex with love and of love with only one other person.

I regard these as two of the more difficult, unresolved issues that our culture faces today in respect to thinking sensibly about the attitudes toward sex and love that we should try to develop in ourselves and in our children. Much of the contemporary literature that advocates sexual liberation of one sort or another embraces one or the other of two different views about the relationship between sex and love.

One view holds that sex should be separated from love and affection. To be sure sex is probably better when the partners genuinely like and enjoy each other. But sex is basically an intensive, exciting sensuous activity that can be enjoyed in a variety of suitable settings with a variety of suitable partners. The situation in respect to sexual pleasure is no different from that of the person who knows and appreciates fine food and who can have a very satisfying meal in any number of good restaurants with any number of congenial companions. One question that must be settled here is whether sex can be so demystified; another, more important question is whether it would be desirable to do so. What would we gain and what might we lose if we all lived in a world in which an act of sexual intercourse was no more or less significant or enjoyable than having a delicious meal in a nice setting with a good friend? The answer to this question lies beyond the scope of this paper.

The second view seeks to drive the wedge in a different place. It is not the link between sex and love that needs to be broken; rather, on this view, it is the connection between love and exclusivity that ought to be severed. For a number of the reasons already given, it is desirable, so this argument goes, that sexual intimacy continue to be reserved to and shared with only those for whom one has very great affection. The mistake lies in thinking that any "normal" adult will only have those feelings toward one other adult during his or her lifetime—or even at any time in his or her life. It is the concept of adult love, not ideas about sex, that, on this view, needs demystification. What are thought to be both unrealistic and unfortunate are the notions of exclusivity and possessiveness that attach to the dominant conception of love between adults in our and other cultures. Parents of four, five, six, or even ten children can certainly claim and sometimes claim correctly that they love all of their children, that they love them all equally, and that it is simply untrue to their feelings to insist that the numbers involved diminish either the quantity or the quality of their love. If this is an idea that is readily understandable in the case of parents and children, there is no necessary reason why it is an impossible or undesirable ideal in the case of adults. To be sure, there is probably a limit to the number of intimate, "primary" relationships that any person can maintain at any given time without the quality of the relationship being affected. But one adult ought surely be able to love two, three, or even six other adults at any one time without that love being different in kind or degree from that of the traditional, monogomous, lifetime marriage. And as between the individuals in these relationships, whether within a marriage or without, sexual intimacy is fitting and good.

The issues raised by a position such as this one are also surely worth exploring in detail and with care. Is there something to be called "sexual love" which is different from parental love or the nonsexual love of close friends? Is there something about love in general that links it naturally and appropriately with feelings of exclusivity and possession? Or is there something about sexual love, whatever that may be, that makes these feelings especially fitting here? Once again the issues are conceptual, empirical, and normative all at once: What is love? How could it be different? Would it be a good thing or a bad thing if it were different?

Suppose, though, that having delineated these problems we were now to pass them by. Suppose, moreover, we were to be persuaded of the possibility and the desirability of weakening substantially either the links between sex and love or the links between sexual love and exclusivity. Would it not then be the case that adultery could be free from all of the morally objectionable features described so far? To be more specific, let us imagine that a husband and wife have what is today sometimes characterized as an "open marriage." Suppose, that is, that they have agreed in advance that extramarital sex is—under certain circumstances—acceptable behavior for each to engage in. Suppose, that as a result there is no impulse to deceive each other about the occurrence or nature of any such relationships, and that no deception in fact occurs. Suppose, too, that there is no deception in respect to the feelings involved between the adulterous spouse and the extramarital partner. And suppose, finally, that one or the other or both of the spouses then has sexual intercourse in circumstances consistent with these understandings. Under this description, so the agreement might conclude, adultery is simply not immoral. At a minimum, adultery cannot very plausibly be condemned either on the ground that it involves deception or on the ground that it requires the breaking of a promise.

At least two responses are worth considering. One calls attention to the connection between marriage and adultery; the other looks to more instrumental arguments for the immorality of adultery. Both issues deserve further exploration.

One way to deal with the case of the "open marriage" is to question whether the two persons involved are still properly to be described as being married to each other. Part of the meaning of what it is for two persons to be married to each other, so this argument would go, is to have committed oneself to have sexual relationships only with one's spouse. Of course, it would be added, we know that that commitment is not always honored. We know that persons who are married to each other often do commit adultery. But there is a difference between being willing to make a commitment to marital fidelity, even though one may fail to honor that commitment, and not making the commitment at all. Whatever the relationship may be between the two individuals in the case described above, the absence of any commitment to sexual exclusivity requires the conclusion that their relationship is not a marital one. For a commitment to sexual exclusivity is a necessary although not a sufficient condition for the existence of a marriage.

Although there may be something to this suggestion, as it is stated it is too strong to be acceptable. To begin with, I think it is very doubtful that there are many, if any, *necessary* conditions for marriage; but even if there are, a commitment to sexual exclusivity is not such a condition.

To see that this is so, consider what might be taken to be some of the essential characteristics of a marriage. We might be tempted to propose that the concept of marriage requires the following: a formal ceremony of some sort in which mutual obligations are undertaken between two persons of the opposite sex; the capacity on the part of the persons involved to have sexual intercourse with each other; the willingness to have sexual intercourse only with each other; and feelings of love and affection between the two persons. The problem is that we can imagine relationships that are clearly marital and yet lack one or more of these features. For example, in our own society, it is possible for two persons to be married without going through a formal ceremony, as in the common-law marriages recognized in some jurisdictions. It is also possible for two persons to get married even though one or both lacks the capacity to engage in sexual intercourse. Thus, two very elderly persons who have neither the desire nor the ability to have intercourse can, nonetheless, get married, as can persons whose sexual organs have been injured so that intercourse is not possible. And we certainly know of marriages in which love was not present at the time of the marriage, as, for instance, in marriages of state and marriages of convenience.

Counterexamples not satisfying the condition relating to the abstention from extramarital sex are even more easily produced. We certainly know of societies and cultures in which polygamy and polyandry are practiced, and we have no difficulty in recognizing these relationships as cases of marriages. It might be objected, though, that these are not counterexamples because they are plural marriages rather than marriages in which sex is permitted with someone other than with one of the persons to whom one is married. But we also know of societies in which it is permissible for married persons to have sexual relationships with persons to whom they were not married, for example, temple prostitutes, concubines, and homosexual lovers. And even if we knew of no such societies, the conceptual claim would still, I submit, not be well taken. For suppose all of the other indicia of marriage were present: suppose the two persons were of the opposite sex. Suppose they had the capacity and desire to have intercourse with each other, suppose they participated in a formal ceremony in which they understood themselves voluntarily to be entering into a relationship with each other in which substantial mutual commitments were assumed. If all these conditions were satisfied, we would not be in any doubt about whether or not the two persons were married even though they had not taken on a commitment of sexual exclusivity and even though they had expressly agreed that extramarital sexual intercourse was a permissible behavior for each to engage in.

A commitment to sexual exclusivity is neither a necessary nor a sufficient condition for the existence of a marriage. It does, nonetheless, have this much to do with the nature of marriage: like the other indicia enumerated above, its presence tends to establish the existence of a marriage. Thus, in the absence of a formal ceremony of any sort, an explicit commitment to sexual exclusivity would count in favor of regarding the two persons as married. The conceptual role of the commitment to sexual exclusivity can, perhaps, be brought out through the following example. Suppose we found a tribe which had a practice in which all the other indicia of marriage were present but in which the two parties were *prohibited* ever from having sexual intercourse with each other. Moreover, suppose that sexual intercourse with others was clearly permitted. In such a case we would, I think, reject the idea that the two were married to each other and we would describe their relationship in other terms, for example, as some kind of formalized, special friendship relation—a kind of heterosexual "blood-brother" bond.

Compare that case with the following. Suppose again that the tribe had a practice in which all of the other indicia of marriage were present, but instead of a prohibition on sexual intercourse between the persons in the relationship there was no rule at all. Sexual intercourse was permissible with the person with whom one had this ceremonial relationship, but it was no more or less permissible than with a number of other persons to whom one was not so related (for instance, all consenting adults of the opposite sex). Although we might be in doubt as to whether we ought to describe the persons as married to each other, we would probably conclude that they were married and that they simply were members of a tribe whose views about sex were quite different from our own.

What all of this shows is that *a prohibition* on sexual intercourse between the two persons involved in a relationship is conceptually incompatible with the claim that the two of them are married. The *permissibility* of intramarital sex is a necessary part of the idea of marriage. But no such incompatibility follows simply from the added permissibility of extramarital sex.

These arguments do not, of course, exhaust the arguments for the prohibition on extramarital sexual relations. The remaining argument that I wish to consider—as I indicated earlier—is a more instrumental one. It seeks to justify the prohibition by virtue of the role that it plays in the development and maintenance of nuclear families. The argument, or set of arguments, might, I believe, go something like this.

Consider first a farfetched nonsexual example. Suppose a society were organized so that after some suitable age—say, 18, 19, or 20—persons were forbidden to eat anything but bread and water with anyone but their spouse. Persons might still choose in such a society not to get married. Good food just might not be very important to them because they have underdeveloped taste buds. Or good food might be bad for them because there is something wrong with their digestive system. Or good food might be important to them, but they might decide that the enjoyment of good food would get in the way of the attainment of other things that were more important. But most persons would, I think, be led to favor marriage in part because they preferred a richer, more varied, diet to one of bread and water. And they might remain married because the family was the only legitimate setting within which good food was obtainable. If it is important to have society organized so that persons will both get married and stay married, such an arrangement would be well suited to the preservation of the family, and the prohibitions relating to food consumption could be understood as fulfilling that function.

It is obvious that one of the more powerful human desires is the desire for sexual gratification. The desire is a natural one, like hunger and thirst, in the sense that it need not be learned in order to be present within us and operative upon us. But there is in addition much that we do learn about what the act of sexual intercourse is like. Once we experience sexual intercourse ourselves—and in particular once we experience orgasm—we discover that it is among the most intensive, short-term pleasures of the body.

Because this is so, it is easy to see how the prohibition upon extramarital sex helps to hold marriage together. At least during that period of life when the enjoyment of sexual intercourse is one of the desirable bodily pleasures, persons will wish to enjoy those pleasures. If one consequence of being married is that one is prohibited from having sexual intercourse with anyone but one's spouse, then the spouses in a marriage are in a position to provide an important source of pleasure for each other that is unavailable to them elsewhere in the society.

The point emerges still more clearly if this rule of sexual morality is seen as of a piece with the other rules of sexual morality. When this prohibition is coupled, for example, with the prohibition on nonmarital sexual intercourse, we are presented with the inducement both to get married and to stay married. For if sexual intercourse is only legitimate within marriage, then persons seeking that gratification which is a feature of sexual intercourse are furnished explicit social directions for its attainment; namely marriage.

Nor, to continue the argument, is it necessary to focus exclusively on the bodily enjoyment that is involved. Orgasm may be a significant part of what there is to sexual intercourse, but it is not the whole of it. We need only recall the earlier discussion of the meaning that sexual intimacy has in our own culture to begin to see some of the more intricate ways in which sexual exclusivity may be connected with the establishment and maintenance of marriage as the primary heterosexual, love relationship. Adultery is wrong, in other words, because a prohibition on extramarital sex is a way to help maintain the institutions of marriage and the nuclear family.

Now I am frankly not sure what we are to say about an argument such as this one. What I am convinced of is that, like the arguments discussed earlier, this one also reveals something of the difficulty and complexity of the issues that are involved. So, what I want now to do—in the brief and final portion of this paper—is to try to delineate with reasonable precision what I take several of the fundamental, unresolved issues to be.

The first is whether this last argument is an argument for the *immorality* of extramarital sexual intercourse. What does seem clear is that there are differences between this argument and the ones considered earlier. The earlier arguments condemned adulterous behavior because it was behavior that involved breaking of a promise, taking unfair advantage, or deceiving another. To the degree to which the prohibition on extramarital sex can be supported by arguments which invoke considerations such as these, there is little question but that violations of the prohibition are properly regarded as immoral. And such a claim could be defended on one or both of two distinct grounds. The first is that things like promise-breaking and deception are just wrong. The second is that adultery involving promise-breaking or deception is wrong because it involves the straightforward infliction of harm on another human being—typically the nonadulterous spouse—who has a strong claim not to have that harm so inflicted.

The argument that connects the prohibition on extramarital sex with the maintenance and preservation of the institution of marriage is an argument for the instrumental value of the prohibition. To some degree this counts, I think, against regarding all violations of the prohibition as obvious cases of immorality. This is so partly because hypothetical imperatives are less clearly within the domain of morality than are categorical ones, and even more because instrumental prohibitions are within the domain of morality only if the end they serve or the way they serve it is itself within the domain of morality.

What this should help us see, I think, is the fact that the argument that connects the prohibition on adultery with the preservation of marriage is at best seriously incomplete. Before we ought to be convinced by it, we ought to have reasons for believing that marriage is a morally desirable and just social institution. And this is not quite as easy or obvious a task as it may seem to be. For the concept of marriage is, as we have seen, both a loosely structured and a complicated one. There may be all sorts of intimate, interpersonal relationships which will resemble but not be identical with the typical marriage relationship presupposed by the traditional sexual morality. There may be a number of distinguishable sexual and loving arrangements which can all legitimately claim to be called *marriages*. The prohibitions of the traditional sexual morality may be effective ways to maintain some marriages and ineffective ways to promote and preserve others. The prohibitions of the traditional sexual morality may make good psychological sense if certain psychological theories are true, and they may be purveyors of immense psychological mischief if other psychological theories are true. The prohibitions of the traditional sexual morality may seem obviously correct if sexual intimacy carries the meaning that the dominant culture has often ascribed to it, and they may seem equally bizarre when sex is viewed through the perspective of the counter-culture. Irrespective of whether instrumental arguments of this sort are properly deemed moral arguments, they ought not to fully convince anyone until questions like these are answered.

Sex and Personal Intimacy

JOHN HUNTER

We have found that while our sex lives are matters of proper moral concern in many ways and cases, sexual activity is not immoral nearly so often as some people would have us believe. In this chapter it will be suggested that there is more than one mode of evaluation of behavior in general and sexual behavior in particular: not all defects are moral imperfections, and not all perfections moral virtues. The specific mode of evaluation with which we will be concerned here is that of personal intimacy. What we will call "personal intimacy" is not something commonly known by that or any other name; but it will be argued that it is something about which many people do care, and which could be recommended to those who so far have not learned to care about it.

Before explaining the concept of personal intimacy, it will be useful to make as clear as possible the idea, and the implications of the idea, that there are various modes of evaluation of behavior, not all of them moral. That will be the task of this introduction.

We may praise or criticize human behavior on moral, aesthetic and intellectual grounds, to name some of the most obvious. People are admired for achieving high standards, and criticized for failing to do so, but the admiration and criticism are of a different kind from case to case. Except in special cases, it is not immoral to paint a picture amateurishly or sing a tune off key. We would criticize but not deplore these things, and certainly not chastise or imprison the person who did them.

We admire people who are witty, perceptive, friendly or warm, and criticize them for being humorless or obtuse or insensitive; but except in special cases, the former are not moral virtues and the latter not moral vices. It is not saintly of a person to be an entertaining conversationalist or a shrewd observer; it is possible for thieves, liars and cowards to be perceptive or witty and for honest, brave and generous people to be dull, gauche or unfriendly. . . .

[This distinction] opens the possibility that some of our sexual activities may be regrettable without being immoral; but if anything is substandard in some nonmoral way, its avoidance will not be something we have a right to require of people, but will be a matter of preference, recommendation, encouragement. We will perhaps teach people to appreciate the preferred way of managing things, in much the way we cultivate taste in architecture or music. The preferred way will be recommended, not as a concession to other people, but primarily as something personally rewarding; and it will be treated as sad, rather than unacceptable, when anyone is slow to learn such things.

WHAT IS PERSONAL INTIMACY?

There are at least three distinguishable ways in which personal relations can be better or worse, and it will be the aim of this section to concentrate on one of these, delineating it as clearly as possible and distinguishing it from the other two.

We might call the first point of view from which our relations with people can be evaluated that of *congeniality*. If two people bore or annoy one another, then given that they have a relationship—for example, if they work at the same place or are members of the same family—it is a poor or unsatisfactory one; while if each finds the other amusing, interesting or merely agreeable, they have a satisfactory or congenial relationship. If they are uncongenial they may also be nasty or deceitful, and then their relationship will involve questions of morality; but an uncongenial relationship is not in itself immoral, nor is a congenial one in itself virtuous. We can be uncongenial without being nasty, and congenial without being helpful or considerate. There is, of course, the case in which it is because someone is immoral in some way that he is uncongenial; but even here there is a distinction between the person interesting enough to be congenial, if he were not so malicious, and the person who would be boring even if he were saintly.

Secondly, a person can be morally upright in his dealings with people, without finding those persons congenial or being found so by them. Indeed, we might say that it is the mark of a virtuous person to be honest, generous and so on toward others regardless of whether they are congenial. A person who is fair or considerate only toward people he likes is to that extent morally defective.

Congeniality and morality are then two of our three ways in which personal relationships can be better or worse; and their distinctness from one another is shown by their independent variability, by the fact that one of them can exist without the other.

The third dimension we will call *personal intimacy*. That expression has no clear ordinary use, nor do we have much else in the way of a standard vocabulary for talking about this quality sometimes found in our relations with people; however, if we describe some examples of its presence and its absence, most of us will recognize something that we care a good deal about; that we rejoice in when it exists and regret when it does not exist.

If two people see a good deal of one another, talk animatedly and enjoy doing things together, each may yet remain somewhat of a mystery to the other. An amusing remark about a serious subject may leave the other person wondering whether the remark was made with no serious intent and merely because it was amusing, or whether it expressed a cynical or sceptical attitude. If questions like that somehow just cannot be raised between them, their relationship may be felt to be defective in being, although extremely congenial, quite superficial.

Similarly, if two people have been on friendly terms and one of them moves to another city for a time and does not write, but resumes the amicable relationship on his return, it may be unclear whether in the interval he missed or thought about his friend, or whether the friendship had no deeper basis than the pleasure of the moment. If that question could somehow not be raised, then although these two people may entirely enjoy one another, and although there need be no deception, unkindness or other moral fault, something is missing.

It is the same thing as is missing sometimes between persons who meet and have a convivial time at a party. They may regard party conversation as a kind of game at which one can be skilled, the object of which is to take on any topic someone raises and make it the subject of a fine display of wit and discernment. Part of the fun is in being able to do something with whatever topic comes up, and poor players are people who are stumped by too many topics. One may very much enjoy this game, and be delighted to meet someone who plays it well, but go away knowing little about the other person, not interested in how he gets along with his wife, what he does on weekends or whether he fears death, and not inclined to help him fix his washing machine or to drop by his place on a Saturday just to say hello. It is not that in party conversation such personal topics as the fear of death are avoided, but they are treated in a way that leaves it unclear what lies behind the display of wit and discernment: whether the good conversationalist has the same thoughts when he is alone at night as he is now offering for our amusement.

We might say that in such cases what is missing is interest in the person. There is interest, not in the person, but in the output: in various capacities that we may find amusing or congenial or useful. We may want good company or good conversation or skill at chess or tennis or lovemaking, and it may not matter who possesses these desired qualities.

We see the same lack of personal interest in commercial relationships, although in these cases it does not usually strike anyone as regrettable. A plumber comes and fixes the water tank; we pay him and he rushes on to his next job. There is perhaps time for a joke or for him to admire the garden, but there is little question of his staying for supper. We are interested in him only in his capacity as a fixer of pipes. This is not because of snobbishness about plumbers: it would be the same with lawyers or doctors. There is just no time in our lives for more than a few close personal relationships.

We should not let the examples of the plumber or the party-goer lead us to think that it is a question of *how many* of a person's capacities we are interested in. Two people may be married and find one another satisfactory mates. They may usually sort out their differences amicably, be proud of one another in public, have interesting conversations about friends, films and books, and enjoy one another in bed—and yet be quite capable of parting with no greater sense of loss than derives from the rarity of such a congenial arrangement. If one mate could immediately be replaced by another equally congenial and there was no sense of a particular personal loss, then there was not an attachment to just this person. Each person was interested, not in the other person, but in that person's conversation, taste, cheerfulness, cooking ability or sexual compatibility.

This extreme case brings out an important point about the concept of being interested in specific persons. As long as we limit ourselves to cases in which we are interested in some one or some few qualities in a person, it can look as if what is missing is just breadth of appreciation: if we were interested in a person not only as an enjoyable lover or a competent plumber or an agreeable conversationalist, but in most of his other qualities and abilities as well, that would be what it is to be interested in him as a person. But in the case of the couple who are entirely pleased with one another, there are no other qualities to be appreciated. Hence the question arises, what is it to be interested in a person? What can there be, over and above all the qualities we are supposing these two people appreciate, in which they might be interested? It would surely be absurd to say that we are interested in something that never shows, something underlying all such things as high spirits and courage and gentleness and wit.

If we seem here to be on the verge of having to suppose that there is something mysterious or hidden that we can appreciate or fail to appreciate, it is perhaps because we are predisposed to think that being interested in a person is a matter of appreciating some good quality or another. Given that supposition, on the one hand, we must find some quality to be appreciated, and on the other, in the case of the couple who like most everything about one another, we can find no ordinary quality to fill the slot, and we have no option but to look for some mysterious or hidden quality. But if being interested in someone is not a matter of appreciating qualities, we will not find ourselves in that peculiar fix.

What then *is* being interested in a person? If we suppose that there is nothing mysterious about it, it ought to be accessible to perceptive observation. As a prelude to trying to say what it is, let us review some significant differences we can notice between personal and impersonal relationships. To do this we can either set before ourselves some extreme cases, or construct a composite out of tendencies noticeable in various moderate cases.

1. The conversation of people whose relation is impersonal will have a kind of showiness about it, as if they were always playing to an

audience; and the topics of conversation will either run to matters of little or no personal involvement, such as films, books, news items, puzzles and scientific curiosities, or, if they extend to such things as the hopes, fears, joys and tribulations of the parties themselves, will be handled in such a way as to conceal attitudes. A person will perhaps be amusing or scientific about his fears, and one will be left wondering whether he is amused by them when they are upon him, and if so what kind of fears they can be.

2. In an impersonal relation, each person's appreciation of the other will run noticeably to concentration on the output, as we have put it: on the joke or the interesting story, for example, rather than on who made the joke or told the story. It is the difference between "What a good joke!" and "How funny you are!" Each will rejoice in the interest of the performance, and it will seem incidental who is performing.

3. In an impersonal relation, tensions, disagreements and disappointments will tend immediately to threaten the connection. If we are interested only in the quality of the output, enthusiasm will diminish to the extent that the quality deteriorates. The attitude will be like the average person's feeling for his car: delighted with it as long as it looks good and performs well, willing to put up with it when it develops faults as long as no other is readily available and able to part with it without a sigh when something better becomes available.

4. By contrast, we tend to dote even on the imperfections of someone in whom our interest is personal. The peculiar plainness of a face or a peculiar awkwardness of manner are welcomed, not as being in general admirable qualities, but just as being so characteristic of a person for whom we care.

5. While people who are impersonally related may stimulate each other to better than average displays of their capabilities, when a relation is personal we draw each other out, reveal ourselves. We express ourselves unreservedly to one another, and if there is uncertainty as to the other person's attitudes or feelings, it is not because they are kept back, but just because there has not happened to be an occasion to express them.

From these observations we might construct the following generalizations:

(a) A test of whether a relationship is personal or not is whether anyone else having the same or comparable good qualities would do as well. A commercial relationship is usually impersonal, and there it makes no difference, as between honest and competent practitioners, whom we employ; and similarly in our friendships if we can move without a sigh from one person to another who is equally congenial, our relationship is impersonal.

(b) The application of this test is complicated somewhat by the fact that it may pain us to lose a friend, not because of a particular attachment to that person, but only because congenial connections can be somewhat rare, or because we have been particularly fortunate in a certain friendship. Then we will experience a sense of loss, and it may not be clear whether that is because there was a particular attachment, or because of the difficulty of finding a replacement. The test may still be useful, however, either in the case in which we are fortunate in replacing one friend by another, or in the case in which, although we enjoyed a friendship and it was not replaced by another, no loss was felt. In other cases, we may have to apply other tests.

(c) There is, paradoxically perhaps, a sense in which a personal relation is objective, and an impersonal one subjective: in the latter case it is just to the extent that I find a person's qualities agreeable or congenial that I am interested, whereas in the former case I care about a person's tastes or hopes or fears *whatever they may be*, just because they are that person's. There is thus a quality of total acceptance about a relationship that is personal, a readiness to let the chips fall where they may.

(d) There are two related character traits that make for personal intimacy, one a disposition to trust other people, so that one will not fear to reveal oneself, and the other a tendency to inspire trust. Conversely, a disposition to fear other people and a tendency to inspire fear will make for such self-concealing behavior as hiding behind a wall of banter and wit, or avoiding such closeness as would create pressures to show oneself.

Being interested in a person, then, is not a matter of appreciating something in addition to various charms and abilities, but of relating to someone in a certain way—a way that is outgoing and trusting, that is not contingent on maintaining any particular standard of attractiveness or agreeability, and that tends to find personal qualities interesting independent of their charm, just because they are the qualities of a given person.

To make perfectly clear that personal intimacy is a quality of human relationships quite distinct from morality or congeniality, we need to show that it varies independently of them, that whatever connections there may be, it is possible to have one without the other.

In the case of congeniality, there is a connection with personal intimacy in that we are not likely to have a very close relationship with someone who is quite uncongenial; but on the other hand, (i) the person with an aptitude for personal intimacy will be undemanding with regard to congeniality, will not always be reviewing friendships as to whether they are sufficiently rewarding; and (ii) clearly there is congeniality without personal intimacy in our cases of the party-goers or the couple who find one another altogether agreeable.

In the case of morality, it seems clear in the first place that there need be nothing morally wrong with a relationship that is impersonal. Take, as the hardest case, the man who engages the services of a prostitute: there need be nothing deceitful, cruel, unfair, selfish or cowardly about such an episode, and hence except in special cases his action, although impersonal, is not immoral. There can, of course, be immorality in such cases; for example, if he is cruel or gratuitously insulting to the woman, or does not pay her, or if he later has sexual contact with someone else without knowing whether he has contracted venereal disease, or if he pretends to deplore the practice of prostitution. But none of these faults must exist, and when they do not it is difficult to see on what ground it could be represented as immoral to use the services of a prostitute. Yet the relationship is normally lacking in personal warmth.

(There is something to be said for the argument that, since it is almost certainly harmful to a person, at least over any length of time, to be a prostitute, anyone employing her services contributes to the degradation of a human being. To do that is certainly immoral; but since prostitutes will generally continue their activities regardless of whether any particular person employs them, it is not perfectly clear whether each customer contributes to their degradation. But even if that is true, it is not because the relationship is impersonal that something immoral is done, but because the life of a prostitute is so afflicted with cruelty, harassment and disease.)

Take a less extreme case: there are people who do not much care for other people, but greatly enjoy the excitement of sex. They may seek out others who are like-minded, and who when called upon most any time will eagerly make love. If these people conscientiously avoid sexual involvement with anyone who shows signs of being in love, or of regarding sexual activity as anything more than a pleasure, and if they are careful not to mislead another person as to their own attitude, there would be nothing dishonest, cruel, harmful or unfair about their practice, and therefore no ground for saying it is immoral. However, such relationships are clearly impersonal.

This is not to say, of course, that no purely sexual relationship is ever immoral, but only that it is not immoral just because it is purely sexual. If there is deception or cruelty, or carelessness about contraception, there will be moral defect; but those faults are independent of the impersonal character of the relationship, and by no means typical of such relationships.

At the other extreme from our first case is the example of our broadly congenial couple whose relation is impersonal. It is obvious here that in spite of the impersonal character of their relationship, there is nothing immoral about it. They may be as fair, honest, generous and considerate as anyone could ask, without revealing themselves to one another, or having any greater attachment than is dictated by the quality of the other person's charms.

Yet there are two reasons why, in spite of the above arguments, some people might hesitate to accept the contention that morality varies independently of personal intimacy:

1. Morality is often (and probably correctly) represented as being at

least in part a matter of respect for persons, of treating other people, as Kant put it, "never merely as means, but always also as ends in themselves"; but personal intimacy appears from what we have seen to require the same attitude. How then is it possible for them to vary independently?

The answer is that the ethical way of treating people as ends in themselves is different from the personal intimacy way. A typical ethical application of the principle might be that if something one considers doing will adversely affect another person, then that fact alone demands to be taken account of in our ethical thinking. The ethical attitude is that it does not matter whether the person in question is a friend or a stranger, rich or poor, saintly or sinful. All we need to know is that a human being would be adversely affected. To have that attitude is to have respect for persons. If I delude someone, even into doing something that is to his advantage, I have not treated him with the kind of respect due to a person: I have not allowed him to decide in a free and well-informed way what he will do. In these cases, it is just because it is a human being we are dealing with that we act in certain ways, not because it is a specific person. It may be a boring and annoying fact that his interests would be adversely affected. We need not be intrigued by it or probe into it; and our actions can be affected by it without there being any personal contact whatever, without the other person knowing that we have changed our plans because of the way they might affect his interests. He can be someone we know of only indirectly; and even where there is personal contact, the transaction need involve none of the colorful interplay between persons that is characteristic of personal intimacy.

In the moral application of the principle, whether we are interested in a person or not, we treat him with respect; whereas the application in the case of personal intimacy is a matter of taking an interest. The interest we take is itself the burden of the principle. We take that interest, not with a view to being able to behave well toward other people, but with a view to appreciating them more, and to having a warmer and richer relationship.

2. It is sometimes said that a person is morally defective if he does right by other people merely from principle, and not out of any kind of affection or personal concern. If this is true, then personal intimacy would perhaps have to be regarded as part of morality, and they could not vary independently; but surely it is not true. A wife may be disappointed if her husband is faithful and considerate, not out of enthusiasm for her, but out of duty, but she can hardly say it is morally defective of him. She is right in thinking that it would be more rewarding if he rejoiced in her as a person, but wrong in thinking it would be morally better. She has not made the distinction we have been trying to draw between two fundamentally different types or scales of evaluation.

Morality requires that we do right by people regardless of whether we know or like them, and therefore it must vary independently of personal intimacy. The quality of life would deteriorate radically if we were expected to be fair or generous only to our friends.

There are, however, relations between the personal and the ethical. Although it is possible to treat another person fairly and with consideration when one feels no personal attachment or enthusiasm, it requires a particular effort and a higher level of concern than is common in the human race. On the other hand, it comes naturally to us to be fair and considerate to someone we rejoice in as a person, because when we care for a person, we become involved in their interests as if they were our own.

In such relations as these between the personal and the moral lies the great strength of any moral perspective in which love has a central place; for example, Christianity. It is easy and natural to do right by someone you love; and one might say that Christianity, recognizing this, chooses to say little about just how to do right, but instead tries to encourage love, which may, if we independently have some understanding of moral virtue, motivate us to do what we know to be right. The weaknesses of such an approach are chiefly two: (i) it tends not to face up to the fact that, while we must do right by everyone, we deceive ourselves if we think we can or do love everyone, and (ii) it offers little guidance as to how to do right, and thus both leaves us ill equipped for the finer questions of right behavior toward those we do love, and quite unprepared for virtuous treatment of people we do not love. It also encourages us to believe that we love people whom we do not love, and so to believe that we are doing right by them when we are not.

If we are right in concluding that it is not a moral question whether our relations with other people are impersonal . . . impersonal relationships are not something we have a right to complain of, and personal intimacy is not something we have right to insist on. If I choose to avoid people who, however amusing they may be, do not reveal themselves and take no personal interest in me, I am expressing a personal preference. I should not despise or deplore such people, and there should be no question of their being penalized or refused entry into the country, as there might be if they were deemed immoral.

If it is not a moral question what kind of personal relationships we have, but a matter of personal preference, is it as much a matter of taste as whether one likes strawberry jam, or are there nonmoral considerations that make one kind of relationship preferable to another?

To put the question just this way suggests falsely that personal intimacy can be achieved at will, that it is as much under our control as what we eat or what we do with our leisure time. There are at least two reasons why this is not true: (i) it is a mutual thing, and depends very much on the reactions and attitudes of the other person, and (ii) one has to have or to cultivate a certain disposition before it is possible, and when one has that disposition, close personal relationships *happen*, rather than being artfully brought about. One cannot turn on the trust, the demonstrativeness or the kind of "objective" interest in people that we described earlier. If it is turned on, either its artificiality shows, defeating one's purpose, or in any case it *is* artificial, and a falsity in the relationship emerges.

Yet it may be possible over a period of time to cultivate these qualities in oneself; and for that reason it is worth asking what sorts of personal relations are preferable. As with most questions of personal preference, the considerations making something advisable or otherwise will relate to individual tastes, capacities and situations, and therefore the wisest and best advised will not necessarily all make the same choice. Some people may be constitutionally ill equipped for close personal relations, and may be happier emphasizing other forms of social relationship. However, since we are all capable of changing, it is difficult to be sure what one's taste or capacity is. Just as a person who initially dislikes chess or mathematics may become an enthusiast, so we may initially derive little satisfaction from friendships, until perhaps some exceptional person breaks through the barriers of reserve and awkwardness and shows us capacities we did not know we had.

What kind of personal relations are preferable is perhaps basically a question of whether one finds a certain picture of oneself acceptable. One can live for a long time without self-examination, but when attention is drawn to the fact that in a sense one's life is perfectly solitary, that other people are nothing but sources of pleasure or annoyance, it is a question whether that fact is disturbing.

It is important here to keep moral considerations out of it. It is not a question of selfishness. It is possible to be quite generous and considerate of other people while taking no interest in them as persons. We should focus on the solitude and egoism of someone of as much moral rectitude as one could wish, who however takes no interest in people except insofar as either duty requires or fancy dictates.

We must all decide for ourselves whether we can live with such a picture of ourselves; but it is evident that many people neither want it for themselves nor like it in other people. This shows in their dismay at the coldness of someone who, however entertainingly, talks at them rather than to them, who loses interest if he is not entertained in return, who shows no curiosity about their hopes and anxieties, and with whom friendship seems a very fragile thing, entirely dependent on maintaining a sufficiently amusing output. It shows also in the desire of many people to reveal themselves: to be demonstrative in the expression of feeling, to share their dreams, discuss their problems or make known their virtues and faults.

We are in many ways afraid of other people, afraid of boring them or appearing foolish, afraid of establishing relationships that may overwhelm or hurt us, and so we withdraw behind facades of manners and safe behavior. But at the same time many of us yearn for warmer and more open personal relationships, and find it immensely gratifying if, with some few persons, this can be achieved.

It might be possible to see more clearly why personal intimacy can be gratifying if we paused here to replace a possible misconception as to its nature with a more revealing understanding of it. We sometimes want very much to be close to another person: to trust, to understand, to share secrets, to know that nothing is held back, and to be confident that if we express ourselves freely, what we say and do will be rejoiced in. While many of us want this, for some of us its achievement is a rare turn of fortune, and most of the time with most people we feel a lack of such intimacy. We are unsure whether we enjoy the confidence of another person, wonder what that person's real thoughts or feelings are, hesitate to let ourselves go for fear of doing or saying unwelcome things.

At such times another person may seem a mystery to us, something concealed behind actions and words, deep inside. It can seem that it is this inner person that we yearn to know; and when we reflect that we can never see behind a person's actions and words, we can come to feel unbearably alone in the world. The inner person is there, we think, but can never be known. Yet the idea of knowing the inner person does not cease to attract us. Any kind of closeness seems to be an approach to it, and it can even seem disappointing that by gazing into someone's eyes we cannot see the soul that lies behind them. Sexual intimacy similarly seems a way of getting close, and this may be one source of the intensity of our interest in sex; but again it is maddening that even here the hidden person is still not revealed.

It can seem to us that people's natures are very imperfectly shown by the way they smile, the things they say, the things that make them angry or sad or jubilant. We are impatient with the (as it seems) crude indications of the real person that we find in smiles and jokes and fits of temper, and we wish we could see right into a person. We of course do not want to see the inner things a surgeon sees, but rather the contents of another person's consciousness. We reckon that a person's true thoughts, desires, hopes and fears appear undisguised on the inner stage of consciousness, and it is for that show that we would like to have tickets.

Yet when we think of it, it should strike us that we do not know *ourselves* the way we would like to know another person. If we concentrate our attention just on what we are conscious of over any randomly chosen interval of time, the show is disappointing: perhaps some feelings of heat or cold, a twinge of pain in the shoulder, a sensation in the throat as we breathe, a slight feeling of weariness, a stray thought here and there about a problem that worries us or a plan we have. Nothing very significant or very revealing. If we could chronicle accurately what we are conscious of over any period of time, even the time when we are doing something that leaves another person mystified, it would be an uninteresting catalogue, and would scarcely satisfy anyone's desire to know the person behind our words and deeds. The fact, however, that the contents of anyone's consciousness are uninteresting does not show that we are all uninteresting people. A person may deliver himself of all sorts of ingenious suggestions, shrewd observations, beguiling fancies and comical remarks, and be most unusual in the things that excite or sadden him, without his conscious states being interesting to know of. The dullest and most interesting people will not likely differ greatly in the true reports they make of their conscious states.

If this seems surprising to you, perhaps that is because you think that everything of which a person delivers himself first appears on the inner stage; that only some of the things that so appear are in fact delivered; and that often what appears inwardly differs from what is delivered, owing either to some want of skill in expressing thoughts, feelings and attitudes, or to some reserve or some deviousness that makes us falsify what we say about ourselves.

If that were the case, there would be much more on the inner stage than is ever revealed outwardly, and in knowing the happenings on the inner stage one would be knowing a person as he is and not as he pretends to be or, through ineptitude, falsely appears to be. Yet are there always two things going on, what we think and what we say; and is it the case that these two things sometimes (perhaps ideally) agree, but all too often differ, either in that we say much less than we think, or in that we say something different from what we think?

Catch yourself in a lively and friendly conversation with someone and you will find that for the most part you just say things: you do not first think them and then say them, but interesting, funny or instructive remarks come forth directly. What you say is, even for you, all there is to your part of the conversation. It does not even *seem* as if something inward showed you what to say, and then you said it.

If the conversation is about a difficult or unfamiliar topic, the flow may not be so smooth. You may have to stop and struggle to find words. You may experience a sense of tension and effort, and may inwardly formulate something to say and decide against saying it because it is not quite true or not sufficiently clear; but if you find the right thing to say you will not generally say it to yourself first, and then aloud; after a time, words will come, and when you have said them you may or may not be pleased with the result of your struggle.

If a conversation is delicate and requires diplomacy, you may find yourself saying something different from what you think; but what you think is not necessarily or even generally spoken inwardly prior to or alongside of what you say: it is just that if you asked yourself whether what you said was quite frank, you would have to say no.

What you said aloud is different, not from what you said inwardly, but from what you would have said had you not been moved by diplomatic considerations.

Is this diplomacy at least something that went on inwardly, concealed from the other person—something that, had he seen it in the flow of your consciousness, he would have found revealing or disappointing? Perhaps some people think out their diplomatic stratagems explicitly, saying to themselves, for example, "I had better say something complimentary to this chap, because he is so sensitive"; but generally a diplomatic person acts instinctively. The artful things he says are not premeditated, but are a direct or prime expression of his sensitivity to another person's fears or foibles. Diplomacy then is not a secret process but a personal trait of certain individuals that is usually quite apparent.

Sometimes a person who knows a great deal about some subject, when talking to a beginner, will say much less than he knows; but the things he knows and does not say are not things that run through his head at such times and are not made public, but rather things he has learned and now could say, if he were talking to someone to whom they would be intelligible or useful.

Through these various cases, we can see that there is something right about the idea that what a person says may be the same as or different from what he thinks; but we go wrong if we imagine that what he thinks is something that goes on prior to or alongside of what he says, and that therefore it would be useful to be able to see into his consciousness. When a person is being frank, he indeed says what he thinks, but that just means that he is not being diplomatic or devious, that he would say the same to his diary or anyone else. When a person is being diplomatic he may say something different from what he thinks, but that just means that what he would write in his diary or say to someone else would not square with what he diplomatically said. When a person explains something to a beginner he tells less than he knows, but that just means that if he were writing a book, he would without further research have a great deal more to say. What is more than or different from what people say is not something that is there but hidden, something that would be fully revealed if only we could see into people's minds, but something they might have said, or done, had circumstances been different.

The things we might do or say, the things we are capable of, the poems we could write, the fun we might concoct, the sympathy or courage we might show, are in a sense hidden all right, but hidden from ourselves as much as from other people. They are not there under wraps: they have not yet been created. We gain access to them, not by somehow going behind behavior, but by letting ourselves go—by behaving more freely. This happens when situations are created in which we are encouraged to be what we are capable of being, situations of trust and mutual appreciation, in which two people draw one another out. When those situations occur, the deeper person we are in search of will be right there in the wistful smiles or imaginative inventions, and will be revealed in what we do as much to ourselves as to anyone else.

That is how two people achieve closeness: when each has the confidence of the other, and each stimulates the other to the inventive things of which we are capable but seldom deliver.

Personal intimacy is thus a rich and unreserved interaction with another person, and therefore even if people's unexpressed thoughts and attitudes were there in their consciousness, and we had some device by means of which we could experience the mental states of other people, personal intimacy would still not prevail. We would not be interacting richly with another person, but rather observing like spectators their conscious processes. Whenever there was any need for the device, that itself would show that there was not intimacy. The way to closeness with and enjoyment of another person is not by coming to know what lies behind the outward shell, but by eliciting from other people the best of which they are capable. For some people and with some people, that is often quite difficult, but it is at least possible; whereas it is neither possible nor what one really wants, to come to know the supposed person behind the smiles and jokes and questions and fits of rage that often seem mere outward show.

An important feature of the picture of personal intimacy we have just sketched is that people appear as sources of creativity that are often dammed up, and that this creativity can be released in some kinds of personal interaction, in which fear and distrust are reduced, self-confidence is generated, and the development and exercise of abilities is stimulated. Creativity here is primarily not a matter of painting pictures, writing books or decorating rooms, but of doing things with another person that are rich and various in their interest and that, unlike party conversation that is designed for universal consumption, expresses the particular interest that two people take in one another.

Hence, to return to our earlier question, "What is good about personal intimacy?" we can now see that wherever it prevails, it releases us from constraints of caution and distrust, which are both thwarting in themselves and tend to make our lives arid. The intimate relationship enriches our lives, both by releasing a creativity of personal interaction that has been inhibited, and by eliciting it from another person.

This, however, still puts it too egocentrically, as if we were talking about an unsuspected way in which another person can be used for maximizing the satisfaction we can get from life. Anyone who approached personal intimacy from this egocentric point of view would not achieve it, because he is not yet so constituted as to find this special kind of relationship good in itself. The slightly paradoxical situation appears to be that the rewards accrue only if one does not aim at them; but this is common to a great many things in life. If we concentrate just on doing something well, the pleasure of so doing it accrues; but if our eye is on the pleasure, our performance will likely be substandard, and whatever enjoyment we derive will not be the satisfaction of a task well performed.

WHY NOT SEX WITHOUT PERSONAL INTIMACY?

So far we have concentrated on explaining the notion of personal intimacy. In doing so it was assumed that this is not an entirely new notion, and that many people care about it, but that it was in need of clarification, both as to what it is and as to what is good about it. Up to this point, except incidentally, we have said nothing as to the bearing of personal intimacy on our sex lives.

In this part of our deliberations it will save a lot of verbiage if we can use expressions like "a purely sexual relationship" or "an impersonal relationship" to mean anything that tends in those directions. Even when sex is put on a commercial basis, it may not always be quite devoid of personal intimacy; and not many of the people who make love casually with near strangers on a Saturday night will be altogether lacking in personal interest in their sex partners. Still, there will not often be much depth of personal interest in such cases, and it would be cumbersome always to construct an expression that allowed for various possible shades and degrees of such interest.

While many people would not want sex without personal intimacy, probably few of those same people, if they had no moral qualms about it, would find sex positively unpleasant just because it lacked personal warmth; and probably many others would not knowingly want and therefore not miss personal intimacy.

It is quite possible to regard sex as essentially a pleasurable activity that happens to require the participation of another person, like dancing. As with dancing, the participants can display skill and style, but it need not matter with whom one is performing, as long as the participants function well together. It would be folly to say that sex, when similarly regarded, need be in any way unrewarding. On the contrary, since it is both a more natural and a more intense pleasure, it is likely to be very much more gratifying than any other activity requiring the participation of someone else.

Yet while sex is not likely to be positively distasteful just through being impersonal, our pleasure in it may be mixed with regrets and dissatisfactions. Whether foolishly or not, many of us are deeply disposed to regard sexual caresses as an expression of affection and enthusiasm for the person who receives them; but when sex is impersonal, caresses come out as an expression of enthusiasm for caressing. If one does not know or care whether the other person is lonely, reads Dickens, likes cats or believes in God, caresses lose their character as expressions of affection. Then there is an emptiness in lovemaking that may be disturbing; and in the case in which one does know and does not like such things about a person, caresses take on the character of falsity.

The disposition to regard sexual tenderness as an expression of affection is not, of course, universal or incurable; but in our culture any other disposition is rare, and it will require either insensitivity or sophistication, when a relationship is primarily sexual, not to wish for personal warmth as well, or to wish one were with someone else with whom there could be such warmth.

From this point of view, when there is personal intimacy between people who make love, they have much the best of it. They want just the person they are with, and have a full relationship with the person they want. There is genuine tenderness in their caresses, which are therefore not only just as pleasant as those of the couple whose love-making is mainly sexual, but satisfying to the deep human wish to demonstrate interest and affection.

Hence it may seem much to be recommended that one adopt a policy of making love only with persons for whom one can whole-heartedly express tenderness. Yet while we might admire and commend the sensitivity and concern about personal relationships of any-one who so resolved, it is not clear whether anything else would be foolish, or would show a regrettable want of sensitivity or of concern about personal relationships. It might be that this is the analogue of what in moral contexts is sometimes called supererogatory conduct: acts of conspicuous heroism or extreme generosity, for example. Although these are altogether admirable, failure to perform them is not regarded as a defect.

Not everyone has any talent or taste for close personal relationships, and those who do will not always find others to share themselves with in an intimate way. Our cultural climate tends to make us so cautious, hurried and pragmatic that close friendships do not develop easily. Hence, although we are passionate fairly constantly, we are on close terms with a suitable person only sometimes; and this can make it seem the better part of wisdom to make love as and when we can, and hope that we will be so fortunate as sometimes to fall into a relationship in which there is also the joy of personal intimacy.

People differ so much, not only in how passionate they are, but in how much they want close friendships and in their aptitude for them, that the answer to the question what is best here will be different from person to person. If one has no interest in personal intimacy there will be no problem, except possibly the question whether one might be turning a blind eye on one of life's joys.

If one does care about the quality of personal relationships, and also requires personal intimacy in one's sex life, then for all but the most outgoing and attractive people, the result will almost certainly be some reduction in the amount of sexual activity one enjoys. However, one may be compensated by the assurance that one's sex life will be rich in the qualities of joy, affection and respect attendant on people's rejoicing in one another as persons.

People who demand personal intimacy in their sex lives may find that having this kind of ideal makes them too self-conscious. They may always be asking themselves, "Is this it? Will my principles permit this?" Not only could these questions be hard to answer with any assurance, the very concern about them could strain the free development of a good relationship. Moreover, the cherished expectation that making love would be particularly splendid might interfere with its spontaneity and cause disappointment.

While not many people would be so deliberate as to encounter this sort of difficulty, perhaps the only general remedy would be the evolution of a cultural climate in which most couples would not make love unless they were on quite special terms, but in which this would not be an ideal that they would list as one of their convictions, or something that was urged upon them by parents and school teachers, but rather something that simply did not happen amongst people who had lived in that climate for any length of time. The thought of making love would perhaps occur to people only when there was an especially warm relationship, or if it occurred to them at other times, it would strike them as a strange or unpleasant idea. Such a cultural climate is not likely to exist soon, but it is perhaps not impossible. Short of that, it is perhaps possible for a person to adopt this attitude deliberately, but over a period of time to make it so much part of the way he functions that it is no longer a principle to which he strives to conform, but instead has become an instinct.

The hardest question is as to the workability of the plan according to which one makes love as fancy dictates or opportunity allows, and hopes that sometimes it will be with someone about whom one cares personally. Clearly this way one might have the best of both worlds: all the sexual satisfaction one wants or fortune provides, some of it under conditions one regards as ideal.

The question as to its workability is whether we can successfully make the switch from one perception of sexual activity to the other; for example, from regarding caresses as a pleasure requiring the participation of another person, to seeing them as an expression of affection and mutual delight. The significance that we can attach to sexual activity . . . is a magic and a fragile thing. It is easy to sustain its reality when it is the only way we perceive sexual intimacies, but the danger is that if we sometimes make love when there is no affection or personal delight being expressed, then even when we are with someone for whom we care, the spell may be broken and our intimacies may remain private pleasures happening to require the cooperation of another person. In that case we will have tried to have the best of both worlds and lost. What we lose is something magic and intangible, which not everyone will miss; and since sex will surely still remain extremely pleasant, it is not a loss which leaves us destitute; but still something splendid will have gone from our lives.

Since it is not a moral issue how we handle these matters, it is acceptable that we should all decide for ourselves about them. We differ widely, both in how much we care about what is at stake, and probably also in how readily we can switch back and forth from one perception of sexual activity to another. If we do not care very much about personal intimacy we will perhaps find the risk in trying to have it both ways well worth taking, while if we care intensely even a slight risk may well seem too great.

What we have called personal intimacy is a dimension of human relations to which many people attach importance, and of whose value many others might be persuaded. It is partly out of concern about personal intimacy that many people deplore sexual promiscuity, and many parents worry about whether their children, in their eagerness to experiment with sex, might not be very particular as to whether there is a good personal relationship between them and their sexual partners, and therefore whether they may grow up insensitive to the possibility and the value of personal intimacy.

What has been suggested is that personal intimacy is indeed an excellent thing, deserving of concern and much to be cherished and promoted, but that we make a mistake if we treat it as a matter of moral concern—except in a way that will be indicated shortly. Personal intimacy is therefore not something on which we have a right to insist. It may be regrettable but it is not sinful to relate to people in a generally impersonal way; and it may be excellent but it is not saintly to be caring, interested in and responsive to people in the way described. Possibly people of the latter disposition are more likely also to be morally virtuous, but their moral virtue is a distinct attribute; and it is both possible and common for people of the other disposition to be as honest, generous, fair and courageous as one could wish.

It is no doubt immoral to do anything likely to destroy or adversely affect a good personal relationship, and morally commendable to further and create such relationships. In this one respect, personal intimacy *is* a matter of moral concern; but it is similarly a matter of moral concern whether what I do adversely affects a person's ability to play the violin, although having that ability is not itself a moral virtue.

Erotic Love: A Final Appraisal

RUSSELL VANNOY

Is erotic love itself "beautiful" and "good"? As we have already noted,[1] Plato argued that it was not since love seeks out beauty and goodness; if it already had beauty and goodness, it would not be necessary to search for what it already possesses. Yet most people would probably hold that a life devoid of love was either worthless or at least sorely missing something that would make it complete.

I have, however, argued in preceding chapters of this book that erotic love is not a viable concept, that it is riddled with contradictions that set up conflicting desires within the lover and cause endless mental torture. This would then refute the claim that love or sex with love results in increased contentment and peace of mind.

Some of these conflicts, of course, can doubtlessly be resolved by a gradual change in what partners demand of a love relationship. For example, the most familiar conflict is, on the one hand, the desire for a sense of oneness with one's partner, involving a unity of heart, mind, body, and soul. On the other hand, there is the desire for freedom and independence; one doesn't want to feel possessed or smothered by one's lover. The sense of oneness with another fulfills an important psychological need that many feel, that of wanting to be lifted out of one's isolation and thus enjoying the feeling of security that one will not have to face the world utterly alone. But to have security and nothing else is deadening to the spirit; one also seeks adventure and variety, and this involves an assertion of one's independence.

Many lovers feel they have worked out a relationship wherein both these demands for security and adventure can be fulfilled. But when the supposed reconciliation of these conflicting demands is put to the supreme test, such as one lover's desire to commit adultery and thus add a little adventure and variety to his sex life, the partner will commonly protest that the sense of total oneness between them is being torn asunder by his giving his body to another. She may very well then threaten to sue for divorce on the grounds of marital infidelity. But then her mate's conflicting desires cannot be fulfilled: on the one hand, he wants the security of a loving wife; on the other hand, he wants the ultimate sexual adventure, which for him is to have an affair.

But perhaps erotic love can overcome the problems posed by this sort of example. The couple will simply reconcile their needs for both freedom and independence by holding that each can exercise his or her independence so long as it does not cause distress to the other or threaten to destroy the marriage. And perhaps even the distress caused by adultery can be overcome by convincing the mate that because two people are in love, it does not follow that they own each other's bodies; their only claim need be to each other's hearts—if even that is necessary. For one's body belongs to oneself alone, and no one has a right to possess it, be he rapist or lover.

Indeed, if love is as truly generous and as concerned for the beloved's happiness as is claimed, then the wife should allow her husband the freedom to engage in a sexual adventure now and then if he feels such a thing is essential to his happiness—and vice versa. Thus the wife should say: "You can give your body to whomever you wish, so long as you do not do so at those times when you know I want sexual satisfaction myself. After all an affair with another woman is only physical fun that is as innocent as any other sport. And by allowing you a little sexual freedom, you will probably love me even more by my granting you this independence. And if you do happen to give your heart as well as your body to another, this only proves that we did not really have a solid love relationship in the first place, so nothing has been lost."

This brief excursion into the problem of adultery shows that, with a more liberal conception of what love implies, one might be able in many cases to overcome the traditional conflict faced by lovers: the desire for oneness with one's beloved and also independence, that is, the desire for both security and adventure. But there are other inherent contradictions in erotic love that cannot be overcome. I will focus on one example I previously analyzed: Love for another claims to be predominantly altruistic, with self-interest either totally absent or, at most, a secondary consideration. And indeed it must presuppose this if it is to justify its claim to be a noble and beautiful thing. Yet I also argued that love is essentially self-interested and indeed presupposes just such essential self-interest. So we have a glaring contradiction.

By one concept of altruism, a lover should be totally free of self-interest and should give his love to whoever needs it most badly, even if that person has no particularly attractive qualities or is even positively disgusting. And he should continue to give his love to such a person even if this person responds by treating him like an animal. Thus he should have no concern for any rewards for himself at all.

But clearly, with perhaps a few rare exceptions, erotic lovers are not like this at all. They will give their love to someone who needs it only if that person also has attractive qualities which stir their emotions and gratify their own self-interest, such as the desire to witness beauty. Or they will completely ignore those who need love badly and give it to someone who doesn't need it at all, such as someone who is already loved by many others; and they will try to seduce such a person into loving them because she has the qualities they want. Furthermore, even if someone has highly attractive qualities, this is no guarantee they will be loved. Those who are extremely intelligent or extremely beautiful are often unable to attract a lover because others feel that their ego is threatened by being in the presence of someone to whom they feel inferior. Thus one's own self-interest is the determining factor in choosing a lover.

In another version of altruism, it is all right to have some self-interest, as long as giving to another is the primary motive. One must have some concern for his own self-interest; otherwise one would become a mere self-sacrificing slave willing to be exploited by others. A truly generous person must have some love for himself and thus some concern for his own interests; otherwise he would only project his own self-hate onto others and could not love them at all. Furthermore, lovers do not want to be loved out of sheer charity anyway; their pride demands that they be chosen because they have certain attractive qualities that appeal to others. They want to "win" the heart of their lover and not merely have love handed to them because they need it. Thus their being loved must be an achievement of which they can be proud.

Can we then reconcile altruism and self-interest by adopting the theory that love is primarily altruistic, with self-interest present but only as a secondary consideration? Clearly the lover does not want a selfish beloved; and on the other hand, she does not want charity. But if she does not want a purely charitable lover, she is going to have to admit that he must have some self-interest. This she would grant, but only as long as the lover is not governed primarily by self-interest; otherwise she is going to be exploited and not truly loved.

Will she be able to find the kind of lover she seeks, one who is primarily generous and only secondarily self-interested? The difficulty is that she does not want to be loved out of sheer charity but wants to merit love by having been selected for the attractive qualities she possesses. But we have already noted that lovers choose only those partners with certain attractive qualities that appeal primarily to their own needs and self-interest. But this means that the one who seeks to be loved will be selected primarily from selfish considerations. Thus the woman's desire to be not an object of charity but an object worthy of love has driven her to require that she be selected primarily for selfish reasons. But this violates her other claim that she wants her lover to be primarily generous.

Furthermore, her wish to be chosen on her merits violates another claim lovers frequently make: to be chosen as a total human being for one's own sake alone. But only a purely charitable lover claims to do this, and she does not want charity. Since she wants to merit love and wants her lover to be selective, she requires that she be viewed not as a mere human being (which we all are), but as someone special who has those unique qualities that appeal to those who are selective. But to be chosen "for one's own sake alone" is, once again, impossible since she wants to be selected for her charming qualities, and those who do select her for such qualities clearly don't do it for her own sake alone. Nor can she claim to be viewed as a total human being, since her desire to be selected for certain special qualities has violated this ideal also. A total human being is always something more than a particular set of attractive traits.[2]

Thus erotic love seems to be caught in a trap: On the one hand we want our lover to be primarily generous in order to avoid being exploited; on the other hand our desire to *merit* love drives us to want to be selected primarily for self-interested reasons. (I do not wish to rest my case on the one particular argument developed here; the additional arguments set forth in previous chapters are necessary to establish my thesis clearly.)

I now wish to continue my attack on the proponent of erotic love's claim to be primarily generous to and concerned for the total human being for his or her own sake alone by philosophically examining some factual data. To do this I will take another look at the research found in Alan Lee's *The Colors of Love*. Alan Lee is a sociologist at the University of Toronto who sent questionnaires to thousands of Canadians asking them to give their own conception of love and to analyze their own personal traits. Lee did not try to impose on his respondents any notion that there is some one thing called "true love." If his respondents claimed that this is what erotic love meant to them, he accepted it at face value and developed his types of love from their reports. Lee is, therefore, a pluralist, who believes there are many different kinds of erotic love. Other than this, however, he did not probe deeply into the philosophical implications of his findings, something which I shall try to do.

He labels the first type the *eros* lover. For this lover, physical beauty is the primary consideration in his choice of a mate. He may enjoy other qualities as well, but unless such persons are physically beautiful he will ignore them, no matter how attractive they may be in other ways. And if the beloved loses his or her physical beauty, it is likely he or she will be dropped cold. Clearly such a lover is motivated primarily by self-interest in his desire to enjoy beholding the beauty of his beloved. And to concentrate primarily on physical beauty is hardly to love the entire person for his own sake. Even if such a lover sublimated his love for physical beauty into love for spiritual beauty, the same criticisms would apply.

Alan Lee labels his second type of lover *ludus* (from the Greek word for game). For the ludus lover, love is a game of seduction to see who can win whom for a temporary intimate liaison. When the game is over he quickly tires of his lover and moves on to another. Ludus is clearly self-interested in that he is interested only in the ego-fulfill-ment of being a successful seducer. And rather than being a loving human being, he seems only to love the game of love. He is, in our jargon, the typical "lover boy."

Lee's third type of lover is the *manic*. The manic is, Lee claims, filled with self-hate and insecurity that he tries to overcome by demanding absolute possession of his lover. Furthermore, he commonly despises his lover as well, perhaps because he secretly resents being so dependent on his lover to give his empty life some meaning. It is clear that he does not love his lover for her own sake, but is merely using her to gratify his desperate desire to be loved so that he can feel that he is of some worth. He is not really in love with a human being at all: he is in love with being loved.

Lee labels the fourth type of lover *storge*. Storge cares nothing for ecstatic emotions, and his love seems to be more like a deep friend-ship. Storge's main goal is to be a family man, and he chooses his lover on the basis of whether she will be a good companion, wife, house-keeper, sexual partner and mother. One wonders if he really loves his mate as a human being for her own sake or whether he is simply see-ing her in terms of the roles he wants her to play to satisfy his desire to raise a family. He seems to be not so much in love with her as he is in love with family life. And if it becomes apparent she cannot play the roles assigned her, he drops her.

Although Lee mentions other types of lovers (none of which avoid the criticisms I have made of the others), he concludes with one type (which he labels *storgic eros*) who seems to be idealistic and unselfish. The storgic-eros lover's main criterion for choosing a mate is that she is someone who needs love. He is utterly lacking in possessiveness or jealousy, is warm and affectionate and does not demand that his love be reciprocated. Nor does he require marriage or their being con-stantly together; he sees her only when she feels she needs loving. And if someone else would serve as a better partner for her, he would graciously step aside without complaint.

However, someone who is loved by this type of person would clearly be dubious of a love that is based on the duty to help those in need of love. Does one really want to be loved out of someone's feel-ing that they are obligated to help those in need? Surely they want to merit love and not be patronized by being an object of charity. Fur-thermore if the storgic-eros lover so readily gives up his beloved if another partner would serve her better and if he does not feel any need for the love to be reciprocated, could he really be said to have any close attachment to her or be deeply involved with her in a erotic way at all? But these are surely things that the one who needs love wants. Thus if one thinks the storgic-eros lover is truly noble (as Lee does), he seems to be giving more of a priestlike love than an erotic love. (Lee notes that this very idealistic type of lover cares little or nothing for sex, perhaps because he feels that lustful desire is selfish). If one thinks he is not so noble, one could say that he is not really in love but is merely using his lover to satisfy his charitable drives. Rather than loving her, he seems to be more in love with the idea of giving love and the enormous ego gratification this yields to this type of person. (It should be noted that only a tiny minority of Lee's respondents claimed to have the self-giving characteristics mentioned above.)

Although Lee does not probe deeply into the philosophical implications of his work, the philosopher would note that there seems to be no one characteristic that all these love types share in common that uniquely defines love and distinguishes love from other types of human relationships. (This confirms a thesis I defended earlier in the book.) But more ominously, it becomes clear that after surveying these love types, the ideal of loving the total person for his or her own sake alone is either clearly absent or at least open to serious doubt in each case. The predominance of self-interest in each type is either obvious or could be detected by a careful analysis of motives.

Lovers, of course, often devote much time and energy to pleasing their beloved. But the owner of a new Cadillac or a fancy sports car devotes endless hours to polishing it or spends considerable money keeping it in working condition. He does these things not out of any devotion to the car but only because the thrill and ego-fulfillment of driving such a beautiful car requires that he do such things for it. And when the car begins to require sacrifices that outweigh the benefits it gives, he trades it in. He has "given" but only in order to "get."

If he continues to hold on to the decrepit car, it is perhaps only because he knows he cannot afford a better one. He might sacrifice much time and energy to "nurse" it back to health and restore it to its original qualities, but this is only so he can have the ego-fulfillment of driving a beautiful car once again. Or he may cling to it because, for some reason, it has him emotionally "hooked" even though it yields no rewards and he would really like to get rid of it. Or he may keep the car for sentimental reasons, for "old times' sake" because its presence brings back delightful memories of all the ego-gratification he once received from it; but this is still a self-interested motive, and he no longer loves the car as it is but only as a memory. Thus ego-gratification or other nonaltruistic considerations were the central motive for remaining loyal to the old car.

This example of the car applies perfectly to lovers as well: They give in order to get and if they think they aren't getting as much as or, hopefully, more than they are giving, they trade the once-beloved in on a new model, even though the rejected partner may need love badly. Or if the lover does not trade her in, it is only for the self-interested reasons analogous to those of the car owner who held on to his decrepit vehicle.

Given these considerations, why is it that most people still want to be "in love," even if they are aware of the self-interested motives for their being loved? The answers, I think, are obvious:

1. One wants to enjoy the ecstasy of the intoxicating emotions that arise from loving or being loved.

2. Either because of pride or because of social conditioning, we feel that we are worthless unless we have had our merits and attractive qualities confirmed by having been able to attract a lover.

3. In a sexist society, the male is faced with the delicious prospect of getting not just as much as he is getting but even more than he is giving. For the female has been conditioned to think that she is inferior and deserves only the minimum of gratification, and that she must honor the supposedly superior male by endless self-sacrifice. This generosity of the female does not, however, rest on any solid foundation of true altruism; it arises only from feelings of inferiority. Once sexism is eliminated, the female's self-interest will start to assert itself, and she will demand rewards commensurate with what she gives, and quite justifiably so. But this then becomes a "you scratch my back and I'll scratch yours" type of relationship, where each partner is on the alert to see that he or she is getting as much or he or she is giving. This can lead frequently to violent lovers' quarrels with one partner feeling that he or she isn't getting a fair share. This grim picture is clearly miles away from any concept of a truly altruistic relationship.

4. The final reason most persons prefer to be loved is that, even if they realize their partner is giving only in order to get, they are at least getting something, which is better than being utterly alone and getting nothing at all. They fail to realize there may be other forms of truly humanistic relationships that do not involve erotic love, which, as we have seen, seems to turn its adherents either into something vicious or at least into something far less than noble. (Despite all I have said, however, most erotic lovers will continue to insist that their love is truly altruistic; but this is only because they are blinded by the emotions of love to their lovers' true motives.)

In my concluding section on love I have chosen to focus on the egoism-altruism controversy, since it gives me an opportunity to show how the second part of my book, dealing with love, supports the central argument of the first part, dealing with sex. There I maintained that sex with a generous, considerate, and sexually adept non-lover committed to humanistic principles can provide a sexual experience that is as good as or even better than sex with a lover.

If my thesis that erotic love is essentially self-interested is correct, it is going to damage seriously the claim that sex with a lover is the supreme experience. Part of the sexual joy lovers experience derives from the feeling that the partner is truly an altruistic person who would be willing to give his all to the act even if he felt he weren't getting very much in return. But if my thesis about the motives of lovers is correct, this joy is based on an illusion.

Lovers, for example, would be on the alert to see that they are getting as much as they are giving, or hopefully, to get more than they give (as with the millions of husbands who leave their wives orgasmically and otherwise unfulfilled). Of course, the lover may do his best to thrill his beloved, but if he is essentially self-interested, this would only be in order to prove to himself that he has the virility or sexual prowess to arouse another person. Furthermore, lovers commonly consider the beloved obligated to satisfy them whenever they wish, even if the beloved isn't in the mood for sex at all.

On the other hand, a generous, considerate non-lover is capable of performing a sex act without engaging in violent quarrels if he fails to be satisfied. Nor will such a generous person so readily threaten to abandon his partner if he fails to be pleased sexually with his partner's performance. Nor will he think that it is his partner's obligation to please him whenever he wishes.

Furthermore, sex between humanistic non-lovers would not be devoid of feeling, for the partners' mutual realization that their motives are truly generous would create enormous feelings of affection for each other. And since a truly generous non-lover would stay with his partner even if he isn't receiving his so-called fair share of sexual pleasure, such a sex act would be devoid of the fears that haunt lovers if they fail to "measure up." (Such tunes as Paul Simon's "Fifty Ways to Leave Your Lover" or "Will You Still Love Me Tomorrow?" or "The Thrill Is Gone" hang over the sexual act like a black cloud.)

Why is the generous type of non-lover more likely to treat his partner better than the erotic lover? The answer, I think, is that he is free of the things I have already claimed that erotic love does to its victims, especially the violence that such a love seems to do to their altrustic nature. I conclude, therefore, that on the whole, sex with a humanistic non-lover is far preferable to sex with an erotic lover.

I now leave it to the reader to judge if I have proved the central thesis about the superiority of sex with a humanistic non-lover. And, while philosophers have traditionally avoided such topics as I have discussed here—perhaps because they could not possibly see how there could be an connection between logic on the one hand and love and lust on the other—I hope this work has also shown that philosophy can have something important to say about such things.

NOTES

1 [The excerpt reprinted here is the concluding chapter of *Sex Without Love: A Philosophical Exploration* (Buffalo, N.Y., 1980)—Ed.]

2 If a lover does insist that he loves the "total human person," all that this means is that he finds all her qualities attractive. And if these qualities were to disappear, the lover of those qualities would disappear.

VII

EQUALITY

Is Racial Discrimination Arbitrary?

PETER SINGER

I

INTRODUCTION

There is nowadays wide agreement that racism is wrong. To describe a policy, law, movement or nation as "racist" is to condemn it. It may be thought that since we all agree that racism is wrong, it is unnecessary to speculate on exactly what it is and why it is wrong. This indifference to moral fundamentals could, however, prove dangerous. For one thing, the fact that most people agree today that racism is wrong does not mean that this attitude will always be so widely shared. Even if we had no fears for the future, though, we need to have some understanding of what it is about racism that is wrong if we are to handle satisfactorily all the problems we face today. For instance, there is the contentious issue of "reverse discrimination" or discrimination in favor of members of oppressed minority groups. It must be granted that a university which admits members of minority groups who do not achieve the minimum standard that others must reach in order to be admitted is discriminating on racial lines. Is such discrimination therefore wrong?

Or, to take another issue, the efforts of Arab nations to have the United Nations declare Zionism a form of racism provoked an extremely hostile reaction in nations friendly to Israel, particularly the United States, but it led to virtually no discussion of whether Zionism is a form of racism. Yet the charge is not altogether without plausibility, for if Jews are a race, then Zionism promotes the idea of a state dominated by one race, and this has practical consequences in, for instance, Israel's immigration laws. Again, to consider whether this makes Zionism a form of racism we need to understand what it is that makes a policy racist and wrong.

First it is necessary to get our terms clear. "Racism" is, as I have said, a word which now has an inescapable evaluative force, although it also has some descriptive content. Words with these dual functions can be confusing if their use is not specified. People sometimes try to argue: "X is a case of racial discrimination, therefore X is racist; racism is wrong, therefore X is wrong." This argument may depend on an equivocation in the meaning of "racist," the term being used first in a morally neutral, descriptive sense, and secondly in its evaluative sense.

To avoid this kind of confusion, I shall accept the usual evaluative force of the term "racist" and reserve it for practices that are judged to be wrong. Thus we cannot pronounce a policy, law etc. "racist" unless we have decided that it is wrong. "Racial discrimination" on the other hand I shall use in a descriptive, and morally neutral sense, so that to say that a policy or law discriminates racially is simply to point to the fact of discrimination based on race, leaving open the question of whether it can be justified. With this terminology it becomes possible to ask whether a given form of racial discrimination is racist; this is another way of asking whether it is justifiable.[1]

If we ask those who regard racial discrimination as wrong to say why it is wrong, it is commonly said that it is wrong to pick on race as a reason for treating one person differently from others, because race is irrelevant to whether a person should be given a job, the vote, higher education, or any benefits or burdens of this sort. The irrelevance of race, it is said, makes it quite arbitrary to give these things to people of one race while withholding them from those of another race. I shall refer to this account of what is wrong with racial discrimination as the "standard objection" to racial discrimination.

A sophisticated theory of justice can be invoked in support of this standard objection to racial discrimination. Justice requires, as Aristotle so plausibly said, that equals be treated equally and unequals be treated unequally. To this we must add the obvious proviso that the equalities or inequalities should be relevant to the treatment in question. Now when we consider things like employment, it becomes clear that the relevant inequalities between candidates for a vacant position are inequalities in their ability to carry out the duties of the position and, perhaps, inequalities in the extent to which they will benefit through being offered the position. Race does not seem to be relevant at all. Similarly with the vote, capacity for rational choice between candidates or policies might be held a relevant characteristic, but race should not be; and so on for other goods. It is hard to think of anything for which race in itself is a relevant characteristic, and hence to use race as a basis for discrimination is arbitrarily to single out an irrelevant factor, no doubt because of a bias or prejudice against those of a different race.[2]

As we shall see, this account of why racial discrimination is wrong is inadequate because there are many situations in which, from at least one point of view, the racial factor is by no means irrelevant, and therefore it can be denied that racial discrimination in these situations is arbitrary.

One type of situation in which race must be admitted to be relevant to the purposes of the person discriminating need not delay us at this stage; this is the situation in which those purposes themselves favor a particular race. Thus if the purpose of Hitler and the other Nazi leaders was, among other things, to produce a world in which there were no Jews, it was certainly not irrelevant to their purposes that those rounded up and murdered by the S.S. were Jews rather than so-called "Aryans." But the fundamental wrongness of the aims of the Nazis makes the "relevance" of race to those aims totally inefficacious so far as justifying Nazi racial discrimination is concerned. While their type of racial discrimination may not have been arbitrary discrimination in the usual sense, it was no less wrong for that. *Why* it was wrong is something that I hope will become clearer later in this article. Meanwhile I shall look at some less cataclysmic forms of racial discrimination, for too much contemporary discussion of racial discrimination has focussed on the most blatant instances: Nazi Germany, South Africa, and the American "Deep South" during the period of legally enforced racial segregation.[3] These forms of racism are not the type that face us now in our own societies (unless we live in South Africa) and to discuss racial discrimination in terms of these examples today is to present an over-simplified picture of the problem of racial discrimination. By looking at some of the reasons for racial discrimination that might actually be offered today in countries all over the world I hope to show that the real situation is usually much more complex than consideration of the more blatant instances of racial discrimination would lead us to believe.

II

EXAMPLES

I shall start by describing an example of racial discrimination which may at first glance seem to be an allowable exception to a general rule that racial discrimination is arbitrary and therefore wrong; and I shall then suggest that this case has parallels with other cases we may not be so willing to allow as exceptions.

Case 1. A film director is making a film about the lives of blacks living in New York's Harlem. He advertises for black actors. A white actor turns up, but the director refuses to allow him to audition, saying that the film is about blacks and there are no roles for whites. The actor replies that, with the appropriate wig and make-up, he can look just like a black; moreover he can imitate the mannerisms, gestures, and speech of Harlem blacks. Nevertheless the director refuses to consider him for the role, because it is essential to the director's conception of the film that the black experience be authentically portrayed, and however good a white actor might be, the director would not be satisfied with the authenticity of the portrayal.

The film director is discriminating along racial lines, yet he cannot be said to be discriminating arbitrarily. His discrimination is apt for his purpose. Moreover his purpose is a legitimate one. So the standard objection to racial discrimination cannot be made in this instance.

Racial discrimination may be acceptable in an area like casting for films or the theatre, when the race of a character in the film or play is important, because this is one of the seemingly few areas in which a person's race is directly relevant to his capacity to perform a given task. As such, it may be thought, these areas can easily be distinguished from other areas of employment, as well as from areas like housing, education, the right to vote, and so on, where race has no relevance at all. Unfortunately there are many other situations in which race is not as totally irrelevant as this view assumes.

Case 2. The owner of a cake shop with a largely white and racially prejudiced clientele wishes to hire an assistant. The owner has no prejudice against blacks himself, but is reluctant to employ one, for fear that his customers will go elsewhere. If his fears are well founded (and this is not impossible) then the race of a candidate for the position is, again, relevant to the purpose of the employer, which in this case is to maintain the profitability of his business.

What can we say about this case? We cannot deny the connection between race and the owner's purposes, and so we must recognize that the owner's discrimination is not arbitrary, and does not necessarily indicate a bias or prejudice on his part. Nor can we say that the owner's purpose is an illegitimate one, for making a profit from the sale of cakes is not generally regarded as wrong, at least if the amount of profit made is modest.

We can, of course, look at other aspects of the matter. We can object to the racial discrimination shown by customers who will search out shops staffed by whites only—such people do discriminate arbitrarily, for race is irrelevant to the quality of the goods and the proficiency of service in a shop—but is this not simply a fact that the shop owner must live with, however much he may wish he could change it? We might argue that by pandering to the prejudices of his customers, the owner is allowing those prejudices to continue unchallenged; whereas if he and other shopkeepers took no notice of them, people would eventually become used to mixing with those of another race, and prejudices would be eroded. Yet it is surely too much to ask an individual shop owner to risk his livelihood in a lone and probably vain effort to break down prejudice. Few of the most dedicated opponents of racism do as much. If there were national legislation which distributed the burden more evenly, by a general prohibition of discrimination on racial grounds (with some recognized exceptions for cases like casting for a film or play) the situation would be different. Then we could reasonably ask every shop owner to play his part. Whether there should be such legislation is a different question from whether the shop owner may be blamed for discriminating in the absence of legislation. I shall discuss the issue of legislation shortly, after we consider a different kind of racial discrimination that, again, is not arbitrary.

Case 3. A landlord discriminates against blacks in letting the accommodation he owns. Let us say that he is not so rigid as never to let an apartment to a black, but if a black person and a white person appear to be equally suitable as tenants, with equally good references and so on, the landlord invariably prefers the white. He defends his policy along the following lines:

> If more than a very small proportion of my tenants get behind in their rent and then disappear without paying the arrears, I will be out of business. Over the years, I have found that more blacks do this than whites. I admit that there are many honest blacks (some of my best tenants have been black) and many dishonest whites, but, for some reason I do not claim to understand, the odds on a white tenant defaulting are longer than on a black doing so, even when their references and other credentials appear equally good. In this business you can't run a full-scale probe of every prospective tenant—and if I tried I would be abused for invading privacy—so you have to go by the average rather than the individual. That is why blacks have to have better indications of reliability than whites before I will let to them.

Now the landlord's impression of a higher rate of default among blacks than among comparable whites may itself be the result of prejudice on his part. Perhaps in most cases when landlords say this kind of thing, there is no real factual basis to their allegations. People have grown up with racial stereotypes, and these stereotypes are reinforced by a tendency to notice occurrences which conform to the stereotype and to disregard those which conflict with it. So if unreliability is part of the sterotype of blacks held by many whites, they may take more notice of blacks who abscond without paying the rent than of blacks who are reliable tenants; and conversely they will take less notice of absconding whites and more of those whites who conform to their ideas of normal white behavior.

If it is prejudice that is responsible for the landlord's views about black and white tenants, and there is no factual basis for his claims, then the problem becomes one of eliminating this prejudice and getting the landlord to see his mistake. This is by no means an easy task, but it is not a task for philosophers, and it does not concern us here, for we are interested in attempts to justify racial discrimination, and an attempted justification based on an inaccurate description of a situation can be rejected without raising the deeper issue of justification.

On the other hand, the landlord's impression of a higher rate of default among black tenants *could* be entirely accurate. (It might be explicable in terms of the different cultural and economic circumstances in which blacks are brought up.) Whether or not we think this likely, we need to ask what its implications would be for the justifiability of the racial discrimination exercised by the landlord. To refuse even to consider this question would be to rest all one's objections to the landlord's practice on the falsity of his claims, and thereby to fail to examine the possibility that the landlord's practice could be open to objection even if his impressions on tenant reliability are accurate.

If the landlord's impressions were accurate, we would have to concede, once again, that racial discrimination in this situation is not arbitrary; that it is, instead, relevant to the purposes of the landlord. We must also admit that these purposes—making a living from letting property that one owns—are not themselves objectionable, provided the rents are reasonable, and so on. Nor can we, this time, locate the origin of the problem in the prejudices of others, except insofar as the problem has its origin in the prejudices of those responsible for the conditions of deprivation in which many of the present generation of blacks grew up—but it is too late to do anything to alter those prejudices anyway, since they belong to previous generations.

We have now looked at three examples of racial discrimination, and can begin to examine the parallels and differences between them. Many people, as I have already said, would make no objection to the discriminatory hiring practice of the film director in the first of these cases. But we can now see that if we try to justify the actions of the film director in this case on the grounds that his purpose is a legitimate one and the discrimination he uses is relevant for his purpose, we will have to accept the actions of the cake-shop owner and the landlord as well. I suspect that many of those ready to accept the discriminatory practice in the first case will be much more reluctant about the other two cases. But what morally significant difference is there between them?

It might be suggested that the difference between them lies in the nature of what blacks are being deprived of, and their title to it. The argument would run like this: No one has a right to be selected to act in a film; the director must have absolute discretion to hire whomsoever he wishes to hire. After all, no one can force the director to make the film at all, and if he didn't make it, no one would be hired to play in it; if he does decide to make it, therefore, he must be allowed to make it on his own terms. Moreover, since so few people ever get the chance to appear in a film, it would be absurd to hold that the director violates someone's rights by not giving him something which most people will never have anyway. On the other hand, people do have a right to employment, and to housing. To discriminate against blacks in an ordinary employment situation, or in the letting of accommodation, threatens their basic rights and therefore should not be tolerated.

Plausible as it appears, this way of distinguishing the first case from the other two will not do. Consider the first and second cases: almost everything that we have said about the film director applies to the cake-shop owner as well. No one can force the cake-shop owner to keep his shop open, and if he didn't, no one would be hired to work in it. If in the film director's case this was a reason for allowing him to make the film on his own terms, it must be a reason for allowing the shop owner to run his shop on his own terms. In fact, such reasoning, which would allow unlimited discrimination in restaurants, hotels and shops, is invalid. There are plenty of examples where we would not agree that the fact that someone did not have to make an offer or provide an opportunity at all means that if he does do it he must be allowed to make the offer or provide the opportunity on his own terms. The United States Civil Rights Act of 1965 certainly does not recognize this line of argument, for it prohibits those offering food and lodgings to the public from excluding customers on racial grounds. We may, as a society, decide that we shall not allow people to make certain offers, if the way in which the offers are made will cause hardship or offense to others. In so doing we are balancing people's freedom to do as they please against the harm this may do to others, and coming down on the side of preventing harm rather than enlarging freedom. This is a perfectly defensible position, if the harm is sufficiently serious and the restriction of freedom not grave.[4]

Nor does it seem possible to distinguish the first and second cases by the claim that since so few people ever get the chance to appear in a film, no one's rights are violated if they are not given something that most people will never have anyway. For if the number of jobs in cake shops was small, and the demand for such jobs high, it would also be true that few people would ever have the chance to work in a cake shop. It would be odd if such an increase in competition for the job justified an otherwise unjustifiable policy of hiring whites only. Moreover, this argument would allow a film director to discriminate on racial lines even if race was irrelevant to the roles he was casting; and that is quite a different situation from the one we have been discussing.

The best way to distinguish the situations of the film director and the shop owner is by reference to the nature of the employment offered, and to the reasons why racial discrimination in these cases is not arbitrary. In casting for a film about blacks, the race of the actor auditioning is intrinsically significant, independently of the attitudes of those connected with the film. In the case of hiring a shop assistant, race is relevant only because of the attitudes of those connected (as customers) with the shop; it has nothing to do with the selling of cakes in itself, but only with the selling of cakes to racially prejudiced customers. This means that in the case of the shop assistant we could eliminate the relevance of race if we could eliminate the prejudices of the customers; by contrast there is no way in which we could eliminate the relevance of the race of an actor auditioning for a role in a film about blacks, without altering the nature of the film. Moreover, in the case of the shop owner racial discrimination probably serves to perpetuate the very prejudices that make such discrimination relevant and (from the point of view of the owner seeking to maintain his profits) necessary. Thus people who can buy all their cakes and other necessities in shops staffed only by whites will never come into the kind of contact with comparable blacks which might break down their aversion to being served by blacks; whereas if shop owners were to hire more blacks, their customers would no doubt become used to it and in time might wonder why they ever opposed the idea. (Compare the change of attitudes toward racial integration in the American South since the 1956 United States Supreme Court decision against segregated schools and subsequent measures against segregation were put into effect.[5])

Hence if we are opposed to arbitrary discrimination we have reason to take steps against racial discrimination in situations like Case 2, because such discrimination, while not itself arbitrary, both feeds on and gives support to discrimination by others which is arbitrary. In prohibiting it we would, admittedly, be preventing the employer from discriminating in a way that is relevant to his purposes; but if the causal hypothesis suggested in the previous paragraph is correct, this situation would only be temporary, and after some time the circumstances inducing the employer to discriminate racially would have been eliminated.

The case of the landlord presents a more difficult problem. If the facts he alleges are true his non-arbitrary reasons for discrimination against blacks are real enough. They do not depend on present arbitrary discrimination by others, and they may persist beyond an interval in which there is no discrimination. Whatever the roots of hypothetical racial differences in reliability as tenants might be, they would probably go too deep to be eradicated solely by a short period in which there was no racial discrimination.

We should recognize, then, that if the facts are as alleged, to legislate against the landlord's racially discriminatory practice is to impose a long-term disadvantage upon him. At the very least, he will have to take greater care in ascertaining the suitability of prospective tenants. Perhaps he will turn to data-collecting agencies for assistance, thus contributing to the growth of institutions that are threats, potential or actual, to our privacy. Perhaps, if these methods are unavailable or unavailing, the landlord will have to take greater losses than he otherwise would have, and perhaps this will lead to increased rents or even to a reduction in the amount of rentable housing available.

None of this forces us to conclude that we should not legislate against the landlord's racial discrimination. There are good reasons why we should seek to eliminate racial discrimination even when such discrimination is neither arbitrary in itself, nor relevant only because of the arbitrary prejudices of others. These reasons may be so important as to make the disadvantage imposed on the landlord comparatively insignificant.

An obvious point that can be made against the landlord is that he is judging people, at least in part, as members of a race rather than as individuals. The landlord does not deny that some black prospective tenants he turns away would make better tenants than some white prospective tenants he accepts. Some highly eligible black prospective tenants are refused accommodation simply because they are black. If the landlord assessed every prospective tenant as an individual this would not happen.

A similar point is often made in the debate over alleged differences between blacks and whites in America in whatever is measured by IQ tests. Even if, as Jensen and others have suggested, there is a small inherited difference in IQ between blacks and whites, it is clear that this difference shows up only when we compare averages, and not when we compare individuals. Even if we accept the controversial estimates that the average IQ of American blacks is 15 points lower than the average IQ of American whites, there is still a tremendous amount of overlap between the IQs of blacks and whites, with many whites scoring lower than the majority of blacks. Hence the difference in averages between the races would be of limited significance. For any purpose for which IQ mattered—like entrance into higher levels of education—it would still be essential to consider each applicant individually, rather than as a member of a certain race.

There are plenty of reasons why in situations like admitting people to higher education or providing them with employment or other benefits we should regard people as individuals and not as members of some larger group. For one thing we will be able to make a selection better suited for our own purposes, for selecting or discarding whole groups of people will generally result in, at best, a crude approximation to the results we hope to achieve. This is certainly true in an area like education. On the other hand it must be admitted that in some situations a crude approximation is all that can be achieved anyway. The landlord claims that his situation is one of these, and that as he cannot reliably tell which individuals will make suitable tenants, he is justified in resorting to so crude a means of selection as race. Here we need to turn our attention from the landlord to the prospective black tenant.

To be judged merely as a member of a group when it is one's individual qualities on which the verdict should be given is to be treated as less than the unique individual that we see ourselves as. Even where our individual qualities would merit less than we receive as a member of a group—if we are promoted over better-qualified people because we went to the "right" private school—the benefit is usually less welcome than it would be if it had been merited by our own attributes. Of course in this case qualms are easily stilled by the fact that a benefit has been received, never mind how. In the contrary case, however, when something of value has been lost, the sense of loss will be compounded by the feeling that one was not assessed on one's own merits, but merely as a member of a group.

To this general preference for individual as against group assessment must be added a consideration arising from the nature of the group. To be denied a benefit because one was, say, a member of the Communist Party would be unjust and a violation of basic principles of political liberty, but if one has chosen to join the Communist Party, then one is, after all, being assessed for what one has done, and one can choose between living with the consequences of continued party membership or leaving the party.[6] Race, of course, is not something that one chooses to adopt or that one can ever choose to give up. The person who is denied advantages because of his race is totally unable to alter this particular circumstance of his existence and so may feel with added sharpness that his life is clouded, not merely because he is not being judged as an individual, but because of something over which he has no control at all. This makes racial discrimination peculiarly invidious.

So we have the viewpoint of the victim of racial discrimination to offset against the landlord's argument in favor, and it seems that the victim has more at stake and hence should be given preference, even if the landlord's reason for discriminating is non-arbitrary and hence in a sense legitimate. The case against racial discrimination becomes stronger still when we consider the long-term social effects of discrimination.

When members of a racial minority are overwhelmingly among the poorest members of a society, living in a deprived area, holding jobs low in pay and status, or no jobs at all, and less well educated than the average member of the community, racial discrimination serves to perpetuate a divided society in which race becomes a badge of a much broader inferiority. It is the association of race with economic status and educational disadvantages which in turn gives rise to the situation in which there could be a coloring of truth to the claim that race is a relevant ground for discriminating between prospective tenants, applicants for employment, and so on. Thus there is, in the end, a parallel between the situation of the landlord and the cake-shop owner, for both, by their discrimination, contribute to the maintenance of the grounds for claiming that this discrimination is non-arbitrary. Hence prohibition of such discrimination can be justified as breaking this circle of deprivation and discrimination. The difference between the situations, as I have already said, is that in the case of the cake-shop owner it is only a prejudice against contact with blacks that needs to be broken down, and experience has shown that such prejudices do evaporate in a relatively short period of time. In the case of the landlord, however, it is the whole social and economic position of blacks that needs to be changed, and while overcoming discrimination would be an essential part of this process it may not be sufficient. That is why, if the facts are as the landlord alleges them to be, prohibition of racial discrimination is likely to impose more of a long-term disadvantage on the landlord than on the shop owner—a disadvantage which is, however, outweighed by the costs of continuing the circle of racial discrimination and deprivation for those discriminated against; and the costs of greater social inequality and racial divisiveness for the community as a whole.

III

A BASIC PRINCIPLE

If our discussion of the three examples has been sound, opposition to racial discrimination cannot rely on the standard objection that racial discrimination is arbitrary because race is irrelevant to employment, housing, and other things that matter. While this very often will be true, it will not always be true. The issue is more complicated than that appealing formula suggests, and has to do with the effect of racial discrimination on its victims, and on society as a whole. Behind all this, however, there is a more basic moral principle, and at this more basic level the irrelevance of race and the arbitrariness of racial discrimination reappear and help to explain why racism is wrong. This basic moral principle is the principle of equal consideration of interests.

The principle of equal consideration of interests is easy to state, though difficult to apply. Bentham's famous "each to count for one and none for more than one" is one way of putting it, though not free from ambiguity; Sidgwick's formulation is more precise, if less memorable: "The good of any one individual is of no more importance, from the point of view (if I may say so) of the Universe, than the good of any other."[7] Perhaps the best way of explaining the effect of the principle is to follow C.I. Lewis's suggestion that we imagine ourselves living, one after the other, the lives of everyone affected by our actions; in this way we would experience all of their experiences as our own.[8] R.M. Hare's insistence that moral judgments must be universalizable comes to much the same thing, as he has pointed out.[9] The essence of the principle of equal consideration of interests is that we give equal weight in our moral deliberations to the like interests of all those affected by our actions. This means that if only X and Y would be affected by a possible act, and if X stands to lose more than Y stands to gain (for instance, X will lose his job and find it difficult to get another, whereas Y will merely get a small promotion) then it is better not to do the act. We cannot, if we accept the principle of equal consideration of interests, say that doing the act is better, despite the facts described, because we are more concerned about Y than we are about X. What the principle is really saying is that an interest is an interest, whoever's interest it may be.

We can make this more concrete by considering a particular interest, say the interest we have in the relief of pain. Then the principle says that the ultimate moral reason for relieving pain is simply the undesirability of pain as such, and not the undesirability of X's pain, which might be different from the undesirability of Y's pain. Of course, X's pain might be more undesirable than Y's pain because it is more painful, and then the principle of equal consideration would give greater weight to the relief of X's pain. Again, even where the pains are equal, other factors might be relevant, especially if others are affected. If there has been an earthquake we might give priority to the relief of a doctor's pain so that he can treat other victims. But the doctor's pain itself counts only once, and with no added weighting. The principle of equal consideration of interests acts like a pair of scales, weighing interests impartially. True scales favor the side where the interest is stronger, or where several interests combine to outweigh a smaller number of similar interests; but they take no account of whose interests they are weighing.

It is important to understand that the principle of equal consideration of interests is, to adopt Sidgwick's suggestive phrase, a "point of view of the universe" principle. The phrase is, of course, a metaphor. It is not intended to suggest that the universe as a whole is alive, or conscious, or capable of having a point of view; but we can, without getting involved in any pantheist suppositions, imagine how matters would be judged by a being who was able to take in all of the universe, viewing all that was going on with an impartial benevolence.[10]

It is from this universal point of view that race is irrelevant to the consideration of interests; for all that counts are the intersts themselves. To give less consideration to a specified amount of pain because that pain was experienced by a black would be to make an arbitrary distinction. Why pick on race? Why not on whether a person was born in a leap year? Or whether there is more than one vowel in his surname? All these characteristics are equally irrelevant to the undersirability of pain from the universal point of view. Hence the principle of equal consideration of interests shows straightforwardly why the most blatant forms of racism, like that of the Nazis, are wrong. For the Nazis were concerned only for the welfare of members of the "Aryan" race, and the sufferings of Jews, Gypsies and Slavs were of no concern to them.

That the principle of equal consideration of interests is a "point of view of the universe" principle allows us to account for the fact that it is a principle upon which it seems virtually impossible to act. Who of us can live as if our own welfare and that of our family and friends were of no more concern to us than the welfare of anonymous individuals in far-away countries, of whom we know no more than the fact of their existence? Only a saint or a robot could live in this way; but this does not mean that only a saint or a robot can live in accordance with the principle of equal consideration of interests, for a principle which is valid from a universal point of view may yield subordinate principles to be acted upon by those who have limited resources and are involved in a particular segment of the world, rather than looking down upon the whole from a position of impartiality.

So subordinate principles giving members of families responsibility for the welfare of others in the family, or giving national governments responsibility for the welfare of their citizens, will be derivable from the principle of equal consideration, *if* everyone's interests are best promoted by such arrangements; and this is likely to be the case if, first, people are more knowledgeable about the interests of those close to them and more inclined to work to see that these interests are catered for, and, second, if the distribution of resources between families and between nations is not so unequally distributed that some families or nations are simply unable to provide for themselves the means to satisfying interests that could be satisfied with ease by other families or nations. In the world as it is presently constituted the first condition seems to hold, but not the second. For that reason I do not think that the subordinate principles mentioned correctly set out our present moral responsibilities, though they could do so if resources were more evenly distributed. Until then, we ought to strive to be more saint-like.[11]

Subordinate principles based on race, giving each race responsibility for the welfare of other members of that race are, I think, considerably less likely to be derivable from the principle of equal consideration than subordinate principles based on family or membership of a nation. For where they are not living together as a nation, races tend to be widely scattered; there is usually little knowledge of the circumstances of other members of one's race in different parts of the world, and there is nobody with the capacity to look after all members of a race as a national government can look after the interests of its citizens. There is, admittedly, often a degree of sentiment connecting members of a race, however widely they are separated. The contributions of American Jews to the support of members of their race in Israel is a well-known example of this, and there are many others. But the intermingling of races still makes it very doubtful that interests could be generally promoted by dividing responsibilities along racial lines.

The fundamental principle of equal consideration of interests, then, pays no regard to the race of those whose interests are under consideration; nor can we plausibly derive from the basic principle a subordinate principle enjoining us to consider the interests of members of our own race before we consider the interests of others; yet it cannot be said that the principle rules out racial discrimination in all circumstances. For the principle is an abstract one, and can only be applied in a concrete situation, in which the facts of the situation will be relevant. For instance, I have heard it said that somewhere in ancient Hindu writings members of the Brahmin or priestly caste are claimed to be so much more sensitive than members of the lower castes that their pleasures and pains are twenty times as intense as those of lesser human beings. We would, of course, do well to be suspicious of such a claim, particularly as the author of the document would no doubt have been a Brahmin himself. But let us assume that we somehow discovered that this extraordinary difference in sensitivity did in fact exist; it would follow that Brahmins have a greater interest in having access to a source of pleasure, and in avoiding a source of pain, than others. It would be as if when a Brahmin scratches his finger he feels a pain similar to that which others feel when they dislocate their shoulder. Then, consistently with the principle of equal consideration of interests, if a Brahmin and an ordinary person have both scratched their fingers, and we have only enough soothing ointment to cover one scratch, we should favor the Brahmin—just as, in the case of two normal people, if one had scratched a finger while the other had dislocated a shoulder we should favor the person with the more painful injury.

Needless to say, the example is a fanciful one, and intended to show only how, within the confines of the principle of equal consideration of interests, factual differences could be relevant to racial discrimination. In the absence of any real evidence of racial differences in sensitivity to pleasure and pain, the example has no practical relevance. Other differences between races—if they were differences between all members of races, and not differences which showed up only when averages were taken—could also justify forms of discrimination which ran parallel to the boundary of race. Examples would be substantial differences in intelligence, educability or the capacity to be self-governing. Strictly, if there were such differences then discrimination based on them would not be *racial* discrimination but rather discrimination on the ground of differences which happened to coincide with racial differences. But perhaps this is hair-splitting, since it would certainly be popularly known as racial discrimination. The kind of discrimination that such differences would justify would be only that to which these differences were relevant. For instance, a respectable argument for benevolent colonialism could be mounted if it really were true that certain races were so incapable of self-government as to be obviously better off on the whole when ruled by people of a different race. I hasten to add that the historical record gives no support to such a hypothesis, but rather suggests the contrary. Again, this fictional example shows only that, given peculiar enough factual assumptions, any acceptable principle of equality can lead to racial discrimination.

On the other hand, the principle of equal consideration of interests does underpin the decisions we reached when considering the three more realistic examples of racial discrimination in the preceding section of this article. Although the principle is too general to allow the derivation of straightforward and indisputable conclusions from it in complex situations, it does seem that an impartial consideration of the interests of all involved would, for reasons already discussed, rule out discrimination by the shop owner and the landlord, though allowing that of the film director. Hence it is the arbitrariness of racial discrimination at the level of the principle of equal consideration of interests, rather than at the level of the particular decision of the person discriminating, that governs whether a given act of racial discrimination is justifiable.

This conclusion may be applied to other controversial cases. It suggests, for instance, that the problem of "reverse discrimination" or "compensatory discrimination" which arises when a university or employer gives preference to members of minority groups should be discussed by asking not whether racial discrimination is always and intrinsically wrong, but whether the proposal is, on balance, in the interests of all those affected by it. This is a difficult question, and not one that can be answered generally for all types of reverse discrimination. For instance, if white communities have a far better doctor-patient ratio than black communities because very few blacks are admitted to medical school and white doctors tend to work in white communities, there is a strong case for admitting some black candidates to medical school ahead of whites who are better qualified by the standard entry procedures, provided, of course, that the blacks admitted are not so poorly qualified as to be unable to become competent doctors. The case for separate and easier entry would be less strong in an area where there is no equivalent community need, for instance, in philosophy. Here much would depend on whether black students who would not otherwise have been admitted were able to make up ground and do as well as whites with higher ratings on standard entry procedures. If so, easier entry for blacks could be justified in terms of the conventional goal of admitting those students most likely to succeed in their course; taking into account a student's race would merely be a way of correcting for the failure of standard tests to allow for the disadvantages that face blacks in competing with whites on such tests. If, on the other hand, blacks admitted under easier entry in a field like philosophy did not do as well as the whites they displaced could have been expected to do, discrimination in their favor would be much harder to justify.

Immigration policy, too, is an area in which the principle of equal consideration of interests suggests the kinds of facts we should look for, instead of giving a definite answer. The relevant questions are the extent to which an immigrant will be benefited by admission, and the extent to which the admitting nation will be benefited. Race certainly does not provide an answer to the first of these questions. A country which chooses to give only those of a certain race the benefit of permanent residence fails to give equal consideration to those not of the favored race who may have a greater interest in leaving their present country than others who are accepted because of their race. While this kind of racial discrimination would in itself be unjustifiable, it has been defended on the grounds that the alternative would be disastrous for citizens of the admitting nation, and ultimately for those admitted too. An extreme version of this kind of defense is the line taken by the British politician Enoch Powell, who prophesied "rivers of blood" if black immigration was not stopped and blacks who had already arrived were not encouraged to go back to where they had come from.[12] Here again, the facts are relevant. If Powell's claims had been soundly based, if it really were impossible for blacks and whites to live together without widespread bloodshed, then continued immigration would have been in the interests of neither blacks nor whites, and stopping immigration could not have been condemned as racist—though the epithet could have been applied to those Britons who were so hostile to blacks as to produce the situation Powell predicted. Despite occasional racial disturbances in Britain, however, there is no sign that Powell's predictions will come true. While a sudden influx of large numbers of immigrants of a different racial (or ethnic) group may cause problems, it is clear that people of different races can live together without serious strife. This being so, there is no justification for immigration policies that impose blanket prohibitions on people of a different race from that of the residents of the country. The most that can be defended in terms of the principle of equal consideration of interests is a quota system that leads to a gradual adjustment in the racial composition of a society.

NOTES

I am grateful to Robert Young for comments and criticism on this paper.

[1] In popular usage, even the term "discrimination" is often used to suggest that the practice referred to is wrong; this is, of course, an abuse of language, for to discriminate is merely to distinguish, or differentiate, and we could hardly get along without doing that.

[2] For a brief and clear statement of this idea of justice, se H.L.A. Hart, *The Concept of Law* (Oxford, 1961), 156-8; see also Joel Feinberg, *Social Philosophy* (Englewood Cliffs, N.J., 1973), Chap. 7.

[3] See, for instance, R.M. Hare, *Freedom and Reason* (Oxford, 1963), Chaps. 9, 11; Richard Wasserstrom, "Rights, Human Rights, and Racial Discrimination," *Journal of Philosophy* 61 (1964) and reprinted in James Rachels, ed., *Moral Problems* (New York, 1975).

[4] See Feinberg, 78.

[5] "In most southern communities . . . the adjustment to public desegregation following the enactment of the 1964 Civil Rights Act was amazing" (Lewis M. Killian, *White Southerners* [New York, 1970]). Similar comments have been made by many other observers; for a more recent report, see *Time*, 27 September 1976, especially the favorable comments of Northern blacks who have recently moved to the South (44). That contact with those of another race helps to reduce racial prejudice had been demonstrated as early as 1949, when a study of U.S. soldiers showed that the more contact white soldiers had with black troops, the more favorable were their attitudes to integration. See Samuel Stouffer *et al.*, *The American Soldier: Adjustment During Army Life* (Princeton, 1949), 594. This finding was supported by a later study, "Project Clear," reported by Charles Moskos, Jr., "Racial Integration in the Armed Forces," *American Journal of Sociology* 72 (1966), 132-48.

[6] The situation is different if it is because of a past rather than a present political connection that one is subjected to disadvantages. Perhaps this is why the hounding of

ex-communists in the McCarthy era was a particularly shameful episode in American history.

[7] Henry Sidgwick, *The Methods of Ethics*, 7th ed. (London, 1907), 382.

[8] C.I. Lewis, *Analysis of Knowledge and Valuation* (La Salle, 1946), 547; I owe this reference to R.M. Hare.

[9] See Hare, "Rules of War and Moral Reasoning," *Philosophy & Public Affairs* 1 (1972).

[10] See the discussion of the Ideal Observer theory in Roderick Firth, "Ethical Absolutism and the Ideal Observer," *Philosophy and Phenomenological Research* 12 (1952), and the further discussion in the same journal by Richard Brandt, vol. 15 (1955).

[11] For a general discussion of this issue, see Sidgwick, 432-3; for considerations relevant to the present distribution of resources, see my "Famine, Affluence and Morality," *Philosophy & Public Affairs* 1 (1972) and reprinted in James Rachels, ed., *Understanding Moral Philosophy* (Encino, Cal., 1976); and Paula and Karsten Struhl, eds., *Philosophy Now*, 2nd ed. (New York, 1975).

[12] *The Times* (London), 21 April 1968.

Freedom and Women

WILLIAM T. BLACKSTONE

The women's liberation movement is a complex phenomenon. Within it there are widely different views of the causes of the oppression of women and, consequently, widely different views of what is required to overcome that oppression. Put in a different way, the movement includes widely different views of what constitutes a free person in the social and political sense and, hence, different views of the sort of society required to assure freedom. The full range of political philosophies are represented in this movement. In this paper I want to focus briefly on some of the more radical claims made in the feminist movement. In order to make my target clear, I will sketch in very general terms several positions within or on the feminist movement.[1]

1. The traditionalist stance can hardly be classified as being *within* the women's liberation movement, but it has many advocates and it constitutes one of the parameters on this issue. The traditionalist holds that everything is all right the way it is (or at least it was all right before the feminists came along). Women are different from men and, in many ways, inferior; they are passive, submissive, and are meant to perform different roles. Sex-differentiated labor, sex stereotyping, and the restriction of females in terms of opportunities and roles are not oppression but the fulfillment of women's nature and necessary for family and social cohesion. Women's real freedom and equality are found within these restrictions, and the state should in no way interfere with those social conventions and practices.

2. The liberal, on the other hand (and I have in mind those like Betty Friedan in *The Feminine Mystique* and John Stuart Mill in *The Subjection of Women*), argues that sex-role stereotyping results in great social injustice, that if a woman wants to be a housewife and mother and perform these traditional roles it is perfectly all right, but she should not be systematically excluded from other alternatives or options on account of her sex. If there are relevant differences between men and women which prevent women from filling certain roles or from performing certain roles well, then discriminatory treatment may be justified, but if there are no relevant differences, then discrimination against women is unjust. Women should have equal

rights with men—social, economic, political, and legal—the liberal holds, and equal responsibilities. They should be judged as individuals and on the basis of their ability and performance—just as men. To permit this freedom and equality, men must be prepared to assume more responsibility in child rearing; and the state, or private enterprise (some liberals are more *laissez faire* than others!), must assist in providing some of the conditions required for genuine freedom and equality for women—day-care centers, for example. The liberal does not require the abolition of all traditional sex roles, nor does he (she) challenge traditional family values, though he insists on other options as life-styles.

3. Whereas the liberal thinks freedom can be had by reforming the system, the radical argues that freedom is possible only with the overthrow of the political system, and the political system is seen in very broad terms.[2] Marriage and the family are political institutions which oppress women. They must go, as well as the more overt social and legal rules. Radical feminists cover a wide spectrum, but those with leftist leanings believe, with Marx, that the state must "wither away" before genuine freedom is possible and that the economic system of capitalism and the class system which it presupposes must be abolished, for that system is the fundamental cause of all oppression. The oppression of women, in other words, cannot be overcome independently of other oppressions. It is part of a package which must be disposed of altogether. As Margaret Bengsten, a radical leftist feminist, puts it, women in a capitalist system are defined "as that group of people who are responsible for the production of simple use-values in those activities associated with the home and family."[3] She continues: "The material basis for the inferior status of women is to be found in just this definition of women. In a society in which money determines value, women are a group who work outside the money economy. Their work is not worth money, is therefore valueless, is therefore not even real work. And women themselves, who do this valueless work, can hardly be expected to be worth as much as men, who work for money."[4] The means of production must be socialized; there must be "a reintroduction of the entire female sex into public industry," as Engels claims; goods and services must be distributed on the basis of needs; and society as a whole, *not* the family, must be made responsible for the welfare of children, as for everyone else. The radical feminist advocates total revolution, then, not mere reform within the system.

4. Some radical feminists do not buy the entire Marxist line, and they should be accorded a category of their own. I have in mind Shulamith Firestone and her followers. I quote: "There is a level of reality that does not stem directly from economics. . . ."[5] Firestone attempts to develop " a materialist view of history based on sex itself," arguing that "for feminist revolution we shall need an analysis of the dynamics of sex war as comprehensive as the Marx-Engels analysis of

class antagonism was for economic revolution. More comprehensive. For we are dealing with a larger problem, with an oppression that goes back beyond recorded history to the animal kingdom itself."[6] Firestone sees economic class analysis of social injustice as secondary to sex analysis. The biological differences between men and women— the general physical strength of men plus the weakness of women due to childbearing—made men dominant and women dependent. Oppression resulted. Liberation for females is possible only by overcoming these biological differences through technology. Contraception and "artificial reproduction" will free women from their biological inequalities and, subsequently, from social inequalities. Liberation requires the abolition of the whole sex-role system (including childbearing), marriage, and the family. It requires, to quote Firestone, "freedom from sexual classification altogether rather than merely an equalization of sex roles."[7] Freedom and equality, within this radical picture, preclude even the choice of a traditional female role.

Within these four inadequately sketched positions, there is wide disagreement on the meaning of freedom (and equality) for women and on what is required to attain it.

Feminist critics, it seems to me, are in general correct in their claim that women in our society (and others) are oppressed as a class. Many of our laws and our extralegal practices discriminate unfairly against women. I will not attempt to provide the data for that assessment here. The sex-based discrimination of many state laws is well known[8]—laws which permit women to be imprisoned for three years for habitual drunkenness while restricting the penalty for the same offense to thirty days for males; laws which "excuse" all women from jury duty; which permit the withholding of credit from married women on the assumption that they are all financially dependent on their husbands; which permit the plea of "passion" killing for wronged husbands but not wronged wives; which make the father, not the mother or the parents, the "natural guardian" of children; which give the husband right of action in divorce in cases of adultery but not the wife; and work practices in which women are paid less than men for the same work; and so on.

Rather than focus on those feminist evaluations which seem so obviously correct, I will examine some of the more philosophically controversial evaluations and theses in the feminist movement. I beg off on those expressed in (3) above. Any treatment of the Marxist feminist position would require an assessment of the cluster of factual and valuational assumptions of the political philosophy of communism.[9] I will focus briefly on only a few of the claims in (4) which can stand independently of these assumptions: the theses that childbearing is a restraint on the freedom of women, that it is an unjustified restraint, and that freedom (and equality or social justice) for women requires biological equality, the total abolition of sexual classification, and the abolition of the traditional institutions of marriage and the family. There are other factual and normative theses within (4) which I will not examine, including the claim that "pregnancy is barbaric";[10] the belief that technology not only will be developed to perform the childbearing function but will also free all humans from the necessity to work;[11] the thesis that all sexual repression ought to cease and will cease with the demise of the biological family (everyone, including children, will be permitted "to do whatever they want sexually. . . . humanity could finally revert to its natural 'polymorphously perverse' sexuality");[12] the claim that wealth should be distributed on the basis of need; and the belief that a communist anarchy is the proper form of government for liberated persons.

First, is childbearing or the capacity to bear children a restraint? The capacity to bear children is a natural capacity which females possess and males do not. We would not say that males are under a restraint because they cannot bear children. Would we say that females are because they can? In neither case is the capacity or incapacity something which is imposed by the social and legal structure. The decision to exercise that capacity for some women may be imposed via an inculcated stereotype image, and that inculcation may properly be seen in some circumstances as a restraint, just as one might view the inculcation of exclusive sex roles in child rearing. These restraints should be lifted or modified and the duties of child rearing shared equitably by men, the liberal believes. But is the capacity to bear children, or the incapacity, itself a restraint? If we stretch the word "restraint" or "unfree" to include the existence or non-existence of such natural capacities, then clearly anything could be counted as a restraint or unfreedom to someone or something, and the concept of restraint or unfreedom would be functionless, at least in the sense of permitting the attribution of responsibility for restraints or unfreedoms. Justified or unjustified complaints about restraints or inabilities presuppose and require that those restraints or inabilities be due to social and legal arrangements controlled (or controllable) by human beings. Consequently, the biological inequalities or differences between men and women cannot be viewed as restraints in the responsibility-attributing sense. They may be viewed as restraints in the sense that they are natural conditions which limit possibilities and which are present in contexts in which there is male domination and oppression of women. One can hardly say, however, that the biological inequalities or differences are responsible for the social inequalities. Granted, if there were no biological differences between men and women there would be no social inequalities between them. This is tautologically true, because there would be no women (or no men, however one wishes to state this). But it is an extreme solution to the problem of unjust discrimination against women to obliterate either the biological differences between men and women (which Firestone does not propose) or the different biological functions of men and women (which Firestone does propose). Even if freedom could be purchased only at the cost of one's sexuality—which is certainly not the case—this would be a terrible price to pay and, in fact, would vitiate a basic purpose for which social and political systems are devised, namely, self-preservation and the fulfillment of each person's interests. For surely a "self" and "interests" cannot be defined completely apart from sex, sexuality, or biological traits—at least not in the world we know. Perhaps they could in some possible world, and Shulamith Firestone may be urging on us this other possible world—in which case we must be prepared to calculate the advantages and disadvantages of that world as compared with our own. In our world, the key factors responsible for oppression are not biological traits but social, economic, political, and legal options or choices. The oppression due to such choices could exist even under conditions in which some biological differences are minimized (strength, for example) or in which certain biological functions (child-bearing) are not performed by women but by machines. Rather than desexualize or asexualize our world through technology (if indeed this is possible), we need to change social and legal systems which discriminate irrelevantly on the basis of sex.

A second radical feminist thesis which is questionable is that freedom for women requires "freedom from sexual classification altogether." As with any claim, everything hangs on its interpretation. If what is meant is that laws and policies which discriminate solely and arbitrarily on the basis of sex (and not on the basis of capacities or abilities to do or become something) are unjust and that a society which has such laws oppresses women (and men), this claim is quite acceptable and follows from the basic democratic commitment to equal rights and equal freedom for all.

However, "freedom from sexual classification altogether" may mean much more than freedom from irrelevant classification based on sex or freedom from unjustified differential treatment based on sex. It may require that sex or sexual characteristics be totally ruled out as ever being relevant to the differential treatment of persons or to according equality of treatment. It may require a system of social justice in which sex and sexually associated characteristics (if they exist and whatever they may be) cannot in principle be invoked. Such a system would increase some freedoms by ridding us of some injustices, for there are many institutionalized practices which discriminate arbitrarily on the basis of sex. At the same time, it would lead to some social injustice *if* there were some differences between the sexes which in certain contexts justified differential treatment. The liberal feminist does not want to rule out such possible differences. Abilities or inabilities due to natural capacities (physical strength or weakness, high or low IQ, blindness, and so on) justify differential treatment in our egalitarian ethic. Firestone rules out such differential treatment with respect to gender in the very name of egalitarianism. Her position on this point would be correct only if all relevant facts, characteristics, or circumstances which could in principle justify differential treatment were independent of gender. One must admit that not all the data are in—perhaps very little which can be trusted—and further that many differences between men and women are enculturated. One might go further and agree that most of the relevant grounds for the differential treatment of persons are independent of gender. But I am leery about prejudging the question before a great deal more research is conducted, and in fact there seem to be differences between men and women (which hold in general) which, whether genetically or culturally caused, justify differential treatment (I am thinking primarily of physical strength).

A third radical feminist thesis which seems to me to be mistaken is that freedom for women requires the utter abolition of the traditional institutions of marriage and the family. There is no doubt that these institutions have oppressed women and continue to do so. But Firestone argues that a free society must preclude the traditional sex-differentiated role for women as a possible option.

However, even if technology will one day permit test-tube babies, even if the state could adequately serve as the custodian of all children, and even if society could function without marriage and the family, the ruling out of traditional options decreases freedom to that extent. Even if freedom were kept as a value (in the sense of the total range of options) distinct from social justice (the proper distribution of goods and services) as a value (though, of course, these values are related), her type of society would limit the range of human options in certain directions and expand it in others. An assessment of her type of society would require a comparative assessment of the range of the options given up and those acquired and the social justice or equality purchased at the cost of limiting human options in her way. Here the liberal feminist's response to the radical is that both social justice for women and the expanded range of options can be had without the preclusion (though not without some alteration) of traditional options (marriage and the family). Marriage and role divisions within marriage are not inherently exploitive and oppressive, though they may be oppressive if predicated on psychological, social, and economic oppression and exploitation (and, of course, many marriages and role divisions are). There is, in other words, no necessary conflict between freedom to choose from a range of options, including traditional roles, and equality or social justice for women. And, with proper modification, the family as an institution need not be a perpetuator of sexist discrimination—though other sorts of inequalities perpetuated by the family as an institution (those stressed in literature from Plato's *Republic* to the Coleman report on *Equality of Educational Opportunity*)[13] are not easily modified.[14]

NOTES

A longer version of this paper was read at a symposium on this topic held at Vanderbilt University in conjunction with the annual meeting of the Tennessee Philosophical Association, 10 November 1973. I am grateful to the members of this association and especially to Stephen White, who served as commentator on my paper, to Robert Bryan and his colleagues at North Carolina State University, where an earlier draft was read, and to my wife, Jean, for valuable discussion.

1 Detailed accounts of various positions within the feminist movement are found in Juliet Mitchell's *Woman's Estate* (Baltimore, 1966); Leslie B. Tanner, ed., *Voices from Women's Liberation* (New York, 1970); V. Gornik and B. Moran, *Woman in Sexist Society* (New York, 1971); and an excellent unpublished essay by Alison Jaggar, "Four Views of Women's Liberation," which was presented at the American Philosophical Association meeting, Western Division, 4-6 May 1972.

2 Margaret Bengsten is an example of a radical leftist feminist; see her "Political Economy of Women's Liberation," *Monthly Review* 21 (September 1969), reprinted in *Voices from Women's Liberation* (see n. 1 above). Mitchell (n. 1 above) spells out in detail the leftist feminist position.

3 Bengsten, 281.

4 *Ibid.*, 282.

5 Shulamith Firestone, *The Dialectic of Sex* (New York, 1971), 6.

6 *Ibid.*, 2.

7 Shulamith Firestone, "On American Feminism," in *Woman in Sexist Society* (see n. 1 above), 686, n. 4.

8 See, for example, Diane B. Schulder, "Does the Law Oppress Women?" in Robin Morgan, ed., *Sisterhood Is Powerful* (New York, 1970), 139-57.

9 I would not write off entirely the Marxist analysis of the oppression of women, but I am not at all convinced that private property is the root of all social evils. If we look at historical realities, unfreedom and oppression (including that of women) are at least as possible under socialist systems as they are under capitalist ones.

10 Firestone, *The Dialectic of Sex*, 226.

11 *Ibid.*, 235.

12 *Ibid.*, 236-7.

13 James S. Coleman *et al.*, *Equality of Educational Opportunity* (Washington, D.C., 1966).

14 See my "Human Rights, Equality, and Education," *Educational Theory* 19, no. 3 (1969), for discussion.

Male Chauvinism:
A Conceptual Analysis

MARILYN FRYE

Some years ago the new feminist rhetoric brought into common use the term "male chauvinist." The term found ready acceptance among feminists, and it seems to wear its meaning on its sleeve. But many males to whom it has been applied have found it rather puzzling. This puzzlement cannot properly be dismissed as a mere expression of defensiveness. In the first place, the term is frequently used as though it were interchangeable with the term "sexist," with the consequence that it can be difficult to see clearly that there may be different kinds of sin here. In the second place, a bit of analysis of the phenomenon called male chauvinism shows that it is not likely to work in male psychology quite as a chauvinism should work, though it bears considerable resemblance to a chauvinism when viewed from the position of the female. As if this were not enough to cloud the picture, male chauvinism involves self-deception, and thus it is bound to escape notice on the first round of self-examination. So for this reason also it is difficult for a male chauvinist, even one eager to repent, clearly to discern the nature of his offense and the extent of his guilt.

One of my tasks here is to disentangle the notions of a male chauvinist and a sexist. The other is to provide the outlines of an analysis of male chauvinism itself. I shall to some extent be describing feminist usage and theory as I understand it and to some extent be developing and improving upon it. There is no sharp line here between description and improvisation.

SEXISM

The term "sexist" in its core and perhaps most fundamental meaning is a term that characterizes anything whatever that creates, constitutes, promotes, or exploits any irrelevant or impertinent marking of the distinctions between the sexes. I borrow the term "mark" here from a use in linguistics. Different distinctions may be "marked" in different languages. For example, the distinction between continuous and instantaneous present action is marked in some languages and not in others, that is, some do and some do not have different syntactic or semantic forms corresponding to this distinction. Behavior patterns very frequently mark the distinction between the sexes. For instance, behavior required in polite introductions differs according to the sexes of the participants. This means, curiously enough, that one must know a person's genital configuration before one has made that person's acquaintance, in order to know *how* to make her or his acquaintance. In general, "correct" or "appropriate" behavior, both nonlinguistic and linguistic, so frequently varies with (that is, marks) the sexes of the persons involved that it is of the utmost importance that a person's sex be immediately obvious upon the briefest encounter, even in conditions relatively unfavorable to observation. Hence our general need for abundant redundancy in sex marking.

The term "sexist" can be, and sometimes is, used in such a way that it is neutral with respect to what, if any, advantage or favor is associated with the marking of the distinction between the sexes and whether such advantage is enjoyed by the female or the male. But it is not standardly used in this neutral sense. As it is standardly used, the unqualified term denotes only those impertinent markings of the sexes that are in some way or sense associated with advantage to the male. To refer to such markings when they are associated with advantage to the female, one standardly must qualify the noun, using some such phrase as "reverse sexism." There is a kind of irony here with which one is now depressingly familiar. The word "sexist" is itself male-centered—one may perhaps say sexist. Nonetheless, for present purposes, I shall use and refer to the term "sexist" in its male-centered sense.

Although the term "sexist" is commonly applied to specific acts or behavior or to certain institutional processes, laws, customs, and so forth when they irrelevantly mark the distinction between the sexes, these uses seem to me to be relatively unproblematic, and I shall not directly discuss them. I shall focus instead on the characterization of persons as sexists—the notion of *a sexist*.

THREE KINDS OF SEXISTS AND AN IMPOSTOR

One would standardly characterize a person as a sexist in virtue of his sexist beliefs, opinions, convictions, and principles.[1] A person might also be called a sexist in virtue of his acts and practices, but in general only if they are seen as associated with sexist beliefs. There may be people whose sexist behavior is nothing but an unthinking adoption of the habits of those around them, for instance, a door-opening habit whose genesis is like that of peculiarities of dishwashing or driving techniques picked up from one's parents. If a person's sexist behavior consisted solely of such habits, perhaps he would be found innocent of sexist belief. In that case I think that though his behavior might be labeled sexist (and he might reasonably be expected to change it), one should probably refrain from labeling *him* sexist.[2] Actually, it is a bit difficult to imagine someone having many such habits and not developing sexist beliefs to link the habits to each other and to various aspects of social life. Perhaps much of our sexist training takes this route, from unthinking habit to conviction.

Speaking quite generally, sexists are those who hold certain sorts of general beliefs about sexual differences and their consequences. They hold beliefs that would, for instance, support the view that physical differences between the sexes must always make for significant social and economic differences between them in any human society, such that males and females will in general occupy roles at least roughly isomorphic to those they now occupy in most extant human societies. In many cases, of course, these general beliefs might more accurately be represented by the simple proposition: Males are innately superior to females.

It is central to most feminist views that these general beliefs (assuming they are beliefs and not mere sentiments) are to be viewed as theories subject to the test of evidence and in principle falsifiable. And one kind of sexist is one who shares this attitude with respect to the epistemological status of such beliefs and differs from the feminist primarily in taking one version or another of them to be true, while the feminist holds that all such theories are false.[3] I call this person a *doctrinaire sexist*. When the feminist and the doctrinaire sexist are both fairly sophisticated, their debates tend to focus on preferred modes of empirical testing and the weights of various kinds of evidence.

There is another kind of sexist who would cheerfully assent to the same sorts of sexist propositions as those accepted by the doctrinaire sexist but who does not view them as mere theories. Such people, who I call *primitive sexists*, are committed to these propositions as a priori truths, or ultimate metaphysical principles. A value-laden male/ female dualism is embedded in their conceptual schemes more or less as a value-laden mind/body dualism is embedded in the conceptual schemes of many people of our culture. Looking at things from the point of view of the primitive sexist, these beliefs or principles cannot simply be refuted by empirical evidence, for they are among the principles of interpretation involved in *taking in* evidence. Even so, there is a point in challenging and haranguing the primitive sexist, for the turmoil of attack and defense may generate a reorganization of his conceptual scheme, changing the role of his sexist beliefs. One may be able to convert the primitive sexist to doctrinaire sexism, which is vulnerable to evidence and argument. (I am inclined to think that much of what feminists think of as unconscious sexism may really be primitive sexism.)

Borrowing a Quinean analogy, we might say that the sexist beliefs of the doctrinaire sexist are relatively near the periphery of his conceptual net, and that those of the primitive sexist have a central position. Sexist beliefs may indeed be anywhere between the center and the periphery of a conceptual net, and accordingly, sexists come in all shades, from empirical to metaphysical.

The stances of the doctrinaire and primitive sexists mark ends of a spectrum. Another spectrum of cases differs from the doctinaire position in the degree to which a person's sexist beliefs are internally coherent and distinct from sundry other beliefs. Certainly, many people would assent (unless the new social pressure inhibited them) to quite a variety of statements the doctrinaire sexist would make; yet they could not in conscience be said to be adherents of a theory. There are those in whom such beliefs are scattered helter-skelter among religious persuasions, racist notions, beliefs and uncertainties about their own excellences and flaws, and so on. These sexist beliefs, though perhaps empirical enough, are not sufficiently organized or distinct from other networks of beliefs to constitute something so dignified as a theory. Sexists such as these I call *operational sexists*. They live pretty much as though they were doctrinaire sexists, but they are not so academic about it. Like the primitive sexist, the operational sexist may be more receptive to persuasion if first educated to the doctrinaire position.

There are other sorts of sexists that would have to be mentioned if we were striving for a complete catalog of members of the species according to the status of their sexist beliefs, but enough has been said to indicate the gist of the list. One other creature, however, should not go unmentioned—the *Opportunist*. The Opportunist is an impostor: he either has no particular beliefs about sexual differences and their consequences or in one degree or another accepts feminist claims about them, but he pretends to sexist convictions in order to gain the privileges and advantages associated with their acceptance by others. Regularly carrying on as though it is one's natural destiny to have some woman tend to one's laundry has, in the context of our present lives, a tendency to bring about the regular appearance of clean and mended clothes without effort on one's own part. Such opportunities abound in our society and are not missed by many persons of normal intelligence and normal distaste for distasteful tasks. (Many of us should recall here that in our youth we took advantage of such opportunities with respect to the rich variety of services our mothers were expected to perform but which we could well have performed for ourselves.) The Opportunist, furthermore, can share not only the advantages but also the excuses of the genuine sexists. The privilege attendant upon the opportunistic pretense of sexism can often be protected by availing oneself of the excuses and sympathy available to the genuine sexist—sexism is, after all, deeply ingrained in our society and in our individual lives, and who can blame the poor soul if he cannot rid himself of it overnight? One may well wonder how many of the people we identify as sexists are really cynical impostors; and while one's speculation on this question may place one on an optimist-pessimist spectrum, it is unfortunately not obvious which end of the spectrum is which.[4]

To accuse a person of being a sexist is to accuse him of having certain false beliefs and, in some cases, of having tendencies to certain reprehensible behavior presumed to be related in one way or another to such beliefs. Those justly accused of being sexists may or may not be blameworthy in this matter; personal responsibility for holding false beliefs varies greatly with persons and circumstances.

MALE CHAUVINISM

The accusation of male chauvinism is a deeper matter than the accusation of sexism. "Male chauvinism" is one of the strongest terms in feminist rhetoric; "male chauvinist pig," which to some ears sounds pleonastic, belongs to a vocabulary of stern personal criticism. In the more extreme instances, persons called male chauvinists are not seen as ignorant or stupid, nor as hapless victims of socialization, but as wicked—one might almost say, perverted. They are accused of something whose relation to belief and action is like that of a defect of character, or a moral defect—a defect that might partially account for an otherwise reasonable and reasonably virtuous and self-critical person holding beliefs that are quite obviously false and behaving in ways that are obviously reprehensible. I believe the defect in question is a particularly nasty product of closely related moral failure and conceptual perversity.

Prior to its new association with the term "male," the concept of chauvinism was connected primarily, perhaps exclusively, with excessive and blind patriotism and closely similar phenomena. Patriotism seems at a glance to be an identification of some kind with one's country. One is personally affronted if one's country is criticized, and one takes personal pride in the country's real or imagined strengths and virtues. A national chauvinism is an exaggerated version of this identification, in which the righteousness and intolerance are extreme. Other chauvinisms will presumably be similar identifications with other sorts of groups, such as religious sects. In any of these cases the chauvinist will be convinced of the goodness, strength, and virtue—in general, the superiority—of his nation, sect, or so on, and will have some sort of psychological mechanisms linking this virtue with his own goodness, strength, and virtue—his own superiority.

Given roughly this view of chauvinisms, it might seem that if we could analyze and understand the mechanisms linking the supposed virtue and superiority of the nation or sect to the supposed personal virtue and superiority of the chauvinist, we could then transfer that understanding to the case of the male chauvinist to see how he is accused of ticking.

But there is a serious obstacle to pursuing this course. An analogy between national and male chauvinisms will not hold up because the objects of the identifications are not relevantly similar. Whatever the mechanisms of national and religious chauvinism might turn out to be, they are mechanisms that associate a person with an entity that is pseudo-personal. Nations and sects act and are responsible for their actions; they are therefore pseudo-persons. Identification with such an entity is identification with a pseudo-person, and its mechanisms therefore will presumably be similar in some fairly important and enlightening ways to those of identifications with persons. Now, if we take the label "male chauvinism" at face value, male chauvinism should be an identification with the group consisting of all male human beings from which the chauvinist derives heightened self-esteem. But the group of all male human beings is not a pseudo-person; it does not have an internal structure that would give it an appropriate sort of unity; it does not act as a unit; it does not relate pseudo-personally to any other pseudo-persons; it is not virtuous or vicious. There cannot be a self-elevating identification with the group of all males the mechanisms of which would be like those of a national or sectarian chauvinism. The group with which the person supposedly identifies is the wrong sort of entity; in fact, one might say it is not an entity at all.

These reflections point to the conclusion that the phenomenon called male chauvinism is not in fact a chauvinism—a conclusion that should not be surprising. There clearly is some kind of mental set in which a male's knowledge that he is male is closely connected with his self-esteem and with the perception and treatment of females as "other," or "alien." But to picture this as a chauvinism is odd. So diverse, varied, and amorphous a group as that consisting of all male members of the species *Homo sapiens* is an implausible peg on which to hang a self-esteem. I do think, however, that this phenomenon, like a chauvinism, critically involves an identification through which one gains support of one's self-esteem. Drawing on a prevalent current in feminist thought, I suggest it is at bottom a version of a self-elevating identification with Humanity or Mankind—a twisted version in which mankind is confused with malekind. Superficially it looks somewhat like a chauvinism, and a female's experience in confronting it is all too much like that of an Algerian in France; but actually the feminist is accusing the so-called male chauvinist not of improperly identifying with some *group* but of acting as though what really is *only* a group of human beings were all there is to the human race. Since that is not a chauvinism and calling it such can only be misleading, I shall hereafter refer to it as *phallism*.

PHALLISM

Feminists have always been sensitive to the tendency to conflate and confuse the concepts of Man and male. We tend (we are explicitly taught) to think of distinctively human characteristics as distinctively masculine and to credit distinctively human achievements like culture, technology, and science, to men, that is, to males. This is one element of phallism: a picture of humanity as consisting of males. Blended with this, there is a (distinctively human?) tendency to romanticize and aggrandize the human species and to derive from one's rosy picture of it a sense of one's individual specialness and superiority.

Identifying with the human race, with the species, seems to involve a certain consciousness of the traits or properties one has *qua* member of the species. In this, we generally focus on those specific differences that we can easily construe as marking our elevation above the rest of the animal kingdom, among which the powers of speech and reason and moral sentiment are prime. Being the highest animals, the crowning achievement of evolution, we feel it morally acceptable to treat members of other species with contempt, condescension, and patronage. We supervise their safety, we decide what is best for them, we cultivate and train them to serve our needs and please us, we arrange that they shall be fed and sheltered as we please and shall breed and have offspring at our convenience (and often our concern for their welfare is sincere and our affection genuine). Every single human being, simply *qua* human being and regardless of personal virtues, abilities, or accomplishments, has these rights and, in some cases, duties with respect to members of any other species. All human beings can be absolutely confident of their unquestionable superiority over every creature of other species, however clever, willful, intelligent, or independently capable of survival.

We are all familiar enough with this self-serving arrogance. It might suitably be called *humanism.* It is just this sort of arrogance and assumption of superiority that is characteristic of the phallist. It is an assumption of superiority, with accompanying rights and duties, that is not seen as needing to be justified by personal virtue or individual merit, and is seen as justifying a contemptuous or patronizing attitude toward certain others. What the phallist does, generally, is to behave toward women with humanist contempt and patronage. The confusion of "man" with lowercase "m" and "Man" with uppercase "m" is revealed when the attitudes with which Man meets lower animals are engaged in the male man's encounter with the female man.

It will be noted by the alert liberal that women are not the only human creatures that are not, or not generally, treated with the respect apparently due members of so elevated a species as ours. This is, of course, quite true. An arrogation of rights and duties fully analogous to humanism is carried out also in relation to infants, the aged, the insane, the criminal, the retarded, and other sorts of outcasts. It turns out that only certain of the creatures that are human (as opposed to equine, canine, and so on) are taken to be blessed with the superiority natural to the species; others are defective or underdeveloped and are not to be counted among the superior "us." The point here is just that phallists place females of the species in just this latter category. The words "defective" and "underdeveloped" and similar terms actually are used, with deadly seriousness, in descriptions of female psychology and anatomy broadcast by some of those assumed to have professional competence in such things.

With this degree of acquaintance with the phallist, I think one can see quite clearly why women complain of not being treated as persons by those who have been called male chauvinists. Those human creatures that we approach and treat with not the slightest trace of humanistic contempt are those we recognize unqualifiedly as fully actualized, fully normal, morally evaluable *persons*. The phallist approaches females with a superiority and condescension that we all take to be more or less appropriate to encounters with members of other species and with defective or underdeveloped members of our own. In other words, phallists do not treat women as persons.

I speak here of "the slightest trace of humanist contempt" and "fully actualized, fully normal, morally evaluable persons." These heavy qualifications are appropriate because much of our behavior suggests that there are degrees of personhood. But for now I wish to avoid this matter of degrees. I propose to simplify things by concentrating on unqualified fully actualized personhood. When in the rest of this essay I speak of persons or of the treatment or recognition of someone as a person, it is "full" personhood that I have in mind. Anything less than that, in any dimension, is covered by phrases like "not a person" or "not as a person." I shall also confine my attention to females and males who are not very young nor generally recognized as criminal or insane.

THE PHALLIST FANTASY—I

The phallist does not treat women as persons. The obvious question is, Does he withhold this treatment in full awareness that women are persons? Are we dealing with simple malice? I have no doubt that there are cases of this transparent wickedness, but it may be more common for a person to shrink from such blatant immorality, guarding his conscience with a protective membrane of self-deception. The phallist can arrange things so that he does not experience females as persons in the first place, and thus will not have to justify to himself his failure to treat them as persons. In this and the succeeding section, I shall sketch out the phallist's characteristic strategies.

What makes a human creature a person is its possession of a range of abilities and traits whose presence is manifest in certain behavior under certain circumstances. Sacrificing elegance to brevity, I shall refer to these traits and abilities as person-abilities and to the behavior in which they are manifest as person-behavior. As with abilities in general, and their manifestations in behavior, certain circumstances are, and others are not, suitable for the manifestation of person-abilities in person-behavior.

Given this general picture one can easily see that the possibilities for self-deceptive avoidances of attributing personhood are plentiful. (1) One can observe a creature that is in fact person-behaving and deceive oneself straight out about the facts before one; one can come away simply denying that the behavior took place. (2) One can

observe certain behavior and self-deceptively take it as a manifestation of a lower degree or smaller range of abilities than it in fact man-
ifests. (3) One may self-deceptively judge circumstances that are
adverse to the manifestation of the abilities to have been optimal and
then conclude from the fact that the abilities were not manifest that
they are not present. I have no doubt that persons anxious to avoid
perceiving females as persons use all of these devices, singly and in
combination. But another, more vicious device is at hand. It is not a
matter of simple misinterpretation of presented data but a matter of
rigging the data and then self-deceptively taking them at face value.

Person-abilities are manifest only in certain suitable circumstances;
so one can ensure that an individual will seem not to have these abilities by arranging for the false appearance that the individual has been
in suitable circumstances for their manifestation. The individual will
not in fact have been in suitable circumstances, which guarantees that
the abilities will not be manifest; but it will seem that the individual
was in suitable circumstances and the deceived observer will perceive
the individual to lack the abilities in question. Then to wrap it up, one
can deceive oneself about having manipulated the data, take the position of the naive observer, and conclude for oneself that the individual lacks the abilities. Parents are often in a position to do this. Presenting their daughters with unsuitable learning situations self-deceptively arranged to appear suitable, they convince themselves that they
have discovered the children's inability to learn those things. A simple
but illuminating example is frequently acted out in a father's attempt
to teach his daughter to throw a baseball. He goes through various
superficial maneuvers and declares failure—her failure—without
having engaged anything like the perseverence and ingenuity that he
would have engaged in the training of his son.

But even this does not exhaust the tricks available to the phallist. A
critical central range of the traits and abilities that go into a creature's
being a person are traits and abilities that can be manifest only in circumstances of interpersonal interaction wherein another person
maintains a certain level of communicativeness and cooperativeness.
One cannot, for instance, manifest certain kinds of intelligence in
interactions with a person who has a prior conviction of one's stupid-
ity, lack of insight, absence of wit; one cannot manifest sensitivity or
loyalty in interactions with someone who is distrustful and will not
share relevant information. It is this sort of thing that opens up the
possibility for the most elegant of the self-deceptive moves of the
phallist, one that very nicely combines simplicity and effectiveness. He
can avoid seeing the critical central range of a woman's person-
abilities simply by being uncooperative and uncommunicative and
can, at the same time, do it without knowing he has done it by self-
deceptively believing he has been cooperative and communicative.
The ease with which one can be uncooperative and uncommunicative
while believing oneself to be the opposite is apparent from the most

casual acquaintance with common interpersonal problems. The manipulation of the circumstances is easy, the deception is easy, and the effects are broad and conclusive.

The power and rigidity of the phallist's refusal to experience women as persons is exposed in a curious perceptual flip he performs when he is forced or tricked into experiencing as a person someone who is in fact female. Those of her female characteristics that in another woman would irresistibly draw his attention go virtually unnoticed, and she becomes "one of the boys." Confronted with the dissonant appearance of a female person in a situation where he is unable to deny that she is a person, he denies that she is female.

The frustration of trying to function as a person in interaction with someone who is self-deceptively exercising this kind of control over others and over his own perceptions is one of the primary sources of feminist rage.

THE PHALLIST FANTASY—II

It has been assumed in the preceding section that it is obvious that women are persons. Otherwise, failure to perceive women as persons would not have to involve self-deception. Some women, however, clearly think there is some point in asserting that they are persons, and some women's experience is such that they are inclined to say that they are denied personhood.

To some, there seems to be a certain silliness about the assertion that women are persons, which derives from the fact that almost everybody, female and male alike, seems to *agree* that women are people. But in many instances this constitutes no more than an acceptance of the fact that females are biologically human creatures with certain linguistic capacities and emotional needs; in accepting this, one is committed to no more than the belief that women should be treated humanely, as we are enjoined to treat the retarded and the elderly. But the personhood of which I am speaking here is "full" personhood. I am speaking of unqualified participation in the radical superiority of the species, without justification by individual virtue or achievement—unqualified membership of that group of beings that may approach all other creatures with humanist arrogance. Members of this group are to be treated not humanely but with respect. It is plain that not everybody, not even almost everybody, agrees that women belong to this group. The assertion that they do is hardly the assertion of something so generally deemed obvious as to be unworthy of assertion.

The other claim—that women are denied personhood—also seems strange to some people. But it by no means emerges parthenogenetically from feminine fantasy. To some, the concept of a person seems somewhat like the concepts that are sometimes called "institutional," such as the concepts of a lawyer or a knight. To some it seems that "person" denotes a social or institutional role and that one may be allowed or forbidden to adopt that role. It seems that we (persons) have some sort of power to admit creatures to personhood. I do not find this view plausible, but it surely recommends itself to some, and it must be attractive to the phallist, who would fancy the power to create persons. His refusal to perceive women as persons could then be taken by him as an exercise of this power. Some phallists give every sign of accepting this or a similar view, and some women seem to be taken in by it too. Hence, some women are worked into the position of asking to be granted personhood. It is a peculiar position for a person to be in, but such are the almost inevitable effects of phallist magic on those not forewarned. Of course, one cannot make what is a person not a person by wishing it so. And yet some vague impression lingers that phallists do just that—and it is not without encouragement that it lingers.

Even apart from the cases of institutional concepts, there is in the employment of concepts, as in the employment of words, a certain collective subjectivity. Every concept has some standard use or uses in some community—the "conceptual community" whose usage fixes its correct application. While admitting that various hedges and qualifications should be made here, one may say that, generally, if everyone in the community where the concept Y is in general use declares Xs to be Ys, then Xs are Ys. For concepts employed only by specialists or, say, used only within certain neighborhoods, the relevant conceptual communities consist of those specialists or the residents of those neighborhoods. In general, the conceptual community whose use of a concept fixes its correct application simply consists of all the people who use it. To determine its correct application, one identifies the people who use it and then describes or characterizes their use of it.

The concept of a person is a special case here. To discover the range of application of the concept of a person, one might identify the conceptual community in which that concept is used. It consists, of course, of all the persons who use the concept. To identify that conceptual community, one must decide which human creatures are persons. The upshot is that the phallist who self-deceptively adjusts the range of application of the concept of a person is also manipulating appearances with respect to the constitution of the conceptual community. Males who live their lives under the impression that only males are persons (and in the belief that this impression is shared by other males) will see *themselves* (the persons) as completely constituting the conceptual community and thence take *their* agreement in the (overt) application of the concept of a person as fixing its correct application, much as we all take our agreement in the application of the concept of a tree as fixing its correct application. We do not have the power to make what is a tree not a tree, but the collective subjectivity of conceptual correctness can be mistaken to mean that we do. Nor could the phallists, if they did constitute the conceptual community, thereby have the power to make what is a person not a person.

But it is here, I think, that one finds the deepest source of the impression that women are *denied* personhood.

The self-deceptive denial that women are (full) persons adds up to an attempt to usurp the community's control over concepts in general by denying females membership in the conceptual community, or rather, by failing to see that they are members of the conceptual community. The effect is not simply the exclusion of females from the rights and duties of full persons but is a conceptual banishment that ensures that their complaints about this exclusion simply do not fit into the resulting conceptual scheme. Hence the phallist's almost incredible capacity for failure to understand what on earth feminists are talking about. His self-deception is locked into his conceptual framework, not simply as his analytic or a priori principles are, but in the underlying determinants of its entire structure and content. The self-deception fixes his conception of the constitution of the conceptual community whose existence makes conceptualization possible and whose collective perceptions determine in outline its progress.

The rejection of females by phallists is both morally and conceptually profound. The refusal to perceive females as persons is conceptually profound because it excludes females from that community whose conceptions of things one allows to influence one's own concepts—it serves as a police-lock on a closed mind. Furthermore, the refusal to treat women with the respect due to persons is in itself a violation of a moral principle that seems to many to be *the* founding principle of all morality. This violation of moral principle is sustained by an active manipulation of circumstances that is systematic and habitual and self-deceptively unacknowledged. The exclusion of women from the conceptual community simultaneously excludes them from the moral community. So the self-deception here is designed not just to dodge particular applications of moral principles but to narrow the moral community itself, and is therefore particularly insidious. It is the sort of thing that leavens the moral schizophrenia of the gentle, honest, god-fearing racist monster, the self-anointed *übermensch*, and other moral deviates. The phallist is confined with the worst of moral company in a self-designed conceptual closet—and he has taken great pains to ensure that his escape will not be abetted by any woman.

POSTSCRIPT

It may seem that I have assumed here that all sexists and phallists are male. I do assume that in the paradigm cases phallists are male, but the suggestion that all sexists and all phallists are male arises innocently from the standard English usage of personal pronouns.

NOTES

I am heavily indebted to Carolyn Schafer, with whom I thoroughly and profitably discussed all parts of this essay at all stages of its development; her contribution is substantial. I also profited from discussion with an audience of philosophers and others at Michigan State University, and an audience at a meeting of the Eastern Division of the Society of Women in Philosophy, in April 1974, at Wellesley College.

1 I will refer to beliefs, opinions, convictions, and principles all indifferently as "beliefs." Not that it does not make any difference; a fuller analysis of sexism would take these distinctions into account.

2 This might be seen as an instance when we condemn the sin but not the sinner.

3 It should be noted that such theories are sexist only if they are false; for if true, they would not count as marking the sexes irrelevantly or impertinently. Consequently my own use of the terms "sexist" and "sexism" in connection with such theories constitutes a certain commitment in this regard.

4 Women are warmly encouraged to view belief in the ubiquity of Opportunists as paranoia. In this connection I refer the reader to a speech by William Lloyd Garrison, included under the title "Intelligent Wickedness" in Miriam Schneir, ed., *Feminism: The Essential Historical Writings* (New York, 1972). He points out that men "manifest their guilt to a demonstration, in the manner in which they receive this movement [feminism] . . . they who are only ignorant, will never rage, and rave, and threaten, and foam, when the light comes. . . ." One cannot but believe that there are also some who, well aware of the point Garrison makes, prudently refrain from foaming in public.

What Is Sexual Equality and Why Does Tey Want It?*

W. E. COOPER

I wish to pose some questions for "the feminist," and in particular for the feminist case presented by Alison Jaggar in "On Sexual Equality."[1] The feminist wants equality because justice apparently demands it. Jaggar declares that "a feminist is one who believes that justice requires equality between women and men."[2] Yet it is not clear that the kind of equality that Jaggar wants is a requirement of justice, and there is reason to believe that it involves injustice. Equality, in Jaggar's sense, means "that those of one sex, in virtue of their sex, should not be in a socially advantageous position *vis-à-vis* those of the other sex."[3]

But what precisely does this mean? Consider one possible interpretation: In a just society there will be no one of one sex who, in virtue of ter sex, is in a socially advantageous position *vis-à-vis* those of the other sex. Jaggar is not expansive on what is involved in the notion of a socially advantageous position, but it is reasonable to assume that A is in a socially advantageous position relative to B if A has greater income than B. Now suppose that this situation obtains: B does not want the higher income level of A, and B does not want it precisely because of ter sex. According to Jaggar's view there is an injustice here, and the only way to rectify it would presumably be to force B to accept the higher income against ter will. But surely this coercion is the real injustice, violating B's right to lead ter life as tey chooses.

My point is that the inequalities Jaggar deplores may arise because of the way that free men and women choose to lead their lives. *If* their choices reflect their conviction that the difference between the sexes is more than simply a physiological distinction, and indeed that the difference makes it fitting for them to introduce inequalities in advantages, *then* they should not be forced to conform to a feminist egalitarian vision. Perhaps such people can be taught to change their minds. But the foundation for persuasion ought not to be the claim that they are acting unjustly, but rather, for example, that they would be happier in a sexually egalitarian society.

In criticizing socialist doctrine Nozick has argued that "the socialist society would have to forbid capitalist acts between consenting adults."[4] In a similar vein, I am arguing that Jaggar's feminist society would have to forbid sexist acts between consenting adults.

Let us consider then another interpretation of Jaggar's notion of sexual equality: In a just society there will be no one of one sex who, in virtue of ter sex, is in a socially advantageous position *vis-à-vis* those of the other sex, unless the disadvantaged one wants to be in that position and wants to be in that position because of ter sex. But this last clause is indefensible. Why should someone be required to have precisely *this* reason for wanting to be in the disadvantaged position? Tey might have any number of reasons, such as love for a sexist spouse, which are in conformity with justice. The fact that tey has this reason or that is *ter own business.*

So let's omit the last clause and examine the remainder, namely: In a just society there will be no one of one sex who, in virtue of ter sex, is in a socially advantageous position *vis-à-vis* those of the other sex, unless the disadvantaged one wants to be in that position. Now it is reasonable to suppose that socially advantageous positions will be attained in a just society on the basis of fair equality of opportunity, understood in Rawls's sense (that is, those with the same natural assets and motivation have the same chances of attaining these positions).[5] On this supposition inequalities in advantages will develop in two ways—from differences in natural assets (natural abilities and talents) and differences in motivation. But it is simply not known that there are *no* sex-relative differences in either of these respects. If there are, then in a just society there *will* be some of one sex who, in virtue of their sex, are in a socially disadvantageous position *vis-à-vis* some of the other. Moreover, sex-relative differences in motivation may emerge through the interaction of the sexes within such institutions as marriage, with the result that sex-relative differences in possession of social advantages occur. The feminist may reply that this is a reason (founded on justice?) for the abolition of such institutions as marriage. But what if people *want* to marry? Does justice require that they be prevented from doing so?

NOTES

* The words "tey" and "ter" used in this article are explained by a footnote in Jaggar's paper: "In this paper I adopt the suggestions of Miller and Swift for a new form of the generic singular pronoun. Instead of using 'he,' 'him,' and 'his,' I employ their suggested common-gender form, derived from the plural, namely, 'tey,' 'tem,' and ter(s)'" (276). In this discussion I adopt it also.

[1] Alison Jaggar, "On Sexual Equality," *Ethics* 84, no. 4 (July 1974), 275-91.

[2] *Ibid.*, 275.

[3] *Ibid.*

[4] Robert Nozick, "Distributive Justice," *Philosophy & Public Affairs* 3, no. 2 (Winter 1974), 59.

[5] John Rawls, *A Theory of Justice* (Cambridge, Mass., 1971), 73 and elsewhere.

Gay Rights

RICHARD D. MOHR

In this paper I will suggest that there are no good moral reasons for exempting gays as a class from the protections which the 1964 Civil Rights Act affords racial, gender, ethnic and religious classes. These protections bar discrimination in private employment, housing, and public accommodations.

I shall assume that it is a reasonable government function to eliminate arbitrariness regarding with whom we make contracts dealing with employment, housing and public accommodations. The reasons for this are diverse,[1] and I shall not discuss them here. All but the most hardened of libertarians would accept this, and even hardened libertarians are likely to hold that consistency demands that if some classes are afforded such protections, all relevantly similar classes should also be afforded such protections. And I take it that it is not in general the claim that one's sexual orientation is dissimilar in relevant respects to one's protected properties (race, religion) that forms the core of possible reasonable objections to the inclusion of gays within the protections of the Civil Rights Act. For on the one hand, if sexual orientation is something over which an individual has virtually no control, either for genetic or psychological reasons, then sexual orientation becomes relevantly similar to race, gender, and ethnicity. Discrimination on these grounds is deplorable because it holds a person accountable without regard for anything *he himself* has done. And to hold a person accountable for that over which he has no control is one form of prejudice. A similar argument from nonprejudicial consistency would seem persuasive for also including the physically and mentally challenged within the reach of the Civil Rights Act.

On the other hand, if one's sexual orientation is a matter of individual choice, it would seem relevantly similar to religion, which is a protected category. We would say that such a personal moral choice is not a reasonable ground for discrimination *even when* the private belief in and practice of it has very public manifestations, as when a religious person becomes involved in politics with a religious motive and a religious intent. And to claim that gay sex is in some sense immoral will not suffice to establish a relevant dissimilarity here. For the nonreligious and the religious may consider each other immoral in this same sense and various religious sects will consider each other immoral, and yet all religious belief is protected.

Now a sufficient moral reason for the protection of private morality from discrimination in the public sphere is the following. In religious and sexual behavior as well as in other types of behavior, like excretory behavior, there is in our society a presumption of an *obligation* that they be carried out in private, even when there is virtually universal acceptance of the behavior, for example non-gay sex in missionary position for the sake of procreation; and this obligation in turn generates a *right* to privacy for these same practices. For society cannot consistently claim that these activities must be carried out in private (despite their manifest public consequences, like population growth) and yet retain a claim to investigate such activity and so make it *pro tanto* public behavior.[2] And by giving up the right to investigate such matters, *a fortiori* society gives up the right to discriminate based on them.

So I take it that there is a *prima facie* case for including sexual orientation within the ambit of the 1964 Civil Rights Act, since sexual orientation is relevantly similar to either race or religion. Now the Civil Rights Act reasonably enough has an exemption clause which allows for discrimination on the basis of a protected category when the discrimination against an otherwise protected category represents a "bona fide occupational qualification." This is a reasonable ground for exemption since it means that the discrimination ceases to be whimsical or arbitrary. Such discrimination would be discrimination in good faith. Two obvious examples of good faith discrimination are the following. It seems to me reasonable that a Chinese restaurant, for the sake of ambience, should choose to hire only orientals. Further, it is good faith discrimination for the director of the movie "The Life of Martin Luther King, Jr." to consider only black actors for the title role.

Now I take it that the possibly reasonable attempt to argue that gays should not be afforded Civil Rights protections is that in the case of gays such exemptions swallow the rule, that is, that pretty much all discrimination against gays is discrimination in good faith, so that it would be disingenuous to include gays within the compass of protected classes. What I wish to argue in the rest of this paper is that virtually all attempts to justify discrimination against gays as discrimination in good faith fail, and therefore that there is nothing remotely approaching a general case to be made for exemptions of gays from Civil Rights protections. I shall take as my examples discriminations in the public sector, where, thanks to the 14th Amendment's equal protection clause, there is already a general presumption against discrimination against gays and where such discrimination is permissible only if it is rationally related to a legitimate government concern.[3]

In trying to give an account of what constitutes good faith discrimination, we enter murky territory. In current practice there is no widely recognized and accepted taxonomy of what constitutes good faith discrimination, nor is there any obvious sufficient set of general principles governing what constitutes a good faith discrimination. Is it, for instance, a good faith discrimination for the new management of a bar that has gone gay to fire all the non-gay union employees of the former management, claiming that only gay waiters will make the bar's new clientele feel comfortable? This is an actual case that occurred recently in Toronto. The outcome of a legal challenge to the firings was that the same court which had ruled earlier that the new management of what was to become an Irish bar could fire all the previous non-Irish employees, ruled against the new gay management, claiming that "being gay is not as substantially different as being Irish." So stated, we seem to have bad grammar, dubious metaphysics, and liberal condescension all masking bigotry; but, I suggest that, for whatever bad reasons the court came up with this ruling, it was the correct ruling.

For I suggest that the following is a valid general principle governing the establishment of good faith discriminations. The principle is that simply citing the current existence of prejudice, bigotry or discrimination in a society against some group or citing the obvious consequences of such prejudice, bigotry, or discrimination can never constitute a good reason in trying to establish a good faith discrimination against that group.[4] Let us call this principle *alfred dreyfus. Dreyfus* tells us that stigmas which are entirely socially induced shall not play a part in our rational moral deliberations. I suggest, for instance, that a community could not legitimately claim that a by-law banning blacks from buying houses in the community was a good faith discrimination on the grounds that whenever blacks move into a heretofore white area, property values plummet. This is illegitimate, since it is only the current bigotry in the society that causes property values to drop, as the result of white flight and the subsequent reduction in size of the purchasing market.

In general, the *fact* that people discriminate can never be cited as a good reason for institutionalizing discrimination.[5] But even more clearly, the current existence of discrimination cannot ethically ground the continuance of the discrimination, when there are reasonable *prima facie* claims against discrimination.

If *dreyfus* is intuitively obvious (once attention is drawn to it) it has a direct bearing on almost every case where people try to justify discrimination against gays as discrimination in good faith. For one of its obvious ranges of application is cases where some joint project is a necessary part of a job. It is in this category of cases that good faith discriminations against gays are most often attempted.

Bans against gays in the armed forces and on police forces are classic cases of the attempt to establish such good faith discrimination against gays. The armed forces, after recently losing a series of court cases, have abandoned the strategy that gays make incompetent soldiers as the basis for their systematic discrimination against gays. In light of the Matlovich case, the Beller case, and others in which gay soldiers were shown to have sterling performance records, the armed forces no longer rest their policy on such contentions as the claims that all faggots have limp wrists; limp wrists cannot fire M16s; and therefore gays reduce combat readiness. Instead the Pentagon has placed renewed emphasis on the contention that gays cause a drop in morale and for this reason reduce combat readiness. As of January 16, 1981, the Pentagon has seven, official, articulated reasons for banning gays:

> The presence of such members adversely affects the ability of the armed forces (1) to maintain discipline, good order and morale, (2) to foster mutual trust and confidence among servicemembers, (3) to insure the integrity of the system of rank and command, (4) to facilitate assignment and worldwide deployment of servicemembers who frequently must live and work under close conditions affording minimal privacy, (5) to recruit and retain members of the armed forces, (6) to maintain the public acceptability of military service, and (7) to prevent breaches of security.[6]

Claims (1) through (6) form a group. I will discuss (7) in a separate context below. What all the first six claims have negatively in common is that none of them is based on the ability of gay soldiers to fulfill the duties of their stations. More generally, none of the claims is based on gays *doing* anything at all. So whatever else may be said for the policy, it lacks the virtue of being a moral stance, since it is a minimal requirement of a moral stance that people are judged and held culpable only for *actions* of their own doing. What the six reasons have positively in common is that their entire force relies exclusively on current widespread bigoted attitudes against gays. They appeal to the bigotry and consequent disruptiveness of non-gay soldiers (reasons 1, 2, 3, and 5) who apparently are made "up-tight" by the mere presence of gay soldiers and officers, and so claim that they cannot work effectively in necessary joint projects with gay soldiers. The reasons appeal to the anti-gay prejudices of our own society (reason 6), especially that segment of it which constitutes potential recruits (reason 5), and to the anti-gay prejudices of other societies (reason 4). No reasons other than currently existing widespread prejudice and bigotry of others are appealed to here in order to justify a discriminatory policy. So all six reasons violate *dreyfus* and are illegitimate.

Gay soldiers are being discriminated against on current Pentagon policy simply because currently existing bigotry and prejudice are counted as good reasons in trying to establish a good faith discrimination. To accept such a reasoning process as sound is to act like a right-wing terrorist who produces social disorder through indiscriminate bombings and then claims that what is needed is a police state. Clearly the social problem created by the bigoted soldiers and the terrorist is not solved by society acceding to their demands. It is soldiers who do not cease to be bigoted, not gay soldiers, who should be thrown out of the armed forces. Practically, of course, the solution to the problem is for the armed forces to re-educate its bigots and to expel those who are incorrigible. It should be remembered that until 1948 the U.S. armed forces were racially segregated on exactly the same grounds as those adduced now for barring gays, and especially on the ground that whites could not work with blacks. That year the forces were racially integrated and the skies did not fall. The West German armed forces have been gay/non-gay integrated in noncommissioned ranks and the skies have not fallen there either.

It is perhaps worthy of note that the current Pentagon policy on gays is simply a mirror image of the long-standing anti-gay policy of the International Association of Chiefs of Police, a policy which for the same reasons is equally illegitimate. That policy reads:

> Whereas, the life-style of homosexuals is abhorrent to most members of the society we serve, identification with this life-style destroys trust, confidence and esteem so necessary in both fellow workers and the general public for a police agency to operate efficiently and effectively; now, therefore, be it resolved, that the IACP . . . endorses a no hire policy for homosexuals in law enforcement.[7]

Despite the bogus appeal to "life-style," gays are here again being discriminated against not for anything they *do,* or on the basis of their ability to carry out police duties, but solely on the basis of the bigoted attitudes of others. If, as is quite possibly the case, the majority of society lacks trust and confidence in the finds abhorrent blacks, Latinos, women, and Jews *as* police officers, the argument would hold equally well against these groups, and yet the argument only singles out gays. So aside from being a bad argument, based entirely on violations of *dreyfus*, the policy fails to treat relevantly similar cases similarly.

I wish to give three other, I hope now obvious, examples of bad faith parading as good faith. The U.S. Civil Service has ceased as a matter of policy to discriminate against gays, but discrimination against gays is still systematic in the State Department, the CIA, the FBI, and the armed forces, on the alleged good faith discrimination that gays are security risks, since they are, it is claimed, subject to blackmail. That gays are subject to blackmail, though, is simply the result of currently existing prejudices and bigotries in the society, some of which are enshrined in law and government practice; so this argument violates *dreyfus.* Further, since it is the fact that one will be thrown out of the CIA (or any of the other organizations cited above) if exposed, that leads to the potential for blackmail, the argument also looks as though it is verging on being circular; for the government policy establishes the situation the government is trying to avoid, and then the government uses this situation as a reason for its policy. The practical solution is for the President to issue an executive order banning discrimination on the basis of sexual orientation in all branches of the government.[8]

Take as another example of bad faith discrimination the arguments used in lesbian child custody cases. Never has there been an area where socially endorsed stereotyping has been so flatfootedly appealed to in forming social policy as in child custody cases. In nearly all jurisdictions, there is a strong presumption in favor of giving custody to the mother, *unless* the mother is a lesbian, in which case the presumption of parental fitness shifts sharply in the direction of the father. Sometimes the argument for this sharp shift is merely a statement of bigotry. It runs: lesbians are evil; lesbians cause their children to be lesbians; and therefore, lesbians cause their children to be evil. When the shift is attempted to be justified as a good faith discrimination, the argument runs as follows; there is nothing inherently evil about mother or child being lesbian, but nevertheless, since, while the child is growing, there will be strong social recrimination from peers and other parents against the child as it becomes known in the community that the mother is a lesbian, only by discriminating against lesbian mothers are their children spared unnecessary suffering.[9] This argument, I take it, is an obvious violation of *dreyfus*. Currently existing bigotry and its consequences are cited as the only reason for perpetrating and institutionalizing discrimination. Note that if one does not think such discrimination is illegitimate *exactly because* it violates *dreyfus*, one would seem equally obliged to argue for the sterilization of inter-racial couples; for, only as such are their "progeny" spared the needless suffering created by the strong social recrimination which is directed against mixed-race children in current society.

Another bad faith argument is the widely held *Time* magazine (8 January 1979) argument for discriminating against gay teachers.[10] It runs as follows: though openly gay teachers do not cause their students to become gay, nevertheless an openly gay teacher might (inadvertently or not) cause a closeted gay student to become openly gay; the life of an openly gay person is a life of misery and suffering; therefore, openly gay teachers must be fired, since they promote misery and suffering. It seems that the second premise, life of misery, if true in some way peculiar to gays, is so as the result of currently existing bigotry and discrimination in society of the very sort which the argument tries to enshrine into school board policy. So the argument violates *dreyfus*. But further, one cannot try to justify a social policy based on the consequences it is supposed to have, then attach negative sanctions or punishments to violations of the policy, and then say one was obviously correct in establishing the policy, citing as evidence that only behavior in conformity with the policy is producing good consequences. Stated more formally: it is illegitimate to give a rule-utilitarian rationale for a law, attach sanctions to the law and then show that one was correct in one's moral ground for the law by observing the consequence of implementing the sanctioned law. Sanctions make rule-utilitarian justifications self-fulfilling prophecies. If one passes sanctions against openly gay people, then obviously if one observes openly gay people beset by these sanctions one is going to claim one wouldn't want one's children to live that way. The solution, though, is to eliminate the sanctions which turn discriminations, based on alleged consequences of being openly gay, into self-fulfilling prophecies.

It should be noted that "purely moral" or religious claims to the effect that gays are wicked seem to bear no weight at all in establishing good faith discriminations. For what sort of job is being a non-sinner an essential job qualification? Nevertheless, most jurisdictions do require "good moral standing" for state and city licensing for a vast number of professional jobs ranging from doctors and lawyers to hairdressers and morticians. How these requirements are held to be reasonable or even desirable qualifications for these jobs is unclear. One wants as a lawyer someone who is shrewd, not someone who is pious. I suspect that eventually the courts will rule that these sorts of moral qualifications are so *vague* as to be incapable of fair application and so violate the due process clause of the Constitution. In the meanwhile, these requirements are abused in the most outrageous ways against gays. For in states which do not have consenting adult laws,[11] gays are selectively discriminated against as systematically violating the laws and so, allegedly, as necessarily lacking in good moral character.[12] Now I think this application of such qualifications against gays should also count as a violation of *dreyfus*. The claim that violating some law was the ground for a good faith discrimination would be legitimate, I suggest, only if the moral ground of the law turned out to be, independently of the enshrinement of the law, a good ground for a good faith discrimination. And on examination arguments against consenting adult laws turn out to be mere statements of prudery or merely religious or aesthetic claims.[13]

My hunch is that all anti-gay arguments that are cast as good faith discriminations violate *dreyfus* or are circular or are illegitimate self-fulfilling prophecies, but I do not presume to outguess human ingenuity in coming up with rationalizations for its hatreds and fears.

NOTES

[Footnotes have been renumbered—Ed.]

A version of this paper was read to the Society for the Philosophy of Sex and Love at the meetings of the Eastern Division of the American Philosophical Association, December 1981. Many people have read and offered useful comments on earlier drafts of the paper. I would especially like to thank Professor Lee Rice of Marquette University and my colleague, Professor James Wallace, for their comments.

1 In unanimously finding the 1964 Civil Rights Act constitutional, the Supreme Court cited the Act's promotion of "personal dignity" as its most noteworthy justification for state action (*Heart of Atlanta Motel v. U.S.* 379 US 241 [1964]).

2 The legal correlate of this moral principle is that the mere presence of a police agent in an action that would otherwise be private or personal does not make the action a public action. This correlate has led the Massachusetts Supreme Court to rule on

procedural due process grounds that the state's sodomy laws are unenforceable, without actually ruling the laws unconstitutional on substantive due process grounds (*Commonwealth* v. *Sefranka* Mass. 414 N.E. 2nd 602 [Dec. 1980]).

3 This "rational relation" test was established for gays in the public sphere generally and the Civil Service specifically by *Norton* v. *Macy* 417 F.2d 1161 (D.C.Cir. 1969). The test for good faith discrimination in the Civil Rights Act is in fact a more stringent test. For "bona fide occupational qualification" is elaborated as that which is "reasonably necessary to the normal operation" of a business. "Reasonably necessary" is a judicial oxymoron. For in equal protection cases, a rational relation or reasonable relation is simply a relation to a legitimate government concern, while a necessary relation is one which is *essential* to a *compelling* state interest. The tension of the phrase "reasonably necessary" notwithstanding, the courts have tended to interpret the Civil Rights Act as establishing a "business necessity test" (*Diaz* v. *Pan American Airways* 442 F.2d 385 [5th Cir. 1971]). If I can establish my claims operating with the weaker test, *a fortiori* my argument will hold for the more stringent test.

4 I take prejudice to be a species of bigotry. A bigot is an adult capable of reason who is willing to act on his moral opinions and who has no reason for his opinion, *or* who has a reason but it is prejudicial, is a rationalization, is merely a personal emotional response or is merely a parroting of someone *else's* reason, *or* who is unwilling to apply consistently the ethical principles which inform and give substance to his reason, once the relevant principles are pointed out to him, *or* whose principles themselves are so specialized as to be arbitrary.

5 See Ronald Dworkin, *Taking Rights Seriously* (Cambridge, Mass., 1977), 248-54.

6 San Francisco *Sentinel*, 23 January 1981. These regulations are published in the *Federal Register* 46, no. 19 (29 January 1981), 9571-8. They were largely constructed out of the holdings of the extremely anti-gay Beller case (*Beller* v. *Middendorf*, 632 F.2d 788 [9th Cir. 1980] denied US cert.). For a military case, though, which ended in a gay re-instatement see *benShalom* v. *Sec'y of Army* 22 F.E.P. 1396 (U.S. D.Ct. E.D. Wis. 1980). This case is important, for in it the court recognized that the Army had violated the plaintiff's First Amendment rights and rights to substantive due process, in particular the right to privacy. In fact, the court recognized a constitutional right to sexual preference within the right to privacy.

7 San Francisco *Sentinel*, 3 October 1980.

8 In military cases and others where "security risk" is adduced as a reason for dismissal, the government has not once brought forth a case where a gay was blackmailed into disclosing secrets. This means that gays are being judged on the basis of stereotypes which have no factual basis. In sex discrimination cases, claims based on stereotypes and unsubstantiated fears and apprehensions have been given no weight in attempts to establish bona fide occupational qualifications (*Weeks* v. *Southern Bell Telephone* 408 F.2d 228).

9 In fact it would seem that children in the custody of lesbian mothers do not suffer. On this subject allow me to recommend the movie on lesbian child custody cases *In the Best Interest of the Children* (Iris Films/Iris Feminist Collective, Berkeley, 1977). For a fairly recent discussion of gay parent custody cases see Donna Hitchens, "Social Attitudes, Legal Standards, and Personal Trauma in Child Custody Cases," in Donald Knutson, ed., *Homosexuality and the Law* (New York, 1980), *Journal of Homosexuality* 5 (Fall 1979-Winter 1980), 89-95.

10 The current judicial status of discrimination against gay teachers is turbid. For an important and generally pro-gay case, see *Acanford* v. *Bd. of Educ.* 491 F.2d 498 (4th Cir. 1974). For a recent anti-gay holding based on religious morality see *Gaylord* v. *Tacoma School Dist. #10* Wash. 559 P.2d 1340 (1981) denied US cert.

11 Approximately 65% of the US population now lives in states with consenting adult

laws. Twenty-two states have revoked their sodomy laws through legislative means: Alaska, California, Colorado, Connecticut, Delaware, Hawaii, Illinois, Indiana, Iowa, Maine, Nebraska, New Hampshire, New Jersey, New Mexico, North Dakota, Ohio, Oregon, South Dakota, Vermont, Washington, West Virginia, and Wyoming. In addition, the highest courts of Pennsylvania and New York have, on the basis of the right to privacy, declared unconstitutional their states' statutes prohibiting private, consensual sodomy between unmarried adults (*Commonwealth* v. *Bonadio* 490 Pa 91, 415 A.2d 47 [1980]; *People* v. *Onofre* 434 N.Y.S. 2d 947, 51 NY 2d 476, 415 N.E. 2d 936 [1980] denied US cert.).

12 A recent landmark gay naturalization case will, it is to be hoped, clear up this area of administrative law: *Nemetz* v. *Immigration and Naturalization Service* 647 F.2d 432 (4th Cir. April 1981). This case ruled (i) that in cases of laws which are national in nature discriminations based on "moral turpitude" cannot be achieved merely by citing the violation of statutes which are peculiarly local, and even more importantly ruled (ii) that determinations of good moral character or moral turpitude can only be made by appealing to public morality and that private sexual acts are not a matter of public morals: "The appropriate test in such cases is whether the act is harmful to the public or is offensive merely to a personal morality. Only those acts harmful to the public will be appropriate bars to a finding of good moral character" (at 436).

13 Anyone who doubts the truth of this claim might usefully read the floor debate surrounding H.Res. 208 (*Congressional Record-House* 6737-62, Oct. 1, 1981), by which the House by a nearly three-to-one margin quashed consenting adult laws which had been passed unanimously by the D.C. City Council.

VIII

JUSTIFIED INEQUALITY?

An Exchange on Preferential Treatment

ROBERT L. SIMON
& SARA ANN KETCHUM

ROBERT L. SIMON
Statistical Justifications of Discrimination

A. 80% of the candidates who score poorly on Test *T* will fail to graduate from the university due to academic deficiencies. Therefore, the university is justified in refusing to admit *any* candidate who scores poorly on *T*.
B. 80% of women lack the physical strength to perform job *J*. Therefore, employers are justified in refusing to consider *any* women as candidates for *J*.
C. 80% of the members of group *G* are victims of past injustice. Therefore, compensatory programs are justified in providing benefits to *all* members of *G*.

Sara Ann Ketchum and Christine Pierce recently criticized arguments of kind *B* (*Analysis* 36, no. 2, 91-5). They allow that "statistical differences between the sexes would indicate that justice does not require equal distribution of women and men . . . within given job categories." But they deny that "all women may justifiably be discriminated against in hiring if sufficiently fewer women than men are qualified" (92, 93). On the other hand, James Nickel has defended arguments of kind *C* (*Analysis* 34, no. 5, 154-60). Nickel argues that while preferential discrimination in favor of black persons as a group may not be justifiable by ideal principles of compensatory justice, it can be justified by administrative or pragmatic factors. Where there is a high correlation between being a member of a particular group and being a victim of social injustice, there is a pragmatic justification for compensating all members of the group in question. It would just be too costly and difficult to evaluate cases on an individual basis. Nickel concedes that the pragmatic approach "may result in a certain degree of unfairness" but maintains that "it does help to decrease administrative costs so that more resources can be directed to those in need" (James Nickel, "Classification by Race in Compensatory Programs," *Ethics* 84, no. 2 [1974], 148; see also his "Preferential Policies in Hiring and Admissions," *Columbia Law Review* 75, p. 534).

Can one justifiably reject arguments such as *B*, which use statistical generalizations to justify discrimination *against* a particular group, yet accept arguments such as *C*, which use similar generalizations to justify discrimination *in favor* of a particular group? I will argue that to the extent that one agrees with Ketchum and Pierce in rejecting the use of statistical generalizations to justify discrimination against persons of a particular sex or race, one is committed to rejection of Nickel's pragmatic defense of preferential discrimination as well. Either there is no difference between the two or, if there are differences, they are not such as to justify any difference in evaluation of the arguments.

Consider an at least relatively benign use of statistical generalizations, such as that found in *A*. Surely, the university's policy is an acceptable one, at least if either it is impossible to tell whether any given candidate of the kind in question will wind up in the 80% who fail or the 20% who succeed, or if it is excessively costly to make such fine distinctions, and no other relevant information about the candidates is easily obtainable.

If such pragmatic considerations are sufficient to justify the use of statistical generalizations as a basis for discrimination in all contexts then *B* and *C* would be as acceptable as *A*. Discrimination for and against particular groups would be justifiable on cost accounting grounds alone. But then, the price of accepting Nickel's argument for preferential discrimination, given the appropriate empirical claims about efficiency, is that we are committed to accepting arguments of kind *B*, given similar empirical claims about efficiency. But if, as is surely the case, arguments from efficiency do not justify discrimination against women or blacks, then arguments from efficiency for preferential discrimination in favor of women and blacks are unacceptable as well (at least where such preferential treatment in favor of group members requires a denial of positions to non-members).

One might reply, however, that there is an important difference between *A* and *C*, on the one hand, and *B* on the other. For it can be argued that discrimination directed against persons of a particular race or sex as such is inherently invidious and degrading and so cannot be justified by arguments that may be acceptable in more innocuous contexts. Although Nickel's pragmatic approach would disfavor some white persons, its *intent* is not to discriminate against whites as such but rather is to extend certain benefits to the unjustly victimized.

Similarly, the intent of the university in A is not to practice systematic and pervasive discrimination against previously low achievers who could nevertheless do university level work. Rather, it is to serve more efficiently the university's high priority educational goals.

This reply will not do, however, for B would remain objectionable even if the intent of employers is not to discriminate against women as such but only to maximize profits. To distinguish in the way suggested between A and C, on the one hand, and B on the other, is to countenance discrimination against a particular race or sex whenever the purpose of such discrimination is in itself benign, e.g. to maximize profits.

Nickel himself argues that correlations appealed to by racists (and presumably by sexists as well) are spurious (*Analysis* 34, no. 5, 156ff.) However, Ketchum and Pierce acknowledge that there may in fact be some statistical differences between the sexes in areas relevant to job qualifications. And some tests used to select among job applicants have had an adversely disproportionate effect on blacks.[1] So the issue of whether statistical generalizations justify discrimination against individuals remains even when false and invidious generalizations cited by racists are left out of the picture.

Perhaps, however, the difference between B and C lies not in the *intent* to discriminate but in actual discriminatory effect. That is, given past invidious discrimination against a group, even benignly motivated discrimination now practiced against that group is likely to stigmatize members of the affected group and, at the very least, continue to perpetuate that group's unfairly imposed subordinate position. Thus, discrimination against blacks is so objectionable precisely because it contributes to or at least perpetuates the effect of past discrimination in creating an especially disadvantaged caste. Discrimination against whites has no such effect, for whites do not constitute an especially disadvantaged caste, nor is preferential discrimination likely to reduce them to such a state.

While such an argument might be quite strong in a world of sharp and clear caste distinctions, contemporary western society is not such a world. For what the argument implies is "that the white majority is monolithic and so politically powerful as not to require the . . . safeguards afforded minority racial groups. But the white majority is pluralistic, containing within itself a multitude of religious and ethnic minorities—Catholics, Jews, Italians, Irish, Poles, and many others who are vulnerable to prejudice and who to this day suffer from the effects of past discrimination."[2] Discrimination against individual members of such groups may perpetuate the psychological, social and economic effects of past discrimination. And while these effects may be more serious on the average for blacks, it is just the propriety of jumping from premises about the average to conclusions about individuals that is at issue.

Finally, it may be suggested that the difference between B and C lies in the difference in cost of obtaining the data that would make reliance on statistical generalizations unnecessary. Thus, it is relatively easy to test individuals for strength but relatively difficult to find out just what degree of injustice a particular individual may have suffered. Thus, B is unacceptable precisely because it is so easy to avoid appeals to statistical generalizations in the context at hand. On the other hand, C at least has a plausible claim to acceptability just because of the difficulty of getting the relevant information about individual cases.

While there may well be this difference between B and C, it is not a significant difference. Thus, we would find arguments of kind B objectionable even if it was quite difficult to verify claims about the strength of particular individuals. This can be brought out by comparing B and A. Surely, the savings in cost would have to be far higher to warrant appeal to statistical generalizations to justify discrimination against women or blacks than to justify the use of standardized tests in university admissions.

This can be brought out more clearly if we consider an alternative to the use of Test T in the admissions process. Suppose that the university finds that the presence in an applicant's background of (i) a family which has been mired in poverty for generations, (ii) a father who lacks a university education and (iii) a family history of diabetes is an excellent predictor of academic failure. Suppose further that it actually is less costly to verify the presence of these factors in particular cases than to administer T. But even given the above suppositions, we surely would think it *unfair* if the university promulgated a rule to the effect that candidates who satisfied (i), (ii) and (iii) would be eliminated from consideration *without even being given the chance to take the test.* On the contrary, each individual at least has a claim to be considered on his or her individual abilities and talents. Even if (i), (ii) and (iii) turn out to be better predictors than T, T is morally relevant to the making of academic decisions in a way that they are not. It is the refusal to allow certain students even to try for admission, when based on ascriptive grounds, that is unjust or unfair. Thus, it is not simply the *cost* of obtaining information that is at stake. The *kind* of information obtained and employed is morally relevant as well. (Similarly, even if it could be shown that certain genetic irregularities were excellent indicators of criminal tendencies in individuals, detention of individuals with such genetic irregularities prior to the commission of any crime would be unfair. This is particularly true if the purpose of such prior detention was simply to cut the costs of police work involved in finding a fleeing criminal.)

Likewise, since B and C replace consideration of morally relevant data with identification of ascriptive characteristics, they are similar in a morally significant way. Each involves a significant degree of unfairness to individuals. Now, it may be that in some contexts avoidance of excessive costs should take precedence over avoidance of unfairness.

But if that is so, avoidance of the same amount of cost will count as much in favor of discrimination against blacks and women as in favor of discrimination benefiting blacks and women.

Accordingly, even if B and C are different in the way suggested, it is far from clear that this difference is sufficient to demonstrate the moral acceptability of C and the moral unacceptability of B. The gains in efficiency involved may not be sufficient to compensate for the unfairness to individuals. And, at the very least, the price of opting for efficiency with respect to C is that of acknowledging that similar gains in efficiency would warrant discrimination against the very groups compensatory policies are designed to benefit. Given the nature of the price, we should be especially wary of accepting the claims of efficiency at the price of fairness.

Isn't there a difference, however, between sacrificing justice to efficiency *in order to right a wrong* and making a similar sacrifice for efficiency's sake alone? And isn't *that* the difference between B and C? That is, Nickel's argument may be interpreted as having moral as well as pragmatic force. The point of using Nickel's approach, on this interpretation, is to minimize injustice by providing compensation to a high proportion of those who are entitled to it at costs which impose a less severe burden on the rest of the community than would implementation of ideal principles of compensatory justice.

However, this kind of response begs one of the crucial issues at stake. For surely one of the major points at issue in the debate over preferential discrimination is whether such treatment creates new injustice by substituting group considerations for evaluation of individual cases. Indeed if, as I have suggested, the substitution of ascriptive criteria for consideration of individual cases does involve a significant degree of unfairness to individuals, then it will not be easy to show that the pragmatic approach minimizes injustice. Nickel is not entitled simply to *assume* that any injustice involved is outweighed *on the scales of justice* by the compensatory benefits provided. That the pragmatic approach cuts costs of administration is indeed initially plausible. That it minimizes injustice as well is far more controversial and thus requires significant additional support.

The price, then, of shifting from a strategy of increasing efficiency to one of minimizing injustice is that of decreased initial credibility and consequent assumption of a far heavier burden of proof.

Perhaps that burden can be met. Or perhaps alternate justifications of preferential treatment for groups are acceptable. It seems to me that those are the issues on which debate should focus. Appeal to statistical generalizations will not help us here. If such appeals are understood as appeals to efficiency, they are vulnerable to the sorts of objections raised earlier. If they are understood as appeals to justice, they simply raise at a new level the very questions about fairness to individuals that the appeal to the administrative approach was designed to help us avoid.

Logically, then, one cannot have it both ways. If purely pragmatic appeal to statistical generalizations can justify preferential discrimination in favor of women and black persons, then, given corresponding gains in efficiency, it can justify discrimination against those groups as well. In each kind of case, fairness to individuals requires consideration of relevant factors, but in each kind of case the appeal is to ascriptive classifications instead. But the price of appealing pragmatically to ascriptive considerations in one kind of case is that of logical commitment to similar appeals in similar contexts in the other kind of case. Even given significant gains in predictive power and efficiency, this sort of commitment is one of which we ought to be exceedingly wary. The moral status of discrimination remains the same, even though its victims and beneficiaries may change.

NOTES

I am grateful to the National Endowment for the Humanities and the Center for Advanced Study in the Behavioral Sciences for their support of my work. I am also indebted to Brian Barry, Elizabeth Ring and the editor [of *Analysis*] for helpful comments on an earlier draft.

[1] Whether such tests are constitutional if there is no intent on the part of those giving it to discriminate is an issue that has been considered by the United States Supreme Court. In *Washington* v. *Davis,* the Court held that it was not sufficient to show simply that more black than white applicants had failed a qualifying examination for police recruits; in addition, the Court required that the plaintiffs demonstrate a racially discriminatory purpose.

[2] This passage, quoted from Professor Lavinsky's contribution to the "DeFunis Symposium," *Columbia Law Review* (1975), 520, 527, was quoted favorably by the Supreme Court of California in *Allan Bakke* v. *the Regents of the State of California* in which it overthrew the University of California at Davis's program of preferential admission to medical school for black applicants.

SARA ANN KETCHUM
Evidence, Statistics and Rights: A Reply to Simon

In a recent paper in *Analysis,* Christine Pierce and I argued that being a member of a group, a high percentage of which are unqualified, is not in itself a disqualification for a job.[1] For example, individual women whose physical strength is not known should not be disqualified from job J on the grounds that, for example, 80 percent of women lack the strength necessary to perform job J. In response to our paper, Robert Simon[2] has charged that this claim is in conflict with an argument for compensatory programs such as the one offered by James Nickel.[3] Nickel argues that compensation is due to victims of past discrimination in the form of programs of special benefits. Although such programs are justified on the basis of injuries suffered, the administrative basis for the distribution of benefits will most likely be a characteristic such as race rather than proof of suffering (155). White males will suffer injustice, according to Simon, "where such preferential treatment in favor of group members requires a denial of positions to non-members" (38).

I

I will agree with Simon that the argument which Nickel presents for compensatory programs would not be a particularly good argument for preferential hiring. However, the major weakness of Nickel's argument is also a weakness of Simon's analysis. That is, they both assume that the connection between being black in a white-supremacist society and having suffered injustice is properly represented by the notion of statistical correlation, that the alternatives are requiring proof of suffering or distributing on the basis of a characteristic which is merely statistically correlated with being a victim of injustice. Thus, as Simon presents Nickel's argument, the relevant characteristic of the group to be compensated is that, for example, 80 percent of its members have suffered injustice.

A comparison of two examples would show that the statistical correlation between group membership and injustice does not represent the connection assumed by defenders of compensatory programs. Imagine the following two societies:

> A. In society A there is an established pattern of white supremacy such that blacks are treated unjustly because they are black. That is, the fact that an individual is black is a reason, either covert or overt, for treating him or her unjustly. By some peculiar accidental circumstance, or by some weakness or failure of the system of white supremacy, 20 percent of the blacks in this society have never suffered an injustice—they are immune not only to racism, but also to any other system of injustice prevalent in the society.
>
> B. In society B, being black is never a social reason for being unjustly treated. There is no history or present practice of racism, black slavery, etc. However, there are practices of discrimination against three groups, and only three groups—for example, people over 65, members of a particular religious group, say, Baptists, and people who come from a particular region. Because of purely accidental demographic patterns, 80 percent of blacks belong to one or the other of these groups and suffer the injustices levelled against these groups. But, within these groups, blacks and whites are treated exactly the same—that is a 70-year-old black would be treated the same as a 70-year-old white and a 30-year-old black would be treated exactly the same as a 30-year-old white, etc.

The argument Simon portrays would entail that we have just as much reason for assigning benefits on the basis of race in society B as in society A. And, although Nickel makes it clear that he intends to be dealing only with A, his analysis does not adequately capture the difference. But the defense of compensatory programs always takes place within a historical context, and Nickel is simply assuming that context. It would be more appropriate to assume that the characteristic which should be connected to the injustice and, hence, relevant to the distribution of compensatory benefits would be something like the following (I will call it C, for short):

C: Being an X in a Y-supremacist society, where the superiority of Y's is defined in terms of the inferiority of X's.

The Y-supremacy might include, but not be exhaustively described by: discrimination in favor of Y's against X's in hiring, access to education and other goods; a systematic ideology of the inferiority of X's and the superiority of Y's; a systematic concentration of political and economic power in the hands of Y's and exclusion of X's from such power, etc.

The connection between characteristic C and the property of having suffered injustice is not a merely empirical correlation. There is a logical or conceptual connection which cannot be captured by any statistical statement. The empirical question is whether or not a given society is Y-supremacist and the degree and pervasiveness of the Y-supremacy. Statistics are relevant as evidence that a specific society is Y-supremacist, but they are not sufficient. The claim that a society is Y-supremacist implies that there are practices, institutions and habits of action and thought which are (i) about the relative social position appropriate to X's and Y's or about the relative capacities of X's and Y's, and (ii) productive of unjust inequalities between X's and Y's.

Thus, I would agree with Simon that, in cases where there is a mere statistical correlation between being X and having suffered injustice it would probably not be appropriate to distribute compensatory benefits on the basis of being X. I disagree, however, with Simon's assumption that this is an appropriate description of either present-day American racism or present-day American sexism. Thus, I would not agree that the failure of this argument would constitute a point against the practice of distributing compensatory benefits on the grounds of being a black in a white-supremacist society such as our own or being female in a male-supremacist society such as our own. In such a program, one would not be distributing benefits on the basis of race or sex *per se* (for example, a black from a black African country might not be due any compensation for racism) but on the basis of one's past and present social status.

II

Simon seems to assume without argument that the white males who would get jobs if there were no policy of preferential treatment have a right to those jobs, and that those jobs would be, so to speak, "stolen" from them by the blacks and women who are hired on such a policy. The first thing to point out is that a policy which is preferential in intent may not be preferential in effect. Employers who are, as one should expect them to be, influenced in their thinking by the society in which they were raised and live might hire qualified blacks only if they thought they were giving preference to blacks, by the same mechanism which leads them to think of themselves as turning down unqualified blacks when they refuse to hire qualified blacks.

The problems that remain even if we assume that the policy is one that has a preferential effect and not just a preferential intent, are perhaps more serious. Let us suppose, for a particular job which requires advanced education, that under a system of blind review or an impartial merit system the proportion of white males to blacks and women hired would be roughly equivalent to their distribution in the candidate pool (that is, people with the appropriate degrees). Say the proportion is 2 percent black and 15 percent female. Suppose further that a policy of preferential hiring would increase those percentages to 5 percent and 20 percent, respectively. Thus, approximately 13 percent of the white males who would have gotten jobs on the policy of blind hiring would not get jobs with preferential hiring. However, even with preferential hiring of this degree the proportion of white males in the profession will be several times their proportion in the population—that is, white males, who are a minority of the population, will hold a large majority of professional positions. If we are not to assume that there are vast differences in innate abilities between blacks and whites and between men and women, then it seems reasonable to believe that the disproportionate number of white males in the applicant pool is a result of discrimination and of white male supremacy. That is, most of the difference between the percentage of white males with the appropriate training and the percentage of white males in the population is a result of past discrimination in their favor and of social and political advantages created by racism and sexism. Since, even with preferential hiring, the proportion of white males hired is considerably larger than the proportion of white males in the population, it is reasonable to assume that even such a policy of preference will grant many white males jobs they would not have received if the system had been non-discriminatory from the beginning.

Let us consider a job candidate, Mr. White, who: (i) will get job X, or some better job Y, if the discrimination in favor of white males continues; (ii) would have gotten job X if a policy of blind review or an unbiased application of the merit principle were used in the hiring practice and were based on present qualifications the possession of which is, in part, related to past discriminatory policies; and (iii) would not have been in the applicant pool at all (that is, would not have received the necessary training) if there had been no discrimination in favor of white males in the process through which he has obtained his education. Thus, he would not have received job X, if there had been no discrimination in his favor.

Simon assumes that Mr. White has a *right* to job X (or that an injustice would be done in denying him job *X*), although not to job *Y*. His assumption implies that, although Mr. White does not have a right to have discrimination in his favor continued, he does have a right to the perquisites of whatever position he has already gained from past discrimination in his favor.

Much is often made of the fact that Mr. White is not morally responsible for the injustices from which he is benefiting. But, surely, this is not sufficient to show that he has a right to benefit from these injustices. His lack of responsibility for such injustices is only relevant to the question of whether or not he should be punished for them or be required to make reparation for them. If Mr. White is prevented from benefiting from past injustices by others in his favor, it is inappropriate to claim that this constitutes his being punished or asked to make reparation. If this analysis is right, then, the suffering that Simon claims the young white males to be paying for the sins of their elders turns out to be the suffering of those who would not be able to benefit as much from past injustices as they had hoped or expected. This may be genuine and even innocent suffering, but it is not the suffering of the victim of present injustice.

Moreover, if the hiring goals are not compensatory—that is, if the goal is to hire roughly the percentage of blacks who are in the qualified applicant pool—Mr. White's position is even shakier. In that case, the white males who do not get jobs under the system of goals will be even more likely to include those who not only would not have had the training had there never been any discrimination, but would also not have gotten the job in question, if, given the present distribution of qualifications, racism were to disappear suddenly and miraculously from the hiring practice. Mr. White is then in a position of having to show that the probability and moral seriousness of his not being hired for extraneous reasons is greater than the probability and moral seriousness of some black's not being hired because of racism if the goals were not present. If we assume that there is a greater probability that white males will be unjustly treated under nonpreferential goals than that members of groups discriminated against will be unjustly treated if we allow past practices to continue, we are presupposing that members of groups discriminated against in the applicant pool are generally less qualified than white males. Unless we assume that employers will not be able to find well qualified blacks or women in proportion to their percentage in the applicant pool, nonpreferential goals should not give us any a priori reason for suspecting unfairness to white males.

Perhaps more important is the fact that Simon's discussion does not even touch on the major use of statistics in affirmative action law as it applies to hiring—that is, the use of statistical comparisons between the qualified applicant pool and hiring decisions as evidence of discrimination.[4] He never explains what system he is comparing preferential hiring to (although his remarks suggest that the alternative he has in mind is a perfect meritocracy run by unbiased ideal observers). Thus, he never confronts the problem of practical means of reducing discrimination. Nor does he offer any argument for the claim that the use of either preferential or nonpreferential goals will produce, for whites, more injustice than any alternative system of preventing racial discrimination would produce or allow for blacks. (He at least suggests that whatever alternative he has in mind would not involve the use of statistical goals even as evidence.)

Thus, although there may be rights which would be violated if a policy of preferential hiring were to be adopted, Simon is obscuring the issue by assuming a priori that the white males who would not get jobs under such a program would, in virtue of that fact, be unjustly treated. Of course there is the more radical criticism that the likely outcome of such programs would be to increase the discrimination against those groups discriminated against which are not included in the compensatory program (for example, white male second-generation immigrants). But this is not an objection to the principle of distributing compensatory benefits on the basis of being a member of a group which has been discriminated against. It is rather a cautionary note about the practical application of such a principle. As such, it would not be appropriate to the conclusion Simon draws from his arguments.

NOTES

An earlier version of this paper was presented at Hamilton College.

[1] "Implicit Racism," *Analysis* 36, no. 2 (1976), 92, 93.

[2] "Statistical Justifications of Discrimination," *Analysis* 38, no. 1 (1978), 37-42.

[3] "Should Reparations Be to Individuals or to Groups?" *Analysis* 34, no. 5 (1974), 154-60.

[4] See Gertrude Ezorsky, "Hiring Women Faculty," *Philosophy & Public Affairs* 7, no. 1 (Fall 1977), 82-91.

ROBERT L. SIMON
Rights, Groups and Discrimination: A Reply to Ketchum

In a recent paper ("Statistical Justifications of Discrimination," *Analysis* 38, no. 1 [January 1978], 37-42) I claimed that arguments like *A* below

> *A.* 80% of the members of group *X* were victims of past discrimination. Therefore, for purposes of administrative convenience, all members of *X* should be regarded as eligible for compensatory benefits.

are logically parallel to arguments like *B*:

> *B.* 80% of women are physically incapable of performing task *T*. Therefore, for purposes of administrative convenience, no women ought to be considered as candidates for *T*.

I concluded that since B is unacceptable, and since A is logically parallel to B, A is unacceptable as well. Accordingly, the so-called administrative defense of preferential treatment, which presupposes the acceptability of arguments like A, fails (see James Nickel, "Should Reparations Be to Individuals or Groups?" *Analysis* 34, no. 5 [April 1974], 154-60).

In reply, Sara Ann Ketchum claims that I am committed to a faulty analysis of race and sex discrimination and that I "seem to assume without argument that the white males who would get jobs if there were no policy of preferential treatment have a right to those jobs and that those jobs would be so to speak 'stolen' from them . . . on such a policy" ("Evidence, Statistics and Rights: A Reply to Simon," *Analysis* 39, no. 3 [June 1979], 150). Since I neither presented an analysis of race or sex discrimination nor advanced a view as to the rights of the most qualified job applicant, I fail to discern why Ketchum attributes these views to me or thinks they are relevant to my original argument.[1] However, as Ketchum's rejoinder does raise substantial questions about the issue I did address, the acceptability of inferences from premises about groups to conclusions about treatment of individuals, I believe her arguments are worth pursuing further.

Ketchum relies on such an inference at a particularly key point. For she argues that since white males as a group have acquired advantages from unjust discrimination against women and minorities, preferential treatment of particular women and minorities over particular white males now is justified. "The suffering that Simon claims the young white males to be paying for the sins of their elders turns out to be the suffering of those who would not be able to benefit as much from past injustices as they had hoped or expected."[2]

At least two questions need to be raised about this argument. First, is it true that *all* white males have secured *net* advantages from unjust discrimination against women and minorities? Second, if such a claim is true, does it follow that preferential treatment of women and minorities is justified as a means of nullifying the unfairly gained advantages of white males?

Surely, there are strong grounds for doubting the claim that all white males have secured net advantages from sex and race discrimination. For one thing, such systematic and pervasive forms of injustice may have contributed to a social climate in which other forms of injustice, some of which have victimized white males, have flourished. Consider, for example, the alleged connection between racial discrimination and economic exploitation of whites in the pre-Civil-War South. Moreover, as Alan Goldman has pointed out, discrimination entails inefficiency (the best candidates are not hired or admitted) and such inefficiency may have harmed some white males more than discrimination against others helped them (Goldman, *Justice and Reverse Discrimination*, 108-9). Still other white males may have to overcome insidious forms of discrimination themselves and may have claims to redress of their own. Indeed, some affluent white females may have benefited more from systems of injustice and exploitation than have some white males.

Accordingly the claim that all white males have secured net advantages from past discrimination (or that they have in all cases secured more of an advantage than any woman) is open to serious objection. Thus unless Ketchum means to advance arguments like A and B, and argue from statistical correlation, her argument appears to rest on a doubtful premise. Even if *most* white males have (however inadvertently) secured net advantages from past discrimination against women and minorities, it does not follow that *every* white male may legitimately be disadvantaged by policies of preferential treatment. For the white male disadvantaged by such a policy may not be among the subclass of white males who have profited from the victimization of others.

Suppose, however, that in fact *all* white males have secured net advantages from past unjust discrimination. It hardly *follows* that the kinds of preferential treatment by race and sex now at issue in hiring or graduate school admission are justified. For one thing, such practices impose the costs of redress arbitrarily. If all white males are liable, it is hardly fair that a small proportion pay the entire cost of restitution while the overwhelming majority give up nothing. More important, even if all white males have benefited, they have not all benefited *equally*. Yet preferential treatment imposes costs according to one's relative lack of qualifications in the market, not degree of benefit received.[3] Indeed, those adversely affected are those with relatively weak records, precisely those who would tend to have benefited least from past injustice or have been victims of it themselves.[4]

What this suggests is that generalizations about groups do not easily lend themselves to direct support of conclusions about the just treatment of individuals. If we are to treat similar cases similarly, we must be sensitive to the differences as well as the resemblances between group members. At the very least, at this point in the debate over preferential treatment much more argument than Ketchum provides is needed if her position is to avoid the kinds of objections sketched above.

At this point, however, it may be objected that I have unjustifiably assumed an individualist framework of discussion. For isn't it Ketchum's point that discrimination of a systematic and pervasive kind affects individuals in virtue of their *group* membership? If so, the very point of so called "reverse discrimination" is not to deal out fair redress on an individual basis but to restore to victimized groups the social and economic position they would have held in the absence of systematic injustice.

If this is Ketchum's point, it seems to me to parallel Paul Taylor's recent defense of group compensation ("Reverse Discrimination and Compensatory Justice," *Analysis* 33, no. 6 [June 1973], 177-82). I will not add to the criticisms of that view that have been advanced elsewhere except to suggest that even if our goal is compensation of groups we must still be as fair as possible to individuals in the process. Thus, Taylor's original proposal calls for *society* to compensate victimized groups. I have argued above, however, that the kind of preferential treatment currently at issue imposes costs arbitrarily on *individuals*. Accordingly, an appeal to group considerations along lines advanced by Taylor will not support Ketchum's position. It is unfair that arbitrarily selected individuals pay the entire cost of promoting equality for groups.

I have suggested, then, that excluding particular white males from consideration for various benefits simply because white males as a group have benefited from past injustice raises serious issues about stereotyping and insensitivity to individual circumstances. Appeal to statistical correlations will not help us avoid these issues for the reasons given in my earlier paper. Accordingly I conclude that, for all Ketchum has said, present recommendations for preferential treatment by race or sex raise many of the same questions of injustice that properly apply to the invidious discrimination practiced for so long against women and minorities.

NOTES

[1] In fact, I find Ketchum's own analysis of systematic and pervasive discrimination quite attractive. And while I do think the most qualified applicant has a *prima facie* right to the job, I do not see that my original argument relies on such a claim. More important, I believe such a right can be overridden for a variety of reasons, including compensatory ones. Finally, in no sense do I believe beneficiaries of preferential treatment have stolen, or "stolen," jobs from the most qualified applicants. For useful discussion of the rights of the most qualified job applicant, see Chapter 2 of Alan H. Goldman's *Justice and Reverse Discrimination* (Princeton, 1979).

[2] Surely the most Ketchum is entitled to claim is that white males expect and hope to profit from a system that in fact operates unjustly. She is not entitled to claim, at least not without providing some supporting evidence, what her language suggests: namely, the entirely different claim that white males intend and hope to profit from what they perceive as injustice.

[3] I have made a similar point about the beneficiaries of preferential treatment in my "Preferential Hiring: A Reply to Judith Jarvis Thomson," *Philosophy & Public Affairs* 3, no. 3 (1974), 315. This point also counts against the acceptability of Ketchum's inference from the claim that every member of certain victimized groups has been injured by systematic discrimination to the acceptability of a system of preferential treatment which awards benefits according to qualifications, not degree of injury suffered.

[4] Goldman makes a similar point about the beneficiaries of preferential treatment, in his *Justice and Reverse Discrimination*, 90-1.

Equality of Opportunity

ALISTAIR M. MACLEOD

A serious obstacle to the resolution of disputes about equality of opportunity is presented by the assumption that the parties to these disputes are normally agreed about what the ideal involves, however much they may disagree as to whether it is either desirable or attainable. The assumption is of course false: "Equality of Opportunity" is no more the name of a single ideal than is "Liberty." Indeed, it is a systematically ambiguous expression and the precautions which need to be taken to render it unambiguous are seldom observed. The purpose of this paper is to direct attention to three of the principal sources of this ambiguity.

I

The first has to do with the fact that opportunity is an indeterminate concept, requiring a certain kind of contextual completion if the claims in which it is embedded are to be fully understood. Opportunity is always opportunity *to x*—that is, to do, be, become or receive something or other; and it is always opportunity enjoyed by some specifiable individual or organization or class, however difficult it may sometimes be to say with precision whose opportunities are in question. Statements about the existence or non-existence of equality of opportunity are thus fully intelligible only if answers are available to two questions: (i) opportunity to what? and (ii) opportunity for whom?

Of course if the answers to these questions were always the same, or if they were always clearly articulated and kept in view, the indeterminacy of the concept of opportunity could not easily be a source of misunderstanding. However, the answers which must be supplied when the ideal of equality of opportunity is under discussion are apt to vary from context to context and since it is often not clear which answers are being taken for granted or how different answers are thought to be related, the risk of serious confusion as to the content of the ideal is in practice quite considerable.

Failure to provide an explicit answer to the question "Opportunity to what?" can be a source of confusion as to the content of the ideal of equality of opportunity partly because it is sometimes taken for granted that some one answer is the only (or the obvious) answer and partly also because the complexity of the relations between opportunities of different kinds is often not appreciated.

It is quite false to suppose that those who discuss the ideal of equality of opportunity always in fact take for granted the same answer to the question "Opportunity to what?" Very often, of course, the focus is on occupational opportunity, especially opportunity to attain to positions of power, wealth or prestige. But opportunities of other kinds receive their share of attention: educational opportunities of various sorts, vocational and non-vocational; opportunities for self-fulfilment through the development and exercise of distinctive natural capacities; opportunities for the pursuit of happiness through the satisfaction of *de facto* wants; opportunities to engage in leisure-time activities; and so on.

How, then, are opportunities of these (and various other) kinds related? The question is a large one and cannot be discussed here. Two contrasting temptations must, however, be resisted if the importance of the question is not to be underestimated. The first is to suppose that the connections are merely fortuitous and that consequently it is possible to seek to equalize opportunities of any given kind without making—or, for that matter, frustrating—attempts to equalize opportunities of other kinds. The second is to exaggerate the systematic interconnections between opportunities of different sorts and to suppose consequently that serious commitment to the equalization of opportunities of any given kind carries with it an automatic commitment to the equalization of opportunities of all the other kinds. The truth, not surprisingly, lies somewhere between these extremes. Opportunities of different kinds are neither all independent of one another nor are they all systematically interconnected. It is for this reason that it is important to the clear delineation of the content of the ideal of equality of opportunity that the complicated causal and logical interrelations between opportunities of different sorts be carefully plotted. Thus, while there is little doubt that job-opportunities cannot be provided effectively for the members of some class if they are not also afforded an opportunity to acquire job-related skills, it is much less clear that non-vocational educational opportunities must be made available to them, and it is even less clear that there is any close connection between the underwriting of equality of job opportunity and equalization of opportunities for the pursuit of leisure-time interests.

A common criticism of the ideal of equality of opportunity illustrates nicely the importance of careful specification of the type of opportunity to be equalized. The ideal is sometimes said to be unduly conservative because, while requiring the elimination of employment and educational practices which militate against occupational mobility, it encourages improper acquiescence in existing social structures by holding out to individuals the prospect of advancement within the system. Now if the principle of equality of opportunity is construed narrowly as applying only to job-opportunities, it certainly looks as though individuals will be able to complain of lack of opportunity only if "open access" is not assured to *whatever jobs happen to exist:* the principle will furnish no basis for complaints about the structure of the social system—the complaint, for example, that jobs exist which should not, or that jobs do not exist which should, or that the scope of existing jobs is too narrow, or too broad. If, however, the opportunities to be equalized are defined as opportunities to develop and exercise latent human capacities, the principle is no longer exposed to this criticism: it is now possible in the name of the principle to stand in judgment upon institutional arrangements of all kinds (including existing job-classification systems) provided they can be shown to be inimical to equalization of opportunities for "self-development."

II

The fact that the concept of opportunity is intelligibly applicable only in contexts in which some answer is available to the questions "Opportunity to what?" and "Opportunity for whom?" and that the answers to these questions vary considerably from context to context does not mean, of course, that the term "opportunity" has more than one sense. It might after all suffice to distinguish different *kinds* of opportunity while insisting that they are all opportunities in the same sense. However there is independent reason for holding that the word "opportunity" is used in two strikingly different ways and that certain misconceptions about the ideal of equality of opportunity are rooted in the failure to take notice of this ambiguity.

Sometimes when we speak of people having, seizing, or passing up an opportunity to do something we assume that it is entirely up to them whether or not the thing is done. To have an opportunity to x is to be in a position to decide whether or not to x: the opportunity to x is seized by deciding *to x* and it is passed up by deciding *not to x*. When A has, in this ("strong") sense, an opportunity to x, the probability of his actually x-ing if he should decide to avail himself of the opportunity approaches 100 per cent. Indeed in those stray cases where he does not manage to x when he decides to take advantage of the opportunity to x, it is a nice question[1] whether he can be said to have had, in the event, an opportunity to do so, at any rate in the sense under consideration.

Often, however, when people are said to have an opportunity to x, what is intended is that they have one chance in N—where N is some number in excess of 1—of (eventually) x-ing. We do not intend to claim that it is within their power to x or that it is entirely "up to them" whether they x or not. Taking advantage of the opportunity to x is emphatically *not* a matter of simply deciding to x. When A has an opportunity to x in this ("weak"—"one chance in N") sense, there will generally (always?) be some action other than x—say, y—which he *is* in a position to decide to perform, and whether or not he (eventually) x-es will normally depend, in part, on whether he does y. (Indeed, typically in this kind of case the way to seize the opportunity *to x* will be to decide *to y*!) But however we add to the complexity of y—the thing (or things) relevant to x-ing which it is wholly within A's power to do and which he is consequently in a position to decide to do or not to do—the doing of y will never be a sufficient condition of his (eventually) x-ing: circumstances over which he has no control, including (often) actions independently performed by other people, will also help determine whether, in the event, he x-es. For example, if there are ten contestants for a prize, each of them can be said to have—in the "one chance in N" sense—an opportunity *to win*; yet obviously none of them has it within his power to secure the prize for himself simply by deciding to avail himself of this opportunity. The things which are wholly within his power—from entering the contest in the first place to doing the various things the rules demand of contestants—will of course *help* determine whether or not he wins. But whether he wins will also depend, crucially, on the performances of the other nine contestants.

It should be clear that the distinction between the "strong" and the "one chance in N" sense of "opportunity" has nothing to do with either the complexity or the difficulty of x. It hinges rather on whether it is wholly within the power of the person whose opportunity to x is in question to determine whether or not he x-es. When he has an opportunity to x in the strong sense, it must be entirely up to him whether or not he (eventually) x-es. On the other hand, when he has an opportunity to x in the weak ("one chance in N") sense, it is (at best) wholly within his power to perform only some action other than x; consequently no amount of diligence on his part in the performance of this action[2] will suffice to ensure that he eventually does what he has an opportunity to do—viz., x.

For some values of x, "opportunity" to x must be understood in the strong sense. In a democratic society, for example, it is in this sense that citizens have an opportunity to participate in the electoral process: it is entirely up to them whether or not they exercise the right to vote. For other values of x, however, opportunity cannot be understood in this way. When we say that the buyers of lottery tickets all have an opportunity to win the Grand Prize or that the students who compete for a scholarship all have an opportunity to win it or that the applicants for a prized job all have an opportunity of getting it, "opportunity" is being used in the weak ("one chance in N") sense. Generally, of course, someone who has in the weak sense an opportunity to x will also have an opportunity in the strong sense to do some thing other than x: buy a lottery ticket, sit the scholarship examination, or apply for the prized job, for example. Indeed, his availing himself of this kind of opportunity—by actually buying a ticket, or sitting the examination, or applying for the job—will normally be a condition not only of his (eventually) x-ing but also of his being said to have, in the "one chance in N" sense, an opportunity to x.

To take note of the distinction between the strong and weak senses of "opportunity" is important in discussions about equality of opportunity for at least two reasons. (i) When "opportunity" is being used in the strong sense, it is impossible to draw any distinction between the claim that all the members of some class have an opportunity to x and the claim that they all have the *same* opportunity to x: since opportunity in this sense does not admit of degrees, their opportunities are necessarily equal if it is certain that they all enjoy the opportunity to x. When "opportunity" is used in the weak sense, however, the two claims are quite likely to diverge. The fact that A and B both have an opportunity to x in the "one chance in N" sense means that their opportunities are the same only if N has the same value for both; but where, given equal expenditure of effort on the part of both, A's chances of x-ing are greater than B's, A will have to be said to have a *better* opportunity of x-ing than B. (ii) Whether failure to x on the part of those who had an opportunity to x can be assumed to be entirely their own fault depends on how "opportunity" is understood. When it is being used in the strong sense, the person whose opportunity it was has only himself to blame for his failure to x; it was after all wholly within his power to x. On the other hand, when "opportunity" is used in the weak sense, no such automatic judgment of blame for failure to x will be in order. It all depends on the explanation for the failure—on whether, for example, it is traceable to lack of serious effort, or to inadequate opportunities for the acquisition of needed skills, or to deficiency in natural capacity.

III

Uncertainty as to how extensively opportunities must be enjoyed if equality of opportunity is to be said to exist is yet another source of ambiguity in discussions of the ideal. According to the most straightforward (and perhaps also the commonest) interpretation, there is equality of opportunity to x in a given society (S) if and only if all the members of S have an opportunity to x. On this view—let us call it *Model 1*—the fact that certain members of S cannot be said to have an opportunity to x is conclusive evidence that the ideal has not been realized in S: its full realization requires the class of those who enjoy the opportunity to be progressively expanded until it coincides with S.

Model 1 is open to objection in at least three sorts of case. (i) Where an individual lacks irremediably the capacity to x, he cannot be said to enjoy the opportunity to x no matter how favorable the circumstances may be for x-ing. (That he cannot unmisleadingly be said to lack the opportunity either is true enough but shows only that having the capacity to x is a condition both of having and of lacking—both of being afforded and of being denied—the opportunity to x.) Consequently if there are values of x in "opportunity to x" for which we must say of some of the members of S that they lack irremediably the capacity to x, we shall not be able to say that every single member of S has the opportunity to x. Since *Model 1* requires that we say just this if equality of opportunity is to be said to exist, we shall have to deny that there is equality of opportunity to x in S if there are any members of S who lack irremediably the capacity to x—which is tantamount to saying that the ideal is in principle unrealizable in any such society. Even if the connection between the ideal and the possible is looser than that between the obligatory and the possible, there is a certain absurdity in the attempt to combine serious commitment to an ideal with the recognition that the ideal is in principle unrealizable. (ii) When x is some role-related task or activity, the opportunity to x cannot be extended to every single member of any society in which there is specialization of function. Since the exclusion of all such values of x from the scope of the ideal is surely out of the question, it looks as though in these (rather central) cases, too, equality of opportunity, on the suggested interpretation, is simply unattainable. (iii) When economic conditions preclude the possibility of every single member of S x-ing and when, in consequence, opportunities to x must denied to some in order to be made available to others, the *Model 1* requirement cannot be met. Yet it is strongly counter-intuitive to suppose that economic scarcity constitutes a decisive obstacle to the achievement of equality of opportunity.

It might be thought that these objections have force only if "opportunity" is understood—gratuitously—in the strong sense. While it is obvious enough that opportunity in this sense cannot be extended to all the members of any society in which there is economic scarcity, or in which there is division of labor, or in which there are differences in natural capacity, perhaps all that is intended by defenders of the *Model 1* account is that all the members of an equal opportunity society must be assumed to have an opportunity to x in the "one chance in N" sense—a much less stringent requirement.

There are at least two difficulties in the way of acceptance of this defense. In the first place, where irremediable lack of capacity is what stands in the way of enjoyment of the opportunity to x, there is no finite value of N which would enable us to say, truly, that persons lacking the capacity to x nevertheless have "one chance in N" to x. The truth is that they must be said to have *no* chance—and therefore no opportunity even in the "one chance in N" sense—of x-ing. Secondly, even when all the members of S can be said to have in this sense an opportunity to x, they can be said to have an *equal* opportunity to x (that is, to enjoy the *same* opportunity of x-ing) only if the value of N is the same for all. Yet the value of N can be held constant only when some strictly random procedure for the selection of x-ers is adopted.

For example, if some kind of competence criterion for the selection of x-ers is employed (as is commonly the case when job-vacancies have to be filled) and if we assume that there is some variation with S in the capacity of individuals to become competent x-ers, it will be impossible to hold the value of N constant. For members of S with quite outstanding ability to x effectively, the value of N may approach 1; while for members of S with meagre ability to x the value of N may approach infinity. It may be a foregone conclusion that the former can become x-ers if they wish to; and it may be clear in advance that the latter "haven't a ghost of a chance" (as we might say) of becoming x-ers no matter how much they may want to or how hard they may try to improve their ability to x. So it looks as though *Model 1* will serve in these cases to account for what we mean when we affirm the existence of equality of opportunity to x in S only if it is a matter of indifference whether or not we can say that all the members of S have the *same* opportunity to x. Yet once a distinction is drawn between (a) the claim that all the members of S have an opportunity to x and (b) the claim that all the members of S have the *same* opportunity to x—and the distinction is needed when "opportunity" is understood in the "one chance in N" sense—it is difficult to hold that it is (a) to the exclusion of (b) which captures more accurately the intended force, on the *Model 1* interpretation, of statements about the existence of equality of opportunity.

The clue to an alternative interpretation of the ideal of equality of opportunity—at any rate for those values of x which prove troublesome for *Model 1*—is provided by the fact that although it is seldom (if ever) possible to say of *all* the members of S that they have the *same* opportunity[3] to x, precisely this can be said about all the members of various sub-classes of S: indeed for any given value of N some subclass of S can in principle be specified all the members of which have the same opportunity (in the "one chance in N" sense) to x. What this suggests is that equality of opportunity is a function, not of the size of the class of those who can be said to enjoy the same opportunity to x, but rather of the criteria for membership in the various sub-classes of S of which this can be said. According to this interpretation—let us call it *Model 2*—there is equality of opportunity to x in S if and only if appropriate criteria for the rationing of opportunities to x are applied in S. Since it is a substantive question what the "appropriate" criteria are for any given value of x, claims about the existence or non-existence of equality of opportunity can no longer be regarded—as they can on Model 1—as evaluatively neutral. Since the question is also controversial, a good deal of variety in *Model 2* views as to the content of the ideal is only to be expected. Something of this variety can be crudely illustrated by contrasting three accounts on *Model 2* lines of what is involved in equality of opportunity to attain to sought-after social positions. According to the first—*A*—there is equality of opportunity of this sort if and only if all who have similar skills have an

equal chance of securing these positions; according to the second—
B—there is equality of opportunity if and only if all who have similar
natural endowments and who are also similarly motivated have an
equal chance; while according to the third—*C*—there is equality of
opportunity if and only if all who have similar natural endowments
have an equal chance. *C*, it will be clear, is a more demanding ideal
than *B*, and *B* than *A*. *A* requires that discriminatory hiring and promotion practices be eliminated, but it does not require the removal of
barriers to the securing of job-qualifications, nor does it require that
action be taken to diminish the differences there may be in the desire
of individuals to make the best of their capacities and opportunities.
B, however, calls not only for the elimination of discriminatory
appointments practices but also for the provision of (at least certain
kinds of) educational opportunities; and *C* requires, in addition, that
measures be adopted to remedy deficiencies in individual motivation.
Despite these (large) differences, all three accounts reflect the conviction that equality of opportunity to x can exist in *S* even though the
opportunities to x of any two members of *S*, selected at random, may
be markedly unequal:[4] the members of *S* need not all enjoy the same
("one chance in *N*") opportunity to x, provided variations in the value
of *N* across *S* correspond to differences in the prospects individual
members of *S* have of satisfying whatever are deemed to be the
"appropriate" criteria for the selection of x-ers.

IV

It has been the purpose of this paper to illustrate the claim that
"Equality of Opportunity" is a systematically ambiguous expression by
identifying three ways in which misconceptions as to its intended
force can arise. Any account of the content of the ideal of equality of
opportunity which is to obviate misunderstanding must consequently
contain answers to the following questions: (i) What are the kinds of
opportunity to be equalized in the name of the ideal? (ii) Is "opportunity" to be understood in the strong sense only, or in the weak sense
only, or in both senses according to context? (iii) How must opportunities be distributed within any given society for equality of opportunity to be said to exist? It is the comparative neglect of these questions
which is responsible in no small part for the perplexingly diverse
claims which have been advanced both in regard to the value and in
regard to the achievability of the ideal of equality of opportunity.

NOTES

[1] This question arises, of course, only when his failure to x cannot be traced back to
lack of serious effort to x on his part.
[2] The action may of course be of any degree of complexity and/or difficulty which is
consistent with his capacities.

[3] When "opportunity" is understood in the weak sense—as indeed it must be if "the same opportunity" is not to be pleonastic.

[4] By contrast, a determined defender of *Model 1* would have to hold that there can be equality of opportunity of this sort if and only if *all* the members of S (and not merely all the members of the various sub-classes of S identified in A, B, and C) have an equal opportunity of attaining to prized positions; and this formulation exposes the ideal to the charge that its realization would require extensive manipulation of the genetic pool for the purpose of eliminating differences in natural capacity among the members of S.

Justice: A Funeral Oration

WALLACE MATSON

THRENODY

Is it any longer possible to talk seriously about justice and rights? Are these words corrupted and debased beyond redemption? There is no need to multiply examples of how anything that any pressure group has the chutzpah to lay claim to forthwith becomes a right, *nemine contradicente.* Nor is this Newspeak restricted to the vulgar. Our most universally acclaimed theoretician of justice has shown at length that justice is a will perpetual and constant to forcibly take goods from those who have earned them and give them to those who have not;[1] and the leading light of Anglo-American jurisprudence has constructed a "straightforward" argument proving that a citizen's right to equal protection of the laws is fully satisfied if only the bureaucrat denying him or her a public benefit on racial grounds shows "respect and concern" while manipulating the shaft.[2]

Linguistic entropy makes it as futile to try to rehabilitate mutilated words as to put toothpaste back in the tube. The semantic battle has been lost; and with it a lot more than perspicuous speech. From Plato onward ideologues have sought to capture the vocabulary of justice, the paradigm of OK words, and tie it to schemes aiming at doing away with rights and justice. Now they have brought it off. A single generation has witnessed the movement of enlightened thought from the position that any discrimination in treatment based merely on race is the most heinous of sins, to consensus that advocacy of forgetting about race and treating people as individuals is proof positive of racism, the culprit to be ostracized and deprived of the protection of the First Amendment. It took the Supreme Court hardly a decade to discover that the Civil Rights Act of 1964, which in the plainest and clearest language ever seen in a statute condemned racial quotas, really encouraged or even mandated them. Scarcely less abrupt has been the transformation of admiration and fostering of excellence into the vice of elitism. The deepest philosophico-legal thinker of the western United States has preached against the immorality of requiring any applicant for any job to possess qualifications for it.[3] At the other end of the country lives another heavyweight moralist who can imagine no worse injustice than paying smart people more than dumb people.[4]

Why then am I writing about justice? What can I say? To whom? To what purpose? Maybe two dozen uninfluential people will read me of whom three or four will agree. What can arguments accomplish anyway? The windmills of the *Zeitgeist* keep right on turning. I write also about the interpretation of Parmenides (5th century B.C.). The one activity is likely to produce about as much change in the world as the other.

But let's get on with it.

• • •

AFFIRMATIVE ACTION

Philosophy is sometimes said to have no practical consequences. If so, the theory of justice is not philosophy, for whether one holds one view or another of justice makes an enormous difference in practice. As an example let us consider the ways in which justice from the bottom up and from the top down deal with the problem of racial discrimination in employment.

First, justice from the bottom up:

In a society recognizing this norm, citizens may make whatever agreements they choose, for any reason or none, as long as they do not infringe on the rights of other citizens. (Please grant me this premiss. I could prove it but I do not have the space.) So if I am a Ruritanian widget-maker, a manufacturer of widgets who detests Ruritanians may legitimately refuse to hire me. And if there are many more of his sort, we Ruritanian widget-makers will be at a disadvantage, we will be being discriminated against just because we are Ruritanians, and that is bad. But happily the problem will solve itself. We will offer our services to non-Ruritanophobe entrepreneurs for wages lower than the bigots must pay; and if we really are just as good workers, our unbiased employers will be put at a competitive advantage over the prejudiced ones. In the not very long run, then, the gap between Ruritanian and non-Ruritanian wage levels will disappear. And in the somewhat longer run the very idea of this sort of discrimination will begin to look silly, and we will be welcomed as fellow club members and sons-in-law by the former meanies. At any rate this is the pattern that has hitherto manifested itself time and again in this country. It is well to note in this connection that slavery in the Southern states was, and South African apartheid is, imposed by government edict, i.e. are interferences with freedom of contract.

Justice from the top down takes a different approach. Everybody is the same as everybody else in all respects (dogma), therefore Ruritanians are just as good at making widgets as anyone else (non sequitur), therefore if Ruritanian representation in the widget industry is not equal to the statistical expectation, it must be the work of prejudice (non sequitur), which if sincerely denied must be an unconscious aversion (absurdity). This is sin, which must be put down by force, viz. the imposition of a pro-Ruritanian quota (called something else) on widget-makers. This will, of course, have two effects: it will disrupt the widget industry, already reeling from Japanese competition, and it will exacerbate resentment against Ruritanians.

. . .

Justice from the top down as I have described it does not sound attractive. I have tried to account for the fact that nevertheless it commands the enthusiastic support of so many clever men and women and is everywhere on the march by showing its emotional basis in the structure of the family, an institution that has been felt to be, at its best, a warm, conflict-free, loving refuge from fear and anxiety. Many people do not really *want* to grow up, and when they do they yearn for a return to blissful dependence in the family or even in the stage of development previous to that. I do not think it can be controverted that this is part of the explanation for the popularity of top-down justice; but nor can it be the whole, for such a complex phenomenon must be due to many factors. Among them are genuine compassion for the unfortunate and altruistic desire to help them; fantasies of omnipotence, to which powerless academic intellectuals are exceptionally liable; and envy. What the proportions are, is anybody's guess.

As there is no hope of lessening the influence of these emotions in human affairs, the triumph of the top-down cannot be stemmed unless there are yet more powerful emotions to pit against them. What might they be? I can think of three possibilities: the desire that everyone has that he himself should be given his due, and the concomitant outrage, with which more and more people are becoming acquainted, when the top-down authority denies it; revulsion from witnessing the actual practical effects of top-down justice, e.g. in Cambodia; and finally the life force itself, Spinoza's *conatus*, the endeavor of each thing to persevere in its being, and not (except in parasites) by sucking forever but by getting proper solid nourishment. I *hope* these are strong enough to prevail and show this funeral oration to have been premature: Justice is not dead, only lying there bound and gagged.

NOTES

[1] John Rawls, *A Theory of Justice* (Cambridge, Mass., 1971), 277-80 *et passim*.

[2] Ronald Dworkin, *Taking Rights Seriously* (London, 1977), 227-9.

[3] Richard Wasserstrom, "A Defense of Programs of Preferential Treatment," *The National Forum* 58, no. 1 (Winter 1978), 15-18. [Reprinted in Thomas Mappes and Jane Zembaty, eds., *Social Ethics*, 2nd ed. (New York, 1982) and in the present volume, 393-8.]

[4] Thomas Nagel, *Mortal Questions* (New York, 1979), 99ff.

Equality

ROBERT NOZICK

EQUALITY

The legitimacy of altering social institutions to achieve greater equality of material condition is, though often assumed, rarely *argued* for. Writers note that in a given country the wealthiest N percent of the population holds more than that percentage of the wealth, and the poorest N percent holds less; that to get to the wealth of the top N percent from the poorest, one must look at the bottom P percent (where P is vastly greater than N), and so forth. They then proceed immediately to discuss how this might be altered. On the entitlement conception of justice in holdings, one *cannot* decide whether the state must do something to alter the situation merely by looking at a distributional profile or at facts such as these. It depends upon how the distribution came about. Some processes yielding these results would be legitimate, and the various parties would be entitled to their respective holdings. If these distributional facts *did* arise by a legitimate process, then they themselves are legitimate. This is, of course, *not* to say that they may not be changed, provided this can be done without violating people's entitlements. Any persons who favor a particular end-state pattern may choose to transfer some or all of their own holdings so as (at least temporarily) more nearly to realize their desired pattern.

The entitlement conception of justice in holdings makes no presumption in favor of equality, or any other overall end state or patterning. It cannot merely be *assumed* that equality must be built into any theory of justice. There is a surprising dearth of arguments for equality capable of coming to grips with the considerations that underlie a nonglobal and nonpatterned conception of justice in holdings.[1] (However, there is no lack of unsupported statements of a presumption in favor of equality.) I shall consider the argument which has received the most attention from philosophers in recent years; that offered by Bernard Williams in his influential essay "The Idea of Equality."[2] (No doubt many readers will feel that all hangs on some other argument; I would like to see *that* argument precisely set out, in detail.)

Leaving aside preventive medicine, the proper ground of distribution of medical care is ill health; this is a necessary truth. Now in very many societies, while ill health may work as a necessary condition of receiving treatment, it does not work as a sufficient condition, since such treatment costs money, and not all who are ill have the money; hence the possession of sufficient money becomes in fact an additional necessary condition of actually receiving treatment. . . . When we have the situation in which, for instance, wealth is a further necessary condition of the receipt of medical treatment, we can once more apply the notions of equality and inequality: not now in connection with the inequality between the well and the ill, but in connection with the inequality between the rich ill and the poor ill, since we have straightforwardly the situation of those whose needs are the same not receiving the same treatment, though the needs are the ground of the treatment. This is an irrational state of affairs . . . it is a situation in which reasons are insufficiently operative; it is a situation insufficiently controlled by reasons—and hence by reason itself.[3]

Williams seems to be arguing that if among the different descriptions applying to an activity, there is one that contains an "internal goal" of the activity, then (it is a necessary truth that) the only proper grounds for the performance of the activity, or its allocation if it is scarce, are connected with the effective achievement of the internal goal. If the activity is done upon others, the only proper criterion for distributing the activity is their need for it, if any. Thus it is that Williams says (it is a necessary truth that) the only proper criterion for the distribution of medical care is medical need. Presumably, then, the only proper criterion for the distribution of barbering services is barbering need. But why must the internal goal of the activity take precedence over, for example, the person's particular purpose in performing the activity? (We ignore the question of whether one activity can fall under two different descriptions involving different internal goals.) If someone becomes a barber because he likes talking to a variety of different people, and so on, is it unjust of him to allocate his services to those he most likes to talk to? Or if he works as a barber in order to earn money to pay tuition at school, may he cut the hair of only those who pay or tip well? Why may not a barber use exactly the same criteria in allocating his services as someone else whose activities have no internal goal involving others? Need a gardener allocate his services to those lawns which need him most?

In what way does the situation of a doctor differ? Why must his activities be allocated via the internal goal of medical care? (If there was no "shortage," could some then be allocated using other criteria as well?) It seems clear that he needn't do that; just because he has this skill, why should he bear the costs of the desired allocation, why is he less entitled to pursue his own goals, within the special circumstances of practicing medicine, than everyone else? So it is society that, somehow, is to arrange things so that the doctor, in pursuing his own goals, allocates according to need; for example, the society pays him to do this. But why must the society do this? (Should they do it for barbering as well?) Presumably, because medical care is important, people need it very much. This is true of food as well, though farming does *not* have an internal goal that refers to other people in the way doctoring does. When the layers of Williams' argument are peeled away, what we arrive at is the claim that society (that is, each of us acting together in some organized fashion) should make provision for the important needs of all of its members. This claim, of course, has been stated many times before. Despite appearances, Williams presents no argument for it.* Like others, Williams looks only to questions of allocation. He ignores the question of where the things or actions to be allocated and distributed come from. Consequently, he does not consider whether they come already tied to people who have entitlements over them (surely the case for service activities, which are people's *actions*), people who therefore may decide for themselves to whom they will give the thing and on what grounds.

EQUALITY OF OPPORTUNITY

Equality of opportunity has seemed to many writers to be the minimal egalitarian goal, questionable (if at all) only for being too weak. (Many writers also have seen how the existence of the family prevents fully achieving this goal.) There are two ways to attempt to provide such equality: by directly worsening the situations of those more favored with opportunity, or by improving the situation of those less well-favored. The latter requires the use of resources, and so it too involves worsening the situation of some: those from whom holdings are taken in order to improve the situation of others. But holdings to which these people are entitled may not be seized, even to provide equality of opportunity for others. In the absence of magic wands, the remaining means toward equality of opportunity is convincing persons each to choose to devote some of their holdings to achieving it.

The model of a race for a prize is often used in discussions of equality of opportunity. A race where some started closer to the finish line than others would be unfair, as would a race where some were forced to carry heavy weights, or run with pebbles in their sneakers. But life is not a race in which we all compete for a prize which someone has established; there is no unified race, with some person judging swiftness. Instead, there are different persons separately giving other persons different things. Those who do the giving (each of us, at times)

---

* We have discussed Williams' position without introducing an essentialist view that some activities necessarily involve certain goals. Instead we have tied the goals to *descriptions* of the activities. For essentialist issues only becloud the discussion, and they still leave open the question of why the only proper ground for allocating the activity is its essentialist goal. The motive for making such an essentialist claim would be to avoid someone's saying: let "schmoctoring" be an activity just like doctoring except that *its* goal is to earn money for the practitioner; has Williams presented any reason why *schmoctoring* services should be allocated according to need?

usually do not care about desert or about the handicaps labored under; they care simply about what they actually get. No centralized process judges people's use of the opportunities they had; that is not what the processes of social cooperation and exchange are *for*.

There is a reason why some inequality of opportunity might seem *unfair*, rather than merely unfortunate in that some do not have every opportunity (which would be true even if no one else had greater advantage). Often the person entitled to transfer a holding has no special desire to transfer it to a particular person; this contrasts with a bequest to a child or a gift to a particular person. He chooses to transfer to someone who satisfies a certain condition (for example, who can provide him with a certain good or service in exchange, who can do a certain job, who can pay a certain salary), and he would be equally willing to transfer to anyone else who satisfied that condition. Isn't it unfair for one party to receive the transfer, rather than another who had less opportunity to satisfy the condition the transferrer used? Since the giver doesn't care to whom he transfers, provided the recipient satisfies a certain general condition, equality of opportunity to be a recipient in such circumstances would violate no entitlement of the giver. Nor would it violate any entitlement of the person with the greater opportunity; while entitled to what he has, he has no entitlement that it be more than another has. Wouldn't it be *better* if the person with less opportunity had an equal opportunity? If one so could equip him without violating anyone else's entitlements (the magic wand?) shouldn't one do so? Wouldn't it be fairer? If it *would* be fairer, can such fairness also justify overriding some people's entitlements in order to acquire the resources to boost those having poorer opportunities into a more equal competitive position?

The process is competitive in the following way. If the person with greater opportunity didn't exist, the transferrer might deal with some person having lesser opportunity who then would be, under those circumstances, the best person available to deal with. This differs from a situation in which unconnected but similar beings living on different planets confront different difficulties and have different opportunities to realize various of their goals. There, the situation of one does *not* affect that of another; though it would be better if the worse planet were better endowed than it is (it also would be better if the better planet were better endowed than *it* is), it wouldn't be *fairer*. It also differs from a situation in which a person does not, though he could, choose to *improve* the situation of another. In the particular circumstances under discussion, a person having lesser opportunities would be better off if some particular person having better opportunities didn't exist. The person having better opportunities can be viewed not merely as someone better off, or as someone not choosing to aid, but as someone *blocking* or *impeding* the person having lesser opportunities from becoming better off.[4] Impeding another by being a more alluring alternative partner in exchange is not to be compared to directly *worsening* the situation of another, as by stealing from him. But still, cannot the person with lesser opportunity justifiably complain at being so impeded by another who does not *deserve* his better opportunity to satisfy certain conditions? (Let us ignore any similar complaints another might make about *him*.)

While feeling the power of the questions of the previous two paragraphs (it is *I* who ask them), I do not believe they overturn a thoroughgoing entitlement conception. If the woman who later became my wife rejected another suitor (whom she otherwise would have married) for me, partially because (I leave aside my lovable nature) of my keen intelligence and good looks, neither of which did I earn, would the rejected less intelligent and less handsome suitor have a legitimate complaint about unfairness? Would my thus impeding the other suitor's winning the hand of fair lady justify taking some resources from others to pay for cosmetic surgery for him and special intellectual training, or to pay to develop in him some sterling trait that I lack in order to equalize our chances of being chosen? (I here take for granted the impermissibility of worsening the situation of the person having better opportunities so as to equalize opportunity; in this sort of case by disfiguring him or injecting drugs or playing noises which prevent him from fully using his intelligence.[5]) *No such consequences follow.* (Against whom would the rejected suitor have a legitimate complaint? Against what?) Nor are things different if the differential opportunities arise from the accumulated effects of people's acting or transferring their entitlement as they choose. The case is even easier for consumption goods which cannot plausibly be claimed to have any such triadic impeding effect. *Is* it unfair that a child be raised in a home with a swimming pool, using it daily even though he is no more *deserving* than another child whose home is without one? Should such a situation be prohibited? Why then should there be objection to the transfer of the swimming pool to an adult by bequest?

The major objection to speaking of everyone's having a right *to* various things such as equality of opportunity, life, and so on, and enforcing this right, is that these "rights" require a substructure of things and materials and actions; and *other* people may have rights and entitlements over these. No one has a right to something whose realization requires certain uses of things and activities that other people have rights and entitlements over.[6] Other people's rights and entitlements to *particular things* (*that* pencil, *their* body, and so on) and how they choose to exercise these rights and entitlements fix the external environment of any given individual and the means that will be available to him. If his goal requires the use of means which others have rights over, he must enlist their voluntary cooperation. Even to *exercise* his right to determine how something he owns is to be used may require other means he must acquire a right to, for example, food to keep him alive; he must put together, with the cooperation of others, a feasible package.

There are particular rights over particular things held by particular persons, and particular rights to reach agreements with others, *if* you and they together can acquire the means to reach an agreement. (No one has to supply you with a telephone so that you may reach an agreement with another.) No rights exist in conflict with this substructure of particular rights. Since no neatly contoured right to achieve a goal will avoid incompatibility with their substructure, no such rights exist. The particular rights over things fill the space of rights, leaving no room for general rights to be in a certain material condition. The reverse theory would place only such universally held general "rights to" achieve goals or to be in a certain material condition into its substructure so as to determine all else; to my knowledge no serious attempt has been made to state this "reverse" theory.

NOTES

[1] For a useful consideration of various arguments for equality which are not at the most fundamental level, see Walter J. Blum and Harry Kalven, Jr., *The Uneasy Case for Progressive Taxation,* 2nd ed. (Chicago, 1963).

[2] Bernard Williams, "The Idea of Equality," in *Philosophy, Politics, and Society,* 2nd ser., Peter Laslett and W.G. Runciman, eds. (Oxford, 1962), 110-31; reprinted in Joel Feinberg, ed., *Moral Concepts* (New York, 1969).

[3] Williams, "The Idea of Equality," 121-2.

[4] Perhaps we should understand Rawls' focus on social cooperation as based upon this triadic notion of one person, by dealing with a second, blocking a third person from dealing with the second.

[5] See Kurt Vonnegut's story "Harrison Bergeron" in his collection *Welcome to the Monkey House* (New York, 1970).

[6] See on this point, Judith Jarvis Thomson, "A Defense of Abortion," *Philosophy & Public Affairs,* 1, no. 1 (Fall 1971), 55-6.

Reverse Discrimination as Unjustified

LISA H. NEWTON

I have heard it argued that "simple justice" requires that we favor women and blacks in employment and educational opportunities, since women and blacks were "unjustly" excluded from such opportunities for so many years in the not so distant past. It is a strange argument, an example of a possible implication of a true proposition advanced to dispute the proposition itself, like an octopus absent-mindedly slicing off his head with a stray tentacle. A fatal confusion underlies this argument, a confusion fundamentally relevant to our understanding of the notion of the rule of law.

Two senses of justice and equality are involved in this confusion. The root notion of justice, progenitor of the other, is the one that Aristotle (*Nichomachean Ethics* 5. 6; *Politics* 1. 2; 3. 1) assumes to be the foundation and proper virtue of the political association. It is the condition which free men establish among themselves when they "share a common life in order that their association bring them self-sufficiency"—the regulation of their relationship by law, and the establishment, by law, of equality before the law. Rule of law is the name and pattern of this justice; its equality stands against the inequalities—of wealth, talent, etc.—otherwise obtaining among its participants, who by virtue of that equality are called "citizens." It is an achievement—complete, or, more frequently, partial—of certain people in certain concrete situations. It is fragile and easily disrupted by powerful individuals who discover that the blind equality of rule of law is inconvenient for their interests. Despite its obvious instability, Aristotle assumed that the establishment of justice in this sense, the creation of citizenship, was a permanent possibility for men and that the resultant association of citizens was the natural home of the species. At levels below the political association, this rule-governed equality is easily found; it is exemplified by any group of children agreeing together to play a game. At the level of the political association, the attainment of this justice is more difficult, simply because the stakes are so much higher for each participant. The equality of citizenship is not something that happens of its own accord, and without the expenditure of a fair amount of effort it will collapse into the rule of a powerful few over an apathetic many. But at least it has been achieved, at some times in some places; it is always worth trying to achieve, and eminently worth trying to maintain, wherever and to whatever degree it has been brought into being.

Aristotle's parochialism is notorious; he really did not imagine that persons other than Greeks could associate freely in justice, and the only form of association he had in mind was the Greek *polis.* With the decline of the *polis* and the shift in the center of political thought, his notion of justice underwent a sea change. To be exact, it ceased to represent a political type and became a moral ideal: the ideal of equality as we know it. This ideal demands that all men be included in citizenship—that one Law govern all equally, that all men regard all other men as fellow citizens, with the same guarantees, rights, and protections. Briefly, it demands that the circle of citizenship achieved by any group be extended to include the entire human race. Properly understood, its effect on our associations can be excellent: it congratulates us on our achievement of rule of law as a process of government but refuses to let us remain complacent until we have expanded the associations to include others within the ambit of the rules, as often and as far as possible. While one man is a slave, none of us may feel truly free. We are constantly prodded by this ideal to look for possible unjustifiable discrimination, for inequalities not absolutely required for the functioning of the society and advantageous to all. And after twenty centuries of pressure, not at all constant, from this ideal, it might be said that some progress has been made. To take the cases in point for this problem, we are now prepared to assert, as Aristotle would never have been, the equality of sexes and of persons of different colors. The ambit of American citizenship, once restricted to white males of property, has been extended to include all adult free men, then all adult males including ex-slaves, then all women. The process of acquisition of full citizenship was for these groups a sporadic trail of half-measures, even now not complete; the steps on the road to full equality are marked by legislation and judicial decisions which are only recently concluded and still often not enforced. But the fact that we can now discuss the possibility of favoring such groups in hiring shows that over the area that concerns us, at least, full equality is presupposed as a basis for discussion. To that extent, they are full citizens, fully protected by the law of the land.

It is important for my argument that the moral ideal of equality be recognized as logically distinct from the condition (or virtue) of justice in the political sense. Justice in this sense exists *among* a citizenry, irrespective of the number of the populace included in that citizenry. Further, the moral ideal is parasitic upon the political virtue, for "equality" is unspecified—it means nothing until we are told in what respect that equality is to be realized. In a political context, "equality" is specified as "equal rights"—equal access to the public realm, public goods and offices, equal treatment under the law—in brief, the equality of citizenship. If citizenship is not a possibility, political equality is unintelligible. The ideal emerges as a generalization of the real condition and refers back to that condition for its content.

Now, if justice (Aristotle's justice in the political sense) is equal treatment under law for all citizens, what is injustice? Clearly, injustice is the violation of that equality, discriminating for or against a group of citizens, favoring them with special immunities and privileges or depriving them of those guaranteed to the others. When the southern employer refuses to hire blacks in white-collar jobs, when Wall Street will only hire women as secretaries with new titles, when Mississippi high schools routinely flunk all black boys above ninth grade, we have examples of injustice, and we work to restore the equality of the public realm by ensuring that equal opportunity will be provided in such cases in the future. But of course, when the employers and the schools *favor* women and blacks, the same injustice is done. Just as the previous discrimination did, this reverse discrimination violates the public equality which defines citizenship and destroys the rule of law for the areas in which these favors are granted. To the extent that we adopt a program of discrimination, reverse or otherwise, justice in the political sense is destroyed, and none of us, specifically affected or not, is a citizen, a bearer of rights—we are all petitioners for favors. And to the same extent, the ideal of equality is undermined, for it has content only where justice obtains, and by destroying justice we render the ideal meaningless. It is, then, an ironic paradox, if not a contradiction in terms, to assert that the ideal of equality justifies the violation of justice; it is as if one should argue, with William Buckley, that an ideal of humanity can justify the destruction of the human race.

Logically, the conclusion is simple enough: all discrimination is wrong *prima facie* because it violates justice, and that goes for reverse discrimination too. No violation of justice among the citizens may be justified (may overcome the *prima facie* objection) by appeal to the ideal of equality, for that ideal is logically dependent upon the notion of justice. Reverse discrimination, then, which attempts no other justification than an appeal to equality, is wrong. But let us try to make the conclusion more plausible by suggesting some of the implications of the suggested practice of reverse discrimination in employment and education. My argument will be that the problems raised there are insoluble, not only in practice but in principle.

We may argue, if we like, about what "discrimination" consists of. Do I discriminate against blacks if I admit none to my school when none of the black applicants are qualified by the tests I always give? How far must I go to root out cultural bias from my application forms and tests before I can say that I have not discriminated against those of different cultures? Can I assume that women are not strong enough to be roughnecks on my oil rigs, or must I test them individually? But this controversy, the most popular and well-argued aspect of the issue, is not as fatal as two others which cannot be avoided: if we are regarding the blacks as a "minority" victimized by discrimination, what is a "minority"? And for any group—blacks, women, whatever— that has been discriminated against, what amount of reverse discrimination wipes out the initial discrimination? Let us grant as true that women and blacks were discriminated against, even where laws forbade such discrimination, and grant for the sake of argument that a history of discrimination must be wiped out by reverse discrimination. What follows?

First, are there other groups which have been discriminated against? For they should have the same right of restitution. What about American Indians, Chicanos, Appalachian Mountain whites, Puerto Ricans, Jews, Cajuns, and Orientals? And if these are to be included, the principle according to which we specify a "minority" is simply the criterion of "ethnic (sub) group," and we're stuck with every hyphenated American in the lower-middle class clamoring for special privileges for *his* group—and with equal justification. For be it noted, when we run down the Harvard roster, we find not only a scarcity of blacks (in comparison with the proportion in the population) but an even more striking scarcity of those second-, third-, and fourth-generation ethnics who make up the loudest voice of Middle America. Shouldn't they demand *their* share? And eventually, the WASPs will have to form their own lobby, for they too are a minority. The point is simply this: there is no "majority" in America who will not mind giving up just a bit of their rights to make room for a favored minority. There are only other minorities, each of which is discriminated against by the favoring. The initial injustice is then repeated dozens of times, and if each minority is granted the same right of restitution as the others, an entire area of rule governance is dissolved into a pushing and shoving match between self-interested groups. Each works to catch the public eye and political popularity by whatever means of advertising and power politics lend themselves to the effort, to capitalize as much as possible on temporary popularity until the restless mob picks another group to feel sorry for. Hardly an edifying spectacle, and in the long run no one can benefit: the pie is no larger—it's just that instead of setting up and enforcing rules for getting a piece, we've turned the contest into a free-for-all, requiring much more effort for no larger a reward. It would be in the interests of all the participants to re-establish an objective rule to govern the process, carefully enforced and the same for all.

Second, supposing that we do manage to agree in general that women and blacks (and all the others) have some right of restitution, some right to a privileged place in the structure of opportunities for a while, how will we know when that while is up? How much privilege is enough? When will the guilt be gone, the price paid, the balance restored? What recompense is right for centuries of exclusion? What criterion tells us when we are done? Our experience with the Civil Rights movement shows us that agreement on these terms cannot be presupposed: a process that appears to some to be going at a mad gallop into a black takeover appears to the rest of us to be at a standstill. Should a practice of reverse discrimination be adopted, we may safely predict that just as some of us begin to see "a satisfactory start toward righting the balance," others of us will see that we "have already gone too far in the other direction" and will suggest that the discrimination ought to be reversed again. And such disagreement is inevitable, for the point is that we could not *possibly* have any criteria for evaluating the kind of recompense we have in mind. The context presumed by any discussion of restitution is the context of rule of law: law sets the rights of men and simultaneously sets the method for remedying the violation of those rights. You may exact suffering from others and/or damage payments for yourself if and only if the others have violated your rights; the suffering you have endured is not sufficient reason for them to suffer. And remedial rights exist only where there is law: primary human rights are useful guides to legislation but cannot stand as reasons for awarding remedies for injuries sustained. But then, the context presupposed by any discussion of restitution is the context of preexistent full citizenship. No remedial rights could exist for the excluded; neither in law nor in logic does there exist a right to *sue* for a standing to sue.

From these two considerations, then, the difficulties with reverse discrimination become evident. Restitution for a disadvantaged group whose rights under the law have been violated is possible by legal means, but restitution for a disadvantaged group whose grievance is that there was no law to protect them simply is not. First, outside of the area of justice defined by the law, no sense can be made of "the group's rights," for no law recognizes that group or the individuals in it, *qua* members, as bearers of rights (hence *any* group can constitute itself as a disadvantaged minority in some sense and demand similar restitution). Second, outside of the area of protection of law, no sense can be made of the violation of rights (hence the amount of the recompense cannot be decided by any objective criterion). For both reasons, the practice of reverse discrimination undermines the foundation of the very ideal in whose name it is advocated; it destroys justice, law, equality, and citizenship itself, and replaces them with power struggles and popularity contests.

NOTE

A version of this paper was read at a meeting of the Society for Women in Philosophy in Amherst, Massachusetts, 5 November 1972.

A Defense of Programs of Preferential Treatment

RICHARD WASSERSTROM

Many justifications of programs of preferential treatment depend upon the claim that in one respect or another such programs have good consequences or that they are effective means by which to bring about some desirable end, e.g., an integrated, equalitarian society. I mean by "programs of preferential treatment" to refer to programs such as those at issue in the *Bakke* case—programs which set aside a certain number of places (for example, in a law school) as to which members of minority groups (for example, persons who are non-white or female) who possess certain minimum qualifications (in terms of grades and test scores) may be preferred for admission to those places over some members of the majority group who possess higher qualifications (in terms of grades and test scores).

Many criticisms of programs of preferential treatment claim that such programs, even if effective, are unjustifiable because they are in some important sense unfair or unjust. In this paper I present a limited defense of such programs by showing that two of the chief arguments offered for the unfairness or injustice of these programs do not work in the way or to the degree supposed by critics of these programs.

The first argument is this. Opponents of preferential treatment programs sometimes assert that proponents of these programs are guilty of intellectual inconsistency, if not racism or sexism. For, as is now readily acknowledged, at times past employers, universities, and many other social institutions did have racial or sexual quotas (when they did not practice overt racial or sexual exclusion), and many of those who were most concerned to bring about the eradication of those racial quotas are now untroubled by the new programs which reinstitute them. And this, it is claimed, is inconsistent. If it was wrong to take race or sex into account when blacks and women were the objects of racial and sexual policies and practices of exclusion, then it is wrong to take race or sex into account when the objects of the policies have their race or sex reversed. Simple considerations of intellectual consistency—of what it means to give racism or sexism as a reason for condemning these social policies and practices—require that what was a good reason then is still a good reason now.

The problem with this argument is that despite appearances, there is no inconsistency involved in holding both views. Even if contemporary preferential treatment programs which contain quotas are wrong, they are not wrong for the reasons that made quotas against blacks and women pernicious. The reason why is that the social realities do make an enormous difference. The fundamental evil of programs that discriminated against blacks or women was that these programs were a part of a larger social universe which systematically maintained a network of institutions which unjustifiably concentrated power, authority, and goods in the hands of white male individuals, and which systematically consigned blacks and women to subordinate positions in the society.

Whatever may be wrong with today's affirmative action programs and quota systems, it should be clear that the evil, if any, is just not the same. Racial and sexual minorities do not constitute the dominant social group. Nor is the conception of who is a fully developed member of the moral and social community one of an individual who is either female or black. Quotas which prefer women or blacks do not add to an already relatively overabundant supply of resources and opportunities at the disposal of members of these groups in the way in which the quotas of the past did maintain and augment the overabundant supply of resources and opportunities already available to white males.

The same point can be made in a somewhat different way. Sometimes people say that what was wrong, for example, with the system of racial discrimination in the South was that it took an irrelevant characteristic, namely race, and used it systematically to allocate social benefits and burdens of various sorts. The defect was the irrelevance of the characteristic used—race—for that meant that individuals ended up being treated in a manner that was arbitrary and capricious.

I do not think that was the central flaw at all. Take, for instance, the most hideous of the practices, human slavery. The primary thing that was wrong with the institution was not that the particular individuals who were assigned the place of slaves were assigned there arbitrarily because the assignment was made in virtue of an irrelevant characteristic, their race. Rather, it seems to me that the primary thing that was and is wrong with slavery is the practice itself—the fact of some individuals being able to own other individuals and all that goes with that practice. It would not matter by what criterion individuals were assigned; human slavery would still be wrong. And the same can be said for most if not all of the other discrete practices and institutions which comprised the system of racial discrimination even after human slavery was abolished. The practices were unjustifiable—they were oppressive—and they would have been so no matter how the assignment of victims had been made. What made it worse, still, was that the institutions and the supporting ideology all interlocked to create a system of human oppression whose effects on those living under it were as devastating as they were unjustifiable.

Again, if there is anything wrong with the programs of preferential treatment that have begun to flourish within the past ten years, it should be evident that the social realities in respect to the distribution of resources and opportunities make the difference. Apart from everything else, there is simply no way in which all of these programs taken together could plausibly be viewed as capable of relegating white males to the kind of genuinely oppressive status characteristically bestowed upon women and blacks by the dominant social institutions and ideology.

The second objection is that preferential treatment programs are wrong because they take race or sex into account rather than the only thing that does matter—that is, an individual's qualifications. What all such programs have in common and what makes them all objectionable, so this argument goes, is that they ignore the persons who are more qualified by bestowing a preference on those who are less qualified in virtue of their being either black or female.

There are, I think, a number of things wrong with this objection based on qualifications, and not the least of them is that we do not live in a society in which there is even the serious pretense of a qualification requirement for many jobs of substantial power and authority. Would anyone claim, for example, that the persons who comprise the judiciary are there because they are the most qualified lawyers or the most qualified persons to be judges? Would anyone claim that Henry Ford II is the head of the Ford Motor Company because he is the most qualified person for the job? Part of what is wrong with even talking about qualifications and merit is that the argument derives some of its force from the erroneous notion that we would have a meritocracy were it not for programs of preferential treatment. In fact, the higher one goes in terms of prestige, power and the like, the less qualifications seem ever to be decisive. It is only for certain jobs and certain places that qualifications are used to do more than establish the possession of certain minimum competencies.

But difficulties such as these to one side, there are theoretical difficulties as well which cut much more deeply into the argument about qualifications. To begin with, it is important to see that there is a serious inconsistency present if the person who favors "pure qualifications" does so on the ground that the most qualified ought to be selected because this promotes maximum efficiency. Let us suppose that the argument is that if we have the most qualified performing the relevant tasks we will get those tasks done in the most economical and efficient manner. There is nothing wrong in principle with arguments based upon the good consequences that will flow from maintaining a social practice in a certain way. But it is inconsistent for the opponent of preferential treatment to attach much weight to qualifications on this ground, because it was an analogous appeal to the good consequences that the opponent of preferential treatment thought was wrong in the first place. That is to say, if the chief thing to be said in favor of strict qualifications and preferring the most qualified is that it is the most efficient way of getting things done, then we are right back to an assessment of the different consequences that will flow from different programs, and we are far removed from the considerations of justice or fairness that were thought to weigh so heavily against these programs.

It is important to note, too, that qualifications—at least in the educational context—are often not connected at all closely with any plausible conception of social effectiveness. To admit the most qualified students to law school, for example—given the way qualifications are now determined—is primarily to admit those who have the greatest chance of scoring the highest grades at law school. This says little about efficiency except perhaps that these students are the easiest for the faculty to teach. However, since we know so little about what constitutes being a good, or even successful lawyer, and even less about the correlation between being a very good law student and being a very good lawyer, we can hardly claim very confidently that the legal system will operate most effectively if we admit only the most qualified students to law school.

To be at all decisive, the argument for qualifications must be that those who are the most qualified deserve to receive the benefits (the job, the place in law school, etc.) because they are the most qualified. The introduction of the concept of desert now makes it an objection as to justice or fairness of the sort promised by the original criticism of the programs. But now the problem is that there is no reason to think that there is any strong sense of "desert" in which it is correct that the most qualified deserve anything.

Let us consider more closely one case, that of preferential treatment in respect to admission to college or graduate school. There is a logical gap in the inference from the claim that a person is most qualified to perform a task, e.g., to be a good student, to the conclusion that he or she deserves to be admitted as a student. Of course, those who deserve to be admitted should be admitted. But why do the most qualified deserve anything? There is simply no necessary connection between academic merit (in the sense of being the most qualified) and deserving to be a member of a student body. Suppose, for instance, that there is only one tennis court in the community. Is it clear that the two best tennis players ought to be the ones permitted to use it? Why not those who were there first? Or those who will enjoy playing the most? Or those who are the worst and, therefore, need the greatest opportunity to practice? Or those who have the chance to play least frequently?

We might, of course, have a rule that says that the best tennis players get to use the court before the others. Under such a rule the best players would deserve the court more than the poorer ones. But that is just to push the inquiry back one stage. Is there any reason to think that we ought to have a rule giving good tennis players such a preference? Indeed, the arguments that might be given for or against such a rule are many and varied. And few if any of the arguments that might support the rule would depend upon a connection between ability and desert.

Someone might reply, however, that the most able students deserve to be admitted to the university because all of their earlier schooling was a kind of competition, with university admission being the prize awarded to the winners. They deserve to be admitted because that is what the rule of the competition provides. In addition, it might be argued, it would be unfair now to exclude them in favor of others, given the reasonable expectations they developed about the way in which their industry and performance would be rewarded. Minority-admission programs, which inevitably prefer some who are less qualified over some who are more qualified, all possess this flaw.

There are several problems with this argument. The most substantial of them is that it is an empirically implausible picture of our social world. Most of what are regarded as the decisive characteristics for higher education have a great deal to do with things over which the individual has neither control nor responsibility: such things as home environment, socioeconomic class of parents, and, of course, the quality of the primary and secondary schools attended. Since individuals do not deserve having had any of these things *vis-à-vis* other individuals, they do not, for the most part, deserve their qualifications. And since they do not deserve their abilities they do not in any strong sense deserve to be admitted because of their abilities.

To be sure, if there has been a rule which connects, say, performance at high school with admission to college, then there is a weak sense in which those who do well at high school deserve, for that reason alone, to be admitted to college. In addition, if persons have built up or relied upon their reasonable expectations concerning performance and admission, they have a claim to be admitted on this ground as well. But it is certainly not obvious that these claims of desert are any stronger or more compelling than the competing claims based upon the needs of or advantages to women or blacks from programs of preferential treatment. And as I have indicated, all rule-based claims of desert are very weak unless and until the rule which creates the claim is itself shown to be a justified one. Unless one has a strong preference for the status quo, and unless one can defend that preference, the practice within a system of allocating places in a certain way does not go very far at all in showing that that is the right or the just way to allocate those places in the future.

A proponent of programs of preferential treatment is not at all committed to the view that qualifications ought to be wholly irrelevant. He or she can agree that, given the existing structure of any institution, there is probably some minimal set of qualifications without which one cannot participate meaningfully within the institution. In addition, it can be granted that the qualifications of those involved will affect the way the institution works and the way it affects others in the society. And the consequences will vary depending upon the particular institution. But all of this only establishes that qualifications, in this sense, are relevant, not that they are decisive. This is wholly consistent with the claim that race or sex should today also be relevant when it comes to matters such as admission to college or law school. And that is all that any preferential treatment program—even one with the kind of quota used in the *Bakke* case—has ever tried to do.

I have not attempted to establish that programs of preferential treatment are right and desirable. There are empirical issues concerning the consequences of these programs that I have not discussed, and certainly not settled. Nor, for that matter, have I considered the argument that justice may permit, if not require, these programs as a way to provide compensation or reparation for injuries suffered in the recent as well as distant past, or as a way to remove benefits that are undeservedly enjoyed by those of the dominant group. What I have tried to do is show that it is wrong to think that programs of preferential treatment are objectionable in the centrally important sense in which many past and present discriminatory features of our society have been and are racist and sexist. The social realities as to power and opportunity do make a fundamental difference. It is also wrong to think that programs of preferential treatment are in any strong sense either unjust or unprincipled. The case for programs of preferential treatment could, therefore, plausibly rest both on the view that such programs are not unfair to white males (except in the weak, rule-dependent sense described above) and on the view that it is unfair to continue the present set of unjust—often racist and sexist—institutions that comprise the social reality. And the case for these programs could rest as well on the proposition that, given the distribution of power and influence in the United States today, such programs may reasonably be viewed as potentially valuable, effective means by which to achieve admirable and significant social ideals of equality and integration.

NEW AND FUTURE PEOPLE

What Should We Do About Future People?

TRUDY GOVIER

There are primarily two kinds of contexts in which the question arises as to whether and how we ought to take into account the interests of people who do not yet exist. One kind of context is that in which an action we are contemplating would significantly affect those people who do not exist at present but are likely to exist in the future. The other is that in which we are deciding whether or not to have children. I shall argue that these two kinds of contexts are importantly different in that the interests of prospective, but non-existent, people bear differently on each. The contrast which is involved here is tied to the contrast between *predicting whether someone will exist*, on the one hand, and *deciding whether to produce him*, on the other. In this paper I shall propose an account of the moral status of prospective, but non-existent, people which is based largely on this contrast.

The account I shall propose fulfills what I think are three very desirable conditions. First, it makes intelligible the moral requirement that we pay some attention to the needs of future generations. Second, it is compatible with an asymmetrical view about reproductive morality: it is wrong to have a child who would likely be miserable if born, but not wrong to refrain from having a child who would be happy if born. And third, though it gives prospective people *some* moral status, it does not entail that their interests should weigh equally in our moral calculations with those of already existent people.

Concerning the second two conditions mentioned, some references to philosophical literature are perhaps in order. First of all, there is the matter of asymmetry. It has been argued that while the very likely unhappiness of a prospective person is a good reason *not* to bring him into existence, happiness which he would be likely to experience if born does not provide good reason to produce him. This view was put forward by Jan Narveson in his book *Morality and Utility* and in several published papers.[1] Critics have questioned whether the asymmetry to which Narveson committed himself in these works can be justified. Recently he himself expressed certain misgivings about it.[2] It might well appear that if we are to consider the pain and unhappiness which a prospective person would likely experience as constituting reason *not* to produce him, then we ought also to consider whatever pleasure and happiness he would be likely to experience as reason *for* producing him. On this issue, I am strongly inclined to agree with the view which Narveson initially held and has repeatedly argued for in print. I think that some of the considerations brought out later in the paper can help to buttress this very plausible asymmetry.

Then there is the matter of weighing the interests of those who do not exist yet against those of people who already do exist. Philosophers have often written as though future people are just as real as present ones. They just happen to differ from present people with respect to the time at which they exist. Time, these philosophers would argue, is no more a morally significant property than hair color or number of freckles. Therefore, this view has it, the interests of future people are every bit as important as those of present people; future people should be accorded all the rights accorded to present people. L.W. Sumner once claimed that if we give a preference to presently existing people in our moral reasoning, if we weight their needs and interests more heavily than those of people who do not exist yet, we are *violating moral canons of impartiality*.[3] I think that it is a mistake to go this far in defending the interests of future generations; the account I shall put forward here provides reasons for the belief that this is a mistake.

Much of the philosophical literature to which I shall allude from time to time concerns the issue as to whether utilitarianism has as its most reasonable interpretation the *total view* or the *average view*. On the total view, utilitarianism directs us to maximize the happiness in the world and minimize the misery in the world. If people could be produced who would be *even slightly happy* and whose existence would not lessen the total happiness of existing people more than their own happiness would increase the happiness in the world, then, on the total view, such people ought to be produced. This consequence does not hold on the average view, wherein it is permissible to produce only those new people whose happiness will result in an increase in the happiness of the whole population *on the average*. The present paper does not address itself to this issue of total versus average utilitarianism. It is intended to be relatively independent of specific moral theories and to be compatible with any moral theory which allows that the rightness or wrongness of actions *depends at least in part on their effects on people's well-being*.[4] My account shares with defenses of average utilitarianism the refusal to allow that there is any obligation to bring people into existence which arises from the likelihood that they would be happy if they existed. However, it departs from some current versions of that doctrine by taking into account the interests of prospective people in other contexts.

In some contexts where we must consider the interests of prospective people, we are making a decision which is *not* a reproductive one. We are making a decision about some non-reproductive activity—say damming a river or using an insecticide. And the problem is that pursuing the activity is likely to change *those who are likely to exist in the future*. In this kind of context, there is a high probability that there will be people to be affected by our action and this probability is *relatively independent of the performance of the action*. If, for instance, we consider damming the river above Peterborough, we ought to consider how that action would affect people who are likely to exist in Peterborough in 100 years' time. Most of those people, whoever they will be, do not exist now, but there *are* likely to be people in Peterborough in 100 years. This likelihood is relatively independent of whether we dam the river or not.

In such a context these prospective people whose interests bear on our decision are possible people, possible in an epistemic sense. By saying this, I mean that there is some likelihood that they will come to exist; that we in effect *predict* their existence with some degree of probability. It is in order to do this when the moral issue which concerns us is *not* a reproductive one. If a moral agent, A, is making a decision, D, about an action, Q_1, wherein the likelihood of the existence of prospective persons, X and Y, is relatively independent of the performance of Q_1, X and Y are *epistemically possible* for A, in the context of that decision.

If, however, an agent is making a moral decision which is a reproductive one, that is a context in which it is inappropriate to think of her prospective child as epistemically possible. Someone who contemplates having a child cannot properly *simply* calculate a probability of her child coming into existence for that probability depends on what she decides to do. Where X is the prospective child, the probability of X's existence is precisely *not* independent of her action. If she decides to have a child and takes steps in that direction, then there is typically a fairly *high* probability that a child of hers will exist. And if she decides not to have one, and takes steps in that direction, there is typically a fairly *low* probability that a child of hers will exist. In this context, the prospective but non-existent child is *volitionally possible*; the agent is deciding whether to produce it, not estimating whether it will come to exist. To be more precise, if an agent, A, is making a decision, D_2, about an action, Q_2, wherein the likelihood of the existence of some prospective person, X, is highly dependent on Q_2, then X is volitionally possible for A, in the context of D_2.

For stylistic convenience, I shall speak of epistemically possible people and of volitionally possible people. But this way of speaking should not be taken to indicate some kind of ontological division among possible people. It is merely a convenience to omit a full reference to the context. However, the distinction between epistemic and volitional possibility *is* one which is relative to context. Persons who might come to exist are *epistemically possible* in that there is some probability of their coming to exist and *volitionally possible* for their prospective parents, or for someone else.

Of course, the clearest and most common case in which possible persons are volitionally possible for us *is* when we are prospective parents. A child is volitionally possible for someone who is deciding whether to use contraceptives or whether to have an abortion. For a god creating a world, its inhabitants are volitionally possible, and if a mad scientist set out to furnish a rocket with sperm and ova which would form developing embryos, the prospective inhabitants of that world would be volitionally possible for him. The god, or scientist, would have to decide whether to produce people and how many to produce. So volitional possibility is not logically tied to prospective parenthood.

There are less fanciful cases in which people are volitionally possible for others who are not their prospective parents, but most have morally problematic aspects to them. A doctor can be in a position where he has effective control over whether his patient has offspring, and in that case her children are for him volitionally possible. A guardian might similarly control whether one of his wards had offspring. And in some circumstances a government could be in such a position that future citizens of a country would be volitionally possible for that government. But the control needed for this would be extraordinary indeed. In any normal case governments only formulate and implement policies which provide incentives or disincentives to parenthood, and they do not decide whether to bring people into existence or not. It is not my purpose in this paper to pursue the question of who should decide whether more children are born. I have a strong inclination to think that prospective parents, and particularly prospective mothers, should make this decision in almost all cases, but I shall not argue for this view here.

Most of the time when we reason about nonexistent people, these people are for us epistemically possible, not volitionally possible. Those future generations whom we believe to have rights to clean air and an aesthetically tolerable environment are epistemically possible; so too are my great-grandchildren, and those people who will grow to adulthood in the northern environment resulting from pipeline construction in the Yukon. Though none of these people exist, all are epistemically possible and there are contexts in which we feel intuitively that their interests should bear on our decisions.

I would contend that it is slightly misleading to talk about future people. Future people are those epistemically possible people the probability of whose existence is very high. We do not know that there will be future generations; we do not even know that there will be human beings alive in 2095, much less in the year 4000. When we speak of future generations, we do so in the belief that it is highly probable that there will be humans at the time in question, and on the assumption that *whether* there will be people then is very largely out of our individual control. For instance, it is highly probable that there will be people living in Peterborough, Ontario, in 2095; those possible people identified as the inhabitants of Peterborough in 2095 are *epistemically possible* for us. They likely will exist, and there is not much that we as individuals can do about this one way or the other. Given the high probability of their coming to exist, and our almost total lack of control over this, it is understandable that we should speak and think of these "future generations" of Peterborough as though they will quite certainly come along. This may explain why some philosophers maintain that "future people" differ from us only in the morally incidental respect that their birthdays just happen to be on dates later than ours and later than the present date.

However, we do not know that there will be any future people, and we cannot know that there will be any. In moral deliberations, the best we can do is to base our decisions on the very best evidence we have. With reference to "future people," this evidence can never tell us that some people *do* have birthdays later than the present date; it can only tell us that it is very likely that people will be born. For the purposes of moral reasoning, it is misleading to think that *there are future people*, who differ from us only with respect to the time at which they exist. Rather, there are people who for us are epistemically possible and whose existence is highly probable.

I shall pause here to try to defend what I am saying, as it is definitely at odds with the view other philosophers have taken. Jan Narveson says:

> Now *future persons*, as the term implies, *are simply persons* whose birth dates lie some temporal distance in the future relative to us. Apart from that, *they are real people*, actual people, flesh and blood people like ourselves. And it would be difficult to think of a more elementary requirement of morality than that the mere fact that someone's birth date is what it is cannot justify treating him in accordance with a quite different basic set of moral rules from others. Whatever we want to claim are the basic rights of persons, we will be committed to the implication that persons existing a hundred or five hundred years hence also have them.[5] (my emphasis)

The italicized statement seems rather at odds with Narveson's later claim, in the same paper, that "it is at any rate in principle (or perhaps 'ideally') always due to a decision (certainly an act) of ours that the next generation contains just the persons it does, and therefore, *partly due to our decisions that any future earthlings exist*."[6] If future persons are as real as we are, and if we have genuine alternatives when we decide, how can it be a matter of our decision whether there are any future persons at all? There seems to be some tension in Narveson's view here. The answer to this dilemma, I think, is that it is not up to anyone *individually* whether there will be future people; nor are there future people who are as real as we are. The word "future" here can be misleading. *If* there are future people, then they are real and have all the basic human rights; but *whether* there will be any such people is not known for certain, it is merely highly probable. In another paper, Narveson repeats his statement that future persons are "just like ourselves"[7] but later seems to recognize the probabilistic element when he says "there is no difficulty identifying future generations, in the ordinary meaning of those terms; they are the collections of individuals who will be living in the future *if any do live*"[8] (my emphasis).

Like Narveson, Derek Parfit contrasts future people whose existence is "merely possible." He says:

> Suppose that we must act in one of two ways. Future people are the people who will exist whichever way we act. Possible people are the people who exist if we act in one way, but who won't exist if we act in the other way. To give the simplest case, the children we could have are possible people.[9]

Parfit goes on to compare people who are distant in time with those who are distant in space, saying that our actions can affect those who do not exist *now* just as they can affect those who do not exist *here*. But Parfit, like Narveson, gets into some trouble with this contrast, as he later argues that, due to the wide-sweeping effects of different social policies, *different specific people* will emerge depending on what action we take.[10] This would entail that there are *no specific people who will exist whichever way we act*, on Parfit's own account.

Parfit's suggestion that future people be compared with past people and with distant people is not a promising one. We can in principle know what people have existed and what people do exist far away. But we cannot know just which people will exist in the future. Indeed, we cannot know that there will be future people at all. In making this claim, I wish to assert more than a simple wholesale scepticism about all future propositions. (Though I think that such scepticism does have much to be said in its favor, I am not basing my case on this doctrine here.)

In saying that we do not know that future persons will exist, I mean to assert the following three propositions:

(1) We do not know that any conceptions which have not yet occurred will occur, be followed by healthy and completed pregnancies, and issue in infants who develop into persons.

(2) We do not know that any conceptions which have occurred will be followed by healthy and completed pregnancies, and will issue in infants who develop into persons.

(3) We do not know that any infants successfully delivered but still very young will develop into persons.

Why do we not know these things? It is not only because these propositions are about the future: special considerations apply. These should be obvious: they have to do with the chanciness of conception; the possibility of natural catastrophes, world war, or accidental nuclear explosion; side-effects from drugs, food additives, pesticides, or any number of other things; the risks of pregnancy and child-bearing; and the possibilities of childhood disease. There are simply too many factors which could intervene, even in cases where we might think that conceptions, healthy pregnancies and deliveries, and nor-mal infancies were virtual certainties. Since world-wide catastrophe as a result of nuclear or germ warfare, or accidents involving sophisti-cated weaponry are among these factors, and since the likelihood of these is not insignificant, it is unreasonable to claim that we *know* now that people not born yet will be born and will develop into persons. This is why I insist that when we speak of future persons, we can only legitimately mean those persons who in all probability will exist after us and whose existence we have no reason to regard as being depen-dent on our individual will.

If the preceding arguments are accepted, then we are left with the basic distinction between those prospective people who are epistemi-cally possible for us in a context and those prospective people who are volitionally possible for us in a context. "Future people" are those epistemically possible people whose existence is highly probable and not properly regarded, in the context in question, as a matter for our decision.

Let us first consider a fairly standard sort of context where con-sideration of the interests of epistemically possible people is morally required. We have an insecticide, which will increase crop production and which is not known to have any harmful effects on people or ani-mals now living. However, it is known that over a number of years, the residue from this insecticide will combine with other chemicals to produce a substance which can cause blindness in human beings. We are deciding whether to use this insecticide. It is certainly *relevant* to this decision that the insecticide is likely ultimately to produce blind-ness in people who probably will exist, though they do not exist now. We run the risk of seriously harming those people likely to exist if we use the insecticide. Although in certain circumstances this might not provide an absolutely *conclusive* reason not to use the substance, it always provides a good reason not to use it. The decision in question is not a decision as to whether there will be people existing at later dates; it is a decision whether to use something now which is likely to harm people who likely will exist at later dates.

In such a case I think that it is natural and correct to take account of the interests of nonexistent, but possible, people. The relevant factors are the likelihood of their coming to exist, the extent and likelihood of effects of one's action upon them, and the cost to existing people of not doing the contemplated action.

What distinction we make between benefiting and harming nonexistent people should depend on the distinction we make for existing people. There is a greater importance to not harming people than there is to benefiting them. Nevertheless, I think that benefits to epistemically possible people should have some bearing on our actions. Imagine a case in which, by spending an extra half hour with my lawyer, I could ensure that my spacious lakeside property would be preserved as parkland for generations-to-come of deprived children. If this could be done, and if there is a significant probability that there will be children in future years who would greatly benefit from having such a park area, then I think that it would be proper to consider the interests of these not-yet-existent children, and that these provide *some reason* to take the trouble to make the arrangement. I shall not say that in this case I would have an obligation to spend the extra time with my lawyer; whether one wants to posit an obligation in this case will depend on one's more general view about whether we have obligations to benefit other people.

It is entirely appropriate here to treat epistemically possible people in a way strictly analogous to the way in which we treat actual people, the difference being only that we should take into account the fact that their existence is only probable. Since the probability that an epistemically possible person will exist is always less than one, the interests of epistemically possible people always count for something less than those of actual people. This is so whenever our decision is not a decision as to whether there will be people or not, and whenever the existence of the people in question is determined by factors other than the matter about which we are deliberating.

When we are the ones who are deciding whether to produce a child or not, it does not make sense to weigh the interests of that prospective child against the probability of his coming to exist. We decide whether he will exist or not. This is why it is crucial to distinguish between contexts of epistemic and volitional possibility when we are reasoning about possible people. There are cases in which people are not exactly volitionally possible for an agent, but wherein the probability of their coming to exist does depend significantly upon his decision. Where there is this interdependence, the model outlined for taking into account the interests of epistemically possible people cannot properly be applied. This is because something which will vary considerably depending upon what our decision is cannot properly be used as a basis on which that decision is made.

Suppose that someone could release a gas which would sharply diminish the safe food supply and make it impossible for human life to survive on the earth in 100 years' time. Those people who might exist in 120 years need not be considered when we assess the morality of this action, for the probability of their existing depends on whether the action is performed or not. Thus their interests cannot be balanced against the probability of their existence. This consequence might seem so implausible as to constitute an objection to the present account. Nevertheless we can arrive at the result that the gas should not be released and that the reason for this is that the gas would affect future people as well as actual people. We can reach this conclusion without including these prospective people in our calculations.

If the gas is released, then there are people alive when it is released, and their food supply will be adversely affected by it. Either they will be able to produce children or they will not. If the former, their children are epistemically possible and their interests in a safe food supply and in being able to reproduce must be taken into account. If the latter, then actual people are harmed in that they are not able to fulfill the very basic and natural desire to have children. There are enough actual and epistemically possible people whose existence is independent of the decision and who will be harmed by the prospective action that we can generate the decision that the gas should not be released. We need not appeal to the interests of those prospective people whose existence depends on the performance of the action in question.

At this point I wish to consider an important argument put forward by Derek Parfit. Parfit considers two alternative policies toward resources which he refers to as Depletion and Conservation. He maintains that there is no future person whose existence is independent of which of these policies is pursued.

> The people who will live more than a century from now would be different on the different policies. Given the effects of two such policies on the details of people's lives, different marriages would increasingly be made. More simply, even in the same marriages the children would increasingly be conceived at different times. This would be enough to make them different children. . . . Depletion would lower the quality of life in the further future. But the people who would then be alive would have existed if instead, we had Conserved. So if we Deplete, *there would never be anyone who is worse off than he would have otherwise been.* Depletion would be worse for no one.[11]

Parfit is not advocating depletion of our resources. Rather, he takes this argument to be a kind of paradox; he does not propose any solution to it. The paradox is that, whereas we would find it natural to believe that future generations will be harmed by depletion, this apparently cannot be true, in that there is no particular person in the future who will be worse off under a depletion policy than under a conservation policy. Because of the variation in which specific people come to exist, it appears that *no one* is harmed by a depletion policy. And this seems paradoxical; would we not want to say that *those who will exist will fare badly if we deplete the resources* and that this, indeed, is why we should *not deplete*? I shall refer to this problem as Parfit's Paradox.

I have said that whenever an action of ours is such that the existence of prospective people is probabilistically independent of the performance of that action, the interests of such people ought to be considered. Given this independence, such prospective people are, on my account, *epistemically possible* in the context in question. Parfit seems to be arguing in effect that no prospective person is ever epistemically possible in this sense, as which specific people come to exist depends on what we decide to do. If we use the insecticide mentioned in my first example, one set of specific people will result in the world of one hundred years hence; if we do not use it, another set of specific people will result. On this account, then, there is no specific person whose existence is (or can be known to be) probabilistically independent of our decision to do anything. Parfit's argument might be seen as generating the conclusion that in effect *all* prospective people are volitionally possible in *all* contexts. But this would be a misleading interpretation: a prospective person is volitionally possible for someone who can decide whether to produce a person, and people do not decide whether to produce *specific* persons. If Beethoven's mother had considered an abortion, she would not have been deciding whether or not to produce Ludwig van Beethoven, but rather whether to carry the child in her womb to term.

Parfit's Paradox is difficult to resolve satisfactorily. My approach to it is along the following lines: people in the future are not to be regarded as volitionally possible in the context of the depletion/conservation issue. This is because in such a context *whether some people will exist in the future* does not depend on whether we deplete or conserve. It is very likely that people will be here on earth in 100 years, and the likelihood of there being some people alive on earth at that time does not depend on this particular social policy.[12] Our concern for people who are likely to exist can never be a concern for some *specific* prospective persons *as opposed to others*, for when we are making decisions which require a reference to prospective persons, we are never in a position to identify *specific* ones. (The first part of what I have said here is acknowledged by Parfit.)[13] The reason we should not deplete the resources *is* primarily that those who are likely to exist will be badly off if we deplete. If someone should say that "the people under depletion" owe their very existence to a depletion policy, and still live a life better than no life at all, the correct reply is "that's irrelevant." It is irrelevant because consideration of *these specific* people who would exist under depletion and will not exist under conservation is logically out of order. First, we cannot sensibly consider *specific* prospective people. Secondly, when we are deciding to conserve, there is *of course* no need to consider specific prospective people identified as "those who would exist if we deplete but would not exist if we conserve." *By definition*, the probability of their existence, given the decision to conserve, is zero. The people we ought to consider when we are deciding whether to deplete or to conserve are *those people who will likely exist at a future time*. Those people will be badly off if we deplete; therefore we ought not to deplete.

We move now to a consideration of contexts where prospective people *are* for us volitionally possible. Typically these are contexts where moral agents are deciding whether to reproduce. If a moral agent is deciding whether to reproduce, then the probability that a prospective child of hers will exist is very largely dependent on what she decides to do. It is not logically appropriate for her to consider the probability that this child will exist as a factor on which her decision is based: that probability depends on the decision. She will have to base the decision on other factors—on the interests of those already alive whose lives would be affected if the child were born. This does not take us yet to the asymmetry which Narveson has argued for. But I think that this asymmetry becomes comprehensible and justifiable if we think about reasons which this moral agent might have for changing her mind, once her decision is made.

Suppose that she has decided to have a child. She ought, then, to consider the interests of this child-that-is-to-be, for if her decision is successfully implemented, he will be an actual person. If there seems to be every chance that he will lead an acceptable happy life, no special problem arises. Since she wants to have a child and after due consideration of the difference this child's existence will make to herself and others, has decided to have one, she can go ahead and do so. The child is likely to be happy and she has judged that any harm or inconvenience to others as a result of his existence is not of over-riding importance. Things are otherwise, though, if it seems likely that the child she wants to bear would lead a miserable life if born. She will have produced a miserably unhappy person; she can anticipate that she will regret her decision, *out of regard for him*, and he could legitimately complain about his miserable fate, perhaps even to bemoan the very fact of his existence. If she implements her decision to have a child, then, if the child will be miserable, this will be the result. So if there is evidence that the prospective child would be miserable, there is reason to reverse the decision to produce him. By "miserable," in this context, I mean so badly off that his life would be worse than no life at all. If one can predict that the child one would have would be so miserable that he would be better off not having been born at all, then there is conclusive reason not to have him. Here it is appropriate to take the interests of the child one would have *into account, since the typical and intended effect of deciding to have a child is that there will be a child to consider.*

But now let us look at the other decision. Suppose that our prospective parent has decided not to have a child. She may then reflect on this decision; can she predict that she will have cause to regret it, or that others will complain of it? She may think of happiness a child of hers could have had; should she anticipate that this can rationally be a source of guilt or sadness? She should not, for if she implements her decision not to have a child, there will be no child; there will be "lack of a happy child," not an unhappy child. And the lack of a happy child should not bring guilt or regret unless the prospective parent wants a child. If she does, she will decide to have one—so that is not the case we are considering. And if she comes to want a child in the future she can decide then to have one. Similarly, if others want her prospective child, this can have a bearing on her decision-making now or in the future. But the child itself can provide no basis for regret, no guilt, and no complaints with regard to a decision not to have it. For the decision is precisely a decision not to have the child. The fact that *if* one had a child, that child would be happy provides no reason to have a child and no reason to change one's mind if one has decided not to have a child.

In this way, I think that we can support the asymmetry for which Narveson has argued. There is reason to reverse a decision to have a child if that child would likely be miserable, and there is no comparable reason to reverse a decision to have a child if that child would be happy. Hence, asymmetry.[14]

This asymmetry is in accord with the pre-philosophical convictions of many people. People do not normally argue that others should produce children on the grounds that those children would be happy if they existed. And yet they do hold it reprehensible to knowingly bring into the world children who will be seriously deformed, in dire poverty, or desperately in need of loving care. Even people who oppose a liberal abortion policy often favor abortion in those cases where the fetus is seriously deformed or handicapped, out of consideration for that person who would exist if the fetus were not aborted.

Before leaving this matter of asymmetry, it is in order to say more about the claim that some prospective persons would be better off if "they" did not exist. For this seems a puzzling assertion. *Who* is better off when "he" does not exist? And just what is better than life: nothingness? The problem may be approached, I think, by comparing birth with death.[15] It is said sometimes that people whose circumstances are absolutely desperate would be better off dead. This is to say that no life at all would be better *for these people* than the life they are leading. And yet, with no life, there is no subject for things to be better *for*. There is no consciousness, no awareness of anything. And yet we do sometimes think that a very desperate life, in which there is no hope at all, is worse *for the person living it* than death. If a person is extremely deprived, or if he is in continual and acute pain, and if there is no hope at all for improvement, then he might very well come to believe that he would be "better off dead." This expression suggests that such a person is making a comparison between two states which he could be in: he could be alive, having these kinds of experiences, or he could be dead, having no experiences at all. And of course this way of looking at the matter is all wrong, for *he won't be* in one of the states. A judgment by someone that he would be "better off dead" should be interpreted as a judgment that his continuance as an experiencing subject should be terminated, because the experiences he has and can expect to have, are so dreadful. People sometimes do judge that they would be better off dead, and when they do this, it is possible that they hold the belief rationally and that what they believe is true.

Let us turn from the context of death to the one which is directly relevant to reproductive morality: that in which we compare the life which we would anticipate for a volitionally possible person with no life at all, *for that person*. Since such a comparison must, of necessity, be made before the prospective person is born, we cannot consult him in the matter. And we cannot go very far in the direction of using his specific interests and ambitions as a basis for making our judgment. We must make the comparison between the kind of life we think he would have and no life at all from the viewpoint of a representative human being, attributed normal, fundamental human emotions and needs. If a prospective parent can anticipate that the child she might have will not have sufficient food, that he will be seriously deformed and in almost constant pain, or that there will be no one interested in loving and caring for him, she can anticipate that he will be miserable, as in his case, fundamental human needs will not be met.

If we say, then, that it would be better, from the point of view of a prospective child, if he did not exist, we define the viewpoint of the prospective child with reference to fundamental human needs. Once this is done, then judging that such a life is absolutely not worth having is similar in principle to comparing a particular life which some particular person is leading with death for that person. It is to say, in effect, that experiences of the type which he could expect just should not be suffered by any human being, and that if these are the only kinds of experiences he is likely to have, then it is better for there to be no subject of experience at all.

There is no insurmountable *logical* difficulty, then, in the judgment that some prospective people would be better off if "they" did not exist. But we must be very cautious in making these judgments, for actual people vary in their needs, and we do not want to underestimate the adjustments which a deformed or handicapped person can make. It is possible to see how to make logical sense of the judgment that a prospective person would be "better off" if "he" did not exist. However, we must take every precaution in particular cases to see that we do not make this judgment insensitively or prematurely.

On the basis of the account just given, I would sum up the moral status of prospective people as follows:

(1) The moral worth of an action, A, depends at least in part on the harm or benefit it is likely to bring to those who exist or who are likely to exist, where in the latter case the probability of their existing is largely independent of whether A is performed or not.

(2) We are never obliged to bring someone into existence merely because he is likely to be very happy if he exists.

(3) We are generally obliged not to bring someone into existence if he is likely to be very miserable if he exists.

(4) It is generally permissible to bring into existence people who are likely to lead happy, or moderately happy, lives.

The word "generally" is used in (3) and (4) to allow for balancing the interests of prospective people against those of already-existing people. It is arguable at least that it would be permissible to produce someone who would be unhappy if his existence would greatly alleviate the unhappiness of people already alive. And certainly the permissibility of producing people who would likely be happy is contingent upon their lives not seriously diminishing the well-being of those who were already alive at the time of their conception.

NOTES

[1] "Utilitarianism and New Generations," *Mind* 76 (1967), 62-72; and "Moral Problems of Population," *The Monist* 57 (1973), 62-86.

[2] At a lecture given at Trent University in March 1977, Narveson said that he did not think that he could adequately defend the asymmetry; however, more recently he has put forward additional arguments in its favor, in a draft paper written in June 1977.

[3] L.W. Sumner, "The Absurdity of Average Utilitarianism," paper presented at the Canadian Philosophical Association meetings in Fredericton, New Brunswick, June 1977.

[4] It may also be used in some of its essentials, in conjunction with moral theories which do not share this presupposition. For instance, Nozick's theory bases morality on respecting rights to life and property. One could deny a right to life for people not yet born or conceived, and who are volitionally possible; and weigh rights of the epistemically possible as less than those of already existing people, on grounds essentially the same as those presented in this paper.

[5] "Harm to the Unconceived?—A Utilitarian (In Spirit) Comment on Professor Bayles' Paper," presented at the Kalamazoo Conference on the Philosophy of Law, Spring 1976, 4.

[6] *Ibid.*, 5-6.

[7] "Semantics, Future Generations, and the Abortion Problem," *Social Theory and Practice* 6 (1975), 468.

[8] *Ibid.*, 473.

[9] "Rights, Interests, and Possible People," in Gorovitz *et al.*, eds., *Moral Problems in Medicine* (Englewood Cliffs, N.J., 1976) 369-75.

[10] Parfit, draft of a paper entitled "Overpopulation," [Cf. section I of his "Future Generations" in this volume, 414-19—Ed.]

[11] "Overpopulation," 12. See also Section IX, 3:

> If we Deplete, the quality of life in the further future will be lower. But the particular people who would then be alive would not have existed if we had Conserved. So if these people's lives would still be worth living, Depletion would be better for them. Since it would also be better for existing people, it would be better for everyone who ever lives.

[12] If one is convinced that the likelihood of there being any people at all depends on whether we deplete, the case then becomes analogous to that of the gas which would affect future food supply, and should be treated in the same way. See above, 12-13.

13 "Overpopulation," 19-20.

14 This line of reasoning is quite similar to that in "Moral Problems of Population," 96-7:

> If you bring these people into existence, then of course you must treat them in accordance with their moral status as human beings. And if you can foresee that it will not be possible to do that, or that no matter how much you or anyone tries, you won't be able to succeed in enabling them to live a worthwhile life, then that is a reason for not starting on the project in the first place. . . . But the solubility of such problems, the fact that one would be able to treat, and that others would be able to treat, the newcomer in a satisfactory way, does not seem of itself any reason at all for having him.

Compare also R.I. Sikora, "Utilitarianism: The Classical Principle and the Average Principle," *Canadian Journal of Philosophy* 5 (1975), 409-17. This reasoning more easily justifies asymmetry when the distinction between epistemic and volitional possibility is kept in mind.

15 I owe a debt here to L.W. Sumner, "A Matter of Life and Death," *Nous* 10 (1976), 145-71.

Future Generations

DEREK PARFIT

I

THE NON-IDENTITY PROBLEM

The Problem

. . . Consider first

> *The 14-Year-Old Girl.* This girl chooses to have a child. Because she is so young, she gives her child a poor start in life. If she had waited for several years, she would have had a different child, to whom she would have given a better start in life.

Suppose that we tried to persuade this girl not to have a child now. We first claimed that, if she does, she will soon regret it. If she waits, that will be better for her. She replied that this is her affair. Even if having a child now will be worse for her, she has a right to do what she wants.

We then claimed that this is not entirely her affair. She should think not only of herself, but of her child. It will be worse for her child if she has him now. If she has him later, she will give him a better start in life.

She disregarded our advice. She had a child when she was fourteen, and, as we predicted, she gave him a poor start in life. Were we right to claim that her decision was worse for her child? If she had waited, this particular child would never have existed. If this child's life is so wretched as to be worse than nothing, we might perhaps claim that this girl's decision was worse for this child. Whether this could be claimed we shall consider later. But we can suppose here that this child's life is worth living. Because his mother was so young, he had a worse start in life than most children do. And this has bad effects throughout his life. But since his life is worth living, and the alternative would have been his non-existence, his mother's decision was *not* worse for him.

When we see this, does this change our moral view? Do we cease to believe that this girl ought to have waited, so that she could give her child a better start in life? This does not change my view. I retain this belief. But this belief cannot be defended in the natural way that we first suggested. We cannot claim that this girl's decision was worse for her child. We must appeal to some other moral principle. What should this be?

Someone might suggest: "There is a clear sense in which this girl's decision *was* worse for her child. In a case like this, when we are trying to persuade this girl not to have a child, the phrase "her child" and the pronoun "he" are naturally used to cover any child that she might have. These words do not refer to one particular child. This is shown by the fact that we can truly claim that, if she does not have her child now, but waits and has him later, *he* will not be the same particular child. If she has him later, he will be a different child. When we use these words in this way, we *can* claim that this girl's decision will be worse for her child. If she waits, he will have a better start in life."

These remarks are true. But they do not solve our problem. This becomes clear after the girl has had her child. The phrase "her child" now naturally refers to this particular child. And this girl's decision was *not* worse for *this* child. We can still claim that, in the other sense, her decision was worse for her child. But we are not appealing to a familiar moral principle.

On one familiar principle, it is an objection to some choice that this choice is worse for some particular person. When we claim that this girl's decision was worse for her child, we are not claiming that it was worse for any particular person. We are not claiming, of the girl's child, that her decision was worse for *him*. We must admit that, in our claim, the words "her child" do not refer to her child. Our claim is not about what is good or bad for any of the particular people who ever live. We are thus appealing to an unfamiliar moral principle. We must explain and justify this new principle.

If we seem to be appealing to a familiar principle, this was a verbal conjuring trick. Here is another example. A general shows military skill if, in many battles, he always makes his the winning side. But there are two ways of doing this. He might win victories. Or he might always, when he is about to be defeated, change sides. A general shows no military skill if it is only the second sense that he always makes his the winning side.

In the Case of the 14-Year-Old Girl, there are other principles to which we might appeal. But the problem arises in many other cases.

We can first describe what these cases have in common. Suppose that we are choosing between two social or economic policies. And suppose that, on one of the two policies, the standard of living would be slightly higher over the next century. This effect implies another. It is not true that, whichever policy we choose, the same particular people will exist two centuries later. Given the effects of two such policies on the details of our lives, it would increasingly over time be true that people married different people. More simply, even in the same marriages, the children would increasingly be conceived at different times. (Thus the British Miners' Strike of 1974, which caused television to close down an hour early, thereby affected the timing of thousands of conceptions.) As we have argued, children conceived more than a month earlier or later would in fact be different children. Some of the people who are later born would thus owe their existence to our choice of one of the two policies. If we had chosen the other policy, these particular people would never have existed. And the proportion of those later born who would owe their existence to our choice would, like ripples in a pool, steadily grow. We can plausibly assume that, after two centuries, there would be no one living in our country who would have been born whichever policy we chose. (It may help to think of this example. How many of us could truly claim, "Even if railways had never been invented, I would still have been born"?)

We can now compare two examples. Consider

> *The Nuclear Technician.* Some technician lazily chooses not to check some tank in which nuclear wastes are buried. As a result there is a catastrophe two centuries later. Leaked radiation kills and injures thousands of people.

We can plausibly assume that, whether or not this technician checks this tank, the same particular people would be born during the next two centuries. On this assumption, this technician's choice is worse for the people struck by the catastrophe. If he had chosen to check the tank, these same people would have later lived, and escaped the catastrophe.

Consider next

> *The Risky Policy.* Suppose that, as a community, we have a choice between two energy policies. Both would be completely safe for at least two centuries, but one would have certain risks in the further future. If we choose the Risky Policy, the standard of living would be somewhat higher over the next two centuries. We do choose this policy. As a result there is a similar catastrophe two centuries later, which kills and injures thousands of people.

The case is, in one respect, implausible. If the Risky Policy might later cause such a catastrophe, it is unlikely that it would be completely safe for the next two centuries. But this simplifies the case in a way that casts no doubt on what I shall be claiming.

Unlike the Nuclear Technician's choice, our choice between these policies affects who will be later born. Because we choose the Risky Policy, thousands of people are later killed and injured. But if we had chosen the alternative Safe Policy, these particular people would never have existed. Different people would have existed in their place. Is our choice of the Risky Policy worse for anyone?

We can first ask, "Could a life be so bad—so diseased and deprived—that it would not be worth living? Could a life be even worse than this? Could it be worse than nothing, or as we might say 'worth *not* living'?" I shall assume that there could be such lives. But we do not yet need this assumption. We can suppose that, whether or not lives could be worth not living, this would not be true of the lives of the people killed in the catastrophe. These people's lives would be well worth living. And we can suppose the same of those who mourn for those killed, and those whom the catastrophe disables. (Perhaps, for some of those who suffer most, the rest of their lives would be worth not living. But this would not be true of their lives as a whole.)

We can next ask: "If we cause someone to exist, who will have a life worth living, do we thereby benefit this person?" This is a difficult question. Call it the question whether *causing to exist can benefit*. Since the question is difficult, I shall discuss the implications of both answers.

Because we chose the Risky Policy, thousands of people are later killed or injured or bereaved. But if we had chosen the Safe Policy these particular people would never have existed. Suppose that we do *not* believe that causing to exist can benefit. We should ask, "If particular people live lives that are on the whole well worth living, even though they are struck by some catastrophe, is this worse for these people than if they had never existed?" Our answer must be No. If we believe that causing to exist *can* benefit, we can say more. Since the people struck by the catastrophe live lives that are well worth living, and would never have existed if we had chosen the Safe Policy, our choice of the Risky Policy is not only not worse for these people: it *benefits* them.

Let us now compare our two examples. The Nuclear Technician chooses not to check some tank. We choose the Risky Policy. Both these choices predictably cause catastrophes, which harm thousands of people. These predictable effects both seem bad, providing at least some moral objection to these choices. In the case of the Technician, the objection is obvious. His choice is worse for the people who are later harmed. But this is not true of our choice of the Risky Policy. Moreover, when we understand this case, we know that this is not true. We know that, even though our choice may cause such a catastrophe, it will not be worse for anyone who ever lives.

Does this make a moral difference? There are three views. It might make all the difference, or some difference, or no difference. There might be no objection to our choice, or some objection, or the objection may be just as strong.

Which of these three views should we accept? The question arises because our choice affects the identities of future people. The people who will later live will not be, whatever we choose, the same particular people. Let us therefore call this *the Non-Identity Problem*.

Some claim

> *Wrongs Require Victims.* Our choice cannot be wrong if we know that it will be worse for no one.

This claim implies that there is no objection to our choice. We may find it hard either to deny this claim, or to accept this implication.

I deny that wrongs require victims. If we know that we may cause such a catastrophe, I am sure that there is at least some moral objection to our choice. I am inclined to believe that the objection is just as strong as it would have been if, as in the case of the Nuclear Technician, our choice would be worse for future people. If the objection is just as strong, it is morally irrelevant that our choice will be worse for no one. As I shall argue later, this may have important theoretical implications.

Before we pursue these questions, it will help to have two more examples. We must continue to assume that some people can be worse off than others, in morally significant ways, and by more or less. But we need not assume that these comparisons could be even in principle precise. There may be only rough or partial comparability. By "worse off" we need not mean "less happy". We could be thinking, more narrowly, of the standard of living, or, more broadly, of the quality of life. Since it is the vaguest, I shall use the phrase "the quality of life." And I shall extend the ordinary use of the phrase "worth living." If one of two groups of people would have a lower quality of life, I shall call their lives to this extent "'less worth living."

Here is another example:

Depletion. Suppose that, as a community, we must choose whether to deplete or conserve certain kinds of resources. If we choose Depletion, the quality of life over the next two centuries would be slightly higher than it would have been if we had chosen Conservation. But we know that it may later, for about a century, be much lower. During this century people would have to find alternatives for the resources that we had depleted. Life at this much lower level would, however, still be well worth living. We can assume that this lower level is that at which, on average, life would be lived over the next two centuries if we choose Conservation. The effects might be shown [as in Figure 1].

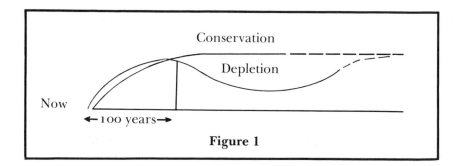

Figure 1

This case raises the same problem. If we choose Depletion rather than Conservation, this may lower the quality of life more than two centuries from now. But the particular people who will then be living would never have existed if instead we had chosen Conservation. So our choice of Depletion is not worse for any of these people. But our choice will cause these people to be worse off than the different people who, if we had chosen Conservation, would have later lived. This seems a bad effect, and an objection to our choice, even though it will be worse for no one.

Would the effect be *worse*, having greater moral weight, if it *was* worse for people? One test of our intuitions may be this. We may remember a time when we were concerned about effects on future generations, but had overlooked the Non-Identity Problem. We may have thought that a policy like Depletion would be against the interests of future people. When we saw that this was false, did we become less concerned about effects on future generations?

. . .

II

POSSIBLE SOLUTIONS

Is it good in itself if an extra person lives, with a life worth living? . . . In some countries, in some periods, it is true that, if more people live, people would be worse off. This raises another question. It would be bad if people would be worse off, or would have a lower quality of life. But could this be morally outweighed by the fact that there would be more people living? Could a decline in the quality of life be made up for by an increase in the number of lives lived? We need some principle, or set of principles, that will both answer these questions and solve the Non-Identity Problem.

Whether Causing Someone to Exist Can Benefit This Person

Before we search for such a principle, we should ask whether causing to exist can benefit. This question has been strangely neglected. Thus, in the Report of a U.S. Senate Commission on Population Growth and the American Economy, it is claimed that "there would be no substantial benefits from the continued growth of the U.S. population."[1] The Report never considers whether, if extra Americans are born, this might benefit these Americans.

We must consider this question if we are to defend some view about overpopulation. If some act is a necessary part of the cause of the existence of a person with a life worth living, does this act thereby benefit this person? I shall argue that the answer Yes is not, as some claim, obviously mistaken.

Some objectors claim that life cannot be judged to be either better or worse than nonexistence. But life of a certain kind may be judged to be either good or bad—either worth living, or worth not living. If a certain kind of life is good, it is better than nothing. If it is bad, it is worse than nothing. We should emphasize that, in judging that some person's life is worth living, or better than nothing, we need not be implying that it would have been worse for this person if he had never existed.

Judgments of this kind are often made about the last part of some life. Consider someone dying painfully, who has already made his farewells. This person may decide that what he has before him, if he lingers on, would be worse than nothing. And he may decide that much of his past life was either worse or better than nothing. If such claims can apply to parts of a life, they can apply to whole lives.

The objectors might now appeal to

The Two-State Requirement: We benefit someone only if we cause him to be better off than he would otherwise at that time have been.

They might say: "In causing someone to exist, and have a life worth living, we are not causing this person to be *better off* than he would otherwise have been. This person would not have been *worse off* if he had never existed."

To assess this argument, we should first ask the following question. If someone now exists, and has a life worth living, is he better off than he would now be if he had died, and ceased to exist? Suppose first that we answer Yes. In applying the Two-State Requirement, we count having ceased to exist as a state in which someone can be worse off. Why can we not claim the same about never existing? Why can we not claim that, if someone now exists, with a life worth living, he is better off than he would be if he never existed? It is true that *never existing* is not an ordinary state. But nor is *having ceased to exist*. Where is our mistake if we treat these states alike when applying the Two-State Requirement?

It might be replied that, when someone dies, there is a particular person who has ceased to exist. We can refer to this person. In contrast, there are no particular people who never exist. We cannot refer to any such person.

This might be a good reply if we were claiming that, in causing people never to exist, we could be harming these people. But we are making a different claim. This is that, in causing someone to exist, we can be benefiting this person. Since this person does exist, we can refer to this person when describing the alternative. We know who it is who, in this possible alternative, would never have existed. In the cases that we are considering, there is not the alleged difference between having ceased to exist and never existing. Just as we can refer to the person who might now have ceased to exist, we can refer to the person who might never have existed. We have not been shown why, in applying the Two-State Requirement, we should not treat these two states in the same way.

The defender of the Two-State Requirement might now change his view about the state of being dead, or having ceased to exist. He might claim that this is not a state in which someone can be worse off. He can then claim the same about never existing.

With this revision, the Two-State Requirement becomes too strong.

It implies that saving someone's life cannot benefit this person, since the person saved is not better off than he would have been if he had ceased to exist. In the case of saving life, it would now be defensible to relax the Two-State Requirement. We understand the special reason why, in this case, the Requirement is not met. We can claim that, because of this special feature of the case, the Requirement need not here be met. If the rest of someone's life would be worth living, we can count saving his life as a special case of benefiting him. And if we can relax the Requirement in the case of saving life, why can we not do the same in the case of giving life? If someone's life is worth living, why can we not count causing him to live as a special case of benefiting him?

The objectors might now turn to

The Full Comparative Requirement: We benefit someone only if we do what will be better for him.

They could say: "In causing someone to exist, we cannot be doing what will be better for him. If we had not caused him to exist, this would not have been worse for him." Unlike the stronger form of the Two-State Requirement, this new Requirement allows that saving someone's life can benefit this person. We can claim that it can be worse for someone if he dies, even though this does not make him worse off. (We would here be rejecting *the Lucretian Claim*: that some event can be bad for someone only if it makes him later suffer, or at least have regrets. Though not absurd, this claim can be rejected.)

Because it covers saving life, the Full Comparative Requirement is more plausible than the stronger form of the Two-State Requirement. But if we can relax the latter, in both of our special cases, it may be defensible to relax the former, in the case of giving life. We can admit that, in every other kind of case, we benefit someone only if we do what will be better for him.[2] In the case of giving someone life, we understand the special reason why the alternative would not have been worse for him. We might claim that, in this special case, the Requirement need not be met. Suppose we have allowed that saving someone's life can benefit this person. If my own life is worth living, it may then have benefited me to have had my life saved at any time after it started. Would it be plausible to claim that, while it benefited me to have had my life saved *just after* it started, it did not benefit me to have had it started?

Causing someone to exist is a special case because the alternative would not have been worse for this person. We may admit that, for this reason, causing someone to exist cannot be *better* for this person. But it may be *good* for this person.[3] In this move from "better" to "good," we admit that the Full Comparative Requirement is not met. But we would still be making two kinds of comparison. If it can be good for someone if he is caused to live, *how good* this is for this person will depend on how good his life is—how much his life is worth living. And we can make interpersonal comparisons. Suppose that

Jack's life is worth living, but not by a large margin. If his bouts of depression became more frequent and more severe, he would begin to doubt that his life was worth continuing. Jill's life, in contrast, is well worth living. We can then claim that, when we caused Jack to exist, this was good for Jack, but it was much *less* good for Jack than causing Jill to exist was for Jill.

We can next repeat that our claims avoid a common objection. When we claim that it was good for someone that he was caused to exist, we do not imply that, if he had not been caused to exist, this would have been bad for him. And our claims apply only to people who are or would be actual. We make no claims about people who are or would be actual. We make no claims about people who are or would remain merely possible. We are not claiming that it is bad for possible people if they do not become actual.

We might end with these remarks. We have considered three things: never existing, starting to exist, and ceasing to exist. We have suggested that, of these, starting to exist should be classed with ceasing to exist. Unlike never existing, starting to exist and ceasing to exist both happen to actual people. That is why, we might claim, they can be either good or bad for these people. The contrary claim is that starting to exist should be classed with never existing, and that neither can be either good or bad for people. The reason sometimes given is that, if we had *not* started to exist, we would never have existed, which would not have been bad for us. But we are not claiming that starting to exist can be either good or bad for people when it does *not* happen. Our claim is about starting to exist *when it happens*. We admit one difference between starting to exist and ceasing to exist. If it is good for someone if his life is saved, it would have been worse for him if he had died. Such entailments generally hold. For almost all events, if their occurrence would be good for people, their non-occurrence would have been worse for these people. But, we may suggest, there is one special event whose occurrence can be good for an actual person, even though its non-occurrence would not have been worse for this actual person. This event, unsurprisingly, is the coming-to-be-actual of the person.

These remarks are not conclusive. Further objections could be raised. My claim is only that, if we believe that causing to exist can benefit, this belief is defensible. There has been a similar debate whether existence is a *predicate*, or a genuine property. Some claim that, because it lacks some of the features of other predicates, *existing* is not a predicate. But others claim that this only shows that *existing* is a *peculiar* predicate. We can similarly claim that causing to exist gives a *peculiar* benefit.

Though this claim is defensible, it can be rejected. I shall therefore consider later how, if we reject this claim, we might hope both to solve the Non-Identity problem and to answer the questions raised by Different Number Choices.

Varieties of Beneficence

If we believe that causing to exist can benefit, we must decide between different versions of the principle of beneficence. We can note first that, unlike a utilitarian principle, a principle of beneficence does not claim to cover the whole of morality. It includes the phrase *if other things are equal*, and thus allows us to appeal to other moral principles, such as principles about equality, or just distribution. We may also claim that we have no duty to benefit others when this would require from us too great a sacrifice, or too great an interference in our lives. This claim can be combined with our chosen principle of beneficence.

It will help to define some more phrases. Suppose that we can do either X or Y. Call the people who will ever exist if we do X *the X-people*. Suppose that we choose X. Call our choice

"worse for people" in the *narrow* sense if the choice of X rather than Y would be either bad for, or worse for, the X-people,[4]

and

"worse for people" in the *wide* sense if the choice of X would be less good for the X-people than the choice of Y would be for the Y-people.

In Different Number Choices "less good for" is ambiguous. Call our choice

"worse for people" in the *wide total* sense if the choice of X rather than Y would give to the X-people a smaller total net benefit than the benefit that the choice of Y rather than X would give to the Y-people.

and

"worse for people" in the *wide average* sense if the choice of X rather than Y would give to the X-people a smaller average net benefit per person than the choice of Y rather than X would give to the Y-people.

We can now distinguish three principles of beneficence. All claim that, if other things are equal, it is wrong knowingly to make some choice that would make the outcome worse, and that the outcome would be worse if it would be worse for people. On the *Narrow Principle* "worse for people" has its narrow sense. This principle condemns some choice only if it would be bad for, or worse for, some of the people who would ever live. On the *Wide Total Principle*, "worse for people" has its wide total sense. To apply this principle, we must compare the possible benefits and burdens to all of the different actual and possibly actual people, and choose the act that produces the greatest total *net* benefit—that is, the greatest sum of benefits minus burdens. In the *Wide Average Principle*, we substitute the words "the greatest average net benefit per person."

. . . Suppose that I can do either X or Y, and wish to apply the Wide Total Principle. In deciding which of my acts would benefit people more, I should compare *all* of the benefits and losses that people would later receive *if and only if* I do X rather than Y, and *all* of the benefits and losses that people would later receive *if and only if* I do Y rather than X. The act which benefits people more is the one that, in this comparison, would be followed by the greater *net* sum of benefits—the greater sum of benefits minus losses. . . . [I]t is irrelevant that many other acts will also be necessary causal antecedents for the receiving of these benefits and losses.

On the Wide Total Principle, if other things are equal, the better of two outcomes is the one which is better for the people who would exist by the greatest total amount. On the Wide Average Principle, if other things are equal, the better outcome is the one which is better for the people who would exist by the greatest average amount per person. These claims will be clearer when we give examples. In applying both Principles, we include, among benefits, that of receiving a life worth living. This benefit is greater if this life is more worth living.

In Same People Choices, the two Wide Principles coincide. And both imply our suggested Claim (A): that, if the same number of lives would be lived either way, it would be worse if those who live are worse off than those who would have lived. As we hoped, the Wide Principles explain this claim in a more familiar way. Why should the first 14-Year-Old Girl wait and have a child later? Because having a child now would benefit this child less than having a child later would benefit that other child. There is a similar objection to our choice of Depletion. This choice will benefit those who later live, since their lives will be worth living, and they would not have existed if we had chosen Conservation. But our choice of Depletion benefits these people less than the choice of Conservation would have benefited those who would have later lived. Similar remarks apply to the choice of the Risky Policy. The objectionable choices in our examples would be "worse for people" in the two wide senses.

These claims do not involve the kind of verbal trick that we dismissed earlier. When we discuss the 14-Year-Old Girl, the words "her child" and "he" may not refer to a particular child. They can be used to cover all of the different children whom this girl could have. This provides a sense in which we can truly claim that, if this girl has her child now, that will be worse for him.

I argued that this claim could not explain why this girl ought to wait. This becomes clear after the girl has had her child. We can claim that, in our special sense, her decision was worse for her child. But this is not a claim about this girl's actual child. We must agree that her decision was *not* worse for this child. Since our claim is not about what is worse for any particular person, it does not appeal to any familiar moral principle. It must appeal to a quite new kind of principle, that would need to be explained and justified.

Could the same be said about our suggested Wide Principles? When we call one of two outcomes "worse for people" in the two wide senses, is our claim about what is good or bad for particular people? Yes. In the case of the 14-Year-Old Girl, we claim the following. If this girl has her child now, this would be good for him, but it would be less good for him than having a child later would be for this other child. The Wide Principles *are* about what is good or bad for particular people.

These principles are not wholly familiar. They cannot claim to be our ordinary principle about effects on people's interests—what I called our principle of beneficence. But this is because we are now assuming that, in causing someone to exist, we can thereby benefit this person. Our ordinary principle does not tell us what is the moral importance of such benefits. We need to extend our ordinary principle so that it answers this question. And there are three answers that seem worth considering. These are the answers given by the Narrow Principle and the two Wide Principles. So these are not principles of some new kind, that need to be explained and justified. They state the different ways in which we can plausibly extend our ordinary principle, as we need to do if we assume that causing to exist can benefit.

Since the Wide Principles are extensions of our ordinary principle, they offer a solution to the Non-Identity Problem. They explain Claim (A) in what seems a satisfactory way. But this does not show that either Principle is acceptable. We must consider Different Number Choices. We may be unable to accept what the Wide Principles here imply.

Let us start with the simplest case:

The Happy Child: Some couple cannot decide whether to have another child. They can assume that, if they do, they would love this child, and his life would be well worth living. And they can assume that, if they have this child, this would not predictably be either better or worse either for them or for other people. They have several reasons for wanting another child. But they also have several reasons for not wanting this, such as the interference it would bring to their careers. Like many others, this couple cannot decide between these two sets of conflicting reasons.

If causing to exist can benefit, having this child would benefit him. Suppose that, as predicted, the existence of this child would not be worse for anyone else. Choosing *not* to have this child would then be "worse for people" in both of the wide senses. Not having the child would give to people *no* net benefit. Since having the child would give him a benefit, it would give to those who would exist both a greater total benefit, and a greater average benefit per person. Both Wide Principles imply that, if other things are equal, this couple ought to have this child.

Can we assume that other things are equal? For this to be so, it must first be true that none of our other moral principles applies to this case. It seems that we can assume this. It must next be true that other things are equal according to our principle of beneficence. We can distinguish here four possibilities. Other things would be equal in the strongest sense if it was true that, whether or not this couple have the extra child, these alternatives would be *equally good* both for them and for everyone else. While this might be true of many choices, it is most unlikely here. What is more likely is that, of the couple's two choices, *neither would be worse than the other* both for them and for everyone else. This is a different possibility if there is only partial comparability, since *not worse than* does not then imply *at least as good as*. Two further possibilities are that neither alternative would be *predictably* worse for the couple and for other people, and that the couple *cannot decide* between their conflicting reasons.

What we would be justified in claiming depends on which of the above is true. Consider

> *The Doctor.* Some doctor can work in either England or India. When she thinks only of herself, she has reasons for choosing England, and reasons for choosing India. She cannot decide between these conflicting reasons. And neither choice would be predictably worse for herself. She also knows that, if she works in India, she could save more lives.

That she could save more lives gives this doctor a moral reason to choose India. Other things are, in a weak sense, equal. We can claim that, if she cannot decide between her other conflicting reasons, she ought to be swayed by this moral reason. She ought to choose India. But suppose that she chooses England. Is she open to moral criticism? It would not be clear that she is. She may have now decided, for example, that going to India *would* be worse for her. If that is so, her choice of England might be morally permissible. She has no duty to save extra lives if this would require from her too great a sacrifice. It would be different if her two alternatives would be *equally good* for her. Suppose that she could prescribe either of two drugs, one of which would save more lives. We could here be confident that, since other things are equal in the strongest sense, she ought do what would save more lives.

Return now to the Case of the Happy Child. Here too, other things are equal only in the weaker senses that the couple cannot decide whether to have this extra child, and that neither choice would be predictably worse either for them or for other people. If the couple do decide not to have the child, it would not be clear that they are open to moral criticism. They may have now decided that they prefer not to have this child, or that doing so would be worse for them. But there is a different question to which our answer can be clear. That our Doctor could save more lives gave her a moral reason to choose India. Do our couple have a moral reason to have the extra child? On the Wide Principles, they do. Since this child's life would be well worth living, having this child would give him a great benefit. If the couple cannot decide between their other conflicting reasons, they ought to be swayed by this moral reason. If other things are equal, they ought to have this child.

Can we accept this conclusion? If we can, we do not yet have grounds for resisting the Wide Principles. But there is another common view. On this view, the case is not like that of the Doctor. The fact that she could save more lives is a moral reason. But the fact that a child would have a good life is no moral reason to have this child. It is no reason even if everything else is equal.

If we accept this common view, we must reject the Wide Principles. We shall then lose their solution to the Non-Identity Problem. But this may still be what we ought to do. The Non-Identity Problem may have a different solution.

To help us choose between these alternatives, let us turn to cases on a larger scale.

Overpopulation

Let us consider various possible futures for one country, or mankind. I shall continue to talk of the quality of life. As before, we could think instead either of the level of happiness, or of the share per person of resources. We can assume that, in our examples, these three would correlate. Our arguments would thus apply whichever we take to be most important. I shall also use a new abbreviation. Lives that are worth living I shall call *worthwhile*.

Different outcomes may be represented [as in Figure 2].

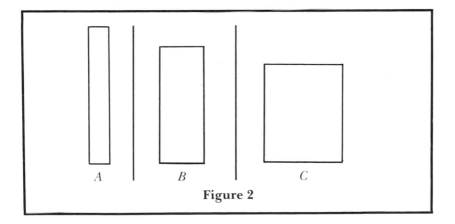

Figure 2

The width of each block shows the number of people living, the height shows their quality of life. I assume, for simplicity, that in these different outcomes there is neither social nor natural inequality. In each outcome no one is worse off than anyone else. And no one would exist in more than one outcome.

In *B* there are twice as many people living as in *A*, and these people are all worse off than everyone in *A*. But the lives of those in *B*, compared with those in *A*, are *more than half as much* worth living. This claim need not assume precision. There may be only rough or partial

comparability. What the claim assumes is that a move from the level in
A to that in B would be a decline in the quality of life, but that it would
take much more than a similarly great decline before people's lives
ceased to be worth living. There are various ways in which, with twice
the population, the quality of life might be lower. There might be
worse housing, more pollution, less natural beauty, and a somewhat
lower average income. If these are the ways in which the quality of life
would be lower, we could plausibly assume that it would take much
more than another similar decline before life ceased to be worth
living.

If we compare A and B, which would be the better outcome? We
can first explain the kind of question we are asking. We are not asking
which outcome would be *morally better*. X can be morally better than Y
only if both are persons, or acts. But one of two outcomes can be better in a sense that has moral relevance. It would be better, in this
sense, if fewer people suffer from some crippling illness. And we can
clearly make such claims about the kinds of outcome we are now considering, involving different possible populations. Suppose that, in
both of two outcomes, there would exist the same number of people.
In one of these outcomes, all of the people would be much worse off.
This would clearly be the worse outcome.

Return now to A and B. Which outcome would be better? It is
clearly bad that, in B, people are worse off. But could this be morally
outweighed by the fact that there would be more people living? Could
the loss in the quality of life be made up for by the gain in the quantity
of worthwhile life lived? As I have said, this is the central question
raised by Different Number Choices.

If B comes about rather than A, this would be "better for people" in
the wide total sense. B would be less good for *each* of the B-people
than A would be for each A-person. But since each B-person would
benefit more than half as much as each A-person, and there are twice
as many B-people, they *together* would benefit more, or would receive
a greater total benefit. In the same sense, if we give one loaf to each of
two hungry people, they together would benefit more than one of
them would benefit if we give him two loaves. The Wide Total Principle thus implies that, if other things are equal, B would be better
than A. By the same reasoning, C would be better than B.

Can we accept these conclusions? Many people would believe that B
would be worse than A, and that C would be even worse. This belief
can be supported by two quite different views.

Some might claim that B would be worse than A because it does not
contain *enough* extra people. On this view, the lower quality of life
could be made up for by the increase in the number of worthwhile
lives lived. But the value of extra numbers is less than that claimed by
the Wide Total Principle. Given the two levels in A and B, A would be
the better outcome if B would have only twice as many people. But B

would be the better outcome if it had some larger number of extra people.

Though this view disagrees with the Wide Total Principle, it is very similar. According to both, a lower quality of life could be made up for by a sufficient increase in the quantity of worthwhile life lived. The difference is only in the relative values assigned to quality and quantity. We can ignore this minor difference.

There is a quite different view which implies that B would be worse than A. On this view, B would be worse than A however many more people it contained. If people are worse off, or have a lower quality of life, this cannot be morally outweighed by the fact that there are more people living. Call this the View *that Only Quality Matters*.

There are two versions of this view. Suppose that the number who ever live had been very small. In one imaginary history, Eve and Adam have lives that are very well worth living, but they have no children. They are the only people who ever live. In a different possible history, millions of people have lives that are well worth living, but none have lives that are quite as good as those that Eve and Adam would have had. In this second possible history, the quality of life is somewhat lower, but the quantity of worthwhile life lived is far greater.

Some would claim that, even here, only quality matters. The first imagined history would have been better. This is the pure version of this view. A qualified version claims the following. If the number who ever live would be very small, it would not be true that only quality matters. There would be some value in the existence of extra people who have lives worth living. When the numbers are small, lower quality can be outweighed by greater quantity. The second imagined history would have been better. But, as the numbers grow, the value in extra numbers steadily declines, and reaches zero. Thus it may have reached zero if the number is several billion. If A is a world with several billion people, B would be worse however many extra people it contained.

Some find it hard to decide between these versions of this view. Because it is simpler, the pure version is theoretically more appealing. But many find it harder to believe. The qualified version might be thought to be an indefensible compromise. It might be objected that, if there is *ever* value in extra numbers, there must *always* be value in extra numbers. But this objection may in turn be too simple. It seems a possible alternative that the value in extra numbers does steadily decline, and reach zero. We accept similar claims in other areas. I shall therefore assume that we cannot simply dismiss the qualified version of this view.

The two versions agree in cases which involve large numbers. And these are the cases which, in the 20th and later centuries, will be of practical importance. With few exceptions, these are the cases that I shall consider. We should thus assume that, in the outcome *A* described above, there would be several billion people living. Since the two versions agree in such cases, I shall cease to mention the qualification in the second version. I shall call both versions the View that Only Quality Matters.

If we accept this view, we believe that *B* would be worse than *A*. We must therefore resist the Wide Total Principle, which implies the opposite.

Does this example provide a fair test for our principles and intuitions? I believe that it does. *A* and *B* are acceptable simplifications of what would in practice be real alternatives. In any possible future there would in fact be some inequality between different people. But it cannot distort our reasoning, on the central question I have raised, if we imagine the simpler case where this would not be so. *A* and *B* then represent two possible futures, for some country or for mankind, given two slightly different rates of population growth over some period like a century. On the Wide Total Principle, *B* would be better than *A*. If we cannot believe this, the principle conflicts with our beliefs in a wholly practical example.

It is worth pausing to describe one particular version of the example. The following can be true, in some country during some period. If the population grows at a certain rate, this will have transitory good effects, and cumulative bad effects. The bad effects might be the steady decline in the share per person of the available resources. The transitory good effects might be on the working of this country's economy. While rapid population growth may be bad for the economy, a slow rate of growth may be better for the economy than no growth at all. There are various technical reasons why, for certain economic systems, this can be true. A remote analogy is the fact that, when we are driving round a bend, we can steer more easily if we accelerate. And population growth may have other, non-economic, transitory good effects. These might simply be that larger families tend to be somewhat happier.

If some rate of population growth would have these two kinds of effect, what would be ideal would be "a population which is always growing, but never getting any bigger."[5] We could attain this ideal only in Alice's Wonderland. In the actual world, the alternatives can be shown [as in Figure 3].

Call this *the Down Escalator Case*. The horizontal line shows the quality of life that would result from keeping a stable population. This can be called *Replacement*. The line of dashes shows the cumulative bad effects of this rate of population growth. This is what would happen to the quality of life if there were no transitory good effects. The sloping line shows the combined effects of this rate of growth. This is what would actually happen to the quality of life, given that there would be transitory good effects.

As the diagram shows, if there is Growth rather than Replacement,

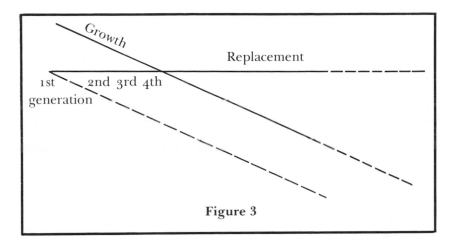

Figure 3

the quality of life would be higher for the first three generations, but would afterwards be increasingly lower. For those who believe that only quality matters, the Down Escalator Case is especially depressing. It seems likely that the actual outcome would be Growth. It seems likely that enough particular couples would prefer to have more than two children. And since Growth would be better for existing people and for the next two generations, it does not seem likely that the community would decide on some policy that would cause a change from Growth to Replacement.

Someone might say: "This is not so. The best policy would be Growth for the first three generations, followed by Replacement. The community should switch to Replacement once Growth begins to produce a lower quality of life. At this point Growth ceases to be better for the existing people. Since this is so, we can expect the community to switch to Replacement."

This is a mistake. If there has been Growth for the first three generations, why is the quality of life still as high as it would have been if there had been Replacement? It is as high as this only because of the transitory good effects of Growth. If the fourth generation switches to Replacement, it would lose these good effects. Its quality of life would drop to the point vertically below on the line of dashes. The diagram therefore shows the alternatives for *every* generation. These will remain the alternatives as long as Growth would have these two effects: the cumulative bad effects and the transitory good effects. While this is true, Growth would always be better than Replacement for existing people and for the next two generations. We can therefore expect that every generation will choose Growth. As a result, the quality of life will continue to decline. If we believe that only quality matters, the Down Escalator Case *is*, as I claimed, especially depressing.

It is worth remarking that this Case is an intertemporal Each-We

Dilemma with two . . . special features. . . . Since it involves different generations, the people involved cannot communicate to reach some kind of political solution, or some joint conditional agreement. And this is a Dilemma of the especially intractable kind *that includes outsiders*.

[Consider] *the Auditorium Dilemma*. If the First Row stands, it will improve its view of the engrossing spectacle on stage. If it is worth standing to get this better view, it would be better for the First Row if it stands. But this would block the Second Row's view. This Row would need to stand to regain the view that it had when all were sitting. Since it would now be standing, but would not have improved its view, this outcome would be worse for the Second Row. Similar remarks apply to all the other Rows.

This case differs from an ordinary Each-We Dilemma. There are two acts: *A* (altruistic) and *S* (self-benefiting). In an ordinary Dilemma, it would be better for each if he does *S*, whatever others do, but if all do *S* that would be worse for each than if all do *A*. In the Auditorium Dilemma, there is a small but fateful difference. It would be better for each Row if it stands rather than sits, but if all stand rather than sit that would *not* be worse for *all* of the Rows. It would be worse for all Rows *except the First*. The First Row is *the Outsider* in this Dilemma.

Because they contain Outsiders, such Dilemmas are especially intractable. The pattern of acts that is worse for everyone else is better for the Outsiders. It would thus be worse for the Outsiders if they helped to bring about a political solution, or joined a conditional agreement. And what the Outsiders do may start a vicious chain-reaction, which makes it worse for everyone to join such an agreement. Thus, in the Auditorium Dilemma, it would be worse for the First Row if all sit rather than stand. It would therefore be worse for this Row if it joins an agreement that all should sit. It may therefore stand. Once the First Row is standing, it would be worse for the Second Row if it joins an agreement that all except the First Row should sit. It may therefore stand. It would then be worse for the Third Row to join an agreement that all except the First Two Rows should sit. It may therefore stand. Similar remarks apply to every Row. The end result may be that all Rows stand rather than sit. This is worse for every Row except the First. The presence of the First Row, the Outsider, here prevents the achievement of the joint conditional agreement. And the same chain reaction may prevent the achievement of a political solution. This special feature makes such Dilemmas less likely to be solved.

Besides being trivial, the Auditorium Dilemma does not have the other depressing feature. It involves contemporaries. This makes it more likely to be solved. The other Rows might use threats to keep the First Row sitting. Or the First Row might sit merely because it expected complaints from the other Rows.

An intergenerational Dilemma does *not* involve contemporaries. This makes it harder to solve. The different generations cannot communicate, and reach a joint conditional agreement. Nor can earlier generations be deterred by threats from later generations. It is therefore a greater problem that this Dilemma contains Outsiders. In an intergenerational Dilemma, which need not involve population growth, the existing generation is always in the position of some Row where the earlier Rows have stood. It has already suffered from the behavior of the earlier generations. And this earlier behavior cannot now be altered by any political or moral solution. Since this is so, it would be worse for the existing generation if it plays its part in such a solution. It would lose from its own act, and it could not gain anything in return. It is thus less likely to play its part in a solution. The same reasoning will then apply to the next, and all succeeding generations.

For those who believe that only quality matters, these facts make the Down Escalator Case even more depressing. Fortunately, this is only one of the possible cases. It may be true for communities with certain economic systems, or for some of the communities where many couples want to have more than two children. But there are other communities where the facts would be different.

. . . [T]here are some communities which face a simpler Each-We Dilemma. In these communities, it would be better for each of many couples if they have more than two children, whatever other couples do. But if all have more than two children that would be worse for each than if none do. If we believe that only quality matters, we could here have more hope that this Dilemma will be solved. This is because it involves contemporaries, not successive generations, and it does not contain Outsiders. Though each of these many couples would prefer to have more children, each may also prefer that none have more children rather than that all do. A system of rewards or penalties, aimed at stopping population growth, may here be democratically adopted.

There are also communities where it would be worse for most couples if they themselves have more than two children. There would here be no Dilemma. And it would here be likely that the population will not grow.

We have described three kinds of case. In all three, population growth would lower the quality of life. In the Down Escalator Case, it would be worse for all except the first *n* generations if the population always grows. But, within each generation, including those *after* the *n*th, it would be *better* for all if the population grows. For those who believe that only quality matters, this is the especially depressing case. It is a Dilemma that is both intergenerational and includes Outsiders. These two features make it much less likely to be solved. In our second kind of case, it would be better for each if he or she has more children, whatever others do, but if all have more children that would be worse for each than if none do. This is an ordinary Each-We

Dilemma, and is thus more likely to be solved. In our third case, it would be worse for each if he or she has more children. There is here no Dilemma. Besides these three, there are many other possible cases. Some would be mixtures of these three; but others would be different in other ways.

The Repugnant Conclusion

Consider now a larger diagram [Figure 4].

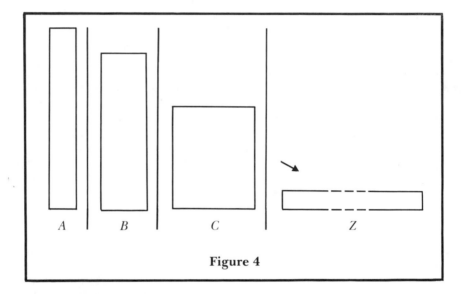

Figure 4

I have claimed that A and B are acceptable simplifications of what would in practice be real alternatives. They could be the outcomes, after some period, of two different rates of population growth. We have been discussing different versions of this common case.

As we saw, the Wide Total Principle implies that B would be better than A. The coming-about of B would be less good for each B-person. But since there are twice as many B-people, they together would benefit more.

By the same reasoning, Z could be best. Z is some enormous population whose members have lives that are not much above the level where life is not worth living. A life could be like this either because it has enough ecstasies to make its agonies seem just worth enduring, or because it is uniformly of poor quality. Let us imagine the lives in Z to be of the second drabber kind. If Z comes about, each of the Z-people would thereby benefit very little. But, if Z is large enough, they together would benefit the most. The Wide Total Principle thus implies

The Repugnant Conclusion: For any possible and large population, say of eight billion, all with a very high quality of life, there must be some much larger imaginable population whose existence, if other things are equal, would be better, and be what we ought to bring about, even though its members have lives that are barely worth living.

As my choice of name implies, I find this conclusion hard to believe.

A and *B* could in practice be real alternatives. But this would not be true of *A* and *Z*. Some claim that, because of this, we need not try to avoid the Repugnant Conclusion. They might say: "Since this conclusion does not apply to any possible choice, it can be ignored. We need not test our principles in cases that that could not occur."

We have distinguished two kinds of impossibility. Call these *deep* and *technical*. An imagined case is deeply impossible if it requires a major change in the laws of nature, including the laws of human nature. There are two grounds for challenging cases that are deeply impossible. We may be unable to imagine what such cases would involve. And some would claim that our moral principles need to be acceptable only in the real world.[6]

It may help to remember here Nozick's imagined *Utility Monsters*. These are people who get "enormously greater gains in utility from any sacrifice of others than these others lose."[7] Such an imagined person provides an objection to act utilitarianism, which "seems to require that we all be sacrificed in the monster's maw, in order to increase total utility."

As described by Nozick, such a person is a deep impossibility. The world's population is now several billion. Let us imagine the wretchedness of all these people if they are denied anything above starvation rations, and all other resources go to Nozick's imagined person. Nozick tells us to suppose that this one person would be *so* happy, or have a life of *such* high quality, that this is the distribution that yields the greatest sum of happiness, or its equivalent in terms of worthwhile life lived. For this to be so, given the billions left in wretchedness that could be so easily relieved by a small fraction of this one person's vast resources, this person's quality of life must, it seems, be *millions* of times as high as that of anyone we know. Can we imagine this? Think of the life of the most fortunate person you know, and ask what a life would have to be like in order to be a million times as much worth living. The qualitative gap between such a life and ours, at its best, must resemble the gap between ours, at its best, and the life of those creatures who are barely conscious—such as, if they *are* conscious, Plato's "contented oysters."[8] It seems a fair reply that we cannot imagine, even in the dimmest way, the life of this Utility Monster. And this casts doubt on the force of the example. Act Utilitarians might say that, if we really could imagine what such a life would be like, we might not find Nozick's objection persuasive. His "Monster" seems to be a god-like being. In the imagined presence of such a being, our belief in our right to equality with him may begin to waver—just as we do not believe that the lower animals have rights to equality with us.

This reply has some force. But even a deep impossibility may provide a partial test for our moral principles. We cannot simply ignore imagined cases.

Let us now return to my imagined Z. This imagined population is another Utility Monster. The difference is that the greater sum of happiness comes from a vast increase, not in the quality of one person's life, but in the number of lives lived. And *my* Utility Monster is neither deeply impossible, nor something that we cannot imagine. We can imagine what it would be for someone's life to be barely worth living. And we can imagine what it would be for there to be many people with such lives. In order to imagine Z, we merely have to imagine that there would be *very* many. This we can do. So the example cannot be questioned as one that we can hardly understand.

We could not in practice face a choice between A and Z. Given some roughly finite stock of resources, we could not in fact produce the greatest sum of happiness, or its equivalent in terms of worthwhile life lived, by producing an enormous population whose lives are barely worth living.[9] But this would be merely technically impossible. In order to suppose it possible, we only need to add some assumptions about the nature and availability of resources. Since it would be merely technically impossible to face a choice between A and Z, this does not weaken the comparison as a test for our principles. Different Number Choices raise the question whether loss in the quality of life could be made up for by a sufficient gain in its quantity. This is the question posed most clearly by comparing A and Z. If we are convinced that Z is worse than A, we have strong grounds for resisting principles which imply that Z is better. So we have strong grounds for resisting the Wide Total Principle.

A defender of the Principle might now say: "This is not so. The Principle includes the phrase *if other things are equal.* And other things never would be equal. We can therefore ignore the Repugnant Conclusion."

This is a weak defense. What other moral principle must be infringed by the coming-about of Z? It might be claimed that this would infringe some principle about justice between generations. But this is irrelevant to our question in its purest form. We are asking whether, if Z comes about, this would be better than if A comes about. We could imagine a history in which only Z-like outcomes occur. The people in Z would then be no worse off than anyone who ever lives. If we believe that Z would be worse than A, this would not here be because Z's occurrence would involve injustice.

If we wish to avoid the Repugnant Conclusion, we should not try to do so by appealing to principles covering some different part of morality. This conclusion seems *intrinsically* repugnant. It is an answer to the central question raised by Different Number Choices: whether, if the quality of life is lower, this can be morally outweighed by its greater quantity. On the Wide Total Principle, the answer is Yes. This Principle implies that, provided that lives remain worth living, any loss in the quality of life could be made up for by a sufficient gain in its quantity. If we cannot accept the Repugnant Conclusion, this is what we must deny. We take a different view, in Different Number Choices, about the part of morality that is concerned with people's interests, or with human well-being. We must resist the Wide Total Principle. We must try to show that, even when it is put forward merely as part of a pluralist morality, this principle gives the wrong account of beneficence.

An obvious move is to appeal instead to the Wide Average Principle. (. . . this is quite different from what is sometimes called the "Utilitarian Average Principle.") If what comes about is Z rather than A, this would be "worse for people" in the wide average sense. Causing Z rather than A would give to the Z-people a smaller average benefit per person than causing A rather than Z would give to the A-people. But this does not solve our problem. The Wide Average Principle does not *directly* imply the Repugnant Conclusion. But it can do so indirectly.

Suppose that we have brought about A. We might now face a new choice. Suppose that in a short time we could change A into B. It might be "better for people" in the wide average sense if we made this change. This would involve adding to the existing population as many new people. And the previously existing half would suffer a decline in their quality of life. So this change would be worse for them. But the change would bring a greater benefit to the newly existing people. Changing from A to B would therefore give to the B-people an average net benefit per person. And it might give them a greater average benefit per person than keeping A rather than changing to B would give to the A-people.[10] The Wide Average Principle would then imply that, if other things are equal, we ought to move from A to B. By similar reasoning, we ought then to move from B to C, and ought then to move from C to D. Z is the population that, in the end, we ought to bring about. The Wide Average Principle could thus indirectly imply one part of the Repugnant Conclusion. We turned from the Total to the Average Principle hoping to avoid this conclusion. We have found that, if we are to do so, we must reject both the Wide Principles.

Let us now review the argument so far. In [Part I] we described what we called the Non-Identity Problem. There seemed to be moral objections to our choice of the Risky Policy, or of Depletion, or to a decision to have a disadvantaged child when by merely waiting one could have a child free from this burden. The problem was to explain these objections, given our knowledge that these choices would be worse for no one.

In this [Part] we first defended one belief that might help to explain these objections. This is the belief that, in causing someone to exist, we can thereby benefit this person. I claimed that this belief is not obviously mistaken. Though controversial, it may form part of an acceptable solution.

We then saw that, if we accept this belief, we have a choice between three versions of the Principle of Beneficence. We had one ground for choosing one of the two Wide Principles. Only these offered a solution to the Non-Identity Problem. But this did not show that we should accept one of these principles. Both may be unacceptable when applied to Different Number Choices.

In asking whether this is so, we began with the simplest case, that of the Happy Child. If we believe that causing to exist can benefit, and accept either Wide Principle, we must agree that our couple have a moral reason to have this child. If other things are equal, this is what they ought to do. If we could accept this conclusion, we did not yet have grounds for resisting the Wide Principles.

We have now turned to another range of cases, that of the possible states of the world from A to Z. Even if we agreed that our couple have a moral reason to have the Happy Child, we may be unable to believe that B would be better than A, or that we ought to change A into B. But this is what the Wide Principles here imply. And we may find it even harder to accept their other implication, the Repugnant Conclusion. I shall assume that most of us would wish to avoid this Conclusion.

If we are to do so, we must reject both Wide Principles. This is done by those who, in the Case of the Happy Child, claim that our couple have no moral reason to have this child. We now have stronger motives to explore this common view. We can first ask whether it survives a well-known test.

The Asymmetry

Consider

> *The Wretched Child.* Some woman knows that, if she has a child, he will be so multiply diseased that his life will be worse than nothing. He will never develop, will live for only a few years, and will suffer pain that cannot be relieved.

It seems clear that it would be wrong knowingly to conceive such a child. Nor would the wrongness primarily lie in the effects on others. The wrongness would primarily lie in the predictably appalling quality of this child's life.

Suppose that we accept the common view that our couple have no moral reason to have the Happy Child. We now believe that it would be wrong knowingly to have the Wretched Child. We thus believe that it would be wrong to have a child whose life would be worth *not* living, but that, even if other things are equal, it would be in no way wrong *not* to have a child whose life would be worth living. These two claims have been called *the Asymmetry*.[11]

How can we explain this Asymmetry? We might deny that causing someone to exist can be either good or bad for this person. But this could explain only half the Asymmetry: why our couple have no moral reason to have the Happy Child. It would imply that, in having the Wretched Child, his parents cannot be doing something that is bad for him. So what should our objection here be? If having this child cannot be bad for him, our primary objection must, it seems, appeal directly to his unrelieved suffering. We must appeal to

> *The Impersonal Suffering Principle*: Other things being equal, we ought not to increase the sum of suffering.

It may be hard to accept this principle but reject

> *The Impersonal Happiness Principle*: Other things being equal, we ought to increase the net sum of happiness.

But if we accept this last principle we still cannot explain the Asymmetry. This principle implies that our couple have a moral reason to have the Happy Child. Even if having this child cannot be good for him, it would increase the sum of happiness.

It may be objected that suffering and happiness are morally dissimilar. Our moral reasons to prevent the former far outweigh our moral reasons to promote the latter. But this cannot explain the Asymmetry unless we have *no* moral reason to promote happiness. And, if we have accepted the Impersonal Suffering Principle, it seems implausible to reject entirely its analogue for happiness.[12]

If we are to defend the Asymmetry, we must reject both Impersonal Principles. We might claim that they take the wrong form, treating people as the mere *containers* of value. Here is a passage in which this feature is especially clear. In his book *The Economy of Happiness*, James Mackay writes:

> Just as an Engineer requires boilers to convert steam into energy, so Justice requires sentient beings to convert the potentiality of happiness in any given land area into actual happiness. And just as the Engineer will choose boilers with the maximum efficiency at converting steam into energy, Justice will choose sentient beings who have the maximum efficiency at converting resources into happiness.

This *Milk Production Model* may be held to be a grotesque distortion of this part of morality. We may thus appeal to

> *The Person-affecting Restriction*: This part of morality, the part concerned with human well-being, should be explained entirely in terms of what is good or bad for those people whom our acts affect.

This is the view advanced by Narveson.[13] As he writes, people are not good because their lives contain happiness. Rather, happiness is good because it is good for people. There are two ways of increasing the sum of happiness. We can make people happier, or make happy people. Only the first is good for people. Since this part of morality only concerns what is good or bad for people, the second way of increasing happiness is morally neutral.

Narveson assumes that causing to exist cannot benefit. Having the Happy Child cannot be good for this child. If we assume this, and appeal to the Person-affecting Restriction, we can revive our claim that our couple have no moral reason to have the Happy Child. But this undermines the other half of the Asymmetry. We must admit that having the Wretched Child cannot be bad for him, and the Person-affecting Restriction disallows any appeal to the Impersonal Suffering Principle. We therefore cannot explain why it would be wrong knowingly to conceive the Wretched Child. More exactly, we cannot explain the primary wrongness, which lies in the appalling quality of this child's life.

If we deny that causing someone to exist can be either good or bad for this person, the Asymmetry seems hard to explain. We might appeal to the rights of the Wretched Child. We might claim that, though it is not bad for this child that we caused him to exist, we did violate his right to a life worth living. We would here be claiming that it would be wrong to do what violates someone's right, even though this right could not have been fulfilled, and we know that what we are doing will not be bad for this person. Perhaps this claim is acceptable.

There is a simpler alternative. We could (i) claim that causing someone to exist can be either good or bad for him, (ii) retain the Person-affecting Restriction, and (iii) appeal to the Narrow Principle. The Asymmetry can now be fully explained. According to the Narrow Principle it is wrong, if other things are equal, to do what would be either bad for, or worse for, the people who ever live. It is therefore wrong to have the Wretched Child. Since his life would be worse than nothing, having this child would be bad for him. But it is in no way wrong to fail to have the Happy Child, whose life would be well worth living. It is true that, if the couple have this child, this would be good for him. But if they do not have this child, this would not be bad for him. And, in the case described, it would not be bad for anyone else. This is why they have no moral reason to have this child.

This seems the best explanation of the Asymmetry. We should note that the Narrow Principle does not involve the familiar claim that our obligation not to harm is stronger than our obligation to benefit. We may wish to add this claim to the Narrow Principle of Beneficence—to add, as Ross did, some stronger principle about Non-Maleficence.[14] But the Narrow Principle makes no such distinction. If there will be someone to whom we have failed to give some benefit, our failure to do so will be worse for this person. If other things are equal, we have acted wrongly according to the Narrow Principle.

We should also note that the distinction between the Wide and Narrow Principles is not the same as that between principles which do and do not appeal only to effects on those who ever live. Suppose that we refrain from conceiving the Wretched Child. We have acted rightly, according to the Narrow Principle. This is because, if we had conceived the Wretched Child, this would have been bad for him. In explaining why we acted rightly, we appeal to a possible effect on someone who might have lived. (But, as we said, the effect would not have been on someone who *remained* merely possible. We never appeal to such effects. The effect would have been on an actual person.)

The distinction between the Wide and Narrow Principles is not, then, reducible to these other more familiar distinctions. It is a new distinction, opened up by the belief that, in causing someone to exist, we can thereby benefit this person. This belief breaks the ordinary entailment that, if some event would be good for people, this event's non-occurrence would be worse for people. With this entailment broken, the Wide and Narrow Principles diverge.

Why We Must Abandon the Person-Affecting Restriction

Let us again review the argument so far. Many people believe that, even if some extra child would be happy, this is no moral reason to have this child. When we considered population size, we were drawn to a similar view. Most of us would wish to avoid the Repugnant Conclusion, and, though perhaps less urgently, the claim that *B* is better than *A*. The simplest way to do this is to appeal, on a larger scale, to this common view about the Case of the Happy Child. On this view there is no moral reason, even if other things are equal, to cause extra people to exist who will have lives worth living.

There were two ways to defend this common view in the Case of the Happy Child. Both appealed to the Person-affecting Restriction. We could then either reject the belief that causing to exist can benefit, or instead accept this belief but appeal to the Narrow rather than either of the Wide Principles. Of these defenses of this view, the first cannot handle the Case of the Wretched Child. But the second defense covers this case. It therefore seemed the better explanation of the Asymmetry.

We may seem to have made progress. But we have not. On both of these defenses we cannot solve the Non-Identity Problem. If we believe that causing to exist can benefit, and appeal to either of the Wide Principles, we do solve that Problem. As we saw, both these Principles explain the objection to the choices we described in [Part I]. The objection is that these choices are in the two wide senses "worse for people." Though these choices benefit those who later live, they benefit these people less than the alternatives would have benefited those who would have later lived. Such claims provided a full solution to the Non-Identity Problem. But we cannot make such claims if we now either deny that causing to exist can benefit, or appeal to the Narrow Principle.

Can we solve the Non-Identity Problem in a different way? Not if we continue to appeal to the Person-affecting Restriction. If we appeal to this Restriction, we believe that the part of morality concerned with well-being should be explained entirely in terms of what would be good or bad for those people whom our acts affect. We cannot then criticize the choices we described except with the claim that, in one of the wide senses, they are worse for people. It is therefore clear that, if we both appeal to the Person-affecting Restriction and reject the Wide Principles, we cannot solve the Non-Identity Problem.

We need to solve that problem. And we want a solution which avoids the Repugnant Conclusion. Since the Wide Principles imply this Conclusion, we must continue to reject these Principles. We must therefore abandon the Person-affecting Restriction. In learning this, we have made progress of a negative kind. We have learned the following. Unless we ought to accept the Repugnant Conclusion, this part of morality cannot be explained in terms of what would be good or bad for those people whom our acts affect.

We may have a second ground for reaching this conclusion. We may not believe that, in causing someone to exist, we can thereby benefit this person. I argued that this belief was not obviously mistaken. But my arguments did not show more than this. After considering the arguments, we may still reject this belief. If we do, it is again clear that, to solve the Non-Identity Problem, we must abandon the Person-affecting Restriction. If causing to exist cannot benefit, there can be no sense in which the objectionable choices in our examples would be worse for people. The Person-affecting Restriction then implies that there is no moral objection to these choices. Though we know that these choices may cause a catastrophe, killing and injuring thousands of people, or may greatly lower the quality of life, we have no moral reason not to make these choices. I assume that this conclusion is unacceptable. If we believe that causing to exist cannot benefit, we can avoid this conclusion only by abandoning the Person-affecting Restriction. We must appeal to principles which are about well-being, or the quality of life, but are not just about what is good or bad for those people whom our acts affect.

Since we have abandoned the Person-affecting Restriction, we must reconsider the two Impersonal Principles given above. We cannot now reject these Principles because they are not about what is good or bad for people. We have learned that these are the kind of principles to which we must appeal.

On both of the Impersonal Principles, it is wrong, if other things are equal, to make the outcome worse. On the Impersonal Suffering Principle, the outcome would be worse if it would involve a greater sum of suffering. On the Impersonal Happiness Principle, the outcome would be worse if it would involve a smaller net sum of happiness—a smaller sum of happiness minus suffering. The second of these principles implies the first, and is the hedonistic form of *the Impersonal Total Principle of Beneficence*.

This principle offers a second solution to the Non-Identity Problem, since it provides objections to the choices we described. But it clearly implies that *B* would be better than *A*, and that *Z* might be best. A greater total net sum of happiness might be found in a vast population, whose lives are barely worth living, just as a greater mass of milk might be found in a vast heap of bottles, each containing only a single drop.

Since it implies the Repugnant Conclusion, most of us would wish to reject the Impersonal Total Principle, whether it is phrased in terms of happiness or in terms of the quality of life. But, if we are not appealing to the Person-affecting Restriction, it becomes unclear on what grounds we should criticize this principle, except that we reject what it implies.

NOTES

[These selections are taken from a draft of a book tentatively entitled *Reasons and Persons*, to be published by Oxford University Press in 1984, and may not correspond exactly to the finished version. I am grateful to Mr. Parfit for permission to use this material. Responsibility for the choice of extracts is my own—Ed.]

This is an early rough draft, and fails to contain the references that would be expected to other people's published work. I shall work these references into the final draft, and add discussions of the relevant arguments. I expect that re-reading other people's discussions will lead me to make many revisions. This draft contains material from my article ["Future Generations: Further Problems"] in *Philosophy & Public Affairs* (Spring 1982), but with extra points inserted, and some new material. I would be very grateful for any comments, of any kind.

1 Reference to the Commission's Report.

2 This is not true on the ordinary use of the word "benefit." But . . . it is true on the use that has moral significance.

3 I owe this suggestion to Jefferson McMahan.

4 To avoid possible contradictions, we must add, "and by more than the amount, if any, by which the choice of *Y* rather than *X* would be either bad for, or worse for, the *Y*-people."

5 Sir Dennis Holmes Robertson, *Lectures on Economic Principles* (London, 1957), 460.

6 See, for example, R.M. Hare's discussion of the different levels of moral reasoning in his "Ethical Theory and Utilitarianism," in H.D. Lewis, ed., *Contemporary British Philosophy* (London, 1976), and his *Moral Thinking* (Oxford, 1982).

7 Robert Nozick, *Anarchy, State, and Utopia* (New York, 1974), 41.

8 *The Philebus* 21 c-d.

9 On some versions of the *Law of Diminishing Marginal Utility*, this is just what is implied. On these versions, each unit of resources produces more utility if it is given to the people who are worse off, so that the most productive distribution will be the one

where everyone's life is barely worth living. There is here an obvious oversight. Large amounts of resources are needed to make each person's life even reach the level where life begins to be worth living. Such resources do not help to produce the greatest causally possible net sum of utility, when they are merely used to prevent *extra* people having lives that are worth *not* living (or have net disutility).

10 To make the point more clearly, let us allow ourselves to assume precision. Let the level in A be 100, and the level in B 80. In the change from A to B, the previously existing half each lose 20, and the newly existing half each gain 80. So the change from A to B gives the B-people an average net benefit per person of 80-20/2, or 30. Keeping A rather than changing to B would give to the each of the A-people a benefit of 20. So changing from A to B would give to the B-people a greater average benefit per person than not changing from A to B would give to the A-people. . . .

11 By Jefferson McMahan, in his "Problems of Population Theory," a Critical Notice of [R.I. Sikora and Brian Barry, eds.] *Obligations to Future Generations* [Philadelphia, 1978] in *Ethics*, October 1981. This Critical Notice discusses many of the questions that I discuss here. In writing these two discussions we are greatly indebted to each other.

12 See, for example, James Griffin's "Is Unhappiness Morally More Important Than Happiness?", *Philosophical Quarterly* 29 (January 1979).

13 In his pioneering "Utilitarianism and New Generations," *Mind* 76 (January 1967), to which much of the recent debate owes its existence. See also Narveson's "Moral Problems of Population," *The Monist* 57, no. 1 (1973).

14 Sir David Ross, *The Right and The Good* (Oxford, 1930), 21.

Selected Readings

The books and journals from which the selections in this anthology were taken are listed on the acknowledgements page. Many of these include other chapters or articles of interest.

GENERAL

Nagel, Thomas. *Mortal Questions*. Cambridge: Cambridge University Press, 1979.

Singer, Peter. *Practical Ethics*. Cambridge: Cambridge University Press, 1979.

Wasserstrom, Richard. *Philosophy and Social Issues*. Notre Dame, Ind.: Notre Dame University Press, 1980.

I. EUTHANASIA AND SUICIDE

Battin, Margaret Pabst. *Ethical Issues in Suicide*. Englewood Cliffs, N.J.: Prentice-Hall, 1982.

—, and David Mayo, eds. *Suicide: The Philosophical Issues*. New York: St. Martin's, 1980.

Ladd, John, ed. *Ethical Issues Relating to Life and Death*. New York: Oxford University Press, 1979.

Perlin, Seymour, ed. *A Handbook for the Study of Suicide*. New York: Oxford University Press, 1975.

II. WAR

Mayer, Peter, ed. *The Pacifist Conscience*. Chicago: Regnery/Gateway, 1967.

Narveson, Jan. "Violence and War," essay in Tom Regan, ed. *Matters of Life and Death*. New York: Random House, 1980.

Shaffer, Jerome, ed. *Violence*. New York: David McKay, 1971.

Stanage, Sherman M., ed. *Reason and Violence*. Totowa, N.J.: Little-field, Adams, 1974.

Wakin, Malham M., ed. *War, Morality, and the Military Profession*. Boulder, Col.: Westview Press, 1979.

Wasserstrom, Richard, ed. *War and Morality*. Belmont, Cal.: Wadsworth, 1970.

Walzer, Michael. *Just and Unjust Wars*. New York: Basic Books, 1977.

III. PUNISHMENT

Acton, H.B., ed. *The Philosophy of Punishment*. London: Macmillan, 1969.

Ezorsky, Gertrude, ed. *Philosophical Perspectives on Punishment*. Albany, N.Y.: SUNY Press, 1972.

Flew, Anthony. *Crime or Disease*. London: Macmillan, 1973.

Goldinger, Milton, ed. *Punishment and Human Rights*. Cambridge, Mass.: Schenkman, 1974.

Hobbes, Thomas. *Leviathan*, Chapters XXVII and XXVIII.

Honderich, Ted. *Punishment: The Supposed Justifications*. London: Hutchinson, 1969.

Menninger, Karl. *The Crime of Punishment*. New York: Viking Press, 1966.

Morris, Herbert. "Persons and Punishment," *The Monist*, October 1968, 475-501.

Sellin, Thorstein, ed. *Capital Punishment*. New York: Harper & Row, 1967.

IV. FEEDING THE HUNGRY

Aiken, William, and Hugh LaFollette. *World Hunger and Moral Obligation*. Englewood Cliffs, N.J.: Prentice-Hall, 1977.

Eberstadt, Nick. "Myths of the Food Crisis," *New York Review of Books*, 19 February 1976. Reprinted in James Rachels, ed. *Moral Problems*, 3rd edn. New York: Harper & Row, 1979.

George, Susan. *How the Other Half Dies*. New York: Penguin Books, 1976. Rev. 1977.

Hardin, Garrett. *Stalking the Wild Taboo*. Los Altos, Cal.: William Kauffman, 1978.

V. ABORTION

Brody, Baruch. *Abortion and the Sanctity of Human Life*. Cambridge, Mass.: MIT Press, 1975.

English, Jane. "Abortion and the Concept of a Person," *Canadian Journal of Philosophy*, October 1975.

Feinberg, Joel. *The Problem of Abortion*. Belmont, Cal.: Wadsworth (forthcoming).

Warren, Mary Anne. "On the Moral and Legal Status of Abortion," *The Monist*, January 1973.

VI. SEX: WITH OR WITHOUT MARRIAGE

Baker, Robert, and Frederick Elliston, eds. *Philosophy and Sex*. Buffalo, N.Y.: Prometheus, 1975.

Firestone, Shulamith. *The Dialectic of Sex: The Case for Feminist Revolution*. New York: Morrow, 1970.

Freud, Sigmund. *Three Essays on the Theory of Sexuality*. New York: Basic Books, 1962.

Fromm, Erich. *The Art of Loving*. New York: Harper & Row, 1956.

Hunter, J.R.M. *Thinking about Sex and Love*. Toronto: Macmillan, 1980.

May, Rollo. *Love and Will*. New York: Norton, 1969.

Taylor, Richard. *Having Love Affairs*. Buffalo, N.Y.: Prometheus, 1982.

Vannoy, Russell. *Sex Without Love: A Philosophical Investigation*. Buffalo, N.Y.: Prometheus, 1980.

Vetterling-Braggin, Mary, Frederick Elliston, and Jane English, eds. *Feminism and Philosophy*. Totowa, N.J.: Littlefield, Adams, 1977.

VII. EQUALITY

Bishop, Sharon and Marjorie Weinzweig, eds. *Philosophy and Women*. Belmont, Cal.: Wadsworth, 1979.

English, Jane, ed. *Sex Equality*. Englewood Cliffs, N.J.: Prentice-Hall, 1977.

Mill, John Stuart and Harriet Taylor Mill. *The Subjection of Women* (1869). Currently available in J.S. Mill and Harriet Taylor Mill, *Essays on Sex Equality*. Chicago: University of Chicago Press, 1970.

VIII. JUSTIFIED INEQUALITY?

Fullinwider, Robert K. *The Reverse Discrimination Controversy*. Totowa, N.J.: Rowman & Littlefield, 1980.

Goldman, Alan H. *Justice and Reverse Discrimination*. Princeton: Princeton University Press, 1979.

Sher, George. "Justifying Reverse Discrimination in Employment," *Philosophy & Public Affairs*, Winter 1975.

IX. FUTURE PEOPLE

Bayles, Michael. *Morality and Population Policy*. University, Ala.: University of Alabama Press, 1980.

—, ed. *Ethics and Population*. Cambridge, Mass.: Schenkman, 1976.

Parfit, Derek. "Future Generations: Further Problems," *Philosophy & Public Affairs*, Spring 1982.

Kavka, Gregory. "The Paradox of Future Individuals," *Philosophy & Public Affairs*, Spring 1982.

Sikora, R.I. and Brian Barry, eds. *Obligations to Future Generations*. Philadelphia: Temple University Press, 1978.